A CAPTIVE
OF TIME

A CAPTIVE OF TIME

My Years with Pasternak

The Memoirs of
OLGA IVINSKAYA

Translated from the Russian
with Introduction and Notes by
MAX HAYWARD

COLLINS and HARVILL PRESS
London
1978

Published in Russian under the title of *U vremeni v plenu*
by Librairie Artheme Fayard, Paris, 1978

ISBN 00-262847-3

Printed litho in Great Britain
by W & J Mackay Ltd, Chatham
for Collins, St. James's Place and
Harvill Press, 30a Pavilion Road, London SW1

'. . . now, as life begins to fade
And I stand by my dear ones' graves
I know I may knock at heaven's gate,
For wasn't I loved by you?'

CONTENTS

ILLUSTRATIONS

All photographs are from the author's personal collection.

PREFACE

Olga Ivinskaya's account of her years with Pasternak begins in 1946, the year of their first meeting. My Introduction is intended to serve as a general outline of Pasternak's life, work, and times up until that moment.

In order to reduce to a minimum editorial intrusions on the text, I have added brief explanatory footnotes only where it seemed of immediate importance; these are marked: (Tr.). All other footnotes are the author's.

Longer or less essential notes and comments (for which the author bears no responsibility) will be found at the end of the book, and are indicated in the text by numbers.

Also at the end of the book are: a Biographical Guide to the large number of persons referred to, and a list of sources for most of the quotations from the works of Pasternak and others.

Occasional minor cuts have been made in the translation. The Russian original of the book is published by Fayard (Paris, 1978). It contains several appendices which have been excluded from this translation as being of prime interest to Russian readers, or to students of Pasternak's poetry.

All the translations of poetry are by me, except in the few cases where otherwise indicated. Michael Harari and Stanley Kunitz have kindly given permission to quote from versions by them.

I wish to express my deepest gratitude to Valerie Jensen for taking on herself the brunt of the research involved in compiling the notes, and for doing it with such care, patience, and proficiency. I have profited in many ways from having been able to consult in manuscript Guy de Mallac's scholarly biography *Boris Pasternak: His Life and Art* (to be published by the University of Oklahoma Press, Norman, 1978); my thanks are also due to Patricia Blake, Martin Dewhirst, George Katkov, and Heinz Schewe for helping to clarify various points.

In its later stages most of the work on the translation was completed in the Mishkenot Sha'ananim, Jerusalem. I am greatly indebted to Mr Teddy Kollek and to Mr Peter Halban for offering me sanctuary and hospitality in these unique surroundings—it eased my labours more than I can say.

MAX HAYWARD
June, 1977

INTRODUCTION

'... life became converted into art, and art
was born of life and experience.'

Boris Pasternak was born in Moscow in 1890, and died in the country
not very far from it seventy years later. Apart from a few brief
intervals, all his life was spent in or near the city.

His father, Leonid Pasternak, had grown up in the Black Sea port
of Odessa and came to Moscow, originally to study medicine at the
University, shortly after his marriage in 1889 to Rosalia Kaufman, the
daughter of a manufacturer. (Leonid Pasternak's father had been an
inn-keeper—one of the few callings open to Jews in the Pale of
Settlement in south-west Russia, to which they were largely confined by law.*) After settling in Moscow, he abandoned medicine for
art and went on to achieve great distinction as a teacher and painter.

Four years or so after the birth of Boris, his first son, Leonid was
appointed to a professorship at the Moscow College of Painting,
Sculpture and Architecture. The College was under the patronage of
the Imperial court, and the appointment was approved even though
Leonid did not go through the usual formality of conversion to
Russian Orthodoxy in order to remove the technical liability of being
officially 'of Jewish faith'. (Before the Revolution citizens of the
Empire had their religion entered in their identity papers, not—as
later in the Soviet Union—their race.)

The Pasternak family lived in quarters allotted to them in the
handsome eighteenth-century building of the College on one of the
principal thoroughfares of central Moscow, not very far from the
scene of many of the events described in this book. Boris, his younger
brother Alexander (later to become an architect), and his two sisters,
Josephine and Lydia, spent their childhood years here.

In his 'An Essay in Autobiography' (written in 1956), Pasternak has
given an account of his early life, and it is also portrayed in many

---

* The Pasternaks were apparently not Ashkenazi, like most of the Jews in
southern Russia, but were descended from a Sephardic family that had settled there
in the eighteenth century. Leonid believed that one of his forbears was Isaac
Abarbanel, the celebrated theologian (1437-1508) who served for a time as treasurer
to Alfonso V of Portugal.

sketches and paintings by his father. He seems to have had an entirely Russian upbringing, hardly distinguishable from what it would have been in any middle-class home in the Moscow of those years. Formal religion apparently played little or no part in the family—as for the liberal intelligentsia in general. But at an early age Boris was taken to church by his nanny to be baptized, and throughout his life he attached much significance to this—particularly in his later years when the symbols and liturgical language of Christianity (outwardly embodied in childhood memories of the gold-and-blue-domed churches of Moscow) came to occupy an important place in his poetry.

The Pasternak household was dominated by art, music and literature. Before her marriage Boris's mother had intended to become a concert pianist, and she sometimes gave private recitals in the apartment at the College. One of his earliest memories was of an occasion in 1894 when Leo Tolstoi came to hear his mother play. Tolstoi was a family friend and, as Pasternak was later to put it, 'our whole house was permeated by his spirit'. His father visited Tolstoi at his country estate in Yasnaya Poliana, where he made a series of notable drawings of him, and—at Tolstoi's request—he also did the illustrations for *Resurrection* as it was serialized in a Petersburg magazine during 1899. In November 1910, when Tolstoi fled from his home and died in the station-master's house at Astapovo, Leonid Pasternak was informed by telegram and he went there immediately, taking Boris with him, and made a drawing of Tolstoi on his death-bed.

Although Pasternak was not appreciably influenced by Tolstoi in his work, he always looked on him as a tutelary spirit and this early personal connection with the great writer must have given him a paramount sense of the legitimacy of his place in Russian literature when, many years later, attempts were made by detractors with no such credentials to banish him from it.

His education, like his upbringing in general, was on completely Russian lines. For a moment it seemed that he might go to the Lutheran school in Moscow (much favoured by Jewish parents), for which he was intensively prepared in German. As a result German became the foreign language in which he was most proficient—until the end of his days he was able to write it with old-fashioned elegance. In the end, however, he was sent (in 1901) to a Russian grammar school, where he received a good grounding in both modern and classical subjects (including Greek). Vladimir Mayakovski, two years Pasternak's junior and later to be ranked with him as one of the great poets of the era, went to the same school, but they do not seem to have been aware of each other's existence at that time.

Pasternak's overriding passion during his school years was music. As he has described in his two autobiographical works, it came to him like a revelation during the summer of 1903, when the family happened to rent a *dacha* (country house) near where the composer Scriabin was living. Of all the many illustrious figures who visited his parents' home in those years, Scriabin was the one who had the most immediate effect and influence on Pasternak. Sometimes to the detriment of his work at school, he began to study composition at the Moscow Conservatory. His parents were delighted, and it seemed a foregone conclusion that he would become a composer. (Three piano pieces composed by him in his last few years at school have recently come to light and were publicly performed in Moscow in 1976.)

But quite suddenly, and at first sight unaccountably, he gave it all up. This happened in 1910, shortly after Scriabin's return to Moscow after a six-year absence abroad, when Pasternak went to play his compositions for him: '[Scriabin's] reaction surpassed all my hopes. He approved . . . encouraged me and gave me his blessing.' Pasternak's explanation for having nevertheless abruptly decided against devoting his life to music is that he did not feel it was his true vocation: it did not come to him with the miraculous ease he believed necessary to the expression of a natural gift, and he had been increasingly tormented by what he considered his inability to bring effortless technical skill to it. 'For six years,' he wrote much later, 'I had lived for music. Now I tore it up and flung it from me as you throw away your dearest treasure. For a while I went on improvising by habit, but I was gradually losing my skill. Then I decided to make a clean break—I stopped playing the piano or going to concerts, and I avoided meeting musicians.' It was, as he said, as painful as an 'amputation'. But this total ban did not last, and throughout his life he was a familiar figure among the audience at concerts in the Moscow Conservatory.

It was impossible to grow up in Moscow in those years without being affected by the great revival of poetry which began at the turn of the century. The decade and a half before the First World War, often referred to as the 'Silver Age', was a time of extraordinary ferment in all the arts. It was one of those moments in history when a sudden quickening of the consciousness coincides with vigorous economic growth. The newly rich Moscow merchants (such as the celebrated sugar or textile 'kings', whose fathers or grandfathers had sometimes been serfs) patronized the arts in lavish fashion—and often with strikingly good taste not always exhibited by their counterparts in the West. In retrospect there seems little doubt that, but for the War and the Revolution, Russia would have developed into a liberal 'bourgeois' democracy in which Moscow and Petersburg might easily have come to outshine the capitals of Western Europe. (The way in which this promise, soon to be aborted, arose out of the abolition of serfdom and the other reforms of 1861, was the theme of Pasternak's last work—his unfinished play *The Blind Beauty*.)

Ironically, the impatient questing of the 'Silver Age' was not only a symptom of the fatal strains in Russian society, but also helped to accentuate them. When they became intolerable under the impact of a virtually lost war in 1917, the fabric crumbled. At the age of fifteen Pasternak witnessed the first ominous signs: the demonstrations in 1905 that led to the establishment of a limited parliamentary system could be seen from the balcony of the College, and some of the fiercest street-fighting went on nearby. He received a glancing blow from a gendarme, and his father made a drawing of a girl wounded in a skirmish. The events and mood of that time were to be graphically recalled in poems and prose written in the 'twenties, and in *Doctor Zhivago*. Like most liberal intellectual families (and some of the merchant tycoons) the Pasternaks sympathized with the revolutionaries.

But for Boris Pasternak the perturbations of the era were refracted mainly through art and the kind of speculative thought so appealing to the Russian intelligentsia—here too there had been a revival, marked by a strong movement away from the somewhat shallow materialism of the preceding age. In 1909 Pasternak entered Moscow University to study philosophy (after at first wishing to study law), but during his student years poetry began to take the place of music as an object of major interest, though still not as an overwhelming passion. A few years previously he had begun to read modern verse and, like all his contemporaries, had been particularly affected by

Alexander Blok, the dominant figure in the Symbolist movement, and of the 'Silver Age' in general. (At about the same time, Pasternak was also greatly impressed by the work of the Austrian poet Rainer Maria Rilke, whose portrait his father had once painted.) By 1912 Symbolism had been challenged by two rival movements, Futurism and Acmeism, and most of Pasternak's contemporaries—such as Mayakovski, Akhmatova and Mandelstam—were associated with one of these conflicting trends, though as major poets they naturally soon came to rise above them. Pasternak was never much concerned with 'programmes' of any kind and, apart from a brief involvement with a late offshoot of Futurism just before and during the First World War, he always stood alone. Rigorous independence was an essential component of his idea of what it meant to be a great poet—which was as much a personal or moral ideal as an 'aesthetic' one, and was embodied for him by Blok: 'He had all the qualities which go to make a great poet—passion, gentleness, dedicated insight, his own conception of the world, his own gift of transforming everything he touched, his own reserved, restrained, self-effacing destiny.'

These words were written by Pasternak towards the end of his life, but they well sum up what was undoubtedly his instinctive feeling from the beginning: that to be a great poet it was not enough to write poetry, but essential—by responding submissively to a high and lonely destiny—to contribute in some vital way to the life of the times. For this reason there could be no question of 'choosing' poetry or anything else as a 'vocation'—it was a matter, rather, of being singled out by destiny in some unmistakable fashion.

When he understood that philosophy could not be the vehicle of his genius and his fate, he gave it up as abruptly as music—and also just at the moment when a brilliant future in it seemed to be assured. In 1912, on the urging of one of his closest friends at Moscow University, Dmitri Samarin (who later served, to some extent, as the prototype of Yuri Zhivago in the novel), he travelled to Marburg to spend the spring and summer studying in the seminar of Professor Hermann Cohen, a neo-Kantian philosopher of international renown to whose lectures people flocked at that time from all over Europe. In Pasternak's first autobiographical work, *Safe Conduct* (1931), he has described how a disappointment in love—the subject of one of his best known poems, 'Marburg'—precipitated the abandonment of his studies. It happened just as he had been invited to lunch with Professor Cohen on a Sunday—a summons which normally augured a successful academic career in the field. Instead, Pasternak went off to see a cousin who had unexpectedly arrived in Frankfurt from Petersburg. Despite this, Professor Cohen persisted in suggesting he should stay in Marburg, and then settle down to teach philosophy in Germany. But he had lost interest in it, and was now, for the first time, overcome by an irresistible urge to write poetry—it had seized possession of him in the days after his rejection by a girl whom he had first got to know in his last year at school, and he began to write it, in his student lodgings in Marburg, as though in a trance: 'Day and night . . . I wrote about the sea, dawn, Southern rain, the coal of the Harz . . .' Before returning home to Moscow, he travelled to Italy, stopping for a short time in Venice and Florence.

The next few years confirmed him in his overpowering sense that poetry 'came naturally' to him. In the summer of 1913, staying with his parents in the country, he wrote all the verse for his first published collection, *A Twin in Clouds* (a title he later described as pretentious, in the spirit of the times). He was inevitably drawn into the literary life of Moscow with its competing coteries, and he got to know some of the leading figures of the older generation—Symbolists such as Valeri Briusov, Viacheslav Ivanov, Andrei Bely, and others. But it is significant that he was not under the personal influence of any of them. There was no question of the sort of dependence which may well have played a part in his decision to give up music and philosophy. The two living poets whose work had made the greatest impression on him remained remote figures: it was not until 1921 that he met Blok briefly for the first (and last) time, and his only significant contact with Rilke was by correspondence in years when his own absolute originality was not in doubt.

He was, however, tremendously affected by one of his almost exact contemporaries—Mayakovski, whom he first met in the summer of 1914. After seeing him on one occasion (in 1917), Pasternak even seriously thought for a moment of giving up poetry himself, and says he would have done so if he had not been too old by then to change direction yet again. It was not a case of jealousy, but of genuine humility: in the presence of Mayakovski he felt he was utterly without talent. But at the same time, he instinctively recoiled from the Bohemian posturing and flamboyant style of public declamation cultivated by the Futurists—most of all by Mayakovski himself. He was by temperament incapable of playing the role of the 'romantic poet' and never thought of writing verse as an exclusive way of life, or as a profession in the ordinary sense. If poetry at times possessed him, he never allowed himself to be consumed by the fact of being a poet, or to 'project' himself as one. All his life he thought soberly—not only out of necessity, but as an article of faith—of the need to support himself and his dependents by the industrious exercise of a craft. In his later years he was often forced by circumstances to devote himself almost entirely to translation, but already well before the Revolution he evidently looked on it as a skill which—in the doubtless regretted absence of any professional training—would enable him to earn his living. (In a letter written to a friend in Moscow from Marburg in 1912, he spoke of translating a work by the Swiss writer Gottfried Keller in order not to be a burden to his by no means wealthy parents when he returned home.) While a student he had also sometimes found employment as a private tutor in rich Moscow families. In the early summer not long before the outbreak of the First World War, he stayed with the family of the poet Baltrushaitis, coaching his son, and working on a translation of Kleist's 'Broken Jug' which had been commissioned by a theatre.

An injury to his leg as a child had made Pasternak permanently lame and he was exempted from military service. In the first three years of the war (apparently only in the summer months) he worked as a tutor in the family of a merchant called Philipp (whose foreign name and connections made him the object of anti-German riots after the outbreak of war—all Pasternak's books and manuscripts were lost in the sacking of Philipp's house). This enabled him to maintain his literary interests and contacts in Moscow which centred round a small, mildly Futurist group started on the initiative of Sergei Bobrov in 1913, and calling itself 'Centrifuge'. The only poets of note to be associated with it were Nikolai Aseyev and Pasternak—who contributed to the several volumes of poetry and criticism put out by it, and whose second collection of lyrics (*Above the Barriers*, 1917) appeared under its imprint. But it is clear from recently published correspondence with Bobrov and other members of Centrifuge that he was lukewarm towards his involvement in collective literary activities and was altogether sceptical about what he called (in a letter of December 1915) the 'poor, sterile epoch', and his own 'meanderings and delusions'. Pasternak's letters of those wartime years also betray his characteristic dissatisfaction with the idea of an existence based on the writing of lyric poetry ('scribbling', as he put it), which could only be the product of intermittent inspiration. Already then he was anxious to attempt something more substantial and of a different order: a work in prose, or a long narrative poem.

Evidently as a form of civilian war service Pasternak spent two consecutive winters (1915-6 and 1916-7) in the Ural Mountains and on the river Kama, where a number of major Russian ordnance factories were located. This was his first important experience of life away from the literary and intellectual environment of Moscow, and his impressions of the region and its people provided the basis, many years later, for several chapters in *Doctor Zhivago*. His duties were administrative and mainly involved the obtaining of military exemptions for men recruited to work in reserved occupations in the local war industry. Towards the end of the second winter he found himself at a chemical factory in a mountain area about two hundred miles from the nearest railway station, at Kazan on the Volga, and it was here that he heard the news of the fall of the monarchy and the Revolution in February 1917. His first piece of prose to be published (early the following year) was the opening part of a never-completed story entitled 'Without Love' in which he described his hectic night-time journey by horse-drawn sleigh through the snowdrifts down from the mountains to Kazan—the first stage of his return to revolutionary Moscow. This fragment is remarkable evidence of how, at the very outset of the new era, he was already preoccupied by the central narrative theme to be unfolded decades later in the novel which made him world-famous: the fate of his generation of the Russian intelligentsia as it would be shaped by the time of great upheavals whose first beginnings in 1905 he had witnessed as a boy.

In the interlude between the February Revolution and the Bolshevik seizure of power in October 1917, it is clear that Pasternak was affected by the general feeling of exhilaration created by the sudden downfall of the autocracy: the description in the novel of Yuri Zhivago's jubilant acceptance of the Revolution during the summer of 1917 is obviously based on his own feelings at the time. But there is no evidence that he was actively involved in what was going on in the country. The summer of 1917 was significant in his own life less for any external events than for a sustained lyrical mood which gave rise to the series of poems later published (in 1922) under the title *My Sister Life*. These immediately established him as a poet of supreme quality and achievement—and at the same time created an impression of such detachment from everything except his own feelings and experiences that he was never able to shake off the reputation (sometimes, in the later Stalin years, held against him in menacing fashion) of a figure largely aloof from the great issues of the day. It is true that the poems contain very few topical references—there is a mention of Kerenski, and of 'soldiers' mutinies', and the word 'revolutionary' occurs once (as the epithet for a haystack), but they nevertheless convey the same heady sense of freedom and of rebirth which in *Doctor Zhivago* was to be described more explicitly in terms of the general mood of intoxication with the great historical changes then taking place. For Pasternak these happened to coincide with a love affair which brought his emotions and perceptions to an exceptional pitch of intensity, releasing an impetuous flow of language hardly to be matched again in his verse for over a decade. By their nature such lyrical eruptions are shortlived and can rarely be repeated, but *My Sister Life* served as the first triumphant assertion of what was always to remain Pasternak's distinctive manner, only slightly modified with the passing years by a serener, more reflective tone, and a conscious striving after greater simplicity.

The months chronicled in the poems of *My Sister Life* were apparently spent between Moscow and various places in the Volga region near Saratov—which accounts for a typical blend of images drawn from both town and country. In many ways this slender volume is a compendium of Pasternak's themes and poetic devices. Although he had his darker moments (in 'An Essay in Autobiography' he confesses that as a child he had at times been 'close to suicide', and in later life he was no stranger to sharp bouts of melancholy or depression), it shows him in his usual and most characteristic mood of eager communion with the world, of grateful acceptance of life as it is. His own changing state of mind is mirrored in nature and merges with it—in this case during the kind of incomparably luxuriant Russian summer, constantly refreshed by sudden downpours and thunderstorms, which is nowhere more nostalgically evoked than in these poems. It is always a domesticated nature, never suggestive of cosmic despair or brooding anguish, but soothing emotional turbulence by its closeness to ordinary, familiar, and human things: the Milky Way leads over towards Kerch, like a dirt road across the steppe, with a herd of cattle raising the dust on it; dead branches resemble the sleeves of a damp shirt hung up to dry; rain weaves like a silk-worm as it beats against the window-panes, cocooning those inside. These are some of the more obvious of the metaphors in which his poetry abounds. His use of language is exuberant, and sometimes he is carried away by it, sacrificing clarity to intricate patterns of assonance which enchant the Russian ear and defy the translator, but he is never guilty of banality and continually surprises by introducing expressive colloquialisms into the most 'poetic' contexts—one of his several ways of 'humanizing' the natural scene. As Nadezhda Mandelstam has said, *My Sister Life* is a 'book of knowledge about the world, of thanksgiving and joy'.

Pasternak remained in Moscow throughout the Civil War (1918–21), making no attempt to escape abroad or to the White-occupied south, as a number of other Russian writers did at that time. No doubt, like Yuri Zhivago, he was momentarily impressed by the 'splendid surgery' of the Bolshevik seizure of power in October 1917, but—again, to judge by the evidence of the novel, and despite a personal admiration for Lenin whom he saw in the flesh at the Ninth Congress of Soviets in 1921—he soon began to harbour profound doubts about the claims and credentials of the new régime, not to mention its style of rule.

The terrible shortages of food and fuel, and the depredations of the Red Terror, made life very precarious in those years, particularly for the 'bourgeois' intelligentsia. In a letter written to Pasternak from abroad in the 'twenties, Marina Tsvetayeva reminded him of how she had run into him in the street in 1919 as he was on his way to sell some valuable books from his library in order to buy bread. He continued to write original work and to translate, but after about the middle of 1918 it became almost impossible to publish. The only way to make one's work known was to declaim it in the several 'literary' cafés that then sprang up, or—anticipating *samizdat*—to circulate it in manuscript. It was in this way that *My Sister Life* first became available to a wider audience.

In 1921, however, with the end of the Civil War and the beginning of the 'New Economic Policy' (NEP), the situation changed radically. The partial restoration of a free market meant that private publishing firms could be launched, and for a time it seemed that Russian literary life had a chance of resuming on much the same lines as before. Several writers (such as Ilya Ehrenburg and Alexei Tolstoi) who had emigrated now returned home, and some of the pre-war literary trends and movements began to reconstitute themselves, often advancing rival claims to special relevance under the new dispensation. Links with the West were re-established, and for a few years it was possible to come and go with relative ease. At the beginning of NEP there was a particularly close connection between Moscow and Berlin—which, being the nearest West European capital, served as a convenient 'half-way house' for those Russian intellectuals and writers who at this time hesitated between permanent emigration or return home to a Russia now apparently in retreat from the revolutionary stringencies of the Civil War. Several émigré Russian publishers in Berlin established connections with Moscow, and for a few years new books were often published in both capitals under the imprint of one of these Berlin firms. The arrangement symbolized the ambiguities of the period—and did much to encourage the more optimistic in the hope that the new Russia would not be isolated from the outside world.

Nobody could really know whether NEP, with the limited economic and cultural diversity it allowed, might lead to permanent relaxation, or whether it was to be merely a breathing space—this indeed was the main question which came to divide the opposing factions in the Bolshevik leadership after Lenin's death in 1924. Several leading writers and poets (such as Tsvetayeva) took no chances and emigrated as soon as it was possible. In August 1921, Pasternak's father (who had retained his position at the College throughout these years) obtained permission to travel to Berlin on the grounds that he and his wife required medical treatment not available in Russia. Although he did not apparently intend to stay abroad for good and later thought of returning, he and his wife and two daughters in fact remained in Germany for a number of years, and then moved to England not long before the Second World War. Towards the end of 1922, Boris also went to Berlin, and for a moment he seems to have toyed with the idea of staying there with his family. He visited Marburg again, but Professor Cohen was dead, and only his former landlady recognized him. In general the sight of post-war Germany was not inspiring—'like a beggar with outstretched hand', as he was to describe it in *Safe Conduct*. Around this time *My Sister Life* was published in Berlin by the same firm which had already brought it out a few months previously in Moscow—to which he now returned early in 1923. He never saw his parents again.

That same year he married his first wife, Yevgenia Vladimirovna Lurye, a painter. His son Yevgeni was born the following year, and he began a more or less settled existence as a writer and poet already of some considerable reputation, and was widely considered to be the equal of such contemporaries as Akhmatova, Mandelstam, and Mayakovski. He shared the general material hardships of the time—a cramped apartment and an uncertain income, but it was at least possible now to make some kind of living by literary work. For a brief time in the mid-twenties, in addition to advances from publishers for his books and translations, he even received a salary as a researcher in the library of the People's Commissariat for Education, where his task was to read through foreign journals and clip out all references to Lenin. The birth of his son had made this regular employment essential—and it also had the incidental advantage of keeping him in touch with Western European literature, since in the intervals of hunting for Leniniana, he was able to read Proust and Joseph Conrad, among others.

Much of the original verse and prose he wrote in these conditions was in form and content as inconclusive as the times themselves, and thus reflected not only his own inner uncertainties, but those of most of the intelligentsia during NEP. As before, it was his ambition to write a substantial work in verse or prose. Apart from translations (of Kleist, Goethe, Hans Sachs, and others) and a further volume of lyric poems (*Themes and Variations*, 1923), he published a lengthy but fragmentary soliloquy in verse on the relation between art and revolution (*A High Illness*, 1923), and attempted a novel, of which only a first part appeared (*The Childhood of Luvers*, 1922). In the second half of the 'twenties he brought out several unfinished narrative poems: *Spektorski* (1925); *Lieutenant Schmidt* (1926), and *Nineteen Hundred and Five* (1927). Their incomplete state underlines how unready he still was for the task he had set himself—which was to give an account of the revolutionary era he had lived through, trying to draw up a balance sheet of what it meant in terms of its effect and claims on uncommitted individuals of his own kind, and on the agents of revolutionary change themselves. Unlike Mayakovski, whom he had so much admired in the previous decade, he was divided in his mind about the new order, and the nearest he came to a nominal display of support for it was by joining Mayakovski's combative LEF (Left Front of Art), together with other former members of Centrifuge. But this was, perhaps, more a gesture of solidarity with old associates than an act of whole-hearted self-identification with LEF's 'revolutionary' programme. As much as he had been impressed by the inimitable verve and audacity of the earlier Mayakovski, he was now repelled by the blustering hyperbole of such long-winded encomia to the Revolution as *150,000,000* (1921) and *Vladimir Ilyich Lenin* (1924). In 1927 Pasternak formally broke with Mayakovski by leaving LEF. It is noteworthy that during the years of increasing estrangement from Mayakovski, he began to correspond with Marina Tsvetayeva, who had supported the White cause in the Civil War before she emigrated. This did not, of course, signify any political preference on Pasternak's part, but only that he now found in Tsvetayeva the same qualities which had once so much attracted him in Mayakovski: overwhelming poetic strength and verbal brilliance in the service of truth to oneself.

In his necessarily unfinished narrative poems of those years Pasternak showed a much greater awareness of the real dilemmas of history than those of his contemporaries who supposed themselves to be 'marching in step' with it. While by no means denying the imperatives of social justice, he knew too well how readily victims turn into bullies and liberating ideas congeal into tyrannical institutions, and how easily revolutionaries may lose control of the processes they set in motion. (As early as 1918 he had published an intriguing dramatic fragment in verse about Saint-Just and Robespierre which suggests how deeply he must have pondered the tragic lessons of the French Revolution for the Russian one.) Yet there is nothing gloomy or pessimistic in his vivid poetic impressions of 1905, in his epic portrait of Lieutenant Schmidt (one of the heroes of the naval mutiny which helped to spark off the events of 1905), or in his semi-autobiographical account of the complex relationship of a Russian intellectual (Spektorski) to the troubled and uncertain times. (The latter was planned as an ambitious 'novel in verse' on the general theme which was much later fully elaborated in *Doctor Zhivago*.) What is common to all three works is the evident belief that the Revolution would be justified and fulfil its promise as long as it remained in harmony with the overriding claims of life as such, furthering rather than stultifying them, and did not demand the total sacrifice of the individual personality. There was nothing deliberately insidious about the doubts implied in posing the question like this, but it needed the experiences of the following decade to resolve them.

The end of NEP and the opening of a completely new phase in Soviet history at the close of the 'twenties happened to coincide with major developments in Pasternak's personal life and, as in the summer of 1917, the resulting mood found expression in a series of lyrical poems—the last such cycle for many years. These poems, written between 1930 and 1931, were published in 1932 as a volume under the eloquent title *Second Birth*, and they offer fascinating insights into Pasternak's view of himself and the world at that crucial turning point.

For all its relative latitude—and to some extent because of it— NEP had been morally debilitating. The suicide of Mayakovski in 1930 (about which there is a remarkable poem in *Second Birth*) was a stunning comment on the toll which its essential ambivalence had taken. It was dispiriting both to those who hoped for a return to the old freedoms and to those who—like Mayakovski—had continued to crave during its 'grey weekdays' for the radical transformations it had deferred. For this reason there was a wide-spread feeling akin to relief (naturally not unmixed with trepidation) when the situation was clarified by Stalin's defeat of his political rivals and the consequent launching of his 'revolution from above': the forced march to industrialization begun by the First Five Year Plan, and the collectivization of agriculture. For a moment, before it turned into unprecedented bloodletting, it looked to many like a return to the 'splendid surgery' of October 1917. The huge sacrifice in life it involved, and the sombre political consequences of Stalin's assumption of absolute power, were not to become fully apparent for some little time.

Pasternak was affected by the singular euphoria which at that moment came over many intellectuals—including some who had originally been opposed to the Bolsheviks. But the prime source of lyrical bravura so evident in *Second Birth* was the ending of an equivocal situation in his own life. By 1929 his marriage to his first wife had virtually collapsed and in the summer of the same year he met and fell in love with Zinaida Nikolayevna, the wife of a well-known pianist, Genrikh Neigaus. Despite the domestic and emotional upsets involved, the whole spirit and tone of the poems of

1930-1 show that the metaphor of their general title accurately defined Pasternak's state of mind at that time. Even the lines addressed to the wife he was soon to divorce, remarkable for their touching candour and elegiac tenderness, do not detract from the buoyancy induced by a passionate new love and the overall sense of a fresh beginning in his own affairs, as well as in those of the world at large. Less frenetic and more disciplined in language than *My Sister Life*, *Second Birth* thus similarly arose from a conjunction of Pasternak's private mood with what he perceived as a public one.

There was a third—and less ephemeral—element in his feeling of regeneration: his discovery of the Caucasus, to which he went for the first time, together with Zinaida Nikolayevna, in 1931. Their journey over the Georgian Military Highway (probably the most breathtaking mountain road in the world) to Tiflis—where they stayed with the poet Paolo Yashvili, later a victim of the terror—is described in poems which have not been equalled since Pushkin and Lermontov wrote on the same theme. For Pasternak the Caucasian peaks, receding in an infinite panorama of unexampled grandeur, offered a simile for a vision of what a socialist future might be like. But, as before, most of his images are domestic and intimate, even in this prodigious setting: the rugged lower slopes, for instance, reminded him of a 'crumpled bed'. Although the use of such topical words as 'plan', 'commune' and 'construction' indicates a greater direct concern than in *My Sister Life* with what was afoot in the country, the paramount source of life and renewal—as usual in Pasternak's eyes—is still nature, and nobody could have been farther from seeing socialism in the Marxist terms of its 'conquest' by man. If it was to succeed, he often seemed to be saying, socialism would have to emulate nature and coalesce with it. What is more, he still insisted on those moral aspects of building a new society which had long been disregarded and were soon to be blatantly trampled on: 'labour in common', he said in one line, must go hand in hand with 'a rule of law'. In view of the future events related by Madame Ivinskaya, there is a particular irony in a passage where he declares his acceptance of the 'revolutionary will' because it had supposedly put an end to the oppression of women—something which had exercised him from his childhood days.

People have occasionally seen naïveté in all this, and it is undeniable that Pasternak shared certain of the misplaced hopes of the moment. But it is also clear that the historical wisdom and prescience displayed in the narrative poems of the previous decade had not in fact deserted him. This appears with particular force in his paraphrase of some famous lines of Pushkin which were addressed to Nicholas I in 1826 with the evident intention of moving the Tsar to show mercy to the rebellious officers arrested after the Decembrist uprising in the previous year. Using the same veiled language as Pushkin, Pasternak expressed the hope that Stalin would likewise spare his defeated opponents. In both cases such a plea was proved by events to be wishful thinking—but of the kind patently aimed at warding off or exorcising clearly perceived dangers. The fact is that in 1931, as in 1917, Pasternak was still prepared to 'accept' the Revolution only on his own terms, and if (in the last poem of *Second Birth*) he elaborately compared it to the spring, this was clearly in the conviction that it would only be worthy of its name if it lived up to the high promise implicit in this and his other figures of speech for it.

In the first half of the 'thirties it was still possible to harbour illusions in connection with Stalin's emergence as the unchallenged master of the country. By 1932 or 1933 it had become obvious that collectivization—during which at least five million peasants died— had been a terrible and irreversible disaster. As Pasternak commented through the mouth of one of the characters in *Doctor Zhivago*: 'I think that collectivization was both a mistake and a failure, and because that couldn't be admitted, every means of intimidation had to be used to make people forget how to think and judge for themselves, to force them to see what wasn't there, and to maintain the contrary of what their eyes told them . . .' Yet at one moment Stalin himself condemned the 'excesses' that had occurred, and for a while he seemed anxious to appease various sections of the population, and to create the impression of a return to 'normalcy'. On his personal initiative a more traditional approach to the teaching of Russian history was adopted in the schools, and the militant, doctrinaire application of Marxism was expressly discouraged in a number of other fields. At the same time, the 'revolutionary' quality of life in the 'twenties was modified by a seeming restoration of certain conventional values (especially marked in family life), and 'class warfare' began to give way to some degree of social reconciliation. But by the time this changed attitude came to be enshrined in the new Constitution of 1936—vaunted as 'the most democratic in the world'—the

terror had begun. Stalin himself was soon calling for an intensifica-
tion of 'class warfare'.

To many writers, it at first seemed a positive step that the 'proletarian' literary organization known as RAPP was disbanded by
decree in 1932 and a 'Union of Soviet Writers' set up in place of all
previous literary groupings and associations. The so-called 'Fellow
Travellers' (that is, those who, like Pasternak, had 'accepted', but not
actively supported the Revolution) were henceforth to be recognized
as legitimate participants in the task of creating a Soviet literature
whose formal continuity with the classical tradition of the nineteenth
century was stressed in the new official doctrine of 'socialist realism'
(first launched in 1932). The rise of Hitler and the consequent policy
of seeking the support of non-Communist public opinion in the West
also seemed initially to work in favour of a 'liberal' approach to
writers and intellectuals in the Soviet Union. Stalin was not unaware
of the useful prestige to be derived from a show of tolerance for
writers such as Pasternak—who by now had a certain reputation in
the West as well. The avowed strategy was, in a word, to 'win over'
the hitherto uncommitted intelligentsia by displaying relative indulgence towards their past attitudes, and—even more importantly,
perhaps—by allowing them to share the material privileges of the
ruling élite.

During the 'thirties (particularly in the second half) the genuine
egalitarianism and informal social behaviour of the previous decade—
when even the leaders could occasionally be glimpsed walking in the
streets—yielded to an increasingly noticeable inequality in the
distribution of goods and services. High officials began to move about
in the sleek chauffeur-driven and discreetly curtained limousines
produced by the new Soviet automobile industry, and obtained their
supplies in special stores open only to them. Luxury apartment blocks
with their own private facilities were built in Moscow for various
groups of functionaries and they were also allotted *dachas* in the
beautiful wooded areas round Moscow. Members of the Union of
Writers gradually found themselves being co-opted into this new
'establishment' and given access to its bounties—including the
medical services of the Kremlin Hospital and its several branches.
Leading writers were offered apartments in a twelve-storey building
put up for them in one of Moscow's most pleasant streets, and *dachas*,
with generous allotments of surrounding land, were set aside for

them in the particularly agreeable country district of Peredelkino, about twenty kilometres south west of Moscow, and easily reached by train or road. In 1936 Pasternak settled here with Zinaida Niko-layevna, whom he had married two years before. (It is interesting to note that Peredelkino had been the estate of the family of Dmitri Samarin, Pasternak's friend from his student days who, as previously noted, was to some extent the prototype of Yuri Zhivago.)

After the difficult existence of earlier years it was perilously easy to succumb to such inducements. A few of Pasternak's friends and neighbours (such as the novelist Konstantin Fedin) found it impossible to resist the temptation of accepting important positions in the apparatus of the Union of Writers, which rapidly became one of the lesser but none the less beguiling avenues of power and influence, if not of glory, in the Soviet system. By the end of the 'thirties it had grown into an awesome corporation which watched over its mem-bers and administered literature on behalf of the state, making its views and wishes known through its newspaper, the *Literary Gazette*. In the 'twenties there had been several private or cooperative publish-ing firms and a number of journals representing the various compet-ing trends in literature, but all this had now come to an end. There was no longer any substantive difference between monthlies such as *Novy Mir* ('New World'), *Znamia* ('The Banner'), and others, and the publication of works of literature in book form was monopolized by *Goslitizdat* (an acronym formed from the Russian words meaning 'State Publishing House for Literature'), and several smaller enter-prises all under the same control. Overall supervision of culture and the arts was exercised by a department of the Party Central Commit-tee, and Stalin himself was notoriously inclined to keep a personal eye on them as well. During NEP censorship had been mainly concerned to prevent the open expression of political dissent and had in any case been relatively lax, but in the 'thirties strict editorial control and surveillance made actual censorship almost a formality: very little that was 'unacceptable' reached the anonymous officials who made the final check.

Whatever grounds there may have been for hopefulness in the early 'thirties vanished completely when the terror began in earnest in 1936-7. (It had started already after the assassination of Kirov in 1934, but it was not until the 'show trial' of Zinovyev and Kamenev in August 1936 that it developed into the frenzied campaign of extermination which literally decimated the Party and government apparatus, the military and the intelligentsia.) By this time Pasternak had certainly lost any illusions he may have had. He was shaken by the arrest of Osip Mandelstam in 1934, and after a further veiled attempt to 'reason' with Stalin in two extraordinary poems published in *Izvestia* at the very beginning of 1936, he drew the melancholy conclusions about the era that were eventually to lead him to the writing of *Doctor Zhivago*.

Ironically, just as he was irrevocably making up his mind as to the nature of the situation, he found that he was the object of attempts to lure him into the role of a literary public figure—a part he was evidently thought fitted for in view of his generally acknowledged status as the greatest surviving poet of his generation who was not in some way politically 'compromised' (like Akhmatova, by the execution of her husband as a counter-revolutionary, and Mandelstam, by his poem denouncing Stalin). In 1934 he was invited to take part in the First Congress of Soviet Writers, at which he heard his praises sung by the official Party spokesman. He knew perfectly well that he was being 'got at', and the behaviour of some of his fellow writers showed clearly enough what the price of giving in to such seductive approaches would be. In a remarkable letter written to his Czech translator at the end of 1935 (and first published in Prague in 1965), he wrote: 'All this time, beginning with the Writers' Congress in Moscow, I have had a feeling that, for purposes unknown to me, my importance is being deliberately inflated . . . all this by somebody else's hands, without asking my consent. And I shun nothing in the whole world more than fanfare, sensationalism, and so-called cheap "celebrity" in the press'.* In June, 1936 he was sent, against his will, as an official Soviet delegate to an international writers' congress in Paris (his last journey abroad). By now the general state of affairs in the country and the pressure on Pasternak to lend his name to it had brought him, as he says in 'An Essay in Autobiography', to 'the verge of mental illness'.

In the following year he resolved the ambiguity of his situation in a bold and unparalleled fashion. At another writers' meeting held in Minsk (February 1936), he told his assembled colleagues how profoundly he disagreed with their view of literature as something that

---

* As quoted by Olga R. Hughes in *The Poetic World of Boris Pasternak*, Princeton, 1974.

could simply be produced in the way one pumps water. He spoke of the need for a new Tolstoi capable of exposing their barren rhetoric for what it was. He then served notice, more or less in so many words, that he intended to part company from them. It was an astonishing performance, clearly born of desperation and occasionally marked by a caustic tone otherwise quite uncharacteristic of him ('I am not aware of anything in our legislation that forbids genius—if so, some of our leaders would have to forbid themselves'). Nothing like this was heard again from a public platform until long after Stalin's death —or at least it has not been recorded. He seemed to be deliberately inviting the virtual ostracism to which he was indeed subjected during the following years. A few months later such plain speaking could have cost him his liberty, or his life. Perhaps he was saved on this occasion by the mildly complimentary tone of his poetic 'message' to Stalin published in *Izvestia* the month before. At any rate, as Madame Ivinskaya makes clear in this book, there is little doubt that he survived the terror of 1936–8 (and then again the equally savage persecution of the intelligentsia in the post-war years) only because it was Stalin's personal whim not to allow his destruction.

After his Minsk outburst Pasternak was left more or less alone. There seem to have been no further serious efforts to draw him into the literary 'establishment'—and he was certainly never again invited to make a public speech. Yet at the same time he was allowed to retain the material privileges of membership in the Union of Writers, including the one he prized most: the house in Peredelkino, which served as a haven for the rest of his life. The chief disability he suffered was probably to experience greater difficulty in publishing original work. But it is likely that inspiration for lyrical poetry was in any case lacking during the second half of the 'thirties: after *Second Birth* he neither wrote nor published any verse to speak of except the *Izvestia* poems and a cycle on a second visit to Georgia which appeared in *Novy Mir* in October 1936. (These poems were subsequently attacked by Stavski, the secretary of the Union of Writers, who ominously denounced them as 'slander on the Soviet people'— part of the price Pasternak paid for his Minsk speech was that he was no longer relatively exempt from this kind of scurrilous abuse.)

Almost the only original work he published in the late 'thirties consisted of unfinished pieces of prose fiction (*From a New Novel about 1905*, 1937; *Journey to the Rear*, 1938; *Aunt Olia* and *The Proud Pauper*, 1939). All these foreshadow *Doctor Zhivago* and show how largely pre-occupied he now was by the themes and ideas which were to find their embodiment after the war in the novel he considered to be the ultimate justification of his whole life as a poet.

During the 'thirties he also turned increasingly to translation. Besides providing an independent means of livelihood, it also often served as an indirect way of giving public expression to what he himself thought or believed. His versions of a number of Georgian lyric poets came out in 1935, and in 1940 he published his *Selected Translations* (two Shakespeare sonnets, verse by Byron, Keats, Verlaine, and others). By the beginning of the war he had completed his version of *Hamlet*—which so pointedly conveyed his view of the times he lived in that he tended to look on it as an essential part of his own work. During and after the war he went on to translate other plays of Shakespeare which were eventually published in two volumes in 1950. (After the war he brought out the first full version of Goethe's *Faust* to be completed in the Soviet Union, and his rendering of Schiller's *Maria Stuart* achieved a notable success on the stage in 1957.)

The Nazi invasion of the Soviet Union in June 1941—as Pasternak was to put it in *Doctor Zhivago*—'broke the spell of the dead letter'. Demoralized and unprepared, the country at first suffered hideous defeats, but for Pasternak, as for many of his compatriots, the real terrors of war in a desperate struggle for national survival were almost welcome after the senseless horrors of 1936–9. As the war went on, and the tide began to turn, there was also a widespread conviction among Soviet citizens of all classes that there could be no reversal to the past.

In October 1941, when Moscow was threatened by the lightning German advance, Pasternak was evacuated, with many other members of the Union of Writers, to the small town of Chistopol on the river Kama—not very far from the places* where he had spent two winters during the First World War. He remained there for about a year with his wife and young son, Leonid (who had been born in 1937), but in 1942 returned to Moscow, where he lived for the remainder of the war. In his *Meetings with Pasternak*, Alexander Gladkov has drawn a most revealing portrait of him during those years. While he continued to work hard at his translations, he

* Including Yelabuga, where Marina Tsvetayeva committed suicide in 1941.

confided to Gladkov that he was anxious most of all to write and publish something of his own which would justify the hopes he believed were being placed in him by the many admirers of his poetry. One of the striking features of the wartime period was that people no longer felt totally afraid to speak their true thoughts and feelings to each other. In this franker atmosphere it was borne in on Pasternak that he would meet with an eager and grateful response if he could find some way of talking directly to his fellow countrymen. He began to regard it as his duty not only to help sustain their patriotism, hatred of the enemy, and will to victory (which he did in a series of poems published in the newspapers between 1941 and 1944), but also to voice their expectations of better times once there was peace again. He first tried to do this in a narrative poem, of which a fragment was even printed in *Pravda* in 1943, but he was forced to abandon it. A plan to write a play also came to nothing. But he vowed to Gladkov that if things did not change after the war, he would speak his mind, whatever it cost him.

Within a year and a half after the victory over Nazi Germany, all hopes for a relaxation in Stalin's régime were shattered (in August 1946) by the notorious Party decree denouncing Akhmatova and Zoshchenko—the first of a number of brutal measures deliberately aimed at reducing the Soviet intelligentsia to the same cowed state as before the war.

It was shortly after this that Pasternak met Olga Ivinskaya for the first time, and her book is a detailed account of the years that followed, until Pasternak's death in 1960. This eloquent, moving and often dramatic testimony gives an intimate portrait of him as he was during the last, crucial years of his life when he wrote *Doctor Zhivago*, and the magnificent verse that goes with it. Here he finally achieved the 'unheard-of simplicity' he had promised in *Second Birth*. Madame Ivinskaya was a direct source of inspiration to him in this crowning achievement: the heroine of the novel, Lara, is in many respects modelled on her, and a number of the poems are about her, or addressed to her.

For the most part *A Captive of Time* speaks for itself, but it may be helpful to give here a brief outline of the author's life, and of the structure of her book.

Olga Vsevolodovna Ivinskaya was born in 1912 in a provincial town where her father was a high school teacher. The family moved to Moscow in 1915. In 1933 she graduated from the Faculty of Literature of Moscow University. Her two marriages ended in tragedy: her first husband, by whom she had a daughter, Irina (born in 1938), committed suicide, and her second husband, the father of her son Mitia, died after an illness. During the War (in 1943), she began to work for the monthly literary journal *Novy Mir*, where she was in charge of the section for young authors. Soon after meeting Pasternak towards the end of 1946, she left the journal and became a free-lance translator of poetry, working in collaboration with him.

In October 1949 she was suddenly arrested and detained for many months in the Lubianka (the headquarters of the secret police) before being sentenced to five years in a forced labour camp.

Following Stalin's death in April 1953, she was released under amnesty, having served four years of her sentence, and came back to Moscow. She now resumed her life with Pasternak and their relationship ended only with his death in May 1960.

About two months later, in August 1960, she was arrested a second time and again held in the Lubianka under interrogation for several months. Her daughter Irina was also arrested. At a secret trial in Moscow on December 7, 1960, she was sentenced to eight years' forced labour, and Irina to three.

When news of this act of posthumous vengeance on Pasternak leaked out to the West, there was a world-wide outcry. The first official Soviet response came only in January of the following year, in a scurrilous English-language broadcast beamed to the West—by which time the two women had been transported to a camp in Siberia. The Soviet authorities were deaf to all pleas on their behalf. After a few years, however, both were quietly released: Irina in 1962, and her mother in 1964.

Since then Madame Ivinskaya has lived in Moscow, still working as a translator. She finished writing this book about her years with Pasternak in 1972.

PART I of *A Captive of Time* opens with an account of the author's first meeting with Pasternak (usually referred to by his initials as BL, for Boris Leonidovich, or by the diminutive form of his first name: 'Boria'), and then goes on to describe the several occasions on which she had previously seen him at public gatherings—

for the first time in her student days, long before the war. We are next told in some detail of their life and work together from 1946 until her arrest in the autumn of 1949, and then again during the later years after her return from the forced labour camp in 1953.

PART II gives the background essential to an understanding of how Pasternak came to his decision to write *Doctor Zhivago* and eventually to have it published in the West. We learn about his complicated view of Stalin, his shortlived attempts in the mid-thirties to come to terms with the system, his reaction to the terror of 1937–8 and to the war, and the shattering effect on him of Madame Ivinskaya's arrest and imprisonment in 1949, which is recounted in detail. After a description of his attitude to Stalin's successor, Nikita Khrushchev, and some observations on his feelings about race and religion, there are chapters on his relations with the four contemporaries who were most important to him as a poet, and whose voices form a counterpart to his own: Mayakovski, Mandelstam, Akhmatova and—most particularly—Tsvetayeva. (PART TWO is entitled 'The Poet and the Tsar'* because of the parallel between Pushkin's life under Nicholas I and Pasternak's under Stalin.)

PART III tells of how Pasternak began to write *Doctor Zhivago* in 1946, of how he sent the manuscript abroad ten years later, and of the way in which the Soviet authorities reacted by launching a systematic campaign of persecution against him after he was awarded the Nobel Prize in 1958. The true facts behind the letter of 're-pentance' which he was induced to write to Khrushchev are revealed for the first time.

PART IV deals with the last year of Pasternak's life—his attempt to pick up the threads of his previous existence as the open attacks on him died away and he was allowed, though still severely ostracized, to go on making a living by his work as a translator; his relations with his family and some of his friends in the strained atmosphere after the *Zhivago* affair; and his work on a play, *The Blind Beauty*. The book ends with a description of Pasternak's death and funeral, and of what happened to the author and her daughter shortly afterwards.

Max Hayward

* The title of a poem about Pushkin written by Tsvetayeva in 1931.

Many years will go by. Many great years. I shall then no longer be alive. There will be no return to the times of our fathers and grandfathers. This would, indeed, be both undesirable and unnecessary. But at last there will appear once more things that have long lain dormant: noble, creative and great things. It will be a time of final accounting. Your life will be rich and fruitful as never before.

Think of me then.

Boris Pasternak

(Translation from the German original reproduced in facsimile in Gerd Ruge's *Pasternak*, Munich, 1958, p. 125)

FOREWORD

Every great poet has no doubt been conscious of the tragic disparity between the mere time in which his life must be lived, and the eternity to which his work belongs. Even an uncommon talent can be stifled and withered by the cares of everyday life to which he is captive, by the rabble of timeservers and intriguers who surround him, by the crassness of ordinary existence.

One of those who had a particularly tragic awareness of the gulf between Time and Eternity was Boris Pasternak:

> You are eternity's hostage,
> A captive of time.*

He knew that his poetry would remain after the age in which he lived had gone by, and that, escaping from time's captivity, it would pass into the future—as Pushkin's poetry has into our day.

All the same, however, he was anxious that something of his life as a 'captive of time' should be recorded for posterity. In his last years he often said to me: 'You must go on living. You must give the lie to all the falsehoods which have been woven around me.'

He could not foresee, alas, that the events of my life were to take a turn which would prevent me from fulfilling his wish for many years.

Those long years are now behind me, but in the meantime things which once seemed completely unforgettable have begun to grow dim in the memory, or to fade from it altogether.

For this reason it is not my aim to attempt a literary or biographical portrait, a study of Pasternak's life and work. All I wish to do is to protect his name from false conjectures, to defend his honour and dignity, and my own as well. I am aware that any individual view of another person cannot be the whole truth. There are people who saw Pasternak in a different light. If they also write down their memories of him, I shall read with interest—and perhaps with pleasure—what they have to say about the Pasternak whom they knew.

* From the poem 'Night' (1957). (Tr.)

But as I now begin my account of the fourteen years I spent at his side and look back on my own calamity-filled life, I hope I can claim to have earned the right to speak of the Boris Pasternak *I* knew, and to record the truth about him as *I* see it.

Olga Ivinskaya

PART I
Novy Mir

Pushkin Square: 1946

In October 1946, *Novy Mir** moved from the fourth floor of the *Izvestia* building to new premises round the corner, on Pushkin Square. In what had been the ball-room, and now served as the office and reception hall of our new residence, the young Pushkin had once danced.

At the time of the move, the wrought-iron statue of Pushkin had still not been shifted from its original spot on Tverskoi Boulevard to the new site where it now stands, almost invisible against the background of the modernist new cinema 'Russia' (this glass palace had still not been built).

The move meant a change of scene—from our windows we could now see, instead of the Square, the little Church of the Virgin 'In the Lanes'; its pilasters ended at the bottom in funny, awkward-looking paws which rested on the pavement in front.

But this was not the only change. At the same time, the journal got a new editor.

He came in, leaning on a stout walking stick and wearing a jaunty cap of some shaggy material. This was Simonov. He hung up his raincoat—of stylish American cut—very different from Shcherbina's black naval greatcoat. He had enormous signet rings on his fingers. He probably found our new office much to his taste: it was painted a rich dark-red and had egregious guilded cornices. Simonov was the dream of all the women of Moscow, as though his famous cycle of poems *With You and Without You* was addressed to each of them personally. He rolled his 'r's' enchantingly in the French manner, had a rich mane of hair already silvery-grey like a beaver skin, and wore a loose-fitting American-style suit of the latest fashion. He loved to receive representatives of our Western allies,† as well as friends he had made not long ago at the front during the war.

He was the first to be given a magnificently decorated private office of his own. For the time being we others, his deputies, did not have separate rooms. I, who was in charge of the section for new

* *Novy Mir* (New World): leading Soviet literary monthly founded in 1925. (Tr.)

† The small colony of Western diplomats, journalists and others living in Moscow were at this time not yet cut off from all local contacts, as happened in the following year (1947), when the 'Cold War' began in earnest. (Tr.)

authors, and my friend Natasha Bianchi, the production manager, sat next to each other at the back of the reception hall. Young authors had to walk timidly across the whole vast length of the hall to reach me at my desk. Often, when Natasha was not doing the rounds of the printing presses, we were visited by old friends we had got to know in the other premises. Life went on as before, rewarding us with new acquaintances, sympathies and attachments, or taking previous ones away. The young, slim and fair-haired Yevgeni Yevtushenko came here with an exercise book full of poetry, written out in semi-capital letters, like a child's. The beautiful Bella Akhmadulina, with rosy cheeks and brown eyes, also turned up here. She breathed an extraordinary freshness, and her favourite colour was salmon-pink. Veronika Tushnova would come in and sit at my desk. She always smelled seductively of good scent, and raised her sculpted eyelids like a Galatea coming to life. We were old friends. Her first husband, the psychiatrist Roginsky, had saved my two-year-old son from meningitis. I still have the picture she gave me of herself with a tender inscription: 'To my dear, kind, understanding and wonderful one. With love, Veronika.' We also shared our intimate secrets.

The boisterous and impulsive Antokolski dashed in and out to see us. We were visited by Zabolotski, his hair slicked down and parted in a slanting line, so unlike the poet who had once described the frenzied signs of the Zodiac—he was much more subdued after his years in the camps. Once Zoshchenko came in, spruced up and still youthfully erect, but sallow-faced with dark shadows under his eyes, and wearing a light-fawn raincoat. It was after all the fuss about him in the newspapers. Simonov received him with open arms, and later reproved me for not immediately announcing his arrival. How impressed we were by the courage of our new editor-in-chief! But it soon turned out that his 'courage' was sanctioned from above.

(Later on, when Pasternak began coming to see us, he once saw Yuri Sher, a translator from French, sitting at my desk, and said in his deep, booming voice: 'This young man reminds me very much of poor Mikhail Mikhailovich Zoshchenko.'* We all looked down at the floor and pretended not to have heard.)

There were many others: Sasha Pismenny, who had been a fellow

* See the note on Mikhail Mikhailovich Zoshchenko in the Biographical Guide at the end of the book, where notes on most other persons mentioned by the author will also be found. (Tr.)

student of mine; Ilya Frenkel, the husband-to-be of Natasha Bianchi; my old friend Sasha Shpirt; the strikingly elegant Nikolai Asanov, adored at that time by both Natasha and myself, who brought carnations to put on my desk; Aliosha Nedogonov, modest and likeable, always in sports shoes, who often brought kagor* from the nearby drug-store and sat drinking it with us; the stern-faced Lukonin; the aimiable Oshanin who would sit for a long time and recite his poetry to us. (At that time he relied very much on my influence with the journal, which had already published his long poem on his friend Boris and gladly accepted his new verses); Mezhirov, with the innocent, rush-coloured eyes of a marsh rusalka, still in his heavy army boots and greatcoat, who read us his beautiful war poems, at first stammering to get the words out, but then taking the plunge, as though diving into water, and swimming along with the greatest of ease.

There was no end to the visitors, both famous and unknown, who came to see us in the Novy Mir office. Some we had inherited from Shcherbina, the previous editor: Boris Solovyev, and our particular favourite, Yan Sashin with his beautiful eyes, like a woman's; and his friend Raskin, decent to the point of being boring, and obviously much attracted to Natasha. Then there were Osip Chorny, Antonovskaya, Mikhalkov, Sergei Vasilyev, and finally, Dmitri Sedykh, who also placed great hopes for his literary future in me. Sergei Vasilyev often invited me to the beer hall which had just been opened on the corner of Strastnaya Square next door to us, and where there was also much discussion of literary business. And all day long we talked about poetry, with one visitor after another—we were head over heels in it. This was the half-famished, but cheerful and youthfully innocent time just after the war, when many things were yet to be revealed and hopes were still high.

At the beginning of his editorship Simonov was very anxious to attract 'living classics': Antokolski, Pasternak, Chukovski, Marshak. It was thanks to him that I met Pasternak. Very soon after Simonov's appointment, our secretary, Zinaida Nikolayevna Piddubnaya, an elderly Hutsul† of whose former beauty nothing remained but her black almond eyes and slender neck (on account of which we gave

* A Soviet imitation of the sweet wine of Cahors, France. (Tr.)

† Member of a small ethnic group in the Carpathians. (Tr.)

her the unkindly nickname of 'The Snake') presented me with a ticket to an evening in the library of the Historical Museum at which Pasternak was to read from his translations. I had not seen him since before the war. I returned from the reading after midnight, and I remember saying to my mother, who was angry at having to get up and open the door for me: 'Leave me alone, I've just been talking to God!' With an impatient wave of her hand she went back to bed.

The next day at work I could talk of nothing else to Natasha. But she was in no mood to listen and made some rather scathing remarks about it all. She often made fun of the way some of us were always mouthing poetry, as though intoxicated by it. I had to mull over my impressions of the evening by myself.

It was, I suppose, the first time I had seen Pasternak at such close range. He was tall and trim, extraordinarily youthful, with the strong neck of a young man, and he spoke in a deep, low voice, conversing with the audience as one talks with an intimate friend or communes with oneself, sometimes fumbling lines or going over them again. In the intermission some privileged people summoned up the courage to ask him to read work of his own, but in his nasal voice, drawing out the words (which ended on an extraordinary kind of mooing note), he said he really couldn't because the evening was supposed to be devoted to Shakespeare, not to himself. He evidently did read his own poetry to those who stayed on afterwards. But I didn't dare to join them, and left.

Until I was to meet him at *Novy Mir*, I had seen him only a very few times. Once, funnily enough, in the days when I had been a member of a literary group for young people at the Komsomol magazine *Smena*, and had been invited with the others by the lordly Georgian Gamsakhurdia to his room in the Metropole Hotel, I fled when I heard he was expecting Pasternak—it was already past one in the morning. Perhaps it was premonition? I was so panicstricken at the thought of sitting at the same table with Pasternak that I ran away like a little girl, followed by Pavel Vasilyev and Smeliakov—who naturally returned to the Metropole after gallantly seeing me home.

On another occasion, while I was still at the Faculty of Literature, a fellow-student called Nika Kholmin, with whom I had my first serious affair, took me over to Herzen House★ (Bulgakov's famous

★ A centre for writers and journalists in Moscow during the 'twenties. It is satirized by Mikhail Bulgakov in *The Master and Margarita*. (Tr.)

'Massolit'), where a crowd of excited enthusiasts were waiting for the
young, tempestuous Pasternak, then still full of the passions and scars
of *My Sister Life*, and already forging ahead *Above the Barriers*★ of
literary tradition. He was supposed to recite 'Marburg'. His raven-
black hair was all ruffled. His response to the applause was mumbled
and rather ill-humoured—he must have been upset by something
that had happened offstage. In the intermission Kholmin said he
would take me up to get a closer view of him and led me into the
corridor, but at that moment the bell rang, and the only thing that
now remains in my memory from the whole evening is a fleeting
glimpse of the nervous, black-haired poet hurrying past me in the
corridor. I decided he must just the moment before have torn himself
away from a passionate embrace, which had left him dishevelled and
on fire. I fancied I heard the sound of rapturous kisses still pursuing
him as he walked to the stage, and this strange echo seemed to linger
in my ears as Nika whisked me back into the hall: so he had been
kissing one of his admirers—probably that one over there, now sitting
in the second row in her enormous wide-brimmed hat! (Subsequently
he denied it all: 'How could you think such a thing, Olia . . .')

When the reading was over, Pasternak was surrounded by the
crowd. A handkerchief belonging to him was torn in shreds, and the
remaining crumbs of tobacco in his cigarette butts were snatched
up. Very many years later, when he and I were driving home in a car
with Ehrenburg after a reading at the Polytechnic Museum at which
he was received with similar wild enthusiasm, Ehrenburg said to
him: 'I hope to God you will not have to pay for this scandalous
success, Boria!'[1]

The first picture I saw of Pasternak in those distant days was the
one in the slender volume of his *Selected Poetry*. This shows him with
a disproportionately elongated face, a nose too short, and negroid
lips. In general Pasternak never comes out well when caught with the
fixed expression of his portrait photographs. They are quite mislead-
ing because they fail to convey the inner fire that constantly played
over his face, the spontaneous, child-like gestures. I realized this when
he first came to our *Novy Mir* office, at Simonov's invitation, and I
saw him as he was at his most natural.

How did he strike me at that moment? He really was almost
completely unlike his photographs—though the fine aristocratic

★ The title of Pasternak's second volume of poetry, published in 1917. (Tr.)

hooked nose was indeed a little short for his face, with its strong, stubborn, and virile jaw, the jaw of a leader. One could well believe that his kisses were made 'with his lips' brass'. His complexion was dark and rosy—the tan of a healthy man. His eyes were the amber colour of an eagle's. Yet with all this he had a feminine elegance about him too. A strange African god in European dress; or perhaps the god to whom Gumilev's Tibetan priests burned their fires?[2]

This god, then, appeared before me, one changeable October day, in our dark-red room. He stood there on the carpet and smiled at me.

Back in those days, in the 'forties, his extraordinary face was still distinguished by another striking and splendid feature: his long, yellowish teeth, like those of a horse, with wide gaps between them in front. I find it hard to write of him as he was in 1946 because he was to become even more classically handsome (much to his own child-like joy) rather late in life, when his African jaw was remodelled thanks to our all-powerful modern technology, and those teeth of his, so unlike anyone else's, were replaced—how hard it was to get used to!—by a perfect set of false ones made abroad. Admittedly, he was no longer able to complain with his usual coyness about the ugliness which had allegedly plagued him all his life. Indeed, by the last year of his life, admiring himself in the mirror, delighted at the unaccustomed magnificence of his appearance and now thoroughly wedded to the idea of his new teeth, as if they had been with him always, he would say, slightly putting it on both to himself and me: 'How late it has all come—good looks, and fame!' Though he didn't really think it was too late . . .

But at that moment long ago, as he first entered my life, walking up the long carpet to my desk, I was struck by the rather outlandish, not quite regular, yet clear-cut way in which his features were carved—evidently by a prodigy ignorant of the laws of proportion. This sculptor of genius had made a man of no particular race, with bright, slightly slanted eyes under brows arching steeply to the temples, a man designed to walk the landscape of the whole wide world. It was an appearance completely to his own taste, and only a small technical modification was needed—a slight scaling down of the jaw and the insertion of evenly placed American teeth between those thick copper lips of an ancient divinity—to produce the Pasternak of the 'fifties.

But at that moment, it was the Pasternak of 1946 who walked into our office.

I was standing by the window, Natasha and I were just about to go off to lunch. Coquettishly holding out her hand for him to kiss, Zinaida Piddubnaya said: 'Boris Leonidovich, let me introduce one of your most ardent admirers'. And now there he was at my desk by the window, the most unstinting man in the world, to whom it had been given to speak in the name of the clouds, the stars and the wind, who had also found eternal words to say about man's passion and woman's weakness. What happiness to partake of such soaring flights and giddy descents—up to the gardens of the stars and down with them again through the gullet into which they flow, swallowed by the nightingales of all the nights of love that ever were! People said that he summoned the stars to his table, and the whole world to the carpet at his bed-side.

But what do I care if this is what other people used to say! I now said it afresh for myself, repeating it for my own ears alone. What happiness, and horror, and turmoil he was to bring into my life, this man . . .

A fine, driving October snow began to fall. I put on my pre-war squirrel coat. It was cold in the room. Pasternak bent over my hand and asked what books of his I had. All I had was one large volume of his collected poetry, inscribed for me by the literary critic Boris Solovyev (part of Shcherbina's legacy to the journal) with the words: 'To Olia from Boris—but not the Boris she loves, the author of this book . . .' A silly joke, but I must say this 'other' Boris had an amazing knowledge of the one I loved! Although Nika Kholmin had already made great efforts to educate me and had succeeded in giving me a feeling for Pasternak's images, even if I didn't understand them, Solovyev also played his part and, despite long since having fallen out with him over his views and tastes, I am still grateful to him for this. He had a phenomenal memory and could recite the most difficult of Pasternak's poems by heart, and delighted in teaching me how to unravel the magical skeins of the metaphors—you just pulled at a thread and they came untangled!

So I told Boris Leonidovich I had only one of his books. He looked surprised: 'Oh, I'll get you some others—though I've given almost all my copies away . . . I'm doing translations nowadays and writing hardly any poems of my own. I'm working on Shakespeare. And you know, I've started on a novel—though I'm not yet sure what kind of a thing it will turn out to be. I want to go back to the old Moscow—which you don't remember—and talk about art, and put down some thoughts.' Then, I remember, he added a little awkwardly: 'How interesting that I still have admirers.' I don't remember exactly what I replied to this, but when Natasha called out to me to go to lunch, I snapped back at her: 'Wait a moment, can't you see I'm busy?' 'Oh, to hell with you,' she said nastily, and went off to lunch by herself.

Pasternak did not stay much longer. He had a word about something with Piddubnaya, kissed the hands of us both, and left.

There is no doubt that one has premonitions—and not merely in the sense of anticipating great changes of some kind or other. I was simply shaken by the sense of fate when my 'god' looked at me with his penetrating eyes. The way he looked at me was so imperious, it was so much a man's appraising gaze that there could be no mistake about it: here he was, the one person I needed more than any other, the very one who was in actual fact already part of me. A thing like this is stunning, a miracle.

I went home, as once before, feeling terribly dazed.

At home I had my mother and two children: my daughter Ira, now seven years old, and a chubby, curly-headed son, Mitia. I had already gone through more than enough horrors: the suicide of Ira's father, my first husband Ivan Vasilyevich Yemelyanov; the death of my second husband, Alexander Petrovich Vinogradov—who had died in my arms in hospital. Then there had been my mother's three years' imprisonment—a quite unexpected and ridiculous business (she had said something about Stalin to somebody). I had had many passing affairs, and disappointments in love.

But all this, it seemed, had probably been a necessary prelude, enabling me to grasp all the more clearly the meaning of the uniquely important and foreordained thing that had happened: the magician who had first entered my life so long ago, when I was sixteen, had now come to me in person, living and real.

How one begins to live by Poetry: Early Years

In my adolescent years my friends at school and everybody else of my age were infatuated with Pasternak. It was Nika Kholmin who first brought his poetry to me. Many a time I wandered along the street that spring, repeating the seductive lines over and over to myself, though their meaning sometimes escaped me.

Closing his dark-blue eyes and tossing back his golden locks, whose resemblance to Yesenin's was deliberately cultivated, Kholmin read me poems from *My Sister Life* and *Above the Barriers*, and it seemed as though he was in a high fever—raving in astonishing words borrowed from someone else's delirium. I still remember how struck I was by the tragic admission of the wanderer in the night:

> This is not the right city, nor yet the right midnight
> And you who bear its message are on the wrong road!

I did not dare admit, as I gazed awestruck into Kholmin's face, that half of it made little sense to me. But I already knew instinctively that these were the words of a god, of the all-powerful 'god of detail' and 'god of love'.

Later there was my first journey to the South and to the sea. Seeing me off at the station, Kholmin gave me a small volume of Pasternak's prose. Lilac-coloured and shaped like an elongated school exercise book, in a binding rough to the touch, it was *The Childhood of Luvers*. Lying on the upper bunk of my sleeping compartment, I again found myself stubbornly trying to fathom a most unusual thing: how could a man have such insight into a young girl's secret world?

After arriving at the sanatorium in Sochi, I often sat by myself reading this extraordinary book. It was then that I wrote in a silly, girlish poem:

> Pasternak's prose, added to my dreams
> Billows cloudlike at my table...

I still cannot understand how I could already feel such a strong urge, as a school-girl, to immerse myself in the deep waters of this unbelievably intricate and original writing. I was simply drawn to it.

I had grown up on Gumilev and one of his lines that had particularly caught my fancy seemed to me at that time to apply very well to

Pasternak: 'Poet, you are granted the gift of sublime inarticulacy . . .'
Later on I found that Boris Leonidovich got very irritated when
people put down the supposed impossibility of deciphering his
immensely complicated poetic hieroglyphs to 'inarticulacy'. He
believed a person could lack feeling for their hidden clarity and interconnection only if he was deaf to poetry, or so blinded by literary
tradition as to be unable to unlock with his own key all the images
and metaphors which seemed so hermetic to him at first sight—and
if he couldn't manage it, why go off and write an article putting the
blame for his own shortcomings on the poet!

At that time, like many others, I was fascinated by the mystery of
something still to be explored, or inaccessible to me. We often found
it hard to understand Pasternak's poetic images because we were
unprepared for them, being too much under the spell of tradition.
But the answers were already in the air all around us. Spring could
be recognized by its 'little bundle of laundry/of a patient leaving
hospital'. Those 'candle-drippings' stuck on the branches in spring-
time did not have to be called 'buds'; and 'the aspen leaf without
lips', or the 'piles of a garden' holding back the sky—it was all
amazingly clear! It was sorcery and a miracle, and may indeed have
been the 'inarticulacy' granted to a great poet. It gave you the feeling
of personally discovering something hitherto unknown and locked
away by a god behind a closed door. Your hands were still too timid
and weak to receive such gifts, but at least a connection had been
established between the great dispenser of them and the timid
recipient.

In my small room in Potapov Street*, I made my first steps
towards understanding these complexities—which later on resolved
themselves into astonishingly precise and simple revelations . . .

* Street in central Moscow, near Chistye Prudy ('Clear Ponds') Boulevard. The
author's family lived here on the top floor of a six-storey apartment building.' (Tr.)

But to return to 1946, a year that was so momentous for me.

The day after our first encounter in the office, I came back to our red-painted room rather later than usual from a meeting of the editorial board, to be greeted by Zinaida Piddubnaya, sitting there at her secretary's post by the door: 'Your admirer called. Look what he's brought you.' On my desk I found a parcel wrapped in newspaper: five slim volumes of his poems and translations.

After this everything began to proceed at a furious pace. He phoned almost every day and, instinctively fearing to meet or talk with him, yet dying of happiness, I would stammer out that I was 'busy today'. But almost every afternoon, towards the end of working hours, he came in person to the office and often walked with me through the streets, boulevards and squares all the way home to Potapov Street. 'Shall I make you a present of this square?' he would ask. 'You don't want it?' But I did . . .

Once he called me at the office and asked: 'Couldn't you give me some telephone number, your neighbour's for example? I'd like to ring you in the evenings, as well as during the day.' I had to give him the number of Olga Nikolayevna Volkova who lived in the apartment below us on the same staircase. I had never done anything like this before.

And now, in the evenings, I would hear a knocking on the hotwater pipe and know it was Olga Nikolayevna calling me to the phone.

Once, during an endless discussion of some very abstruse subject, he managed (a little slyly, as though just by the by) to slip in something to the effect that despite his 'hideous looks' he had often been 'a cause of heartbreak'. But at the moment, he gave me to understand, he was going through the same kind of thing he went through many years ago, when he had been obliged to work as a private tutor to a certain young lady called V.[3] He had told the story in *Safe Conduct*, and I reminded him a little of this first love of his. It was she of whom he had written that he had learned her 'off by heart, like a play of Shakespeare, from the combs in the hair to the tips of the toes'. It was her rejection of him that had made him break into sobs and exclaim: How beautiful you are! . . . Why go on?

Come to your senses! It's over. You're not wanted.

V's relatives were alarmed by the young poet's lack of firm prospects and got her to turn him down. They say that she died in poverty.

'I hope you will never weep over me,' BL* now said to me, 'but our meeting will not be without its effect—both on you and on me.' When I got home, I wrote him a poem:

> Hardly had I forced my eyes open,
> still only half-seeing from our first day,
> than that one who once refused her love
> came between you and me . . .
> The telephone wires, tautly stretched,
> carried overhead, above this city
> that does not believe in God, the
> story, like a storm, of your young love . . .

and so on in the same vein.

The conversations we had during our long walks half-way across Moscow were very disjointed, and it would scarcely have been possible to make any record of them. He needed someone to talk to, and the moment I arrived home I would hear a metallic tapping on the pipe leading to the radiator and rush downstairs to go on listening at the point where he had left off, while the children stared after me in bewilderment.

One day I had a telephone call at *Novy Mir* from a very pleasant-sounding young woman whose voice I did not recognize. It was someone by the name of Liusia Popova calling on behalf of BL. Not long afterwards she came to see me at home. She was tiny, fair-haired, and doll-like, with the face of an an angel by Leonardo. (Liusia Popova had been a student of acting at the Moscow Institute of Drama, and later became a painter. In 1944, after an evening of poetry reading at the Polytechnic Museum, she had waited for Pasternak at the exit and gone up to him to make his acquaintance. But she was overcome by embarrassment and fright, and began to stammer out something quite incomprehensible. BL introduced his son to her and then said, with a smile of encouragement—as though assuring her it was just as hard for him to get his words out: 'I am tired, and can't speak to you now, please excuse me. Here is my telephone number. Call me, and we'll meet and have a talk. All the

* Boris Leonidovich—Pasternak's first name and patronymic. (Tr.)

best'. And even after he had started to walk away, he turned round and repeated: 'You really must call me—Wednesday is the best day...')

Much later she told the story behind her phone call to me: 'I got a postcard from BL asking me to come and see him because he very much needed to talk with me. I went and found him looking like the picture of an unfaithful husband. "You know, Liusia," he said, beaming all over, "I'm in love". "But how will this affect your life, Boris Leonidovich?" I asked, imagining the look on Zinaida Niko-layevna's* face when she heard. "But what is life?" he answered. "What is life if not love? And she is so enchanting, such a radiant, golden person. And now this golden sun has come into my life, it is so wonderful, so wonderful. I never thought I would still know such joy. She works at *Novy Mir*. I would very much like you to tele-phone her and then go and see her." "Of course I will see her," I said. So I called you at *Novy Mir*.'

'My life, my angel ...'

In the New Year, on January 4, 1947, I got a note from him:

Once again I send you all best wishes from the bottom of my heart. Wish me godspeed (cast a spell over me in your thoughts!) with the revision of *Hamlet* and *1905*, and a new start on my work.

You are very marvellous, and I want you to be well.

B.P.

This was the first note from him—the first time words in his hand, so much like cranes soaring over the page, had come flying to me ... But there was a slight coolness in the wafting of their wings: sub-consciously I had been expecting something more, warmer words than these. That 'new start on my work' sounded suspicious. Was it by way of warding me off?...

So there I was at our New Year's table with the children, my mother, and Dmitri Ivanovich (my step-father) ... And this first note.

In the meantime I was beginning to have trouble in the office. I had gone a little further than anyone expected in speaking up for the

* Pasternak's wife. (Tr.)

verse of Zabolotski, who had recently been released from a camp. To make matters worse, I had had several clashes with Simonov's deputy, Krivitski, over an abortive new section in the journal originally proposed by Simonov: it was to have been called 'Literary Moments' and the idea was to invite living poets to send us verse they had written 'on the spur of the moment' and had then put away in their desk drawers.

Pasternak, I remember, brought us 'Winter Night' ('Snow swept over the earth . . .') written after a visit we had made together to Maria Veniaminovna Yudina.* I also remember how furious we were, Lidia Chukovskaya (at that time a literary adviser to *Novy Mir*) and I. Simonov had promised to publish it, but had not done so. Pacing his office nervously, he told us he would give five years of his life to have written 'Winter Night'. But he nevertheless did not publish it, and the new section in fact came to nothing. (On the other hand, the candle from 'Winter Night' began to light up repeatedly in Simonov's own verse of that period . . .)

I couldn't refrain from telling BL about my difficulties at work. My colleagues realized that my relations with him had gone a stage beyond the normal ones between editor and author. Krivitski had begun making remarks such as 'I wonder where it will end, this little game of yours with Pasternak?' At the same time he kept trying to flirt with me, as he did with all the women in the office.

When I told all this to BL, perhaps exaggerating a little in my distress, he was indignant: 'You must clear out of there at once. I will make it my business to see you are looked after'.

The next day he called me at the office and said in a rather distraught tone: 'I have to see you at once to tell you two very important things. Can you walk over to the Pushkin statue?'

When I got to the statue, our usual meeting place, BL was already pacing up and down in great agitation. In a tone of voice quite unlike his normal one, he said: 'Don't look at me for a moment while I tell you briefly what I want: I want you to say 'thou' to me, because 'you' is by now a lie . . .†'

'I cannot call you "thou", Boris Leonidovich,' I pleaded with him. 'It's just impossible for me, I'm afraid still . . .'

---

* Famous pianist. See Biographical Guide. (Tr.)

† As in French and other European languages, 'thou' is commonly used as the familiar form of address. (Tr.)

'No, no! You'll get used to it . . . Very well, then, go on saying "you" to me for the time being, but let me call you "thou" . . .'

All confused I went back to my office . . . I had a feeling that something very crucial was still to come before the day was over!

At about nine in the evening I heard the familiar tapping on the hot-water pipe in our apartment . . .

'I didn't get to the second thing I wanted to tell you,' I heard him say in an agitated, hollow tone of voice, 'and you didn't ask me what it was. Well, the first thing was that we should say 'thou' to each other. The second thing was: *I love you.* I love you, and this is my whole life now. I won't come to your office tomorrow, but to your house instead—I'll wait outside for you to come down, and we'll walk round the town.'

I went back upstairs to our apartment, in great torment, and sat down to write him, with utmost frankness and not sparing myself in the least, a letter—or rather, not a letter, but a confession which filled a whole school exercise book.

I described how my first husband Yemelyanov had hanged himself because of me, and how I had then married his rival and enemy Vinogradov. There were many rumours about Vinogradov. He seemed a charming, generous person, but some people alleged it was none other than he who had written a lying denunciation of my mother, saying she had 'slandered the Leader' in a conversation in her apartment—as a result of which my poor mother had spent three years in a camp during the war, the most terrible and hungry years of all. But even so I had stayed with Vinogradov—we had a small son, and he treated Ira like his own daughter—and it was only with his death that this nightmare had come to an end. (I only went out to look for my mother after his death. I travelled without a ticket, in a soldier's greatcoat, to the terrible station known as Sukho-Bezvodnaya.[4] I took her the special ration I received as a blood donor, and even managed to get her out of the place after she was released as an invalid incapable of work—such a thing was still possible then. I brought her back illegally, more dead than alive, to Moscow. Life was one endless horror: deaths, suicides . . .)

'If you have been a cause of tears,' I wrote—still addressing him as 'you'—'so have I! Judge for yourself the things I have to say in reply to your "I love you"—which gives me more joy than anything that has ever happened to me . . .'

The next day, when I went down, BL was already waiting by the abandoned fountain in our courtyard. There was a comic little incident. Consumed by curiosity, my mother came after me to look out of the window on our landing, but she leaned out so far that when I got down, BL said to me in some alarm: 'A woman up there nearly fell out of the window just now . . .'

Our meeting was brief this time: BL could not wait to read my exercise book.

By half-past eleven that night I was summoned by a knock on the pipe and was greeted in the downstairs apartment by a rather grumpy Olga Nikolayevna: 'Of course I called you, Olia, but it's late, and Mikhail Vladimirovich has already gone to bed.' I felt terribly embarrassed but did not have the heart to tell BL not to ring at such an hour. The sound of his voice at once made up for it: 'Olia, I love you. I try to spend my evenings alone now, and I think of you sitting in your office—where for some reason I always imagine there must be mice—and of the way you worry about your children. You have come tripping right into my life. This note-book will always be with me, but you must keep it for me—I dare not leave it at home in case it is found there.'

And so I kept the note-book with my 'confession'. Two years later, after my arrest, it found its way into the hands of my interrogator.

In this manner BL and I crossed a boundary-line beyond which there was nothing else for us except to come together completely. But the obstacles seemed insuperable.

It was a period of endless discussions between us as we wandered round the dark streets of Moscow. Several times we parted never intending to meet again. But it was impossible for us not to meet again.

I was living with my mother, her husband Dmitri Ivanovich Kostko, and my two children by different fathers who were both long since dead. Because of the war they would have had no proper childhood at all if Dmitri Ivanovich had not cared for them like his own. But all the same, not having a real father had told on them— particularly on the older one, Irina.

The day came when my children saw BL for the first time. I remember how Irina, stretching out her thin little arm to hold on to the table, recited one of his poems to him. It was a difficult one, and Lord knows when and how she had managed to learn it:

You, so concerned with our balance sheet,
With the drama of the SCPE
Who used to sing like the Flying Dutchman
Over the gangway of whatever verse you like.

A sailcloth tempest of tents
Billowed out, a flooding Dvina★
Of movement when you, oh winged one,
Came alongside me gunwale to gunwale.

And you go on prating of oil?
While I, lost and bewildered,
Dream of a therapeutist
Who could restore your fury to you.

I know: your way is your own.
But how could you fetch up
Under such workhouse vaults
On your so authentic path?[5]

BL wiped away a tear and kissed her: 'What extraordinary eyes she has! Look at me, Ira. You could go straight into my novel!' The description of Katenka, Lara's daughter in *Doctor Zhivago*, is a portrait of her: 'A little girl of about eight came in, her hair done up in finely braided plaits. Her narrow eyes had a sly, mischievous look and went up at the corners when she laughed.'

But BL was tormented by his feelings about his own family and, torn between us and them, did not know what to do. He told me over and over again that whenever he went home and found his no longer young wife waiting for him, he thought of Little Red Riding-hood abandoned in the forest and just could not get out the words he had rehearsed in his mind about how he wished to leave her. He made it quite clear, incidentally, that I had nothing to do with his indifference towards her—not only indifference, but even fear of her iron character and voice. 'She comes from the family of a gendarme colonel,' he told me with a sigh. The present state of affairs had begun long before he met me. The whole thing sounded rather preposterous: 'It was just my fate,' he explained, 'and I realized my mistake during my first year together with Zinaida Nikolayevna. The fact is that it

★ River in Russia and Latvia, noted for the spring floods (sometimes a mile across) in its lower course. (Tr.)

was not her I really liked, but Garrik'—as he called her first husband, Genrikh Gustavovich Neigaus—because I was so captivated by the way he played the piano. At first he wanted to kill me, the strange fellow, after she left him. But later on he was very grateful to me!' This was just like BL and it is quite possible that what he really fell for was indeed Neigaus's playing on the piano, fancying that the moment of bliss it gave him could only have been inspired by passionate love for a woman! It meant the break-up of two families. Though it was no easy matter, BL left his first wife, Yevgenia Vladimirovna and their small son, and set up house with Zinaida Nikolayevna—and 'in this hell', as he put it, he had now been living for more than ten years. He told me all this with such anguish that there was no question of not believing him—which I was ready enough to do in any case!

On April 3, 1947, we sat up until midnight in my tiny room, alternating between elation and despair. Our parting was sad: BL said he had no right to love. The good things in life were not for him. He was a man of duty and I must not deflect him from his set way of life—and his work. But all the same he would look after me for the rest of his life.

I could not sleep that night. I kept going out on the balcony, listening to the sounds of daybreak, and watching the streetlamps grow dim under the still young lime trees of Potapov Street . . . It was of these that he was to write later:

> Like gauze butterflies the streetlamps,
> Touched by the morning, trembled . . .

At six in the morning the doorbell rang. It was BL. He had gone out to his house in the country and then come back and walked the streets of Moscow all night. We embraced in silence . . .

It was Friday, April 5, 1947. My mother and her husband went off with the children for a day's outing to Pokrovskoye-Streshnevo.* As newly-weds spend their first night together, BL and I now had our first day together. I ironed his crumpled trousers. He was borne up and jubilant over this victory. It is indeed true that 'there are marriages more mysterious than those of man and wife.'

Later on he wrote and spoke about it quite simply and straight-

---

* Picturesque spot on the outskirts of Moscow, with an old park and eighteenth-century house. (Tr.)

forwardly in *Doctor Zhivago*: 'He did not believe in "free love", or the "right" to be carried away by his senses. To think or speak in such terms seemed to him degrading. He had never "sown wild oats", nor did he regard himself as a superman with special rights and privileges.' In a letter to Renate Schweitzer of May 7, 1958 he said: 'I am neither a judge in matters of morality nor an active opponent of its various forms. I am sickened in every way by all theorizing about "the rights of the senses", "free love" or any other kind of intimate human relationship . . .' To a woman who visited him on November 2, 1959 he said (according to her note of the conversation): 'I am against any kind of rules: whether it is a matter of a family modelled on the *Domostroi**, or of free love, every case is different. There can be no rules about such things: life itself is the only arbiter . . .'

And finally, there is what he had written long before:† 'And how much the two have in common: . . . a kind of consummate "you-and-I" relationship binds them together with all conceivable earthly bonds, and proudly stamps their twin profiles on the same medallion.'

On the morning of that happy day, he inscribed a small red volume of his verse for me: 'My life, my angel, I love you truly. April 4, 1947.'

This red volume had its subsequent history. After my first arrest in 1949—of which more later—all the books he had given me were taken away. When my interrogation was over and the *troika*‡ in the shape of a pimply young lieutenant had pronounced sentence on me, BL was summoned to the Lubianka,§ and handed the books belonging to me. He then tore out the fly-leaf with the inscription. The morning after I returned from the camp, and we were again happy in each other's company—even happier than ever before—I could not refrain from chiding him over this: how could he have done such a thing? In reply he now wrote—on the inside cover this time: 'I tore out the inscription when I brought it home.¶ What does it matter to you?' I read this without a word and added my comment below: 'A fine thing to do, I must say: if you hadn't torn it out, this book would

---

* Sixteenth-century Russian code for the strict regulation of domestic life. (Tr.)

† In *Safe Conduct*, about Mayakovski and a woman he loved. (Tr.)

‡ A tribunal of three which in Stalin years frequently laid down sentences in secret, without the accused even being present. (Tr.)

§ The headquarters of the secret police, where the author was first held. (Tr.)

¶ i.e. for fear his family should see it. (Tr.)

be a reminder of happiness, but now it is a reminder of unhappiness, of disaster . . .' He then took a photograph of himself he had brought and wrote on the back, word for word, the same inscription as in 1947, with the same date under it, and underneath he added: 'This inscription is eternal and valid for ever. And can only grow stronger.' This was written in 1953.

'Beckoned by the passion to break free'

So our 'Summer in Town'* began on April 4, 1947. Both my apartment and his were empty except for ourselves. We met almost every day. I often opened the door for him, at seven in the morning, in my Japanese dressing gown decorated with little houses, and with a long train at the back. It is all in one of the *Zhivago* poems:

> I have let my family scatter,
> All my dear ones are dispersed,
> And the loneliness always with me
> Fills nature and my heart . . .
> You fling off your dress
> As a coppice sheds its leaves.
> In a dressing gown with a silk tassel
> You fall into my arms.
> You are the good gift of destruction's path,
> When life sickens more than disease
> And boldness is the root of beauty—
> Which draws us together so close.

The lime trees were particularly laden with blossom that summer, and the boulevards seemed almost to have the fragrance of honey. His lines about the 'lack of sleep' of the ancient lime trees on Chistye Prudy Boulevard were born of our marvellous wakefulness at first light, in those days when we were in love. He would come into my room at six in the morning, still sleepy, of course—which meant that the boulevard, the houses and the streetlights hadn't had enough sleep either . . . Once I did up my hair with a tortoise-shell comb of my mother's, and this inspired the line about the 'helmeted woman'

* Title of one of the *Doctor Zhivago* poems. (Tr.)

looking in a mirror . . . We have long ceased to exist as we were at that moment, but the tortoise-shell in my hair, still luxuriant then, and the lime trees which had not slept enough, entered into his poetry and now exist quite apart from me, BL, or the little room in Potapov Street.

Those days that we spent 'under high tension', despite the underlying note of tragedy, had their moments of light relief. Once, right at the beginning (on his second visit to me at home, I think), after walking the cold streets for a long time, BL was sitting in the warmth of my room when he suddenly got up from the sofa to come over to my chair. The sofa was very old, one of its legs broke and it collapsed. BL jumped back in alarm and became quite flustered: 'It's the hand of fate pointing to my bad behaviour!'

Another time, much later on, when we were having things out and quarrelling much more often than usual, there was another little incident which still makes me smile. BL was bent on getting his own back for some scene I had made the previous evening, but I wanted to make it up and had put cornflowers in vases all round the room as a peace offering. 'Those are cornflowers,' he said crossly, at the sight of them, 'and they are weeds.' I now learned that he did not like flowers in a room—though he was always sending them to his women friends.

He hated scenes—he had obviously had enough of them before I came into his life—and whenever I began to talk seriously with him, he always tried to fend it off: 'No, no Olia, that's not like you and me! It sounds like a bad novel! This is not you!' But I wouldn't give in and insisted: 'Yes, it *is* me—I'm a woman of flesh and blood, not a figment of your imagination!' Neither of us would give way.

The tittle-tattle of relatives was no help. They were always nagging me about the need for BL to make a clean break and leave his family, if he really loved me.

I don't like to speak badly of my mother, but she too was very much at fault. She made absurd scenes—ringing BL, for example, to say I was ill because of him, when I simply had 'flu, or going on about his heartlessness if he was unable to come and see me for a day or two. 'I love your daughter more than my life, Maria Nikolayevna,' he said to her, 'but don't expect our life to change outwardly all at once.'

My mother was, of course, only responding to her maternal instinct and simply wanted me to be happy in her understanding of the word. It made no sense to her if we spent one day together like a married couple, and then he didn't show up, perhaps for a day or two. She naturally wanted to give us her blessing straightaway, but all this was like the portrait of Lazhechnikov in Chekhov.[6]

But I thought of Boris as more than a husband. He had entered my life and seized possession of it entirely, leaving no corner untouched. I was overjoyed by his tender, loving treatment of my two children, particularly Irina, now rapidly growing up. During the first stage of this tragedy of ours, my mother's attitude to BL affected Irina too, and whenever she saw me hang up his photograph only to take it down again, she pursed her lips scornfully, and said: 'Where's your pride, Mama?' But everything changed as she became a grown girl. 'I understand you, Mama,' she said one day, seeing me put BL's picture back on the wall for the umpteenth time. On some occasion an older person had said: 'You should treasure every minute you spend with our classic, children!' The pompous word 'classic', with its respectful, deferential intonation, was at once transformed by Ira into a sweet, affectionate nickname 'Classoosha' . . . Before long, 'Classoosha' had become closer to her than anyone else in the world, and nobody had a more sensitive understanding of his comic, endearing weaknesses, of his greatness and generosity.

But at the beginning it was not the children who posed a problem. I was often just not up to the situation myself and ruined many of the good moments we spent together. The harangues I got from my family had their effect on me, and I was always trying to make some womanly demand or other on him. I am still distressed and ashamed at the thought of those stupid scenes between us. This is how he wrote about it all himself, after we had once tramped the streets for ages, stopping in the entrances to the courtyards of strange houses to bicker for a while or make things up again:

> . . . Again I rehearse my excuses,
> Or again grow weary of it all,
> Once more a woman from next door
> Skirts the courtyard wall, not to disturb us.
> . . . . . .
> Don't cry, don't purse your swollen lips,
> Don't draw them together like that—
> You'll make them just as sore and cracked
> As they were from last spring's fever.

Take your hand from my breast:
We are cables under high tension
Watch out—or once again
We'll be flung together willy nilly ...
. . . . . .
But strongly as I may be bound
By the aching shackles of our nights,
The pull away is stronger still,
And I'm beckoned by the passion to break free.

'No, no, Olia, it's all over,' he kept repeating, during one of his attempts to 'break free'. 'Of course I love you, but I must stop seeing you because I cannot go through with all the horrors of leaving my family.' (By this time Zinaida Nikolayevna had heard about me, and was also beginning to make his life a misery.) 'Unless you can accept that we must exist in a kind of higher world and wait for some still unknown force to bring us together, it would be better not to see each other again. We cannot live a life together on the ruins of somebody else's.'

But, as he says, we were 'cables under high tension', and were by now simply powerless to leave each other.

Once, when his younger son Lionia fell seriously ill, Zinaida Nikolayevna extracted a promise from him, as they stood by the boy's sickbed, that he would not see me again. He asked Liusia Popova to tell me about this, but she refused point-blank and told him he must do it himself.

At the time, I remember, I was lying ill in Liusia Popova's house in Furmanov Street, when suddenly Zinaida Nikolayevna turned up there. But I became so ill through loss of blood that she and Liusia had to get me to hospital, and I no longer remember exactly what passed between me and this heavily-built, strong-minded woman, who kept repeating how she didn't give a damn for our love and that, although she no longer loved BL herself, she would not allow her family to be broken up.

After my return from hospital, Boria came to visit me, as though nothing had happened, and touchingly made his peace with my mother, telling her how much he loved me. By now she was pretty well used to these funny ways of his.

There was one more attempt to 'break free' later on—in 1953, not

long before I was due to return from the labour camp. Even from the
touching postcards he wrote to me in Potma*—which were made to
look as though sent by my mother and which I was luckily able to
bring back with me—it is very clear how much he longed for me,
and what great efforts he made to try and get me released. His first
heart attack (in 1950) was certainly brought on by our enforced separation—which is the subject of one of his finest poems at that period:

> A man stands and peers across the threshold
> And does not recognize the room inside . . .

The idea of our reunion appeared to him in his dreams as something that would be in the nature of a miracle if it came to pass:

> When the snow covers over the roads
> And lies heavily on the rooftops
> I'll go outside to take a walk
> —and find you standing at the door . . .

But then suddenly, when our reunion was actually in the offing,
he got it into his head that neither I nor he were what we had been
before, that he had recovered from his heart attack only thanks to
Zinaida Nikolayevna, and that he must therefore sacrifice his personal feelings on the altar of devotion and gratitude to her. With this
in mind he summoned Ira, now fifteen years old, to meet him on
Chistye Prudy Boulevard, and charged her with a very peculiar
errand: she was to tell me, her mother, when I returned from the
camp after my four years there, that he still loved me and that all was
well, but that a change might now come about in our relationship.

It is a pity Ira never made a note of the conversation to preserve
the full flavour of his words—the mixture of candour, guileless
charm, and undeniable heartlessness.

I knew that he had a horror of changes in people who were dear
to him. He was very reluctant to see his sister Lydia whom he had
known as a beautiful young girl. 'How terrible,' he said to me once,
'if she turns out to be an awful old woman, someone completely
foreign to us.' I am sure he expected me to come back from the camp

---

* Small town and rail junction about 400 kilometres east of Moscow in the
so-called 'autonomous region' of Mordovia inhabited by a small people related to
the Finns. The author was sent to a forced labour camp there after being sentenced
in 1949.

like that—hence the delicate message entrusted to Ira that our lives might not be the same as before. But then he saw that I was just the same—though a little thinner perhaps. And my love for him and closeness to him somehow always brought me back to life in an astonishing way. In short, our life, after being torn apart by sudden separation, now bestowed an unexpected gift on him—so once more nothing mattered except the 'living sorcery of hot embraces', the triumph of two people alone in the bacchanalia of the world.

We were both seized by a kind of desperate tenderness, and a resolve to stay together for the rest of our lives. Ira told me about her conversation with him on the boulevard only many years after his death.

As a poet he was ruled by his 'passion to break free', but it was overridden by the ordinary human attraction which drew us together, as though we could not breathe without each other. Every time we met after being apart, I would press his head to me, without saying a word, and listen to his heart beating wildly. This is how it was right until that last fateful May of 1960. While I was with him it was not given to him to grow old.

I remember how he wrote his allegorical 'Fairy Tale'* about my captivity and release when I returned from the camp after Stalin's death. He depicted me here as the traditional maiden in the clutches of the dragon, and perhaps imagined himself as the knight in the poem who traverses 'fords, rivers and centuries' to resue her. He certainly liked to think it was ultimately his name which had delivered me from my five years' imprisonment. 'It was I who unwittingly brought it on you, Olia,' he said, 'yet as you say yourself, they were afraid of going too far—five years is nothing, after all, by their standards, when they measure sentences in tens of years! They wanted to punish me through you . . .'

It is impossible for me to reproduce all he said during those extraordinary first minutes after my return from the camp, or convey the manner in which he spoke. He was ready to 'turn the earth upside down', and we were to 'kiss like two worlds'.

I was overjoyed to feel that he now thought of me as part of his family, and I could see that he was lifted up and inspired by the business of caring for me and mine. 'Olia,' he often said, 'I am leaving you only to go and work.' And if he had worked well during the

* One of the *Zhivago* poems. (Tr.)

day, he returned to me in my room as though to share in some richly earned festivity, and we were both so happy that none of life's hardships seemed to exist . . . But he also kept reminding me that we must not try to force the pace, that everything would come of its own accord, like our meeting at *Novy Mir*:

You are a gift of the spring, my love—how good that God created you a woman . . . Let it always be like this: we fly to each other, and never want anything so much as to meet! And we need nothing else. Let's not look ahead, or complicate matters, or hurt other people's feelings . . . Would you want to be in the place of that unfortunate woman? For years now we have been deaf to each other . . . and of course she is only to be pitied—she has been deaf all her life—the dove tapped at her window in vain . . . And now she is angry because something real has come to me—but so late in life! . . .

At such moments all our squabbles were forgotten. The only pity is I still had fits of female tantrums from time to time. Happy as I felt at being his chosen one, I had to listen to narrow-minded reproaches and expressions of sympathy, and this upset me . . . I suppose I longed for recognition and wanted people to envy me. Eventually my mother began to leave us in peace.

Our 'Shop'

When Boria insisted, early in 1948, that I leave *Novy Mir*, he began to instruct me systematically in the art of literary translation. I had written poetry ever since I was a child, loved it and had a feeling for it. As BL said, 'the trains of all the poetry written in the national languages* are just waiting for us to board them', and he thought me quite capable of taking a seat in one of the front coaches and establishing myself as a verse translator.

He had always been used to working hard—which in his case, providentially, was synonymous with writing poetry, with making

* Non-Russian languages of the Soviet Union; translating from them, with the help of literal versions prepared by linguists, is often an important source of income for Soviet writers. (Tr.)

his miracles—and he appreciated a similar love of work in others, whatever their field. He had no patience with amateurism—which is perhaps why he considered his first wife's painting as nothing more than an idle way of filling in time, and placed a much higher value on what he regarded as Zinaida Nikolayevna's sensible house-keeping talents, the loving care with which she looked after the garden. This is also perhaps why he gave up music: he realized he would not achieve the heights he aspired to, as became clear to him when Scriabin made the brilliant mistake of playing one of BL's youthful *études* written at the age of seventeen, while he was still setting out to be a composer.

At the time we first met, he was translating Sándor Petöfi—and in such a way that he seemed to be writing him anew:

My love is no nightingales' retreat,
Where with singing one awakes from sleep
While the earth still drowses on,
Flushed from the dawn's first kisses.

My love is no quiet woodland pool
Where swans' reflections ripple
As, sailing by, necks curved
Before the moon, they bow in greeting to it.

My love is no sweet abode of riper years
In a sheltered cottage among thick willow trees
Where serene contentment rules the home,
Nurturing happiness as a mother tends her daughter.

My love is a dark and brooding forest
Where jealousy, the ruffian, lurks in ambush
And desperation, like a cut-throat, dagger drawn,
Loiters to waylay me behind every tree I pass.
. . . . . .
A night without end gleams in the window opened wide
—A starlit night, a bright-blue night it is,
And boundless it stretches out, the world between these shutters.
My angel's beauty is no less than that of all the stars.
. . . . . .
Time to lie down upon the bed again
And leave the window now. But sleep is needless.

Why should I sleep? What dream could I dream
That may compare with what I see awake?'

I still have here before me the little volume of Petöfi with a
dedication in Boria's cursive hand, the words flying over the page
like cranes:

Petöfi served as a code in May and June 1947, and my close
translations of his lyrics are an expression, adapted to the require-
ments of the text, of my feelings and thoughts for and about you. In
memory of it all—B.P., May 13, 1948.

And in 1959 he wrote on the back of a photograph of himself:

Petöfi is magnificent with his descriptive lyrics and pictures of
nature, but you are better still. I worked on him a good deal in 1947
and 1948, when I first came to know you. Thank you for your help.
I was translating both of you . . .

During all of our years we addressed each other through our
translations of poetry. Petöfi was thus a first declaration of love, and
when I went with a note from BL to collect his honorarium for it,
I felt as though I was presenting a bill of exchange entitling me to
receive happiness in return.

In my small room on Potapov Street, BL explained to me the basic
principles of the art of translation, and I began to try my hand. It is
funny to remember how at first I would pad out a dozen lines into at
least two score. He laughed at me for taking such liberties and
taught me how to preserve the sense by discarding words—how to
strip an idea bare and clothe it in new words, as concisely as possible,
without striving to prettify it. You had to pick your way gingerly
along the boundary between translation in the strict sense and im-
provisation on the theme suggested by the original.

When he felt I had learned my lessons sufficiently well, he took me
along to *Goslitizdat* (State Publishing House for Literature) where he
introduced me to Alexandra Petrovna Riabinina.* I was given Gafur
Guliam† to translate. Alas, BL had to do virtually all of it for me: I

* Alexandra Petrovna Riabinina: head of the section for the 'national' literature
in *Goslitizdat*.
† An Uzbek poet; see Biographical Guide. (Tr.)

still tended to make five lines out of one. For some reason this translation of Guliam was never published.

In a letter dated May 23, 1942, BL had written to one of his editors, Anna Naumova, as follows:

I am completely opposed to contemporary ideas about translation. The work of Lozinski, Radlova, Marshak, and Chukovski is alien to me, and seems artificial, soulless, and lacking in depth. I share the nineteenth-century view of translation as a literary exercise demanding insight of a higher kind than that provided by a merely philological approach...

In his conversations with me he often condemned the tendency of modern translators to try and reproduce their literal versions too exactly. This, he thought, ultimately led to an inadmissible obfuscation of the sense. The way to render the original more faithfully was to stand back from it, look at it from a distance, and rid it of everything superfluous. 'The farther back you stand, the closer you will get to it', as someone (I don't remember who) has put it in a nutshell —which was exactly what BL advocated. Sometimes, giving me his blessing as I started on some new piece of work, he wrote down various helpful suggestions—for example:

1 Bring out the theme of the poem, its subject matter, as clearly as possible.
2 Tighten up the fluid non-European form by rhyming internally, not at the end of the lines.
3 Use loose, irregular metres, mostly ternary ones. You may allow yourself to use assonances.

Later on we began a partnership (our 'shop', as we called it). He often started a translation and I would then take over, leaving him time to work on his novel. I was soon making a good living out of it as well.

Here is something he wrote on the manuscript of our translation of Vitězslav Nezval's poem 'The Call of Time':

Try to continue in the same way. Alternate lines stressed on the final syllable with lines stressed on the penult. Use the literal version only for the *meaning*, but do not borrow words as they stand from it: they are absurd and not always comprehensible. Don't translate every-thing, only what you can manage, and by this means try to make the translation more precise than the original—an absolute necessity in the case of such a slipshod, confused piece of work. The whole transla-tion, including the first part, will be your work and appear under your signature.

I was particularly happy collaborating with him during our work-ing summer of 1956. He was then preparing a large one-volume edition of his poetry, and an autobiographical outline to go with it, while I was busy translating Rabindranath Tagore, going at it for all I was worth. We needed money, and nothing could have been better than earning it by this congenial work, which was turning out well. One quiet August evening at dusk, I remember BL came over to the verandah of the room we had rented in Peredelkino,* and I read out to him the poem Tagore had written just before his death:

> A clock strikes in the distance, and I scarcely hear
> The city's noise outside my walls.
> The March sun has risen high above
> The flat roofs, to face me once again . . .
> . . . . . .
> The heat drones away on a drawn-out mid-day note.
> All I have ever seen on the roads
> Of my long life has come back to me today—
> Such must be the law of our existence.
> Forgotten scenes slowly return
> To take their leave
> At my dying hour, and over my long life
> A clock strikes somewhere at the city's edge.

I regarded this as my first really crucial test. Hardly able to hold back his tears of emotion, BL said: 'It's inspired, Olia! Very good, magnificent! You've really mastered the art.'

Exaggerated praise of this kind was typical of him. He did not

---

* Peredelkino: a village about twenty kilometres southwest of Moscow. For-merly the estate of the Samarin family, it was turned into a 'writers' colony' in the mid-thirties. Pasternak had a country house (*dacha*) here from 1936 until his death. (Tr.)

change a single line. In the following year the seventh volume of
Rabindranath Tagore's collected works was published and I was
happy to see my name side by side with his. This publication was a
landmark for us. And then, in 1958, thirty-two of my translations of
Galaktion Tabidze appeared in the one-volume edition of his work,
also without a single change. Among them were many of my
favourite lines:

> When the forest's sailcloth
> Is swollen by the wind,
> I always hear the aspens
> Whisper of wondrous things,
> And their tales of long ago,
> Calling me back again,
> Intoxicate like vintage Tsinandali*
> Or the resurrected scent of roses
> Which someone sang of
> Many years ago ... But who? And where?
> The vault of branches only has to stir,
> Lightly brushed by a passing breeze,
> For the sail of life itself to reel
> Under the weight of wind and woe:
> Perhaps it means old age is near,
> Or that you and I are long since gone?

(This is exactly the same theme we hear in BL's 'Meeting':

> But who are we, and whence
> If of all those years
> Nothing but idle gossip's left
> And the two of us have vanished from the earth?)

And also:

> As a reflection and likeness
> Of great events
> Above a white tombstone of clouds
> The setting sun glowed red,
> And without you, among the ruins
> I wandered on alone,

* A Georgian wine. (Tr.)

While the wind blew the dust around
Behind me.
Suddenly I see the outline of a bridge
Of silver—
To make it easy for the stars to climb
Up into night, till morning . . .

The work of our 'shop' had its moments of comedy. When editors had begun to accept and recognize my work and I was receiving, with pride, my first payments for it, BL one day put a translation done by himself among some of mine and submitted it under my name with the rest. He was as happy as a small boy when the publisher turned down this particular one and sent it back to me for revision!

In the seventh volume of the works of Tagore (*Goslitizdat*, 1957) the translation of the long poem 'A Single Voice' was described as BL's, though it was entirely my work, and in the eighth volume there was a note correcting this ('For "Pasternak", read "Ivinskaya"'). BL insisted on this since he had not changed a single word in the poem which he felt had come out particularly well. He was always very pleased at any success of mine.

In the volume of Titian Tabidze's *Selected Poems* (Tbilisi, 1957), one of the six translations contributed by me ('Verses on the Valley of Mukhran') is signed by BL—this was essential to ensuring my association with the book, over which, incidentally there was a rather unpleasant incident. This is how it is described by Maria Yefremovna Struchkova, who was an editor with *Goslitizdat* at the time:

We were about to publish the volume of Titian Tabidze, in which many of the translations were done by Pasternak and Ivinskaya. Tabidze's widow, Nina Alexandrovna, had spoken very well of them. But the day before the book was due to be sent to the printers, I had a call from Boris Leonidovich who said to me: 'Maria Yefremovna, I want you to remove my translations. I have just heard that Nina Alexandrovna is against Olga Vsevolodovna's versions being used. If even a single one of hers is dropped, you must take me out altogether.' 'But Boris Leonidovich,' I pleaded, 'it's quite impossible: the book is completely ready.' 'No, no, I tell you! Olga

Vsevolodovna and I are one and the same, she is my own soul, my second life, and anything said by her is said by me. So I beg you, please—if there is any interference with her translations, you must take out all mine as well. I wish to state this formally, to avoid any misunderstanding later on.' Almost immediately after this conversation Nina Tabidze walked into our office. She said she was not happy about Olga Vsevolodovna's translations and they must be left out. (As appeared later, she was not uninfluenced by Zinaida Nikolayevna, with whom she was on particularly close terms just at that time.) But, with Boris Leonidovich's words still ringing in my ears, I told Nina Alexandrovna about his decision in rather emotional language. She was terribly upset and we both went in to talk with the managing editor. Needless to say, the question was settled in accordance with BL's wishes.

The professional aspect of our relations was very typical of BL. A poet of genius—and recognized as such by the world—he behaved towards me, a mere beginner in the art of translating, as though we were professional equals. I still have a note he wrote about one of our translations, I no longer remember which one:

Dear Olia: I expect that in the original all this somehow stood up and didn't sink to the ground—rather as similar inspired gibberish in our early work, in Mayakovski's or in mine, got entangled in the thickets of the language, like a child's kite in the treetops, instead of dropping down to earth to be revealed for the arrant nonsense it was. But in the literal version and my rhymed adaptation of it, it comes out as unbelievably rhetorical and tasteless stuff, so do forgive me for putting these unspeakable ravings under the protection of your shining literary name. It really is drivel, isn't it?

Not wanting to trade too much on his own prestige, BL sometimes got third persons to suggest me as a translator. This is what happened in the case of Simon Chikovani's poetry which BL passed on to me without the author's knowledge, then suggesting we get somebody else to write in support of my versions—as he put it to me in a note at the time:

Alexandra Petrovna should write personally to Simon Chikovani and say: 'Pasternak declined with apologies and regrets to translate your poetry because the writing of his novel leaves him no free time at all, and I have therefore asked a woman translator I know to take it on. I am sending you what she has done. I have compared her versions with the literal translations and I find them satisfactory. Please tell me what you think. What really matters after all is not so much the name of the translator as the quality of the work.' You should tell Alexandra Petrovna that you have shown your versions to me, that I made slight changes in one or two places but otherwise spoke highly of them. She should not mention my part in your work, even though it amounted to so little.

BL was always fondly looking for resemblances between women characters in Goethe, Shakespeare or Petöfi and myself—no doubt fancifully projecting me into them. The classics thus became a living discourse between us. This started during his work on *Faust*, after my release from the camps, when he said to me: 'I speak to you, Olia, through the lips of Faust, in his words to Margarita—"how pale you are, my beauty, my guilt"—all this is addressed to you.' Later on, when his *Faust*, with Goncharov's engravings, was published, he wrote on the copy he gave me: 'Olia, step for a moment out of this book, stand aside from it and read it. November 18, 1953.'

Later still, he fancied he saw something of my character in Maria Stuart and therefore worked with particular enthusiasm on his translation of Schiller's play about her.[7] Unfortunately, there were snags over the publication of this. The trouble was that just as BL finished work on his *Maria Stuart*, another translation was submitted by N. Vilmont, a relative of BL's by marriage. I have kept the 'brief' which BL wrote out for my guidance when I went to speak with B. S. Weissman, an editor in the foreign literature section of *Goslitizdat*:

1. Let him [Weissman] do what he wishes. I will incorporate all his suggestions. This can be done in the proofs.
2. I had not seen Vilmont's translation. I have just now taken a look at the beginning—two or three pages. It is much better than I thought. I don't understand why the Arts Theatre turned it down. Since we were working from the same original and given the similarity of our language and style, there may well be places where Vilmont's

translation is identical with mine. If there are many, it will look bad and we must try to remedy the situation—or it will seem like plagiarism. Perhaps Bor. Sav. [Boris Savelyevich Weissman] can take it on himself to compare the two and note places that are alike, and I will then change them in mine.

3. If the difference in quality between the two versions is not *evident*, and if mine is not superior, or not noticeably so, it is not too late to reconsider: I can recompense *Goslitizdat* for the 16,000 [roubles] received from them by doing other work, and forgo publication.

4. I have tended in my translation to condense, whenever possible, in places where the original is unnecessarily long-winded, and I wish to abide by this.

In the event, as is well known, BL's translation was a great success, and after the triumphant first night at the Arts Theatre, he was inspired to write the cycle of poems called *Bacchanalia*:

> . . . She is all life, all freedom,
> A pounding of the heart in the breast,
> And the prison dungeons
> Have not broken her will.
> . . . . . .
> She too could have gone
> —An unattended queen—
> And laid down her head
> On the executioner's block.
> . . . . . .
> Before her in the drawingroom
> He falls to his knees,
> And the pictures on the walls
> Look down sternly at their deeds.
>
> But what are pity, conscience or fear
> To the brazen pair, compared
> With the living sorcery
> Of their hot embraces?
>
> In their madness they throw
> Caution to the winds
> And the whole world means less to them
> Than their short moment together . . .

Every word here is about us . . .

Whenever BL was provided with literal versions of things which echoed his own thoughts or feelings, it made all the difference and he worked feverishly, turning them into masterpieces. I remember his translating Paul Verlaine in a burst of enthusiasm like this—*L'Art poétique* was after all an expression of his own beliefs about poetry. 'In his verse,' BL said of Verlaine, 'he was able to imitate the pealing of bells. He conveyed the smells of all the main flowers and plants of his homeland, echoed the singing of its birds and went through the whole register of stillness, both inner and outer—from the silence of a starlit winter's night to the torpor of a hot summer's day at noon. Like nobody else he expressed the long, gnawing, relentless pain of loss—whether of a God no longer there, of a woman who has jilted you, of a place dearer than life itself which you have been forced to leave, or of peace of mind.'

Was translation a genuine vocation with BL, or was it forced on him by the conditions of his life and the impossibility of devoting himself entirely to work of his own? In his later years he often said that translation had become a wide-spread form of literary work because it enables one to live at the expense of other people's ideas—which was particularly important if you were unable to come out openly with your own. And then, in a letter of May 25, 1950, he wrote to a close friend: '. . . translating, I find, is not worthwhile—everybody has learned how to do it.' In one moment of exasperation he said: 'Better be a talented loaf of black bread than a talented translator . . .' Whatever he really thought about it, however, the fact is that for a long time translating was his basic means of earning his living.

One day somebody brought him a copy of a British newspaper in which there was a double-page feature under the title 'Pasternak Keeps a Courageous Silence'. It said that if Shakespeare had written in Russian he would have written in the same way he was translated by Pasternak, whose name was much respected in England, where his father had lived for some years until his death. What a pity, the article continued, that Pasternak published nothing but translations, writing his own work only for himself and a small circle of intimate friends. 'What do they mean by saying my silence is courageous?' BL commented sadly on reading all this, 'I am silent because I am not printed.'

But this was another matter, and it takes us beyond the narrow world of our 'shop'.

Domestic Arrangements

Boria always preferred not to meddle in problems of everyday existence. And besides, he was quite sure that the good Lord would sort out the muddled situation that had arisen between the mistress of his house in the country and myself, thereby deciding for him what mode of life would be most suitable.

But the good Lord was in no hurry, and meanwhile life didn't stand still, so we were forced to look, almost blindly, for some way of putting things in order. We simply could not go on without a proper place of our own. I am talking now about the time after my release [from the labour camp] in 1953, the wild joys of our reunion and the complete peace of mind which followed. We then decided we would live together, come what might, in any manner possible.

In 1954 I sent my mother and children to spend the summer with my aunt in Sukhinichi. I was glad not to have Ira around: it was becoming hard to hide the fact that I was pregnant, and I could not imagine how she would take it. Boria's view of it could not have been more clear-cut: 'This is just as it should be: it will make everything fall into place, bring things to a head, and a solution will somehow suggest itself. In any case, surely there can be no question that the world is large enough for your and my child?'

During this first summer after my release I was beginning to take in, with some difficulty, the joy of a return to the world after nearly four years of being excluded from it. *Doctor Zhivago* was taking shape, and life was kind to us that summer. But in the autumn, as often before, it took a turn for the worse. At the end of August I went out to the country in a pick-up to look at a *dacha*. It was a very bumpy ride and, feeling unwell, I stopped at the pharmacy in Odintsovo,* where they called an ambulance. On the way to hospital I gave birth to a still-born child.

One might have thought that no one would have been particularly upset by this: Ira, whose reaction to my having a child I had feared

* 24 kilometres west of Moscow. (Tr.)

most of all, would have no cause for concern, or so I imagined. BL
had shown no sign of wanting to change his mode of existence and
was happy enough for us to live from meeting to meeting—something which would obviously have been complicated by the birth
of a child . . .

But I was quite wrong: everybody was cross with me. Ira was
distressed that I had lost my baby, and Boria sat weeping at the foot
of my bed, repeating bitterly what he had said before: 'Do you really
think there would have been no room in the world for our child?
How little faith you have in me!'

It was as though a black cat had run across the path of us all.*
Apart from this, there was the continued frustration throughout the
long winter of not having a place of our own in which to live. In the
spring I did something unbelievably foolish: taking the advice of a
woman friend I rented a *dacha* out on the Kazan road.† This made
matters even worse: it meant a change of trains to go twice a week to
see BL in Peredelkino. He had to wait for me at the station there,
miserably pacing the platform. In the summer I had the better idea of
going out to Peredelkino and renting half a *dacha* for the whole
family on the shore of the Izmalkovo‡ lake. BL could walk here from
his house across a long plank bridge over the lake—which in a poem
of 1956 he describes as being 'like a dish'.

More by accident than by design my mother and the children
settled into the two rooms of the *dacha*, while I moved into the
glassed-in verandah. The first time Boria came there, he was quite
taken aback: 'But I asked you to find us a refuge, not a glass-house—
you must admit, it looks very odd, Olia!' I had to put things right as
quickly as possible and went to Moscow where I bought some red
and dark-blue chintz to cover over the whole of the glass-sided
verandah. We brought in a table and a large bed—which was also
covered with chintz. This gave us the illusion of having our own nest,
but BL was still unhappy: he hated those large panes of glass, through
which you could hear every sound.

The summer of 1955 was very hot and sunny, with lots of thunderstorms, and the wild roses blossomed luxuriantly. When September
came round, BL began to fret: 'You will go away and I'll be here

* Reference to Russian superstition—a black cat brings bad luck. (Tr.)
† Road leading due east from Moscow. (Tr.)
‡ A village adjacent to Peredelkino, formerly part of the Samarin estate. (Tr.)

alone again . . . the thought of all those trips into Moscow and living for nothing else! If only all the others would go away and we could stay here!'*

So I decided to stay on in Izmalkovo and simply go to Moscow on visits. BL would not then have to wait for me at the station, wandering forlornly about the platform, and would be able to come and see me twice a day at the *dacha*.

At first I tried to persuade our summer landlady, Nadezhda Vasilyevna, to let me go on renting the same part of her house for the whole winter; but there would have been many inconveniences about this, and she herself advised me to take another house nearby which had a room properly insulated against the cold and was equipped with a cooking stove. Her husband helped me to carry my things over to it: a blue-painted outdoor table, a typewriter, and some canvas chairs. I thus took up residence in part of a house belonging to Sergei Kuzmich, as our landlord was called. (In 1959 I moved to a larger place with its own garden plot on the hill opposite the 'Fadeyev tavern'.†) But the best years were the ones spent in Kuzmich's house. We had a small room leading out onto a verandah which served as a dining-room in summer and a porch in winter. Sergei Kuzmich's plot of land was bordered by huge poplars, but in the neighbouring areas the trees were being mercilessly cut down to make way for the growing of vegetables.

The room was quite tiny and very warm, though a little dingy to begin with. In the spring we had it done up.

If there has been any part of my life which could be described as truly happy, it was during those years between 1956 and 1960. It was the happiness of daily communion with someone I loved, of all the mornings and winter evenings spent together, reading to each other or entertaining people we liked. It seemed like one long, never-ending feast . . .

* In his poem 'Autumn', he wrote:
> 'I'll stay here with you till the spring
> Looking at these wooden walls,
> We'll not lead any one by the nose,
> And go openly to perdition . . .'

† Local nickname for the tavern frequented by Fadeyev, secretary of the Union of Writers, who committed suicide in 1956. See Biographical Guide. The Russian word used for 'tavern' here is *shalman*, a colourful expression from underworld slang, suggestive of a drinking place frequented by criminals. (Tr.)

BL no longer wanted to make regular trips into Moscow, and he entrusted the whole of his literary business to me. I typed and edited his manuscripts, read proofs for him, and later handled the whole saga of *Doctor Zhivago*.

BL now began to view even a brief separation from me—my day trips into town on business or rare overnight stays at the apartment in Potapov Street—as almost a slap in the face. He managed to have a telephone installed in the Moscow apartment and whenever I spent the night there he rang at nine o'clock in the evening from Peredelkino to tell me about his day and ask about mine. The children were not supposed to use the phone at this hour. He always began by saying: 'Olia, I love you! Don't get stuck there tomorrow.' And every return journey was a new, rapturous homecoming to the little room in Kuzmich's house, which now seemed so cosy to us with its blue table, the summer chairs, the ottoman covered by red and dark-blue chintz, and the wall hangings of the same material. The window was hung with an ample, well-fitting curtain which kept out draughts, and there was a thick red carpet on the floor. The door to the unheated verandah (which I also used for cold storage) was upholstered on the outside with felt. A small stove made to look like a fireplace crackled away in one corner of the room, and the 'fiery skin' of the lampshade—an orange-coloured tulip of satin—swayed gently above the table on its cord.

Kuzmich became an inseparable part of our life—and even, as chance would have it, appears in a *Paris Match* photograph side by side with Bulat Okudzhava and Naum Korzhavin coming down the steps of the Pasternak *dacha* after paying his last respects at the funeral.

But why anticipate events? Before his death I still had almost five years of Boria's love—blissful years of walks together, shared joys and anxieties, working on translations, meeting friends, learning from him and listening to everything he had to say.

On Sundays we were visited by my mother, Ira, and our friends and acquaintances. It was very agreeable to be able to receive them all in a home of one's own. These occasions on which we kept open house sometimes turned into regular literary gatherings. We also held our little 'family' celebrations here. I particularly remember a birthday party for me with my family and several friends—among them Nikolai Vasilyevich Bannikov, an editor at *Goslitizdat*, who was later to play an important part in the business of the novel. He read out a poem in my honour in which he compared me with Madame Récamier and Princess Volkonskaya, and went on to say that I would be quite capable of halting a galloping steed in its tracks! After dinner I went out for a walk with him down to the lake where a horse with hobbled front legs was grazing. A little tipsy by now, we went up and patted it. But the horse suddenly reared up on its hind legs and lashed out at the air with them. Both of us fell flat on the ground in terror. Everybody thought it was very funny.

In brief, we had a room of our own, a home, an anchorage. I often reproached myself for not setting up house like this earlier, so we could have lived and worked together from the beginning in complete independence, instead of Boria having to travel wearily back and forth to Moscow...

Our household gradually expanded to include Kuzmich (whom we took on as our handy-man), and Olga Nikolayevna, an elderly God-fearing peasant woman from a family deported during collectivization, who cleaned for us. She had had her share of suffering, and became very attached to both of us.

An account of these happy years would be glaringly incomplete without a mention of the animals which formed an essential part of our domestic life. No, it was not a question of livestock, only of small creatures with whiskers. One day, when Boria happened to leave his jacket lying on the divan, Kuzmich's cat Murka bedded down in it to give birth to two kittens. We were re-reading O. Henry's *Kings and Cabbages* at the time, and BL christened them Dinkie and Pinkie. In six months one of them grew up into a splendid light-blue angora tom, and BL referred to him as the Cat Prince. He was still not oppressed by the sheer number of cats in the place, and the Prince really was very handsome, particularly in winter when he came and stood upright on the windowsill outside, asking to be let in. He would leap into the room through the *fortochka*,★ blue, cold, and affectionate. Boria was enchanted by him, as he was by anything beautiful.

Pinkie was involved in several rather comic incidents. Once, for instance, in spring, he came up to the house along the path, rolling along on the ground with his paws and nose an egg which had obviously been stolen from our neighbours' hen-coop. He repeated his 'exploit' more than once, and BL said we must reimburse the

★ Small window to let in air during winter. (Tr.)

neighbours for these pranks. But I was terrified of betraying Pinkie in case they killed him and thought it better to keep quiet. Before long, however, Pinkie died of distemper. Dinkie, the female, lived on for a long time after him. She loved anything that glittered and stole the decorations from our Christmas tree, hiding them in her lair. Boria said that she was really a little woman turned into a cat by witchcraft. Once, to the great distress of Olga Nikolayevna, she seized my gold wrist-watch in her mouth and jumped out of the *fortochka* with it, but was caught before she could get very far. 'A prostitute, that's what she is,' Olga lamented to me, 'always galli-vanting instead of staying at home! If I hadn't seen her, you'd have thought it was me went off with the watch, wouldn't you?' Olga just couldn't get over it, though Boria and I assured her that it would never have entered our heads to suspect her. He then launched into a long philosophical disquisition about how it was even good to lose things, including manuscripts, and how one should never grieve for them. (But I knew only too well how much he regretted losing Marina Tsvetayeva's letters to him!)[8]

At Christmas we got a tree which took up almost the whole of the table at which I worked. We laughed when Dinkie stole decorations from it and took them off to her hideaway outside. We were so happy at the thought of it all: *our* Christmas tree, *our* table, a place to call our own. In general, however, my fondness for cats had always been a little worrying for BL right from our early Moscow days. Once, at the Potapov Street apartment, one of them got lost and I had raised the alarm, just before Boria was due to call and pick me up to go to a literary evening. As he was coming up the stairs to the sixth floor he saw a boy bringing up a cat in his arms. 'Where are you taking that?' he asked. 'To apartment eighteen,' the boy replied: 'there's a notice downstairs saying they'll give 100 roubles to anyone who finds their cat.' 'Here's a 150 roubles,' BL said, pulling out his wallet, 'if you'll take it away again ...'

But when we lived in Izmalkovo, he got on well enough with my animals—until there became rather too many of them. I remember a comic episode from our last years. Heinz Schewe (the Moscow correspondent of the West German *Die Welt* and a frequent visitor at that time, of whom I shall have a lot more to say later) got us to take in a stray cat he found in the snow in the Bakovka* forest. 'The

* Village near Peredelkino. (Tr.)

snow is no place for a lone cat to be,' he said with feeling as he
scrambled out of a ravine in his wet boots. Ira, too, was touched, so I
took the cat, saw her and Heinz off to Moscow, and went back to the
dacha. Coming out of the door to meet me, Boria was incensed: 'I'll
tell him just what I think of him!' he threatened. 'Such a nice man,
and he brings us a cat! Next Sunday I'll tell him to his face!' But on
Sunday, as could have been expected, all he said was: 'A very fine
cat: it settled down with us straightaway . . .' Another time, I heard
him shooing something away from the verandah. When I said, 'How
dare you!' he replied: 'But, Olia, you can't even tell the colour of this
one . . . Lord knows what it is!' It turned out to be our neighbour's
tabby . . . BL always nicknamed our cats after people he didn't like.
At a time when he had fallen out with the head of V.U.O.A.P.*
Grishka Khesin, he gave his name to an unprepossessing grey cat
which had several times misbehaved in front of visitors.

On the other hand, looking at his beloved dog Tobik, BL once told
me he was the spitting image of the Arts Theatre actor Vladimir
Yershov. I don't remember Yershov, so I can't say . . .

Autumn in Peredelkino

In the spring, with the help of my cousin, Militsa Nikolayevna
Gotovitskaya, I redecorated our room and it immediately began to
look much cosier. Militsa papered over the walls in light-blue and
bought me some thick material to cover the divan and make curtains.
A vase of flowers appeared on the blue table next to my Olympia
typewriter and manuscripts. It was now that the poem 'Miss Touch-
me-not' was born—evidently in honour of the new lampshade which
so transformed the room. I remember the evening when he wrote it.
I had just returned from Moscow where I had visited the 'Art'
publishing house to discuss the publication of his translations, and
was telling him about it all, while he sat at one corner of the table,
listening not very attentively and writing something down. Later he
read it out to me:†

* Authors' rights department of Union of Writers (Tr.)
† This translation is by Michael Harari. (Tr.)

Miss Touch-me-not's on fire,
The prude of everyday,
In the dark turret of a poem
I'll lock your looks away.

The lampshade's fiery skin
Transforms the room, makes free
With cramped walls, window sill,
Our shadows, you and me.

You tuck your feet beneath you
Like a Turk on the divan,
Reason (you always do)
As only children can,

Daydream, threading the beads
That spilt across your dress,
Look much too sad and chatter
With too much artlessness.

You're right, I must rename love;
It's a word we have all worn through.
If you like, I'll christen the world
And all its words, for you.

But how can dark looks show me
What ore of feeling lies
At the hidden mine of your heart?
Why do you cloud your eyes?

This is just exactly how it was: our shadows, grotesquely enlarged, on the blue walls—I with my feet tucked under me on the
divan and BL on a chair next to the table with the pages on which he
was writing in pencil spread out in front of him, and even the dark
beads of my grandmother's old garnet necklace on my lap.★

In this way, much of the poetry which is now the proud possession
of us all was born in the tiny room of Kuzmich's house on the rush-
grown banks of the Setun in Peredelkino, or close by the silvery
willows of the Izmalkovo lake and the weeping birches of our little

★ In a volume of translations of his poetry, 1956–59, published in Germany
Fischer Verlag, 1960), he later wrote: 'Olia, the poem on p. 69 is yours. Feb. 17,
1960.' This was 'Miss Touch-me-not'.

village. The poem 'Intoxication'* was written by BL as we sat on a raincoat spread out under the sparse branches of the trees in the Peredelkino graveyard:

Under a willow entwined in ivy
We seek shelter from the rain,
Our shoulders covered by a coat
And my arms entwined round you.

I was wrong: these thickets
Are wreathed not in ivy but in hops.
So perhaps better spread out the coat
Beneath us on the ground.

This raincoat, 'spread out on the ground', was our great stand-by before we had the more permanent shelter of our room in Kuzmich's house. In the same place Boria had written:

The world is ruled by pity,
By pity born of love,
By its own singularity
And the novelty of life.

Women and girls
In the palm of the hand
Hold birth and death
From beginning to end.†

And once, during a sleepless night, away from me at the 'big' house‡ he wrote the poem 'Insomnia':

What is the hour? It's dark. Must be three.
Again, I fear, I shall not sleep a wink.
The cowherd in the village will crack his whip at dawn,
And a cold breeze blow through the window
That looks out on the yard.
And I'm alone.
But no: engulfing me in all your whiteness
You are with me here.

* The Russian title is 'Khmel', which has the double sense of 'intoxication' and 'hops'. (Tr.)

† From 'Under the Open Sky' written in 1953, i.e. not long after the author's return from the camp. (Tr.)

‡ Where BL's family lived. (Tr.)

By next morning the poem had been written down in pencil and brought over to me at Kuzmich's.

Almost all the poems in the cycle *When the Weather Clears*[9] were written between Izmalkovo and Peredelkino. I well remember the day when BL brought 'August'* to me. To allay his own superstitious fears (and mine too) he tried to explain away this clearly premature farewell to life.

'You must understand,' he said, 'that it's only a dream, and now I've put it down on paper it won't come true. But even so—how good it would be to die at this God-given time of year, when the earth pays people back a hundredfold, makes good its debts in full and rewards us with unbelievable generosity. The sky is as blue as it can ever be, the water so eagerly reflects the fantastically coloured rowan trees, turning them upside down. The earth has given its all and is ready for a breathing-space . . .'

When BL first read me the poem, his voice broke with emotion. Later on he left out one or two stanzas, including the following one:

> Farewell the counsel and aid of women,
> Of girlfriends, wives and companions
> —how underrated, taken for granted
> this compassionate gift of fate . . .

Particularly significant for BL at this time was his work on the autobiographical introduction to the one-volume edition of his work being prepared by *Goslitizdat*—it took him back to the time of *Safe Conduct*, of his own and Mayakovski's young days. He was moved in this connection to start revising some of his early poems, and both I and his editor Nikolai Bannikov (who was spending that summer nearby) quarrelled with him about it. When we both shouted at him for daring to mutilate some old favourites known to everybody, he was quite indignant: 'But for heaven's sake, why do you want to keep such things?' He stubbornly insisted on taking out 'the charred pears of rooks' from 'February',† and was already about to make changes in 'Marburg'. But we would have none of these 'improvements'.

At the same time, thanks to the writing of the introduction he was

---

* In which Pasternak described his own death. See p. 348. (Tr.)

† One of Pasternak's first published poems (1913). (Tr.)

able to re-live, so to speak, his meetings with Tabidze and Yashvili, and to undertake a re-appraisal of Mayakovski.

In the midst of all this he was summoned one day by the Public Prosecutor to give evidence in connection with the rehabilitation of Meyerhold. When he came back, he immediately sat down and wrote a polemical poem. But a little later he had second thoughts: 'No, one must not write verse like this. One must not give way to such things. A poet cannot descend to the level of the publicist. Poetry touches on everything under the sun, but in its own way— only then will it pass the test of time.' It was for this reason, no doubt, that in his later years he so much preferred Fet and Tiutchev to Nekrasov or Mayakovski.

On dark nights, guided by the crisscrossing beams of our electric torches, we often left our warm burrow for a walk, skirting the vegetable gardens of Izmalkovo or walking over the bridge to Peredelkino, to the sound of the water lapping underneath, and in summertime to the croaking of frogs; in winter we went back and forth over the ice, leaving our uneven tracks in the snow. We went out walking in rain or blizzards, indifferent to the weather or the season, content at having found each other and fearful only that we might not be able to preserve this way of life, or that someone or something might bring it to an end. 'If only it could always be like this ...', BL was never tired of saying to me.

In these last years he found Tiutchev the most congenial poet not only because of his verse, but also because of a resemblance in their personal life. Once he read to me, with a catch in his voice:

> Now I walk along the highroad
> In the waning day's soft light,
> My feet are heavy, my heart oppressed
> Beloved one, do you see me still?
>
> The earth grows darker, ever darker ...
> The last lingering ray has fled ...
> Here is this world where you and I have lived,
> My angel, do you see me still?

'Love also came to him late in life,' BL said to me. 'After you were taken from me that time long ago,* I could never read these lines

---

* i.e. in 1949, to prison. (Tr.)

without tears. I used to read them to Liusia Popova.' He was overcome in the same way whenever he read one of the stanzas of Blok's
'To the Muse':

> . . . And when you mock at the faith,
> that same nimbus seen by me before
> at once glows above you, faint and purple-grey.

During this same period, however, he also often went back to
Pushkin, never failing to be delighted by the brilliant precision and
gaiety of Pushkin's diction:

> Powdered silver by the frost
> His beaver collar glistens . . .

'That's the way to write!' BL exclaimed once as we walked along
the road under the branches weighed down by snow and he was
suddenly reminded by the deep hush of winter over Peredelkino of
his own lines about 'the princess sleeping in her tomb'. But in 1957
the snow lying on the hills like white mist and shrouding the trees
suggested a new vision of winter to him: 'a dead woman of white
plaster' who had fallen to the ground.

There are now convenient steps leading to the door of our last
refuge, but in those years BL had to pick his way among twisted tree-
roots up a treacherous, ice-bound path which rose far too steeply for
comfort. And on the other side we could hear the noisy revellers of
Izmalkovo in the 'Fadeyev tavern' which still exists there today. Cars
would glide past us on their way to and from Moscow.

The Eccentric

The word 'eccentric' is usually applied, it seems, to people who have
left the beaten track of ordinary convention and seek a path of their
own beyond the understanding of their contemporaries. In the eyes
of any right-thinking average person, BL was certainly an eccentric
in this sense. Of such right-thinking persons—the kind who, in
Marina Tsvetayeva's words, dismissed as lunacy the most rational,
elementary, and legitimate things—there were more than enough.

One could write a whole book about BL's 'oddities' and what follow are just a few examples picked out at random.

If anybody was unfriendly towards him, BL would get his own back in a naïve, child-like way. Once, for example, he took a dislike to Lukonin, who became boss of *Novy Mir*'s poetry section under the editorship of Simonov. I was still working at *Novy Mir*, when one day BL needed to speak to Lukonin about some matter of business or other. I could hear his voice coming over the telephone and asking for 'Lutokhin'. 'There's no such person,' replied someone who happened to be sitting at the secretary's desk. 'Oh, really?' BL came back at him. 'Well, Lutoshkin then! . . . No? Very well: Lukoshkin!' This was evidently his way of conveying what a poor view he took of the man. About Simonov he once said to me: 'He's the best of those ruffians!'

He had a peculiar sense of humour. He once decided it was very funny, for instance, to say *gladi-oaf-us* instead of *gladiolus*, and laughed so loudly and infectiously himself that everybody else began to laugh as well just at the sight of him.

Pelageia Vasilyevna Balashova, who as a young woman presided over the board of the Moscow Party committee, has told me about an incident which happened at the end of the 'twenties, when a very well-educated young woman came to see her on a 'personal matter': she wished to complain about her husband, a writer, who was leaving her and their young son for another woman. Warning that, though he was not a member of the Party, he could evidently count on the support of Lunacharski, she asked Balashova to try to use her influence with him. The husband, it turned out, was Pasternak. Balashova decided to summon the 'non-Party' husband for a serious talk in her office. To her astonishment he came straightaway, listened calmly to her exhortations, and then asked in the most matter-of-fact way what she wanted him to do. Encountering so little resistance, she suggested he sign a pledge undertaking to mend his ways. He sat down and wrote it out at her dictation without more ado, said goodbye, and left . . .

I do not think Balashova can have invented this story in her old age, and even if it is a legend, it sounds very plausible: it was so entirely in character for him to stand his ground without bothering to argue the rightness of his case (particularly when he thought it was obvious), and even accepting without demur any reproaches that might be heaped on him. He simply looked with disdain on people who thought they knew best. Later on, in *Doctor Zhivago*, speaking through his hero, he put it like this: 'I don't like people who have never fallen or stumbled. Their virtue is lifeless, and it isn't of much value. Life hasn't revealed its beauty to them.'

Liusia Popova tells of two curious episodes:

We were once at his house, drinking tea. For some reason there was no sugar in the house. BL smeared mustard on black bread and drank it down with tea. A beggar knocked at the door. BL emptied his pockets of all the small change in them and gave it to the man, but feeling it was not enough, he began to fuss so much that the beggar became visibly embarrassed and tried to leave. But BL wouldn't let him: 'You must forgive me, but we have nothing in the house,' he apologized, 'they're bringing supplies tomorrow, so come back then and I'll give you something. But at the moment we haven't even got any money . . .' The beggar was desperately trying to get through the door, but his way was barred by BL. At last he managed to slip past him and literally fled, followed by a last booming command to 'come tomorrow without fail'. But for a long time afterwards BL went on lamenting: 'How unfortunate, how embarrassing—someone comes to us and we have absolutely nothing to give him . . .'

The second episode was this:

BL told me that once, at an evening gathering at his home, a tall, well-dressed man whom he didn't know came up and introduced himself. 'I understood him to say he was Vyshinski. And then suddenly he started saying how much I was loved and appreciated by the émigrés, and what pleasure I gave them, these people torn from their native country. I was taken aback: why should Vyshinski be so concerned about émigrés? Next I started asking his advice about the problems I was having with my apartment—and it was his turn to be astonished. Then I was told that it wasn't Vyshinski at all but Alexander Vertinski, who had just returned from emigration . . .' Later on Alexander Nikolayevich told me:* 'I was at Pasternak's at Easter. He is so cut off from life he really has his head in the clouds all the time—he should try to come down to earth a little . . .' When I

* Liusia Popova knew Vertinski well.

subsequently asked BL about this visit of Vertinski's to his house, he
was rather embarrassed: 'Yes, he actually did come, you know, and
he read his verse. But I said to him: you should give it up, it has
nothing to do with art. And I think he took offence. He should have
come a little earlier, before we'd all had something to drink . . .'
'But Boris Leonidovich,' I said to him, 'his verse is made to be sung,
not to be read. And the last thing he should do is give it up—Vertinski
is Vertinski after all, and there's nobody else like him in the whole of
Russia.' 'Well, I suppose I shouldn't have hurt his feelings . . . He
didn't say anything, but he looked upset.' He certainly was upset!

The writer Alexander Raskin has told the story (after BL's death)
about what happened when there was once a burglary at a house near
Pasternak's in Peredelkino, and his family, very alarmed, asked him
to take some kind of precautionary measures. He got an envelope,
wrote 'To the Burglars' in large letters on the outside, and put 600
roubles in it, together with the following note:

Dear Burglars: I have put 600 roubles in this envelope. It is all I have.
Do not go to the trouble of looking for more: there is none left in
the house. Take this and go away. It will be better like this for both
you and us. You do not have to count the money. Boris Pasternak.

As Raskin tells it, the sequel was as follows: 'The envelope had been
put under the mirror in the front hall. The burglars gave no signs of
life, and after a while BL's wife began to take money on the quiet out
of the envelope for her household expenses—by way of a loan, as it
were, and always eventually putting it back. But one day, BL
happened to check the envelope and found some of the money
missing. He was beside himself: "How dare you take the burglars'
money!" he shouted, "how can you rob my burglars? Suppose they
come tonight? What sort of a position will that put me in? What
shall I say to them? That they've been robbed?" Thoroughly
frightened, the family quickly raised the missing sum among themselves and put it back in the envelope. The 600 roubles lay there for a
long time still, but the burglars never came for them.'

In our last year at Peredelkino (1959–60), when we were living
opposite the 'Fadeyev tavern', our neighbour Marusia who worked as
a caretaker was heavily involved, together with a jolly boyfriend of

no fixed occupation, in the distilling of moonshine—something done, incidentally, by most of the local peasants. After several cases in which people had died of paralysis after drinking such stuff, Marusia became worried about police raids and asked us whether she could hide a three-litre flagon of their *pervach** in our cellar. The trap-door leading to it was in our room. BL not only agreed, but was terribly pleased: 'Excellent, Olia—now we are all in the same boat! They know we're wise to their crimes, and they are in on ours!' By 'our crimes' he meant all our meetings with foreigners and our conversations about the novel which by this time was well and truly launched on its progress through the world. Friends had warned us about microphones planted in the walls, and BL had taken to bowing down before ours and making mock speeches of welcome to it. We were so used to the idea of its existence that we somehow couldn't help thinking of it as a kind of third, invisible partner in our conversations, and BL referred to it fondly as the 'dear little mike'.

One day during this same last year of his life we were told that two Russian ladies who had long been living abroad wanted to visit BL. They had arrived in Moscow either as tourists or as correspondents of some big newspaper or other. One of them, Vera Trail, was the granddaughter of Guchkov, who had been Minister of War in the Provisional Government, and the other was the no less celebrated Maria Ignatyevna Zakrevskaya (otherwise known as Countess Benckendorff; and also as Baroness Budberg).

BL was particularly thrilled by the prospect of a visit from Maria Ignatyevna Zakrevskaya, a woman with an unusual and checkered past, who had once been very close to Maxim Gorki and was the official widow of H. G. Wells. Anastasia Tsvetayeva, who had once stayed on Capri with Gorki, had written about her: 'Tall, graceful and slim with a rather round (but not full) face, a huge, dominating and intelligent forehead, and large, dark eyes. Her dark hair is brushed straight back. She is a highly well-educated and cultivated woman ... With a magnificent knowledge of languages, she has translated Gorki into English. (And also, I believe, Pasternak's *The Childhood of Luvers*.)'

BL invited the two ladies to have lunch with him at the Potapov Street apartment and began hectic preparations for their reception. He came in from Peredelkino at seven in the morning and went to his

* Home-distilled vodka 'of first quality'. (Tr.)

apartment in Lavrushinski Street* where he first summoned a barber, and then began phoning us. Ira was asleep near the phone when he woke her up with his first call at eight and asked for me. 'Olia,' he enquired anxiously, 'do we have H. G. Wells?' I told him we had the two-volume edition. 'Open it up and put it out in a place where it can be seen.'

At half-past nine he rang again: 'And do we have Gorki? Just leave him lying around somewhere. One of his things is dedicated to Zakrevskaya!'

When he called a third time at eleven, Ira, robbed of her sleep, shouted out to me tearfully: 'Mama, she's had a very long life. Just stay by the phone—"Classoosha" will phone ten times more.' But he had to give up with the international adventurer who had supposedly been Maria Ignatyevna's first lover:† we didn't have a copy of his memoirs.

We had a large jar of pressed caviar for the guests. I suggested we put it out on the table as it was, but BL said something about laying some small bowls to eat it out of. He was soon to discover how absolutely right I had been.

All spruced up, with his hair newly trimmed, BL duly arrived, to be followed shortly afterwards by the two ladies—who for some reason preferred to walk up to the sixth floor of our apartment instead of using the lift. It was easy enough for the younger of the two, but it was harder for the Baroness. Large and corpulent, she struggled for breath, refusing to let BL help her off with her fur coat, and all the while searching persistently for something in her bottomless pockets. At last she produced a present for Boria: a large, old-fashioned tie—something she may well have inherited from H. G. Wells. But this was not all: after a further search she came up with yet another tie for Boria, and a pair of large gold-plated ear-rings for me.

Eventually our two guests got their breath back and took off their coats. BL, thanking them profusely for their gifts, invited them into the dining room, where the table was laid for lunch. They said the

* In central Moscow; in the late 'thirties a twelve-storey building with apartments and various facilities (barber shop, a bank etc.) for Soviet writers was put up here. (Tr.)

† This apparently refers to Bruce Lockhart, author of *Memoirs of a British Agent.* (Tr.)

main purpose of their visit was to interview him. It was decided that they would conduct the interview over lunch.

Boria was most affable and courtly, talking about Wells, Gorki, and literature in general. The Baroness, taking no note at all of the books by Wells and Gorki, tucked into the pressed caviar for all she was worth. Between this and listening to Boria's gushing eloquence, the two ladies managed to get in some questions—all of which seemed to us completely absurd, for example: 'What kind of jam do you like?' or 'What colour tie do you prefer?' BL decided that these questions were clearly meant in jest and responded with laughter, trying to get the conversation back to more serious topics, mainly literary ones.

When the two had departed, I suggested diffidently that their questions had been put in all seriousness, but Boria waved his hands in the air and laughed at me for failing to appreciate, in my ignorance, the Western sense of humour displayed in the conversation . . . How embarrassed he was a month or so later with the arrival of some British and American newspapers which informed their readers that the Nobel Prize winner Boris Pasternak liked strawberry jam best of all, wore ties with coloured designs, and never touched black caviar.

Many stories are told about BL's absent-mindedness. Once (in March 1950) he wrote to a close friend: 'I wrote an airmail letter to you today, but I took it to the post office with other things to mail, and I now simply have no recollection of putting it in the mail-box. It is possible that it may have been thrown in some waste-basket and got lost there among all the pieces of torn wrapping paper, instead of being sent to you.' From another letter to the same person: 'I wrote to you the other day in such a state of gloom, and hence probably of mental debility too, that I am not at all sure I did not offend against sense and the laws governing agreement between different parts of speech, so please pay no attention to that letter.' But this was not so much the usual kind of 'professorial' absent-mindedness as the self-absorption without which a man of such creative powers as BL (whether in art or science) is unthinkable. Anastasia Tsvetayeva puts it very well in her memoirs—she saw BL in Moscow after her return from Capri: 'When he looks at you, his eyes go past you (or through you, perhaps). He is absorbed not by you, but by something of his own—in which you too may be swallowed up. But you may equally well not enter into this "something" during the whole conversation.'

In 1935, after the Paris Congress,* something happened (or rather did not happen), the memory of which tormented him literally till the last days of his life.

His parents were living then in Germany, in Munich. He had not seen them for twelve years—since his departure from Berlin, after the whole family had moved there in 1921. His parents hoped he would now visit them in Munich on his way home from Paris. But, as he later explained: 'I didn't go to see them out of a stupid sense of false pride. I didn't want them to see me in such a pitiful, dejected state . . . I had thought of seeing them on the return journey, but I travelled back through England. True, my sister came to the train to see me in Berlin, but I never saw my mother and father again.' At the end of 1935, Marina Tsvetayeva wrote to him:

I cannot for the life of me understand how anyone could travel past his parents on a train, after they have waited twelve years for him. And your mother will never understand it—not a hope. It is beyond my understanding, my human understanding. In this I am the opposite of you: I would carry a whole train on my back to see my parents—though I am, perhaps, just as afraid of the idea and would enjoy it just as little . . . And now your excuse is: only *such* people create *such* things. Goethe was the same—not going to say farewell to Schiller, or not travelling to Frankfurt to see his mother because he was saving his strength for the second part of *Faust* or something else, yet at the age of seventy-four thinking nothing of falling in love and getting married—not sparing his (physical!) heart this time. For in this people like you are spendthrifts . . . since your only cure for everything (for everything in yourselves—for all this awesome side of you, the non-human, the divine) is the simplest one of all: love . . .

Much later (in May 1950) BL wrote to Marina's daughter, Ariadna, as though in answer to this letter:

. . . during my journey to the anti-Fascist Congress, I didn't want to meet my parents because I felt in such a terrible state and would have been embarrassed. I firmly believed there would be another chance in more suitable conditions, but then they both died—first my mother, and then my father, so we never saw each other . . . there has

* i.e. the International Writers' Congress (see also pp. 75-76). (Tr.)

been much of this kind of thing in my life, but I swear it is not from lack of concern or love!

In this connection BL's relations with his sisters are significant. The younger of the two, Lydia Leonidovna, wrote nice letters to her brother, and to me and Ira. We exchanged photographs of our children. Our friend Georges Nivat, who became Ira's fiancé, was a welcome visitor to her home in Oxford. After the visit of the Arts Theatre to London in 1958, the actress Zuyeva (to whom BL's poem 'The Actress' is dedicated) brought back with her a long letter to BL from his sisters, and in further correspondence between them there was talk about Lydia wanting to come and see him in Moscow. But, though he gave instructions to his publisher in Milan to transfer a large sum of money to her (and to the elder sister, Josephine), he was afraid of an actual meeting with her. Only after Lydia again wrote about coming to Moscow, on hearing he was dangerously ill, did BL suddenly warm to the idea and encourage her to do so. The nurses in attendance at his bedside reported him as saying: 'Lydia will come and see to everything.' The sense of the words was clear: he believed that Lydia was well disposed towards us, his second family, and not unduly prejudiced in favour of the first one, and that she would therefore be able to achieve a 'reconciliation' between me and Zinaida Nikolayevna. He very much wanted this.

By the time the visa formalities had been completed, the worst had happened. And since Lydia could not bring herself to fly, she arrived in Moscow only the third day after the funeral. She rang me, and we agreed to meet in Peredelkino at the cemetery. I went there with Ira. We recognized her immediately in the distance: an elderly, tired woman who in some ways looked very much like Boria.

PART II
The Poet and
The Tsar

'Stalin has gone to his grave,
—and so now has Pasternak:
poet and Tsar, tyrant and heavenly spirit . . .'
                                   Grigori Pozhenyan

The names of Pasternak and Stalin always seem to stand for exact opposites or antipodes. At the end of the 'forties the young poet Naum Mandel (Korzhavin) wrote the following lines:

> In the Kremlin, at the heart of darkness
> Lives someone harsh and cruel
> A man who claims to understand these times
> But has never made sense of Pasternak ...

Yet at the height of the campaign against BL at the end of 1958, when somebody tried to console him by suggesting that in Stalin's day 'Doctor Zhivago would soon have turned into Doctor Mertvago'* (i.e. that if Stalin had still been alive, the business of the novel would have ended with the liquidation of the author), BL replied: 'But perhaps not'.

It is indeed hard to say how Stalin would have reacted to the novel. The man who could 'never make sense of Pasternak' did in fact occasionally try to do so. And it is perhaps only owing to this that BL survived during the years of the wholesale destruction of the intelligentsia, when even convinced supporters of Stalinism such as Mikhail Koltsov and Sergei Tretyakov went to their doom.

During the fourteen years of our life together BL often found occasion to speak or write about Stalin. His judgments were very contradictory and subjective, often reflecting the influence of later events on the past. The theme became particularly insistent in 1956 when he was summoned to the Prosecutor General's office in connection with the rehabilitation of Meyerhold, and made a written statement saying that Meyerhold was much more Soviet than he, Pasternak. And, of course, the subject of Stalin cropped up again during the campaign of persecution after the award of the Nobel Prize in 1958.

Since then many years have gone by and my memories of that time have been overshadowed by later ordeals. I shall try to write about the main points in the history of BL's relations with Stalin by drawing on BL's own recollections and those of his close friends.

---

* Zhivago is derived from the Russian word for 'alive', and Mertvago from the word for 'dead'. (Tr.)

Pasternak, Yesenin and Mayakovski had a personal meeting with Stalin which seems to have taken place at the end of 1924, or the beginning of 1925.* Recalling this occasion, BL described Stalin as the most terrifying person he had ever seen in his life:

A man looking like a crab advanced on me out of the semi-darkness. The whole of his face was yellow and it was pitted all over with pockmarks. His moustache bristled. He was dwarfish—disproportionately broad and apparently no taller than a twelve-year-old boy, but with an old-looking face.

I believe that at the time and for some period afterwards BL's impression may have been a little different—as one may judge from the verses inspired by Stalin of which I shall speak a little further on.

The conversation was about the question of which Georgian poets should be translated into Russian. Stalin evidently found BL promising and had decided to enlist the talent he sensed in him for the cause of promoting Georgian poetry, and it was in the hope of doing so with the help of Russian poets that Stalin, in BL's view, had called this meeting with Mayakovski, Yesenin, and himself. Needless to say, this aspiration of Stalin's did not prevent him in later years from causing the deaths of many of the Georgian poets, including such close friends of BL's as Titian Tabidze and Paolo Yashvili.

Although Yesenin, Mayakovski and Pasternak were invited together, Stalin spoke with each of them separately. Doing his best to try and charm them, he said that everybody expected them to create truly inspired works, and that they must assume the role of 'spokesmen of the epoch'.

In those years BL still looked on Stalin as a leader in the real sense, and referred to him as such in several stanzas of part of a cycle of poems published in *Izvestia* under the title 'Two Poems' on New Year's Day, 1936. As he was preparing his final one-volume collection for the press (in 1956), BL wrote the following note on the manuscript: 'On pages 3, 4, 5 I was referring to Stalin and myself. This is how it was published in *Izvestia*. Bukharin very much wanted some-

---

* Some people who have read these memoirs of mine in manuscript doubt whether such a meeting can really have happened. I am only reproducing here something that BL told me *repeatedly*.

thing of this kind to be written, and the poem pleased him greatly.'
The stanzas in question are omitted from the 1965 edition of BL's
poetry, and I quote some of them here.[10]

> And in these same days, apart,
> in the ancient citadel
> lives—no, not so much a man as action
> incarnate on the whole globe's scale.
>
> To him destiny assigns
> everything the past omitted;
> he does what the boldest dreamed
> but never dared in previous times.
>
> Labouring prodigiously, he yet spares
> the old familiar scheme of things,
> not soaring, comet-like,
> only to go astray or end in smoke.
>
> In the Kremlin, this great reliquary
> and hoard of legends afloat above the city,
> the centuries now know him just as well
> as they do the clock-tower's chimes.
>
> For all this he remains a man—
> when he hunts a hare
> in wintry fields his gun
> is echoed in the woods like yours or mine.
>
> And by this genius of action
> his opposite, the poet, is absorbed so much
> that he grows heavy as a sponge,
> drinking in whatever drop he may.
>
> In the fugue of both their voices
> the poet's part is infinitely small and piteous,
> but he trusts in the knowledge shared
> between even such extreme polarities.

These 'extreme polarities', I am sure, will always be an object of
much study ('Some later historian will write a most learned work'),
and it is with this in mind that I am now offering what evidence I
have of the relations between them. I hope it will prove to be useful.
About BL's celebrated telephone conversation with Stalin in 1934,

The Telephone Call: 1934

Akhmatova has written, '. . . there is a whole folk-lore. A certain *Trioleshka** has even had the nerve to write (needless to say, during the Pasternak affair) that Boris was the cause of Osip's [Mandelstam] doom. Nadia [Mandelstam] and I consider that Pasternak came off with a good "four"'.† I feel it is important to go into this matter at some length, not only recording what I remember of BL's account of it, but also discussing what Akhmatova and Nadezhda Mandelstam have to say on the subject.

I never met Mandelstam, but whenever I recall BL's stories about him, I am struck by their similarity to Yuri Olesha's description of a figure 'made unnaturally bulky by a fur coat clearly too big for him—and which he was wearing even though it was not winter. Between the massive coat and the high pinnacle of his cap—also of fur—his face glowed like a tiny jewel . . . Mandelstam was clean-shaven, toothless and prematurely aged, but his appearance was majestic. His head was always thrown far back, and his hands engaged in executing some unpractical gesture not of this world.'

Mandelstam was evidently the first of the poets to perceive the monstrosity latent in the character of the man of destiny who was 'action incarnate on the whole globe's scale', and he wrote a short poem about him, drawing a terrifyingly realistic portrait of the despot and of the 'half-men' who served him. He decided he must read his lines about Stalin to the poet whom he regarded as his equal, and one evening at the end of April 1934, when BL ran into him on Tverskoi Boulevard, Mandelstam recited it to him:

> We live, deaf to the land beneath us,
> Ten steps away no one hears our speeches,
>
> But where there's so much as half a conversation
> The Kremlin's mountaineer will get his mention.
>
> His fingers are fat as grubs
> And the words, final as lead weights, fall from his lips,
>
> His cockroach whiskers leer
> And his top boots gleam.

* Contemptuous Russian diminutive for *Triolet*. See Biographical Guide. (Tr.)
† Next to top mark in Russian schools. (Tr.)

Around him a rabble of thin-necked leaders—
Fawning half-men for him to play with.

They whinny, purr, or whine
As he prates and points a finger,

One by one forging his laws, to be flung
Like horseshoes at the head, the eye, or the groin.

And every killing is a treat
For the broad-chested Ossete.[11]

'I didn't hear this, you didn't recite it to me,' BL then said to him 'because, you know, very strange and terrible things are happening now: they've begun to pick people up. I'm afraid the walls have ears, and perhaps even these benches on the boulevard here may be able to listen and tell tales. So let's make out that I heard nothing.'*

Talking of his motive in writing the poem, Mandelstam said that more than anything else he hated Fascism in all its forms.

Every word in the poem is a realistic detail based on actual observation. In her memoirs Nadezhda Mandelstam tells us the origin of some of them. Demyan Bedny wrote once in his diary that he did not like lending his books to Stalin because they always came back with greasy finger-marks on them. Bedny's secretary, needless to say, reported on him and Bedny fell into disfavour. The story provided Mandelstam with a line for his 'subversive' poem. 'Thin-necked' was suggested by the appearance of Molotov's neck: 'Just like a tomcat's', as Mandelstam remarked to his wife.

On the night of May 14, 1934, Mandelstam was arrested in his home on a warrant signed by Yagoda himself. The search of the apartment lasted throughout the night. All this took place in the presence of Anna Akhmatova and—as she recalls—to the miauling strains of a Hawaiian guitar being played next door by Kirsanov. They did not discover the poem, for the simple reason that it had never been committed to paper.

* Later, when the Mandelstams were already in Voronezh, BL complained to Nadezhda Yakovlevna: 'How could he write a poem like that when he's a *Jew*?' Nadezhda Yakovlevna in her memoirs comments: 'I still do not see the logic of this, and at the time I offered to recite the poem to him again so he could tell me exactly what it was wrong for a Jew to say, but he refused with horror.'

BL was terribly upset by Mandelstam's arrest, not only out of concern for Mandelstam's fate, but also because he was anxious in case it might be thought that he, BL, had talked about the poem to anyone else. He raced frantically all over town, telling everybody he was not to blame and denying responsibility for Mandelstam's disappearance, which for some reason he feared might be laid at his door.

Before describing (in the words of Akhmatova) how BL helped Mandelstam, I will put down what he himself told me about his conversation on the telephone with Stalin.

When the phone rang and a voice from the Kremlin said, 'Comrade Stalin wishes to speak with you', BL was almost struck dumb. He was totally unprepared for such a conversation. But then he heard *his* voice, the voice of Stalin coming over the line.

The Leader addressed him in a rather bluff, uncouth fashion, using the familiar 'thou' form: 'Tell me, what are they saying in your literary circles about the arrest of Mandelstam?'

As was usual with BL, instead of answering straightaway to the point, he started off on a rambling disquisition: 'You know, they are not saying anything, because . . . what literary circles do we have now? There are no literary circles, nobody says anything, because they don't know what to say, they're afraid . . .' and so on. There was a lengthy pause at the other end of the line, and then Stalin said: 'Very well. But now tell me your own opinion of Mandelstam. What's your view of him as a poet?'

At this BL, in the eager, fumbling manner characteristic of him, launched into an explanation of how he and Mandelstam were poets of completely different schools: 'Of course, he is a very great poet, but he has no points of contact at all with us—we are breaking up the old verse forms, whereas he belongs to the academic school', and he went on for quite a time in this vein. Stalin gave him no encouragement whatsoever, not interjecting, or uttering a sound of any kind. At last BL came to a halt. Stalin then said, in a mocking tone of voice: 'I see, you just aren't able to stick up for a comrade', and put down the receiver.

BL told me that at this moment his heart missed a beat. It was so humiliating, the receiver being put down like that. He really had proved a poor friend, and the whole conversation had just not turned out as it should. Acutely upset and dissatisfied with himself, he had then rung the Kremlin number and begged the telephone operator to connect him with Stalin again. The whole business now became quite ludicrous. He was told he could not be connected ('Comrade Stalin is busy'), but futile as it was, he went on insisting that Stalin had just been on the telephone to him, they had not finished their conversation, and it was all very important!

In a state of extreme agitation, he frantically began to walk round the communal apartment,* where he then lived on Volkhonka Street, saying to one neighbour after another: 'I must write to him [i.e. to Stalin] and tell him: injustices are being committed in your name. You didn't let me get to the end of what I wanted to say—that all the bad things happening now are linked with your name, and you must look into it all ...' He actually did send off a letter of this sort.†

On the day of Mandelstam's arrest both BL and Akhmatova acted jointly to intercede for him. In Akhmatova's words:

Pasternak, whom I visited that day, went to Bukharin at *Izvestia* to plead on Mandelstam's behalf, and I went to Yenukidze in the Kremlin. To get into the Kremlin in those days was almost a miracle. It was arranged by the actor Ruslanov, through Yenukidze's secretary. Yenukidze was fairly polite, but asked straightaway: 'Perhaps it's over some verse?' . . . In this way we probably hastened the verdict and mitigated it . . . Stalin ordered the case to be reviewed and . . . then phoned Pasternak . . . Stalin told him a decision had already been made and everything would be all right as regards Mandelstam. He asked Pasternak why he hadn't tried to do anything for him: 'If a poet friend of mine were in trouble, I would do anything to help him.'

Pasternak replied that if it weren't for the fact that he *had* tried to

* Standard type of Soviet apartment consisting of rooms connected by a corridor and in which the tenants share the kitchen and bathroom. (Tr.)

† In his 'An Essay in Autobiography', BL mentions one of his subsequent letters to Stalin: 'There were two famous pronouncements about the era: one, that life was getting better and more cheerful; and the other, that Mayakovski was and continued to be the best and most talented poet of our times. For this second pronouncement I wrote personally to thank its author because it protected me from the inflation of my own importance which had begun with the Writers' Congress in the mid-thirties.'

do something, Stalin would never have heard about the matter. 'Why didn't you approach me or the writers' organizations?' Stalin asked. 'The writers' organizations haven't bothered with cases like this since 1927.'[12] 'But he is your friend isn't he?' Pasternak hesitated, and after a slight pause Stalin continued the question: 'But he's a genius, a genius, isn't he?' To this Pasternak replied: 'That's not the point.' Pasternak thought Stalin was trying to sound him out to see if he knew about the poem and explained that this was why his replies were so guarded. 'Why do we talk about Mandelstam, Mandelstam all the time, I have wanted to speak with you for such a long time.' 'About what?' 'About life and death.' Stalin hung up.

Much more astonishing things about Mandelstam are produced by X in his book on Pasternak: the description here of the story of Stalin's telephone call and the circumstances in which it took place is preposterous. It all smacks of information supplied by Zinaida Nikolayevna Pasternak who loathed the Mandelstams and considered that they were compromising her 'loyal' husband. Nadia never went to Boris Leonidovich, and never begged him for anything, as Robert Payne alleges.★ This comes from Zina, who is famous for her immortal phrase: 'My sons love Stalin most of all—and then their mummy . . .'

Nadezhda Mandelstam gives a similar account in her memoirs:

Pasternak was called to the phone, having been told beforehand who wished to speak to him. He began by complaining that he couldn't hear at all well because he was speaking from a communal apartment and there were children making a noise in the corridor . . . Pasternak began any conversation with this complaint. Whenever he was talking on the phone to one of us, Akhmatova and I would quietly ask the other—whichever of us happened to be on the phone with him: 'Has he stopped carrying on about the apartment yet?' He talked with Stalin just as he would have talked with any of us.

Stalin began by telling Pasternak that Mandelstam's case had been reviewed, and that everything would be all right. This was followed by a strange reproach: why hadn't Pasternak approached the writers' organizations, or him [Stalin], and why hadn't he tried to do some-

★ i.e. in his book *The Three Worlds of Boris Pasternak*, New York, 1961, p. 149. 'X' apparently also refers to Payne. (Tr.)

thing for Mandelstam? 'If I were a poet and a poet friend of mine were in trouble, I would do anything to help him.'

Pasternak's reply to this was: 'The writers' organizations haven't bothered with cases like this since 1927, and if I hadn't tried to do something you would probably never have heard of it.'* Pasternak went on to say something about the word 'friend', trying to define more precisely the nature of his relations with M, which were not, of course, covered by the term 'friendship'. This digression was very much in Pasternak's style and had no relevance to the matter in hand. Stalin interrupted him: 'But he's a genius, he's a genius, isn't he?' To this Pasternak replied: 'But that's not the point.' 'What is it, then?' Stalin asked. Pasternak then said that he would like to meet him and have a talk. 'About what?' 'About life and death', Pasternak replied. Stalin hung up . . .

Just as I have not named the one person who copied down M's poem about Stalin, because I believe he had nothing to do with the denunciation and arrest of M, so there is one remark made by Pasternak in this conversation which I do not wish to quote since it could be held against him by people who do not know him. The remark in question was entirely innocent, but it had a slight touch of Pasternak's self-absorption and egocentrism . . .†

Pasternak himself was very unhappy about his talk with Stalin, and to many people, including me, he lamented his failure to follow it up with a meeting . . . Like many other people in our country, Pasternak was morbidly curious about the recluse in the Kremlin . . . This was another extraordinary feature of the times: why were people so dazzled by absolute rulers who promised to organize heaven on earth, whatever it might cost? Nowadays it would never occur to anyone to doubt that in their confrontation with Stalin, it was M and Pasternak who came out on the side of right, displaying both moral authority and a proper sense of history. But at the time Pasternak was very upset by his 'failure' and he told me that for a long time afterward he could not even write poetry . . . I believe that Pasternak still

* Yevgeni Yevtushenko distinctly remembers BL describing this part of the conversation in a slightly different way: *Stalin*: 'If a comrade of mine had been arrested, I would beat my head against the wall till I broke through it.' *BL*: 'But the very fact that you are phoning me, Iosif Vissarionovich, means that the matter will be decided favourably, and that Mandelstam will be released.'

† This evidently refers to the remark about not having any 'points of contact', which I have quoted earlier.

regarded Stalin as the embodiment of the age, of history, and of the future, and that he simply longed to see this living wonder at close quarters.

Rumours are now being spread that Pasternak lost his nerve during the talk with Stalin and disowned M. Not long before his [Pasternak's] final illness I ran into him on the street and he told me about this story. I suggested we both make a written record of his conversation, but he didn't want to. Perhaps things had now taken such a turn for him that he no longer had any time for the past.

How can Pasternak possibly be accused of such a thing—particularly since Stalin started off by telling him he had already exercised mercy? According to the present rumours, Stalin asked Pasternak to vouch for M, but Pasternak supposedly refused to do so. Nothing of this kind happened, and the question of it never even arose.

When I gave M an account of the whole business, he was entirely happy with the way Pasternak had handled things, particularly with his remark about the writers' organizations not having bothered with cases like this since 1927. 'He never said a truer word,' M said with a laugh. The only thing that upset him was that the conversation had taken place at all. 'Why has Pasternak been dragged into this? I have to get out of it myself—he has nothing to do with it.' Another comment of M's was: 'He [Pasternak] was quite right to say that whether I'm a genius or not is beside the point . . . Why is Stalin so afraid of genius? It's like a superstition with him. He thinks we might put a spell on him, like shamans.*' And yet another remark: 'That poem of mine really must have made an impression, if he makes such a song and dance about commuting my sentence.'

Incidentally, it's by no means certain how things might have ended if Pasternak had started praising M to the skies as a genius— Stalin might have had M killed off on the quiet, like Mikhoels, or at least have taken more drastic measures to see that his manuscripts were destroyed. I believe that they have survived only because of the constant attacks on M as a 'former poet' . . . As a result the authorities felt that M had been so discredited and was such a has-been that they did not bother to track down his manuscripts and stamp them out completely. If they had been led to think more highly of M's poetry, neither his work nor I would have survived. It would have been a case, as they say, of scattering our ashes to the winds.

* Witchdoctors among aboriginal Siberian tribes. (Tr.)

The version of the telephone call that has been told abroad is completely absurd. According to accounts published there, M supposedly read his poem at a party in Pasternak's apartment, after which the poor host was 'summoned to the Kremlin and given hell'. Every word of this shows a total ignorance of our life . . .

During Mandelstam's exile in Voronezh, BL and Akhmatova went to Katanian to petition for his transfer to some other town, but they met with a refusal.

Finally, Nadezhda Yakovlevna recalls in her memoirs that: 'The only person who . . . visited me [after Mandelstam's death] was Pasternak—he came to see me immediately on hearing of M's death. Apart from him nobody . . . dared to come and see me . . .'

(A different version of how the telephone call from Stalin ended has been recorded by Zoya Maslennikova,* who kept a diary of her conversations with BL, noting the exact dates on which they took place. In an entry dated September 7, 1958, she quotes BL as having described the final part of the exchange to her in the following terms: *Stalin*: 'What do you want to talk with me about?' *BL*: 'Well, all kinds of things—about life, about death.' *Stalin*: 'Very well. Some time when I have more free time, I'll invite you here, and we can talk over a cup of tea. Goodbye.' Further on Maslennikova says BL told her: '. . . When I later went over the conversation in my mind, I found nothing in my answers that I would have wanted to change.' I do not believe that BL could simply have forgotten his sense of agonized dissatisfaction with himself and the humiliating way in which Stalin put down the receiver. I do not think he could possibly have forgotten this, and what is most likely is that in this conversation with a person he liked but did not know all that well he simply had no wish to 'rake up the past'. Needless to say, the testimony of Anna Akhmatova and Nadezhda Mandelstam, who heard the story directly when it was still fresh—not to mention what I heard from BL—is much closer to the truth.)

* A sculptress who made a bust of Pasternak in his last years. (Tr.)

'Do not sacrifice your personality . . .'

In the middle of August 1934, I went into the Institute of Editing and Publishing, where I was due to attend courses in my final year. Studies were about to begin, and it was all very hectic and crowded. I looked in at the Dean's office, where a nice surprise was waiting for me: I was handed a ticket to the opening session of the First All-Union Congress of Soviet Writers.[13]

On the evening of August 17, I was among the first to take a visitor's seat in the Hall of Columns of the House of Unions★ in the centre of Moscow. For the first time I saw Gorki in the flesh and heard him speak. He was tall and round-shouldered, kept rubbing his hands together, and pronounced his o's broadly. He looked like a life-size statue of himself. I was so absorbed by his appearance that I paid little attention to what he was saying. I knew that Pasternak was on the platform as well, but from my seat right at the back I couldn't make him out at all well.

There were not enough visitors' tickets to go round for all the people in the Institute who wanted them, so I was unable to get to any of the subsequent sessions, but I followed everything written about them in the newspapers with the closest attention—especially, of course, anything that had to do with my favourite poet, Pasternak.

The opening address on poetry was given by Nikolai Bukharin who expressed the highest regard for Pasternak:

He is a poet of that old intelligentsia which has now become the Soviet intelligentsia . . . Pasternak is original . . . and this is his strength: he is infinitely remote from the hackneyed, the stereotyped, from rhymed prose . . . Such is Boris Pasternak, one of the most extraordinary masters of verse in our time, who has not only threaded a whole row of lyrical pearls on the string of his art, but has also given us a number of profoundly sincere revolutionary works.†

★ Formerly the Assembly Hall of the Moscow Nobility, and now used for important meetings and formal occasions (and, in the late 'thirties, for the 'show trials'). (Tr.)

† *Stenographic report of the First Congress of the Union of Soviet Writers*, State Publishing House for Literature, 1934, pp. 494–5.

Olga Ivinskaya, 1936

Boris Pasternak in school uniform, with his parents, his younger brother
Alexander, and one of his sisters in the arms of her nurse

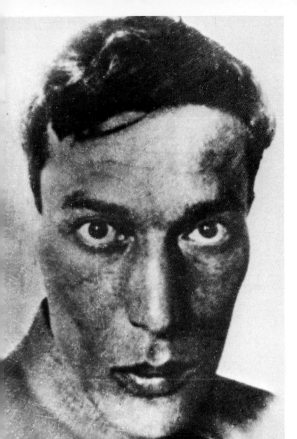

Boris Pasternak, 1934

André Malraux, Vsevolod Meyerhold and Boris Pasternak, 1934, at
the First Congress of Soviet
Writers

Marina Tsvetayeva, 1940,
Moscow

Anna Akhmatova and Boris
Pasternak, 1946

During one of the sessions there was an incident that has been described by several authors, among them Ehrenburg:

Pasternak sat on the platform, a constant smile of delight on his face. When a delegation of Metro workers arrived, he jumped up and tried to relieve one of the girls of a heavy tool she was carrying. She began to laugh, and so did the audience.

Other witnesses of this scene—an extremely typical one for BL— say that it lasted quite a time, because he kept on stubbornly trying to remove the heavy pick-axe from the girl's shoulder while she just as stubbornly refused to part with it. Could this have been the charming play-acting so typical of him, or did he rush to help because he genuinely believed that the girl had just come off the job?

On the evening of August 29, he went up to the rostrum to address the Congress:

... my appearance at this rostrum is not something that has happened of its own accord: I was afraid you might take it amiss if I did not speak.

... When I was unaccountably moved to try and take that miner's tool, the name of which I do not even know [laughter], from the shoulder of the girl from the Metro, the comrades here on the platform who laughed at me for being an oversensitive intellectual could not have been aware that in some immediate sense I felt she was my sister and I wanted to help her, as though she were someone close to me whom I had known for a long time.

Poetry is prose ... the voice of prose—prose in action, not at second-hand. Poetry is the language of organic fact, that is, fact in all its living consequences ...

... Pure prose in its pristine intensity—this is what poetry is ... Do not sacrifice your personality to your position ... With all the enormous affection lavished on us by the people and the state, there is all too great a danger of one turning into a literary office-holder. Shun favours for the sake of their direct source, for the sake of a great, practical and fruitful devotion to the country and the very great men of these times.*

* Ibid. p. 349.

The last phrase was evidently a concession to the incipient style of glorifying Stalin, but there is nothing blatant about it.

BL's constant 'smile of delight' which so stands out in Ehrenburg's memory of him at the Congress, seems to have escaped the notice of other observers, such as Emil Mindlin, for instance, who writes in his book about a conversation he had with Andrei Platonov:

He listened to my account of Boris Pasternak's complaints about the First Writers' Congress . . . Pasternak had told me he hoped to hear something quite different from what people had dwelled on in their speeches. He had expected that there would be speeches of great philosophical import, that the Congress would prove to be a gathering of Russian thinkers. Maxim Gorki's speech had seemed to him the only one of its kind. But the things he felt to be vital for the future of Russian literature had not been discussed. He was disappointed. 'I am mortally disheartened,' he had repeated several times over, 'you understand, mortally!' To this Platonov said in a low voice: 'It's not because of the Congress that Pasternak is feeling so dispirited. I think he would be in just the same state whatever people said in their speeches. It is a matter of Pasternak's own character, not of how the writers are speaking at the Congress. Of course, it's hard for Boris Leonidovich . . . but so it is . . . for everybody.'

BL did not stay to the end of the Congress and on the evening of August 30, after the speech by Stetski, the head of the Central Committee's cultural section, he went off to the Odoyev* rest home. On September 1, at the suggestion of Fadeyev, the Congress elected BL to the board of the Union of Writers.

Could one speak of a relationship between Stalin and Pasternak? 'You'd think we wrote letters to each other and exchanged postcards on holidays,' BL once observed crossly. But he was a member of the Union of Writers and of its Board. Acting on Stalin's behalf and in his name, this organization determined the country's literary policy— and the instruments for carrying it out were real live people: Fadeyev, Stavski, Surkov, Sobolev, Fedin. Among such as these, BL was condemned to spiritual isolation.

* A small town south of Moscow. (Tr.)

In June 1935 an international Congress of Writers for the Defence of Culture took place in Paris. The participants included Heinrich Mann, André Gide, Barbusse, Brecht, Malraux, Aragon . . .

In the fourth volume of his memoirs, Ehrenburg says that a few days before it was due to open, the French writers approached the Soviet ambassador in Paris with a request to send Pasternak and Babel —neither of whom had been included in the Soviet delegation. Both of them arrived in Paris by air after the Congress had already begun its work. There is also a reference to this in one of Marina Tsvetayeva's letters:*

. . . Boris Pasternak, towards whom for many years now I have always turned, from hundreds of miles away, as though to my second self, whispered to me at the Writers' Congress [in Defence of Culture] 'I didn't dare not to come: Stalin's secretary came to see me, and I was frightened.'

Further she says that BL did not want to travel without his wife, but 'they put him on an aeroplane[14] and sent him off'.

I do not remember BL ever mentioning this episode to me, but, needless to say, there is no reason to doubt Tsvetayeva's words. It is very noteworthy indeed that a year after his telephone call to Pasternak, Stalin should again have remembered him and sent his secretary to see him.

When he arrived in Paris, BL told Ehrenburg that his doctor found he had psychasthenia, that he was suffering from insomnia and had been in a sanatorium at the moment when he was ordered to fly to Paris.

Much later (in the summer of 1958) BL explained his state of mind at that time as being the result of a journey he had made to look at the collective farms: 'At the beginning of the 'thirties there was a movement among the writers to visit the collective farms and gather material for books about the new countryside. I wanted to be like everybody else and also went off on a trip with the idea of writing a book. There are no words to describe what I saw there. It was such

* In the book, *Letters to A. Tesková*. Publishing House of the Czechoslovak Academy of Sciences, Prague, 1969, p. 135.

an inhuman, unimaginable misfortune, such a terrible calamity that it was on the way to becoming an abstraction, as it were—the mind could simply not take it in. I fell ill. For a whole year I couldn't sleep.'

After returning from the Paris Congress, in a letter dated November 15, 1935, he wrote to G. V. Bebutov:*

I find it difficult now to understand myself what was wrong with me, but it was something in the nature of psychasthenia, and it lasted from April till the end of August. I had to go to Paris when it was at its height . . .
After such a prolonged spell of insomnia—which seemed so deep-seated that I thought I would never get over it—I could not of course remain the same as I had been before it. I was bound to change, and I do not regret it. I have become more sober and more composed, and you will be unjust if this letter strikes you as unfeeling.†

André Malraux introduced BL at the Congress with the words: 'Before you is one of the very major poets of our time.'

In his address BL spoke mainly about his illness, and said only a few words about poetry. But how significant they were, these few words:

Poetry will always remain that celebrated peak, higher than all the Alps, which lies in the grass at our feet, so that one only has to bend down to see it and pick it up from the ground; it will always be too simple to be discussed at meetings; it will always remain an organic function of the happiness of men endowed with the blessed gift of rational speech—thus, the more happiness on earth, the easier to be an artist.

André Malraux, who acted as interpreter for Pasternak's speech, then read out a French translation of the poem 'Thus one begins . . .' The hall responded with a long ovation.

Next, Tikhonov spoke about BL:

. . . Boris Pasternak introduces us to a complex world of psycho-

---

* A literary scholar and the editor of the last of BL's books to come out while he was still alive: *Verses on Georgia. The Georgian Poets.* Tbilisi, 1958.

† *Literary Georgia*, no 3, Tbilisi, 1966, p. 73.

logical dimensions. What a flow of verse, so swift and taut! What an art that breathes without pause! What a poetic and deeply felt endeavour to perceive and bring together so many intersecting artistic qualities!

In an article on Tikhonov's speech in *Izvestia*, Ehrenburg wrote: 'When Tikhonov went on to give his view of Pasternak's poetry, the audience got to its feet and gave a prolonged ovation to the poet who has shown that artistry of a high order and conscience of a high order are by no means incompatible.' (Six months later *Komsomol Pravda* would accuse Ehrenburg of having acclaimed Pasternak as 'the only one with a conscience'!)

War: 1941

Many people have testified that BL's spirits rose greatly with the beginning of the war. When the air-raids on Moscow started in July 1941 he immediately began to serve as a firewatcher on the roof of the writers' building in Lavrushinski Street, and on more than one occasion dealt with incendiary bombs that fell on it:

> ... The pavement underneath—
> A terrible drop to the skyscraper's base—
> Seemed an island of the dead
> On the far side of the tomb.
>
> And when rubble leapt in the air,
> Hurled skyward by a bomb,
> Anatoli Glebov★ and I
> Were standing there above.
>
> What is it that lifts me today
> Up to the seventh heaven,
> As though from the nether world
> I had climbed out on the roof?

★ The pseudonym of Anatoli Glebovich Glebov-Kotelnikov (1899–1964), the author of stories about Turkey (where he served as a diplomat) and of a number of plays.

Now I'll go down to the tenants
And, fingertips touching faces,
Blind and intoxicated,
I'll tell them it's 'all clear'.

Writers who knew him at that time say he always went up for firewatching duty as though to take part in a festivity, to perform an act of service to his fellow-men. But it was a festivity full of mortal dangers.

At the beginning of September 1941, BL wrote: 'I am doing the same things as everybody else: firewatching, drill and shooting practice.' And three days later: 'Yesterday was a happy day: In the morning I shot better than anybody else in our squad (every bullet on target) and got an "excellent."' In December 1942 he wrote: 'Three weeks ago I mentioned my wish to visit the front to Fadeyev, and have also spoken to the editors of *Red Star* about it—for the last two weeks I have been ringing them every night (they only work at night), and every time they say they will be sending me any day now.' In another letter written in 1942 he said: 'I did firewatching duty on the roof of a twelve-storey building on nights when there were air-raids—once it was hit by two incendiary bombs while I was on duty; I dug a foxhole out at my house in the country and went through a course of military training,—which unexpectedly brought out my natural talent as a marksman.'

He did everything in his power to try to get to the front, but it was only on August 28, 1943, that he was able to go with a group of other writers to visit the divisions which had liberated Orel.

According to those who were there with him, BL bore up very well under the strain of life on the march and was always eager to go where it was most dangerous. He read his verse to the wounded and spent a lot of time talking to the troops. Before the writers left, BL wrote an address to the troops in the name of them all:

Soldiers of the Third Army! For the last three weeks we, a group of writers, have lived among your divisions and taken part in your marches ...

As common sense has taught us through the ages, and as comrade Stalin has often repeated, a just cause is bound sooner or later to conquer. The time has now come: right has triumphed. It is too early to speak of the enemy's flight, but his ranks have faltered and he is retreating under the blows of your victorious arms, under the now clear and evident certainty of his inevitable defeat, under the pressure of our allies, under the crushing weight of his unexampled historical guilt.

Pursue him without mercy and may your ancient good fortune and glory remain with you for ever. Our thoughts and our concern are always with you. You are our pride. We look at you in admiration.

The result of his journey to the front was the cycle *Verses on the War*, and two pieces of prose, *A Liberated City* and *A Visit to the Army*. Apart from this, however, BL also drew on his recollections of the front, using them in an almost documentary way, in the epilogue to *Doctor Zhivago* which begins:

Gordon, recently promoted lieutenant, and Major Dudorov were returning to their units, the one from a service assignment in Moscow, the other from three days' leave. This was in the summer 1943, after the break-through on the Kursk bulge and the liberation of Orel. They met on the way and spent the night at Chern, a small town which, although mostly in ruins, had not been completely destroyed, like most of the inhabited places in this 'desert zone' left in the wake of the retreating invader.

And in *A Visit to the Army* BL wrote about this same small town:

These were the ruins of Chern, the main town of the district, and the point at which we began our subsequent endless journey through a devastated and burned-out land, the first gateway to what in the language of the enemy's orders-of-the-day is described with such disarming simplicity as the 'desert zone'.

BL also visited 'the town of Karachev which had been razed to the ground', and describes it both in the novel and in *A Visit to the Army*.

. . . *and Peace*

The war ended in a victory such as had never been seen before. The peace for which everybody had longed so much, both at the front and in the rear, was with us at last. We all imagined that the war had put an end not only to the crimes of Fascism, but to those of the Yezhov terror★ as well. We had hoped that peace would bring mercy to the millions of our fellow-citizens returning from the German prisoner-of-war camps. Very much was expected from the great victory . . .

But trains full of prisoners again began to move in the direction of the camps. It was not only a case of men who had fought under Vlasov or Bandera, but (to a much greater extent) of ordinary Soviet soldiers and officers. They now found themselves being transported directly from Nazi captivity to their 'own' Soviet concentration camps. Soon they were joined by others: Russian émigrés from many countries in East and West who had been moved to return by the Motherland's promise of 'forgiveness'; thousands of 'homeless cosmopolitans' (that is, in plain language, Jews from the Anti-Fascist Committee and other organizations); thousands and thousands of party officials involved in the 'Leningrad Case' and similar affairs . . . Then there was the deportation of whole peoples to Siberia; the pillorying of Anna Akhmatova and Mikhail Zoshchenko; the persecution of Shostakovich and other composers; the anti-Semitic affair of the 'Doctors' Plot' with its grimly mediaeval flavour. On top of it all we now had the total deification of the Leader—'the greatest military commander of all ages and nations', 'the coryphaeus of all the sciences'.[15]

It took a little time for most people to understand that thanks to Stalin and Beria, victory against an external foe had turned into a defeat for the country's population. Many years later a well-known Soviet poet put it very bluntly:

> . . . And for all our laurels won in war,
> Laying our own country waste,
> We were defeated by ourselves
> —As Rome destroyed itself . . .

At the time, immediately after the war, our friend Kostia Boga-

★ The Great Terror of 1937–8. See Yezhov in the Biographical Guide. (Tr.)

tyrev (of whom I shall have more to say later) translated a poem by the German poet Erich Kästner entitled 'The Other Possibility':

> If we had won the war,
> Then, to the thunder of drums and guns,
> We'd have turned the whole of Germany
> Into a vast insane asylum.
>
> . . . . . .
>
> If we had won the war,
> Setting ourselves above all other races
> We'd have kept the world away
> By putting up a barbed-wire fence.
>
> If we had won the war,
> Beating all our enemies,
> Our country would be so rich
> —in cretins, lackeys, and soldiers.
>
> . . . . . .
>
> Then we'd have tried all thinking people
> And packed them off to fill the jails—
> If only we had won the war . . .
> But, luckily, we lost it.

This was written after the defeat of Kaiser Wilhelm's Germany in the First World War. We had won the Second World War, but BL sometimes felt that the kind of misfortunes described in this poem as hypothetical possibilities had, as the result of our victory, come upon us in actual fact . . .

We realized how futile it was to expect changes for the better from what was going on in literature and art. After Stalin (the 'Coryphaeus'!) had made several pronouncements laying down the law in matters of literature and the writing of history, the clouds began to gather directly over BL himself. From the beginning of March 1947, his name began to get abusive mentions at various literary gatherings, and at a meeting of young writers he was sharply attacked by Fadeyev. But the worst was on March 22, 1947, when the newspaper *Culture and Life* published an article, 'On the Poetry of B. Pasternak', by Alexei Surkov, who wrote:

[Pasternak] flaunts his aloofness from the modern era . . . has adopted the pose of a recluse living outside time . . . upholds the complete separation of poetry from man's social feelings . . . a subjective and idealistic attitude . . . speaks with undisguised enthusiasm about the bourgeois Provisional Government . . . lives at odds with the new reality . . . speaks with obvious hostility and even hatred about the Soviet Revolution . . . direct slander against the new reality . . . Soviet literature cannot be reconciled with his poetry . . .

This was, in effect, not an article, but an open political denunciation. ('In our days political denunciation is not so much an activity as a whole philosophy . . .' BL had once said.)

After reading Surkov's article, BL rang his friends, and even mere acquaintances, and said to them: 'Have you seen what a public whipping I've been given? But it doesn't matter: I feel none the worse.'

But just as it was enough, in the Middle Ages, to denounce a woman as a witch for her to be burned at the stake without more ado, so in Stalin's Moscow of the post-war years it only needed a few words of denunciation from someone such as Surkov for a man to be packed off to a camp or simply done away with. Nobody was immune to being branded with the terrible name 'enemy of the people'.

Even earlier than this, in 1943, there had been rumours in Moscow that Stalin had expressed his dismay at the idea of the Arts Theatre putting on *Hamlet* in Pasternak's translation. In his book *Meetings with Pasternak*, Alexander Gladkov writes: 'This of course was enough for it to be taken out of rehearsal at once. Stalin was probably against it for the same reason that he was against putting on *Macbeth* or *Boris Godunov*: such portraits of rulers whose road to power had been strewn with corpses did not appeal to him in the least.'

BL had foreseen what was to come. Already in 1942, he had said to Gladkov in Chistopol: 'If things remain the same after the War as they were before, I may well land up somewhere in the Far North among many of my old friends, because I shan't be able to go on not being myself . . .' And, on another occasion: 'We could do with a new Tolstoi to hit out . . . by speaking the plain, unadorned truth . . .'

Original verse by BL was now rarely published. Once again, as in 1937, he was forced to give up his own work and seek refuge in translation. As he wrote to someone in Georgia in a letter dated December 10, 1948: 'Translating means establishing myself in a secondary, subordinate capacity—something that, combined with my present, even more acute, struggle for existence and the dual nature of my daily life, is harmful, not to say disastrous for me.' And in a letter to his Georgian editor, written on August 23, 1957: '... I should have given up translating a long time ago and done only work of my own ... My friends should have prevented me from doing translations ... Translation has taken up the best years of my active life and now I must make up for lost time ...'

Akhmatova recalls in her memoir of him how Mandelstam in her presence (in the only apartment he ever had in his whole life, on Nashchokin Street) said to Pasternak: 'Your collected works will consist of twelve volumes of translations, and only one of your own work.' And she adds her own comment: 'Mandelstam knew that translating is a drain on creative energy, and it was almost impossible to get him to do any.'

But what could a writer do if his original work was subjected to such ideological scrutiny that he had no free choice in the matter? Either he had to 'adapt' or earn his living by translation.

Yevgeni Zamiatin said he would prefer to find a job as a street cleaner, rather than do violence to his own soul by engaging in a substitute for literary work. And he emigrated to the West—something Pasternak would not have been able to bring himself to do.

BL knew that the alternative way—conformism—led to the decline and impoverishment of a writer's talent. Much later, in the mid-fifties, Marina Tsvetayeva's daughter Ariadna Efron made the following note of a conversation she had had with BL:

Pasternak once asked me: 'Do you know X?* He has been to see me several times and tried to help me—to get my verse published, and so on. It's possible to talk with him. He understands everything. He's a *very* good man and undoubtedly a *very* talented one. And then, you know, he suddenly gave me his book to read. I never read anything—I value my time too much to read what is written nowadays. But this I decided to read—I liked the man himself so much!'

'Well, and how was it?'

* The person in question was a very well-known and widely published prose writer.

'Just imagine—it was very second-rate. I can't believe he couldn't have done better. But of course if they publish you, you can't write as you please. And if you write as you please, they won't publish you...'

The only thing left, then, was to translate for a livelihood and keep to himself any original work he might write. To Ariadna Efron he wrote: 'My need to earn a living—which, God willing, will still be with me for a long time to come—justifies my existence in my own eyes, and I shall continue to depend on literary translation for it'. (letter of February 1950).

But even this solution was by no means plain sailing. In 1950, the August number of *Novy Mir* published a violent attack on BL's translation of *Faust*:

... the translator clearly distorts Goethe's ideas ... in order to defend the reactionary theory of 'pure art' ... he introduces an aesthetic and individualist flavour into the text ... attributes a reactionary idea to Goethe ... distorts the social and philosophical meaning ...

In conclusion, the author of the review, Tamara Motyleva, delivers her devastating verdict: 'The task of creating a first-rate Soviet translation of *Faust* remains unfulfilled.'

Commenting on this shortly afterwards, BL wrote to Ariadna (who was then living in exile)*:

There has been concern over an article in *Novy Mir* denouncing my *Faust* on the grounds that the gods, angels, witches, spirits, the madness of poor Gretchen and everything 'irrational' has been rendered much too well, while Goethe's progressive ideas (what are they?) have been glossed over. But I have a contract to do the second part as well! I don't know how it will all end. Fortunately, it seems that the article won't have any practical effect.

How much sadness there is in the following passage from a letter BL wrote the year before his death to Boris Zaitsev in Paris:

* In Soviet usage, 'exile' can mean banishment within the country—a measure often applied to persons released from camps. Ariadna lived in Siberia until after Stalin's death. (Tr.)

I have sent my *Faust* to your daughter. For me work of this kind is always accompanied by pain and unhappiness. I have never once been allowed to write introductions to . . . books. Yet it was perhaps only for this that I translated Goethe and Shakespeare—I always made rare and unexpected discoveries in the process, and every time I so much longed to put into concise and living form all the new things I derived from them! But . . . we have other specialists for 'ideas', and my job is only to pick rhymes . . .

Every link in the chain of events that had led to this situation was a source of great anguish to BL and he brooded on it constantly, talking about it with all and sundry, whether or not they could be trusted. He was so appalled by the renewed 'power of the lie' and the continued dominance of the 'spell of the dead letter' that once, in the autumn of 1949, he said to me: 'If, in a bad dream, we had seen all the horrors in store for us after the war, we should have been sorry not to see Stalin go down together with Hitler: an end to the war in favour of our allies—civilized countries with democratic traditions—would have meant a hundred times less suffering for our people than that which Stalin again inflicted on it after his victory . . .'

It was in fact thoughts such as these that finally determined the underlying idea of *Doctor Zhivago* as it is known to the reader. Alexander Gladkov has recorded in BL's own words the reason why he wrote the novel as he did:

I started to work on my novel again when I saw that all our rosy expectations of the changes the end of the war was supposed to bring to Russia were not being fulfilled. The war itself was like a cleansing storm, like a breeze blowing through an unventilated room. Its sorrows and hardships were not as bad as the inhuman lie—they shook to its core the power of everything specious and unorganic to the nature of man and society which has gained such a hold over us. But the dead weight of the past was too strong.

BL's constant preoccupation with the war and its aftermath, and with Stalinism, is also reflected in the following passage in *Doctor Zhivago*:

I think that collectivization was both a mistake and a failure, and because that couldn't be admitted, every means of intimidation had to be used to make people forget how to think and judge for themselves, to force them to see what wasn't there, and to maintain the contrary of what their eyes told them. Hence the unexampled harshness of the Yezhov terror, and the promulgation of a constitution which was never intended to be applied, and the holding of elections not based on the principle of a free vote.

And when the war broke out, its real horrors, its real dangers, its menace of real death, were a blessing compared with the inhuman power of the lie, a relief because it broke the spell of the dead letter.

Not only [people] . . . in concentration camps, but everybody without exception, at home and at the front . . . took a deep breath and flung themselves into the furnace of this deadly, liberating struggle with real joy, with rapture . . .

Among the many manuscripts and other papers of Pasternak which have survived all the tribulations of the years after his death, and which I have managed to keep right until the present day, is a typed copy of the cycle which opened with the 'Two Poems' published in *Izvestia* on January 1, 1936. On the last three pages of the typescript, there is the following comment on these poems written in pencil in BL's hand:

A sincere and one of the most intense of my endeavours—and the last in that period—to think the thoughts of the era, and to live in tune with it. Today (February 17, 1956), going through what few additional materials I have, and coming across this, I am vividly reminded that I wasn't always what I am now, as I finish the second book of *Doctor Zhivago*. It was actually in 1936, when all those terrible trials began (instead of the years of cruelty coming to an end, as I had believed in 1935), that everything snapped inside me, and my attempt to be at one with the age turned into opposition—which I did not conceal. I took refuge in translation. My own creative work came to an end. It awoke again just before the war, perhaps as a premonition of it, in 1940 (*On Early Trains*).[16] The tragic and harrowing wartime period was a *living* [twice underlined by BL] one, and in this sense a free and blissful restoration of a feeling of community with everyone else. But when, after the magnanimity of Providence had expressed itself in victory—even one bought at such a cost—and history had proved so generous, there was a return to the brutality and chicanery of the darkest and most imbecilic pre-war years, I experienced for the second time (since 1936) a feeling of shocked revulsion for the established order of things—now even stronger and more categorical than the first time. I should like to convey something of this in the autobiography which is supposed to serve as an introduction to the one-volume edition. It is very important as regards the development of my outlook and its true nature.

BL was not embittered by all the official harassment and the slander of ill-wishers during 'the bleak autumnal season' that dragged on for so very many years of his life. Both in his own heart and in his writings he never lost the main and most needed thing: hope. The reason he looked on *Doctor Zhivago* as his principal life's work was that in showing his readers a part of their own destiny—a harsh destiny, often tragic, and dreary without end—he always offers a ray of hope. It is a hope, however, that does not depend on unquestioning faith in God, or in miracles. This is how Yuri Zhivago speaks to the dying Anna Ivanovna about death, consciousness and resurrection:

Resurrection: in the crude form in which it is preached for the consolation of the weak, the idea doesn't appeal to me ... life, always one and the same, always incomprehensibly keeping its identity, fills the universe and is renewed at every moment in innumerable combinations and metamorphoses. You are anxious about whether you will rise from the dead or not, but you have risen already—you rose from the dead when you were born and you didn't notice it ... You in others are yourself, your soul ... You have always been in others and you will remain in others. And what does it matter to you if later on it is called your memory? This will be you—the you that enters the future and becomes part of it ...

There is no death. Death is not our business. But you mentioned talent: that's different, that's ours, that's at our disposal. And to be gifted in the widest and highest sense is to be gifted for life ...

There will be no death because the past is over; that's almost like saying there will be no death because death is already done with, it's old and we are tired of it. What we need is something new, and that new thing is life eternal.

And, finally, there is what BL says in the novel about death and art:

... Art has two constant, two unending preoccupations: it is always meditating upon death and it is always thereby creating life ...

One and the same event could been seen by Pasternak as both defeat and victory, as loss or redemption, as death or resurrection. The defeats suffered by the characters of the novel in their ordinary lives could turn into undoubted victories in terms of the Spirit:

> But between victory and defeat
> You should not yourself distinguish.

This is expressed most clearly of all in the endings of three of Yuri Zhivago's poems:

> But at midnight beasts and men fall silent,
> Hearing the spring rumour
> That as soon as the weather changes
> Death can be vanquished
> Through the travail of Resurrection.
>
> ('In Holy Week')

> Those three days will pass
> And I shall be cast down into such a void
> That in the terrifying interval
> I shall grow up to the Resurrection.
>
> ('Mary Magdalene', 11)

> And on the third day I shall rise again.
> Like rafts down a river, like a convoy of barges,
> The centuries will float to me out of the darkness.
> And I shall judge them.
>
> ('Gethsemane')

The Day of the Arrest

The post-war terror was gradually stepped up more and more and with it the harassment of Pasternak. It was a time, in the words of Akhmatova, when 'only a dead man smiled, / glad of his peace.'

October 6, 1949. On this day Boria and I met at *Goslitizdat*, where he had to collect some money. Before this, we had talked about my listening to some new chapters from the first part of *Doctor Zhivago* and he now said to me: 'Olia, let me see you this evening and read to you. There'll be nobody out at Peredelkino, thank goodness, and I can read you another chapter.'

By this time our relations had settled into an extraordinary phase of tenderness, love, and understanding. He was now wholly absorbed by the novel, by the need to complete *Doctor Zhivago* as his main life's work—a design summed up in one sentence in a letter to a correspondent in Georgia: 'One must write in a way never known before, make discoveries, so that unheard-of things happen to you—that is life, and the rest matters nothing.'

We sat down for a short while on a bench in the public garden near *Goslitizdat*. It looked very autumnal. The present statue of Lermontov had not yet been put up there. I noticed we were being looked at closely by a man in a leather overcoat who had sat down near us on the same bench. I remember how I said: 'You know, Boria—they've arrested Ira's English teacher, Sergei Nikolayevich Nikiforov.'

I must say a little more about this person since he was later to play an ominous part in my life.

In 1948, when my children returned from Sukhinichi, where they had been staying with my aunt, Nadezhda Ivinskaya, I put them in a house in Malakhovka—this was at the time when Boria and I were spending our 'summer in the town' . . . One evening I went to take some food out to the children, and as I was walking from the station, I stopped to transfer my bag from one hand to the other when suddenly I saw a huge, pinkish-coloured cat sitting in the road—it was easily the size of a dog. Never having seen its like, I was quite taken aback and began to call loudly to it, 'Puss, Puss, Puss,' whereupon a lady in an old-fashioned lace dress similar to a dressing-gown came out of a garden-gate and said: 'Do you like this cat? She's a Siamese, but a special breed—the fluffy variety. In a little while you might be able to have one of her kittens.'

And so, through this offer of a kitten, I became friends with her and her husband, Sergei Nikolayevich. Olga Nikolayevna was an unusually obliging woman who said she worked as a cosmetician 'at the Moscow Soviet'—where, as she told me, she knew the people responsible for the allocation of apartments. When I told her about BL, she made a strange suggestion: 'If you like, Olga Vsevolodovna, I will arrange for you and Boris Leonidovich to get a separate apartment. All I need is some money, and I'll put you on the list . . .' When I mentioned this to Boria, he wouldn't hear of it: '. . . what's this strange list? Don't have anything to do with it, or even talk about it.'

And then, all of a sudden, we heard that Olga Nikolayevna had been arrested. It was only later that we learned she was a professional confidence trickster who had been in and out of prison. 'You see, Olia,' Boria said to me, 'I told you this was a very funny business—a cosmetician finding apartments for people. You're always taking everything on trust—and it all ends in folly.'

The news of Olga Nikolayevna's arrest was brought to us by her husband, who was quite shaken by it. He was an elderly man whom I had invited to give English lessons to Ira—he came to us at the apartment, was very nice and anxious to please, and Ira made good progress. He had supposedly suspected nothing of his wife's activities. But before a month had gone by, there was news that he too had been arrested—of which I now informed Boria as we sat in the public garden.

We got up and walked towards the Metro station. The man in the leather raincoat came after us.

I did not want to leave Boria even for a few minutes—and he also had a feeling that we should stay together that day. But it so happened that just then I was translating a volume of Korean lyrics, and I had arranged for the author, Won Tu-Son, to come and see me in the evening with his corrections. For this reason I would be able to go out to Peredelkino only much later on. This was what we were talking about as we went into the Metro and got on a train. Boria had to change at the Lenin Library, and I had to get out at Kirov Station. I looked round and saw that the man in the leather coat was still there. 'Very well, Olia,' BL said, 'if you can't manage it tonight, I'll come in to see you tomorrow. And this evening I'll read the new bit to Aseyev.'

Everything seemed just then to be going very well for us, and I was enjoying a peculiar feeling of freedom which came from the closeness that had grown up between us. He had just dedicated his translation of *Faust* to me, and I had said I would give him a poem by me in return. He begged me to write it out for him. When I now went back alone to my apartment in Potapov Street and sat down at the typewriter to do so, I was suddenly overcome by a strange feeling of anxiety which seemed quite out of keeping with the happiness I had felt earlier in the day.

When some strange men burst into my room at eight o'clock that evening to take me away, breaking the thread of my life, the unfinished poem remained in the typewriter:

> Play on the whole keyboard of pain,
> and may conscience not prick you
> if, though ignorant of the parts,
> I act the role of Juliet and Margarita . . .
> Or if I've forgotten even the faces of those
> who came before you: from birth I'm yours.
> And twice you've opened up my prison—
> though still you have to bring me out of it . . .

I had not believed that such a thing could ever happen to me. I suddenly was unable to swallow because of a pain in my throat. I wondered what on earth it could be for. For my connection with Olga Nikolayevna, perhaps? And then, the quite preposterous thought: on account of Boria?

I remembered the strange feeling we had both had earlier in the day that we should stay together this evening . . . Now *they* began to rummage in my things, throwing them all over the place and I shall never forget how Mitia, who had run home from school to feed the hedgehog he kept on the balcony, looked on, his eyes round with amazement. One of the men searching the apartment put his hand on Mitia's head and said 'good boy'—and I remember how Mitia, in an unchildlike gesture, pushed the hand away from him. Ira was still at school. But my mother and step-father were at home. And it so happened that Alexei Kruchenykh had just come to visit me.

The most shaken of all was my step-father who had once been through the business of my mother's arrest. He stood weeping on the staircase and kept saying to me through his tears: 'You'll soon be back, you haven't robbed or killed anyone!'

While the search was still being conducted in my presence, I noticed that in going through books and papers they laid aside everything connected with Pasternak. All his manuscripts and every scrap of paper with a note by him were picked out and gathered together. The many books that Boria had given me, with the unstinting, generous dedications in his hand, often covering all the blank pages, were now being pawed by these strangers. They also seized all my letters and notes.

I was soon taken away, and the search went on without me.

When he learned of my arrest, BL telephoned Liusia Popova and asked her to come and meet him on Gogol Boulevard. She found him sitting on a bench near the 'Palace of Soviets' Metro station. He began to cry and said: 'Everything is finished now. They've taken her away from me and I'll never see her again. It's like death, even worse.'

After this, in conversation even with people he scarcely knew, he always referred to Stalin as a 'murderer'. Talking with people in the offices of literary periodicals, he often asked: 'When will there be an end to this freedom for lackeys who happily walk over corpses to further their own interests?' He spent a good deal of time with Akhmatova—who in those years was given a very wide berth by most of the people who knew her.* He worked intensively at the second part of *Doctor Zhivago*.

Ira's Account

Many years later my daughter Ira wrote down her memories of that night and the following days:

One day in October 1949 when I came home from school and rang the bell, the door was flung open by a man in military uniform who smiled brightly at me. Hanging on the stand inside there must have been about ten elegant greatcoats with blue epaulettes, and as many caps. Thick clouds of blue cigarette smoke were drifting out of my Mother's room, and people were talking in low voices there. Since I

* i.e. because of the official attack on her in 1946; see Biographical Guide. (Tr.)

was then in the second shift at school* it must have been after eight. It was already dark outside. The ceiling light had been switched on in our room—something that happened very rarely indeed. Only eleven years old, I was overwhelmed by terror and a premonition of doom. I hung up my coat and, peering through into the living room, saw my Grandmother, her face wet and swollen with tears, my Aunt Nadia, who was like a ghost, and my Grandfather looking the picture of misery.

But that was not all. Apart from these there were yet other persons in the room, and only now do I realize, after reading the memoirs of people who have gone through the same experience, that this was not at all strange, but simply the usual thing. Our janitor with his large moustache sat in his quilted jacket and apron on a chair, his head bowed—he was here as the inevitable 'witness' on behalf of the authorities. Nearby, on a small sofa, was Kruchenykh, a regular visitor to Mother's 'at homes', and clearly frightened to death; next to him was Grandfather's brother—Uncle Fonia, as we called him then —who must have got caught here while paying a visit, and now sat with his light-blue eyes almost starting out of their sockets with terror.

I went through into the room where Mitia and I slept, and Grandmother's sister, Aunt Milia, told me in a very distraught tone of voice that there was a search going on, and that Mother had been taken away in a car to the Lubianka an hour ago. What was I to do? In a demonstrative manner, I picked up a book, lay down on my bed and began to read. In the meantime matters pursued their course, as I learned later, in tragi-comic fashion. At one point they were all asked to show their papers. At that time Uncle Fonia happened to be working as a nightwatchman at the Cocktail Hall† on Gorki Street and often used to bring us cocktail straws and paper napkins, or anything else he could lay his hands on (he was already not quite right in the head). Now, when he was suddenly asked for his 'papers', he just couldn't understand what they wanted and decided they must be investigating him for stealing at work, so he burrowed into his pockets and began to pull out paper napkins.

* In the post-war years, because of severe overcrowding, Soviet schools worked in two shifts. (Tr.)

† A unique institution (now abolished) in Moscow during and after the war. Frequented by foreigners and members of the Soviet élite, it served as a useful listening post for the secret police. (Tr.)

At eleven o'clock Kruchenykh, whose day was divided up according to a very strict timetable (it was simply a mania with him) announced that he must at all costs go home to take his sleeping pills and spend the night in his own bed, as he was accustomed. But they wouldn't let him, and he became very obstreperous. But eventually he took a tablet and lay down on our tiny sofa.

I still remember how terribly worried I was the whole time because the fishes' water hadn't been changed. We had one huge fish (a non-tropical one) which had to have its water changed every day—towards evening it used to swim up to the surface, blowing bubbles out of its great, tragically gaping mouth, and this always alarmed me very much. But now I was not allowed out into the kitchen to fetch water. Grandmother just sat in total silence. Doors banged and people came and went. Then we began to get some scraps of news: Grandfather heard from the soldier who had driven Mother to the Lubianka that it had been 'a bad ride', that she had cried in the car. Aunt Nadia from Sukhinichi was deaf and couldn't understand what was meant when the others bellowed something about 'a bad drive' into her ear. By two o'clock in the morning everything seemed to be over—our light was put out and we were told to sleep. Mitia and I lay in the darkness pretending to sleep, and we could hear Grandfather and Grandmother talking something over with the soldiers.

I kept hearing the words 'children's home'—in which, from what they were saying, we would have to be put under Soviet law because we had no father or mother. We would be all right, they said, in a children's home, whereas Grandfather and Grandmother would find it hard to bring us up when all they had was his wage of sixty-six roubles a month and she earned nothing at all. But Grandfather and Grandmother replied rather non-committally to this, because they already had the thought at the back of their minds that Boris Leonidovich would come to our rescue and not let us be sent to an orphanage. We were certain the help he had already been giving us would not stop now. But Grandmother was evidently fearful of putting our cards on the table and telling them outright that sixty-six roubles a month was not the sum total of our resources, and that we therefore had a chance of surviving at home. The men in uniform did not seem to press the point too much, and the next morning Grandmother told us that she and Grandfather had signed a paper saying they wanted to take us into their care and not put us in an orphanage. This is the most vivid memory I have of that first occasion when Mother was arrested.

How did we get news of Mother? The men in uniform had been given the telephone number of our neighbours, and the interrogator in charge of her case occasionally phoned Grandmother. He was extremely polite—of which she was very glad indeed, since we were now social outcasts and such politeness seemed like a gift or a favour. Because of it we went on hoping . . . Grandmother was allowed to hand over some money and parcels at the prison . . . Once, an unknown woman rang us to say she had been in the same cell as Mother and would like to see us. Grandmother went to visit the woman and we waited for her to come back and tell us what she had learned— which was that things were very bad: Mother was pregnant and ill.

After this we heard nothing more until we received a letter from Mordovia*—and from that day on Mordovia entered into our life as a permanent feature. We began to get regular letters and requests for things. It was forbidden to send parcels from post offices in Moscow, so Grandmother used to go out with Mitia (who was then only eight) to mail them from Perovo.† We bought cans of soup and mashed peas—not that we had no money for anything else, but because Grandmother thought they would be the most suitable. It was all done up in packages and taken out to Perovo once a month. When she returned, Grandmother would describe what a terrible wind had been blowing and how the package had nearly been torn from her grasp—altogether, she liked to tell tales of woe.

I wrote letters to Mother, but my link with her as a real live person had been completely broken, and I must admit that I only wrote because Grandmother forced me to.

We were indeed not abandoned by BL. Although he rarely visited the apartment, I believe we now lived entirely off what he gave us. Many years later, when I too was in the Lubianka, my interrogator wanted to know what had so bound me to Pasternak, and I replied that without him we would not have survived—in the direct physical sense of the word. We always had something to eat, and there was enough left over to go to the cinema. Grandmother was

* See note to p. 26. (Tr.)

† A large town about ten kilometres south east of Moscow. Parcels to the camps had evidently to be mailed from here, rather than from Moscow, in order to attract less attention. (Tr.)

even able to rent us some kind of a *dacha* for 800 roubles. Until BL
fell ill (he had a heart attack in 1952) he used to come and bring us
money himself. But there was always something embarrassing about
it.

I remember one occasion when he came in his black fur coat (the
one he wore to the end of his days, I believe) and black astrakhan hat
and sat at the table with Grandmother while she told him the most
terrible things (the kind of thing she was prone to do, as I have mentioned): Mother was dying of hunger, she had podagra, pellagra,
scurvy, and so forth. It all seemed to me terribly humiliating. BL
said he was hard up at the moment, but would keep it all in mind.
At this point I made a face and buried my nose in a book. Then, very
spontaneously as always, not taking the least account of the difference
in our ages (which was just right in the circumstances and the reason
it so sticks out in my memory), he said to me: 'I realize of course, Ira,
that you don't want me to leave, and that's not the reason why you
are reading a book, but I really am in a hurry.'

Not long after this Grandfather died, and one day Grandmother
came rushing up to our apartment on the sixth floor, and sinking into
a chair, all out of breath, told us in horror-struck tones that it was all
over with us now: BL had had a heart attack. We were overcome by
panic. I now know from letters and certain other documents that as
soon as BL was brought to hospital and was able to hold a pencil in
his hand, he scrawled a note to Marina Baranovich* instructing her
to hand over 1000 roubles to us and to stay in constant touch with us.
And the money did indeed continue to come in, keeping us alive.
Later, when he recovered, but still could not walk up the six steep
flights of stairs to our apartment, Grandmother would go down to
meet him on the Chistye Prudy Boulevard. Once she took me along
with her, and I remember seeing him again for the first time after his
illness—it was spring, and he was sitting on a bench in the same old
black astrakhan hat. We ran up to him over the snow. It was so long
since I had seen him and suddenly, after all these long months of his
absence, right there on the boulevard, I felt there was a very special
bond between us. I raced up to him and kissed him. 'Irochka,' he said,
'it's so long since I've seen you: how pretty you've grown, and your
eyes have evened up now!'

* Marina Kazimirovna Baranovich, a typist who typed out most of Pasternak's
work.

And so for the first time, in October 1949, I crossed the fateful boundary, the Rubicon which divides ordinary humans from prisoners. Female guards subjected me to a humiliating examination. Everything I had was removed from me: all the little things a woman values so much—my ring, my wrist-watch—were seized by them. Even my brassière was taken away: as was later explained to me, it can be used to hang yourself with.

Sitting in my solitary cell all I could think was: what if I don't see Boria? My God, what can I do to warn him? How terrible it will be for him, that first moment when he learns I'm gone! And then the thought flashed through my mind that he too must surely have been arrested—they would have picked him up on the way home after we parted! (He was soon to write to Ariadna Efron who had just been released from a labour camp but was still condemned to exile: '. . . my poor dear is in a plight like the one you have been in.')

I don't remember how long I was kept in solitary confinement—about three days, I think. All that stays in my mind is how at one moment, when I took hold of the hem of my shift, put it round my neck and began to pull it up in some peculiar fashion towards my ears, two men suddenly burst into the tiny 'box',* hauled me off a long way down a corridor and pushed me into a cell in which there were already fourteen other women. The beds were screwed to the parquet floor and had good mattresses on them. The women had all covered over their eyes with white material, trying to protect them from the blindingly bright light of the lamps. I soon understood that this was part of a refined method of torture by deprivation of sleep: interrogations were at night, sleeping was 'not allowed' in daytime and a dazzling light shone in your face continuously. The Inquisition was a backward affair compared with this: that was before the days of electricity . . .

This cunningly contrived ordeal was terribly oppressive. The prisoners began to feel that time had come to a halt and their world had collapsed about them. They ceased to be sure of their innocence, of what they had confessed to, and which other persons they had compromised apart from themselves. In consequence, they signed

* The English word 'box' is the term used for the minute cells in which prisoners are briefly confined while waiting to be 'processed'. (Tr.)

any raving nonsense put before them, and named the names needed by their tormentors to fulfil some fiendish plan for the liquidation of 'enemies of the people'.

All this I was to understand in the following few days, but in the meantime, after the stultifying horror of the tiny 'box' without light or air, what should I see in the new cell but a table, with a teapot and a set of chessmen . . . The other women bombarded me with questions, asking about everything under the sun. I told them about my children and said how I couldn't for the life of me understand why I had been arrested—and that I was sure I would be released in a day or two, once 'they' had understood what a complete mistake it all was. Like everybody else in prison for the first time, I said many such comic things.

The long, monotonous days of waiting dragged on. I was not summoned out for interrogation; nobody, so it seemed, was in the least concerned with me. Only the other women were called out at night to be questioned.

One of my fellow-prisoners was an elderly woman by the name of Vera Sergeyevna Mezentseva, a pleasant person with pale-blue eyes and rosy cheeks. She had been a doctor in the Kremlin Hospital. At a New Year's Eve party somebody had proposed a toast to the 'immortal Stalin'. But someone else had remarked that the 'immortal' one was very ill—supposedly from cancer of the lip through smoking a pipe—and that his days were numbered; a third doctor then claimed he had once treated Stalin's double. After being denounced by an informer—in those days there was inevitably one present at any gathering—this whole group of incautious doctors had landed in our cell and the one next to it. Vera Sergeyevna, who had taken no part in the conversation, faced a minimum of ten years in jail, and she knew it. From my very first day in prison she took a friendly interest in me, questioning me closely about the circumstances of my arrest, and about my last moments with Boria, when we had both had the uncanny feeling that we shouldn't leave each other, even though we were supposed to meet again in only a few hours' time. Vera and I wondered how he would have taken the news of my arrest when he went to look for me at home, and what he would do now. Later on, after my interrogation had begun, I was always very glad to be able to get back to the cell and unburden myself to Vera Sergeyevna.

I also remember a young, very beautiful girl with eyebrows that met at the bridge of her nose, extraordinarily bright grey eyes, and long lashes. I stared at her so intently that she at once asked: 'Do you think I look like someone else?' 'For some reason,' I said, 'you remind me of Trotski.' At this she laughed: 'Well, as a matter of fact, I'm his granddaughter—and I actually do look like him, as everybody notices.' This was Sasha Moglin, the daughter of Trotski's daughter who had left the country with her son. Sasha's father, one of the editors of *Pravda*, had then married someone else called Katzman. When Moglin was arrested and executed by firing squad, Sasha's step-mother had needless to say been called in for questioning and she soon lost her nerve and admitted that she was bringing up Trotski's granddaughter. At this time Sasha had just finished her studies at an institute of geology. Once she looked in her mail box and found someone had pushed into it a foreign newspaper with a report that her brother had been murdered by unknown persons and her mother had committed suicide. She herself, still barely out of her teens, had been arrested on the formal pretext that she had copied out into a notebook some verses by Margarita Aliger which had been published only two years previously:

> Lighting the stove and warming her hands,
> As we settled in to start our lives again,
> My mother said: 'We are Jews,—
> How could you forget?'*

On the day when Sasha was called out of the cell 'with belongings', it was a terrible wrench for us both. (She was sent off for five years somewhere to the Far North with her mother, who was in the next cell, as a 'socially-dangerous element'.) Many things have by now faded from my mind, but I shall never forget how she wailed as they pulled her away from me: it still rings in my ears even now. It broke my heart to hear her cry. Nowhere do you come closer to a person than in prison. Nobody listens and speaks to you like the cell-mates who see their own fate reflected in your own, and from nobody else do you get such sympathy.

* From the long poem 'Your Victory' in *Selected Works*, Soviet Writer Publishing House, 1947, p. 177.

One night, a month or two after my arrest, a comic-looking figure was pushed into our cell. She was a thick-set woman of small height with a disproportionately large face and brown slits of eyes. She was tear-stained and frightened. She told us she was a member of the Piatnitski choir, and indeed she had a marvellous, soft voice—as we heard when she managed to sing Russian songs in the cell. Even the guards outside listened to them, giving her time to finish before they burst into the cell and shouted 'Singing not allowed: you lose your exercise period!'

This woman, whose name was Lidia Petrovna, had landed here because of her husband Petrunka, a wretched drunk who worked as an accountant—and he had been arrested because of her. They had gone somewhere out of Moscow (to Zagorsk, I think) to visit Petrunka's relatives. He and his brother got drunk and she locked herself and her small daughter in the bedroom to escape from him. But Petrunka would not have it—he wanted to spend the night with his wife, instead of all alone on a campbed. He began hammering on the locked door. But Lidia Petrovna would not open up. To his undoing, the poor man now felt an upsurge of masculine strength and began to bluster and threaten. 'Open up, you slut!' he shouted, swearing obscenely, 'you'd better open up! I could not only break this door down, I tell you, I could blow up the Kremlin as well!'

The next morning at breakfast Lidia Petrovna told his relatives how he had made this drunken threat to blow up the Kremlin and begged them to take him in hand before he got into serious trouble for blurting out things like that. One of the relatives did indeed 'take action'—with the result that Petrunka was now being intensively questioned, somewhere not far from us, about what terrorist organization he belonged to and precisely when it planned to blow up the Kremlin. His silly wife, weeping tears of pity for him, confirmed to her interrogator that Petrunka actually had made an attempt on the seat of government—but only in words. As things were in those days Petrunka stood to get a sentence of eight years, and she could have got five for 'failure to report'. But for her co-operation—unwilling though it was—in unmasking an evildoer she was told she would be released. And, strange to say, she actually was set free. Before she left us, she pricked out our addresses on a handkerchief with a needle made of a fish-bone.

Anticipating a little, I should mention that around this time it became clear that I was pregnant—a fact of which Lidia Petrovna, after her release, informed my mother, thereby creating a tragi-comic imbroglio with Boris Leonidovich. As soon as my pregnancy was confirmed, I began to receive white bread, purée instead of *kasha*,* and salads—they were handed to me through the hatch in the cell door. At the same time I was allowed to buy twice the usual amount from the prison store. But the chief and most tangible concession was of another kind. Prisoners were not allowed to sleep in the daytime, even after spending the night under interrogation; in the daytime all you could do was pace the cell or sit and brood. The moment you began to doze off, a guard rushed in and woke you up. But now, after we got up in the morning, the warder on duty came in without fail and, prodding me with his finger, said in a respectful tone: 'You are allowed to sleep. Lie down again.' And I would go back to sleep, —a sleep without dreams, into which I fell as though into an abyss, interrupting in mid-sentence anyone who happened to be telling me about her interrogation during the night. My kind cell-mates talked in whispers not to disturb me, and I would wake up again only to eat the mid-day meal.

Interrogation by the Minister

Of course not all my cell-mates were so nice. There was one, for instance, called Lidochka (I don't remember her surname)—an odd, mysterious person who had been in jail for six years already. She was in fact a 'stool pigeon' working for the Lubianka authorities and reporting on everything we said in Cell No. 7.†

'Olia,' she kept assuring me, 'you'll certainly be released if they haven't yet called you out for an interrogation after all this time, it must mean they have nothing on you.'

* A porridge usually made of buck-wheat. (Tr.)

† Later on she was brutally killed in a labour camp by fellow prisoners when they discovered what she was up to: they ducked her head in a cesspool and held her there till she drowned. Such was the terrible end of this girl with her waxen complexion and carefully kept silk dresses who dreamed of earning a pardon. During the war her husband had worked for the Germans as a *politsai*. In her six years in the Lubianka she was always spying on someone and got cigarettes from the interrogator as a reward.

On the fourteenth day after my arrest, Sasha Moglin, Vera
Sergeyevna and I had just eaten our supper of potatoes and salted
herring, and after our usual conversation about our relatives, about
what might be in store for us—and even about the most recent films
we had seen before our arrest—we lay down on our beds. But before
I had managed to fall asleep, the guard on duty rushed in suddenly
and said: 'What are your initials? Get dressed for interrogation!' I
gave him my initials. 'Initials *in full*,' he said—when asked for our
'initials', we were always ordered to give them 'in full'.

Very agitated, I began to pull on the dark-blue crepe de chine dress
with large white polka dots which had been brought from home and
handed in for me at the prison. It had been a favourite of BL's. Seeing
me in it, he had often said: 'Olia—that's how you should look, that's
how you came to me in my dream.' I was now putting it on with a
particular feeling of expectation and hope that a very special new
page was about to be turned over in my life, after which I would
certainly walk out of this place into the streets of Moscow—what a
surprise for Boria when he came to Potapov Street in the morning
and found me there!

But in the meantime here I was being led down the long corridors
of the Lubianka past all the closed, mysterious-looking doors from
behind which all one could hear were occasional muffled and incomprehensible cries. My escort stopped at a door with the number
271. It led not into a room, but into what looked like a cupboard.
When I went in, I suddenly felt it revolve, like the 'house on chicken's
legs' in the fairytale, and at once I found myself in a large room
where there were at least ten men in uniform with shoulder boards
and insignia of rank. But I was taken right past them to another door
—they stopped talking and stood aside to let me by.

I was now in a vast, brightly-lit and comfortable office with walls
lined in some grey velvety material—or so it seemed to me. At an
angle to one wall was a huge desk covered with green baize. Behind
it, facing me, there sat a handsome, portly figure—my first impression
at least was of a well-groomed, good-looking man with brown eyes,
sleek, steeply-arching eyebrows, and dressed in a long military tunic
of the Caucasian type with small buttons up to the neck.

He motioned me to sit down on a chair some way from him. On
his desk I saw a pile of the books which had been taken from my
apartment during the police search. One, of which I was particularly

fond, had been brought back from abroad by Fadeyev.[17] The title page was entirely covered by a dedication to me in BL's flowing hand (the words always looked like a flock of cranes sailing across the sky): 'To you as a memento—even if imperilled by all these pictures of my ugly mug.' The book opened with a beautiful sketch of a boy —one leg was dangling from a chair and he was writing something in an exercise book at a table just barely indicated by a single line. This was Boria at the age of seven, as drawn by his father, Leonid Osipovich Pasternak. It was followed by the artist's self-portrait, showing him as a handsome, grey-haired man in a soft-brimmed hat. In the kindly, wise, and serene face with its inspired look one could see the firm, irregular, and expressive features of his son Boria—the features of an ancient African deity.

I could also see the small red volume of verse in which Boria had written the blissful words: 'My life, my angel, I love you dearly'. They were dated April 4, 1947, the year when our closeness had begun to seem to him like some stupendous victory or gift.

Then there were other signed books of his verse and translations which he had given me in recent years. There were also many books in English.

All of these beloved books now lay here on this desk in the world's most dread building to be fingered by alien, unfriendly hands. I sat there in my chair, ready to meet my fate, telling myself to cast all hopes aside, to await the end and not lose my human dignity. The man at the desk asked sternly: 'Tell me now, is Boris anti-Soviet, or not, do you think?'

And before I could reply, in a half-bantering tone: 'Why are you so bitter? You've been worrying about him for some reason! Admit it now—we know everything. You've been worrying, haven't you?'

'You always worry about a person you love,' I replied. 'If he goes out on the street, you worry in case a brick falls on his head. As regards whether Boris Leonidovich is anti-Soviet or not—there are two few colours on your palette, only black and white. There is a tragic lack of half-tones.'

The man at the desk arched his eyebrows and asked, nodding towards the pile of books confiscated from me: 'How did you come by these? You no doubt realize why you are here at this moment?'

'No, I don't. I am not aware of having done anything.'

'Then why did you plan to get out of the country? We know all about it.'

I replied indignantly that I had never in all my life thought of leaving the country, but he brushed this aside impatiently: 'Now listen here, I would suggest you think very carefully about this novel Pasternak is passing round to people at the moment—at a time when we have quite enough malcontents and enemies as it is. You are aware of the anti-Soviet nature of the novel?'

I again contradicted him hotly and in a rather disjointed way tried to describe the contents of the part of the novel already completed, concentrating on the chapter 'Boys and Girls' which BL had read not long before at Ardov's house, where his listeners had included Akhmatova and Ranevskaya. (The title of this chapter was subsequently changed.)

The man at the desk again interrupted: 'You will have plenty of time to think about these questions and how to answer them. But personally I would just like you to appreciate that we know everything, and that your own as well as Pasternak's fate will depend on how truthful you are. I hope that next time we meet you will have nothing to conceal about Pasternak's anti-Soviet views. They are clear enough from what he says himself.' Then, pointing at me imperiously, he said to my escort who had come back into the room at that moment: 'Take her away.' The clock in the endless Lubianka corridor showed that it was three o'clock in the morning.

'I am your humble interrogator . . .'

Three hours' sleep under the blinding lights of the cell were not restful and the following day went by in a haze. I began to understand the effect of this ordeal by deprivation of sleep and bright lights. I was becoming confused in my mind and felt exhausted. Just at the moment when we were allowed to go to bed, and I had covered my face with a kerchief to shield my eyes from the powerful lamps, the door opened with a clang: 'Your initials in full . . . .'

And again I was led down the long corridor, this time to a much simpler office occupied by a man in a military tunic whom I had not seen before. In reply to his preliminary questions I said I had already been called out for interrogation and that somebody else was evidently in charge of me.

'Not at all,' he said. 'I am your humble interrogator. Allow me to introduce myself: Anatoli Sergeyevich Semionov. The person who interrogated you yesterday was the Minister, Abakumov himself. Come now, don't you see what a modest office I have? There's nothing here like what you saw yesterday. Well then, let's hear what you have to tell me.'

'What do you want me to tell you about?' I countered.

'Well—about how you and Pasternak have been planning to escape abroad, how you have been running down the Soviet system, saying you don't like the government, and listening to foreign lies. And then tell me: what is this novel of Pasternak's? He has of course shared his thoughts with you. On what lines is he thinking of continuing it? Who are your friends? These are the things you must go over in your mind and which we have to look into together.'

'Very well, I'll do as you say and write it all down, but I have to go home,' I replied with the most grotesque naïveté. 'It really is quite preposterous, you know—I have my children to look after and I'm not aware of having done anything wrong.'

It was only later on that I was to understand through direct experience the basic principle of the MGB's* activity in those years: 'Give us a man, and we'll make a case.' Or rather, I had hitherto known it only in the abstract—even though the arrest of innocent people at night had long been a terrible everyday reality for me, particularly since many military people (including Gamarnik) had lived in our building. But as BL had once aptly observed: 'There is a law by which things that happen all the time to other people can never happen to *us*.' Now my turn had come, and it was very hard to get used to the idea.

Semionov smiled ironically: 'Ah, but it will take six or eight months for us to establish whether you've done anything wrong or not.'

I went cold all over. This was the crossing of a boundary: the door had slammed shut and there was no question of going home.

My interrogation now went on night after night. Semionov was not particularly rough with me. He spoke in an ironical, mocking tone, endlessly repeating the same stereotyped phrase about how

* Ministry of State Security. (Tr.)

Pasternak sat down at table with the British and Americans, but ate Russian bacon. This formula got on my nerves right from the start and I had to keep hearing it over and over again. Eventually he stopped beating about the bush and told me that to all intents and purposes Pasternak had long since become a British spy.

I think it was at our second session that he gave me a few sheets of paper and asked me to put down briefly what *Doctor Zhivago* was about. I started to write, describing it as the story of an intellectual, a doctor who had found life difficult in the years between the two revolutions.* He was a man of artistic temperament, a poet. Zhivago himself would not survive to the present day, but some of his friends would. There would be nothing discreditable to the Soviet system in the novel. What was to be written was the truth, an account of the whole era such as might be expected from any genuine writer who, instead of retreating into his own personal world, decided to bear witness to his times.

I had already covered several pages in illegible handwriting when Semionov casually picked one of them up and glanced through it: 'It's no good, what you're writing,' he said, making a face. 'You must simply say that you have actually read this work and that it constitutes a slander on Soviet life. You know perfectly well we have seen some bits of it. So don't try to play the innocent. Look at this poem "Mary Magdalene" for instance—is that the work of one of our poets? What era does it refer to? And why have you never told Pasternak that you're a Soviet woman, not a Mary Magdalene, and that it's simply not right to give such a title to a poem about a woman he loves?'

'What makes you think it's about me?'

'But it's obvious—and we know all about it, so there's no point in denying it! You must speak the truth: this is the only thing that might make things easier for both you and Pasternak.'

Unhappy with my description of the novel, Semionov began to look through some sheets of paper he had in front of him with verses and various notes on them . . .

I was now summoned for interrogation on these lines practically every night. It became a matter of ordinary routine for me during my stay in the Lubianka—even in hell, it thus appeared, life could be quite humdrum.

* i.e., those of 1905 and 1917. (Tr.)

If I managed to hold out after a fashion it was only because I was allowed to sleep until the mid-day meal on account of my pregnancy. After eating we whiled away our leisure hours (these too exist in hell) in various ways—sewing with the help of a fish-bone needle in which an eye had been made for the thread, or 'ironing' our dresses in preparation for the next interrogation by sprinkling them with water and sitting on them. But most of the time we just talked and recited poetry. A constant topic of conversation was a certain Doron who supposedly thought it his duty to hand out savage sentences even in the most trifling cases.

A little variety was sometimes brought into our life by the arrival of a new prisoner. One woman came in crossing herself and weeping, and another cursing and swearing—because her interrogator had apparently slapped her in the face several times during the very first session.

In the course of endless night-time interrogations, Semionov and I even grew quite accustomed to each other. We sometimes talked about poetry in general and Pasternak's in particular. I once recited several passages from memory for him from *Lieutenant Schmidt*, and he said: 'There now, the way he used to write, your Pasternak! It's you who've spoiled him, you see! Now you need a dictionary to read him—otherwise you just can't make head or tail of it. What is this word "nard", for example, in "Mary Magdalene"?:

> "With *nard* from a little pail
> I wash your most pure feet."

What is it, I'd like to know?'

I said tartly that I was under no obligation to tell him, but then I did all the same try to explain that 'nard' is a fragrant ointment obtained from the roots of an aromatic plant. (In a later version of the line BL replaced the word by 'myrrh'.)

Once, confusing Mary Magdalene with the Madonna, Semionov said: 'Why are you trying to make yourself out to be a Magdalene? You've been the death of two husbands, both of them honest communists, and now you turn pale at the very mention of this scoundrel who eats Russian bacon but sits down at table with the British . . .' I was so sick and tired of hearing about this wretched 'Russian bacon' that I angrily suggested it had actually been paid for by *Lieutenant Schmidt*, and even by the translations of Shakespeare and Goethe.

On another occasion Semionov began to cast doubt on my love for BL: 'But what have you got in common?' he asked impatiently. 'I can't believe that a Russian woman like you could ever really be in love with this old Jew—there must be some ulterior motive here!' (As Remarque once noted, Jews are always 'old': they are born old, marked at birth by two thousand years of persecution.) 'I've seen him myself. You can't love him. He's just mesmerized you, or something. You can almost hear his bones creak. A fine specimen! You must have some ulterior motive.'

And then on a different tack: 'If only your Pasternak would write something of the right kind, he'd be appreciated by the Motherland...'

As in the case of Radishchev, Pushkin, or Polezhayev in the old days, so now with Pasternak policemen were trying to set themselves up as the best judges of the work of the writers, all the time keeping secret dossiers on them, and sometimes throwing them in jail—or if not the writer himself, then a relative or close friend. Anna Akhmatova's son, Lev Gumilev, was arrested three times and spent a total of eleven years in prisons and camps, as well as several more years in various places of exile. Akhmatova has written that 'for three months he was beaten by his interrogator, Barkhudaryan, and forced to sign a monstrous statement that I, Akhmatova, had incited him to murder A. A. Zhdanov . . . I have never felt so bad as now. Every day of separation [from my son] brings the end nearer.' Apart from this, Gumilev was further accused of the atrocious 'crime' of having criticized the Party decree* on the journals *Zvezda* and *Leningrad*—though, as Akhmatova insisted, he had never breathed a word on the subject to anyone, fearing beforehand that he might be accused of just this. Nadezhda Mandelstam has described how Andrei Bely spent a lot of his time seeing off people who were being deported, or meeting them when they returned after completing their sentences (until 1934 there were such cases). Bely's wife was also hauled off to the Lubianka more than once. 'Why do they take her and not me?' he used to complain.

I remember how once, some time in the middle of 1959, Boria put 1000 roubles into an envelope and, after writing an address on it, gave it to Ira to take to Bely's widow, Claudia Nikolayevna Bugayeva. It

* In which Akhmatova was denounced in 1946. See entry on her in the Biographical Guide. (Tr.)

appeared that efforts on the part of Kaverin, Paustovski, and Vigdorova to get a pension for her had not been successful. I do not know whether she was eventually given one before she died. Ira went to her together with her fiancé, Georges Nivat, who was very interested in Bely's work and was writing a dissertation on him. They arrived at some building on Gogol Boulevard. Georges waited outside while Ira went in to see her. She described later how she found herself in a huge old-fashioned apartment piled high with dust-covered junk. She was met by an old woman—evidently Bugayeva's companion—who explained that Bugayeva was ill and could not see visitors. Through an open door Ira caught a glimpse of a figure lying under a pile of rags on an antiquated bed. Ira left the money and went back outside to Georges, whose hope of seeing Bely's widow was thus disappointed . . .

Ten years before this, in 1949, as I sat in the Lubianka prison fearing for the life and freedom of the man I loved, I was haunted by the spectres of those who had never come back: Osip Mandelstam, Isaac Babel, Titian Tabidze, Yegishe Charents, Pavel Vasilyev, Boris Kornilov, Ivan Katayev, Benedict Livshits, Bruno Jasienski . . . How many more were there—'martyred', put before the firing squad, turned into 'graveyard mould'? ('. . . the sentries will no longer set on them/ or the escort guards hound them, /Now only the stars of Magadan/ will glisten, standing overhead'—Zabolotski.)

During one interrogation session a loud banging could suddenly be heard on the iron gates of the Lubianka. Semionov looked at me with a smile and said: 'Hear that? It's Pasternak trying to get in here! Don't worry, he'll make it before long . . .'

To this very day I still cannot imagine that Semionov was not well aware of the utter absurdity of my case. He may even have thought Pasternak's name and my complete innocence made it likely I should be let free in a relatively short time. Perhaps this was why I was not maltreated by him, as other women in my cell were by their interrogators. With his assent I was allowed the one-volume edition of Pasternak, among other rare books from the prison library. It was probably he who saw to it that I was able to keep this until the end of my time in the Lubianka.

The Meeting

These weary days dragged on inexorably until my examination at last stretched out beyond the six-month period Semionov had predicted for me at the very beginning. It was then that a third person suddenly appeared at one of our sessions. This was another interrogator. In his presence Semionov spoke much more sharply to me than usual. 'Well now,' he said, 'you have so often asked for a meeting, and we are going to let you have one. Get ready for a meeting with Pasternak!'

I went cold all over. Yet at the same time I felt very happy, not even thinking of the distressed state BL would probably be in—I had no doubt that he too must have been arrested. But I was simply overcome with joy at the thought of being able to embrace him, of being able to say a few tender words of encouragement.

Both interrogators now signed a piece of paper, wrote out a pass and handed it to a guard. Hardly able to walk straight from sheer happiness, I went out with my escort. I was put into a windowless prison van and driven off somewhere—to the premises of the *oblast* Lubianka,* as I was told later. Here I was led along endless, unfamiliar corridors with frequent staircases sometimes leading upwards—but more often further and further downwards. This too was evidently one of the techniques for wearing a person out and breaking his powers of resistance

It was quite clear now that I was being taken down to some basement area. When I had almost reached the end of my tether, I was suddenly pushed through a door in the semi-darkness and heard it close behind me with a sepulchral, metallic clang. I looked back in terror, but there was no one there. When my eyes got used to the gloom, I could make out a whitewashed floor with pools of water, tables with zinc tops—and on them the outlines of motionless bodies covered by sheets of grey tarpaulin. There was the unmistakable sweetish smell of a morgue. Could it be that one of these corpses was the man I loved?

I sank down to the whitewashed floor, my feet in one of the pools of water. But I scarcely noticed. And oddly enough, I suddenly felt completely calm. For some reason, as though God had put it in my mind, it dawned on me that the whole thing was a monstrous hoax, and that Boria could not possibly be here.

* i.e. branch of the Lubianka 'serving' the Moscow region (*oblast*). (Tr.)

It subsequently appeared that almost on that very same day, he happened to write these lines in 'Meeting':

> As though a rasp
> Dipped in acid
> They have drawn
> You over my heart.
>
> . . . . . .
>
> And this is why the snowy night
> Appears double to my gaze,
> And I cannot draw a boundary line
> Between myself and you.
>
> But who are we, and whence,
> If of all those years
> Nothing but idle gossip's left
> And the two of us have vanished from the earth?

But at that moment neither of us had yet in fact 'vanished from the earth'. He was in Peredelkino and I was in the Lubianka morgue.

I do not know how much time passed before I heard the door grind open again, and I was taken on by my escort for the next stage of my 'meeting'. I was led along the endless corridors, going up and down stairs, and I was trembling—not from terror any more, but from a chill which had suddenly come over me in the cold and damp of the morgue, and which was not to leave me for a very long time.

At last I was brought into a brightly-lit room where Semionov was waiting for me. 'Please forgive us,' he said, with a meaningful little smile playing over his face, 'we made a mistake and took you to the wrong place altogether. It was the fault of the escort guards. But now prepare yourself: we are waiting for you.'

Another door opened, and there, to my utter astonishment, I saw not BL, but Sergei Nikolayevich Nikiforov, Ira's English teacher, whom I have described earlier on.

The elderly Sergei Nikolayevich, always so neat and tidy in appearance, had now changed out of all recognition: he had a growth of beard, his trousers were unbuttoned and his shoes had no laces.

'Do you know this man?' Semionov asked. So this was it, my 'meeting' with my beloved!

'I do,' I replied. 'It is Nikiforov, Sergei Nikolayevich.'

'There now,' said Semionov mockingly, 'you don't even know what kind of people come to visit you: he is not Nikiforov at all, but Yepishkin—the former merchant Yepishkin who fled abroad! You're not very discriminating—Lord knows who else comes to see you in your apartment.'

(It later emerged that Yepishkin had gone to Australia during the First World War, but after the Revolution returned to Russia, where he got married and took the name of his wife.)

'Tell us, Yepishkin,' the interrogator said to him, 'do you confirm the evidence you gave yesterday that you were present at anti-Soviet conversations between Pasternak and Ivinskaya?'

'Yes, I do. I was present,' Yepishkin answered without hesitation.

'Sergei Nikolayevich, aren't you ashamed to say such a thing!' I burst out angrily. 'You have never even seen me together with Boris Leonidovich!'

I was immediately put in my place: 'Don't talk out of turn: only speak in reply to questions!'

Everything said by Yepishkin was too ridiculous for words, and the way in which he was being questioned in my presence was utterly outrageous.

'Now you told us that Ivinskaya informed you of her plan to escape abroad together with Pasternak, and that they tried to persuade an airman to take them out of the country in a plane. Do you confirm this?'

'Yes, that is so,' Yepishkin answered vacantly.

Again I was furious at such a barefaced lie, and though Semionov motioned me to be silent by putting his finger to his lips, I couldn't contain myself: 'Aren't you ashamed, Sergei Nikolayevich?' In my indignation I could find no other words.

'But you've confirmed it all yourself, Olga Vsevolodovna,' Yepishkin mumbled.

Now I understood: he had been induced to give false evidence by means of a flagrant provocation—they had probably told him that I had in any case already owned up to all these 'crimes'—none of which had even occurred to us, never mind taken place.

'Tell us how you listened to anti-Soviet broadcasts at the home of Ivinskaya's friend Nikolai Stepanovich Rumiantsev,' continued Yepishkin's interrogator, a glib and brazen young man with a pimply face.

But by this time Sergei Nikolayevich must have realized that during my interrogation I had given no false evidence against him, and now he became confused and began to shift his ground ('But that's not actually so, I think', etc.).

'So you were lying to us, were you?' his interrogator snapped at him.

Yepishkin began to whine and prevaricate. There was now no trace of his previous air of stolid calm.

I now stated that Nikiforov-Yepishkin had seen Pasternak in the flesh only twice—and then at public poetry readings which I had made it possible for him to attend.

Yepishkin and his interrogator left the room, and Semionov said to me smugly: 'You see, not all interrogators are like yours. Let's go home. There's no place like home . . .'

Again I walked those long corridors and was then driven back in the police van . . . No sooner had I reached my 'home' cell than I was suddenly racked by fearful pain. I was having a miscarriage. Waiting for my 'meeting' with Boria, the nightmarish minutes (or hours?) spent on the whitewashed floor of the morgue, the grotesque confrontation with Yepishkin—all this had put me in a state of nervous shock and I was now paying the price.

I was taken to the prison hospital. Here Boria's and my child perished before it even had a chance to be born.

Years later, after Stalin's death, when the nightmare of the labour camp was already behind me, I received a letter from Yepishkin. The return address on the envelope was a post office box number at Yavas* in Mordovia. I reproduce part of it here, with all its peculiarities of style:

I recently learned by chance that you are back at home. I have pondered for a long time whether to write to you. In the end, the conscience of an honest man . . . prompts me to account for the situation in which I put you—believe me, against my will, given the conditions then existing. I know that these conditions were familiar to you, and that to some extent they were experienced by you as well. But they were of course applied to us men more forcefully and severely than to women. Before our meeting at that time, I had

* Near Potma. See footnote on p. 26. (Tr.)

repudiated two documents, even though I had signed them. But how many people are able to go boldly, and uprightly, to the scaffold? Unfortunately, I do not belong to their number because I am not alone. I had to think of my wife and shield her.

To put it more clearly, the times were then such that by virtue of the situation, as it were, one person dragged another after him into the same abyss. In repudiating and disowning the two documents signed by me, I did so in the firm knowledge that they were false and had not been drafted by me. But, as I have said, I was compelled, if only for a time, to save myself from the scaffold with which I was threatened...

When I read over this letter and view Yepishkin's behaviour (and that of many thousands like him) in the light of my own confused state during the first days after my arrest, and when I think of my feeling of terror in the morgue, I understand very well indeed that a prisoner is only to be condemned if he bears false witness simply to please his jailers, or to save his own skin. But he cannot really be blamed for losing his head or giving way to terror. Yepishkin was not the only one. All too many others, during the first few days of their imprisonment, were turned into informers, witnesses for the prosecution and, in general, servants of the inquisition. Yepishkin at least felt pangs of conscience, even if rather late in the day.

For this reason, Boria and I, my mother and children all forgave Yepishkin when he came back to Moscow after Stalin's death. Until recently—while he was still able to work—my mother helped him to find English lessons. He is dead now, I believe.

Pasternak and the Lubianka

Tragedy and comedy often go hand in hand.

I have already mentioned that Petrunka's wife, Lidia Petrovna, kept her promise: as soon as she was released she went to tell my mother that I would soon be giving birth to a child. Then came my 'meeting' in the morgue, and the child was still-born. But nobody outside knew this had happened, and that the child was not destined to come into the world. Boria, therefore, went all over Moscow, telling friends or even slight acquaintances that I would soon be having a baby in jail, and enlisting their sympathy.

In the meantime, after a month in the prison hospital, my interrogation was resumed and went on in the same old way—though Semionov, apparently trying to make up for lost time, now began to invent new accusations, spinning them out of thin air.

Eventually, we began to go through all the papers with poems and notes which Semionov had collected together. The bulk of them were afterwards destroyed, though some were returned to my relatives. In particular, however, my interrogator ruled that certain books with inscriptions 'of a personal nature' should be returned to Pasternak—who was duly summoned to appear at the Lubianka for this purpose.

This was where the farce began. After receiving the summons, BL rang Liusia Popova. This is her account of the conversation:

'You know, I am going to such a terrible place,' BL said. 'You can guess where, but I deliberately don't want to say . . .' It would have been obvious even to a deaf-mute where he was going! 'You know, they say I must go there straightaway because they want to hand something over to me. I suppose they're going to give me the child. I have told Zina we must take it in and care for it until Olia comes back.' 'And how did Zinaida Nikolayevna react to that?' I asked. 'She made a terrible scene, but I just had to put up with it: it's only right I should suffer too in some way . . . What kind of a life can the child have in there? Of course, they want me to go and pick it up. But in case I don't come back, I just wanted you to know where I'm going.' 'Perhaps I should come and stand around somewhere nearby, until you come out,' I suggested. 'No, I don't know where to tell you to wait, and I'm going right away. If I come out, I'll ring you.'

And so BL went to the Lubianka, where he immediately began to remonstrate with Semionov, demanding that 'my child' be handed over to him. But instead of a child, he was given a bundle of his own letters to me, and several of the books inscribed by him, including the ill-fated one in the red binding, with the dedication dated 'April 4, 1947' on the title page.

A number of interrogators found an excuse to look into the room where this loud argument with Semionov was going on—they wanted to see Pasternak with their own eyes.

Utterly confused and bewildered at not being handed the child, BL demanded pencil and paper and there and then wrote a letter to the Minister of State Security, Abakumov.

The first lines of this letter were later shown to me by Semionov. Covering up the rest of it with his hand, he said: 'You see, even Pasternak himself admits you could have done something wrong from the point of view of the State.'

In fact, BL had written that if they thought I had done something wrong, he was willing to accept this, but that in such a case he was guilty too, and if his standing as a writer counted for anything, they should take him at his word and put him in prison instead of me.

I realized that in this totally sincere letter to the Minister there was of course also a certain characteristic element of playing the innocent, but whatever he did was dear to my heart and came only as a further proof of his love.

He rang Liusia Popova and told her: 'They didn't give me the child, but asked me to take away some of my letters. I said they were addressed to her and should be given back to her. But in the end I had to take a whole bundle of them, and some books with dedications as well.'

'So instead of the child,' said Liusia, 'you'll take home some love letters and other such things—which will be just as bad.' And she advised him not to take the whole lot back with him, but first to read them through and sort them out.

'Yes,' he answered, 'you always take a sensible view and it's a joy to talk with you, but nobody's going to read my things any more.' All the same, however, he tore out some dedications—which he restored after I came back.

The day came when a pimply lieutenant read out my sentence, which had been pronounced by a *troika* (three-man tribunal) without my being present: five years in a hard labour camp 'for close contact with persons suspected of espionage'.

All these months of interrogation, and all the vast expenditure of paper had been aimed at only one person: Pasternak.

Just as a dossier was kept on Pushkin in the Third Section in the days of Nicholas I, so during the whole of his active life there was a file at the Lubianka on Pasternak in which not only everything he wrote was entered, but also every word ever uttered by him in the presence of innumerable informers. Now we had 'progress' of a kind: Pasternak was not merely a subversive poet, but a British spy, no less. There was a kind of logic here: his father had lived and died in England, and his two sisters were still there. In other words: a British spy. From this it followed that if not Pasternak himself, then at least I must be packed off to a camp.

Years later Boria wrote this about me to Renate Schweitzer* in Germany:

She was put in jail on my account, as the person considered by the secret police to be closest to me, and they hoped that by means of a gruelling interrogation and threats they could extract enough evidence from her to put me on trial. I owe my life and the fact that they did not touch me in these years to her heroism and endurance . . .
(Written in German and dated May 7, 1958)

And now I was taken to the 'transit' jail of Butyrki†—a veritable paradise compared with the Lubianka. After a short 'vacation' in Butyrki I was sent to a labour camp together with other 'harmful elements' who had been transferred here from Lefortovo and the Lubianka. We were packed like sardines into a passenger coach. We had no idea where we were going. The stench was suffocating. I got a berth on the luggage rack at the top of the compartment and from there I could see an astonishingly bright and free new moon sailing in the sky. A monarchist called Zina pressed up close to me and whispered in my ear that a soothsayer (once the abbess of a forcibly disbanded nunnery), on whose account she had been imprisoned, had foretold that a great upheaval would soon come, bringing freedom

---

* At the beginning of 1958 BL received from West Germany a libretto for an opera based on the novel by E. T. A. Hoffmann, *The Devil's Elixir*. It was the work of a young poetess, Renate Schweitzer, until then completely unknown to BL, and the music had been composed by her father. They wanted to know his opinion of this work, which they had dedicated to him. BL said it was 'written in good verse' and that 'the overstatement of Hoffmann's nightmares only serves to clear the air'. His letter to her was the beginning of a friendly correspondence which she later published in German under the title *Friendship with Boris Pasternak* (Munich, 1963).

† See note 53 on Moscow prisons, p. 436. (Tr.)

with it. Sick at heart, as I gazed out at the moon, I mentally composed a poem about separation. I very much hoped Zina was right.

The last stage of the journey was a forced march across country. I found myself walking next to an old general who tried to comfort me by saying: 'Everything will soon be over.' Finally we arrived at the camp.

'Cranes' over Potma

Nowadays, when I hear the words of Galich's song about the clouds sailing over Kolyma* and the tale of the prisoner, released after twenty years, who hacked at the frozen ground with his pick, I see a different picture in my mind's eye. I remember one of my days in the camp in 1952 . . .

The sky blazed above the parched Mordovian fields, where 'the knout dances over the corn' . . . Admittedly, the corn had still not started to come up. The earth was grey and cracked, and we 'politicals' sentenced under Article 58 still had to turn it over, driven on by the knouts and curses of our overseers and the lackeys they recruited from among those of us who had been corrupted.

Clouds, creamy-white and sultry, sailed slowly over Potma—above the dry, unyielding earth. It was noon, and we had been working since seven in the morning. Before the end of the working day we would have to spend another eight hours under the hot sun. I was in a 'brigade'† led by a woman agricultural expert, herself a prisoner, called Buinaya. She was a small, scrawny woman with a sharp nose, and looked just like a bird of prey. She was proud of enjoying the confidence of the camp authorities. 'Ladies' like us from Moscow were regarded by her with intense hatred. It was a real punishment to be put into her brigade—which had happened to me after I had lost my own position as a brigade-leader for failing to cope with my duties. (At the beginning, I had been appointed to this and similar jobs because my sentence was only five years—such short-term prisoners were a rarity and the camp authorities were always at

* A vast area in the far north east of the Soviet Union, notorious for its forced labour camps under Stalin. (Tr.)

† Usual word for a work-team on a collective farm. (Tr.)

a loss what to do with them.) In Buinaya's brigade, the only ones to 'keep their end up'—though never, of course, making the output quota in full—were hefty women from the Western Ukraine* who had worked in the fields all their lives. They had all been with Bandera or Vlasov. One of them, already an old woman, had received her twenty-five-year sentence for giving milk to a stranger who later turned out to have been a Bandera man.

Buinaya had been shrieking at us all morning. She grabbed me by the arm and thrust the pick back in my hands whenever I dropped it. I would again gloomily scratch at the earth, but it was labour in vain. There was not a hope of making the quota, or even half of it.

The only thing was to sweat it out to the end of the day, cursing the sun, which was now flaming white-hot in the June sky and took such a very long time to go down. Oh for a breath of wind! But even the wind, when it blew, was hot and brought no relief . . . If only we could go 'home', to the compound!

Buinaya was serving a ten-year sentence. She had somehow got into trouble on a collective farm. Her two sons were in camps for common criminals in the North. She worked for all she was worth and was always being commended as a 'shock-worker' on the camp's bulletin board. It was her job not to let anyone have an easy time of it. She had to earn her right to her privileged status, continually giving even the escort guards a lesson in how to take it out of pampered creatures like myself. In the end she died of tuberculosis in the camp infirmary.

I remember my desperation. My quota was there in front of me: a few cubic metres of soil baked hard by the sun which I was supposed to turn over and hoe with my unpractised hands, finding it hard even to lift up the pick.

To prevent ourselves being completely stupefied by the heat some of us covered our heads with weird-looking hats made of gauze stretched over pieces of wire. Buinaya despised us for this—she herself never tried to shield her face from the sun and her skin was leathery and wrinkled, though she was still no more than forty.

We worked in rows, straggling out over the dry, scorching earth. Our grey prison smocks, with numbers marked on the back and the hem with chloride of lime, were made of a shiny stiff material known

* Annexed to the Soviet Union in 1939 and the scene of partisan activity in the post-war years; see Bandera in the Biographical Guide. (Tr.)

as 'Devil's skin' which did not let the air through. The sweat poured off us, prickling our breasts, and the flies crawled over us. There was no shade. At such times:

> The road swims in a white haze
> And the corpse of a God dead of thirst
> Hangs, head drooping, from his cross.

Snatches of verse hammered in my temples. I kept remembering and repeating over and over lines from my prison poems:

> . . . It can sometimes be that an eagle's iridescent eye
> Is clouded over suddenly by a dark film,
> Or that a molten mass turns into glass . . .
> This is so . . . But miracles can never happen . . .

My pick was too heavy to lift. My shoes of imitation leather, which were size 44 and might have been given me as a mockery (even size 36 is too big for me), seemed glued to the ground. There was no God. Miracles could never happen.

Buinaya snatched the pick from my hands, hissing angrily and threatening to write a report denouncing me as a slacker. 'These pampered ladies from Moscow! You have to work and earn your ration! . . .' In the blazing heat I felt utter despair. How many more days like this? The Mordovian summer was never-ending and without mercy. Oh for the slush of autumn—how much better to wade through the mud over these Mordovian roads! Let me soak in a rain-sodden quilted jacket, anything rather than swelter in a smock of 'Devil's skin'. This was hell on earth! This was surely what it must be like in hell!

And there was no question of making the quota, or even half of it—which meant no parcels and no letters. This was 'disaster twice over', in the words of Galich's song.

I had to memorize my poems—there was no point in writing them down. We were thoroughly 'frisked' every evening, and they were always taken away and destroyed. I tried to remember them:

> . . . I shall walk as far as the shadow on the road
> Cast by your high cross . . .

I did not know how Boria was. There had been no letter. It was a long time now since I had found a postcard from him—lying on a

windowsill in the bath-house dressing room of all places, almost as
though it had been left there by accident.* Suddenly, I saw it with
my name in Boria's easy flowing hand, and his words flying in like
cranes from the world outside . . . It had been ages ago, this unexpected message. And it made no sense at all.

At last the day ended and we trudged home, raising the dust as we
went. The wooden gates of the camp were silhouetted by the sunset,
which promised another day just as hot. The women guards came
hurrying out to 'frisk' us and make sure we carried nothing inside.
During the night I lay awake and tried to think of ways of getting out
of work the next day. I was still plagued by haemorrhages after my
miscarriage in the Lubianka. This became unbearable in the heat, but
it was not something they would willingly let you off work for. I
decided to risk it and simply not go out. I put my only frock to soak
in a basin of water next to my bunk. My other one was being mended
by some nuns. I longed for a day in the compound, in the shade of the
barracks. I remembered how I had recently been sent a blue dressing-
gown of light-weight material. But I had been made to hand it in:
because of a tightening up in the regulations, all our personal
belongings were now kept in the camp storeroom, and we were not
allowed to take them out.

I lay there in my shift. I had nothing to put over it now, so how
could I go out? But roll-call was still going on, and I was petrified
with fear. When my brigade was called out, I was immediately
missed, and Buinaya reported me. I was dragged outside and
threatened with all the punishments in the book as I stood with the
rest in my wet smock which had been hastily wrung out. It was at
once covered by a fine, grey dust and began to turn stiff in the pitiless
sun—even at this hour in the morning it was already scorching, so
what would it be like later?

Fourteen hours to go before returning to the barracks. I shall never
forget standing under the mocking stares of the camp officers on the
steps of the guard-house as they waved through the brigades on the
way to work in the fields. So there I was, going out after all! I was
frightened I might not be allowed my letters from home. I envied
the nuns, who were ready for anything. They were dragged out like

* Evidently a prisoner whose duty it was to distribute our mail to us after it
had been censored by the camp authorities had simply left it there and forgotten it
during a visit to the bath-house.

sacks and flung down in the dust next to the guard-house, where they lay under the broiling sun exactly as they had fallen. Impassively, the soldiers tossed them over towards the walls of the guard-house—all of them equally pitiable, the pretty young women as well as the old ones. The nuns refused to report for work, preferring to go to the punishment block with its stifling cells which crawled with bedbugs. They could do without letters from home. They had their faith, and were happy. They openly scorned their tormentors and just went on chanting their prayers, whether in the barracks or the fields, on the occasions when they were dragged out there by force. The camp authorities hated them and were quite baffled by the firmness of spirit shown by these women they were so cruelly mistreating. The nuns, for example, even refused to take the meagre sugar ration we were given, and the camp officials simply couldn't understand what kept them alive. In fact, they were kept alive by their faith. Once, I remember, a cocky young fellow in charge of discipline in the barracks (he was later demoted for having an affair with a woman work-supervisor) came into the punishment block where the nuns continued to say their devotions without paying the slightest attention to him. Then one of them said sharply: 'Take your cap off while people are praying!'

The young officer looked about him in confusion and then pulled off his *kubanka*,* cursing and swearing like the devil. There was nothing to be done with them!

During a period when I had worked inside the camp compound in the CES† I had often witnessed such brutal treatment of the nuns that I usually needed no encouragement to go out to the fields.

Now there was this horror as we paraded for work: the stony faces of the officers on the guard-house steps, and the living bundles lying on the ground just where they had been thrown. Those considered capable of work were dragged off to the punishment cells by the arms or the legs. But we were weak-willed: we needed our letters from home.

It is pointless to try and describe such things. All one can do is curse the evil men by whose orders they were perpetrated.

There was an unexpected ending to that day of particular shame and humiliation, when I was forced out to work in my wet smock

* A kind of military fur cap. (Tr.)

† Cultural Educational Section. (Tr.)

clinging to my body. The Mordovian sunset was blood-red and there were clouds of an ominous colour—promising yet another sweltering day. We came up to the gates and I hardly had the strength to wait for the blissful word of command: 'Stop work! Stand in formation!' The tongues of the guards' sheepdogs were hanging out—they were overcome by heat and exhaustion. Clouds of dust swirled in front of the gates. There was one more agonising procedure: the body search. You pressed forward eagerly to the hands waiting to feel you up and down—anything to get into the compound as fast as possible, splash water on your face, and collapse on your bunk, without bothering to go for the evening meal . . .

I dropped down on my mattress just as I was, in my out-size shoes which were tied with white tape instead of laces. My feet throbbed. I scarcely had strength enough to throw off my clothes and wanted only to sleep—who could tell, I might even dream of a bird, a sure sign you were going to be released? But suddenly I felt a hand on my shoulder. It was the security officer's woman orderly who had been sent to bring me to him . . .

Why on earth? . . .

I got dressed again under the hostile gaze of the women in the bunks next to me—all Western Ukrainian peasant women who hated a Muscovite like myself with such a ridiculously short sentence. Five years! In their eyes I was scarcely better than our jailors. And it was true that people like myself were always pathetically hoping their cases would be revised, trusting in good luck instead of in God. We were ready to sell ourselves for the sake of letters from home and to work on Sundays. We took part in the camp's wretched 'cultural' occasions—imagine a choir made up of 'political criminals' singing 'Broad is my native land . . .'* We had no pride. None of these women from the Western Ukraine would ever go to work on a Sunday or any other religious holiday—even if they were dragged out and flung on the ground like the nuns. Not on your life. But we did! . . . It was from among us that the lesser camp minions were recruited: overseers, orderlies, *starostas*,† the staff of the CES—and all the other 'trusties'. The Western Ukrainians were right to despise us! And now here I was being called out at night to the security

---

* A patriotic Soviet song with the refrain 'I know no other country / Where man breathes so freely.' (Tr.)

† 'elders' (persons appointed to represent the prisoners in the barracks). (Tr.)

officer . . . It was bound to be taken to mean I was working as a 'squealer'. I left my bunk, trying not to look at the other women. Outside it was a beautiful Mordovian night. The moon was low in the sky and the freshly-watered flowerbeds smelled sweetly. How would anyone looking down from above at the white-painted barracks, pleasant enough on the outside and surrounded by flowers, ever have guessed at the suffocating stench, the groans of the wretched, lonely outcasts crammed into these prison cells? When he returned from the camp, Nikolai Asanov wrote: 'It suits me, this brotherhood of others as lonely as myself . . .' But here, even the feeling of brotherhood had broken down: we never had real friends, or only very few and in any case we were always too tired to seek each other out in the compound.

I walked under the trees. In a cosy-looking house with a green-shaded lamp in the window was the dragon's lair of the security officer, the '*kum*'.*

I went in, and after questioning me about my particulars, the security officer, a thickset corpulent man with bumps on his face, said to me in a surly tone of voice: 'Here is a letter for you, and a note-book. Some poems or other. It's not allowed to take them away, you must sit and read them here. Sign afterwards to say you've read them . . .'

He buried himself in the reading of a file, while I read:

> When the snow covers over the roads
> And lies heavily on the rooftops
> I'll go outside to take a walk
> —and find you standing at the door . . .

Boria's 'cranes' flying over Potma! So he missed me, and loved me —just as I was now, in my smock with its convict's number, my size 44 shoes, and my sun-scorched nose . . .

> . . . Trees and fences retreat
> Into the distant murk.
> Alone among the snowdrifts
> You're standing at the corner.

And there was much else, including the cycle on gospel themes,

* Literally 'god-father'—camp slang for the officer whose duty is to organize surveillance of the prisoners, recruit informers among them, etc. (Tr.)

which is no doubt why I was not allowed to keep it. But for some reason proof was required that I had read the twelve-page letter and the poems—an entire little green notebook filled with them. 'There are no instructions to let you have them,' the security officer muttered when I begged and begged him: 'Give them to me, give them to me...'

So evidently somebody had issued instructions about them? Somebody was concerned with our case? In his letter Boria wrote: 'We are doing everything we can and will go on doing it.' What they robbed me of, the fiends, by not letting me have this letter! I sat there reading for a long time, till the early hours, and walked back to the barracks as the stars were beginning to fade before dawn. I didn't lie down, but kept trying to look at my face in a small piece of tarnished mirror. My eyes had not lost their blueness, but my skin had coarsened, and my nose had peeled over and over again. A real sight! And one of my teeth was chipped at the side. Boria was writing to my loving self as he had known me before: 'I write to you, my joy, and wait for you . . .' But one more year of this, and I would be an old woman.

Lord, it was almost time to parade for work again—another sweltering, merciless day, guards, size 44 shoes, Buinaya . . .

But now I could stand it. It looked, I thought to myself, as though my case was not quite so simple and that Boria was badgering my tormentors, and they were not sure what to do about the whole business. In his letter he said: 'I am telling them that if we have done something wrong, then the guilt is mine, not yours. They should let you go and take me instead. I have some literary standing after all . . .' I remembered how every time a sound of banging came from the courtyard of the Lubianka, Semionov had said with a smile: 'Hear that? It's Pasternak trying to get in here . . .', and how he had told me that BL must be aware of his guilt in the eyes of the Motherland to be able to write: 'if I am guilty, arrest me!' And he was still writing this to them now. It was clear, then, that the all-powerful Ministry of State Security was making some kind of exception for us . . . There were 'no instructions' to hand the poems over to me, but there had been instructions to let me read them! All those twelve pages full of love, longing, hopes, and promises had been kept by the security officer. But no matter: Boria's 'cranes' had flown over Potma! Now I would find the strength, after my sleepless night, to go out for work—despite the withering stares I would get as a suspected informer from the Ukrainian women. It would be a happy day, and when I slept that night, I prayed to God I might dream of cranes.

When you dream of birds, it means freedom ...

Letters

I brought back from the camp one note and four postcards written to me there by Boria. The note was put in a letter from my mother sent on November 4, 1952:

My darling, my angel! How are you, how are you? I speak to you all the time, do you hear me? It's terrible to think what you have gone through and still have to face—but I'll say not a word about this! Keep your spirits up and have courage: we have been doing all we can, and are not giving up. Do not lose hope. How marvellously you wrote your postcard—you put everything into a few lines. I don't know how to do that. I will get news of you from your mother. I won't write to you myself—it will be better like that. And what's the need anyway? You know everything.

But BL did write, and more than once. The letters he wrote at first never reached me ('It is not permitted to write to persons who are not close relatives'), so he began to send postcards ostensibly written by my mother. I found them enchanting—and very funny: it was hard to imagine someone like my mother ever writing things which were so poetic and involved. All of them were sent from Potapov Street and had my mother's signature: Maria Nikolayevna Kostko.

May 31, 1951. My dear Olia, my joy! You are quite right to be cross at us. Our letters to you should pour straight from the heart in floods of tenderness and sorrow. But it is not always possible to give way to this most natural impulse. Everything must be tempered with caution and concern. B. saw you in a dream the other day dressed in something long and white. He kept getting into all kinds of awkward situations, but every time you appeared at his right side, light-hearted and encouraging. He has decided it must mean he is going to get better—his neck is still giving trouble. He sent you a long letter and some poems, and I sent you a few books. But it has all gone astray, it seems. God be with you, my darling. It is all like a dream. I kiss you endless times. Your Mama.

My darling! Yesterday, the 6th, I wrote you a postcard, but it dropped out of my pocket somewhere on the street. I am going to play a guessing game: if it does not get lost, but reaches you by some miracle, then it means you will soon come back and all will be well. I wrote you in that postcard that I will never understand BL and am against your friendship with him. He says that if he were to speak his mind, he would say that you are the most supreme expression of his own being he could ever dream of. The whole of his past life, the whole of his future no longer exist for him. He lives in a fantastic world which he says consists entirely of you—yet he imagines this need not mean any upheaval in his family life, or in anything else. Then what does he think it means? I hug you, my purest dear, my pride, I long for you. Your Mama.

(Postmarked July 7, 1951)

April 10, 1953. Olia, my little girl, my darling! How close we are now, after the decree* they've just published, to the end of this long and terrible time! What a joy that we have lived to see the day when it is behind us! You will be here with the children and with us, and your life will stretch out before you again like a broad highway. That's the main thing I wanted to say and share our delight in. The rest is so unimportant! Your poor BL has been very ill—I have written to you about this before. In the autumn he had a heart attack and spent three months in hospital. After that he stayed in a sanatorium for two more months. Now, more than ever, he is possessed by only one thought: to finish his novel, so that nothing is left undone, in case the unforeseen happens. We just met him on Chistye Prudy. This was the first time after a long while that he has seen Irochka. She has grown a lot, and become very pretty.

April 12, 1953. Olia my angel, my baby girl! I am finishing the card

* i.e. granting amnesty to some prisoners after Stalin's death. (Tr.)

I began the day before yesterday. Yesterday Ira and I sat with BL on the boulevard. We read your letter, wondering when we may expect you here, and going over our memories. How marvellously you write, as usual, and what a sad, sad letter! But when you wrote it, the decree on the amnesty had not yet come out, and you did not know of the joy awaiting us all. Our only concern now is that this longed-for happiness should not cause us to pine away with impatience, that the deliverance about to come should not overwhelm us by the very fact of being so near at hand and momentous. So arm yourself with patience and remain calm. At last we are nearly at the end of the way. From now on everything will be so wonderful. I am feeling fine and am glad to see BL looking well. He thinks that Irochka's eyes, which used to turn up at the corners, have evened out now. She has become very pretty. Forgive me for writing such silly things. Your Mama.

My years in the camp were a great ordeal for BL as well. He took it on himself to care for my family, though he had very few resources. Without him my children simply would not have survived.

He had his first heart attack not long after my arrest.* He had then just turned sixty, but was still in extraordinarily good health, both from the physical and moral point of view.

Later, recalling our enforced separation, he wrote:

> ... In years of tribulation, in times
> When life was unimaginably harsh
> A wave of destiny brought her from the depths
> And cast her up before him.
> . . . . . .
> And now she is departed, gone—
> Against her will, it may be.
> This separation will devour them both,
> Grief will gnaw away their very bones.
> . . . . . .
> And pricking his finger on a needle
> Where she had left it in her sewing
> He suddenly sees the whole of her
> And weeps softly to himself.

* In 1950. Pasternak had a second heart attack in 1952. (Tr.)

My mother has kept a letter written to her by BL as soon as he had begun to recover from his heart attack:

January 2, 1953
Dear Maria Nikolayevna! I took the liberty of asking Marina Kazimirovna [Baranovich] to open your letter and read it to me over the telephone. How I recognized and felt you in it! How much of your warmhearted self there was in it, how much feeling and life! I send lots and lots of kisses for it! I could hardly refrain from phoning you right away—I am still trying to keep myself in hand now, because I am not supposed to get worked up. Thank you, thank you! Irochka, my darling girl, thank you, and thank you as well, Mitia, for all your concern and tears. I owe part of my recovery to both of you, dear children, and to your hopes and prayers, Ira.

But now at once to practical matters, dear Maria Nikolayevna. I am enclosing with this a letter authorizing payment of money to you at *Goslitizdat*. I don't know how much is owing: if a lot, then it will see you through the next few months, if not, then it will do for January. We shall only know exactly how much there is when they pay it out to you. I have spoken on the phone about making it over to you with two people in different departments of *Goslitizdat*: with Nikolai Vasilyevich Kriukov in the editorial section for Russian literature, and with Valentina Vasilyevna Miasnikova in the accounts department. Ring up the first so he can arrange payment and speed things up, and find out from the second how much will be paid, and when. Tell both of them *not to phone me at home* about these earnings, say I have a friend (a man) who has been in trouble and has been away for four years, his children are still at school and on their own, you are their grandmother and this money has been earmarked by me specially for them.

Apart from this I've asked Maria Khrisanfovna to let you know that the 'Soviet Writer' Publishing House has brought out the poems of Won Tu-Son* in a translation which they describe in their advertisement as 'authorized'. It's very possible that this is Olga Vsevolodovna's translation—we should ask about this, and then perhaps you can get some money out of them for the children— unofficially, perhaps.

* The author was translating him at the time of her arrest. See p. 90. (Tr.)

When I get home I'll make some enquiries myself, but this won't be for quite a while.

I must finish. Forgive me for this short and skimpy letter—I'm still not supposed to write and it's bad for me.

Because of lying flat on my back for the last two months, the nonsense with my head and neck has worsened again—I had almost ceased to notice it in the autumn after all that work in the garden.

Even at the most critical moments during the night they brought me to hospital I never ceased to thank Providence for the life I have lived, and didn't wish it to have been otherwise. I felt calm, and was moved to tears at how merciful and gentle my end was, if this was it. I had faith that the forces I called on to help you and my other friends, and to protect my family, would still be at work after I was gone. Once again, I send lots of kisses to you, Ira and Mitia.

Z.N. [Zinaida Nikolayevna] saved me. I owe my life to her. All this, and everything else as well—everything I have seen and gone through—is so good and simple. How great are life and death, and how insignificant the man who does not know it!

The parallel with the late D.I.* was of course ever present to my mind. And it did not frighten me.

Yours, B. P.

[The author was released under amnesty, like many others, after Stalin's death in March, 1953, and she returned from the camp to Moscow.]

'If only they knew how to keep silent . . .'

When the campaign against Dmitri Shostakovich was launched,† BL decided he must write him a letter to cheer him up. He drafted something and showed it to me. But I remember saying: 'Wait a little before you send it. You'll see: tomorrow he'll recant and start beating his breast.'

But BL sent it off without telling me. How mortified he was when my words turned out to be all too true. I recall a very characteristic

---

* Dmitri Ivanovich Kostko—my step-father who had died in 1952.
  † In 1948; see Shostakovich in the Biographical Guide. (Tr.)

comment by BL: 'Oh Lord, if only they knew how to keep silent at least! Even that would be an act of courage!'

Liusia Popova remembers what BL said during the days when Akhmatova and Zoshchenko were being hounded: 'I am against this decree* first and foremost because it's illiterate,' he said. 'What has Acmeism got to do with it? In general I dislike all these labels and don't accept them, and I just can't agree with all this.'

But BL was a member of the Board of the Union of Writers, and a messenger came with a summons for him to attend a meeting at which the two would be denounced. 'I cannot be there,' he said. 'I'm not well. I have radiculitis.' To this the reply was: 'You'll have to think of something else. Fedin already has radiculitis.' So he then took the summons and wrote on the back: 'I shall try to come if I am well and nothing else prevents me.' But he just didn't go, saying: 'Anna Akhmatova is my friend and I do not consider it possible to behave like this towards her.'

He was then expelled from the Board of the Union of Writers, but nobody ever heard a word of complaint or regret from him on this score.

Speaking of Eisenstein's *Ivan the Terrible*, BL expressed his indignation at this attempt to vindicate and glorify the *oprichnina*†: 'How vile! What swine they are: Eisenstein, Alexei Tolstoi, and all the rest. I could never have any dealings with them, and for many years I have practically refused to meet such people. I cannot stand our intelligentsia for its servility towards power, for its faintheartedness. They are just half-people!'

BL hated '. . . every kind of triumphant official church', as he put it. His own civic sense and patriotism had nothing in common with the standard 'optimism' and tub-thumping nationalism. It is astonishing that to this very day even some people who knew him very well are unaware of the social content of his poetry. Nikolai Bannikov, for example, maintains that BL 'did not think on social lines'. Maxim Gorki, on the other hand, once said in a letter: '. . . This is the voice of a real poet—and of a social poet in the best and deepest meaning of the concept'.

* i.e. the Party decree of August 14, 1946, denouncing two literary journals *Zvezda* (Star) and *Leningrad* for having published work by Zoshchenko and Akhmatova. (Tr.)

† Ivan the Terrible's special forces which he used to commit atrocities against the population. (Tr.)

Could the following lines have been written by someone who 'did not think on social lines'?:

> I threw in my lot at one time with the poor—
> Not from conviction or highmindedness,
> But because I found that only they
> Led lives without display or pomp.
>
> Although a friend of noblemen
> And no stranger to the best of circles
> I took a poor view of the idle rich
> And stood up for the lowest of the low.
>
> And I tried to be good friends
> With people from the working classes
> For which my peers did me the honour
> Of thinking me a down-and-out myself.
>
> The way of life in basement hovels
> And attics with uncurtained windows
> —So unadorned and forthright,—
> Was earthy, real, and ponderable.
>
> But I have never been the same
> Since our times were spoiled by blight
> And poverty was held up as a shame
> By narrow-minded spirits feigning optimism.
>
> To those in whom I once believed
> I've long since ceased to bear allegiance
> And I miss the common human touch
> Now everybody round about has lost it.*

'My soul is in mourning . . .'

'An artist,' BL once said, 'should find some response during his lifetime . . . fame, or recognition, or some other kind of answering echo from life must come to him—it is essential . . . because art lives in others . . .'

Boria's reward came at the right time: not too early, but not too

* Written in 1956, and hitherto unpublished in the Soviet Union. (Tr.)

late either. And it was a rich one: he sensed—or rather, he even
knew—that he was a living classic, that his work would have a
permanent place in history and in people's hearts.

> Fame is the pull of one's native soil:
> Oh, if only I were rooted more directly there!
> Yet even so—not as a homeless vagabond
> But as a trueborn son I'll go down in my mother tongue.

Pasternak was not alone of his kind in knowing his own worth. As
Marina Tsvetayeva said: 'All true poets have known their own worth,
beginning with Pushkin—the worth of their creative powers.'

Pasternak was fully entitled to say of himself:

> . Like a songbird I shall be echoed,
> The whole world will make way for me . . .

Ariadna Efron once noted that '. . . Pasternak had the vanity of any
man of true talent who, knowing he will not live to see himself
acknowledged by his contemporaries, and hence snapping his fingers
at them for their failure to understand him, nevertheless craves *their*
recognition more than any other—he knows perfectly well that the
posthumous fame of which he is assured is about as much use to him
as a wage paid to a worker after his death . . .'

Yes, BL certainly had a high opinion of himself—but the demands
he made of himself also became progressively higher. Describing
BL's account of how he first came to the idea of his novel, Gerd
Ruge quotes him as saying literally the following: 'I thought to
myself: you must stand at attention before your own name. I felt
that I still had to earn this name by writing not verse, but prose—
something which would demand a greater amount of work, time,
and effort and might even cost me a good deal more besides.'

I find it difficult to imagine, of course, that BL would ever stand
at attention before anything whatsoever, but the underlying thought
is true: he always felt hopelessly in debt not only to his readers, but
simply to people in general—to all those together with whom he
lived and suffered on earth.

The ordeals and hardships of his own country were reflected both
in his actions and in his writings.

He could feel only horror for the 'man-crab', or rather, the man-
spider who had enmeshed the whole country in his web of denunciation, demagogy, and repression. He used to recall how he had been

overcome by this horror with particular force when Anna Akhmatova had rushed to see him with a plea for help after the arrest of her husband, Nikolai Punin. The next morning BL wrote a letter to Stalin in defence of Punin, and not long afterwards Akhmatova was told that her husband would be allowed home on her responsibility. (When Punin later left Akhmatova, BL was most indignant at such ingratitude!)

Always aware of the danger threatening himself, BL openly showed his sympathy for those confined in Stalin's concentration camps.

In 1937 the Georgian poet Titian Tabidze was arrested. He and BL were bound together by deep personal affection, by the friendship of two poets. At the First Congress of Soviet Writers Titian had said: '. . . just as the title of the acknowledged poet of the Revolution is Mayakovski's, so that of the flawless master of his craft is Boris Pasternak's.' And in 1936, when political purges became the order of the day and the threat of the terror hung over everyone, BL wrote to Titian: '. . . rely only on yourself! Bore down with your drill as deeply as you can, without fear or mercy, but into yourself, into yourself. And if you do not find the people, the earth, and the sky there, then give up the search—in that case there is nowhere else to look . . .'[18]

For a long time there was no news about what had happened to Tabidze. Only in October 1955 did it become known that he had been brutally put to death two months after his arrest. For years BL worried about his fate—a dangerous thing to do in those times, when it was customary to put a person out of one's mind the moment he disappeared. But right until the day the truth came out, BL continually returned to this dangerous question both in conversation and correspondence. Here are a few passages from letters written to people in Georgia:

My thoughts about him are all too close to my thoughts about myself, although he, poor fellow, is no longer with us, whereas I am alive, still cursing the scandalous nature of my situation.

(March 21, 1941)

Titian is for me the best image of my own life—he embodies my

own view of the earth and of poetry, as it came to me in the happiest
of dreams . . .

(May 30, 1944)

From time to time BL was seized by hope of a happier outcome to
Titian's case. On January 28, 1944, he wrote to his friend in Lenin-
grad, the poet Sergei Spasski (also soon to be arrested): '. . . [Yevgeni
Dmitrievich*] was recently here and brought the joyful news that
Titian is still alive, and that his case will be reviewed.'

But hope was succeeded by despair: '. . . I have long since ceased
believing in the possibility of Titian being alive. He was too big, too
exceptional a man, and radiated too much light for it to have been
possible to hide him, to prevent all signs of his existence from filtering
out of even the closest confinement.' (July 7, 1953.)

And this is what BL wrote when he at long last learned of Titian's
death in one of Stalin's dungeons: '. . . poor, poor Titian, who was
doomed to go through this martyrdom; I always knew it in my
heart, I suspected it.' (October 4, 1955)

But it was not only Titian's fate that caused such great sorrow to BL.
He suffered untold anguish on behalf of all the victims of persecution
and terror.

When the playwright Alexander Gladkov told BL about a letter
he had received from his brother in a camp in Kolyma thanking him
for a 'precious gift of a volume of Pasternak's poetry,' BL became
very agitated and began to question Gladkov in a loud voice (the
conversation was in a tramcar) about his imprisoned brother: 'Thank
you for telling me. This is very important to me. I am grateful to him
for writing about it. I am grateful to them all for remembering me . . .'

A few years later, after Gladkov himself had returned from serving
a sentence in the Obozersk† camp, he met BL again and told him
that during his own years of imprisonment he had always kept a
volume of BL's verse by him and used to wake up in the barracks
earlier than his fellow prisoners in order to be able to read it: 'If ever
something prevented me from doing so, I always felt as though I had
not washed.' 'Oh, if only I had known this then, in those black
years,' BL replied, 'life would have been so much more bearable just
to think that I was *out there* too . . .'

* Spasski's brother (Tr.)   † Near Archangel (Tr.)

Many prisoners wrote to BL from the camps and he replied to them, sending them food packages, books, and poetry.

Several of his letters had an unusual fate. One of them is the subject of a short story by Varlaam Shalamov, published in 1971 in the New York Russian-language *Novy Zhurnal* (New Review) under the title 'For a Letter'. After serving his sentence in a camp, the author stayed on in a remote part of wintry Kolyma as an exile and one day he received a radiogram from Magadan saying: 'Come for letter.' He had to travel five hundred kilometres on sleighs drawn by dogs and reindeer, or by getting lifts from passing trucks—it took him five days and nights in the bitter Kolyma cold! And at the end of it: 'The next day I knocked on the door of an apartment, and when I went in I was handed a letter written in a hand which I knew very well— a swift, flowing hand, yet at the same time clear and legible. It was a letter from Pasternak.'

Liusia Popova recalls: 'BL several times showed me the letters he kept getting from various prisoners. He gave them to me in whole sheaves and said: "Look how these people write to me—I'm glad they do, it gives me a way of easing their lot. I can make up for my guilt at not being together with them, for being at liberty. The people in my circle have been wiped out by fate, but I am at liberty and in good health and can have as much as I like to eat. This oppresses me terribly and I feel guilty."'

Once, when BL was offered an additional sum of royalties on his collected Shakespeare translations, he turned it down: 'I have been given a great deal as it is'. They were very surprised in the accounts department of the publishing house, but they cancelled the payment —which even did something to improve their financial position.

In the period just after this, however, BL began to receive fairly frequent letters from prisoners. So he went to the director of *Goslitizdat*, Kotov, and said: 'Anatoli Konstantinovich—give me those royalties for the Shakespeare translations. People are being jailed, and I have no way of helping them. I'll send the money to prisoners.'

There was no longer any provision in the accounts for the royalties in question, but some money was nevertheless paid out to him, and not telling his family anything about it, he used it to help luckless people who had been sent to the labour camps.

He regularly sent sums of 2–3,000 roubles to Ariadna Sergeyevna

Efron (the daughter of Tsvetayeva) who was in exile in the Turuk-hanski region.* He had been very upset by the fate of Tsvetayeva and her family—particularly as he himself had not discouraged her from returning to Russia.[19]

I remember yet another typical case. A girl whose father was in a camp came to see BL. After getting a letter from the father, BL had sent him a signed book of his poetry and a food parcel. And now the daughter had come to thank him at her father's request. With great difficulty BL got her to accept another food parcel for him, and he wanted to give her some money as well—but this she refused out-right. He then persuaded her on some pretext or other to go and see Liusia Popova—whom he immediately phoned to say that he feared the girl might not have the fare for her journey back: '. . . find out tactfully, and then give her some money as though from yourself—she will take nothing from me and I just can't give her any.'

When BL learned about the arrest of Kostia Bogatyrev in 1951, he immediately offered his parents material help. Kostia's father, whom BL had known for a long time, was a well-known authority on folk-lore, a university professor, and was not short of money. His son had been sentenced to death by shooting (which was later com-muted to twenty-five years in a penal camp) 'for terrorism against the Leader of all progressive humanity'.

So BL sent out to Kostia in the camp a large volume of the selected works of Shakespeare:

To dear Kostia with best hopes, and a warm embrance. B. P. (These are mere trifles, but in a month's time *Faust* is coming out. Keep up your courage, Kostia, you are a brave boy, as I always thought.)

The 'mere trifles' were BL's translations, included in this volume, of *Romeo and Juliet, Henry IV, Hamlet, Othello, King Lear, Macbeth, Antony and Cleopatra*.

When *Faust* came out at last, BL at once sent him a copy in which he wrote:

Dear Kostia! You do not have to wait much longer now! Keep up your courage, hold firm. With all my heart I wish you strength and

* In Siberia. (Tr.)

health in the measure needed—no, in abundant measure, more than needed. And patience, patience.

> Ever yours B. Pasternak. January 27, 1954, Moscow.

This copy of the book has survived. Underneath Boria's signature there is a dark-blue official stamp and the words: 'Permitted for personal use. Head of camp section 14, Major Fadeyev. August 12, 1954.'

On all those years and their sorrows there is BL's poem 'My Soul, You Are in Mourning':

> My soul, you are in mourning
> For all those close to me,
> Turned into a burial vault
> For all my martyred friends.
> Keeping their remains embalmed,
> Enshrining them in verse,
> Grieving over them
> With sobbing lyre,
> In these selfish venal times
> You stand, fearfully, for conscience sake—
> A funeral urn that holds
> And rests the ashes of them all.
> The sum of all their sufferings
> Has left you bowed, prostrated;
> You reek of the dust of mummies
> In some Egyptian tomb.
> My soul, you are a charnelhouse,
> And everything our eyes have witnessed
> You grind down like a mill
> And mingle all together.
> Go on grinding as before
> All that has happened in my life
> For these last forty years or so,
> And make it into graveyard mould.*

* Although this poem has still not been published in the Soviet Union, it has been set to music in worthy fashion by the composer Sviridov. A recording of the song (and of two others based on Pasternak's poems 'Snow is Falling' and 'Night') performed by the women's choir directed by Yurlov, has been on sale.

Of all the people imprisoned in the camps or sent into exile in remote parts of the country the one whom BL was most deeply concerned and distressed about was Ariadna Efron, Marina Tsvetayeva's daughter.

Long before she returned from her many years of exile in the Turukhanski region I had come to know her—in absentia, so to speak—through everything that BL told me about her.

He wrote to her, in her place of exile, about the disaster that overtook us when I was torn from him on that terrible autumn night of 1949. Long before we finally met, BL said to me: 'You will be like sisters. I must care for her till the end of my life. I have let her into our Holy of Holies, and told her about my second life—and, you know, she is very glad for me, and writes in such a remarkable way about it!'

I read the superb letters she wrote to Boria, who was so close and dear to her. And I could picture her trudging a vast distance to the post office through the snow in her felt boots on a cold starry evening to collect the precious, loving letters he sent to her. Every month, apart from words of encouragement—her only link in the boundless wastes of Turukhanski region with the forbidden world beyond—he also sent her money and books. I wrote to her as well, and got back replies.

Her letters to BL—from which he drew great comfort—were written in a firm, straight and legible hand which mirrored a strong, straightforward character—the character of a woman who was clear about everything in her own mind. Once, when I asked him to tell me what she looked like, he hesitated for a moment, and then said: 'Well, she is like nobody else. Don't let it put you off, but she is not pretty. She is not like Marina. Her head is somehow disproportionately small. But on the other hand what a character she has, how clever she is!'

What he said about her looks turned out, of course, to be nonsense—though he was right about her character, which later on he even found a little daunting. Like her mother Marina, she could be a little too forthright and categorical, even in her disapproval of the confusion in his domestic affairs—something which could hardly appeal to a person as easy-going in such matters as BL.

When I at last met Ariadna, I was struck by her very large and beautiful deep-blue eyes—it may well have seemed that her head was disproportionately small in relation to these. I must say that in general Boria's ideas on women's looks seemed to me peculiar. The pale, round-faced Olga Berggolts, with her bobbed hair, for example, he regarded as a great beauty, while Ariadna struck him as ugly. When I told him indignantly that I found her marvellous even in her appearance, he smiled happily: 'How good that you like each other! How magnificent!'

As soon as she returned from exile Ariadna became part of our household, as though she had lived with us unseen all the time. Of course her long years in extremely harsh conditions had affected her: she had begun to neglect her appearance as a woman too soon, and now she devoted herself entirely to her mother's posthumous affairs —and also to our tangled domestic situation, for which she blamed BL to his face. She scolded me as well for not being firm enough with him—she evidently regarded me as too weak, as too much of a 'silly woman'. She was much fonder of Irina than of me. Not having any children of her own, she probably saw in her some fulfilment of her own dreams. She in fact became closer to Ira than I was, and found fault with her (as I did) for only one thing: namely, that she denied herself the enormous pleasure one gets from a love of animals. Ariadna took a more delicate and sensitive interest in Irina's problems as a young woman than I did. In my defence it must be said that, being happier than everybody because I was so much in love with Boria, I was that much more unfeeling towards the others—who realized how much he loved me. And it was recognized that I had a special understanding for him. At the height of our 'time of troubles', when everybody believed I was making obvious blunders, Ariadna always stood up for me: 'Olia has a sixth sense about Boria—she knows best what to do.'

With great courage and fearlessness she shared in all our tribulations, keeping her nerves calm by knitting innumerable scarves. Even when she and I were not on speaking terms for a while, she maintained her contact with me through Irina and would ask her about me ('Well, how's your mother? Not squawking? Everything must be all right then!').

After Boria's death I remember how in my dazed state of despair and foreboding, I was instinctively driven to go and see Ariadna in Tarusa.* We felt completely at one with each other. We went and

* Small town near Kaluga, south of Moscow. (Tr.)

stood in the evening on the bank of the haze-covered Oka and in the daytime wandered through the fields, meeting people who talked of her father, Sergei Efron, in tones of veneration. Her sober talk about practical matters brought me back to a sense of reality and the need to face what had to be done. She urged me to plunge into the day-to-day business of living: 'This will help you. You must!'

But later on, after my second arrest (in 1960, after BL's death), she began to take a poor view of me for my behaviour during my interrogation—she thought I had been foolishly gullible and trusting, agreeing with everything and not attempting to deny the charges, thereby willy nilly involving Irina (for whom her feelings, as I have said, were like those of a mother) and dragging her into jail in my wake. As she said to Irina with alarm and disapproval: 'Your mother has gone mad—she's made a clean breast of everything!' By her very nature Ariadna was incapable of making allowances for weakness or forgiving it. She probably had no sense of the depth of my despair and apathy. Boria was dead, and nothing else mattered for me now. The core of life had gone. I was driven to distraction by loneliness (though at the same time saved by it, because it forced me to move to new surroundings). It was not only that Boria had died—with his death I had lost my place in life. Ariadna could not understand this: those she loved were deathless in her eyes, even after their departure from the world, and never for a single moment did she cease to carry out her obligations towards them as though they were living persons.

'Do not touch this cloud-dweller . . .'

BL often talked about various attempts which were made to get his signature to collective statements expressing approval of the latest death sentence on some 'enemy of the people' or other—and which led him to feel obliged to write another letter to Stalin. One of his accounts of such an attempt was written down word for word by two visitors, independently of each other, as he gave it to them sitting on the verandah of his *dacha*:

In 1937, at the time of the trial of Yakir, Tukhachevski and others, the writers were asked to put their signature to a statement endorsing the death sentence. They came to try and get mine as well. I refused to give it. This caused a tremendous hue and cry. The chairman of the Union of Writers at that time was a certain Stavski, a great scoundrel. He was scared stiff he would be accused of not watching things more closely, the Union of Writers would be called a hotbed of opportunism, and he would have to pay the price. They tried to put pressure on me, but I wouldn't give in. Then the whole leadership of the Union of Writers came out to Peredelkino—not to my *dacha*, but to another one, where they summoned me. Stavski began to shout at me and started using threats. I said that if he couldn't talk to me calmly, I wasn't obliged to listen to him, and I went home.

At home there was a painful scene. At that time Zinaida Niko-layevna was pregnant with Lionia, and was soon going to give birth. She threw herself at my feet, begging me not to destroy her and the child. But there was no arguing with me. It later turned out that an agent was sitting in the bushes under our window, and that he heard every word we said . . .

We expected I would be arrested that night. But, just imagine, I went to bed and at once fell into a blissful sleep. Not for a long time had I slept so well and peacefully. This always happens after I have taken some irrevocable step. My close friends urged me to write to Stalin—as though we were regular correspondents and exchanged cards at holiday seasons! But I actually did send him a letter. I wrote that I had grown up in a family with very strong Tolstoian convictions, which I had imbibed with my mother's milk, and that my life was at his disposal, but that I could not consider I had a right to be a judge in matters of life and death where others were concerned. To this very day I cannot understand why I was not arrested there and then . . .

BL thus did not bow to pressure from the authorities and his own family, to the threat of losing his freedom or his life, and refused to give his signature. Imagine his indignation, then, when he saw the statement published in the newspaper with his name under it all the same! His protests and denials were in vain. The power of tyranny was greater.

It is hard to say why Pasternak's persecutors went no further than scurrilous public denunciation of him and my imprisonment—why, in fact, they did not do away with him, like Mandelstam and millions of other people. Even in the 1937-9 period he was treated with a certain indulgence. As regards my imprisonment—by the standards of the time, a sentence of five years in the camps was an act of mercy rather than a punishment. After all, not only I (I was a mere nobody —just the woman friend of an unruly poet), but even the lawful wedded wife of our All-Union *starosta*, Kalinin,* was put in a camp —from which she was graciously let out for the funeral of her husband, only to be sent back behind barbed-wire once it was over.

There were rumours (which BL once mentioned to Liusia Popova) according to which Stalin, on being presented with documents giving grounds for the arrest of Pasternak, is supposed to have said: 'Do not touch this cloud-dweller ...'

There may have been some truth in this rumour. At any event, BL himself believed that Stalin had no wish to destroy either him or me —as witness what he said to me after my return from the camp in 1953: 'It was really my lucky star that saved you.' And he says as much in his allegorical 'Fairy Tale' as well.

In literary circles nobody doubted that BL's arrest was a foregone conclusion. But—why, nobody knew—he was not arrested. Alexander Gladkov writes in his memoir:

... he could have no possible illusions: he had lost too many close friends and in the Stalin years he had too often waited on some desolate night for the agents of Yezhov and Beria to knock on the gate of his house in Peredelkino. What saved Pasternak in those days? It is hard to say. All we know for certain is that in 1955 the young procurator R., who was going into the case of Meyerhold, was astonished to discover that Pasternak was still at liberty and had never been arrested: according to the papers in his hands, Pasternak was marked down to figure as an 'accomplice' in an imaginary conspiracy supposedly hatched by people connected with the arts, and for which both Meyerhold and Babel paid with their lives. Another name which cropped up fleetingly in this 'case' was that of Yuri Olesha, who also in the upshot escaped arrest ... At some stage during the preparation

---

* The nominal 'President' of the Soviet Union. (See the Biographical Guide.) As the supposed representative of the people, he was sometimes called *starosta*—the 'elder' of a village. The term is here ironical, since it was also used of the representative of the prisoners in the barracks of a forced labour camp. (Tr.)

of this infamous frame-up it was evidently decided to make do with Meyerhold and Babel, who had already been arrested . . .'

In his *People, Years, Life*, Ehrenburg has the following to say: 'When I think of the fate of my friends and acquaintances, I can see no logic at all in it. Why did Stalin not touch Pasternak, who maintained his independence, while he destroyed Koltsov, who dutifully did everything he was asked to do?'

'. . . *two things that never go together* . . .'[20]

BL once described Stalin as a 'giant of the pre-Christian era.'[21] Perhaps these words explain his cycle of poems on Gospel themes. They were a form of protest—the strongest kind of protest available to his genius: a 'remembrance of all that immeasurable greatness which has been created in the world in . . . thousands of years . . .'

The head of the prose section in *Novy Mir*, the old, respected literary critic Nikolai Zamoshkin, once said to me: 'Just wait, Olga Vsevolodovna, these poems will be studied by our descendants as one of the wonders of the twentieth century.'

He was the first to draw attention to the universal character of the landscape in 'Christmas Star': . . . winter, steppe, a snow-covered field, camels, donkeys, a rooks' nest, sheepdogs. This is a Christmas scene outside time, or any particular geographical setting, yet even so, it is a landscape which is inevitably connected in the mind's eye with the Russian winter and the Russian countryside. At one point in the novel, Yuri Zhivago remarks that one should 'paint a Russian version of a Dutch Adoration of the Magi with snow in it, and wolves, and a dark fir forest'.

No, 'Christmas Star' is not Judea, but the whole world—and Russia as well. And how concise and comprehensive the definition of what legend means for mankind and art:

> . . . And, an awesome vision of future times,
> Everything to come rose up in the distance.
> All the thoughts of centuries, their dreams, their worlds,
> The whole future of galleries and museums,

All the pranks of goblins and feats of wizardry,
All the Christmas trees, all the children's dreams.
All the shimmering candles, all the paper chains,
All the splendour of coloured tinsel . . .

By the official critics, however, this cycle of poems—obviously Pasternak's crowning achievement—was greeted with blank hostility —as it would have been by the militant, blaspheming atheists of the 'twenties.

I believe that between Stalin and Pasternak there was a remarkable, silent duel. BL, who had studied philosophy at Marburg, did not like works devoted exclusively to the subject: 'I think a little philosophy', he wrote, 'should be added to art and life by way of a spice, but to make it one's speciality seems to me as strange as feeding on nothing but pickles.'

Our century of progress, driven on by the engines of space missiles, is not equipped with the brakes of morality—hence all that is so 'tragically typical of modern man: his shrill textbook admirations, his forced enthusiasm, and the deadly dullness conscientiously preached and practised by countless workers in the field of art and science in order that genius should remain extremely rare . . .'

Everything of this kind thought, said, or written by Pasternak was not by way of reply to actual catchwords or pronouncements, or to Stalin personally, but rather to the whole pitiful intellectual world of Stalinism, and it may be that Pasternak survived simply because something as poverty-stricken as this does not fear what it fails to understand. Yet Pasternak made his point very clearly: '. . . he would not have made a scientist of the sort who breaks new ground. His intelligence lacked the capacity for bold leaps into the unknown, the sudden flashes of insight that transcend barren, logical deductions. And if he were really to do good, he would have needed, in addition to his principles, a heart capable of violating them—a heart that knows only of particular, not of general cases, and which achieves greatness in little actions.'*

* This is said of the revolutionary Strelnikov, in *Doctor Zhivago*. (Tr.)

'Nationality'*

A Jew by origin, but a Christian by baptism, BL believed in assimilation:

It's so strange that these people who once brought about the liberation of mankind from the yoke of idolatry and so many of whom now devote themselves to its liberation from injustice, should be powerless to achieve their own liberation from themselves, from the yoke of their loyalty to an obsolete antedeluvian designation which has lost all meaning—that they should not rise above themselves and dissolve among all the rest whose religion they have founded and with whom they would have so much in common if they knew them better.

Of course, it's true that persecution forces them into this futile and disastrous pose, this shamefaced, self-denying isolation, which brings them nothing but misfortune. But I think some of it also comes from a kind of inward senility, the fatigue of centuries. I don't like their ironical whistling in the dark, the workaday poverty of their outlook, their timid imaginations. It's as irritating as old men talking of old age, or sick people about sickness.†

A writer from Czechoslovakia, an acquaintance of BL's, told him that after the publication of *Doctor Zhivago* in Israel, the local critics attacked him on account of his assimilationist point of view. Boria only smiled: 'No matter. I am above race...'

But he also wrote in *Doctor Zhivago*:

You can't imagine what this wretched Jewish population is going through in this war. The fighting happens to be in their Pale of Settlement. And as if punitive taxation, the destruction of their property, and all their other sufferings were not enough, they have to put up with pogroms, insults, and the charge that they lack patriotism. And why should they be patriotic while the enemy offers them equal rights and we do nothing but persecute them? There is something paradoxical at the very root of this hatred of

* The term used in the Soviet Union for ethnic origin or race—which is entered in a person's identity papers. (Tr.)

† *Doctor Zhivago*, Chapter 9. (Tr.)

them. It is stimulated by the very things which should arouse sympathy—their poverty, their overcrowding, their weakness and their inability to fight back. I can't understand it. There is something fateful about it . . .

Later, when I came back from the camp and told him of all the anti-Semitic jibes made about him in the Lubianka ('How could you, a Russian woman, fall in love with this old Jew?' etc.) he at first said nothing but then remarked with a sigh how fortunate Sholokhov was to have nothing 'questionable' about his background.

On another occasion he said jokingly (and repeated it several times later) that it would not be at all a bad idea to swop his 'nationality' for Sholokhov's.

On May 2, 1959, he wrote to Jacqueline de Proyart:

I was baptized as a child by my nanny, but because of the restrictions imposed on Jews, particularly in the case of a family which was exempt from them and enjoyed a certain reputation in view of my father's standing as an artist, there was something a little complicated about this, and it was always felt to be half-secret and intimate, a source of rare and exceptional inspiration rather than being calmly taken for granted. I believe this is at the root of my distinctiveness. Most intensively of all my mind was occupied by Christianity in the years 1910–12, when the main foundations of this distinctiveness— my way of seeing things, the world, life—were taking shape . . .

I believe that Pasternak's religious feelings were akin to those of Leo Tolstoi or Albert Einstein. He himself indicates their nature in the novel:

. . . he listened to the [funeral] service as if it were a personal message to him, affecting him directly. He attended to the words and expected of them a clear meaning, as of any other serious communication, and there was nothing merely pious in his feeling of continuity with the supreme forces of heaven and earth, which he venerated as his great precursors.

In a conversation with the Swedish scholar, Nils Åke Nilsson, he said:

... We have learned that we are only visitors in this world, travellers between two stations. During our short sojourn on earth we must ourselves discover what relationship we have to existence, what our place is in the universe. Otherwise life is inconceivable. This means ... a revival of our inner world, a revival of religion—not religion in the sense of church dogma, but as a feeling about life ...

He thought of the Bible as being mainly an inexhaustible source of creative inspiration, as the starting point for an infinite number of ideas in literature and art: 'The Bible is not so much a settled text as a notebook for the whole of mankind.'

So much for BL's feelings about religion. The matter of his origins, however, was a sore point with him. It wasn't that he was embarrased by them—there was no question of this. But as a Russian poet to the core of his being, he was at a loss what to do or say whenever he was brought up against the fact that his Jewish descent would never be forgotten or forgiven. What was to be done if, in the words of Marina Tsvetayeva's poem:

> In this most Christian world
> Poets are Yids! ...

Here Marina was conveying the anguish she suffered on behalf of poets who—with very few exceptions—are always and everywhere persecuted and hounded in the same way as 'Yids'. And when she wrote about Christ's passion, she thought first and foremost of his sufferings as a Jew:

> In all the world, from end to end,
> He is crucified and taken down from the Cross.
> Only with the last of your sons, O Israel,
> Shall we truly bury Christ!

BL's attitude to the whole problem was, it must be said, complicated—and at times contradictory, or even at first sight naïve and comic. I remember how once, when I was already in charge of all his dealings with publishers, he phoned me one day at the Potapov Street apartment while he was busy working at Peredelkino and said (in connection with a contract for a translation of Calderón): 'You may have to fill out a form, Olia, so write down the particulars from my identity card.' He read them all out to me, but when he came to 'nationality', he hesitated and then mumbled: 'Nationality: mixed—write that down. Date of birth: 1890. I know I've sometimes added four years to it, but let's keep it as I have it here—it's not worth making an issue of.'

And, laughing, I did exactly as the dear man wanted—as though I cared at all what he put down on forms or gave as his age! For me he was always young and handsome, and eternally naïve and funny, like a spoiled child.

Needless to say, his deeper feelings about the question of his personal background were much more complicated—as he tried to show in one of his letters (written in July 1958) to Jacqueline de Proyart:

. . . Why do I avoid giving precise biographical information about myself, why do I try to get out of it? Whenever you talk about yourself, you create the impression of voicing approval of what you are or were, of justifying it. Or if not, it means you are in open revolt against what you are, disapprove of yourself, regret being what you are and build up a whole philosophy condemning yourself. I have no wish to do either. I have no desire to discuss any of the things which have a bearing on my life—the Jewish question, or the reasons for Slav nihilism and submissiveness; current theories of art, revolution, or counter-revolution; my marriage or my friendships. All my dislikes were and are unjust. In all my disagreements I have been wrong, not my opponents. But can I, or would I wish to mend my ways? Absolutely not. This is something hopelessly incorrigible. The fabulously small part of me that represents me in my true essence I have distilled into my essays and my novel . . .

And in another part of the same letter, he defines very precisely 'the list of dramatis personae' in his life: 'God, woman, nature, work, death . . . These are the really close partners, friends, and companions. Everything of significance is limited to these . . .'

The poem 'The Cult of Personality . . .' was written immediately after the suicide of Fadeyev, and is an expression of BL's attitude to Khrushchev and the men around him.

BL's feelings towards those who, unlike himself, had been unable to preserve their integrity, were compounded of great compassion, forbearance, and even anguish on their behalf. One such person was Alexander Fadeyev. BL's relations with this man who had unreservedly put his unquestioned talent at the service of Stalin's régime were complex.

Fadeyev had once spent a good deal of time and energy getting Pasternak to stop work on his long poem 'Nightglow', in which a polemical note about the pseudo-art of the Stalin era was all too explicit:

> Self-advancement was not sought
> By the writer of an earlier day. . .
> By not embellishing his every thought,
> Now, too, he could become a Priestley or a Hemingway.[22]

In the 'raw materials for the one-volume edition' the text of 'Nightglow' has been preserved with the following note on it in Pasternak's hand: 'Nightglow. Full text: the introduction as published in the press and the never published first chapter of a projected long poem which was begun and then abandoned. It was its very appearance in *Pravda*, for which it was being written, that put me off the idea of carrying on with it.'

During the war, in Chistopol, BL told Gladkov:

In Peredelkino, Fadeyev sometimes used to come and see me and after a few drinks he would begin to take me into his confidence. I was embarrassed and upset that he felt he could do this with me, of all people . . . Fadeyev is well disposed to me personally, but if he received orders to have me hung, drawn, and quartered he would carry them out conscientiously and make his report without batting an eyelid—though the next time he got drunk he would say how sorry he was for me and what a splendid fellow I had been. We talk about people having a 'split personality', and there are many such in this country. But in Fadeyev's case I would put it differently: his personality is divided off into a number of watertight sections, like a submarine. Only alcohol breaks down the bulkheads and mixes everything up together . . .

We knew that Fadeyev was very fond of BL's poetry and could go on reciting it by the hour. In his memoirs Ehrenburg mentions an occasion of this kind:

I remember meeting Fadeyev after his report denouncing the 're-moteness from life' of certain writers, including Pasternak.★ I happened to run into him on Gorki Street, near the house where I live. He persuaded me to go to a café on the corner, ordered a cognac and said: 'Ilya Grigoryevich, do you want to hear some real poetry?' He began to declaim Pasternak from memory and could not stop— except once to ask: 'All right?'

And then, when Stalin died, and—in Ehrenburg's phrase—the 'thaw' began, the unexpected happened: Kuzmich's granddaughter, the eight-year-old Verochka, raced into the yard of the little house we rented from him, and told us, all out of breath, that *Fedin* had shot himself. Nobody would ever have expected the high and mighty, two-faced Kostia Fedin to do such a thing. But it soon transpired that not Fedin but Fadeyev had shot himself.

'This one can understand,' said BL, 'it absolves many of the wrongs he did, willingly or unwillingly.'

He later said the same thing in public, when we went to the House of Unions† where Fadeyev's body lay in an open coffin in the Hall of Columns. I stayed outside at the service entrance while Boria went in. I heard about what followed from two writers who were standing at the time in the guard of honour by the coffin. BL stood at the head of it, and looked closely for a long while into the face of the dead man. And then, in a loud, distinct voice, for everybody round about to hear, he said: 'Alexander Alexandrovich has rehabilitated himself!' And, bowing low, he walked away to the exit . . .

★ At a meeting of young authors in Moscow in 1947. (Tr.)
† See footnote on p. 72. (Tr.)

I believe that Fadeyev's tragedy was somewhat similar to Maya-kovski's. Mayakovski, however, shot himself in 1930 already,* whereas the talented young prose-writer not only put himself at the service of the 'cult of personality', but actually did so in various bureaucratic capacities. In the meantime Pasternak, his older contemporary, with whom he had been associated in the first years after the Revolution when Soviet literature was at the height of its achievement, remained true to himself as a writer—despite all the time-serving accommodation to Stalin's dictatorship he saw round about him, he preserved both his talent and his conscience. This is perhaps why Fadeyev would go in his cups to pour out his soul to Pasternak, and also why, through drunken tears, he lavished such praise on his poetry. A man's betrayal of himself almost always ends with his own spiritual destruction. This is what happened in the case of Fadeyev. He summoned up the courage to pronounce the death sentence on himself.

Now a few words about the second of the two principal sources of inspiration for the poem 'The Cult of Personality . . .'

BL always gave credit to Khrushchev for denouncing Stalin and for rehabilitating his innocent victims on a mass scale—whatever motives he may have had in preparing the Twentieth Congress.

But Boria was staggered by Khrushchev's verbosity and blustering boorishness. And he was not the only one—even our landlord, an ordinary worker, spoke derisively of Khrushchev, and said to his wife: 'We truckled to that one for so many years, and now we're supposed to truckle to this one. Better keep our mouths shut!'

BL had no faith in any 'thaw'. As we had seen, it too easily gave way to frosty weather again—or turned the ground under our feet into impassable, sticky mud:

> The roads have turned to mire
> And I make my way along the verge,
> Churning slush and clay like dough
> I plod through liquid sludge.

Another comment was: 'For so long we were ruled over by a mad-

---

* i.e. only at the beginning of the period marked by the glorification of Stalin (denounced as the 'cult of personality' by Khrushchev at the Twentieth Party Congress in 1956). (Tr.)

man and murderer—and now by a fool and a pig. The madman had his occasional flights of fancy, he had an intuitive feeling for certain things, despite all his wild obscurantism. Now we are ruled over by mediocrities...'

At this period BL was reading George Orwell's *Animal Farm* in the English original and he hugely enjoyed this merciless satire about a society of animals which mutiny against their human masters, and then gradually revert to a wretched caricature of their original condition. The animals were presided over by a fat hog who vividly reminded BL of our head of state. Sometimes he said laughingly that Khrushchev put his collar round the wrong part of his anatomy.

It was thoughts such as these, as well as the official story about Fadeyev having killed himself because of alcoholism that prompted BL's extempore lines on the 'cult of personality'—though they never actually took final shape as a poem:

> The cult of personality's been unthroned
> But the cult of hollow words holds sway
> And the cult of faceless Philistines, perhaps,
> Has magnified a hundredfold.
>
> The cult of personality's been vilified,
> But in this fortieth year of grace
> The cult of evil and the cult of uniformity
> Are just as ever present as they were.
>
> And every day brings with it, grossly,
> Always the same group photographs
> —Truly more than can be borne—
> Of all those porcine visages.
>
> And, it seems, the cult of Philistines
> Is honoured as it always was
> —So people shoot themselves from drunkenness,
> Because they cannot stand it any more.*

BL often returned to the question of the contrast between Stalin and Khrushchev in those autumn days of 1958, when he was being hounded over the Nobel Prize. There were moments when the campaign reached such a pitch of tragic intensity that the whole logic

* This poem has never been published before. (Tr.)

of the situation seemed to demand the intervention of Khrushchev. But this was not forthcoming: lesser officials were delegated to deal with the matter instead.

BL now remembered the way in which Stalin had called him on the phone about Mandelstam: however a poet may have ended then —as an enemy of Stalin, an 'enemy of the people', an inmate of prison or the death cell, a suicide—he remained a poet nonetheless. The man who wielded absolute, arbitrary power understood that poetry was also power of a kind:

> In days when great councils meet
> And seats are assigned to higher passions,
> One should not leave a place for poets:
> This vacancy is dangerous if filled.*

While Pasternak was alive, the vacancy in Russian poetry was never unfilled. Shunning honours (he received no prize or any other distinction in the whole of his life), enduring the constant jeers and affronts of the Philistines, he patiently and bravely, with great self-sacrifice, played his predestined part:

> The noise is stilled. I come out on the stage.
> Leaning against the doorpost
> I try to guess from the distant echo
> What is to happen in my lifetime.

> The darkness of the night is aimed at me
> Along the sights of a thousand opera glasses.
> Abba, Father, if it be possible,
> Let this cup pass from me.

> I love your stubborn purpose,
> I consent to play my part.
> But now a different drama is being acted;
> For this once let me be.

> Yet the order of the acts is planned
> And the end of the way inescapable.
> I am alone; all drowns in the Pharisees' hypocrisy.
> To live your life is not as simple as to cross a field.†

* From 'A High-Illness', 1924 .(Tr.)
† Hamlet, 1946. (Tr.)

On the day of Stalin's death, Boria and I were still separated from each other: I was in the Potma camp, and he in Moscow. In both places—in Potma as well as in the capital city, and in the country at large—there were waves of panic. The vast majority, millions of people, wept for Stalin and asked each other through sobs: what will happen now? Others rejoiced—but in silence, furtively, and looking over their shoulders. Only very few were bold enough to give open expression to their joy.

BL had been right to say: 'Men who are not free . . . always idealize their bondage.'

Pasternak's feelings about Stalin were extremely complex and contradictory, taking on various nuances and occasionally undergoing influences of a diametrically opposed kind. But at all times he could never be reconciled in his mind with arbitrary despotism as a system of rule. It was in his very nature to strive constantly after complete freedom for the spirit to roam at will.

He had been utterly sincere when he wrote:

> . . . in the ancient citadel
> lives—no, not a man, but action
> incarnate on the whole globe's scale.

But he was no less sincere in May 1956 when he was preparing his *An Essay in Autobiography* for the one-volume edition of his poetry and summed up Stalinism in the following laconic phrase, which could not be more definitive: 'It seems to me that Paolo Yashvili was utterly confused, spellbound by the Shigalevism of 1937 as by witchcraft . . .' Anybody who has read Dostoyevski's *The Possessed* will understand what is meant by Shigalevism,[23] and the connection Pasternak saw between it and Stalinism.

It is said that the true measure of a country's civilization is the kind of men it produces. The same country, in the same era, gave us Pasternak, and gave us Stalin. Both are the measure of their age: the measure of its humanity, and the measure of its cruelty; the measure of its greatness of mind and spirit, and the measure of its perfidy and baseness . . . Measures at opposite poles. Principles at the utmost remove from each other, and as contradictory as the age which brought them forth.

On which side are the hearts of the best people in our day, and on which side will they be in times to come? Need one ask?

'There are few of us. Perhaps only three . . .'

BL had no time for the catchword once launched by Mayakovski:

> More and more poets
> —good ones and various!

In Pasternak the 'all-powerful god of detail' always, it seems, revolted against the idea of turning out verse for its own sake or in order to convey vague personal moods. If 'eternal' themes were to be dealt with yet again, then only by a poet in the true sense of the word —otherwise he should have the strength of character not to touch on them at all.

Poetry so tightly packed (till it crunched like ice) or distilled into a solution where 'grains of true prose germinated', a poetry in which realistic detail cast a genuine spell—only such poetry was acceptable to Pasternak; but not poetry for which indulgence was required, or for which allowances had to be made—that is, the kind of ephemeral poetry which is particularly common in an age of literary conformism.

BL could weep over the 'purple-grey circle' which glowed above Blok's tormented muse and he never failed to be moved and astonished by the terseness of Pushkin's sprightly lines, but rhymed slogans about the production of tin cans in the so-called 'poetry' of Surkov and his like, as well as the outpourings about love in the work of those young poets who only echo each other and the classics—all this left him cold at best and for the most part made him indignant.

The Nekrasov tradition was at one time simply not of much interest to him, while the parallel one of Tiutchev's and Fet's lyrics seemed to him supreme in its poetic vision and truly miraculous.

No wonder he avoided the literary gatherings to which he was always being invited by young poets longing to read him their verse. It was this sort of thing that moved him to say: 'Who started the idea that I love poetry? I can't stand poetry.'

In a letter to M. G. Weinstein* of December 15, 1955, he wrote:

. . . my readers and admirers fail to understand the main thing about me: that I do not like 'poetry in general' and am not an expert on

---

* A young Leningrad poet who had sent BL some of his verse; I do not know what became of him.

poetry as it is generally understood; that I am not a judge, or a connoisseur in the field.

And further on:

If you divide people into members of the Party and non-members of it, into men and women, into the villainous and the virtuous—these are still not such radically opposed categories, the difference between them is not so great as between me and that antithetical world in which people love, appreciate, understand, relish and discuss poetry, write it and read it.

And finally:

. . . the belief in the idea that there is such a thing in the world as poetry, which one is driven to write by talent, and so forth and so on, is like faith in black magic or alchemy.

But in his last years, when his need of simple human kindness had grown particularly strong, he could be moved to tears by the pathos of Staniukovich, whose *Sailor Chizhik* he happened to see in a television production or, even more, by such favourite lines of mine as the following from Nekrasov's 'Knight for an Hour':

> This night I should like to weep
> On the distant grave
> Where lies my poor mother . . .
> . . . . . .
> Yes, I see you, house of God!
> I see the inscription over your portal
> And the Apostle Paul with his sword,
> Clothed in shining raiment . . .

'The way they could write!' he once exclaimed—by 'they' he meant the Russian classics. And immediately afterwards, reading or, rather, glancing through some verse in the *Literary Gazette*: 'Just look how tremendously well they've learned to rhyme! But there's actually nothing here—it would be better to say it in a news bulletin. What has poetry got to do with this?' By 'they' in this case he meant the poets writing today.

Quite often he was no doubt unfair. Once, for instance, reading a few lines from Tvardovski's long narrative poem *Far Distance*, which he had himself given me, he said: 'It's all very smooth, everything is in place, and better than we could do it, but it's long-winded, and I don't see why it need be rhymed.' I remember timidly objecting and saying that Tvardovski was a real poet, with his own way of seeing the world, his own themes and manner. BL listened to me dubiously, but then read it again and agreed with me.

What he could not stand at all was any kind of striving after effect. For example, in the late and, in my opinion, splendid verse of Zabolotski, he disliked the starlings singing 'in the birch wood's very throat.' This may have been because he saw here echoes of his own style of imagery—but employed by someone else in such a way as to make it suddenly sound to his ear high-flown, or even cloying.

On May 10, 1952, BL wrote the following dedication:

To Anna Andreyevna Akhmatova, to the soul of finesse and finality, to that which has always cheered and delighted me, to that which is congenial and close to me, as well as higher and greater. B. Pasternak.

But he did not like Akhmatova's later verse, or, rather, he simply found it hard to read. He was evidently put off by the mannered way in which the subject matter was organized. On receiving a type-written copy of 'Poem Without a Hero', which she had signed for him, he said to me, in a half-questioning, half-affirmatory tone: 'Read this. I've looked through it. Very beautiful, but altogether a bit 'da-di-da-di', and what's it all about?'

This did not prevent him from telling Akhmatova herself how delighted he was by the 'Poem'. Perhaps his feelings towards her were particularly tender at that time, because of the campaign against her. But it must be admitted that there was a certain engaging hypocrisy about him.* Sometimes, in my presence, he would tell someone how wonderful his work was—having previously expressed a contrary view of it—and wink at me conspiratorially.

Sometimes I read out aloud to him verse that had been sent to him

---

* No wonder—as Nikita Struve reports in his article 'Eight Hours with Anna Akhmatova'—that during her visit to Paris in 1966 Akhmatova described BL as a 'divine hypocrite'!

in manuscript or in published form, for his opinion. But he was always rather guarded when I did so: 'Don't try to win me over with your voice.' For some reason he always liked my voice, but was mistrustful of it—and not only of mine. I remember the good impression made on him by the verse of Andrei Voznesenski at a time when he was still unknown and simply 'Andriusha' to us, a familiar visitor of whom we were very fond, and always present at our gatherings.

Once in the summer of 1957, on our small verandah, Andriusha read his then new poem 'Tbilisi', showing off his talented verbal conjuring tricks, with all the characteristic assonances and alliterations. BL told me later that although he wasn't sure 'what will come of him', and 'even making all due allowances for his voice', he sensed in Voznesenski a secret link with the language of the early Tsvetayeva. BL loved her more than any of his contemporaries and, whether because of this affinity, or because Andriusha stood out from other poets of his generation by virtue of his own original qualities, the fact is that BL really did like him.

As regards Yevtushenko, BL was in two minds.

'You know,' he said to me once, 'he's terribly fashionable with everybody. But I'm not very sure of him. We must watch him: he may be one of those poets who 'rhyme summertime with Lermontov and snow and geese with Pushkin.'*

But I stood up for Yevtushenko—I had thought of him as a protégé ever since my days in *Novy Mir*, when I had been so delighted to sense a real poet in the diffident youth.

Before long one of BL's Georgian friends brought him a copy of Yevtushenko's volume *Bow and Lyre*, published in Tbilisi. Here, in BL's view, there were things of true quality, and Yevtushenko was astonished when BL, happening to see him at a concert by Stanislav Neigaus, went up and quoted from memory four lines he thought particularly successful:

> All the world's largesse is not enough for me,
> Day and night are too short for me,
> Who have been reared by insatiability
> And suckled by thirst.

* Line from a poem of Pasternak's (1931) which evidently refers to facile or far-fetched rhymes. (Tr.)

And he said he liked the comparison of the lights of Tbilisi with the multicoloured speckles on a trout's back.

Yevtushenko has described in his *Autobiography* how he first met Pasternak:

Almost bumping into me, a grey-haired man with a dark complexion and dressed in a white canvas jacket suddenly came out from behind a tree at the bottom of the garden. 'How do you do?' he said in a voice that drawled slightly, shaking my hand and looking at me with brown eyes in which there was a surprised look, though it was clear at the same time that nothing could ever surprise him. And suddenly, without letting go of my hand, he said with a smile:

'I know who you are . . . you are Yevtushenko . . . Yes, yes: this is exactly as I imagined you: thin, tall and pretending not to be shy . . . I know everything about you—even that you sometimes miss lectures in the Literary Institute★ . . . and all sorts of things . . . And who is this here behind you, a Georgian poet? I like Georgians very much . . .'

I explained that it was not a Georgian poet, but the Italian professor Ripellino, and I introduced him. 'Well now, that's very good. I like Italians too. And you have come exactly at the right moment: our lunch is just ready. Come along now, you must be hungry.' We at once felt completely at ease and were soon sitting at table, eating chicken and drinking brandy.

To look at him one would not have given Pasternak more than forty-seven or forty-eight. He radiated an extraordinary, sparkling freshness, like a newly cut bunch of lilac with the garden dew still shimmering on its blossom. He was all iridescence, with a constant flurry of hands in movement and an astonishing child-like smile always lighting up his animated features and displaying his white teeth. There was a little of the actor about him. But, as he had once said in a poem to Meyerhold:

'Even if this is only a part you've entered into,
Good for you: that's just the way to act it.'

After lunch BL and Yevtushenko recited poetry until five o'clock in the morning. (Zinaida Nikolayevna kept coming in and making a fuss: 'You're killing him—he's not supposed to stay up so late . . .')

★ Yevtushenko was a student here, 1951-4. (Tr.)

BL read 'Bacchanalia' and Yevtushenko a number of his own things. 'Weddings' did not much appeal to BL, but he was very enthusiastic about 'Prologue'—so much so that he presented Yevtushenko with a copy of the 1930 edition of his poems, *Two Books*, and wrote the following dedication in it:

To Y. A. Yevtushenko.
Dear Zhenia, Yevgeni Alexandrovich, today you have read your poetry here and have moved me and many others present to tears with the proofs of your talent. I am confident that you have a bright future ahead. I wish you further such successes, and may all you have undertaken come to fruit in final, comprehensive shape, leaving the way clear for new ventures. Continue to grow and advance. B. Pasternak. Peredelkino, May 3, 1959.

But since this was just around the time that BL embraced the 'unheard-of simplicity' to which he had come via the complexity now suddenly seen by him as evidence that in the old days he and Mayakovski simply 'didn't know how to write', he was really no longer receptive to the mannerisms of fashionable poets and their way of using rhyme.

I remember what a genuine interest he took in the work of the young Chuvash* poet Gennadi Lisin (Aigi), who was then a fellow student of Ira's at the Gorki Institute. He listened attentively to literal translations of his work and preferred it to rhymed verse. (But here again, it must be said, he was dependent on the author's voice.) In Lisin's work he found what he so much valued: a keen eye and an individual way of seeing things.

Yura Pankratov and the late Vania Kharabarov, also friends and fellow students of Ira's, were closer than the others to BL not so much from the literary as from the human point of view. Active members of the 'Timur group'[24] created by Ira, they helped to make life easier for BL during the difficult days of the Nobel Prize.

I should probably say a little more about the relations between Pasternak and Tsvetayeva. It was to her and Mayakovski that he addressed the lines, extraordinary in their tragic quality:

* A people of mixed Finnish and Mongolian origin living in the middle Volga region. (Tr.)

> There are few of us. Perhaps only three
> —Donetsian,[25] burning, infernal . . .

It is clear that already then, in 1921, BL realized what an explosive force was concealed in the three of them—the force that resides in any truly original poet:

> We were people. Now we're epochs . . .

And there was so much prescience in the line:

> . . . You'll realize it too late . . .

I cannot attempt here any analysis of this poem, or of the relationships which lay behind it. The myriad threads binding (and separating) these three people—Pasternak, Tsvetayeva, and Mayakovski—were simply too complicated, subtle, and elusive in their multiple strands of significance. So all I can give here is a rough sketch, a few clues.

Of Tsvetayeva, Pasternak said, addressing her directly: '. . . you are building a world which is crowned with the mystery of genius'.* And, dedicating a copy of his *Themes and Variations* to her, he wrote: 'To the incomparable poet Marina Tsvetayeva "Donetsian, burning, infernal."' To which Tsvetayeva responded with the words: 'I need nobody's praise and recognition except yours.' And in verse:

> In a world where
> All are hunched, in a sweat,
> I know: only you
> Are on a par with me.
>
> In a world where
> We want so much
> I know: only you
> Have my power.
>
> In a world where
> All is mould and rust
> I know: only you
> Are of the same stuff
> As I.

---

* He generally disliked this 'grand' word, which, as he put it further on: 'when used in private has about it something of a comment made from the gallery or in the barber's shop'.

Then, in an article on literature, she wrote of him: 'In Russia I maintain that the greatest of the poets and prose-writers—I insist on this last as well—is Boris Pasternak who has brought forth no new form, but a new essence (and consequently a new form as well).' One could almost think the words had been said after reading *Doctor Zhivago*—but this was thirty years before it was written.

Although Mayakovski and Tsvetayeva also valued each other very highly, it was not comparable at all to this . . .

As to BL and Mayakovski: at the beginning of the 'twenties both of them were most anxious that the Revolution should not pass them by and that they should not miss, through their own short-sighted-ness, all the grandiose things taking place before their eyes. BL's opinion of the Mayakovski of those years was the highest that one poet could possibly have of another—as he shows in *Safe Conduct*, 'An Essay in Autobiography', and various poetic tributes to him. It is the opinion he put into the mouth of Yuri Zhivago in the novel:

I've always liked Mayakovski. He is a sort of continuation of Dostoyevski. Or rather, he's a Dostoyevski character writing lyrics —one of his young rebels, the 'Raw Youth' or Hippolyte or Raskol-nikov. What an all-devouring poetic energy! And his way of saying a thing once and for all, implacably, straight from the shoulder! And above all, the way he takes a good bold swing and chucks it all in the face of society and even further somewhere into outer space!

Mayakovski also spoke of there being only two or three poets of true quality:

> These
>   verses and odes
>   bawled out
>   today
>   amidst applause,
>   will go down
>   in history
>   as the overhead expenses
>   of what
>   two or three of us
>   have achieved.

And in an article he wrote: 'Boris Pasternak is a lyric poet of genius . . . good things can never be hidden . . .'

But opinions that remained static would not be worth very much, and to the end of their days Mayakovski and BL carried on an inner debate one with the other, occasionally trying to draw preliminary conclusions from it. Mayakovski, for example, speaking at a public meeting in March 1927, did so by quoting the critic Lezhnev on the difference between them: 'At a time of radical change in art, when there is a need for drastic innovation of a kind that loudly and explicitly calls everything into question, then the age brings futurism to the fore, with Mayakovski as its standard-bearer, and Pasternak remains in the background . . .' To which Mayakovski added his own corollary: 'When the age brings Pasternak to the fore, Mayakovski remains in the background . . .'

I remember many occasions on which BL reflected aloud about the different roads travelled by Mayakovski and himself. From what he said I gathered that the parting of the ways had come after the end of their collaboration in LEF. BL was able to learn from life and history, and his views on certain basic events of our age underwent a substantial change. This was sometimes demonstrated in unexpected ways—as for example, in an incident which—anticipating a little—I will mention here, though it happened many years later, at the time when *Doctor Zhivago* had already appeared abroad and there was general confusion while the authorities made up their minds exactly what course of action to take and we were still in negotiation with them, wondering what would happen next and full of forebodings.

Once, in the midst of it all, Boria, more than usually upset and bewildered, clambered up over the gnarled roots (which served as steps) to the door of our little house in Peredelkino, and began to tell me something even before he had come inside: 'You know, I had a very strange meeting after I left you yesterday and went back home—right here on the main road, by the lake. Just imagine—some person in a padded jacket came running up to me and said he'd recently returned from a camp. I thought he might want money and offered him some, but he said he didn't need any and that he'd travelled a very long way just in order to come and ask my advice. Then he starts telling me about all the horrors of the camps under Khrushchev: how they now torture you by starvation—in the old days you got packages from home, but now he tells me, they allow only five kilograms every six months! But do you know why he had come such a long way to see me? He had been trying to find me for several days already, but had only just managed to track me down. And what he wanted to ask me was: "What is your attitude to terrorism— wouldn't there be a change for the better, for example, if there were somebody capable of sacrificing his own life to kill Khrushchev?" Knowing what an oppositionist I am by nature, he said, he just had to come and consult me about this! And he'd come such a long way—as though he wanted to seek my blessing!'

'Oh God,' I said, 'and what did you reply?'

'Well, I replied that not only do I not regard terrorism as a solution or a means of salvation, but that I even take a different view of revolution than I did in my youth, when we all welcomed it with such wholeheartedness. I believe that changes for the better can be brought about only in an evolutionary manner . . . And now I'm beginning to wonder whether this man might have been put up to it. What do you think? . . .'

BL showed even more clearly how his attitude had evolved in the major epic and lyrical work which sums up his philosophical and historical views, *Doctor Zhivago*:

. . . it turns out that those who inspired the Revolution aren't at home in anything except change and turmoil: that's their native element; they aren't happy with anything that's less than on a world scale. For them, transitional periods, worlds in the making, are an end in themselves. They aren't trained for anything else, they don't know about anything except that. And do you know why there is this incessant whirl of never-ending preparations? It's because they haven't any real capacities, they are ungifted. Man is born to live, not to prepare for life. Life itself—the gift of life—is such a breathtakingly serious thing!

This is said about Strelnikov, whose description in the novel embodies many aspects of Mayakovski's personality, though it is in no sense a portrait of him, and is quite remote from the actual facts of his biography.*

* Solzhenitsyn once stated that the figure of General Samsonov in *August 1914* reflects the 'spiritual reality' of the poet Alexander Tvardovski. (*continued overleaf*)

Like Mayakovski, Strelnikov represents an idea taken to extremes. As his wife, Lara, says of him: 'It was . . . as if a living human face had become an embodiment of a principle, the image of an idea . . .' And in the words of Yuri Zhivago: 'He is a doomed man. I believe he'll come to a bad end. He will atone for the evil he has done. Revolutionaries who take the law into their own hands are horrifying not because they are criminals, but because they are like machines that have got out of control, like runaway trains.' And when Strelnikov speaks of himself, it sounds like Mayakovski: '. . . for us life was a campaign. We moved mountains for those we loved, and if we brought them nothing but sorrow, we never meant to harm a hair of their heads and in the end we suffered more than they . . .'

Such fanatical faith in an idea, an utter failure to take the facts of real life into account, was bound to lead to catastrophe. Strelnikov ends by shooting himself . . .

The final summing up of the relations between Mayakovski and Pasternak, it seems to me, was made by the first with a bullet, and by the second with the chief work of his life, *Doctor Zhivago*.

Mayakovski 'set his heel on the throat' not only of his song, but of himself as well.[26] Was it because this had finally dawned on him that he fired the fateful shot? The bullet he put through his head may be seen, perhaps, as his own laconic and merciless verdict on his poetic career. Marina Tsvetayeva once said: 'The only judgment on a poet is his own'.

Despite the blinkers put over the eyes of even many talented writers during the Stalin era, Pasternak on the other hand was able to preserve his individuality as a poet, his spiritual independence—and hence his integrity, his distinctiveness, his unique poetic vision of the world. This fully entitled him in his later years to define what it was to which Mayakovski sacrificed both his gift of poetry and his life. Merciless in his judgment both of himself and the friends he loved, BL wrote down the following harsh thoughts over which he had brooded and agonized for decades:

I could see no point in his propagandist zeal, in his determination to force himself and his companions on the attention of the public, in

---

In the same way the 'spiritual reality' of Vladimir Mayakovski comes out in the image of the Red General Strelnikov.[27]

his waging of campaigns, his appeal to the collective spirit, or his submission to the voice of topical events . . . I could make nothing of Mayakovski's later poetry . . . of its clumsy rhyming dictums, its elaborate triteness, its hackneyed commonplaces expressed in such an artificial, confused and impenetrable manner. None of this, to my mind, had anything to do with Mayakovski—there was no Mayakovski in it. And yet astonishingly, it is this non-existent Mayakovski who came to be regarded as revolutionary . . . Mayakovski began to be introduced forcibly, like potatoes under Catherine the Great. This was his second death. He had no hand in it. ('An Essay in Autobiography')

Marina Tsvetayeva put it even more succinctly:

. . . for twelve years Mayakovski the man was engaged in killing Mayakovski the poet, but then in the thirteenth year the poet rose up and killed the man. If his life ended in suicide, it was not what people think it was, and it lasted not the time it takes to pull a trigger, but for twelve whole years. (*Art in the Light of Conscience*)*

BL did not betray Mayakovski, as some people have alleged, by writing of him in such words. There is deep understanding here of the fact that Mayakovski, by putting politics above poetry, betrayed himself. He thereby lost his own identity as a poet and it was this, if anything, that killed him.

In his view of Mayakovski, written down at the end of the 'fifties, Pasternak thus expressed in final form what he had already foreseen in the 'twenties—that of the three of them, only two would actually prove to be 'Donetsian, burning, infernal' to the very end of their days. Of the two who did ('Serfs of the Lyre'†) I must speak separately and in detail.

But before I do so, I must first say a little about another 'triangle'—the poetic trio Pasternak-Mandelstam-Akhmatova. Although it has the same apex—Pasternak—as the first, this second 'triangle', if I understand it rightly, stands in a certain opposition to it. Mandelstam and Pasternak have been described as 'antipodes'—not only by

* An essay published in Paris, 1932. (Tr.)
† An expression used by Tsvetayeva in one of her letters. (Tr.)

Nadezhda Mandelstam but also by Nikolai Otsup, who wrote as follows: 'In the first [Mandelstam], the rays of Latin, and in the second those of German culture are gathered and focussed; in the first, through the crystal clarity typical of him one sees chaos in a captive state (here Mandelstam bears a very slight resemblance to Tiutchev), whereas in the second, through an outer chaos (which, incidentally, is more and more subordinated to the laws of simplicity) we see a pure and wholesome soundness of spirit . . .'

Already before the Revolution, Kornei Chukovski noted the 'antipodal' relationship between Mayakovski and Akhmatova, who were, in his words, 'just as hostile to each other as the eras that gave birth to them'. But the remarkable thing is that poets who were thus generally regarded as such opposites to him and each other nevertheless loved and valued Pasternak in equally great measure. Mandelstam, for instance, wrote many extraordinary things about his work, such as: '. . . When they stood on Sparrow Hills* as boys, Herzen and Ogarev had a physical sense of holy awe at space and the flight of birds. Pasternak's poetry is also about such moments—it is a brilliant Nike transported from the Acropolis to Sparrow Hills . . . the two elements in which Pasternak's poetry moves are discovery and memory . . . Pasternak is not an inventor conjuring things up out of thin air, but the first to sing in accordance with the new harmony and structure of Russian verse achieved now that the language has grown up and reached manhood. With this new harmony it is possible to say anything one wants—and henceforth it will be used by everybody, willy-nilly, because it is now the common property of all Russian poets.' And then, writing of those Russian poets who belong 'not to yesterday or today but to all times', yet who are rewarded by their contemporaries with 'monstrous ingratitude', Mandelstam mentioned Pasternak as an example.

Whenever BL spoke about Mandelstam, it was always in connection with the notorious telephone conversation with Stalin, which had caused him such anguish. 'You don't know how to stand up for a comrade!' Stalin had said to him. The charge was not only not entirely just, but also wounding. If ever the conversation turned to Mandelstam, BL would always hark back to the same thing: that he was not to blame for his misfortunes, and that if he had not written

* A Low range of hills overlooking the Moscow River. Now Lenin Hills. (Tr.)

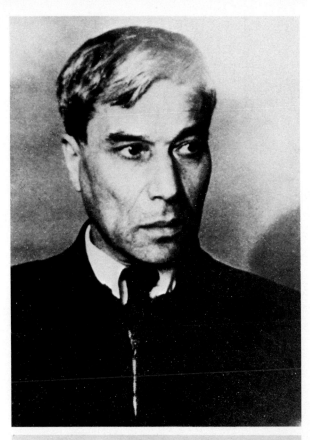

Boris Pasternak, 1953

Inscription on the back
of the above photo
(originally written in a
book in 1947)

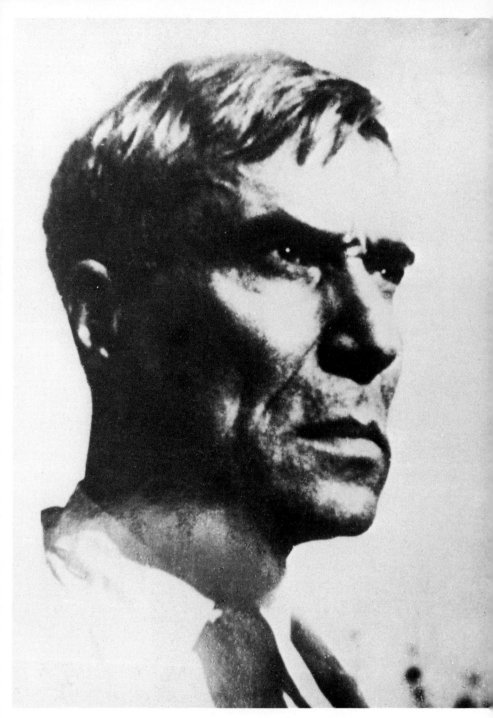

Boris Pasternak, 1957

Olga Ivinskaya in Potapov Street apartment, 1958

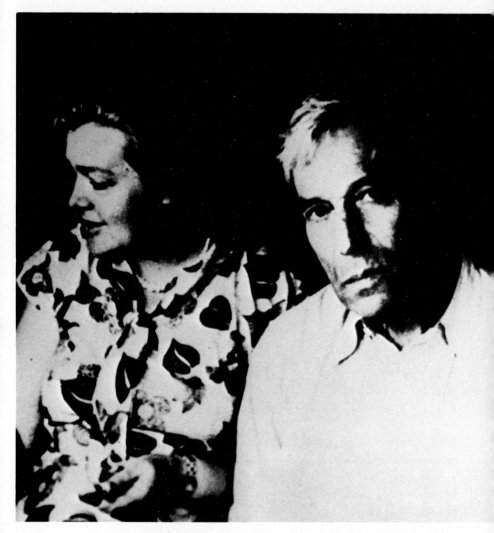

Olga Ivinskaya and Boris Pasternak, 1958

to Bukharin and in general made a great fuss about his arrest, then perhaps Mandelstam would not even have had the respite, brief as it was, which was granted to him—with the result that the *Voronezh Notebooks* might never have been written. It was clear, however, that BL himself felt he had not come as well as he should out of his unexpected conversation with the Leader. He had done something not quite right . . .

But this was thanks only to the peculiarities of BL's character. He really had wished to do everything he possibly could for Mandelstam and had been utterly fearless in interceding for him. The fact is, however, that during the fateful conversation matters of universal concern had seemed more important to him than the fate of individuals. When he heard Stalin's voice coming over the line at that historic moment the main thing he had wanted to do was to tell this man who held everybody's life in the palm of his hand about the injustices being committed in his name. He was seized by the overwhelming impulse to try and engage the Superman in an ordinary human conversation—to pour out his heart, to put everything right by saying what needed to be said. And for a moment Mandelstam had evidently taken second place for him. It no doubt seemed to BL, with his special poet's way of thinking, that his response to the trust implied by this telephone call from the highest quarter must be sincere and unreserved. And so he began—the 'all-powerful god of detail'—by going on about the difference between Mandelstam and himself in their approach to poetry. Of course, he said, Mandelstam was a great poet, but they had nothing in common because of Mandelstam's academic manner and exact rhymes whereas 'we believe in assonance and are breaking down the old dogmas and forms'. But none of this, he continued, was important anyway—only matters of life and death were important, the fact that people had no conscience and even that 'literary circles' had ceased to exist . . .

I often asked BL what Mandelstam, this extraordinary poet and one of those I loved most of all—was really like. As BL described him, he was a lyric poet of the greatest subtlety who out of a hidden feeling of terror displayed the highest courage and heroism. He was a beggar prince, an asthmatic in an aristocrat's fur coat who could refract in crystalline verse the rays of light falling on a woman's translucent fingers. Terrified of the strong, he gave a public slap in the face to the almighty Alexei Tolstoi with the words 'I am punishing the scoundrel who licensed an assault on my wife!'* People accused him of being as cowardly as a rabbit, but he had not been afraid to write the poem about Stalin and the 'thin-necked half-men' around him, and then to read it to the dumbfounded BL as they sat on a bench on Tverskoi Boulevard. In his verse he conveyed as nobody else the oppressive and humiliating sense of fear which hung over the whole era. He was a classic, a great Russian poet who wanted not to love his 'bitter land', but was unable not to love it:

> Oh allow me to be just as misty
> And allow me not to love you!

From what BL told me about him, I was able to form a good picture of him: a frail, sprightly man—majestic, child-like, tender, and desperate . . .

A final word on the two poetic 'triangles': I believe that if BL stood at the apex of both of them, it was because he embodied for the others not only poetic genius but moral integrity of the highest order as well. These were the qualities which probably made him into the unifying figure.

'And both of us will go to heaven'

BL first got to know Marina Tsvetayeva in the 'twenties, and after that their meetings were brief and infrequent. But they always felt very drawn to each other—a feeling that was strongest when they were far apart, as they were for most of the time. I know how Marina felt about BL from her letters to him: they convey all the burning sense of pain and sorrow at being separated from him by such a distance, at being denied the chance of direct human contact with him. I know of his attitude to her from his stories about her—stories always tinged with sadness and full of admiration. As he used to say to me: 'Marina's poetic talent could have been divided into ten parts and each part would have been enough for one man to earn the complete recognition of his contemporaries.' Perhaps this was not the actual form of his words, but it is the essence of them. During

---

* Mandelstam believed that Tolstoi had exonerated Sergei Borodin after the latter had insulted his wife, Nadezhda Yakovlevna.

the whole of his life he liked Marina more than any other poet.

Nobody who loves Russian literature will be unfamiliar with the impassioned 'romance in letters' between BL and Tsvetayeva—this was not simply a correspondence in the ordinary sense, but the kind of heart-to-heart exchange which goes beyond the letters themselves, as though their writers were able to look into each other's eyes and feel the living presence of each other.

During my years with BL I heard him speak over and over again about his sense of responsibility for Marina's return to Russia, for her feeling that she was utterly abandoned, and for her death. Till the end of his life he never ceased to mourn her. There are now absurd rumours to the effect that at the time of her death, during her ordeal as an evacuee, BL behaved like all the other venerable writers who lived nearby and left her to her fate, even refusing to help her. This is a wicked and shameless lie. Marina herself, as she wandered round Chistopol during her last days begging for help, said that she was now quite alone because she no longer had 'even Boria's letters'. But his letters did not reach her because of the war, and he was far away—in Moscow. On the day when he learned of her death, he wrote to Zinaida Nikolayevna in Chistopol:*

. . . Yesterday I was told by Fedin that Marina has killed herself. I cannot believe it. She must be somewhere not far from you, in Chistopol or Yelabuga . . . But if it is true, what a horror! In that case you must look after her son—find out where he is and what has happened to him. What a stigma on me, if it's true! . . . I shall never be forgiven for it. During this last year I no longer showed any interest in her. She was very highly thought of among the intelligentsia and was becoming fashionable among people who understand poetry—my friends Neigaus, Asmus, Kolia Villyam—not to mention Aseyev—had taken her up. Since people were flattered to be numbered among her friends, and for many other reasons, I had drifted away from her and didn't impose myself on her—and during the last year almost completely forgot about her. And now this! . . .

Such were the terrible accusations which BL levelled against himself, and they did not fade from his mind with the years. But was he

* Pasternak's wife was evacuated to Chistopol soon after the German invasion in June 1941, and he followed her later, in October. (Tr.)

really so much to blame? With the help of Marina's own letters and notebooks, the stories of her daughter (and my close friend) Ariadna Efron, the memoirs of Tsvetayeva's editor at *Goslitizdat*, Zinaida Kulmanova, and various materials published abroad (for instance, Tsvetayeva's letters which came out in Paris in 1972), I shall try to trace, even if faintly, the path which took her from the painted wooden house on Trekhprudni Street in Moscow where her life began to the other wooden house on Zhdanov Street in Yelabuga where it ended. (What singular coincidences there are in life: Marina hanged herself on a street named after the 'friend' of literature Zhdanov and 'a certain'* Pasternak lived on a road—in Peredelkino—named after the 'famous' writer Pavlenko.)

Already well before the Revolution, when she was only sixteen years old, Marina had expressed her forebodings about the precarious nature of life and the upheavals to come:

> Soon this world will perish!
> Steal a look at it while you can
> Before the poplar's been cut down
> And our house put up for auction . . .

The house was not in fact sold, but looted, sacked, and then burned down. Marina was to see the death of one of her daughters ('. . . Irina died from hunger, in a children's home just outside Moscow', in Kuntsevo), and was to live as an émigré in penniless obscurity, wandering first from one village to another in Bohemia, and then settling near Paris. The appalling business of simply keeping alive, the constant illnesses of her husband and his inability to find work swallowed up all her time and strength. At the same time her relations with other émigrés grew worse and worse. Even her fellow poet, the Acmeist Georgi Adamovich, failed to understand or appreciate her while she was still alive. Only after her death did he realize how unjust he had been, how irreparable what had happened was:

> . . . In her lifetime it was not to be. I am not to blame.
> Literature is a summons to descend to hell,
> Which I obeyed joyfully, I'll not deny it,
> And from which no one finds a way back again.

---

* An epithet often applied in Soviet polemical writings to persons – even if well known—who are 'in disgrace'. (Tr.)

I am not to blame. How much pain in the world.
But neither do I blame you for anything.
Everything happens by accident, by fate.
How marvellous life is. How badly we live it.

Yes, that is how it was with Marina—everything was by accident,
by fate. Very few people here understood Marina's lot as an émigré
as well as BL:

A distant foreign land. Foreign rain
Pouring down on hats, in ditches,
And turned into an oak by sheer forlornness
The poet stands, a stranger, like Pushkin's miller.[28]

At the same time she was neither able nor willing to fight for any
improvement in her way of life: 'Understand that on the roads of
life I always give way to others'.

On top of it all there was her distress at not having a reading public
for her poetry, and her constant anxiety for her children growing up
in a foreign country: '. . . Moor—the son of an émigré—that's what
it will say in your papers. A wolf's papers* they will be . . .' Of the
young Ariadna, when she was thirteen, she wrote: 'Alia is enormous . . . with long braids, clever and tiring (because of her laziness
and inborn slowness of movement). She has a very hard life, but she
has a generous nature and does not reproach me for having brought
her into this world. From the age of four she has known nothing but
buckets and brooms—she will have something by which to remember
this planet of ours!' Marina did not then know how terribly prophetic
her words would turn out to be: Ariadna (of whom her mother also
wrote: 'I was proud of Alia when she was a child, even boastful
about her') lived to see her father's execution, her mother's suicide,
the death of her brother, and her own wanderings through the circles
of Stalin's inferno—she was to spend sixteen years in various camps
and places of exile. ('All equally, unerringly, are beaten by God's
flail.') She has indeed had something to remember our planet by—or
rather, that part of it occupied by her native country . . .

BL's letters to Marina during her years in emigration are well
known. Here I would only like to recall the end of the poem he
dedicated to her at that time:

* Russian expression for the identity papers of a social outcast, e.g. an ex-
convict. 'Moor' was the nickname of Tsvetayeva's son. (Tr.)

... I am indifferent to changes
In the fashions of the present age:
All that is will be swept away,
Fading like a dream, immuring the poet in itself.

Then, wreathed like smoke
He will move, curling from
The holes of his own fateful era
Into yet another impassable dead-end.

He will escape, billowing from the chasms
Of his own crushed existence,
And his grandchildren will say—as of smouldering turf—
The age of so-and-so still burns.

I have already written about BL's meeting with Marina in Paris in
May 1935. She and her family were at the moment undecided
whether or not to return home to Russia. According to BL (in 'An
Essay in Autobiography'): 'Tsvetayeva asked me what I thought about
it. I had no definite opinion. It was hard to know what to advise
them . . .' But one might have thought, given the mass purges
following the assassination of Kirov, that BL could have offered her
clearer and more definite guidance. (This is no doubt why, after
Marina and most of her family had perished, he was so full of self-
blame in his poem to her memory: 'In the silence of your going /
there is an unspoken reproach.')

Soon there were sinister developments about which there are
many stories, not all of them true. But the basic fact, on which they
all agree, is that in order to earn the right to return to Russia,
Marina's husband, Sergei Efron, allowed himself to become seriously
involved in the murder (September 1937, in Switzerland) of a former
Soviet agent, Ignace Reiss, who had defected. In connection with
this Marina was subjected to a merciless interrogation by the French
police. But her ignorance of the whole business was so obvious that
they soon left her alone. Efron had already been forced to flee to the
Soviet Union, where Ariadna had also returned a little earlier.
Marina remained behind near Paris with their son, Moor. Relations
with other Russian émigrés became still worse, and now that Ariadna
was gone they no longer had even the income from the hats which
she knitted and sold to help the family.

To show how hard it was for them, one detail will suffice. The bulk of their income was swallowed up by the rent for their lodgings and whenever they were so short of money that the situation became critical, Marina would somehow manage to hire (or more often, get someone to lend her) a small hall, to seat 80 or 120 people at the most, and sell tickets for a public reading of her poetry. Many people will remember the letter she once wrote to Anna Tesková in Prague begging her to send a decent dress for her to wear on one of these occasions—she had nothing suitable in which to appear before even the most 'simple' audience . . .

Moor, now growing up, was not much inclined to take his family's material difficulties to heart. Like any young Parisian of his age, he wanted to keep up with the fashions and buy something 'smart' for himself more often than he could afford. Marina loved him very much and was proud of him, and the lack of money to buy what he wanted upset her terribly. (Alexei Eisner*, who saw a good deal of Marina and her family during those years in Paris, recalls that Moor was a very plump, good-looking, intelligent boy, though many people felt there was something unpleasant about him. But Marina doted on him and was always particularly distressed by her inability to cater for his needs.) 'Indignation—this is what grows in me by the year, the day, the hour. Indignation. Contempt. A lump of outrage growing ever since childhood. It's unjust, unreasonable, ungodly. Blok strikes this same note in his line: "Is *this* how things must be among people?"'

To make matters worse, there was no news from her husband† and daughter. A month went by, then a year, but still no word. After another six months or so Marina decided on a last, desperate step: to return home herself . . .

Zinaida Shakhovskaya remembers her words at the time: 'There's nothing else for it. The emigration is driving me away! . . . One thing

* Alexei Vladimirovich Eisner (1905–) was taken to Paris by his step-father and mother after the Revolution. He took part in the Spanish Civil War, serving as adjutant to General Lukacz (Maté Zalka). In 1940 he returned to the Soviet Union, where he was soon arrested. He was released and rehabilitated only after Stalin's death. As is clear from one of Marina's letters to Anna Tesková, he became a close friend of her family at the beginning of the 'thirties.

† This is what Mark Slonim says in his articles in *Novy Zhurnal* (New York). But according to Alexei Eisner, Marina did in fact receive some letters from Efron in one of which he told her how much he missed the French cinema.

you can be sure of: there too I shall be with the persecuted, not with the persecutors, with the victims, not with the executioners . . .' When the woman poet Alla Golovina asked her whether she would miss France, she replied with these impromptu lines:

> I love no country more than France
> And I have been granted tears to bid her farewell.
> Like pearls they hang on my eyelashes:
> The farewell of a Mary Stuart.

Almost two years after Sergei and Ariadna had left, on June 12, 1939, Marina and Moor left Paris for Le Havre, where they took a boat for Poland. They travelled on to Moscow via Warsaw, arriving there on June 18. In the West people have gained the impression that Sergei and Ariadna were no longer at liberty by the time Marina reached Moscow. But this is not so. In fact, the whole family was reunited, and they all went to live in a tiny house in the village of Bolshevo near Moscow. Things were hard for them and there wasn't enough room (Ariadna settled on the unheated verandah to make room for her brother), but for a brief while—a little over two months—they were happy: they were all together again and had hopes for the future.

BL took Marina to *Goslitizdat* and introduced her to the editors there (two of them, Sophia Khitarova and Zinaida Kulmanova, remember this very well and still talk about it). Marina was immediately given a lot of work to do: she was asked to translate some of the Georgian poets (in particular Vazha Pshavela), Yiddish ones from Byelorussia, and some others.[29] She received payment on completion of the work, without having to wait for publication. But she translated slowly. As she wrote later (in the spring of 1941): '. . . nothing can ever force me to deliver a manuscript until the last full stop is in place. But the time this may take is known only to God—to the God of poets.' For this reason, she did not earn a great deal, but she was helped out by Ariadna who had a job, if I remember rightly, in the Society for Cultural Relations with Foreign Countries.* Sergei is also said to have been given some kind of work. Everything, in a word, would have been all right—if it had not been for the arrest of Ariadna, which took place on the night of August 27, 1939. About

---

* Official agency, founded in 1925 and commonly known by its initials as VOKS, for the channelling and control of contacts with other countries. (Tr.)

a month later Sergei was arrested as well ... It was just as Akhmatova wrote in a poem after meeting Marina in 1940, putting these words into her mouth:

> ... Today I came back to my home:
> Look and marvel, my native fields,
> At what has been done to me.
> My dear ones have been swallowed by the pit,
> And my parents' house is plundered ...

In 1955 Ariadna returned from exile* to Moscow and went to live with her aunt, Elizabeth Efron, in a tiny room in Merzliakov Street where she slept on a trunk—the same trunk on which she had slept for a time after first arriving in Moscow from Paris in 1937, and which was then, after her arrest in 1939, taken over by her mother, Marina. This is what Ariadna wrote down at the time of her second return to Moscow (1955): 'I used to take Mother's notebooks out of the trunk at random—both the early ones and the last ones in which, wedged in among the painstaking columns of translations, there were notes about the packages [handed over at the prison] for Father and me, drafts of hopeless appeals to everybody from Stalin to Fadeyev, and the words "I shall never again write poetry. It is all finished."' (Further on Ariadna says about these notebooks: 'I read them at night when everything was quiet in the large communal apartment.† I was wrong in thinking that I had no more tears left to weep—though *this* was beyond tears ...')

Marina found it hard to live after the arrest of her husband and daughter. To put it more precisely: though she felt she ought to go on living, she had already made her decision to die: 'Washing-up, dishwater, and tears ... Nobody sees, nobody knows that for the last year (roughly) I have been looking for a hook [to hang by], but there aren't any, because everything is done by electricity nowadays. There are no chandeliers ... For about a year I have been thinking of death. Everything is monstrous and terrible ... I do not wish to die. But I wish not to be.' Apart from anything else there was also the ordeal of trying to find a place to live. Everything was either unsuitable or only temporary. Sometimes she stayed with Moor in the tiny room of Sergei's sister Elizabeth Efron and her companion Zinaida Mitrofanovna on Merzliakov Street, and sometimes in a room at the

* i.e. from exile in Siberia. (Tr.)   † See footnote on p. 67. (Tr.)

Writers' Club on Herzen Street, or at the writers' rest home in Golitsyno . . .

It is said that in the memoirs left by the late Emmanuil Kazakievich (who helped Ariadna after her return to Moscow from exile and also had a hand in getting the first Soviet edition of Tsvetayeva published) there is an account of an episode shortly after Marina's return to Russia when BL went to see Fadeyev in Peredelkino and asked him to help her—in particular, to find her a place to live. BL of course, spoke in his usual agitated, rambling manner. Fadeyev affected not to understand what he was driving at, or even about whom exactly he was talking. All the same, a few evenings later he came round to the Pasternak house, as though just 'dropping in' by chance, and met Marina who was there on a visit at the time. He did thus make her acquaintance, and it was scarcely BL's fault if nothing came of it.

Marina also turned for help to *Litfund*,* and to the highly influential Pavlenko, but it was all in vain. No wonder she spoke with such bitterness: '. . . Moscow has no room for me . . . I cannot rid myself of the idea that I have a *right* to it. We gave so much to Moscow, but now it casts me out, rejects me.' She was here referring to the fact that her father had taken the initiative in founding the Museum of Fine Arts (now called the Pushkin Museum), and that three collections of books of immense value belonging respectively to her grandfather, her father, and her mother had been presented by them to the Rumiantsev Museum (now the Lenin Library).

On the last day of August 1940, she wrote: '. . . as I move from place to place I am gradually losing the sense of my own reality: there is less and less of me, rather as with a sheep that leaves a tuft of wool on every hedge it crosses . . . All that remains is my basic nothingness . . .'

Whenever she was able to live for a short while in someone's *dacha* in relatively decent conditions, she felt terribly guilty at the thought of those dear to her languishing somewhere in jail: 'I am ashamed to be still alive . . . the only thing Russian about me is my conscience, and it will never allow me to enjoy fresh air, peace, and the blue sky knowing, and never for one second forgetting, that others are

* 'Literary Fund', a subsidiary organization of the Union of Writers, which caters for the writers' material welfare. It is possible to remain a member of it, even after expulsion from the Union of Writers—as happened in the case of Pasternak. (Tr.)

suffocating at this very moment from the heat behind stone walls . . .'
The 'others' in question were of course her husband and daughter,
and her sister Anastasia, who was already living in a place of exile
when Marina returned from Moscow, so that they had not even seen
each other.

And so it went on: 'My life is very bad—my non-life' (August 31,
1940); 'I have now been *killed*, at the moment I do not exist, and do
not know whether I ever shall again . . .'; 'Very lost and unhappy . . .'
(June 10, 1941).

Yet at the same time, even though slowly, she continued to work
on translations, and a book of her own verse: '. . . So I am putting
together a book of my poems, adding things, checking them, paying
to have them typed out, correcting them again—but I am practically
certain that they won't be accepted [for publication], I would be
astonished if they were.' (October 24, 1940).

Needless to say, the book never appeared. But in the March
number of the magazine *30 Days* an old poem of hers, written in
1920, was published—one with the first line 'Yesterday you still
looked into my eyes' and with the refrain: 'My dear, what have I
done to you?' (One wonders whether this was the magazine's way of
marking International Woman's Day, on March 8!)

There was one other important event: Marina was made a member
of the branch of the writers' organization at *Goslitizdat*.[30] She wrote
to Ariadna in the labour camp about this on April 12, 1941: '. . . the
other day I was made a member of the writers' organization at
Goslitizdat. Unanimously. Altogether I am doing my best.'

But in fact it had not gone through quite as smoothly as that.
Zinaida Kulmanova remembers very well how Marina burst into her
room that day, deeply hurt and upset because some other woman in
the office had attacked her on standard lines as a former émigré and
a close relative of people who had been arrested. Kulmanova
remembers how she tried to calm her and went to the cupboard to
get a glass to pour her some water, but before she had time to bring
it, Marina had already snatched a bakelite container, thrown out all
the pens and pencils in it, and poured the water herself . . .

When the first German bombs rained down on the city and
shrapnel from anti-aircraft shells, as well as small German incendiary
bombs, began to drum on the roofs of Moscow's buildings, all
Marina's misfortune and fears were compounded by anxiety for

Moor, by now a grown boy, who had been put in a fire-watching squad with the task of throwing fire bombs off the roof of the high apartment building on Pokrovski Boulevard where she had rented a tiny room on the top floor. At this very same time BL did fire-watching duty on the roof of the Writers' House in Lavrushinski Street. Marina went to see him and ask his advice about what she should do to save Moor. She had already formed the idea of going off to the Tartar region—where the Union of Writers was then being evacuated. As though foreseeing the calamity to come, BL did his best to dissuade her, but he did not make the alternative proposal which she was expecting from him. As she remarked bitterly to Kulmanova at *Goslitizdat*, telling her about this visit to Pasternak: 'Boris could have invited me to stay out at Peredelkino with him, if only for a little while.'

Years later BL told me that he had not invited Marina to stay— the thing he would really have liked to do—partly because of his own indecisiveness and partly because of the domestic situation at the Peredelkino house. So she decided on evacuation. When she said goodbye to Kulmanova, she remarked half-jokingly that since her family had been arrested and the Germans were now advancing towards Moscow, it would in any case be as well for her to leave the city—so as not to be suspected of hoping for their arrival.

BL saw Marina and her son off at the Khimki River port.* This was their last farewell.

BL and Marina judged each other by the highest possible criterion —by their quality as poets. Apart from this, they were bound together in the intellectual and cultural sense by a thousand invisible threads—beginning with the similarity in their family backgrounds. Marina's father had been professor of Fine Arts at Moscow University and a director of the Rumiantsev Museum (and also the founder of the Museum of Fine Arts, as already mentioned); BL's father was a painter, the director of the College of Fine Arts in Moscow, the author of superb literary memoirs on Leo Tolstoi, Rilke, and many others. Both their fathers had deep roots in Russian art, but at the same time were closely connected with European culture in general.

Marina's mother was a pianist and painter, a favourite pupil of Muromtseva (who in her turn was the best student of Nikolai

* On the outskirts of Moscow: it is possible to go by steamer from here to Chistopol and other towns on the river Kama, and the Volga.

Rubinstein) and of Nikolai Clodt. As Marina said: 'Mother suckled us from an open vein of lyricism . . .' Her last words before her early death were: 'I shall miss only music and the sun'; BL's mother was a talented pianist remarkable not so much for her technique as for her 'rare artistic temperament and understanding of the score'.

But the direct affinity between Boris and Marina was even greater than that between their parents—they had a common view of the nature and spirit of poetry, they were alike in their non-ritual, unobtrusive sense of religion, in sharing an 'equal loneliness'*, and in very many other things quite impossible to describe here.

Yet despite all this, their 'equal loneliness' all too often proved to be not so equal, and their way of looking at the world to be in fact rather different (for instance, the peculiar attitude which each had to Peter the Great). Both in their own way were deeply conscious of the greatness of the other, and each was anxious to understand and accept the antagonism inherent in their relationship, but neither was able to entirely . . . I believe the reason for their failure to become really close to each other in spirit—if they had done so, they would have come together and never parted—was to be found in their different attitude to something very tenacious that has a great hold over most mortals, namely the idea of ordinary domestic life. A person may either rise above it, spurn it, or wholly submit to it. In my view the reason for the parting of the ways—in effect, for the break—between these two poets of perhaps different creative strengths (which, however, converged at a certain point) was due to the simple fact that Marina was bold, decisive, and peremptory in a masculine way, while BL was soft and feminine in his approach to family life, or, as Marina herself put it, 'tortuously meek'. And although he was drawn by the 'passion to break free', in practice it was, for the most part, only the subject of daydreams or poetry. Whenever Marina, on the other hand, wanted to 'break free', she put all her soul into it: with her it was unbridled and uncompromising, as witness the following passionate plea addressed to BL (in June 1926) during their 'romance by correspondence':

Boris, Boris, how happy you and I would be . . . both in this world and the next, which is already *all here within us* . . . We would sing in the same voice. My dear one, pluck the heart filled with me. Do

* A phrase used in one of Tsvetayeva's letters to Pasternak's father. (Tr.)

not distress yourself. Live your life. Do not fret over your wife and son. I give you complete absolution from all and everything. Take everything you can, while there is still the desire to take it! Remember that our blood is older than we ourselves—particularly in a Semite like you. Do not try to tame it. Take everything from lyrical—no, from epic heights!

But Ariadna often told me that though her mother longed with all her being for the day when she would see Pasternak again, she was never really inwardly ready for it, and even secretly feared it. A little before she wrote the letter quoted above, she had foreseen that '. . . all the same I could never live with him—because I love him too much.' And later: 'I could never live with BL, but I want a son by him, who would *live in him through me*. If this does not happen, then my life, its very concept, has come to nothing.'

When the meeting she had wanted for so long at last came about* it was evidently as big a disappointment as she had always feared. For one thing both of them by now had their hands tied: Pasternak already had a second family and since he had taken his break with the first one very tragically, he was terrified of any repetition, of any further upheavals of this sort. Apart from this, I believe it was not without some significance that they had already had their lengthy 'romance by correspondence'—both of them must have realized, perhaps instinctively, that something of *such* a kind could only happen once in a lifetime, and could never be renewed in a personal encounter. I thought it odd that during the whole of our fourteen years together, BL never once gave me any coherent account of his first meeting with Marina after her return to Moscow from emigration on June 18, 1939. He clearly did not like to recall it, and once, when I said to him jokingly, not without malice: 'You should have married Marina then,' he was very vehement in his reply: 'Olia, we could never have lived together—Marina combined every kind of female hysteria in concentrated form. I could not have taken it.'

· * i.e. after Tsvetayeva's return to Russia in 1939. Before this they had met only fleetingly—once after the Revolution, before Tsvetayeva's emigration in 1922, and again in 1935 during Pasternak's visit to Paris. Both these meetings are mentioned in Pasternak's 'An Essay in Autobiography', where he also describes how he wrote her a long letter in the early 'twenties—this was the beginning of a long and active correspondence that went on for several years. (Tr.)

Marina—'condemned to write verse as a wolf is to howl' (as she put it herself)—was also condemned to experience one misfortune after another. It was almost as though her poetic instinct unfailingly led her to disaster, painful separations, and storms of passion, as a result of which new notes and revelations in her verse were born— struck like sparks from a violent clash of temperaments, the rupture of precious bonds, or unexpected blows of fate.

In her three years in Czechoslovakia she found herself constantly on the move, going with her family from one village to another, all with names like Horni Mokropsy or Novy Dvory, until they finally got to Prague. In each of these villages they often had to trudge under the rain along muddy Czech country roads, her poor husband Sergei pushing a wheelbarrow with their belongings, as they moved from one lodging place to another. No, it was not really that Marina sought out hardships and distress, but rather that they found her:

> Friend, rain beats on my window,
> Sorrows and follies on my heart . . .

But all the same, of nobody is it truer to say than of her that pain served as the mainspring of her life, forging the link between her and poetry. What she described as her 'mad love of life, a frantic, feverish hunger for it' constantly alternated with thoughts of death—'better to hang myself', she once wrote—not in 1941, but already in 1920.

Apart from her love for Sergei (of whom she wrote to Vasili Rozanov: 'We shall never part. Our meeting is a miracle.'), there was not only her 'romance by correspondence'—no more than that!— with Pasternak, but also her very real and tempestuous affair with Konstantin Rodzevich (who later fought in the Spanish Civil War and the French Resistance).* This was widely known at the time, and Marina wrote poems about it:

> . . . Love is flesh and blood,
> A flower watered by your own blood.

---

* Rodzevich's father, Boris Kazimirovich, had been the general in charge of the medical services of the Tsarist army. After the Revolution he commanded a Bolshevik military flotilla on the Southern Dnieper. He was captured by the Whites and sentenced to death, but General Slashchev (the prototype of Khludov in Bulgakov's play *Flight*) reprieved him and persuaded him to join the Whites— for which he was then condemned to death in absentia by the Bolsheviks.

> Do you think love
> Is polite conversation at table? . . .
>
> . . . . . .
>
> And in that same blissful air,
> While you still can, sin!

This storm of passion gave birth to her immortal cycle of lyrics *The Poem of the Mountain*, but before a year was out it was all finished:

> A man's tears are cruel:
> Like a blow to the head with a hammer!
> Weep—you'll make up with others
> For the sense of shame you lost with me . . .

Her break with Rodzevich produced a new flight of lyrical inspiration in *The Poem of the End*, and as soon as it was written, all her passion died away, and Marina introduced him to Maria, the daughter of her close friend, the priest Sergei Bulgakov, helping to bring about their marriage. She gave the bride a white wedding dress, and soon she was writing to Tesková that '. . . they are our neighbours, we see each other all the time. Relations are amicable, benevolent, and impassive—we go to the cinema together . . .' And in another place she noted of herself: 'I treat the human side of myself like a dog—when I'm tired of it I put it on a chain'.

To the hypocritical busybodies who wanted to save Marina from her 'bad ways', she replied in verse with a pride and disdain worthy of a Polish *panna*:*

> Do not hasten to judge:
> Human judgment is frail!
> Do not blacken a jackdaw
> By making it white as a dove.
>
> All who wanted kissed me!
> But, perhaps on that blackest day
> When I've loved the last one,
> I'll wake up whiter than you!

Of course Marina's life did not consist entirely of these stormy and passionate affairs which served as the source of her creative impulses.

---

* Polish noblewoman. Tsvetayeva was partly of Polish descent. (Tr.)

There was also life at a much more humdrum level—the daily round of keeping body and soul together. This comes out in her letters: '. . . I work away at my drudgery. I am like that goat which the slaughterers don't quite finish off. I am like the stew that is for ever simmering on my primus stove'. '. . . Do you remember Katerina Ivanovna in Dostoyevski? That's me: harassed, ill-humoured, cantankerous . . .' And again: '. . . Re-read the parts about Katerina Ivanovna in *Crime and Punishment*—that's me . . .' This last quotation is from a letter to BL.

As I have said, BL's attitude to domestic life, the daily round was quite different from Marina's. He was not a man to go out seeking causes to fight for—though neither did he try to hide from all the storms and troubles that descended on him (as is clear enough from the affair of his novel)—but the chief source of his poetic inspiration, as I understand it, was ordinary everyday life. Whatever he wrote about—love, nature, or social upheavals—his art was rooted in the interaction of his poetic vision with life at its most down-to-earth, as lived in an ordinary domestic setting, or in the work-a-day world round about. As he said himself: '. . . Only in nature and the daily round of life does one find novelty, the eternally unusual; the whole universe resides only in work and poverty . . .'

In BL's unique manner of describing human existence, its most important, crucial, and momentous aspects are shown through things incidental to it, through what appears at first sight to be secondary or of little significance. But by these means he is able to show the movement of the human spirit in such a graphic way that one is quite justified in speaking of the portrait of a whole generation —a portrait in which the harmony of composition is all the more telling for being so unobtrusive.

In order to write poetry, BL had no need to wander the face of the earth, to transfer his affections as often as he changed apartments or to engage in dramas of conflict and separation in his personal life—he saw poetry everywhere around him, wherever he was and whatever he was doing. I have already quoted his words about poetry at the Paris congress: 'Poetry . . . lies in the grass at our feet, so that one only has to bend down to see it, and pick it up from the ground . . .' For BL everything was eternally new—every love, every parting, every season of the year. Nature constantly gave him joy:

Winter—all for the first time again.
Into the grey distances of November
The willow trees retreat, like blind men
Without sticks or guides to lead them.

The river's iced over, osiers are frozen,
And right across, resting on the naked ice,
Like a mirror on its supporting table
The black horizon rises up above it.

Or:

And at noon the skies turn blue again,
Again the hay-ricks look like clouds,
Again, like vodka mixed with aniseed,
The earth's fragrance goes to the head.

Even a cold and gloomy street, through which the few passersby
hurry on their way to get as quickly as possible to the warmth of their
homes, causes Pasternak to linger in admiration—he likes it there:

The City. A winter sky.
Darkness. Arched gates.
At the church of Boris and Gleb
Light, and a service . . .

BL took a completely different view than Tsvetayeva of the
ordinary comforts of life. He did not want luxury, only a certain
minimum of the ordinary amenities: peace and quiet, a desk to write
at and a study were *essential* to him, not as mere creature comforts
but for the sake of his poetry, which demanded an orderly way of life.

One might think—as some people do—that this was out of
egotism. I believe that it was rather out of an instinctive wish to
protect his Muse, to create the right conditions for his work. If one
understands BL's attitude to domestic life from this point of view,
then much about his relations with the women close to him—at least
in the last twenty years of his life—becomes clearer. Zinaïda Nikolayevna managed to create for him a kind of 'Olympus' at the 'big'
house in Peredelkino—everything there could not have been better
arranged for living and working. BL very much appreciated this, as
is evident from a lot of what he writes about Tonya in *Doctor*

Zhivago, and even from a letter he wrote to my mother.* I think Zinaida Nikolayevna understood very well that by making a good home for BL, she strengthened her position as his legal wife and the mistress of the 'big' house—which made it easier for her to reconcile herself to the open existence of the 'little' house (that is, mine), and she knew that any ill-considered attempt to put pressure on BL would have meant disaster for her.

But it was not quite as simple as that. In his last years, the study with his favourite books and his desk had its due place in his heart, but he often said to me: 'I am going off to work. I have to be worthy of you. My place of work is over there.'

Nikolai Liubimov has told me how heart-rendingly lonely BL seemed to him when he once saw him coming down the stairs from his study at the 'big' house to join him in the drawing room, where his wife and some of her women friends were playing cards. They all cast disapproving glances at him—the man who had jeopardized this comfortable existence by publishing his novel. Yet he did not make a clean break with it all, as Marina would certainly have done. This does not suggest the behaviour of a self-satisfied egoist. As Ariadna put it to me with some impatience, BL was so tormented by compassion and pangs of conscience because he no longer loved Zinaida Nikolayevna, this uncouth woman who had failed to respond to his love, that he saw her as a Little Red Ridinghood who had lost her way in the forest, and wept tears of pity for her. Speaking about her to me, he said: 'I do not pity you, and I hope to God it will always be like that with you and me. Let us save our pity for others. I saw that ageing woman standing by the fence, and thought: you wouldn't want to change places with her, would you? So let us bestow the blessing of mercy on those around us ...'

It is absurd to imagine that he sat in an ivory tower, preserving an Olympian calm. If he never took any desperate steps, it was only because of this sense of pity, particularly in regard to someone he had ceased to love—and thereby wronged, as he felt. Even at a particularly difficult time, when the alien spirit of the 'big' house had become intolerable, and we both felt so stifled by the hostility emanating from it that we had decided to clear out and settle in Tarusa,† Boria could simply not bring himself to—again, it was not a question of putting

* For the text of this, see p. 130. (Tr.)
† A small town south of Moscow, on the river Oka. (Tr.)

his own well-being first, but of the overwhelming compassion he felt for those who could only suffer uncomprehendingly.

I believe that the estrangement between BL and Zinaida Nikolayevna had started long before my appearance on the scene. It was because of it that he didn't invite Marina to come and stay with them during her wartime troubles—he evidently decided he must find some other solution for Marina, rather than impose her unwelcome presence on Zinaida Nikolayevna.

Another similar example from a much later period: when the Hamburg Drama Theatre visited Moscow in December 1959, BL very much wanted to invite its director, Gustaf Gründgens, and the leading actors out to the 'big' house at Peredelkino, but he felt unable to do so because of his domestic situation (as noted even in the posthumous appreciation of BL written by Gerd Ruge*). On this occasion too, he did not want to go against Zinaida Nikolayevna's wishes.

As regards my own relations with BL during our fourteen years together—the main topic of my book—I can only say in this particular connection that there was much of the same kind of thing as I am describing here, and that it was the cause of many of our quarrels . . . I was sometimes infuriated by his tolerance and soft-heartedness.

After this digression from my outline of Marina's life, I can now return to where I broke off at the moment of her final parting with BL, as the boat bore her down the Moscow River farther and farther away from the landing stage at Khimki, until he disappeared from her sight—in the words of her poem:

> . . . into hollow waves
> of mist, hunched, my equal,
> silently, without trace—
> as a ship sinks.[31]

On August 21, 1941, Marina and her son arrived in Yelabuga and found lodgings in the house of a couple called Bredelshchikov, who, learning after her death what sort of person they had had in their house, described her as 'tall, bent, thin, and grey-haired—just like a witch'. (She herself has written a long time before:

* In his book *Gods Die* (Poets of the world as remembered by their friends), published in Western Germany, 1961.

The gold of my hair
Turns slowly to grey.
Don't pity me: all is fulfilled,
All is confused in my soul; all songs are sung.

And in her last letter to her daughter Ariadna, written on April 12, 1941, she said: 'Moor said to me indignantly the other day: "Mother, you look like a terrible old country crone!"')

She was dressed very badly—in a long dark dress, an old brown autumn raincoat, and a beret of a dirty-blue colour she had knitted herself.

She tried to find work, and made unsuccessful attempts to sell the remnants of a silver table service. The only offer of work she got was as a cleaning woman in a cafeteria. She wrote a letter to the Tartar branch of the Union of Writers in which she asked them to '. . . employ me as a translator, because I have no skills outside my profession as a writer.'* Before she left Moscow, Zinaida Kulmanova had already asked the Tartar poet Alehmed Yerikeyev (the chairman of the Tartar branch of the Union of Writers) to find Marina work as a translator in Kazan; she had also asked P. Chagin to help. But it was to no avail: nobody replied or did anything.

For three days Marina went to Chistopol, where Aseyev and Fadeyev were already staying. She asked them to find her a place to live and what was most important of all—to obtain a residence permit for her . . . Again, nobody responded or did anything.

Whenever he spoke of Marina, BL repeated to me many times: 'Do they really think I wouldn't have paid them back?'—he was indignant that his fellow writers, and chief among them Fadeyev, as well as his close friend 'Kolia' Aseyev, had not at least lent her some money until he arrived in Chistopol. He was all the more outraged because he had heard from someone or other that not only had Aseyev refused to help Marina, but had actually told her off for coming from Yelabuga to pester them.

Somebody also reported to BL Marina's remark that she would rather freeze into the ice on the Kama than return to Yelabuga. Telling this to Gladkov, BL commented: 'Actually, winter was still far off, even though people were already thinking of it with dread, and

* Quoted by R. Mustafin in his article 'The Last Address of a Poetess' (published in the newspaper *Komsomolets Tatarii* of March 20, 1966).

the barges were sailing endlessly down the river, one after another.'

So Marina returned to Yelabuga empty-handed.

On Sunday, August 31 (ten days after her arrival from Moscow), the landlady of the house where she was staying found Marina hanging from a large nail on the left side of the entry-way:

> . . . a bleak entrance, dark, where
> the hempen rope held firm,
> where, for the last time,
> from a ewer she wet her lips
> with chilling water from the Kama.
>
> Not a hook, a nail—square-sided, stout,
> for hanging up horse-collars, fishing tackle.
> It was too low there just to hang yourself,
> —easier to do it by strangulation.
> . . . . . .
> Grandma, I'm frightened here in this passage,
> in this room,
> I want to cry on your shoulder.
> Remember now: people are only killed,
> they never kill themselves.
>
> (Yevgeni Yevtushenko)

Before her death she did not even take off the apron with the large pocket in which she had been doing her housework that morning after sending Moor off to his job on the site of an aerodrome that was being made nearby. Who knows what went through her mind in her last moments? (The letters she wrote before her death have been kept secret.) Did she think of her own definition of suicide as '. . . the cowardice of the soul turning into heroism of the body. To live is heroism of the soul; to die is heroism of the body.'?

She left behind the food supplies she had brought with her from Moscow and 400 roubles in cash (though at that time a small loaf of bread cost 140 roubles in the market and a *pood** of potatoes 200 roubles). The landlady's comment was: 'She could have held out a bit longer . . . She could have done it when they'd eaten everything up . . .'

No, it was not hunger that drove Tsvetayeva to hang herself, but

---

* About 36 pounds (Tr.)

loneliness. ('For years I've been alone—a human wasteland.') She did not even get on with her son. He did not bother to go to her funeral. Nor did anyone else.

In May 1934, while she was still in Paris, Marina had written: 'I should like to lie in the *khlyst*★ cemetery at Tarusa, under an elder bush, in one of those graves with a silver dove on it, where the wild strawberries are larger and redder than anywhere else in those parts. But if this is not possible, then . . . may a stone from the Tarusa quarry be put up saying:

Here MARINA TSVETAYEVA
would have wanted to lie'

But this wish was not fulfilled. She was buried in an unmarked grave, and under one of the pines in the old Yelabuga cemetery her sister Anastasia has put up a metal cross with the inscription:

ON THIS SIDE OF THE CEMETERY IS BURIED
MARINA IVANOVNA TSVETAYEVA
SEPTEMBER 26 (O.S.) 1892–AUGUST 31, 1941

Having followed Marina's path from the house on Trekhprudni Street where she was born to the one on Zhdanov Street in Yelabuga, we may now ask: Was Pasternak right to reproach himself in such a way, and if so, what was the nature of his guilt as far as Marina was concerned?

A good and brief (though indirect) reply has been given to the question by Marina's daughter, Ariadna. Some people think that everybody shared the blame, 'but Pasternak,' writes Ariadna, 'felt guilty because what happened to me had never happened to him.'†

Ariadna also has something interesting to say about BL's readiness and ability to help his fellow men: 'The ability to help people simply and straightforwardly is the rarest of human talents. All of us, or nearly all of us help others, and ourselves receive help as well. But in helping, we expect something in return—if only gratitude, or the easing of our own conscience: by making life happier and easier for others, we make it happier and easier for ourselves. Pasternak was unusually kind and quick to help—but his kindness was simply a

★ Russian religious sect. Tsvetayeva's family spent their summers in Tarusa before the Revolution. (Tr.)

† i.e. he was never imprisoned in the Stalin years. (Tr.)

supreme form of egocentricity: as a kind person he found it easier to live and work, and he slept the sounder for it; by being so responsive to the misfortunes of others, he alleviated his own—both past and future; he washed away his own sins, both real and imagined. He knew this himself and used to speak about it.'

I think that if egocentricity always took such a form, then one would hope and pray that everybody might become an egocentric: the whole world would be filled with kindness and generosity.

BL's poem on Marina's death was not written immediately after the event.* He felt he must say something to her—and he did, but it took time and was not easy for him, nor was he happy with the result himself. The poem to her ends with the following lines:

> Your face turned to God,
> You reach out to Him from earth—
> As already in those days before
> Your final reckoning here was made.

It is noteworthy that people close to Marina—as Ariadna and Anastasia have told me—were even annoyed by what they felt was the cold, 'classical' tone of BL's response to Marina's death. But he needs no defence other than the lines Marina herself once wrote about him:

> We'll be measured—for sure!—
> By the very same measure:
> And both of us will go to heaven,
> —The heaven I believe in!

* The poem was written in 1943 but was not published until several years after Pasternak's death, in 1965. (Tr.)

PART III
A Novel about A Novel

'There are no low truths and sublime
untruths: only low untruths and
sublime truths.'

Marina Tsvetayeva

'All will pass, only
The Truth will remain.'

Alexander Tvardovski

'Boys and Girls'

It is not my intention to write the history of how the novel came into being. Even if I wanted, I should not be able to: all my notes were taken from me at the time of my arrest in 1949, and then I spent more than three years in a camp. By the time I returned, *Doctor Zhivago* had been almost completed.

I heard of the novel from BL at the time when I first met him.

'You know,' he said to me once, as he was walking with me from the *Novy Mir* offices, 'I have suddenly had a marvellous thought, though perhaps it will seem marvellous only to me. Let me take you to see a woman pianist I know. She will play the piano and I have promised to read her a little from a new prose work of mine. It won't be a novel as the word is generally understood. I shall skim through years and decades, perhaps dwelling on trivialities. I think I may call this new thing "Boys and Girls", or "Pictures from Fifty Years of Daily Life". I have a feeling that you will write your page in it as well! We really must go out there!'

So we went to see Maria Veniaminovna Yudina, right in the middle of a Christmas blizzard. We drove out in somebody else's car and lost our way among snowdrifts. In addition to us there was the niece of Shchepkina-Kupernik and one or two other people as well. We found ourself in deep snow, under which all the roads had disappeared, among some isolated houses beyond Sokol, and we could not find the one we wanted. Going round in my head were the lines:

This is not the right city, nor yet the right midnight,
And you who bear its message are on the wrong road!

I watched BL's profile. He was sitting next to the driver and kept turning to me with a smile: 'I don't remember the number of the house, I've forgotten the address! It'll be funny if we get lost—and they've been waiting for us for ages.' We really had lost our way, and BL, in felt boots that were grotesquely oversize for him, kept jumping out of the car. Suddenly, among the houses, we saw the flickering light of a lamp shaped like a candle. This proved to be the window of the house where we were expected.

The light of a candle suddenly gleaming at us out of the night through a snowstorm in an unfamiliar place played a symbolic part in the whole of our life after this.

Maria Veniaminovna played Chopin for a long time. BL was particularly affected by the music and his eyes shone. I was beside myself with happiness.

At last BL began to read. The lights on the Christmas tree at the Sventitskis' glowed before us, and the student Yuri Zhivago danced with his fiancée Tonya: the janitor Markel made his first appearance, and we heard about the heavy wardrobe, the epitome of the old Moscow life . . .★

It was first light when we came out into the glittering, fleecy snow. And as we got into the car, BL said to me: 'Now a poem has come to me that I can give you for your journal. It will be called "Winter Night".† It was funny, getting lost like that, wasn't it?'

The next day BL brought the poem to me at the office:

> Snow swept over the earth,
> Swept it from end to end.
> The candle on the table burned,
> The candle burned . . .

Later on, seeing me home, he told me that somebody's candle, a candle seen from outside in the cold and leaving the mark of its breath on a frosty pane of glass, had been needed as a symbol in his poetry. And now there had been this window gleaming in the night. He had felt, he said, exactly the same about it as the young Zhivago: beyond this window with its candle there was a life certain to be linked in the future with his own life, though for the time being it was only beckoning. He also saw in the candle what was perhaps an even deeper meaning: 'Just as a lighted candle is not hidden under a bushel, but put in a holder to give light to everybody in the house— so, in just the same way, a word must be uttered.'

This was how Doctor Zhivago came into my life.

The name 'Zhivago' itself was chosen as a result of the merest chance. Walking along a street, BL happened to see a round manhole cover with the name of the manufacturer on it: Zhivago. He decided that this would do very well—someone quite unknown who had be-

★ Chapter 3 of *Doctor Zhivago*. (Tr.)

† BL had been asked to let us have his latest poem for a new feature, 'Literary Moments', which K. Simonov had suggested, but then failed to go through with. See p. 16.

longed either to the merchant class or to the semi-intelligentsia, perhaps. This would be the hero of his novel.

Doctor Zhivago is an autobiography—concerned, however, not with the externals of the author's life, but with his spiritual history. There has been much speculation about the identity of the novel's characters. As early as 1948 BL wrote to a student of literature (he always answered any letter that stirred or moved him, sending new unpublished poems to complete strangers who had written to him, and telling them about his work):

I was very pleased to have your letter. Thank you. In order to return your kindness, I am sending you with this letter my latest poems which will form a chapter in a prose novel I am writing now. It describes the life of a circle of people in Moscow (though the Urals will also come into it). The first book deals with the years 1903 to the end of the 1914 war. In the second, where I hope to take events up to the last war, the chief character, a doctor by profession, but with a very strong literary bent as well, like Chekhov, will die in the year 1929 or thereabouts. When his half-brother, of whom he knows only by hearsay and has always regarded as his mortal enemy, puts his papers in order after his death, they turn out to include notes of philosophical interest and a whole book of poems, which the half-brother publishes and which will form a separate chapter, consisting entirely of verse, in the second part of the novel. The hero will be something intermediate between me, Blok, Yesenin, and Mayakovski, and whenever I write poems nowadays they go into the notebook of this man, Yuri Zhivago. Do not be upset if you find them weaker than my previous ones or simply like them less, and do not be afraid to let me know as much—I shall not take offence. There is no secret about them, and you may show them to other people . . . Let me know, please, when you get them and the letter—my things are always going astray. I have nothing to complain of and am happy with life, but I would like to finish off the novel as soon as possible, or at least the first book, which is almost complete, and until I have done this, I shall feel fretful and inwardly consumed by haste to a certain extent. Thank you for your good wishes—I need them. Yours, B. Pasternak.

In the autumn of 1958, BL said to the Swedish professor, Nils Åke

Nilsson: 'Lara, the heroine of the novel, is someone in real life. She is a woman very close to me.'

There is also a mention of the origin of Lara in a letter written to Renate Schweitzer on May 7, 1958:

In the post-war years I got to know a young woman, Olga Vsevolodovna Ivinskaya . . . She is the Lara in the work which I had just begun to write at that time (with interruptions to translate Schiller's *Maria Stuart*, *Faust* and *Macbeth*). She is the soul of cheerfulness and self-sacrifice. She gives no sign of all she has gone through in life (in previous days). She also writes verse and translates poetry of our national minorities—working from literal versions, in the same way as some people here who do not know Western European languages. She is privy to my inner life and to all my literary affairs as well . . .

In an interview with the British journalist Antony Brown at the end of January 1959, BL said:

She [Ivinskaya] is my very good friend. She has been a great help to me in the writing of the book, and in my daily life . . . She was sentenced to five years for her friendship with me. In my youth, there was no one, single Lara . . . The Lara of my youth is based on general experience. But the Lara of my late years is inscribed on my heart in her blood and her imprisonment . . .

When he had finished the first four chapters, BL could already visualize the book as a whole and the dedication he would one day write in it for me: 'To Lara from Yuri.' All the same, I am probably not 'absolutely' Lara, any more than he is absolutely Yuri. He often used to tell me there was no need to identify the characters completely with their prototypes. They were to be seen as composite images—Tonya having something of me and of Zinaida Nikolayevna, just as Lara would also have elements of both of us, and of somebody else as well. But the main thing was to show me and himself, and his own way of looking at life, literature, and art.

All his life he worshipped women:

> . . . What can compare with woman's strength?
> Who has such reckless courage?

> She has rented the world, like a house,
> And settled it, burning her boats behind her . . .'

No wonder, then, that he lavished such care and attention on the portraits of the two women, Tonya and Lara. Although there are scarcely any direct biographical resemblances to Zinaida Nikolayevna and me, there is more of Zinaida Nikolayevna in Tonya's character, and of me in Lara's.

When he learned that I am a quarter German and half Polish, BL made Lara non-Russian by origin as well and gave her a foreign name: Guishar.

My childhood years were spent in Kursk, and this is alluded to in one of the poems of Yuri Zhivago:

> . . . Daughter of a small landowner of the steppes,
> You had come from Kursk to be a student . . .

And in the image of Tonya certain aspects of Zinaida Nikolayevna appear quite distinctly. Yuri says of Tonya in the novel: 'I have noticed how quick, strong and tireless she is, how cleverly she plans her work so as to waste as little time as possible between one job and another.' In a letter to Renate Schweitzer, BL wrote about Zinaida Nikolayevna: '. . . my wife's passionate love of work, her eager skill in everything—in washing, cooking, cleaning, bringing up the children—has created domestic comfort, a garden, a way of life and daily routine, the calm and quiet needed for work.'

Many such similarities of character can be found, just as there is a good deal of himself in Yuri Zhivago. Yuri, for instance, '. . . ever since his schooldays . . . had dreamed of writing a book in prose, a book of impressions of life in which he would conceal, like buried sticks of dynamite, the most striking things he had so far seen and thought about. He was too young to write such a book; instead he wrote poetry. He was like a painter who spent his life making sketches for a big picture he had in mind.'

Another parallel: Yuri 'considered that art was no more a vocation than innate cheerfulness or melancholy were professions . . . and believed that a man should do something useful in his practical life.' This was why Zhivago, as we know, became a doctor, not making the writing of poetry his profession. Although BL himself made his living only by writing, he took every opportunity (particularly when budding young poets turned to him for advice) to warn against choosing art as a profession—though of course he was not against 'professional' standards of skill in the practice of it. A good example is his well-known letter of December 15, 1955, to M. G. Weinstein, who was then only just starting on his literary career: '. . . I would rather that the writing of verse or even poetry did not exist as an occupation—however "divinely inspired"—of and for the many . . .'

BL had his own idea of what was 'typical' about his characters, and his views had not changed since *The Proud Pauper*, where he said:

Already as a child I was taught by experience to believe that the 'typical' is tantamount to the artificial, and that only those persons can actually be 'typical' who do violence to their nature by deliberately striving to be so. Why, I wondered, should the 'typical' be dragged out onto the stage when it is already theatrical enough in real life?

In the novel he wrote:

It's a good thing when a man is different from your image of him. It shows he isn't a type. If he were it would be the end of him as a man. But if you can't place him in a category, it means that at least a part of him is what a human being ought to be. He is free from himself, he has a grain of immortality.

It is no accident that BL wrote the main work of his life in prose. On August 29, 1934, speaking at the First Congress of the Union of Soviet Writers, he had said: 'Poetry is prose . . . pure prose in its pristine intensity is what poetry is.' A quarter of a century later (December 23, 1959), he wrote in a letter to E. D. Romanova*, thanking her for her comments on the novel:

. . . what it can be, real prose, what a magic art—bordering on alchemy! While the giants of Russian literature were still alive, the Russian reading public, too, kept its sense for prose, for its charms and its secrets. This is now completely lost, and it astonished me to find signs of such an understanding in you, not simply with reference to

* A member of the staff of the Lenin Library in Moscow.

myself, but as the general, inviolate foundation of your taste . . .
'Beautiful as prose', Karamzin used to say of real poetry—perhaps of
the young Pushkin's—when he wished to praise it.

'All my life I have wanted to write prose,' he often said, 'writing
verse is easier!' He thought of his poetry simply as a preparation for a
major prose-work. Even Shakespeare, he suspected, wrote verse only
by way of making 'rough drafts for prose'.

Small wonder, then, that almost throughout the whole of his life
as a writer he brooded on his future novel and prepared for it. In a
letter written to him from Berlin (June 29, 1922) Marina Tsvetayeva
recalled how: 'Once, in the spring of 1918, you and I were sitting
next to each other at supper with the Tsetlins.* You said: "I want to
write a big novel—with a love story and a heroine, like Balzac."
And I thought: "How good. How exact. How beyond vanity. A
poet."'

The Childhood of Luvers and *Without Love* (1918), *Aerial Ways*
(1924), *From a New Novel about 1905* (1937), *A District in the Rear*
(two extracts from a chapter for a novel, 1938), *Aunt Olia* and *The
Proud Pauper* (1939) are all clear milestones on the road to the 'big
novel'.

Leafing through the volume of Pasternak's prose writings, one
fancies that Zhenia Luvers could be the Lara of the future. Alexander
Alexandrovich Gromeko, professor at the Petrovskaya Academy,†
figures already in *The Proud Pauper*, *Aunt Olia*, *From a New Novel
about 1905*, and in *A District in the Rear*. We find his brother Nikolai
(also a professor) and his daughter Tonya appearing in the early prose
under the same names. Only his wife, Anna Ivanovna, is called
differently—Anna Gubertovna. But the unfortunate incident of the
wardrobe is foreshadowed almost word for word in *From a New
Novel about 1905*, where Anna Gubertovna moans that 'It's my death,
not a cupboard'. In this same fragment we find a description, later
repeated in the novel, of an attempt to hide armed workers in the
Gromeko house.

Zhenia Luvers reappears, this time under the married name of

---

* Mikhail Osipovich Tsetlin (1882–1945), poet and prose writer, founder and
first editor of the *New Review* (Russian language journal in New York); author of
novels *The Decembrists* and *The Five and Others* (on the Russian composers).

† A college of Forestry founded in 1865. (Tr.)

202 A CAPTIVE OF TIME

Yevgenia Istomin, in *A District in the Rear*. Her father, Luvers, has shot himself after going bankrupt, and her husband, Vladimir Istomin, a teacher of physics and mathematics at the Yuriatin secondary school goes to the front as a volunteer, leaving her with their six-year-old daughter, and is assumed to have been killed in action. How similar they are to Lara, Pasha Antipov, and their daughter Katia ...

And then there is Lev Polivanov in *Aerial Ways* and Yuri Koval-evski in *Without Love*—could these be precursors of Antipov-Strelnikov? And is it possible that Antipov was originally intended to be the hero of the novel?

In his essay on Pasternak, 'Realism in Four Dimensions', Victor Frank suggests that Zhivago's friend Innokenti Dudorov is based on Mayakovski. But he also thinks that in his most affecting aspect Mayakovski may be reflected in the figure of Antipov-Strelnikov as well:

One of the crucial antitheses in the novel is that between Strelnikov and Zhivago, two diametrically opposed types, who love the same woman. Strelnikov tries to conquer both the world and the woman he loves by putting his iron will at the service of abstract principles— which he then seeks to impose on life. Zhivago on the other hand believes in submitting to life, in surrendering himself to others in an act of love:

> And life itself is only an instant,
> Only the dissolving
> Of ourselves in all others
> As though in gift to them.

The following words spoken by Lara about her husband seem in Frank's view to apply equally well to what he calls 'the meta-morphosis undergone by Mayakovski after 1918':

It was as if there was something abstract in his expression—it made him colourless. As if a living human face had become an embodiment of a principle, the image of an idea ... I realized that this had happened to him because he had handed himself over to something lofty, but deadening and pitiless, which wouldn't spare him in the end.

And indeed, Victor Frank concludes, these 'lofty, but deadening and pitiless' forces spared neither Antipov nor Mayakovski.

Akhmatova's Judgment

BL never made any secret of his novel, even long before it was finished. He was often eager to tell me what was going to happen in a chapter he was still writing. 'Boria, how can you write if you always tell the story beforehand? I don't see the point,' I would say in astonishment. 'But it makes it easier for me—I can just go on in the way I tell it to you . . .'

As soon as a few chapters were ready, he was always glad to read them out to people. I was recently reminded of this by something connected with that far-off time . . .

Sceptics always say that miracles do not happen. But occasionally I think they do: people come back after being away for twenty-five years, mountain meets mountain (despite what the proverb says),* and everything 'returneth again according to its circuits'—as did the top copy of a typescript of *Doctor Zhivago* made in 1948, with a neat dedication written in pencil on the first page in BL's flowing hand, the letters looking like black birds: 'This copy belongs to poor Olechka, the strongest person in the world, from her B.'

It came about in the most simple, yet unexpected way. Almost a quarter of a century ago I lent this copy to Alexandra Vasilyevna Krooming. We had become close to each other in the 'forties because of a tragic event in her life, which was in a way similar to what had happened in mine: her husband, a talented young actor of the Vakhtangov Theatre, had hanged himself because he could not get on with her son by a previous marriage who had come back home after the war from a P.O.W. camp. He did this because she took the side of her son, Tolia, who was almost the same age.

I shall not go into all the complicated twists and turns in her life, and it would be out of place here to do so. I only wish to tell how after a quarter of a century (during which she has died and I have

---

* The Russian proverb says, 'Mountain never meets mountain, only man meets man.' (Tr.)

become old and grey-haired) the bell suddenly rang one day at my
apartment and when I went to the door, it was Tolia, Alexandra's
son, who had come to say that, now his mother was dead, he wanted
to return a manuscript with an inscription by Pasternak, which was
no doubt precious to me. I went to see him, and the manuscript is
now back with me. At the sight of it, I was immediately reminded of
how the unusual pencilled dedication came to be written.

It was a very long time ago. *Zhivago* was not yet finished, but I
had given the first four parts to BL's great friend Marina Kazimirovna Baranovich, who always did his typing for him. She typed
them out and then bound the copies, or rather stapled them together.
I brought them to BL who at once generously gave them all away to
people to read. As a result, there was no copy left for me, so naturally
enough, I complained: 'Of course you expect me to get them ready
and bring them to you, but there's no copy for poor me!' A week
later, evidently feeling a little ashamed of himself, he brought me the
top copy of the four which had been made—he had recovered it from
some woman reader and admirer—and wrote this dedication to his
'poor' deprived Olechka, saying to me as he did so: 'Don't hesitate
to lend it to anyone who asks you for it—it's very important for me
to know what people think of it.'

So I lent it to Alexandra Krooming. After my sudden arrest in
1949, many of the books and manuscripts given me by BL were
confiscated—but this one, as it turns out, was fated to survive and
come back to me.

It is interesting that on reading these first four parts again, I found
not a single divergence from the text in its final, completed form—
except that in addition to the title, *Doctor Zhivago*, there was a sub-
title: 'Scenes from half a century of daily life.' But there was no other
difference—which goes to show, I think, that the whole novel had so
completely taken shape in BL's mind before he began to put it on
paper that it required no subsequent modifications. Such things
happen . . . But to return to those distant days.

In the autumn of 1949 he invited me to go with him to the
Ardovs. For many months afterwards the evening we spent there
was to be a matter of deep concern to the State Security Services. We
were given a friendly welcome by Ardov's wife, Nina Alexandrovna.
Bronze and cut glass gleamed on the old-fashioned mahogany table.
Aliosha Batalov, at that time still an unknown young actor just

beginning to make his way in the theatre, had managed to install himself inconspicuously in a recess between two windows.

Anna Akhmatova sailed in from the next room in her legendary white shawl and, wrapping herself in it with a slight shiver, sat down regally in the middle of the room in a chair placed there specially for her. Also present were Nikolai Erdman, Faina Ranevskaya, and others I do not remember.

BL sat by a lamp and read in the extraordinary way he always did when he felt people were listening with attention. I still have a clear memory of the inspired look on his face, the convulsive movements of his throat, and the suppressed tears in his voice. He took delight in imitating the popular manner of speech and various kinds of jargon, and was scarcely able to refrain from laughing as he did so. Finally he finished, and took a sip of his tea. After a long pause, Akhmatova began to speak.

I remember her saying she thought the prose style superb and as concise as verse. But she felt literature should raise its heroes above the crowd, in the tradition of Shakespeare, and could not agree with BL's own view of Zhivago as an 'average' man. I was surprised when she went on to say how she had never understood the universal admiration of Chekhov, considering that his principal characters were ordinary people—about whom it was always easier to write. Chekhov's low-key manner, she declared, had a strange ring about it in that atmosphere of 'the gathering storm before Lenin'. In her view it was important to speak for and depict only major movements in human affairs. She advised BL to think carefully before making Zhivago a plaything of historical events instead of into a personage who tried to influence them in some way—this was the kind of poetic solution she expected from a novel by Pasternak . . .

In the presence of such people I didn't dare utter a sound, but I was surprised that BL who adored Chekhov and wept over him, as he did over Levitan's watercolours, eagerly agreed with everything Akhmatova said, and altogether saw fit to be the soul of tact. As soon as we left I said: 'Boria, aren't you ashamed to be such a Pharisee?' He smiled artfully and winked at me: 'Oh really now, let her have her say, for heaven's sake! And she may be right after all! I don't like people who always think they're right, and it could be that I am wrong. I don't want to make out I am right.'

After the reading Erdman, as I remember, said nothing. Ranevskaya,

who sat by BL's side at the tea table, kept saying in her remarkable low, deep voice: 'Heavens above, I have to pinch myself: here
I am, sitting next to the real live Pasternak.' BL looked bashful,
of course, and protested ('Goodness me, what are you saying!'), but
he was obviously flattered and pleased by the success he was having—
particularly since it was in my presence. I could see very well that at
this time he needed to grow both in my eyes and in his own.

For three or four years, during which he was all the time distracted
by translating, he reworked individual chapters and whole parts of
the novel. Later he was to say:

Much more was written than went into the novel—about a third was
discarded. It was not that these pages were inferior to the others, but
simply a question of limiting myself: I was overwhelmed by material
. . . one must try to be merciless in throwing out everything superfluous! One must strive for a miracle, so that people cannot believe
the result is the work of human agency, but seems like something not
man-made! The main problem is what to regard as the finished work
. . . What I used to think of as completed now seems only just
begun . . . And one must try to make everything sound plausible, so
the characters and the period come to life, and the author retreats into
the background . . .

Of the passages thrown out, one I particularly remember was a
chapter on flowers. It was conceived as an attempt to define the place
of flowers in a person's life and death: at one's birth, wedding, funeral
and all the other crucial moments of human existence. Every flower
speaks in its own language and has its particular meaning. Chrysan-
themums, for example, are associated with death. Who knows, perhaps a flower's scent is its language? The main theme of the chapter
was the interconnection between life and death. BL believed that the
dead are able to give a kind of arcane sign to the living through the
flowers growing on their graves . . . It was an important, deeply
philosophical and lyrical chapter, but it was a digression from the
narrative and was discarded. It was only lightly crossed out in the
manuscript copy of the novel and I hope it may have been preserved
somewhere in the archives of the State Security Services. Perhaps it
may come to light one day!

What did he hope to achieve by the endless revision of chapters

already completed? I believe that apart from trying to make everything ring as poetically true as possible, he was also concerned with
the kind of originality—organic, unobtrusive, unforced—of which
he speaks in the novel:

It had been the dream of his [Zhivago's] life to write with an originality so covert, so discreet, as to be outwardly unrecognizable in its
disguise of current, customary forms of speech. All his life he had
struggled after a language so reserved, so unpretentious as to enable
the reader or the hearer to master the content without noticing the
means by which it reached him. All his life he had striven to achieve
an unnoticeable style, and had been appalled to find how far he still
remained from his ideal.

In a conversation with Alexander Gladkov at the end of June 1947,
BL said:

I am not by any means saying I am for giving up originality of
expression, but I aim at a kind of originality which is unobtrusive . . .
and unassuming—so that the subject matter is absorbed by the reader
without his even noticing . . . I dream . . . of an inconspicuous style
in which nothing intervenes between the idea of a thing and its
depiction . . .

In *Doctor Zhivago*, BL sometimes has no qualms in skipping over
important historical events, but will dwell lovingly, in great detail,
on some small point that may appear of little significance at first
sight—a few phrases, and a whole vista opens up in the lyrical life of
a character.

With the help of 'parables from everyday life', bringing out the
truth in the light of everyday reality, BL shows that 'communion
between mortals is immortal'. History is written in his novel as it
appears through the life of the undying creative spirit.

In that final period of work on the novel, BL read out many
chapters to people, and listened to their criticisms, but I remember
none of any particular substance. On the other hand, some people
wrote very significant comments in the form of letters, and a few of
these have survived. Soon after I returned from the camp BL showed
me one such letter he had received from the Leningrad poet Sergei

Spasski, with whom he had been friendly ever since they first met in Moscow at the beginning of the 'twenties. After Spasski had moved to Leningrad in 1925 they had started a correspondence which went on right until his death in 1956. BL was now sending him each new part of the novel as soon as it was completed and was always eager to hear what he had to say.*

In the spring of 1954, something happened which gave us particular joy: after a very long interval of time, original verse by BL was at last published again—in the April issue of *Znamia*. The selection was entitled: 'Verses from a novel in prose, *Doctor Zhivago*'. Of course, none of the poems on Gospel themes was included; neither was 'August', or 'Hamlet'. But at least BL's prefatory note was printed:

The novel is expected to be completed this summer. It treats of the period 1903 to 1929, and has an epilogue which relates to the Great Fatherland War.†

The hero, Yuri Andreyevich Zhivago, a doctor, a thinking man, a seeker after truth with a creative and artistic cast of mind, dies in 1929. He leaves behind papers written in his younger years; among them is a collection of poems, some of them reproduced here, which will appear in its entirety as the final, concluding chapter of the novel.

That same April was marked by another happy event. The well-known art historian, Mikhail Alpatov, by whose judgment BL set great store, asked to be permitted to read what was ready of the novel. BL gave him the almost completed manuscript and at the end of the month, Alpatov wrote him a letter about it.‡

A day came when BL phoned me from Peredelkino and, sounding shaken, began to speak in a voice choked by tears. 'What's wrong?' I asked in alarm. 'He's dead, he's dead, I say!' he groaned several times over. It turned out that he was talking about the death of Zhivago: this harrowing chapter was now finished.

By the summer of the following year (1955) copies of the first book of the novel had been bound in a handsome brown binding, and BL was as pleased as a child with it. Soon the second book was bound

---

* For the text of Spasski's letter see Appendix B. (Tr.)

† The usual Soviet way of referring to the Second World War. (Tr.)

‡ For the text of Alpatov's letter see Appendix B. (Tr.)

as well. I then took the impressive-looking brown volumes round to the publishers. These fully edited and corrected copies of *Doctor Zhivago* were ready for publication.

(In May or June 1956, BL was to write in 'An Essay in Autobiography' which he was preparing for *Goslitizdat**: '. . . I have just finished my chief and most important work, the only one of which I am not ashamed and for which I take full responsibility, a novel in prose with a section in verse, *Doctor Zhivago*. The poems scattered over the past years of my life and collected in the present book are steps preparatory to the novel. And it is as a preparation for the novel that I regard their publication in this book.'

Only someone with personal experience of the unrivalled demands BL made on himself can appreciate the full weight and sincerity of these words.)

The Fateful Day

The summer of 1955 was going by, and the hot, golden days of August were already upon us. The novel was with several publishers, but there was no word from any of them. At last, at the very end of August, A. Krivitski at *Novy Mir* agreed to see me and was quite friendly—although I had left the journal after a row between us, and could not hope for any good to come of these renewed dealings with him. However, speaking officially on behalf of the editorial board, he said that although they regretted the novel was too long for them to cope with, Simonov, who was away at the moment, had taken with him several chapters (which was possible because *Novy Mir* had an unbound copy—we had given the bound volumes to *Goslitizdat* and *Znamia*), and he thought it might be possible for them to publish some excerpts from the novel.

Some years previously (in 1948) BL had signed a contract for the novel with *Novy Mir*, but when he began to doubt that they would ever be able to publish it, he had asked them to cancel the contract and returned the money they had paid him as an advance. This happened because, as the idea of the novel began to evolve in his

---

* i.e., as the introduction to the projected one-volume edition of his poetry which, in the upshot, was never published. (Tr.)

mind, a certain element of 'subversiveness'—at first almost imperceptibly—began to enter into it. It was not that he brought it in deliberately, but simply that he was bent on telling the truth—and the truth, as he knew, would lead to situations and notions which would hardly be pleasing to those in power.

On a warm evening that autumn of 1955, after one of my regular trips to Moscow, Boria and I were walking over the long bridge across the Izmalkovo lake, when he said to me: 'You mark my words—they will not publish this novel for anything in the world. I don't believe they will ever publish it. I have come to the conclusion that I should pass it round to be read by all and sundry—it should be given to anyone who asks for it, because I do not believe it will ever appear in print.'

While he was still writing the book, Boria thought about nothing but the supreme artistic truth he wished to convey and the need for utmost honesty with himself. But when he now read it all through in the two handsomely bound brown volumes, he suddenly saw that 'the Revolution is not shown at all as the cake with cream on top which it has always been made out to be as a matter of course.' It was natural enough, therefore, that although *Novy Mir* spoke of publishing excerpts (they were evidently in the process of choosing chapters which would be suitable for publication), BL had no hope of ever seeing his novel actually brought out.

Time went by and it was soon the beginning of 1956, but the novel was not published. Nor were there any negative reactions to it.

If I may anticipate a little and refer to the criticism made of the book at the time of the 'scandal' in 1958, I would say that—apart from the scurrilous abuse some people heaped on it because they were told to—this criticism could be divided into two kinds. The first came from writers who thought that as a reward for attacking *Doctor Zhivago* they might be able to get something of their own into print; the second type was that of people—and these were the majority among those who disapproved of the book—whose intellectual level was below the minimum needed to understand a work of art of such scope and novelty of form.

BL had foreseen this once when he said about his work: '*Doctor Zhivago* is an attempt to write in a quite new idiom—one free of previous literary and aesthetic conventions . . . In a word, the book is not for those who lack the necessary preparation . . .'

On the deeper content of new forms and the misgivings they arouse he had written already in *Safe Conduct*: 'I agreed [with Scriabin] that . . . extravagant wordiness may be all the more comprehensible for being without content; that, corrupted by the emptiness of hackneyed stereotypes, we will mistake unique richness of content, after long being unaccustomed to it, for pretentiousness of form.'

It is ludicrously naïve to reproach Pasternak for having allegedly departed from the tradition of Tolstoi and Chekhov. Victor Frank is clearly right when he sees it as Pasternak's great achievement to have got the Russian novel out of its rut, taking it 'not in the direction mapped out by Bely, Proust, or Joyce, but in a completely new, still uncharted one' . . . 'Can one demand of a great artist,' Frank goes on to ask, 'that he should reproduce the mannerisms of a previous age and view the world as it was viewed by his predecessors? It would be the same as to complain that Tolstoi did not write like Karamzin, or Pushkin like Lomonosov!'

Despite everything, we had one pleasant surprise at this time (early 1956): *Goslitizdat* told us it was ready to bring out a large one-volume edition of BL's verse, and he decided he would include the entire cycle of poems from the novel in it. He started to work with enthusiasm at 'An Essay in Autobiography', which he intended as an introduction to the volume. Nikolai Vasilyevich Bannikov was appointed as his editor.

One thing I can say with certainty about this period: the thought of publishing the novel abroad never even occurred to Boria or myself at this stage. But events had a logic of their own, quite outside what any of us may have wanted.

At the beginning of May 1956, the Italian-language service of Moscow Radio mentioned in a broadcast that Pasternak's novel *Doctor Zhivago*, the action of which covered a time span of three-quarters of a century, ending with the Second World War, was about to be published. The dramatic consequences of this broadcast were not long in making themselves felt. It was in fact the beginning of an affair which became world-famous . . .

One evening at the end of that same month, returning to Peredelkino after going the rounds of the publishers in Moscow, I was greeted by a startling piece of news: Boria, who had come out along the road to meet me, told me he had just handed over the novel to someone. Seeing him in the distance and hurrying towards him, I was just wondering in what words I should tell him the good news that *Novy Mir* had again confirmed its intention of publishing some excerpts, when suddenly I heard him saying to me: 'I had a visit today, Olia, from two young people who arrived here at the house while I was working. One of them was very pleasant—handsome, youthful, and charming . . . You would have been delighted by him! And, you know, he had such an extraordinary name: Sergio d'Angelo. He came here with someone who is supposedly a member of our Soviet Embassy in Italy—I think he's called Vladimirov. They said that they had heard the announcement on Moscow Radio about my novel and that Feltrinelli, one of the biggest publishers in Italy, was interested in it. D'Angelo is Feltrinelli's *emissario*—of course, that is his private part-time job,' BL added with a smile. 'He's actually a member of the Communist Party, and he is here in an official capacity with the Italian section of Moscow Radio.'

BL obviously realized he had done something a little odd, and was worried about how I would react. From his manner, which was even somewhat ingratiating, I could see that he was pleased and at the same time uneasy, and very anxious to have my approval. But my reaction was not the favourable one he hoped for:

'What have you done?' I said reproachfully, not giving in to his blandishments. 'Just think how they'll go for you now! I've been in prison once, remember, and already then, in the Lubianka, they questioned me endlessly about what the novel would say! Krivitski has good reason for saying the journal can only publish chapters from it. It's because they *can't* accept it all, of course—they simply want to leave out the awkward parts and publish what they needn't be afraid to print. You know how they always try to cover themselves! I'm really amazed you could do this! And then don't you realize how furious Bannikov will be that you've given the novel to the Italians without consulting anyone—this may put paid to the poetry volume!'

'Really now, Olia, you're overstating things, it's nothing at all,' he remonstrated weakly. 'Just let them read it. If they like it, let them do what they want with it—I said I didn't mind!'

'But Boria—that was giving permission to publish, don't you understand! They will certainly seize on it! There's bound to be a great rumpus, you'll see!'

I am far from wanting to claim I was being all that far-sighted, but

I had the sad experience of the camp behind me and I knew from what nonsense the case against me had been concocted: 'closeness to persons suspected of espionage', indeed! There was in fact only one such person—Boris Leonidovich, and he was left at liberty because they evidently feared to touch him. I remembered what a great interest my interrogator had taken in what the still unwritten novel was about: would it be an expression of literary opposition?

Boria was upset and put out by our conversation: 'Well then, Olia, you must do what you think best, of course: you can even phone this Italian—because I am not going to make any move without you—you can even phone this Italian and ask him to give the novel back, if you're so upset about it. But in that case we should at least play the fool a little: "It's just like Pasternak," tell him, "the way he's given you his novel, but what do you think yourself?" It may even be a good idea for you to sound out the ground a little about what sort of an effect the news of it will have.'

But the fact is that by now he had made up his mind that the novel must be published—if it could not be done at home, then let it come out in the West!

Around this same time (the end of May or beginning of June 1956) Kostia Bogatyrev told me he had been present at a conversation in the 'big house' between BL and the Italian scholar Lo Gatto (the author of histories of Russian literature and of the Russian theatre) during which BL said he was ready to face any kind of trouble, as long as the novel appeared. And when Zinaida Nikolayevna said: 'I've had enough of such trouble,' he merely brushed her aside with an impatient gesture.

On the tenth anniversary of all the memorable events still to come, Sergio d'Angelo published a long article about the affair of the novel. (It appeared in German in the journal *Ost-Europa*, July 1968, under the title 'Roman eines Romanes', clearly inspired by our conversations in Moscow at the time. I had told him that BL kept saying how he felt as though he were 'living through a novel about a novel', and that I intended one day to write something under this title.) In his article d'Angelo describes his fateful visit in the following words:

I had already been living for two months in the Soviet Union, where I had been sent by the Italian Communist Party to work in the Italian section of Moscow Radio. In my spare time I devoted a good deal of attention to authors and books of possible interest to the rich young Milan publisher Feltrinelli, a Communist with ambitious plans for the future . . . He had asked me to keep him informed of any interesting new works of Soviet literature. The news of Pasternak's novel *Doctor Zhivago* was not, of course, a matter of indifference to me. If I could obtain the manuscript of the novel before it appeared in the USSR, then Feltrinelli would have an advantage over possible competitors in the West. Without more ado, I went out to Peredelkino . . . It was a beautiful day in May. I found Pasternak working in the garden, and he welcomed me in warm and simple fashion. We sat out in the open on the verandah and talked for a long time. When I came to the purpose of my visit, he seemed taken aback (it had evidently never occurred to him before to have dealings with a foreign publisher). As we continued to talk, he looked thoughtful, as if undecided what to do. I asked him whether any member of the [Soviet] publishing house concerned had pronounced unfavourably on the book or raised any objection of principle against it? No, there had been nothing like that. I suggested there could be an official announcement beforehand about publishing the novel, saying that the political climate had changed and that his misgivings seemed to me unfounded. At last he yielded to my pressure. He excused himself, disappeared into the house for a moment, and came back with the manuscript. As he showed me to the garden gate and said goodbye, he again voiced his concern in what seemed a joking way: 'You have invited me to take part in my own execution.'

Boria never used these words to me, but I am sure d'Angelo did not make them up.

Everybody takes Fright

In the days when it had already become known in literary circles what had happened, the writer K., while talking with Ariadna Efron, suddenly burst out into loud laughter, apparently for no reason at all, and then said: 'I can just imagine the look on their fat faces when *they* get to know about it: how they will fuss!' But in the meantime, it was I who had to do all the 'fussing' . . .

From the writers' colony in Peredelkino it was possible to take a taxi into town, and instead of going on the nice walk with Boria I had been so much looking forward to on the way out, I now travelled back into Moscow to see Bannikov on New Basmannaya Street.* I was in something of a state as I went into his office. Things were not going all that smoothly for him as it was: the one-volume poetry edition was still being held up and people were still reading and re-reading the introductory 'An Essay in Autobiography', insisting that whole passages must be changed. It all made the outlook for the volume look very uncertain, and Bannikov and I were worried. His personal situation in the publishing house was also rather difficult at that moment since he was at loggerheads with a certain strange woman called Vitashevskaya who had once been the commandant of a forced labour camp and for some reason had now been given a job as an editor. In the hope of getting on close terms with BL, she had arranged for me to translate Tagore for *Goslitizdat* and was always trying to make up to me by doing other favours, without even being asked. I still have a note Boria jotted down about her at that time:

Vitash[evskaya], Bannik[ov]—I trust poverty more than riches. O[lia]'s impression on first visit: this solicitousness not to be trusted. A rich apartment and expensive clothes, but a poor and empty life that has to be filled out with concern and worry over others. Try to fend off these friendly incursions, even if disinterested, and gifts: we are too preoccupied just now with vital matters already launched and gathering momentum, and there is no room for anything else.

This morning begrudged having to block up my ears against the clamorous outside world so full of advice and suggestions and at having to respond while I am working by writing these stupid letters.

When I told him about the Italian, Bannikov became terribly agitated: 'But what has he done! Doesn't he know this is a period when the novel might eventually be published? It's an abstract, philosophical novel, full of magnificent descriptions of nature. But now he may even have wrecked the chances of the poetry volume with the autobiography . . .'

* Street on which *Goslitizdat* (State Publishing House for Literature) is situated. (Tr.)

Upset by this conversation with Bannikov, I went straight to Vitashevskaya's apartment. I told her too about what BL had done— you never knew, I said, what he would do next: these Italians had come to see him, and he had taken it into his head to give them the novel—just gone and handed it over! Vitashevskaya expressed great sympathy: 'I tell you what, Olenka,' she said in a soft, purring voice —she was a woman of enormous bulk, covered in rolls of fat, 'let me show the novel to someone high up. It is quite possible that everything will then fall into place.'

Later I learned that the 'someone high up' she had in mind was none other than Molotov, with whom she had some personal connection. I don't know whether she in fact showed it to him or gave it to someone else (she had one of the unbound copies). Most likely she simply passed it on to the same institution which had once, after arresting me, shown such extreme interest in the contents of this 'seditious' work—and in whose view nothing by Pasternak could be other than 'seditious'.

On returning home to my apartment in Potapov Street, I was given a sealed envelope by the woman lift attendant. It was a note from Bannikov in which he summed up his attitude to BL's action: 'How can anyone love his country so little? One may have one's differences with it, but what he has done is treachery—how can he fail to understand what he is bringing on himself and us as well?' (I may not have remembered the exact words correctly, but this was the sense.)

I realized that this note was an expression of Bannikov's troubled state of mind. Foreseeing the scandal to come, he may also have wished to 'cover' himself by putting down his opinion of BL's action in good time and condemning it.

After spending the night at Potapov Street, I took the note out to BL the next day. He said that if I was so upset by the handing over of the novel, and our friends reacted to it so violently, then I should go and try to get it back. He found d'Angelo's address for me, and I decided to go and see him.

I arrived at a large building near the Kiev station, easily found the right apartment, and rang the bell. The door was opened by a charming woman who might have come straight out of an Italian film: long-legged, dark, with ruffled hair, a sculpted face, and eyes of astonishing blueness. This was d'Angelo's wife, Giulietta. She knew a few words of Russian, but spoke them incorrectly, with an accent. But I could say even less in Italian, so we had to make do with gestures for the most part.

Actually, she was pretty quick to understand the reason for my visit and, waving her arms, began to tell me with tremendously expansive gestures, how well she understood my concern, but that her husband had never intended to cause any problems for Boris Leonidovich, but never! After about an hour and a half of such 'conversation' in which there was much more noise and gesticulation than meaning, d'Angelo himself appeared on the scene. He was indeed young and handsome—a tall man with jet-black hair and delicate features such as one sees on icons. My first thought was that a real adventurer should be just as charming and attractive as this.

He spoke Russian magnificently, with only a slight accent. He nodded sympathetically as I explained how this whole business might end for BL. Then he said: 'You know, it's now too late. I got the novel to the publisher that same day. Feltrinelli has already managed to read it and says he will certainly publish it, come what may.'

Seeing how upset I looked at this, he went on: 'Don't worry. I'll write to Giangiacomo, or even speak to him on the phone. He is my personal friend, and I will be sure to tell him how alarmed you are by this, and perhaps we will be able to find a solution. But you must realize that a publisher who has obtained such a novel will be reluctant to part with it! I don't think he will give it up so easily.'

I asked him to propose to Feltrinelli that he should wait for the publication of the novel in the USSR: he had a prior claim to publication abroad, but let him be the second, not the first to bring the novel out.

'Very well, I'll tell all this to Feltrinelli,' d'Angelo agreed.

This was the beginning of our long and complicated relations with d'Angelo. I gave him my address, and before long he came to see me and got to know my daughter (to whom it was all of great interest). I hoped that d'Angelo would help us avoid an international rumpus. He had a better understanding of things, after all, than a publisher living in Milan could possibly have; and he knew that I had recently suffered for much less serious reasons.

I did not, however, let matters rest here, and decided, after a little thought, to go and see Vadim Kozhevnikov, the editor of *Znamia*. This was the journal that had already published some of the verse from *Doctor Zhivago*, and they had a copy of the whole novel, which Kozhevnikov must have read. I had known him ever since my student days when I had attended the Higher State literary courses, and I hoped to be able to speak with him not merely as an editor, but as a man who was not indifferent to my personal fate.

I found Kozhevnikov alone in his office, and I told him what had happened.

'Oh, how like you this is!' he sighed. 'Of course, you had to go and get involved with the last romantic left in Russia, and now we all have to think how to get you out of the mess! You're never satisfied, nothing is ever good enough for you! Now listen here: why not help to get us all out of trouble? I shall be blamed for being the first to publish verse from the novel, and now people will start going through it and picking on everything subversive. A good comrade of mine, Dmitri Alexeyevich Polikarpov, works in the Central Committee. I will speak to him on the phone and he will ask you to go and see him. Tell him what you have just told me.'

Very soon afterwards I got a phone call at Potapov Street from the Central Committee, and was told that a pass had been made out for me there to see the head of the cultural section, Polikarpov.

The man who greeted me had a haggard, rather frightened, and prematurely aged look about him. His eyes were bleary. He listened to what I had to tell him, and then said I must try to reach an understanding with d'Angelo: 'Go on meeting him, reason with him, beg him to return the manuscript. And we really can promise him that we will eventually sort the matter out and publish the novel here— whether with cuts or not we'll have to see. But in any case we'll make it possible for them to publish after we do.'

I then told Polikarpov that the novel had been with various publishers for a long time already and had been read by them, that nobody seemed to be able to make up his mind about it, that I felt the novel would not be published here, and that the Italians would probably not return the manuscript.

'See what you can do, see what you can do,' Polikarpov replied, 'you must have a proper talk with d'Angelo.'

I again tried to persuade him that the only solution was for the novel to be printed here at once—we would then be first with it, since translating it into Italian would be a big job, demanding much time and effort.

'No,' Polikarpov replied, 'we must get the manuscript back, because it will be very awkward if we cut out some chapters, and they print them. The novel must be returned at all costs. So do what you can—come to an agreement with d'Angelo, tell him that he will be the first to get a copy of the novel in proof to pass on to his publisher, and that they will have no cause for complaint. In any case, the question of what happens to the novel has to be settled here, and we will do everything we can about it.'

After several further conversations with d'Angelo, I went to see Polikarpov a second time and told him I had learned that Feltrinelli had kept the manuscript only to read it, but had also stated he would not part with it—he was ready to take responsibility for this, and the 'crime' would be his. He did not believe we would ever publish the manuscript here and felt he had no right to withhold a masterpiece from the world—this would be an even greater crime.

Dmitri Alexeyevich lifted the receiver of his phone and called *Goslitizdat*. The director was now A. K. Kotov, formerly the literary adviser to the publishing house, a nice and well-meaning man. We had once both eked out our salaries by advising on manuscripts together.

'Anatoli Konstantinovich,' said Polikarpov, 'Olga Vsevolodovna will be coming to see you in a short while to arrange a time when she can bring Pasternak to see you. You must have a look at the novel, appoint someone to edit it, and make a contract with Pasternak. The editor should think about what passages to change or cut out, and what can be left unchanged.'

When I told Boria about this conversation, he at first made no comment. Later, after thinking about it, he wrote the following memo, which I still have in my possession:

I am glad that Anat[oli] Konst[antinovich] will read the novel (though he will not like it). I am by no means intent on the novel being published at the moment, when it cannot be brought out in its original form.

I have other wishes:
  1. That my translation of *Maria Stuart* should be published. (Why does Yemelyanikov* object? Doesn't he like the translation?)

* Presumably another editor at *Goslitizdat*. (Tr.)

2. That the volume of my selected verse should be brought out in a large edition.

All the same, Boria and I soon went to see Kotov. I well remember how Kotov, not realizing I had overheard his conversation on the phone with Polikarpov, pretended he had taken the decision to publish the novel on his own initiative.

'My dear Boris Leonidovich,' he said, getting up from his seat to greet him, 'you have written a most magnificent work, and we shall certainly be publishing it. I shall appoint an editor for you, and we will draw up a contract. True, we will have to shorten a few things, and perhaps add some. But at any event you will have an editor to work with you, and everything will be all right.'

An editor was indeed appointed. He was Anatoli Starostin, a passionate admirer of Pasternak's work.

'I shall make this into something that will reflect the glory on the Russian people,' Starostin announced triumphantly. Alas, this was not to be. Starostin and I went through the whole ordeal of the battle for the novel together, but we did not come out the winners.

The Proofs

It seems self-evident that the novel ought to have been published in the Soviet Union. But the fact is that those who should have made the crucial decision were simply paralyzed by fear. A well-known writer, E.G. (who had several times been awarded Stalin and State Prizes★), spoke of the situation in the following terms:

The most terrible thing about them is that they are cowards—like all timeservers. They are frightened themselves and try to intimidate everybody else. It is a chain reaction of fear. A coward is incapable of taking rational decisions: he acts out of confusion and panic, and then takes great trouble to justify his panic by providing cast-iron (and at the same time elastic!) ideological reasons for it. The only solution is to publish the novel at once in this country! Even if only in a small edition, to keep up appearances—as long as it is published!

★ After Stalin's death the 'Stalin Prize' was renamed the 'State Prize'. (Tr.)

Is it possible they will do this? Will they have the courage? When it comes to making fools of themselves in front of the whole world—then they have enough courage. As much as is needed.

In the upshot they chose the second course. But this happened only after the long and dreary battle over publication of the book which now began—though perhaps it would be better to use the word 'fuss' rather than 'battle'. On one side was *Goslitizdat*, which was anxious to bring out both the novel and the one-volume edition of verse as soon as possible, and on the other the people in control of the Union of Writers, who did not even want the verse to come out, never mind the novel. Opposed to Pasternak's well-wishers (Kotov, Puzikov, Starostin) was Surkov, who hated him. Already at the First Congress of the Union of Writers in 1934, Surkov had replied to high praise of Pasternak's poetry by saying, with reference to the younger generation of poets: '. . . Pasternak's work is an unsuitable guide for them in their development.'

It was perhaps by way of taking issue with Surkov that André Malraux said at the same Congress: '. . . art does not submit, art conquers . . . You should know that only works which are truly new can maintain the cultural prestige of the Soviet Union abroad—as Mayakovski maintained it, as Pasternak continues to maintain it.'

I have already written about Surkov's violent denunciation of Pasternak in *Culture and Life* (March 22, 1947), and I shall not describe here all the stages in the shameful campaign waged by this literary bureaucrat against a poet of genius. The story is well enough known. In hounding genuinely great artists the Bulgarins of every age have, I imagine, always used the same well-tried method of alleging that their victims wish to undermine the existing system. Pushkin had good reason to describe the police spy Bulgarin, who envied and vilified him, as 'the blackguard of our literature'. Nowadays he is mentioned in the histories of literature only as the enemy of Pushkin, and one wonders how Surkov relishes the prospect of being remembered only as the persecutor of Pasternak . . .

On top of everything else BL now had trouble of a different kind: in the spring of 1957 he fell ill with arthritis and was put in a branch of the Kremlin Hospital at Uzkoye (the former Trubetskoi estate, where Vladimir Soloviev died). He found the terrible physical pain very hard to bear, and thought he was dying. But even this did not

prevent him from working on the one-volume edition of verse—
together with myself and Bannikov—whenever the pain died down
sufficiently for him to be able to hold a pencil. I still have nine letters
which he wrote to me from the hospital at this period (see items 1–9
in the Appendix), and also a note on the question of the proofs:
'. . . how can we find out about when to expect the proofs and make
sure that we get them on time? When, approximately, would it be
best to go and enquire? It will take me about two days to check the
prose part.'*

But he need not have worried about getting the proofs on time.
There was no delay and we received them when they were due. But,
alas, to this very day the book exists *only* in the form of these proofs
and is always referred to accordingly, with capital letters, as the
'Proof Copy'. This is how it is identified, for example, in the notes
to the edition of Pasternak's verse which came out in 1965. It must be
said that there can be few books whose proofs have been honoured
in such a way . . .

The arrival of the proofs marked the beginning of a more acute
phase in the battle over the publication of both the poetry volume
and the novel.

'*The whole world will make way for me*'

Aware that my attempts to reach an agreement with d'Angelo were
not producing results, the authorities made moves at a completely
different level. We knew nothing of them at the time. The scene now
shifted to Italy, where, according to d'Angelo in the article already
quoted:

Officials of the Italian Communist Party were asked to persuade
Feltrinelli not to go ahead with the publication of *Doctor Zhivago*. To
this end Togliatti had a personal conversation with the publisher, but
Feltrinelli assured him that he intended to have friendly talks with the
responsible Soviet authorities and in this way succeeded, without
causing any offence, in leaving matters exactly where they had stood

---

* i.e. the autobiographical introduction ('An Essay in Autobiography') to the
poetry volume. (Tr.)

before. At the beginning of 1957, by which time the atmosphere in the Soviet Union had considerably worsened because of the Hungarian uprising, the Moscow publishing house *Goslitizdat* sent Feltrinelli a letter informing him that *Doctor Zhivago* would be coming out in the Soviet Union in September that year, and asking him not to publish it in Italian before then. Feltrinelli replied in conciliatory fashion that he would have no difficulty in complying with this request. That the letter from *Goslitizdat* was nothing more than a manoeuvre to gain a breathing space is evident from its timing, as well as from subsequent events that clearly expose it for what it was. It was, for example, inconsistent with the fact that months earlier, in September 1956, five members of the editorial board of *Novy Mir*, the writers B. Agapov, B. Lavrenev, K. Fedin, K. Simonov, and A. Krivitski had written a long letter criticizing Pasternak and expressing their conviction that the novel had serious ideological flaws and should not be published.[32] Is it possible, one wonders, that *Goslitizdat*, at the time of writing to Feltrinelli, was unaware that five authoritative representatives of official literary circles had already vetoed the novel several months before? On the other hand, the fact that it was published the day after the award of the Nobel Prize to Pasternak (in the *Literary Gazette* of October 25, 1958) makes one suspect that this letter—which, despite the unambiguously negative conclusions expressed in it, is couched in a reasoned and friendly tone—may have been given an earlier date in order to lead people in the West to believe that *Doctor Zhivago* had been examined in literary circles and discussed objectively before the change in the political climate. This suspicion is actually quite well founded, since Pasternak never spoke to me of this letter from the writers, although we often saw each other until the end of 1957 to exchange news and views regarding the publication of the novel.

D'Angelo's suspicions about the date on the *Novy Mir* letter may have something in them. I also have the feeling that this letter was sent to BL not in September 1956, but sometime later, after the novel had been published abroad. But I cannot swear to it; although I remember the circumstances in which it was sent, the exact dates now escape me. It happened in the following way:

A woman friend of mine (whom I will refer to as N.) had continued to work at *Novy Mir* after I left. At the end of one very hectic day she was summoned by the editor-in-chief, Konstantin Simonov, and sat for a long time in his office while he paced up and down, reading some papers and consulting his deputy, Krivitski, who was sitting nearby and writing something. N. had to go on waiting for ages and thought it would never end. At last Simonov turned to her with a bulky envelope in his hand and said: 'Don't be angry with me, but I have a rather strange favour to ask of you. Will you please take a car and go out to Peredelkino as quickly as possible. This letter must be signed today by Agapov, Lavrenev, Katayev, and Fedin. I can't entrust it to anyone else, so I am asking you to take it. Read it so you know what it's all about.'

After reading the letter, N.'s first impulse was to refuse to go on such an errand. There was something strange and suspicious about her being asked to do it when Simonov had a secretary who was perfectly capable of performing the most delicate tasks on his behalf. It then occurred to N. that there was a good reason for her being asked to do it: Simonov knew very well that she was my friend and his motive was clearly to ensure that BL had advance notice, via the person closest to him, of the *Novy Mir* letter. N. decided to go.

The journey in an official *Novy Mir* car did not take long. Katayev signed at once, without even looking at it. Agapov read it carefully, but made no comment; Lavrenev also read it and muttered some disapproving phrases. The last was Fedin, but he was ill and could not see her. The letter was taken into him by his daughter. N. waited for a long time in a passageway—about an hour. 'Will he refuse to sign?' she wondered. How interesting that would be! But no, he signed. He was the last.*

The driver asked: 'Where do we go now?' N. did not remember exactly where my house was, and for a while the car cruised almost at random round Peredelkino. Quite by chance I happened to see it with N. inside by the bridge across the Izmalkovo lake. She invited me into the car and showed me the letter. I read through it slowly and

---

* It is a mystery why the other members of the editorial board of *Novy Mir* as it then was (S. Golubov, M. Lukonin, A. Maryamov, and E. Uspenskaya) were not asked to sign. Is it because the composition of the board was different at the actual moment of the signing of the letter? Or were only those asked who were sure to sign? In the text of the letter as published in the *Literary Gazette*, Katayev's signature is absent. He was not a member of the editorial board, and I do not understand why he was asked to sign in the first place.

deliberately, trying to remember as much as possible to be able to tell Boria. As soon as I had finished, N. returned to *Novy Mir*, where Simonov was waiting for her, despite the late hour. Without asking a single question, he took the letter, thanked her, and left.

When I reported the contents of the letter to Boria, he simply shrugged his shoulders. The wrath of the literary establishment had begun the moment he handed the novel to the Italians. He had long since given up hope of seeing it published at home. It was not his political but his literary enemies who were to blame for this—first and foremost jealous persons of the type of Surkov. People in the actual political leadership, on the other hand, such as Polikarpov, the head of the cultural section of the Central Committee, were interested in preventing a scandal from breaking out by having the novel published here in some form more or less acceptable to them.

If the term 'anti-Soviet' can be applied to anything connected with Pasternak's novel, then surely only to this *Novy Mir* letter of condemnation which is far more a political than a literary document. I am sure that one could equally well pick out passages from *Quiet Flows the Don* in order to represent this officially approved work as 'anti-Soviet'. If Pasternak expresses pity for the young men of the White Army killed in action, Sholokhov is no less guilty in voicing his horror at the slaughter of White officers. From the point of view of common sense it is ludicrous that the novel was not published once this *Novy Mir* letter had been printed in the *Literary Gazette* and thus made available to millions of Soviet readers—the letter, after all, reproduces in concentrated form, in order to put a tendentious interpretation on it, everything in the novel that could possibly be considered 'subversive' by the orthodox. In other words, the *Novy Mir* letter tells the Soviet reader exactly what its authors were so anxious to conceal from him!

In the summer of 1957 *Znamia* was negotiating with us for the publication there of a selection of BL's new verse, as was also the non-periodical almanac *Literary Moscow*[33] which wanted to publish 'An Essay in Autobiography' as well. In a note written to me at the time, BL commented:

I shall have to give my verse to the 'Almanac'. Furthermore, it would go unnoticed in *Znamia*. As a general rule, however, I prefer 'official' journals and publishers to new 'cooperative' ventures started by the writers themselves—they permit themselves so little, and differ so little from the 'official' ones. This is a familiar way—by means of a doubly contemptible fraud—of palming off what is required as something ostensibly 'freely expressed'. This was the case with the *Literary Gazette* after the war, which was to have been the voice of the nation, or of the literary community, in whose opinions the government supposedly had no right to interfere. You should tell Krivitski about this preference of mine for *Novy Mir* as against the Almanac. He should warn Aliger or Kaverin* without fail that I have definitely decided the 'Introduction' should appear not with them, but in *Novy Mir*. If he [Krivitski] agrees, let him give it the title 'People and Circumstances'. And there should be an asterisk and footnote saying: 'This essay is to appear in a volume of selected verse being prepared by *Goslitizdat*.'

We had already read and corrected the proofs, and made some additions in them. But there was still no word about actual publication.

Next came the business of the telegram which BL was obliged, under insistent pressure, to send to Feltrinelli telling him not to publish the novel in Italian. D'Angelo gives an interesting account of this:

... Olga came to see me about the telegram Pasternak was being told he must sign, and she asked me to call on him straightaway and persuade him to do so, since he was refusing to agree. This was no easy task. Anyone who knew Pasternak at all well was aware how warm, kindly, sensitive, and broad-minded he was, but also how proud, and how easily moved to anger and indignation. Because of the pressure he was now being subjected to, he was in a very stubborn mood and responded to our pleas with irritation. Neither our friendship nor sympathy for him, he said, almost shouting, entitled us to speak in favour of this move: we did not respect him and were treating him like a man without dignity. And what would Feltrinelli think of him after he had just written to say that the publication of *Doctor Zhivago* was the main aim in his life? Wouldn't he think him either a fool or a coward? At last, however, he came to understand that the telegram would not be believed, and it was in any case

* Aliger and Kaverin were both editors of *Literary Moscow*. (Tr.)

already impossible to stop publication, since many Western publishers had made photo-copies of the original and contracts had been signed for versions in the countries concerned. So the telegram was sent.

The author of one memoir on Pasternak quotes him as saying about the telegram: 'I did it with an easy mind, since I knew it would immediately be understood from the way it was phrased that it had not been written by me.' I do not believe he did it 'with an easy mind' at all. In talking with people he did not know well he generally spoke light-heartedly, with a smile, about what he was going through —hence the image in some memoirs of the unworldly poet to whom it was all like water off a duck's back. But in fact all such episodes (and there were very many!) left scars that never healed, as he himself said of the unforgettable hurts inflicted on him.

It soon became clear to everybody that Feltrinelli had indeed taken no notice of BL's telegram. (Feltrinelli once told Yevtushenko that he did not believe it because it was written in Russian, and he had an understanding with BL that he should believe only telegrams sent in French.)

That October a group of Soviet poets was supposed to visit Italy, and Surkov, not originally scheduled to go with them, now crossed somebody off the list and went himself instead. There were persistent rumours in Moscow that the one crossed off was Pasternak. Possibly so, but I do not know for certain.

The newspaper *Unità* of October 22, 1957, reported that at a press conference in Milan on October 19 Surkov had said:

Pasternak has written to his Italian publisher asking him to return the manuscript for revision. As I have read yesterday in the *Corriere* and today in the *Espresso*, *Doctor Zhivago* will nevertheless be published against the author's will. The cold war thus invades literature. If this is artistic freedom as understood in the West. then I must say that we have a rather different view of it.

Someone reported to Boria that Surkov had also described the novel as 'anti-Soviet'.

'He is right,' BL commented, 'if by "Soviet" one means seeing life not as it is in actual fact. We are made to rejoice in what brings us unhappiness, to declare our love for things we do not love, and to behave contrary to our instinct for the truth. So we stifle this instinct like slaves, and idealize our own bondage ...'

At around this time, Alexander Gladkov made a note in his diary of a conversation in which BL said to him:

They want to make a new Zoshchenko out of me ... Yes they do, I assure you. No, there's nothing to be done about it now; the order from above has already been given. On Friday I was summoned to a meeting of the Secretariat [of the Union of Writers]. It was supposed to be behind closed doors, but I didn't go and they took great offence and passed a fearful resolution denouncing me. Some of them are going out of their way to inflate the whole thing and heighten the tension—K.*, for instance. Even Panferov is taking it more calmly than K., and his like. I suddenly find I have a lot of enemies. At this meeting of the Secretariat, by the way, they appointed a committee to have things out with me ... No, no, don't you believe it, I'm in for trouble this time: my turn has come. You really have no idea— it's a complicated business, involving the pride and prestige of all kinds of people. It's a clash of rival authorities. The novel itself is hardly at issue—most of the people concerned with the matter haven't even read it. A few of them would gladly just drop the whole affair—not out of sympathy for me, mind you, only because they want to avoid a public scandal. But this is no longer possible. I'm told that somebody at the meeting accused me of being hungry for publicity, of wanting to create a great hullabaloo and scandal. If only they knew how foreign and hateful I find such things!

In November 1957, *Doctor Zhivago* was duly published in Italy. It appeared in the bookshops of Milan, first in Italian and then in the original Russian.[34] After this its progress round the whole world began—by now independently of the author's wishes, and much to his astonishment. In the first six months alone it went through eleven printings. And in the space of two years it appeared in twenty-three languages: English, French, German, Italian, Spanish, Portuguese, Danish, Swedish, Norwegian, Czech, Polish, Serbo-Croat, Dutch, Finnish, Hebrew, Turkish, Persian, Hindi, Gujarati, Arabic, Japanese, Chinese, Vietnamese.[35] As a curiosity, I should mention that the novel appeared in another Indian language: Oriya.†

* Probably Katayev. (Tr.)   † Spoken in the state of Orissa. (Tr.)

On March 21, 1960—it was a bright, sunny day, already spring-like—there was a gathering of some of our close friends at the Potapov Street apartment (N. Liubimov, K. Bogatyrev, M. Sizova, M. Polivanov—and others I don't remember). BL was in very good form and told us at some length about this edition. A firm which put out books in Oriya had decided they must publish a version of this novel which had caused such a stir. They felt they should add some kind of illustration, if only a specimen of the author's handwriting. They put an advertisement in the newspapers asking anyone who might have something of this kind to send it to them. The only response was from a Swiss lady living in Zurich—Elisabeth Kott-meier, who had translated Pasternak's verse into German. She sent them a photocopy of a dedication to her in BL's hand on a small type-written collection of his verse. The novel soon came out in Oriya with this dedication reproduced in facsimile. A copy of it was brought from India by K. Voroshilov, who passed it on to BL through somebody else. It was a rather poor edition, printed on bad paper, but the most remarkable thing about it was that because of the way the facsimile was placed, it looked as though the novel was dedicated to Elisabeth Kottmeier!

On May 7, 1958, BL wrote to Renate Schweitzer in Germany:

The appearance of the book will not give only pleasure but will provoke a certain hostility as well: political from circles with Communist sympathies, and also aesthetic on account of its un-modern naïveté, simplicity, and transparent language, its boring commonplaces and flatness. You yourself will be bored as you read, and see the truth of what its critics say. But you should not be put out by this. Do not take it too much to heart. If I were not reluctant to tire both of us by writing a long letter, I would explain to you why a book about the crucial matters for which our age has paid such a price in blood and madness had to be written clearly and with utmost simplicity.

And on June 8, he wrote to Jacqueline de Proyart in France:

. . . I have heard that *Doctor Zhivago* may be expected to appear in Paris at the end of June. This is already half of the joy to come. I am sure I shall weep from tenderness, from transports of bliss when I touch with my own hands this living miracle—the inspired work done by all of you* in a year of difficulties and setbacks. But I should not write in my ludicrous and abominable French of these things which are of such significance for the greatness of life in general—not only ours . . . The [forthcoming] publication of *Doctor Zhivago* in France, the remarkable personal letters, dizzying and breathtaking, which I have received from there—this is a whole novel in itself, a special kind of experience which creates a feeling of being in love . . .

'One of us' or 'not one of us'?

The novel thus went on its way round the world, and was greeted with controversy or with fanfare. But for the time being, in the Soviet Union itself, there was only an ambiguous silence. And BL was left in peace.

That spring of 1958 (as often in other years) he fell ill again and had to go to hospital. I still have two letters from this period. The first was to the senior editor of *Goslitizdat*, A. I. Puzikov:

Dear Alexander Ivanovich,

I am so tired myself of my frequent illness and of being in hospital that you and my close friends must be even more so. I have no faith in the faint stirrings that have again begun in connection with my poetry volume, nor in the rumours about possibilities of publishing my novel. This will never happen, and such talk will lead nowhere.

But the myths about my supposed affluence are also groundless. Sooner or later, and perhaps rather soon, I shall need a lot of money. How good it would be if, as in former years, instead of placing hopes in unfeasible things, the publishers [*Goslitizdat*] would agree to reissue my translations of Shakespeare's tragedies, as in the 1953 collection. Let O.V. know what you feel in general about my affairs, and whether anything can be thought of. Cordial greetings.

Your devoted B.P.

March 4, 1958

* The French version of *Doctor Zhivago* was done by a group of translators working together. (Tr.)

The second letter, written to me from hospital, was concerned with a proposal by Panferov, the editor of the journal *Oktiabr*. Panferov had asked me to go and see him and he went on for a long time about how 'we won't give him up to the foreigners . . . Let him go to Baku and see the building of the oil rigs there out in the sea . . . and write something new . . . I'll let him have a car for the trip . . .', and so on. He said he would go and visit BL in hospital.

Boria's comment on all this was as follows:

If there is so much talk about the more distant future, then let him [i.e. Panferov] take steps in the immediate future—not through his own efforts, but armed with some very forceful instruction from higher up (N.S.?)*—to have me placed as the *only* patient in a two-bed ward in the first section, with a guarantee that this arrangement will last till I leave, and no one else will be put in with me. Although this seems (even to me) an excessive request and something quite unheard-of, I have done enough to merit an exception of this kind being made for me. Then I will be able to spread out my books and papers in this separate ward and gradually start work on something, and return, God willing, from sickness to health. The only thing is that before Thursday, when I shall expect him here, Fiodor Iv. [Panferov] should obtain the necessary firm authority from above, and perhaps also, in the meanwhile, even come to an agreement over the phone with the main people in charge of the hospital. Now this—getting me put as the only patient in a small ward— would be interesting, but the rest is for the moment of little importance.†

'One of us', or a 'foreigner' etc. It is curious that in order to qualify as 'one of us', as a Russian, you have to be subject to violent fits that keep you travelling around and looking at things, but if you don't go anywhere and just sit quietly at home, you could be a Dutchman or an Argentinian. The only way to show genuine goodwill towards someone is to leave him in peace and cease to concern oneself with him in such a complicated and ambiguous fashion.

Almost as soon as he was out of the hospital, BL wrote to G. V.

* i.e. Nikita Sergeyevich Khrushchev. (Tr.)

† My recollection is that Panferov did not come to see BL in the hospital after all—something prevented him—and BL was not transferred to a private ward.

Bebutov, one of his Georgian editors: 'I do not like reminiscences about the past, particularly my own. My future looms immeasurably larger, I cannot but live by it, and have no reason for looking backwards.' (May 24, 1958).

It was not till long after BL had handed a copy of the novel to d'Angelo that he was eventually summoned to a meeting at the Union of Writers, called to look into the affair. (I do not remember the exact date or agenda of the meeting.) I went instead of him, with a note giving me his authority to represent him, and was accompanied by Starostin, the editor who had been appointed by *Goslitizdat* to deal with the novel. Much later BL wrote to Renate Schweitzer: 'During the endless unpleasantness over the Zhivago affair, I was only twice made to appear personally in connection with it. The higher authorities regard O.V. as my representative who is willing to take on herself the whole brunt of every blow, and of talking with them.' On this occasion, too, I was afraid to let BL go in person—he could easily have got very worked up and had a heart attack or something worse. So I left him in Potapov Street with friends, and went off to the Union of Writers together with Starostin.

It was, I believe, a so-called 'enlarged' meeting of the Secretariat and it had been called to discuss Pasternak's unseemly behaviour in sending the manuscript of his novel abroad—by now more than two years had gone by since he had given it to d'Angelo in May 1956. The meeting was presided over by Surkov. At first he greeted me in friendly fashion, called me into his office and questioned me gently about how it could all have happened.

I tried to explain to him. One had to know BL, I said—he was a generous man who really thought, with the spontaneity of a child (or a genius?), that frontiers between countries are of no account and must be crossed by people who stand outside ordinary social categories—poets, artists, scholars. He was convinced that the interest of one person or nation in another should not be forcibly impeded by frontiers. He was sure that cultural communion among people could not be regarded as a crime, and that instead of merely paying lip-service to it, one should promote it in a practical way.

I told him that when these two young people (one apparently a member of the Soviet Embassy in Rome, and the other an Italian Communist) had come to see him, he had given them the novel to read, not to publish. He had not made any agreement regarding publication, taken any payment or discussed the question of rights—there had been nothing of this kind. And no secret had been made of it—which would have been necessary if the manuscript had been deliberately handed over for publication. On the contrary, we had informed all the official bodies concerned, right up to the Central Committee of the Party.

Surkov agreed with me. 'Yes, yes,' he said, 'it was quite in character. But it was so untimely.' (I was tempted to quote Zhivago's phrase 'Only real greatness can be so misplaced and untimely'*, but refrained.) 'You should have prevented him—he does, after all, have a good angel like you . . .' (I could never have imagined at that moment, heaven help me, how Surkov would soon be slinging mud at Pasternak's 'good angel'.)

This was the end of our conversation and we went out into the hall. There were many people. I remember the young Lukonin, Narovchatov, Katayev (who had just become a Party member), Sobolev, Tvardovski . . .

Surkov began to give an account of what had taken place between Pasternak and the Italian. Alas, there was no trace now of the friendly attitude he had shown only a little while before, and after reading out the *Novy Mir* letter in a calm enough tone, he gradually began to work himself up more and more, until at a certain moment in his speech he came out with the word 'treachery'. Needless to say, he took no account of what I had told him. Sobolev kept egging him on from where he was sitting among the others, and Surkov became more and more impassioned. The novel, he said, had been discussed and condemned, but Pasternak had paid no attention to the views of his comrades, and was now negotiating to receive money for the novel from abroad. (The writer K. had accurately foretold this: 'Our cretins will pin political and mercenary motives on him—the very motives they're so prone to themselves . . .') 'Now what are you making things up for?' I burst out indignantly. But I was not allowed to speak: 'I must ask you not to interrupt me!' Surkov shouted. I remember that Tvardovski tried to intervene on my behalf: 'Let her speak. I want to understand what happened. Why do you want to muzzle her?' But now Katayev, sprawling insolently in his chair, butted in and said to me: 'What sort of person have you

* These words are spoken by Zhivago about the Revolution. (Tr.)

come here to represent, may I ask? I'm blessed if I know what world I'm living in—novels being sent abroad, and all these money deals going on...'

Azhayev was interested mainly in the 'method' by which the novel had been sent out of the country. 'But how did he actually get it out?' he kept asking. 'If we had known, we could have intercepted it...'

Sobolev, dressed in overalls and looking like a small podgy boy, said he felt defiled and insulted that a poet who was so little known should suddenly become world-famous in such a monstrous way.

'Will you let me speak or not?' I again broke in angrily.

'Why are you here instead of him?' Surkov now bawled at me. 'Why does he refuse to talk with us?'

'Yes,' I replied, 'it's hard for him to talk with you. But I am able to answer all your questions.'

I then repeated more or less what I had told Surkov before the meeting began. As I spoke, there were constant rude interruptions. When at one point I turned to Surkov and said, 'Here is the editor of the novel, Starostin,' Surkov shouted, 'Novel, you say? I'll give you novel! I'm going to put a stop to this romance of yours* with *Goslitizdat*!'

'If you won't let me speak,' I said, 'then there's no point in my being here.' At this, Katayev, who for some reason was more heated than anyone else, chimed in to say: 'There really is no point in your being here! Who do you think you're representing? A poet or a traitor? Or doesn't it bother you that he's a traitor to his country?'

It was impossible for me to go on, and I sat down.

It was then announced that the editor of the novel, Anatoli Starostin, wished to speak. Before he could begin, Katayev again spoke up: 'Just fancy that—the *editor*, if you please! How can something like *this* be edited!'

'I may tell you,' Starostin began in a calm, quiet voice, 'that what has been put in my hands is an impeccable work of literature which could reflect glory on the Russian people. But you wish to make it the object of a campaign of abuse...'

I do not remember the exact words of his speech and can only reproduce the gist of it, which was as follows:

Pasternak did not regard the text of the novel as final, and had not

* There is a pun here: *roman* in Russian means both 'novel' and 'romance'. (Tr.)

insisted on keeping in it any passages that might be contentious. He had expressed his willingness to accept editorial changes made by Starostin.* But the leaders of the Union of Writers were still opposed even though there had been clear encouragement from the cultural section of the Central Committee of the Party. Instead of trying to win the poet over to their point of view they had cold-shouldered him, not giving him a chance to make the changes that could be made. By his political accusations against Pasternak, which were most ugly and Bulgarin-like, Surkov had misled everybody, forced the novel to be sent out of the country, and instigated a campaign of persecution against a great Russian poet . . .

> But can devotion to the Motherland be thought
> The same as strict adherence to the truth?

Pasternak had been tormented by the rival claims of 'devotion to the Motherland' and 'strict adherence to the truth'. He had often said he would like to be proven wrong in his judgments and that things might turn out to be better than depicted in the novel. He had often been inclined to believe that many of its misfortunes had come on the nation not because of the nature of the system, but through the evil will of those people—by no means the best—whom chance had placed in power.

In a word, it would have been possible to edit the novel and put everything in proper perspective in a judicious editorial note at the end—the author had been agreeable to all this. But it could not be done unless Surkov showed genuine concern for the country's literature instead of for his own exalted official position in it, which he maintained by means of petty political intrigue. For the sake of this he had struck a blow not so much at Pasternak (whose significance was not in the least diminished—if anything his popularity had even grown in consequence), as at Russian literature in general. He had deprived the nation of a great work of literature . . .

Surkov now announced that the Secretariat had to discuss matters concerning the internal affairs of the Union of Writers, and that the presence of outsiders was undesirable at this point. I had no alternative

---

* In so doing, however, he had said: 'Cross out what you please, but I don't want to know about it, or have anything to do with it. And don't "bridge over" the gaps—I don't want anything added.'

but to leave. Saying that he too was an 'outsider', Starostin also got up and went out with me . . .

By way of comment on this unseemly meeting, one of the people present wrote the following lines, which he asked me to pass on to BL:

> Like witches gathered for a ritual
> The evildoers on this vile occasion
> Hound a champion of principle
> And vilify his noble reputation.
>
> Drunk on words, they fume and rant
> —The fury fills their bloodshot eyes—
> How dare he spurn the usual cant,
> And contradict their never-ending lies!
>
> How dare he write this work
> For which, while they will leave no trace,
> The multitudes will flock in thousands
> To bow down at his resting place.
>
> They do not understand, the scoundrels,
> Their fatal limitation
> That, rage, as they may—the baying pack—
> They've all been dead for ages.

'You're right,' BL said, after I had given him an account of what had happened. 'I should not go to these meetings.'

A short time after this (September 13, 1958), there was an evening of Italian poetry in Moscow (in the Polytechnic Museum, I think). In reply to notes sent up to him asking why Pasternak was not present, Surkov, who was in the chair, explained that Pasternak had written an anti-Soviet novel against the spirit of the Russian Revolution, and had sent it abroad for publication.

This was the first time the accusation was made in public—but for the moment still only verbally.

'One must write in a way never known before, make discoveries, so that unheard-of things happen to you—that is life, and the rest matters nothing'—these are the words I have already quoted which BL said to me at the time when we were first getting to know each other and he was beginning work on the novel. And now a 'thing never done before' had indeed not only been written, but had been printed in vast editions throughout almost the entire world, and its author was being proposed as a candidate for the Nobel Prize of 1958.

People have forgotten that BL's candidature for the Nobel Prize was first put forward in 1947, before the name Zhivago had come to him, and the novel was still conceived of under its original title of *Boys and Girls*. His name was put forward then by some British writers, who considered that he was a legitimate candidate for the prize on the strength of his lyric poetry. (See P. Olbert: 'Sweden and Boris Pasternak'.) In 1954 there had again been talk about the Nobel Committee considering Pasternak, but in the event they decided in favour of Ernest Hemingway.

Now, in 1958, BL wrote to Renate Schweitzer:

Some people believe the Nobel Prize may be awarded to me this year. I am firmly convinced I shall be passed over and that it will go to Alberto Moravia. You cannot imagine all the difficulties, torments, and anxieties which arise to confront me in my mind at the mere prospect, however unlikely, of such a possibility. There are situations in life when only a certain lack of movement can assure stability for those around one. One step out of place—and the people closest to you will be condemned to suffer from all the jealousy, resentment, wounded pride, and disappointment of others, and old scars on the heart will be re-opened . . .

And, only two days before the award of the prize to him, he wrote in another letter to Renate:

. . . it seems the hunger in the whole world for freedom and simplicity is so great, that everybody is glad of *Dr. Zh.* as a happy excuse for a kind of self-emancipation . . .

A little earlier he had written to her:

... Soon you will read my book. Then you will weep uniquely justified and uniquely grateful tears—such as I could not restrain myself when I began to read the French translation ... it *did* exist, that time before the [First World] War, when the great cities were crowded almost as in nature, like forests, saturated by the light of the skies.... Even merely to wander round the streets was to experience the delights of art: the throngs of people, the traffic, the store fronts; railways and journeys, brightly lit nights. And a rich, deeply affecting art of the sort found in the ancient world, or during the Renaissance. ... But then came the reign of the House Manager,* the imperious stamping of his foot; the unbelievable collapse of society (ours and yours), whose victims and witnesses we have been; the destruction of thousands of towns.

I feel almost as though I have done nothing new—in the sense that my teachers and forerunners, our great Russian novelists (and the Scandinavians) did—but have simply re-lit the candle of Malte Laurids† which had been standing extinguished and unused, and gone out with this light of Rilke's into the darkness of the streets, into the midst of the ruins. To think that when he wrote his novel (like Proust) he had nothing to apply his brilliant insights to—but now look at the mountain of subject matter around us ... the terrifying pretexts for art begging to be used. How grimly in earnest it is, this reality, how tragic and stern—but it is nevertheless the reality of our earth, a defined poetic entity. And so we want to weep from joy and awe...

On October 23 the Swedish Academy announced its award of the Nobel Prize for Literature to Boris Pasternak, 'For his important contribution to contemporary lyric poetry, as well as to the great traditions of the Russian prose-writers'.

That same day, BL sent a telegram to the permanent secretary of the Academy, Anders Østerling saying: 'Infinitely grateful, touched, proud, surprised, overwhelmed.'

Correspondents of foreign newspapers in Moscow flocked out to

* The person appointed to manage apartment blocks after the Revolution and a symbol of the new régime's petty tyranny in everyday life. Compare Markel in *Doctor Zhivago*. (Tr.)

† The hero of Rainer Maria Rilke's novel *The Notebooks of Malte Laurids Brigge*, 1910. (Tr.)

the house in Peredelkino with their cameras: in one photograph we see BL reading the official telegram from the Swedish Academy, in another he sits bashfully with raised glass, replying to the congratulations of Kornei Chukovski and his granddaughter, and of Nina Tabidze . . . And then, in a photograph taken only about twenty minutes later, he is sitting at the same table, with the same people, but, heavens above, looking so woebegone, his eyes sad and his mouth turned down at the corners! What had happened in the intervening twenty minutes was that Fedin had come to see him and, without congratulating him, had said that in order to avoid serious trouble he must 'voluntarily' repudiate both the prize and the novel.

BL came over to see me in the 'little' house. He was in an agitated state: 'Just imagine, Olia, I have been given this prize and now I must talk to you. Fedin is waiting for me and I believe Polikarpov has been to see him. What do you think, can I say I repudiate the novel?'

The words sounded so strange—'repudiate the novel'!

He talked for a long time, as though trying to persuade himself of something, told me about his telegram of thanks to Stockholm, and then went back to the 'big' house.

That evening he phoned Ira in Moscow. Her recollection of events that day is as follows:

Mama and BL were out in Peredelkino. On October 24, in a little public garden near the Byelorussian Station, I met the correspondent of *Unità*, Giuseppe Garritano. He had a 'Torpedo' typewriter for me to take to Mama—it had been bought for BL. He handed me the typewriter and asked me whether I knew that the day before the Swedish Academy had awarded the Nobel Prize to BL. Garritano looked worried, and I felt terribly scared. I had only a vague idea what the Nobel Prize was. What would happen next? It seemed that something forbidden, compromising, and utterly needless had happened.

I went home feeling quite at sea, and almost at once had a call from BL in Peredelkino:

'Ah, you know already!' he said in a disappointed tone. 'I just tried to get your grandmother on the phone, but Sergei Stepanovich answered, so I told him about it, and he didn't even congratulate me.' (Only now did it occur to me that it might be a subject for congratulation, not only something to make you die of fright!) 'And of course the fat is in the fire now! Fedin has been round and tells me I must give it up. He looked as though I'd commited a crime, and didn't congratulate me . . . Only the Ivanovs did . . . what marvellous people they are! Tamara Vladimirovna gave me a great kiss—what a nice woman! But those others . . . I wouldn't speak to Fedin. Was I right?'

Now I suddenly understood that I was probably the first person he had told of his decision, of the 'line' he was going to take, and that Mama, even if she knew about it, must be in a state of total confusion and quite unable to give him any support. So then I said with enormous enthusiasm: 'Of course, of course! Tell them all to go away, the miserable, wretched slaves! There's no point in talking to them.' 'Yes? So I'm right?' BL repeated joyfully.

That same night I had a phone call from a friend in the Literary Institute, the young poet Pankratov, who was very devoted to BL; he told me a demonstration was being planned, with posters demanding Pasternak's expulsion abroad and all kinds of scurrilous caricatures . . .

This was on Friday, October 24.

'. . . Like a beast at bay . . .'

The next day, Saturday, October 25, it all began . . .

Two whole pages of Saturday's edition of the *Literary Gazette* were devoted to denunciation of BL—a long leading article, and an open letter from the newspaper's editors ('the life-story of a malignant petty bourgeois . . . open hatred for the Russian people . . . a paltry, worthless, and vile piece of work . . . a rabid literary snob . . .').

The same day there was a 'spontaneous' demonstration at the Literary Institute against BL. It was very carefully organized and there was great pressure on the students from the heads of the Institute. The director stated that the attitude they took to Pasternak would be a 'litmus test' for them, and they were told they must turn up at the demonstration and sign a letter denouncing Pasternak in the *Literary Gazette*. According to Ira:

Of the more than three hundred students in the Institute, only a little over a hundred signed this letter. The people collecting the signatures came round the dormitories and it was hard to escape them. Some of our girls took refuge in the toilets or in the kitchen, and pretended they weren't in. My friend Alka simply chased them out of her room. But not everybody could afford to do this.

Ira's friends Pankratov and Kharabarov described the demonstration to us. It was led by two writers, Vladimir Firsov and N. Sergovantsev. Despite all their efforts and the threats of the Party committee it was a pitiful display—only a few dozen people turned up. They went over to the Union of Writers* with their posters. On one of them there was a caricature showing BL reaching for a sack of dollars with crooked, grasping fingers. Another said: 'Throw the Judas out of the USSR!' The demonstrators leaned their posters against the wall. Voronkov came out to see them. They handed him the letter (which was subsequently published in the *Literary Gazette* of November 1, under the heading 'A Shameful Act') and said they would now go out to Peredelkino and 'continue the demonstration' in front of Pasternak's house.

Voronkov said that he appreciated their feelings, and that a decision on the matter would be taken in the next few days—so they need not go to Peredelkino and could now bring their demonstration to a close . . .

The next day, Sunday, October 26, all the newspapers reproduced in full the materials that had appeared in the *Literary Gazette* the previous day. There were of course some new items as well—such as a long article by David Zaslavski, 'Reactionary Propaganda Uproar Over a Literary Weed', which took up half a page in *Pravda*. This was the selfsame Zaslavski of whom Lenin had once spoken in terms which can hardly be bettered: '. . . these filthy gentlemen of the Zaslavski type . . . such scoundrels as Zaslavski' . . . 'blackmailing hired pens, such as Zaslavski and Co.', and, finally, '. . . one should make a precise distinction in law between the concept of polemicist, and that of a scandal-monger and slanderer.'

We learned that the next day, Monday, there was to be a combined session of the writers' organizations which would decide BL's fate.

Ira recalls:

* The Literary Institute is opposite the Union of Writers on Vorovski Street. (Tr.)

. . . I was very glad that BL did not read the newspapers—the monstrous cheapness of it all would have stung him to the quick and wounded him—he would not have been able to treat it aloofly, with contempt, as we could. He might well have taken all this wretched filth to heart, and tried in a desperate (and also comic) manner to justify his actions both to himself and everyone else. I had often noticed—and it was particularly evident at this time—that he was unable to take an ironical view of things that seemed almost idiotic to others. For example, somebody thought to cheer him up during those days by telling him about an exchange between two women in the Metro: 'Why are you shouting at me like that?' said one to the other. 'Do you take me for a *Zhivago*, or something?' When he later re-told the story to us, BL put on a great show of finding it very funny, but I, for one, sensed—and I had an unusually heightened capacity to enter into his feelings during those days—that it was in fact all very painful to him . . .

I went out to Peredelkino with Pankratov and Kharabarov. It was clear that BL was going to be hounded, that a witch-hunt had been mounted against him, and it was impossible to say where it might end. But at least there was no doubt about the part we would play—and so off we went to Peredelkino, I and these two friends, who were afraid and quaking in their shoes, but nevertheless overflowing with eagerness to help. We came to the Kuzmich house, where BL happened to be at the moment. He seemed in very good heart, but was not all that glad to have visitors—he wanted to be alone. We walked with him towards the 'big' house. He was ready to 'drink his cup of suffering to the end'. It was really impossible to foresee how the whole business would end—after all, only five years had gone by since the end of Stalin's reign of terror.

One had a clear impression of his loneliness—a loneliness borne with great courage. He was still dressed in his usual get-up—a cap, a mackintosh, and wellingtons—which Mama and I loved so much. In the following days, when he had to go and see high officials, he took on a different aspect—obviously a very rare occurrence—by donning a formal suit, an overcoat and hat.

We went with him as far as the electric substation, at which he would have to turn off to his house, and stopped for a moment. We could hear the electric trains hooting by the cemetery. Pankratov recited some lines from one of BL's poems:

That is the reason why in early spring
My friends and I foregather,
Our evenings are farewells
Our revelries are testaments,
So that suffering's secret flow
Should warm the cold of being.

BL was visibly moved. He thanked the two boys for coming to see him, pulled out a checked handkerchief and, almost in tears, walked off towards his house . . .

We heard that Bella Akhmadulina and many young people close to her—as well as others quite apart from her—sympathized with BL and wanted to help in some way, but hesitated to approach or bother him, and did not know in what way they could show their love and sympathy. Because of their friendship with Ira, Pankratov and Kharabarov were more successful in doing so, and were thus able to give BL some moral support. But even in this there was a sour note. As BL told Yevgeni Yevtushenko:

Yura [Pankratov] and Vania [Kharabarov] came to see me and said that if they refused to sign Firsov's letter demanding my expulsion from the country, they would be thrown out of the Institute, and they asked me what they should do. 'Really now,' I replied, 'what does it matter? It's an empty formality—sign it.' And when I looked out of the window I saw them skipping with joy as they ran off hand in hand. How strange young people are now, what a strange generation! In our time such things were not done.

I myself saw how hard it was for BL to reconcile himself to this behaviour, or to anything else he regarded as disloyalty.

Mark Twain once said that a man is admitted to the Church for what he believes, and expelled from it for what he knows.

The time had now come for Boria to be expelled from the Church because of what he knew. He had broken the basic rule of the age in which we live: the rule that requires you to ignore realities. And he had usurped the right, claimed by our rulers for themselves alone, to have an opinion, to speak and think one's own thoughts.

'Doctor Zhivago has no right to make any pronouncements what-soever on the Revolution,' Surkov once said in conversation with Nadezhda Mandelstam.*

In all ages, geniuses have been dangerous because they lay bare the truth. On January 26, 1837, on the eve of his fatal duel, Pushkin wrote to Count Karl Fiodorovich Tol: 'Genius lays bare the truth at a single glance, and truth is stronger than the Tsar . . .' This is why dictators cannot forgive poets their moral superiority, their 'precious awareness of poetic rightness'. As Yuri Zhivago says in the novel:

Ordinary people are anxious to test their theories in practice, to learn from experience, but those who wield power are so anxious to estab-lish the myth of their own infallibility that they turn their back on truth as squarely as they can. Politics means nothing to me. I don't like people who are indifferent to the truth.

*We'll remember by his name
Everyone who raised his hand'* †

'Wherever a great spirit speaks his thoughts—there is Golgotha' (Heinrich Heine). The day of Boria's Golgotha had now arrived. It was Monday, October 27. A meeting had been called for 12 o'clock to consider 'the Pasternak affair'. It was a combined meeting of the Presidium of the Board of the Union of Writers of the USSR, of the Bureau of the Organizational Committee of the Union of Writers of the RSFSR, and of the Presidium of the Board of the Moscow Section of the Union of Writers of the RSFSR.

BL came in that morning from Peredelkino to the Potapov Street apartment. Koma Ivanov came too. Koma, a literary scholar and linguist, is the son of the writer Vsevolod Ivanov. For old times' sake, I shall refer to him by his nickname 'Koma', as in those years.) And of course Ira and Mitia were there. The question immediately arose: should BL go to his 'execution' or not? I think it was Koma who was the first to say that he should not go on any account. He loved BL

---

* See *Hope Abandoned*, p. 592. (Tr.)

† A. Galich, 'To the memory of Pasternak'. These lines refer to those who voted to have Pasternak expelled from the Union of Writers. (Tr.)

very much, watched over him, and helped him in every way he could. We all supported Koma. BL agreed, but asked us to ring Voronkov to say he would not be present, and then went into the next room to write a letter of explanation addressed to the meeting. For some reason, Koma went to the next-door apartment to phone Voronkov. He told him he would be bringing a letter from BL. By the time he came back to our apartment, Boria had emerged from the next room with the sheets of paper on which he had written his letter in pencil. It was an unusual kind of letter in which he had listed all his points in summary form. It was quite undiplomatic, without any beating about the bush or compromises, and had been dashed off without a moment's hesitation. It was criminal of us, I need hardly say, that no one took a copy of this letter or preserved the exact text in some way. I reproduce it here partly from memory, and partly from notes taken by people who heard it read out at the meetings of October 27 and 31:

1. I have received your invitation, and intended to come, but knowing what a monstrous display it will be, I have decided against it . . .
2. I continue to believe that it was possible to write *Doctor Zhivago* without ceasing to be a Soviet writer—particularly as it was completed at the time of the publication of V. Dudintsev's novel *Not by Bread Alone*—which created the impression of a thaw, of a new situation . . .
3. I gave the manuscript of *Doctor Zhivago* to an Italian Communist publisher, and expected that the translation would be censored. I was willing to cut out [unacceptable] passages . . .
4. I do not regard myself as a parasite . . .
5. I do not have an exaggerated opinion of myself. I asked Stalin to let me write as best I can . . .
6. I thought *Doctor Zhivago* would be the object of friendly criticism . . .
7. Nothing will induce me to give up the honour of being a Nobel Prize winner. But I am ready to hand over the money to the Peace Committee . . .*

* The ostensibly 'international' Committee set up in support of the Soviet-inspired Stockholm Peace Appeal in 1950 as an instrument of Soviet propaganda in the post-war years. (Tr.)

8. I do not expect justice from you. You may have me shot, or expelled from the country, or do anything you like. All I ask of you is: do not be in too much of a hurry over it. It will bring you no increase either of happiness or of glory.

We listened in silence. Koma then said in his usual manner: 'Well now, it's very good!' One of us suggested he cut out the reference to Dudintsev, but to no avail.

Koma and Mitia took the letter off by taxi to get it there in time for the start of the meeting.

The next day, October 28, the *Literary Gazette* had a headline in huge letters: 'On Actions by Member of the Union of Writers of the USSR B. L. Pasternak Incompatible with His Calling as a Soviet Writer'. Then, in smaller letters: 'Resolution of the Presidium of the Board of the Union of Writers of the USSR, of the Bureau of the Organizational Committee of the Union of Writers of the RSFSR, of the Presidium of the Board of the Moscow Section of the Union of Writers of the RSFSR.' The text of the resolution took up two columns:

. . . these actions . . . were directed against the traditions of Russian literature, against the people, against peace and socialism . . . [Pasternak] has become a tool of bourgeois propaganda . . . of those circles . . . who endeavour to slander all progressive and revolutionary movements . . . has joined the struggle against the progressive advance of history . . . the author's boundless self-conceit combined with poverty of thought . . . [*Doctor Zhivago*] is the cry of woe of a frightened Philistine who is aggrieved and dismayed because history has not followed the crooked paths which he would have liked to dictate to it . . . has severed his last links with his country and its people . . . the same forces are organizing military blackmail against the Arab peoples, provocations against the People's China, and raising a rumpus around the name of B. Pasternak . . . renegade . . . in view of . . . his betrayal of the Soviet people, the cause of socialism, peace, and progress, for which he has been rewarded, in the interests of stoking up the Cold War, by the Nobel Prize . . . [the Presidium of the Board of the Union of Writers of the USSR, etc.] divest B. Pasternak of the title of Soviet writer, and expel him from membership of the Union of Writers of the USSR.

Those listed as being present were: G. Markov, S. Mikhalkov, V. Katayev, G. Gulia, N. Zaryan, V. Azhayev, M. Shaginyan, M. Tursun-Zade, Y. Smolich, G. Nikolayeva, N. Chukovski, V. Panova, M. Lukonin, A. Prokofyev, A. Karavayeva, L. Sobolev, V. Yermilov, S. Antonov, N. Gribachev, B. Polevoi, S. S. Smirnov, A. Yashin, P. Nilin, S. V. Smirnov, A. Ventslova, S. Shchipachev, I. Abashidze, A. Tokombayev, S. Ragimov, N. Atarov, V. Kozhevnikov, I. Anisimov.

All of them, according to the *Literary Gazette*, '. . . unanimously condemned the treacherous behaviour of Pasternak, angrily rejecting the attempts of our enemies to represent this internal émigré as a Soviet writer.' An editorial comment ('Unanimous Condemnation') mentioned that the meeting had been presided over by N. S. Tikhonov—the same 'Kolia' Tikhonov who on August 29, 1934, speaking at the First Congress of the Union of Writers, had said:

Pasternak's very difficult and impetuous flow of language, this avalanche of words restrained only by a most delicate sense of measure, this at first sight cryptic onrush, which overwhelms the reader and frightens him off, has given birth, through the magic power of his skill, to utterances of a new kind:

> A kinsman of all that is, a confidant
> and friend of the future in our daily life,
> in the end you cannot but succumb,
> like a heretic, to unheard-of simplicity . . .

Once upon a time, BL had given a magnificent portrait of himself, painted by his father Leonid Pasternak, to Ilya Selvinski. Quite recently Selvinski had publicly recognized his debt to BL in a poem:

> . . . all my teachers,
> From Pushkin to Pasternak.

But now, at a critical moment in the life of his 'teacher', Selvinski sent him this letter from the Crimea:

Yalta, October 24, 1958
Dear Boris Leonidovich,
Today I learned that the British Radio has reported the award of the Nobel Prize to you. I immediately sent you a cable with my

congratulations. If I am not mistaken, you are the fifth Russian to have received the prize—before you were Mechnikov, Pavlov, Semionov, and Bunin. So, as you see, you are in fairly good company. The situation over your book, however, is such that it would be simply provocative on your part to accept the prize. I know that for you my advice has always been *nihil*, and that you have never forgiven me for being younger than you by ten years, but all the same I now take it on myself to tell you that to *ignore the view of the Party*, even if you think it wrong, is equivalent, in the international situation of the present moment, to delivering a blow at the country in which you live. I beg you to trust in my political sense, which may not be very accurate, but is fairly so.

With a friendly embrace, yours affectionately, Ilya Selvinski.

This letter was the first in an avalanche which from now on began to descend on BL from all over the world and never ceased until his death.

But having written his letter, Selvinski did not stop there—suppose its contents remained unknown? On October 30 he went together with Victor Shklovski, B. S. Yevgenyev (deputy director of the journal *Moskva*), and B. A. Dyakov (head of the literature section of the 'Soviet Russia' publishing house) to give an interview to the local Yalta newspaper, where he was quoted as saying (in its issue of October 31, 1958): '. . . Pasternak has always had one eye on the West, has always stood apart from the community of Soviet writers, and has perpetrated a low act of treachery.'

Shklovski had this to say to the newspaper:

When people criticized his *Doctor Zhivago*, Pasternak would admit there was 'some truth' in what they said, but then went on to ignore it. Not only is the book anti-Soviet, but it also betrays the author's total failure to understand the essence of Soviet life and the direction in which our country is moving. His isolation from his fellow writers and from the Soviet people has led him into the camp of rabid imperialist reaction, whose charity he eagerly accepts . . .

(Selvinski felt that even this was not enough. In *Ogoniok* No. 11, 1959, he published a poem about a bad son who has had a thrashing from his mother, and then decides to take revenge by beating her with a cudgel borrowed from a neighbour. After some moralizing on this theme, he continues:

And you, poet, on whom the enemy lavishes such favours,
Just to indulge your caprices to the full,
Have made it possible for the lowest scum
To prance and caper gleefully.
What price today that generous display
Of a passion once so pure
When now, to earn the fame of a Herostratus,
You expose your Motherland to taunts and jeers?)

The Noose Tightens

The campaign of persecution against us had begun almost immediately after the publication of the novel in Milan—that is, a long time before the public outcry unleashed following the award of the Nobel Prize. I have already described one of the first semi-official hearings on the matter in a previous chapter. Although the newspapers had not yet begun to hound BL as they did after the award of the prize, they were not entirely silent. In the *Literary Gazette* of September 9, 1958, for example, the critic Victor Pertsov, in an article entitled 'The Voice of Truth', spoke of '. . . the decadent religious poetry of Pasternak, which reeks of mothballs from the Symbolist suitcase of 1908-10 manufacture . . .' (This of BL's cycle of poems on Gospel themes!)

But from the very beginning it was clear to our persecutors that since all newspapers and publishing houses in the Soviet Union—in a word, all sources of income—are in the hands of the state, the easiest way of dealing with intellectuals like us was simply to starve us into submission. Soon after the appearance of the novel abroad, therefore, we began to receive notices terminating various contracts for translations. By the time of the award of the Nobel Prize and the public scandal that broke out as a consequence, I was left completely without work, and all contracts with BL had also been cancelled—except, I believe, the one for his translation of Juliusz Słowacki's verse and his play (*Marja Stuart*). It was impossible to see how we would live.

At the same time—or so I thought—we had firmly decided on the line that the prize was deserved and must be accepted, and there was to be no retreat, whatever happened. But then there came the moment when we were all gathered in the Potapov Street apartment towards evening (as far as I remember, it must have been Wednesday, October 29), and Boria arrived, still in his best suit, to tell us something startling. He announced that now the first reaction of the authorities was clear and all their plans were based on the fact that the prize had been awarded, this was just the moment for him to renounce it—what would they do then, he wondered? . . .

I was terribly angry: how could he, when our course of action had been decided, and the authorities too had settled on their line already! . . .

But he said he had already sent off a telegram, to Anders Østerling in Stockholm, and he showed us a copy of it:

In view of the meaning given the award by the society in which I live, I must renounce this undeserved distinction which has been conferred on me. Please do not take my voluntary renunciation amiss . . .

As in the case of the first telegram (the one in which he had sent thanks for the award) we were dumbfounded. This was just like him—first to act, and only then to speak about it and ask what people thought. I think it was only Ariadna who went up to him at once and kissed him, saying, 'Good for you, Boria, good for you!'—not, of course, because this was what she really thought, but because it was an accomplished fact and the only thing left was to support him.

But he had yet another surprise in store for us. We now learned that, apart from the telegram to the Swedish Academy, he had also sent one to the Central Committee. No copy of this second one has been preserved, but the general sense was: I have given up the Nobel Prize. Let Olga Ivinskaya be allowed to work again.

When I now look back on the whole business, I have the feeling that this decision on BL's part to renounce the prize did not suit the book of the authorities, including Polikarpov. It was not what they had in mind at all. The huge sum in foreign currency involved would have been quite welcome to them. They were aiming at something else, not BL's repudiation of it.

What they really wanted, as I understood only later, was to humble the poet, to force him to grovel in public and admit his 'errors'—in other words, to score a victory for brute force and intolerance. But in moving first as he did, BL took them by surprise.

The tension at this time was increased by the fact that we were now being followed—wherever we went, our footsteps were dogged by suspicious-looking characters. Their methods were extremely crude —they even dressed up as women, and sometimes pretended to hold drunken parties (together with dancing!) on the landing right outside our apartment in Potapov Street. And I learned that a microphone had been installed somewhere in the 'little' house in Peredelkino.

'Good day to you, microphone!' BL would say, bowing low to the wall, and hanging his cap on a nail next to the place where, as we discovered later, the microphone really had been hidden. Boria did not actually believe in it, but all the same, the mere thought that there might be one helped to create a feeling of being harassed on all sides, so we spoke mostly in whispers, frightened of our own shadows, and constantly glancing sideways at the walls—even they seemed hostile to us. Many people turned their backs on us and did not want to know us any more.

Two days before BL renounced the prize, on Monday, October 27, Ariadna and I went to see Bannikov, but both of us gained the firm impression that he had lost his nerve and wished to have nothing more to do with BL—he was clearly unhappy that we had come to see him. After we left, Ariadna went on at me for a long time for going in the first place—we should have had more sense! When we got to Potapov Street I could see our sleuths (some of them we already knew by sight) hanging about near the entrance. I decided there and then that it was time to try and save our letters and manuscripts, and also to burn certain things.

I told BL on the phone that I should be coming out to Peredelkino the next day. So the following day, Tuesday, October 28, Mitia and I put our papers in some bags and took them out to the Kuzmich house. BL arrived there very soon afterwards, and straightaway, still in the doorway, he began to speak in a trembling voice: 'Olia, I have to say something very important to you, and I hope Mitia will forgive me. I cannot stand this business any more. I think it's time to leave this life, it's too much. There's no way now for you to get out of it all. If you think we must stay together, then I'll write a letter, and we'll just sit here this evening, the two of us—and that's how they'll find us. You once said that eleven tablets of Nembutal is a fatal dose— well, I have twenty-two here. Let's do it. That's what the Lanns did, didn't they?★ . . . And it will cost them very dearly . . . It will be a slap in the face . . .'

Mitia, a well-behaved boy, overhearing the beginning of this extraordinary conversation, had immediately gone outside. Boria now ran after him: 'Mitia, forgive me, don't think too badly of me, my precious child, for taking your mother with me, but we can't live, and it will be easier for you after our death. You'll see what an uproar it will cause—they'll never hear the end of it. But we can't go on—what's happened already is enough. She can't live without me, and I can't live without her. So please forgive me. Now tell me, am I right or not?'

I remember that Mitia was as white as a sheet, but he replied stoically: 'You are right, Boris Leonidovich, Mother must do what you do.'

Sending Mitia out again to fetch a basket of wood chips, I now rushed to Boria and said: 'Wait, let's try and look at things more calmly, and find the courage to go on a little longer . . . tragedy may still turn into farce . . . and our suicide would suit them very well: they will say it shows we were weak and knew we were wrong, and they will gloat over us into the bargain! . . . You know how much you trust my sixth sense—let me try once again to go and find out what more they want from you and how they are thinking of dealing with you now. Only don't ask me where I mean to go—I am still not sure myself. And now just go back to your study and don't worry, and try to write a little. I'll find out what the position is, and if it's something we can laugh at, then better just laugh at it and bide our time . . . But if not, and I see there really is no way out, then I'll tell you honestly . . . and we'll put an end to it, we'll take the Nembutal. Only wait till tomorrow, don't do anything without me!'

When I read through these words of mine as I have put them down

★ A few days previously I had told him about the terrible suicide of Lann and his wife. Lann's real name was Lozman (Yevgeni Lvovich, 1896–1958); he was a literary scholar, the author of a historical novel *Old England*, and of books on Voloshin, Joseph Conrad and Charles Dickens. Tsvetayeva once said of him: 'An exasperating and delightful man! His poetry is quite alien to me, but what an avalanche!'

here I am astonished how feeble and unconvincing they sound. I suppose I must instinctively have spoken them in such a tone of voice that he was won over by them. At any rate, he agreed: 'Very well, go wherever it is today, and stay the night in Moscow. I will come out tomorrow morning early with this Nembutal, and we'll decide then. I cannot stand up anymore to this hounding.'

At that we parted. He went up the path towards the other house, turning round to wave back at me and Mitia as we trudged through the thick mud in the opposite direction: to Fedin's house. If I had told BL where I was going, he would never have agreed for anything in the world ...

There was slush and mud on the ground, and the roads were awash with a dirty-brown mixture of the two. A nasty autumn sleet was coming down. I couldn't help thinking of a passage in *Doctor Zhivago*:

It was a bleak, rainy afternoon with only two colours to it—wherever the light fell it was white, everywhere else it was black; and Yuri's mood was one of the same bleak simplification unsoftened by halftones.

Our clothes soaking wet and crumpled, our feet covered in mud, Mitia and I went into the hallway of Fedin's well-appointed house. For a long time his daughter Nina would not let us any further, saying that her father was ill and wanted to see no one. 'I am Ivinskaya, and he will be sorry if he does not see me now,' I replied. At this moment Fedin appeared on the landing above and shouted down to me: 'Come up, come up, for heaven's sake, Makarchik, come up!' (Once when we had both been on vacation at the *Izvestia* rest-home Adler, he had nicknamed me 'Makarchik', because every time something went wrong for me, I always quoted the Russian proverb: 'Every pine-cone falls down on poor Makar's crown'.) But suddenly he checked himself, put on a formal manner, and took me along to his study.

I told him BL was on the verge of suicide, and had just proposed this to me as a way out: 'BL does not know I have come to see you,' I added. 'You are an old friend of his and a man of intelligence—you must understand that with all this hue and cry going on, a word from you could be very important for him. So tell me: what do they still want from him? Do they really want him to commit suicide?'

Fedin went over to the window, and I thought I saw tears in his eyes at that moment.

But then he turned round: 'Boris Leonidovich has dug such an abyss between himself and us that it cannot be crossed,' he said with a sort of theatrical gesture. And then after a short pause, and in a completely different tone: 'You have told me a terrible thing. Can you repeat it in another place?'

'In hell to the devil himself, if needs be,' I replied. 'I do not wish to die myself, and even less to be witness to the death of BL. But all of you are driving him to suicide.'

'Just wait a moment, please. I am now going to make a phone call so you can see someone to whom you must tell everything you have just told me.' He called a number and spoke to Polikarpov—the same Polikarpov as ever was! 'Can you come to the Union of Writers at three tomorrow?' Fedin asked. 'Dmitri Alexeyevich will see you there, instead of at the Central Committee.'

'At the Union of Writers, the KGB, or the Central Committee,' I replied, 'it's all one to me. I'll be there.'

'You realize, don't you,' Fedin said, as he showed me out, 'that you must restrain him—he mustn't inflict a second blow on his country.'

This made it clear to me that they didn't want him to kill himself. Leaving dirty footmarks on Fedin's spotless parquet floor, Mitia and I left.

I know that later on Fedin described my visit and conversation with him as a wild gamble. But in fact I was prompted by the sixth sense which always guided me whenever BL was in danger (this was something Ariadna understood very well). To outsiders my actions sometimes seemed unbelievably stupid, but they were dictated by an instinct of self-preservation, and they did indeed preserve Boria. It was a matter of having faith in me.

When BL came to Potapov Street the next morning (Wednesday, October 29), I greeted him with the words: 'You may want to murder me, but I went to see Fedin.'

'Why to Fedin of all people, to Kostia Fedin who even puts his smile on as though it were an item of dress!' he replied. It turned out that the evening before BL had been to see Kornei Chukovski and had a long talk with him. This had cheered him up, and he was calmer now: 'Let's just wait and see what happens next!'

So that's what we decided—to wait and see . . .

BL took me in a taxi to the premises of the Union of Writers, where I was to meet Polikarpov, and went by himself back to Peredelkino.

Polikarpov was already waiting for me.

'If you allow Pasternak to commit suicide,' he said, 'you will be aiding and abetting a second stab in the back for Russia.' (Oh, these stabs in the back!) 'This whole scandal must be settled—which we will be able to do with your help. You can help him to find his way back to the people again. But if anything happens to him, the moral responsibility will be yours. Don't pay too much attention to all the shouting, just stay at his side and don't let him get silly ideas into his head...'

To my question about what was to be done in concrete terms, Polikarpov gave me to understand rather vaguely that BL 'must now say something'. His renunciation of the prize clearly wasn't enough, and they expected something else. But what? The next day I was to understand what it was. But for the moment this conversation with Polikarpov had somewhat calmed my fears. I had felt death was very close, but once I knew this was the last thing 'they' wanted, I was enormously relieved...

Feeling in a comparatively good mood, I hastened out to Peredelkino, where I had an excellent talk with Boria. I gave him a light-hearted account of my meeting with the high official, stressing the humorous side. 'We must certainly wait and see what happens next,' he said.

I now went straight back to Moscow—I had to set the children's mind at rest, and talk to Ariadna and Starostin. Boria kept ringing me up from Peredelkino. I was very tired, not having slept properly for several nights, and was beginning to see everything that was going on through a strange kind of haze. I was longing to have a good sleep that evening, and I asked the children not to disturb me.

But despite this, in a short while Mitia came and woke me up: 'Mother, Ariadna Sergeyevna says you must come to the phone at once.' 'I'm sleeping,' I answered. 'What the devil does she mean by it?' But, all the same, I went to the phone. 'How can you!' Ariadna said crossly, 'you went to bed too early!' When I retorted that I had done so because I was tired, she explained: 'You must switch on the television set immediately!'

Semichastny was just making his speech: '. . . in the shape of

Pasternak we have a mangy sheep . . . he has spat in the face of the people . . . even a pig does not do what he has done . . . He has befouled the place where he eats . . . Let him become a real émigré and betake himself to his capitalist paradise . . .'

So the whole thing had started up again with a vengeance! Again I would have to go into action, seeking advice and taking steps to try and defend us.

BL read Semichastny's nice remarks in *Komsomol Pravda* the next morning.

For a short time we now toyed with the idea of actually leaving the country—if they were telling us to get out, why not do so? The first to speak her mind was Ira: 'You should go,' she declared boldly, 'there's no reason not to!'

'Perhaps, perhaps I should,' BL agreed. 'And then I'll get you out through Nehru'. (We had just heard rumours that Nehru had supposedly announced his readiness to offer political asylum to BL.) And then he suddenly said to me: 'Perhaps we should go, yes?' There and then he sat down to compose a letter to the government. He wrote that since he was regarded as an émigré, he would like to be allowed to go, but at the same time he did not wish to 'leave hostages' behind him and therefore would like me and my family to be allowed to go with him as well.

When he had finished, he at once tore it up, and said: 'No, Olia, I couldn't go abroad even if they let us all out together! I have always dreamed of going to the West as though on holiday, but I couldn't possibly live like that day in day out. I must have the workaday life I know here, the birch trees, the familiar troubles—even the familiar harassments . . . and hope. I shall put up with what I have to suffer.'

It was thus a mood that lasted only a few moments. The question whether to go or not never seriously arose. BL had always thought of himself as a Russian, and deeply loved his country.

My Fault

On the morning of October 30, I went to Lavrushinski Street to consult Grigori Khesin, the head of the department for 'authors' rights'. We had always thought him a cultivated, agreeable person, and he seemed to be extremely well-disposed to BL, and to me as well. Whenever I came to his office to see him on business, he had always kissed my hand, put me in a comfortable chair, and asked me lots of questions—the epitome of kindness and readiness to be of service.

This time, alas, when my need of advice and help were greatest of all, Khesin greeted me icily. He was cold, formal, and aloof. He bowed stiffly and stared at me, waiting to hear what I had to say.

'Grigori Borisovich, I have come to ask your help. Tell me now, what are we to do! Yesterday I went to the Union of Writers, and was told they were very worried about BL, and that I must stay with him all the time. This made me begin to feel much calmer, but now suddenly there is this dreadful speech by Semichastny. What *are* we to do?'

'Olga Vsevolodovna,' Khesin replied, for some reason speaking very loudly, and carefully articulating every word, 'there is now no further advice for us to give you. I consider that Pasternak has committed an act of betrayal and become an instrument of the cold war, an internal émigré. There are certain things one cannot forgive —for the country's sake. No, I'm afraid I cannot give you any advice.'

Shaken by the change in Khesin's manner, I got to my feet and went out into the corridor, without saying goodbye, and slammed the door behind me. With unseeing eyes, I stared at some pictures on the bulletin board in the lobby, trying to calm down and pull myself together. And almost at that very moment I heard a pleasant, youthful voice behind me: 'Olga Vsevolodovna, please wait a moment—I was afraid you had gone already!'

It was one of the young lawyers in the office. Always referred to as 'Zorenka' (later I learned that his surname was Grimgolts), he was a handsome boy, a friend of one of Ira's teachers, Inessa Zakharovna. He had delicate, almost girlish features, innocent eyes, and was altogether beguiling in his appearance.

'I would do anything I can to help you,' said Zorenka. 'For me Boris Leonidovich is a saint! It's hard for you to understand the situation at the moment. Let's agree to meet somewhere so we can talk about it all.'

Overjoyed by this sudden offer of help, I gave him my mother's address in Sobinov Street* and suggested he come there in two hours' time.

He arrived on the dot.

'You must understand that I love Boris Leonidovich and that his name is holy for me,' were his opening words (how could I not take them on trust?), 'but there is no time to waste! The only advice I can give is that he should write a letter to Khrushchev—otherwise he may be expelled from the country, even though he has renounced the prize. I can help you draft the text of such a letter right now.'

Many years later I read somewhere: 'When a great moment comes and knocks on the door, the sound is at first no louder than the beating of your heart, and only the keenest of ears can make it out in time.' This was just such a moment. But I failed to distinguish it . . .

Appalled at the thought of BL being forcibly expelled—given his attachment to the habits of a lifetime it would certainly have killed him—I asked our well-wisher to compose a draft letter to Khrushchev and in the meantime phoned Ira at Potapov Street, asking her to get our friends together.

When I arrived home, they were all sitting there: Ira, Mitia, Koma, Ariadna. We discussed the letter at great length, arguing back and forth, until my ears began to ring. Ariadna talked about it for a long time, and Ira insisted that the letter must not be sent, that there was no need to express repentance in any shape or form.

It is clear now that this was the only right attitude to take. But at the time everything looked different, and even some people whose opinion I very much valued—such as Alexander Yashin and Mark Zhivov—urged the opposite view.† But the main point was how terrifying the whole situation had become: threatening letters, a student demonstration, rumours that the house in Peredelkino would be sacked, the foul abuse by Semichastny and threat of expulsion to

---

* In 1956 my mother married Sergei Stepanovich Bastrykin, and went to live with him in a large room on Sobinov Street.

† Zhivov called me on the phone and invited me to go and see him at his apartment (near Herzen Street), where I found him with Yashin. They both recommended that BL should give in and 'renounce the novel' since they felt that continued resistance on his part would lead to a new clamp-down on the writers.

the 'capitalist paradise'—all this filled me with alarm and had to be taken seriously. And then, I was quite simply afraid for BL's life.

It seemed clear to me that we had to give in, that there was no other way. I made up my mind. We re-worded the text provided by Zorenka, trying to make it sound more like Pasternak. Ira and Koma took it out to Peredelkino for his signature.

Looking back on it now, it seems monstrous that we should have made up this letter, before BL even had any idea of what was going on. But we were in a great hurry, and in the bedlam around us nothing seemed very extraordinary any more.

BL signed the letter, making only one change at the end. He also signed a few blank pages, in case I needed to make further revisions to the text. He sent them with a note in red pencil, saying: 'Olia, keep it all as it is, only if you can, write that I was born not in the Soviet Union, but in Russia.'

After all this, the final text of the letter read as follows:

Dear Nikita Sergeyevich,
I am addressing you personally, the C.C. of the C.P.S.S., and the Soviet Government.
From Comrade Semichastny's speech I learn that the government 'would not put any obstacles in the way of my departure from the USSR'.
For me this is impossible. I am tied to Russia by birth, by my life and work.
I cannot conceive of my destiny separately from Russia, or outside it. Whatever my mistakes and failings, I could not imagine that I should find myself at the centre of such a political campaign as has been worked up round my name in the West.
Once aware of this, I informed the Swedish Academy of my voluntary renunciation of the Nobel Prize.
Departure beyond the borders of my country would for me be tantamount to death and I therefore request you not to take this extreme measure against me.
With my hand on my heart, I can say that I have done something for Soviet literature, and may still be of service to it.
          B. Pasternak.

The next day (Friday, October 31), Ira and Nina Ignatyevna

Bam* took the letter to the Central Committee building on Old Square. They handed it in through a hatch, from which, as Ira told me, an officer and a soldier leaned out to look at them with great interest.

The Jesuitical trick of our persecutors had succeeded perfectly. If it had been made head on, any demand that BL recant would have been angrily rejected; but when an 'admirer' and 'well-wisher' advised him to do so, and we all backed him up, giving our blessing to the text he had foisted on us, it worked beautifully.

At the time when the Nobel Prize was awarded to another Russian writer—Alexander Solzhenitsyn—I was carried back again to those terrible days at the end of October 1958, a year that now seems so far away. It made me feel with particular keenness our own lack of resolve, perhaps even our folly, our failure to recognize the 'great moment', which instead turned into one of shame.

Looking back on it now, it is hard to say whether the renunciation of the prize was an act more of defiance or of faintheartedness. And it was certainly only a state of panic that could have allowed me not to see through Zorenka, and to draft the letter to Khrushchev after falling for such a cheap provocation.

If one tries to look for excuses (though there probably are none), then all one can say is that Solzhenitsyn was twenty years younger than BL at the time when he was awarded the prize—and also that he had been toughened, probably like no one else in the world, by the triple ordeal of four years of combat duty in the war, five years of forced labour in the camps, and cancer. How could Boris Pasternak, a typical member of the 'spineless' Russian intelligentsia, have been expected to behave comparably? It was at least something that he died in his own bed, not on the street at a tram stop, like the hero of his novel . . .

That letter should never have been sent—never! But we sent it. It was my fault.

---

* The widow of a well-known Soviet literary scholar S. Romov who was arrested in the purges of 1937 and died in prison. She edited the *Memoirs* of A. S. Alliluyeva (the sister of Stalin's wife who killed herself in 1932) which appeared in Moscow in 1946. We first met in 1955, when she came out with a mutual friend to see me in Peredelkino.

'Victory through renunciation'

Yes, it was my fault, and I cannot remain indifferent when the blame is put on the man who was dearer to me than anybody else. This is not only unreasonable, but simply unfair as well. Yet the injustice is done to him by no means infrequently and I should like to interrupt my story of the affair of the novel to tell of one actual instance, a particularly upsetting reflection on his memory that happened in quite recent times.

On one dark cold night in spring, at the beginning of the 'seventies, I left Leningrad for Moscow by train. Thanks to the efforts of my Leningrad friends I had been lucky enough to get a ticket on the de luxe 'Arrow', which is almost beyond the reach of ordinary Soviet citizens. The compartments in its 'international' coaches have only two berths and it is equipped with every comfort—lamps on the tables, a restaurant, and so forth. For ten minutes before the train left I stood in the corridor and joked through the window with my friends who were seeing me off. All I needed to complete my happiness was for another woman to share the compartment with me★. We would have put on our dressing gowns, dabbed cream on our noses, read a little, and gone to bed. But the fates willed otherwise. Glancing round, I glimpsed two men in the compartment where I had expected to travel in such bliss. Only the backs of their heads were visible—one was evidently seeing off the other, whose bald pate gleamed from the depths of the dimly-lit, velvet-upholstered lair. A little put out, I went along the corridor, looking into each compartment in the hope of finding another woman and arranging an exchange of berths. But, alas, the privileged persons about to journey to Moscow in this exclusive coach were all males. I said goodbye to my friends, and then waited for the man who was seeing the other one off to leave the compartment. Apologizing for keeping me from my seat, he left at the very last moment; he was carrying a violin case in his hands.

The other man rose to his feet as I came in. He was tall, his crumpled shirt was unbuttoned at the neck, and his tie askew. On the small table behind his back I could see black caviar sandwiches set out on a piece of newspaper, an empty champagne bottle lying on its side, and glasses with something still in them.

★ In the sleeping compartments of Soviet trains there is no segregation of the sexes. (Tr.)

Despite his venerable-looking bald pate, he was actually quite young and had a nice face with the slightly pouting lower lip of a naughty child, and grey eyes of the kind one refers to as 'innocent'—also like those of a child.

He greeted me as though I were an old friend who had suddenly dropped in on him out of the blue.

'Do please forgive me,' he said, helping me off with my coat, 'my friend and I didn't manage to have dinner—we had to dash here right after his performance. He's a very good musician, you know—the public love him. We scarcely made the train and had to have a bite to eat here . . . They have champagne in the buffet, would you like some?'

'I had a very good dinner, thank you,' I replied, trying to conceal my unhappiness. It was all too obvious that this was not someone who would quickly settle down and leave me in peace—and there was quite clearly no question of being able to swap him for a woman. I unpacked my things, and took out a magazine where a work by a well-known Soviet author was appearing in instalments.

'How can you possibly read such rubbish?' he asked. 'I never look at magazines like that—you know exactly what everything's going to be about! . . .'

This was how our conversation about literature began.

'Now the only modern authors I can read,' my travelling companion continued perkily, 'are those who are not published.'

'For example?' I asked.

'Well, Solzhenitsyn, for example! I rate him higher than Tolstoi. But you don't read him, I suppose? You think it would be wrong? You haven't read his latest things?'

He was clearly doing his best to be provocative, but when I assured him that I would not deny Solzhenitsyn's literary quality, and that I respected him as a writer, my new friend jumped up looking very pleased, and said: 'I say, that calls for a drink! I'll go and see what they have,' and he went along to the restaurant car. He came back carrying more caviar sandwiches and bottles of champagne in both hands.

'I'm called Slava*,' he now introduced himself. 'We may as well get acquainted, since we're going to be together in any case. Don't you think so?'

* The common short form for a number of Russian first names ending in -slav e.g. Vladislav. (Tr.)

'Of course!' I agreed. I had taken a great liking to Slava. He was the sort of person who wore his heart on his sleeve: spontaneous, frank, and trusting. Not only did he not hesitate to speak his mind, but he actually flaunted views which other people keep shamefacedly to themselves, even though they might in fact also share them.

'And I wanted to exchange you for a woman,' I now confessed, laughing, as we drank to each other from the cut-glass goblets provided on this train.

'What an idea! But it wouldn't have come off. I believe in fate.'

We sat up the whole night, drinking champagne and talking about Solzhenitsyn, and the people who supported him. We argued and even quarrelled. Looking back on our conversation, I now realize how Slava started dropping broad hints right at the beginning that he himself was Solzhenitsyn's main protector. But it was only in the morning as we were saying goodbye, and Slava—who was by now addressing me tenderly as Olenka—wrote down on a piece of paper his telephone number and full name (Mstislav Leopoldovich Rostropovich) that I suddenly realized the reason for many things. The freedom with which he expressed himself, the way he aired his opinions—this was something that came easily to him, as a natural right. He could do anything! What a fool I had been not to guess—and the fact that his cello was there on the luggage rack above his head left me with no excuse at all. I think that my response to certain things he said may also have led him to suspect who I was.

When we began to talk about what had happened to winners of the Nobel Prize, he was scathing and categorical, clearly identifying himself with Solzhenitsyn: 'He was not someone to disown himself, like Pasternak. Solzhenitsyn was simply indignant at such shameful, cowardly behaviour, at those idiotic letters of renunciation Pasternak allowed himself to write! One really mustn't be frightened of them—if you show you're frightened of them, then you're finished! If only you knew, Olenka, how Alexander Isayevich [Solzhenitsyn] condemned him for that! No, Alexander Isayevich is not one of your pitiful intellectuals. He really went to war on behalf of the truth, and knew how to fight for it! He was perfectly ready to die for it!'

To this I replied, unable to restrain my anger, that people always forgot at what period Pasternak's tragedy took place, and also that he was the first to tread the path now taken by all the others. It was good, I said, that Solzhenitsyn had friends and protectors who stood up for him. But who did Pasternak have? In those days it had been heroism merely to keep silent, and to speak out on his behalf would have meant being denounced as a 'cold warrior'—which was to be condemned to total ostracism.

'Now, who do you think Solzhenitsyn's friends are?' Slava asked, screwing up his eyes cannily.

'Well, for heaven's sake—there's Chukovski, Sakharov . . . and then, there's also Rostropovich . . .'

At this Slava burst out, quite beside himself: 'Ah, *also* Rostropovich, you say? Really now! Do you know that after Rostropovich had seen Solzhenitsyn only once at a recital in Ryazan, he invited him to come and stay in his home, and shared everything he had with him? And now he's not only going to get him a residence permit to live in Moscow, but permission to have a *dacha* there as well! He'll go right up to the people at the top and won't stop at anything! But what has Sakharov done?'

For a long time Slava went on heatedly like this about the friendship between Rostropovich and Solzhenitsyn—little did I know at the time that I was hearing about it from none other than Rostropovich himself . . .

I remember that I then told him, with equal vehemence, and clearly giving away my own involvement in Pasternak's 'disgrace', how the letter of repentance had been concocted by Polikarpov and myself from various genuine phrases of BL's to make it sound in character and like his style. BL, I said, had signed this letter out of inner weariness and pity for the frightened, disheartened women who trembled for his life . . . He had done it because he was so sorry for the people close to him who could be used as hostages, because he feared and worried for them so much. And then, I went on, it was pointless to compare him with a fighter like Solzhenitsyn who had gone through the school of the forced labour camps, and even survived cancer! BL's motive in signing the letter had been to protect and reassure others. Despite everything, however, he had left his novel behind to speak for him!

'Yes, I see . . .' Slava said thoughtfully. 'It was all because of women, naturally . . . God, these women! Well, of course, that gives me a rather different picture . . . But Solzhenitsyn would never have allowed himself to be run by women . . .'

He now began to tell me a long story about how he had brought in forbidden books by his favourite author through the Soviet customs, who were quite dumbfounded by the sheer brazenness of it. He was indeed capable of anything . . . But what had he actually achieved? . . .

Soon after this, I was able to get hold of what Solzhenitsyn himself had written about Pasternak in his autobiographical work, where he describes the effect on him of reading BL's letters* of 'repentance' in the newspapers. At that time Solzhenitsyn was still an obscure teacher of physics in a Ryazan secondary school—which did not prevent him from confidently considering the question of what *he* would do when he was awarded the Nobel Prize (he evidently had no doubts that this would happen):

I measured him [i.e. Pasternak] by my own aims, by my own criteria —and squirmed with shame for him, as though for myself: how could he have taken fright at abuse in the newspapers? How could he flinch before the threat of exile and humbly plead with the government, mumbling about his 'mistakes and failings', about his 'own fault' as regards the novel, renouncing his own ideas, his very spirit— simply in order not to be sent out of the country. And then all this about the 'glorious present', 'pride in the age I live in', and, of course, 'bright faith in the common future'. And this is not a professor being pilloried in some provincial university, but our Nobel Prize winner —in full view of the whole world! We really are hopeless! . . . Heavens, if you are called to battle—in such superb conditions, at that!—then go and serve Russia! I condemned him with harsh reproaches, unable to find any excuse for him. Already as a youth— and even more so as a dyed-in-the-wool *zek* [forced labour camp prisoner]—I had never been able to forgive or understand the putting of personal ties before duty.

Very well put—in form; but in substance strikingly unfair. It is unfair on two counts. In the first place, no allowances are made for the situation and the period in which Pasternak, by means of his novel, chose to engage in one of the most stirring contests to be fought in the middle of this century between the human spirit and

* Pasternak wrote a second letter to *Pravda*, described below, and this is the one quoted by Solzhenitsyn in his autobiographical work *The Oak and the Calf*. (Tr.)

tyrannical rule; in the second place, Solzhenitsyn did not understand the motives behind BL's signing of the letters of repentance.

But first a few words about the moral climate which had arisen by the end of 1946, when Pasternak finally decided to write the novel. In August of that year, not only writers but all thinking people had been shattered by the Party decree on the journals *Zvezda and Leningrad*.* The tone of the whole thing may be fully judged by a few such phrases as: 'The cheap literary scum Mikhail Zoshchenko', 'the disgusting thing *Before Sunrise*', 'the physiognomy of Akhmatova is well known', 'the questionable review by Yuri German of Zoshchenko's work', and so forth.

In this atmosphere of intellectual oppression, which was particularly hard to bear for people of a creative bent, in a situation in which 'literature does not . . . help to educate people but to bamboozle them with assurances no more truthful than statements such as "fire does not burn", or "you can't drown in the sea"', Pasternak remained himself and was utterly devoted in his writing to 'unwavering attachment to the facts', to historical truth.

Despite the times in which he lived, BL retained a boundless sense of his own inner freedom. The West German literary scholar Gerd Ruge was later to write of BL that he was 'the freest person with whom I have ever spoken.'

The very fact that in these conditions of lack of creative freedom BL continued his search, untrammelled by dogma, for truth, harmony, and beauty made him into a tragically isolated figure.

He was, of course, only a writer, not a politician. But disregarding the base political standards of the age, BL never sought easy ways out, and never curried favour with those in power. He had no time at all for the mawkish official rhetoric about the Motherland and the Party, or for all the immoderate bombast about 'victories', real or imagined, which many of his fellow writers indulged in without qualms.

Typical of these other writers was Alexei Tolstoi, whom Bunin described as a 'cynic fascinating in his candour, a clever rogue' possessing 'the great gift of being able to supply the literary market only with what would do well on it'.

In the worst months of the infamous year 1937, in those months when, in the words of Akhmatova,

* See footnote on p. 131. (Tr.)

The stars of death stood over us,
And Russia, guiltless, writhed
Under the crunch of bloodstained boots,
Under the wheels of Black Marias,*

Alexei Tolstoi often spoke on the radio and wrote in the newspapers, singing hymns of praise to the executioners and blackening the names of their victims. Here is just one example of his 'humanism'—very characteristic for the atmosphere in the literary and political world of those days:

Stavrogin in Dostoyevski's *Possessed* . . . is the prototype of those of our contemporaries who harbour scepticism and double standards in their breasts—those who are 'a hundred percent loyal' at public meetings or at their place of work, but at home are mangy wolves pining for the forest . . . This is a fertile breeding ground for Trotsky-ism, treachery, and espionage . . . any citizen who does not love his Motherland is a Trotskyist, saboteur, and spy.

And yet, this was the same man who in the early days of the Soviet régime had written to Bunin in Paris: 'the whole of life [in Russia] is built on sand, on politics, on a gamble—the Revolution was simply ordered from above.' But not long afterwards, Tolstoi, now a Soviet citizen, could boast to Bunin on meeting him in a Paris street: 'I have a whole estate in Tsarskoye Selo, and three motor cars . . .' A year after this meeting we find him safeguarding his estate and motor cars in the simplest possible fashion— by singing the praises of the terror against the people of his own country, by identifying love for the Motherland with love for its rulers, and by threatening all who refused to love them with the firing squad. Worst of all was his suggestion that the whole nation constituted a 'breeding ground for espionage'—by this invitation to universal suspicion, denunciation, and betrayal he was corrupting his fellow citizens for the sake of his own well-being. Anybody who cares to look at the thirteenth volume of Tolstoi's works can read to his heart's content all the fairytales he concocted to order about 'germs in tin cans' supposedly placed in railway trains by 'enemies of the people'. This and similar fantasies were written not by some oaf devoid of talent and education, but by a Russian count.

* From *Requiem*, translated by Stanley Kunitz. (Tr.)

Many other writers were no less eager to demonstrate at every moment of the day their patriotism, loyalty, and solidarity with the 'people'.

Against this background BL's behaviour stood out in remarkable contrast. I have already described how he refused to sign a statement of approval for the latest death sentence, and how he subsequently wrote to Stalin saying he could not set himself up in judgment over others. And in a letter to someone else he wrote: 'As the years go by . . . I live more and more as though in an attic . . . I feel ashamed that we still walk around, converse, and smile . . .'

Such, then, was the difference in attitude of two Russian writers towards the same national catastrophe—the Great Terror. One displayed the greatest lack of conscience and cynicism, acclaiming the executioners in order to keep his estate, motor cars, and social status. The other maintained a stubborn silence: all the forces of brutish coercion would not induce him to lie in support of injustice. But when he found it impossible to go on being silent, he bravely spoke the truth, knowing full well the risk not only to himself, but also to the life and freedom of his family.

The first was declared a *national* writer and showered with prizes, medals, and material rewards. The second was denounced as an *anti-national* writer, a self-seeker, an 'internal émigré', and was finally hounded 'like a beast at bay' . . .

BL could not be forgiven for his unprecedented act—for passing, by virtue of his astoundingly emancipated spirit, beyond enforced silence, to the free literary expression of *Doctor Zhivago*. He wrote it, after all, at a time when literature was still totally suffocated by falsehood.

From 1928 to 1940 Mikhail Bulgakov wrote his novel, *The Master and Margarita*, but this became known only towards the end of the 1960s. He wrote it in secret, and in literary circles there was not even a whisper of it. The novel was published twenty-six years after his death (and then, at first, with extensive cuts).

BL, on the other hand, from the end of 1946 and during all the following years of Stalin's mass terror, was not only not afraid to write *Doctor Zhivago* openly, but even read chapters from it to groups of listeners, never particularly concerning himself as to who exactly was present. The consequences were not long in making themselves felt. But even the shock of my arrest and imprisonment did not make him more cautious or prevent him from going on with the novel. My interrogator had pages from the first part lying on the desk in front of him—and he was extremely interested in reports by informers about readings from the novel which had taken place in certain Moscow homes...

One must not forget that in those years BL was not only the first, but perhaps the only professional writer in the Soviet Union to do something of this kind. In this sense—as indeed Solzhenitsyn allows in his autobiographical work—BL was the one who 'opened the way for literature and blocked the path of its enemies', and who 'looked on present reality from the point of view of eternity'.

At the same time one must also bear in mind that he realized, of course, that things would not end with my imprisonment, and that the day would come when the persecution against him would be launched head-on, in a form that would brook no argument. Instead of argument there would be primitive words of command perfectly accessible to the mind of a dog: 'Go for him—he's not one of us!' As we know, that day did indeed arrive.

It seems to me, therefore, that when Solzhenitsyn—who is also, furthermore, not a delicately nurtured Russian intellectual, but as he puts it himself, a 'dyed-in-the-wool *zek*'—came into literature years later, after the death of both Stalin and BL, he was treading a path already opened up by BL in very much more terrible times.

Solzhenitsyn has no need, therefore, to 'squirm with shame' on behalf of the man who long before him braved those terrifying, inhuman forces, so brutish, pitiless, and crushing, and was beyond any doubt the first to do so.

So much for the situation before and during the actual writing of the novel.

Now as for the later aspect of the question—BL's renunciation of the Nobel Prize and his letters of 'repentance'—Rostropovich and many others consider this to have been a defeat for Pasternak. But he himself looked at it differently—as comes out most clearly of all in a letter he wrote to Jacqueline de Proyart in France:

... they are trying to make life hard for us in every way—sometimes by means of direct threats, sometimes by imposing obnoxious restrictions on us; however, not only do we rise above it all, but we are even immensely helped by this hostile force, which afflicts and impedes us, because it is none other than this that preserves every-thing most alive, valid and deeply felt about our victory—without this it might easily degenerate into an abstract nothing, into high-sounding phrases . . . I do so wish to tell you how marvellous everything is, and how full of the future, even at this late hour, a few steps, possibly, from the end!

Yes, he understood victory or defeat in this unequal contest mainly in terms not of external appearances and prestige, but of the final results. If I, Ariadna Efron, Koma Ivanov, and Ira had not drafted those letters of 'repentance' and put them in front of him for his signature, he would never have signed them. This is precisely why the idea was broached by an *agent provocateur*—so that it would come to BL through us, and he would sign because of our fears for him, and because of our influence with him.

And the pressure on us was suffocating. It has now been admitted even in a Soviet publication that in those days Pasternak '. . . thanks to the long-standing efforts of our local political Philistines, was caught in a thick web of falsehood, incomprehension, and slander' (*Literary Georgia*, No. 11, 1972, p. 22). In such conditions it was easiest for him to sign anything I brought him, almost without looking at it, as long as he and I were left in peace. When all is said and done, it is true, as someone has put it, that 'each of us has the right to his own, personal Golgotha, but nobody is entitled to drag others along to it as well.' This was why BL decided not to leave for the West, abandoning us all as hostages to 'Golgotha' here.

So he simply signed the letters I brought to him. He did it all the more easily for having not the slightest doubt as to his ultimate victory. The main thing was that he had already accomplished his aim: the novel had been written and published, and was being read if not in his own country, at least in the whole world outside. The deed was done, and *Doctor Zhivago* had been launched round the planet on its 'journey into space'—to use BL's own expression. But even apart from this, he already understood at the time something now clear to almost everybody else as well, namely that these letters of repentance would reflect only on those who extorted them from him. He was later to put it quite clearly and unambiguously: '. . . when a person one suspects is being martyred says that he is flourishing one begins to wonder whether he may not have been forced to make such statements by the torments inflicted on him.' That is just how it was.

Marina Tsvetayeva once talked in a letter about one of the ways in which an intellectual may achieve victory—a way she called 'victory through renunciation'. This was a case in point.

Yes, dear Alexander Isayevich and Mstislav Leopoldovich, you are mistaken in thinking that his renunciation of the Nobel Prize and the signing of those letters meant surrender on BL's part. Today, in the 'seventies, it is already clear to everyone that this was a true 'victory through renunciation'.

'Manikins and Men'

Now came the culminating moment in the 'novel about a novel'—Friday, October 31. The action unfolded on several stages simultaneously: at Film House, the Central Committee, Peredelkino, Potapov Street, in cars. It is impossible to follow them all at once, so first: Film House on Vorovski Street...

Here on that day a general meeting of the writers of Moscow took place. The aim was to 'rubber-stamp' in the name of the whole literary community of the capital the decision taken on October 27 to expel BL from the Union of Writers.

Apart from this—and more importantly—it had been decided somewhere at higher levels that since BL found the idea of leaving Russia intolerable, they would 'put the screws' on him even more by threatening to strip him of his Soviet citizenship. It was to set the usual machinery of 'public approval' in motion that this meeting had been called in Film House.

Needless to say, neither BL nor I attended it, but there were people present who took notes and later sent them to us.*

The chairman was Sergei Sergeyevich Smirnov, who was said to be a decent enough person in the sense that he would never have done anything vile deliberately and on his own initiative—but he was always ready to do whatever was ordered by higher authority. He opened the meeting by reading out the text of a letter approving

---

* A verbatim transcript of the proceedings at this meeting has also been published in the Russian-language periodical *Novy Zhurnal* (New Journal), New York, No. 83, 1966. (Tr.)

Pasternak's expulsion from the Union of Writers and demanding even sterner measures:

. . . a group of Moscow writers, indignant at Pasternak's behaviour, have written this letter with a view to its publication in the newspapers, and it has been signed by a large number of Moscow writers [*reads the list of names*] . . . But the question arises: why has it been signed only by a section of the Moscow writers? Surely the Moscow branch as a whole would like to express its opinion? . . .

. . . There is no poet more remote from the people . . . he was fated to have only a narrow circle of readers . . . And this narrow circle of admirers gradually put a halo round his head, and the legend of Pasternak became very widespread among us. It was the legend of a poet who was completely un-political . . . among Pasternak's friends were people who said that whenever his name was mentioned at meetings, everybody should get to their feet . . . This legend has now been exposed and finally laid to rest by Pasternak's novel and by his behaviour . . . *Doctor Zhivago* is a highly political work . . . Pasternak sent a telegram to the Swedish Academy saying: 'Infinitely grateful, touched, proud, surprised, overwhelmed'. And in an interview with foreign journalists he said: '. . . I am happy . . . I should like to go to Stockholm for the prize . . .' . . . Note what company this puts him in: the reactionary French writer Camus, Winston Churchill . . .

Last Saturday students from the Literary Institute came to the Union of Writers with posters demanding that the Judas be expelled from the USSR. On Monday, October 27, there was a joint meeting of the Presidium of the Board of the Union of Writers of the USSR, the Bureau of the Organizational Committee of the Union of Writers of the RSFSR, and the Presidium of the Board of the Moscow branch of the Union of Writers. Pasternak was invited to attend, but he did not do so, although he had come to Moscow from Peredelkino, and sent a letter instead.

[Smirnov then read out the letter summarized in an earlier chapter but did so very rapidly and indistinctly, as though he was loath to read something from such a contemptible person—and also, perhaps, in order to make it impossible for anyone present to note it down verbatim. He replied to some of BL's points, including his offer to donate the prize money to the Peace Committee.]

He is trying to buy himself off. Fedin once tried for four days to get him to sign the Stockholm Peace appear* . . . Readers came to the house of the traitor Knut Hamsun† and threw his books over the wall . . . When I finished reading this novel, I somehow couldn't help agreeing with what Comrade Semichastny said at the plenum of the Central Committee of the Komsomol. Perhaps his words—the comparison with a pig—were a little harsh, but they were in fact to the point . . . I particularly liked the second part of Comrade Semichastny's remarks in which he said that Pasternak should be transformed from an internal émigré into one in the real sense . . . We should approach the government with the request that Pasternak have his Soviet citizenship taken away from him. [*Loud applause*] There are rumours that he has renounced the Nobel Prize, but we know nothing of this‡ . . . abroad they have published a statement from him saying: 'In view of the reaction of Soviet society I am forced to give up the prize . . .'

For forty years now this hidden enemy, full of hatred and spite, has lived among us, and we have shared our bread with him.§ To my mind it would even have been better if he had first joined the ranks of the Soviet Union's open enemies, and then been awarded a prize . . .

Lev Oshanin [reading from a piece of paper]:
Pasternak has been an object of interest to our enemies. The award of the Nobel Prize is a cunning, calculated blow . . . When in 1945 members of the Union of Writers were being presented with the medal 'For Valiant Work during the Fatherland War', he was invited to come and get his, but he said, 'Oh, perhaps I'll send my son for it . . .' . . . Andronikov spent many hours trying to get him to

* See footnote on p. 245. (Tr.)

† Norwegian novelist (1859–1952) who gave his support to the Quisling régime during the Second World War. (Tr.)

‡ Two days before this, on October 29, the world press had published BL's telegram renouncing the prize, and on the same day he had sent a telegram informing the Union of Writers of it, yet the chairman of this meeting—one of such great consequence—could say he 'knew nothing of it'.

§ During the campaign against him, BL was several times reproached in this way for the bread he ate, and once he said to me: 'Have they forgotten the proverb "Eat bread and salt, but speak the truth"?' [Bread and salt are the traditional symbols of hospitality in Russia. Tr.]

sign the Stockholm Peace Appeal . . . I regard him as an internal
émigré . . . Pasternak is the clearest example of a cosmopolitan in our
midst . . . We do not need a citizen like this!

K. L. Zelinski [without notes]:
I have read *Doctor Zhivago* carefully, with pencil in hand . . . I felt as
though I had been spat upon . . . There is a mass of religious stuff . . . I
had respected Pasternak as a poet . . . in the West his name has
become a synonym of the cold war . . . His picture is printed on the
front pages of [Western] newspapers together with that of another
traitor—Chiang Kai-shek . . . The award of the Nobel Prize to
Pasternak [is compared in one American paper to] a literary atom
bomb, a slap in the face for the Soviet Government.

In Naples there was a meeting of writers from twenty-two
countries. Nobody mentioned Pasternak's name—it would have been
the same as making a rude noise in company . . . It is the people round
him who are to blame—they created the cult of his personality . . .
Once, because of an article I wrote criticizing Pasternak, V. V.
Ivanov, the deputy editor of *Questions of Linguistics*★, refused to shake
hands with me . . .

We must say to Pasternak: Go, receive your thirty pieces of silver
over there! We do not need you here today, as we build the world
to which we have devoted our lives!

V. Gerasimova:
As a former member of the Komsomol, I cannot excuse that scene
where Doctor Zhivago shoots at a tree instead of at the enemy . . .
He is Doctor Mertvago†, not Doctor Zhivago . . . Not he, but
Makarenko, Timiriazev, are the flower of the intelligentsia . . .

V. Pertsov:
Even though a week has gone by, indignation has still not died down
. . . I was particularly struck by one thing in Pasternak's letter: he
regards it as a mitigating circumstance that he finished *Doctor Zhivago*
at the time when Dudintsev's novel came out. But these are quite
different things!

★ This is 'Koma' Ivanov. See Biographical Guide. (Tr.)
† A pun: Zhivago is derived from *zhivoi* ('alive'); *mertvy* means 'dead'. (Tr.)

I met Pasternak in the company of Mayakovski . . . I never sang his praises, but neither did I think him capable of such a low act . . .

Apart from some young people of over-refined taste, nobody reads Pasternak . . . Pasternak is an individualist . . . His literary credo may be defined as 'eighty thousand miles round his own navel' . . . As a young man I published an article on Pasternak under the title 'An Invented Figure'—thereby provoking the anger of Aseyev and Shklovski . . . I think he is not only an invented figure, but a vile one too . . . He has published his autobiography[36] in Paris. I know nothing more outrageous than what he says here about Mayakovski . . . He wrote a letter to Stalin thanking him for having said of Mayakovski that he was 'the best, most talented poet of our epoch . . .'*

What are we to do with Mister Pasternak? I think Comrade Semichastny is right . . . Let him clear off over there. It is hard for me and many other comrades to imagine that such people can live in the writers' colony [at Peredelkino]. I cannot conceive of continuing to have Pasternak as a neighbour . . . He should not be included in the census about to be taken.

We were late in publishing the letter from the editors of *Novy Mir*. When it became known that he had passed the novel to a bourgeois publisher . . . the letter should have been printed then, and we would have been in a better position to engage in a dialogue with the bourgeois world about it . . . We must remember this mistake . . . Let us try to do things properly.

A. Bezymenski:

. . . Today our long argument with Pasternak is over . . . Already in 1934 a group of proletarian writers rose up in arms against Bukharin for saying that everyone should take their cue from Pasternak . . . Now, by his vile novel and his behaviour Pasternak has placed himself outside Soviet literature and outside Soviet society. [At this point Bezymenski went into ecstasies over Semichastny's speech.] Pasternak is an internal émigré, so let him become a real émigré, and clear off to his capitalist paradise. I am convinced that no obstacles will be put in his way either by the public or the government, but that, on the contrary, it will be felt that his departure from our midst can only clear the air . . . Weeds should be uprooted!

* Isn't it strange that this 'outrageous' passage should have been published nine years later in *Novy Mir*?

A. Sofronov [speaking from notes]:

. . . even in Chile, one writer said to us: 'It's odd the way you're dealing with Pasternak—he's your enemy, after all' . . . Out of our country with him! [Sofronov spoke badly and incoherently, using only newspaper clichés.]

S. Antonov:

. . . The prize is for forty or fifty thousand dollars. Nobel would turn over in his grave if he knew where his money had gone . . . and it is a great pity that in 1958 it is Pasternak who has been chosen as a puppet to carry out a dirty anti-Soviet task! . . . The decision we have taken to expel Pasternak from the Union of Writers was very much over-due—it could have been done a year ago . . .

B. Slutski:

A poet should seek recognition from his own nation, not from its enemies. A poet should look to his native country for glory, not to a rich transatlantic uncle . . . All the Swedish Academicians know about our country is that it was the scene of the hated Battle of Poltava*, and of the even more hated October Revolution . . . The prize was awarded to Pasternak only out of hatred for us . . . Pasternak is the winner of the Nobel Prize against communism . . .

G. Nikolayeva:

. . . I am among those people who accepted and liked some aspects of Pasternak's work—what he has written about nature, about Lenin . . . I thought he might find a new path . . . But the story of Pasternak is a story of treachery . . . With *Doctor Zhivago* he spits in the face of the people . . . I had cherished the hope that he might find the courage to confess his error . . . The letter from *Novy Mir* is too lenient . . . I support the view that there is no place for this person in the Soviet land . . .

V. Soloukhin [quoting some of Pasternak's verse from memory and drawing conclusions from it]:

. . . the sense of all these lines is that a real poet must be in opposition

---

* At which Charles XII of Sweden was crushingly defeated by Peter the Great in 1709. (Tr.)

to the society in which he lives! For this reason *Doctor Zhivago* is not something exceptional in Pasternak's work as a whole. Everything here is all of a piece . . . it is the deliberate championship of individualism to be expected from an internal émigré . . . The entire book is a weapon in the cold war against communism . . .

When our Party criticized the revisionist policies of Yugoslavia, the wise Mao Tse-tung* said that these policies were needed by the Americans only as long as Yugoslavia remained in our camp. Pasternak will be needed 'over there' only as long as he continues to live here. But when he becomes an émigré in actual fact, he will cease to be of use to them, and they will soon forget him . . . He will be able to tell them nothing of interest, and after a month they'll throw him away like an empty egg-shell or a lemon which has been squeezed dry. This will be the main punishment for the act of betrayal he has committed.

S. Baruzdin:
Comrades! Tomorrow a week will have passed since our people learned about the Pasternak case . . . Our people never knew Pasternak as a writer, but now they know him as a traitor . . . This is the most shameful thing about Pasternak . . . There is a good Russian proverb: 'You can't change the ways of a dog!' It seems to me that the best thing is for Pasternak to clear out of our country as soon as possible. [*Applause*]

L. Martynov [reading his whole speech from notes, and systematically mispronouncing BL's name as 'Pasterniak']:
. . . there is no conflict of opinion among those present here as to Pasternak's behaviour . . . No living person who wants a better future is on the side of the author of *Doctor Zhivago* . . . So let Pasternak stay with those spiteful ill-wishers of ours who have curried favour with him by awarding him a prize, while progressive mankind is and will remain with us.

[Martynov also said that in Italy, in Rome, most people present in a crowded hall had greeted the Soviet view of the Pasternak affair with applause, and only one person had spoken against it.]

* It would be interesting to ask Soloukhin what he thinks *now* of the 'wisdom' of Mao Tse-tung.

B. Polevoi:

'An Anti-Communist in the Communist camp' says 'The Voice of America', 'The Greatest Blow at Communism' is the headline in the West German magazine *Der Stern* . . . The cold war has also produced its traitors, and in my view Pasternak is in essence a literary Vlasov.[37] General Vlasov was sentenced to shooting by a Soviet court [voice from the floor: 'to hanging!'] . . . I think that a traitor in the cold war should also have the greatest possible suitable punishment meted out to him. We must say to him, in the name of the Soviet public: 'Out of our country, Mister Pasternak! We do not wish to breathe the same air as you.' [*Applause*]

S. Smirnov:

There is a proposal that we bring the discussion to a close. The following comrades have put themselves down to speak: Y. Dolmatovski, S. Vasilyev, M. Lukonin, G. Serebriakova, P. Bogdanov, P. Arski, P. Luknitski, S. Sorin, V. Inber, A. Amegova, V. Dudintsev, R. Azarkh, D. Kugultdinov (on behalf of the students of the higher literary courses).

V. Soloukhin:

I propose that Dudintsev speak, since in his letter Pasternak has equated his novel with Dudintsev's.

Smirnov said this would be undemocratic and put it to the vote. The majority was for ending the proceedings. The text of the resolution was then read out and, after some argument about wording, was passed unanimously. The *Literary Gazette* published the resolution under the heading 'The Voice of the Moscow Writers':

. . . Boris Pasternak . . . an aesthete and decadent in love with himself . . . an enemy of what is holy for all of us . . . betrayal of Soviet literature, of the Soviet land, and of all Soviet people . . . a dirty lampoon . . . has stretched out his hand for his thirty pieces of silver . . . the meeting requests the Soviet Government to strip B. Pasternak of Soviet citizenship . . . all who value the ideals of progress and peace will never shake hands with him, as a man who has betrayed his Motherland and its people!

The claim that the resolution was passed 'unanimously' was not entirely correct. I could mention the names of writers who, while not having sufficient courage to stand up for BL, at least had enough to get up while the vote was being taken and go out into the buffet, the toilet, or any old place just to avoid taking part in this shameful mockery of a trial conducted by ignorant literary bureaucrats.

It was probably such people Yevtushenko had in mind when shortly afterwards he wrote the following lines:

> ... when they appeared as false accusers
> who should themselves have been arraigned,
> you were too kind to add your voices
> and made off to the lavatories.
> But later, how surprised you were
> when—to discourage such unwisdom—
> like so many blundering seals,
> you yourselves were knocked off one by one.

At that time Yevtushenko was secretary of the Komsomol organization of the Union of Writers. Before the meeting he was summoned, together with the Party Secretary Sytin, to the First Secretary of the Moscow City committee of the Komsomol and urged at great length to speak. But he did not do so.

Ilya Ehrenburg (as his secretary told BL and me) insisted on answering the phone himself during those days of the witchhunt, and when he was invited to various meetings in connection with it, he replied (not bothering to disguise his voice): 'Ilya Grigoryevich has gone away and will not be back for some time'. This was his way of dealing with the situation—and it was by no means the least risky for those times.

Re-reading the transcript of the writers' meeting I am reminded of Yuri Zhivago's diary, which he called 'Manikins and Men' and which consisted of 'prose and verse, and every kind of odds and ends coloured by his feeling that half the world round him had ceased to be itself and was playing goodness only knew what part'.

But I can see quite clearly that there has been some progress since the year 1920, to which the diary relates: not just half, but the majority of the speakers were 'manikins', and were not saying what they really thought. How can one imagine that all those who spoke, eagerly offered to speak, or merely applauded, really believed that

280 A CAPTIVE OF TIME

Pasternak was a traitor, or that the novel was a piece of hackwork, etc.? No, I have a rather better opinion of them. They *understood* what it was all about, but the 'rules of the game' overrode any kind of understanding.

Almost none of them, needless to say, had read the novel, and most of those who spoke either hoped to advance their careers through this sordid affair or, with the Stalin terror still fresh in their minds, were simply frightened and wanted to save their own skins. ('The great misfortune, the root of all the evil to come, was the loss of faith in the value of personal opinions. People imagined that it was out of date to follow their own moral sense, that they must all sing the same tune in chorus, and live by other people's notions, the notions which were being crammed down everybody's throat. And there arose the power of the glittering phrase . . .')*

Later on another writer,† in another context, said: 'It is a short-sighted calculation that one can live always putting one's faith in force, never listening to the voice of conscience.' Not everybody found it easy to ignore their own moral instinct, to disregard their qualms of conscience. Vera Figner's daughter, Marina, has described how Sergei Smirnov told her while they happened to be travelling together on the Moscow-Leningrad train: 'The blot on me can never be washed away. It will be with me for the rest of my life.'‡

I do not bear grudges against people, and it would be possible to forgive someone who had been forced to stoop to a despicable action by the threat of imprisonment or loss of livelihood. But everybody who heard Smirnov on that black Friday remembers the nasty, mocking tone in which he read out BL's letter, clearly trying to give a malicious imitation of his way of speaking . . . Smirnov may have had no option but to be chairman of the meeting, but nobody can have forced him to make fun of the letter and its author in such a fashion.

After the meeting he published an article entitled 'The Philosophy of Betrayal' in the journal *Agitator*, No. 22, 1958, where he expanded on his opening speech and, among other things, described Albert

* *Doctor Zhivago*, Chapter 13. (Tr.)

† Solzhenitsyn (Tr.)

‡ This expression of 'penitence' did not, however, prevent Smirnov, many years later, from proposing the expulsion of Okudzhava from the Union of Writers.

Camus, who had sent a telegram congratulating BL, as a 'writer of Fascist tendencies with whom . . . no decent French writer would shake hands'.

In 1970, Yevgeni Yevtushenko happened to be in a small town called Leticia, in the Colombian jungle, where most of the inhabitants make their living by hunting crocodiles. He was astonished to see here, among the books of a local self-educated poet Díaz, a copy of *Doctor Zhivago* in Spanish. But the most extraordinary thing of all was that the volume had been touchingly inscribed for Díaz, also in Spanish, by the only Soviet writer to visit Colombia before Yevtushenko—Sergei Smirnov . . . 'But', said Yevtushenko, taken aback, 'Smirnov presided over the meeting at which Pasternak was expelled from the Union of Writers!' At first Díaz wanted to tear out the page with the words written by Smirnov, but after thinking about it, said: 'In that case, perhaps my copy with this inscription is unique and acquires a special value.'

I was acquainted with Boris Slutski and recognized him as a poet, though it was said that he did not like BL's poetry. BL once told Yevtushenko in a half-joking way how, after he had read 'Bacchanalia' at the Ivanovs, Slutski had come up and made the strange comment: 'Well now, it's not the worst of your poems.'

But nobody expected Slutski to play such a low trick on BL. Indeed, Yevtushenko, as he sat with Vinokurov at the back of the meeting in Film House, was convinced that Slutski would speak in defence of BL and was worried at the possible consequences to Slutski himself. For this reason he said to him in the interval: 'Be careful, Boris.' 'Don't worry,' Slutski replied, 'I shall know how to make my point in the right way.'

Everybody now knows what his 'point' was. According to Yevtushenko this speech caused Slutski enormous distress—until then his reputation had been unsullied and nothing like this had ever happened to him before. One person, it is said, demonstratively returned a hundred roubles he had borrowed from Slutski, almost literally throwing the money at him—he didn't want to be under any obligation to him.

Ariadna Efron, describing Slutski's remorse, told us how indignant she felt when he came out to see her in Tarusa after the infamous meeting, and wept. But he apparently got no sympathy from her and she angrily cut short his tale of woe.

This act of Slutski's plunged him into a deep crisis during which he was unable to work.

Many other active participants at that meeting would give anything if the whole affair could be consigned to oblivion—particularly such of them as understand that Pasternak's name has in no way grown dimmer while those who hounded him are shown up in an even more unflattering light by the passage of time.

To Nikita Sergeyevich

To continue with the story of that very long Friday, October 31, 1958. Exhausted by the stirring events of the previous day and the business of writing the letter to the Central Committee, I had again got to bed late the night before and slept badly. On the Friday afternoon I therefore went to my mother's apartment in Sobinov Street to try and get a little sleep. But it was a vain hope. Soon my mother came and woke me: 'You're wanted on the phone—they say it's from the Central Committee, on a very important matter.'

I had to get up. It turned out to be Khesin on the line. He spoke in an excited, friendly tone—as though that last conversation, after which I had left and slammed the door behind me, had never taken place: 'Olga Vsevolodovna, my dear, you're a good girl. They have received the letter from BL and everything will be all right, just be patient. What I have to say is that we must see you straightaway—we will come right along now.'

'I don't even want to talk with you, Grigori Borisovich,' I answered with irritation. 'It's very strange to hear you approaching me like this. At the most difficult moment for me you showed what sort of a friend you are! I can have nothing to do with you any more.'

After a long pause Khesin said he was handing the receiver to Polikarpov.

'Olga Vsevolodovna,' I heard Polikarpov say in an affable tone of voice. 'We must see you. We'll drive over to Sobinov Street now, you put on a coat and come down, and we'll go out together to Peredelkino: we must bring Boris Leonidovich to Moscow, to the Central Committee, as soon as possible.'

The letter addressed to Khrushchev had been delivered to the

Central Committee only two hours previously and here they were already summoning BL to the Central Committee, as though it had all been prepared beforehand, and they had only been waiting for the letter.

My first thought was to find Irina and get her to race out to Peredelkino ahead of us to warn BL that they were coming from the Central Committee to fetch him—and, even more important, to assure him that the worst was over and the rest could be regarded as mere farce. I realized that with the letter we had passed the climax and would now have an easy passage. All that remained was the formality of a 'personal talk'. With whom? There seemed no doubt that if Polikarpov was going to Peredelkino to fetch him, it must mean he would be received by Khrushchev himself.

I got through to Ira on the phone, and she agreed to go—so I would have to play for time a little to enable her to carry out her errand. But soon after we spoke I heard a car sounding its horn out-side—a black government ZIL* stood at the gate in the street down below with Polikarpov and Khesin inside.

I came down and told them I still had to get something, and went back in to my mother for a little while—all in order to give Ira a head start.

But it was hopeless. Our limousine went out along the special lane for government cars and did not stop at the lights. We drove at top speed to the turn-off for Peredelkino with scarcely a single halt.

On the way Khesin started whispering to me: 'You never know who's an enemy and who's a friend. You never know—you see it was I who sent Zorenka to help you . . .'

I simply gasped. So that was it! Not content with BL's renuncia-tion of the prize, they had wanted publicly to humiliate him as well— this was, after all, what a letter of this kind amounted to. The only problem had been: how to get him to sign it? They knew BL was stubborn and incapable of acting on orders. So they had found a way through me, taking advantage of my fears and thoughtlessness. Knowing that no official person would ever have won me round, they had put this 'nice boy', an 'admirer' of Pasternak, onto me, and it had worked.

* Largest Soviet car produced by the Likhachev works (formerly Stalin works, when the car was known as ZIS. (Tr.)

Without replying to Khesin, I leaned forward to Polikarpov and began to say something to him in a deliberately loud voice.

'We're now relying entirely on you,' Polikarpov said, turning round to me with a smile. 'You must set his mind at rest. The government will give him a reply to his letter in a little while. There mustn't be a word out of place while we're there. You mustn't make any more trouble now. At the moment the main thing is to get him out of Peredelkino—I only hope and pray he won't refuse to come with us.'

When I later went over in my mind all the events of that Friday, I was struck by how afraid they had been that BL might not go with them. Given such a superiority of forces, not every commander in the field would have prepared a military operation with as much care as they did this business of getting Pasternak to the Central Committee.

Our first stop was at the 'Fadeyev tavern', which was right near our house on the main road. There were already some cars parked there, with G. Markov, Voronkov, and yet others standing next to them (the forces they had mustered!). Polikarpov said I must transfer to another car and drive on, while he would wait near the tavern. As soon as he saw me coming back in the direction of Moscow with BL, he would follow behind. The plan he suggested was that Ira should go into the house and ask BL to come outside and join me. I was then to persuade him to go to the Central Committee, after which we would drive to my apartment in Potapov Street and spend a little time there—on the grounds that I had to change and we could all have some tea. The car was to wait outside and eventually take us to the Central Committee where passes would already have been made out for us. It was clear, in a word, that for some reason or other they needed to gain a little time.

By the time we drove up to the house it was already getting dark and had begun to rain slightly. There was no sign of Ira's taxi near the house—I was extremely angry and upset, since I thought she must have had a forty-minute start on us by now . . . There was nothing to be done, if we were to stick to the plan, except to wait—which we did for fifteen minutes, silently staring through the gathering gloom at the road. At last Ira's taxi appeared. It turned out that she had chased all over Moscow trying to find Koma—a fine time indeed to do this! . . . She now went up towards the house, and a frightened-looking Zinaida Nikolayevna came out to meet her and say that BL would get dressed at once. Evidently sensing something, or alarmed by Ira's sudden arrival, he came out in the grey overcoat and hat he always put on to travel in.

Sizing up the situation at a glance, he cheerfully got into the car, complaining only that Ira had not given him time to change his trousers.

'You know,' he said, 'I have put on a magnificent jacket—this dark-blue Argentine one which suits me so well, but Ira didn't give me a chance to put on another pair of trousers.'

Then turning to Ira, he said: 'Well now, Irochka, my girl, I'm really going to show them. I'll make such a fuss and tell them everything I think, everything—you'll see.'

'But Boria, they won't give her a pass,' I said. 'There's no point in dragging her there and making scenes.'

'Well, I just shan't go in without her. Don't worry, Olia, I'll get a pass for her.'

I now whispered in his ear that it wouldn't be a bad idea for us to go to Potapov Street so I could change and we could all drink tea—and then go off to the Central Committee in our own good time. He liked the idea very much—not even suspecting, poor man, that this 'liberty' had been suggested by Polikarpov and was part of his strategic plan.

Once or twice, nudging him gently and pointing towards the chauffeur, I whispered: 'Boria, not so loud—he's a spy,' but nothing could stop him. He went on complaining in a very funny way about how bad his appearance was—he hadn't slept properly, and he was wearing his country trousers. How would he be able to explain it in the Central Committee? He would tell them he had been out walking when they came for him and hadn't had time to change. But what worried him most of all was the way he looked himself. He peered over at the driving mirror and said: 'Good God, when they see me they'll wonder why the world should make all this fuss over someone with a mug like mine.' He kept us laughing all the way.

Behind us came the cavalcade of government cars. I knew that Polikarpov was in one of them.

When we arrived at my apartment, Boria took off his coat, walked up and down the room, and drank strong tea. He asked me not to wear any jewellery or put much make-up on ('Olia, you have good

286 A CAPTIVE OF TIME

natural looks, don't put anything on'). This was something we always clashed over.

BL asked Ira to get medicines for him—a huge bottle of tincture of valerian, and some Valokordin. This would be needed for first aid in case the talk became heated. Since the car was waiting for us outside, we were not worried about being late, and our mood was one of almost hysterical gaiety . . .

We drove along the Pokrovka to the fifth entrance of the Central Committee on Old Square. BL went up to the guard and started to explain that he was expected, but had no documents with him except his writer's card—'the membership card of this Union of yours, which you've just thrown me out of,' he explained to the soldier, and then immediately went on to talk about his trousers in exactly the way he had said he would: 'They came for me while I was out walking, you see, which is why I have these trousers on!' The guard listened with great astonishment, but he was friendly enough: 'It's all right, it's all right,' he said, 'it doesn't matter, it's quite all right.'

Just as I had thought, Boria and I were taken through into the cloakroom, and then up the stairs, but Ira was not allowed to go with us. 'Don't worry, my girl,' Boria whispered to us, 'wait here a little while and I will get you a pass in a moment—I won't go without you.' As we went up the stairs, Boria winked at me and whispered: 'It will be interesting now, you'll see . . .' Needless to say, he had not the slightest doubt that it was Khrushchev he was going to see.

But when the door to the inner sanctum opened, the person we saw sitting at a huge desk was none other than Dmitri Alexeyevich Polikarpov again. The only thing was that he was freshly shaved, and looked in better shape—as though the hectic business of the day had never happened. It was clear that after our trip out to Peredelkino, he had managed to smarten himself up—for which reason, as it now emerged, he had got us to linger on the way at Potapov Street. One could not help feeling even a little embarrassed at the thought of all the trouble he had gone to in order to get BL here and at the same time to create the impression that he had never left his office that day, and could not have cared less whether BL came or not. (He rather reminded me of the officer in Kafka's *Penal Colony* who invents a torture machine, and then gets into it himself.)

Next to Polikarpov sat a thin man whom I thought I recognized from pictures of him, but he kept silent throughout, and there is nothing I can really say about him. Another person appeared at one moment with a file, but he did not stay. In fact, the only personage in the room who counted was Polikarpov. Boria and I were invited to sit down—which we did, in soft leather chairs, facing each other.

Boria was the first to speak and he began, of course, by demanding a pass for Ira: 'She will give me my valerian.'

Polikarpov frowned: 'I hope you will not need to be given valerian, Boris Leonidovich. And why involve the girl? Lord knows the sort of things she has to listen to as it is!'

'I request that she be given a pass,' BL persisted. 'Let her arrive at her own judgment!'

'What does it matter, Boria?' I now butted in. 'We shall soon be out of here, so just let her wait.'

When the exchange about Ira was over, Polikarpov cleared his throat, rose solemnly to his feet, and in a voice befitting a town crier announced that in view of his letter to Khrushchev Pasternak was to be allowed to remain in the Motherland, but that it was now up to him to find a way of making his peace with the Soviet people. 'There is nothing we can do at the moment to calm the anger of the people', Polikarpov went on to explain. 'We simply have no way, for example, of stopping tomorrow's issue of the *Literary Gazette* . . .'

'Aren't you ashamed, Dmitri Alexeyevich?' Boria interrupted. 'What do you mean, "anger"! You have your human side, I can see, so why do you come out with these stock phrases? "The people! The people!"—as though it were something you could just produce from your own trouser pockets! You know perfectly well that you really shouldn't use this word "people" at all.'

Poor Dmitri Alexeyevich gasped loudly for breath, walked up and down his study for a moment, and, mustering all his patience, came over to Boria: 'Now look here, Boris Leonidovich, the whole business is over, so let's make things up, and everything will soon be all right again . . .' And then he suddenly gave him a friendly pat on the shoulder: 'Goodness me, old fellow—what a mess you've landed us in . . .'

But Boria, angered by being addressed as 'old fellow' in my presence—he thought himself young and healthy, and the hero of the hour into the bargain—impatiently pushed Polikarpov's hand aside: 'Will you kindly drop that tone! You cannot talk to me like that.'

But Polikarpov still went on in the same familiar manner: 'Really now, here you go, sticking a knife in the country's back, and we have to patch it all up . . .' (Again that unspeakable 'stab in the back'!)

Boria jumped to his feet: 'I will ask you to take those words back! I do not wish to speak with you any more'—and he made abruptly for the door.

Polikarpov threw me a desperate look: 'Stop him, stop him, Olga Vsevolodovna!'

'You bait him like this, and expect me to stop him?' I said, not without a little malicious pleasure. 'You must take your words back!'

'I do, I do,' Polikarpov mumbled. He was clearly rattled.

BL hesitated by the door, and I told him to come back. The conversation was now resumed in a different tone.

As we were leaving and after he had said goodbye to BL, Polikarpov kept me behind for a moment: 'I shall have to get in touch with you again before long. There'll be no more trouble now for a couple of weeks, but then, by the look of things, we shall have to write another letter for Boris Leonidovich to sign. You and I will work it out together, here in this room. But that will only be after the October holiday,* so you can spend it in peace and quiet. You must admit that this is a great load off your mind as well, isn't it?'

'Oh, I'm not so sure,' I replied.

'There you see, Olia,' BL said as we went down the stairs, 'how badly they manage things . . . They should have held out their hands to me, and everything would have been different, but they're unable to: they are so mean-spirited, always afraid of giving something away—that's their basic defect. They could have spoken to me like human beings just now. But they have no feelings. They are not people, but machines. See how terrible they are, these walls here, and everybody inside them is like an automaton . . . But all the same I gave them something to worry about—they got what they deserved!'†

So all three of us—BL, Ira, and myself—were now driven back to Peredelkino at top speed in a huge official car. As on the way out to

* Anniversary of the October Revolution celebrated, because of the change in the calendar, on November 7. (Tr.)

† A very well-informed writer has told me that before his fall from power Khrushchev invited Ehrenburg to visit him, and expressed his regret that Pasternak had been hounded. He had entrusted the whole business to Polikarpov and Surkov, but when he had found time to look through the novel himself he realized that he had been misled—but by then it was too late.[38]

Moscow, Boria was in high spirits and very talkative. With great gusto he acted out the whole conversation with Polikarpov for Ira's benefit. However much I plucked his sleeve and motioned with my head in the direction of the chauffeur, nothing could stop him. But then, during a lull in the conversation, Ira recited some lines from *Lieutenant Schmidt*:

> In vain, in years of turmoil,
> One seeks a happy ending—
> Some are fated to kill—and repent—
> While others go to Golgotha . . .
> I suppose you never flinch
> From wiping out a man.
> Ah well, martyrs to your dogma,
> You too are victims of the times . . .
> I know the stake at which
> I'll die will be the boundary mark
> Between two different epochs,
> And I rejoice at being so elect.[39]

BL's mood of elation, all his exuberance, vanished in a flash. Until now he had been in a frenzy of high spirits, but when he heard his own verse, tears even came into his eyes: 'Just think—how right, how true it is!'

We left him at the 'big' house and said goodbye to him. We had to go back to Moscow, but our large car now turned out to be firmly stuck in the mud. We all joined the chauffeur in trying to push it clear, but without success. Ira had to go up to the house to get assistance. The domestic help, Tatiana Matveyevna, and BL's younger son Lionia came out. Tatiana Matveyevna particularly distinguished herself in the work of getting the car out of the mud, and Ira said there was even something symbolic about this . . .

This was the end of that very long day, Friday, October 31.

The next day the 'wrath of the people' promised by Polikarpov duly descended on our heads—in the form of a full-page feature in the *Literary Gazette* under a headline in letters an inch high: 'Anger and Indignation'. It was accompanied by an editorial note saying that the newspaper had been 'literally flooded' by letters and telegrams in the last few days.

This was of course true. But by no means all the letters condemned BL. We ourselves received hundreds of letters from many parts of the Soviet Union and from abroad expressing indignation at the campaign of persecution and offering moral support. Many of these letters were copies. The originals had been sent to the Union of Writers and the *Literary Gazette*. But none of them was printed.

Pride of place was given in the *Literary Gazette* to the comment of an excavator operator called F. Vasiltsev under the title 'A Frog in a Bog'. It well conveyed the sense of all the other statements, articles, and resolutions by means of which the *Literary Gazette* gave vent to the 'just anger' of the people.

But before giving examples of this 'just anger', I would like to quote some words from a millennial source of wisdom:

Then he said unto his disciples, 'It is impossible but that offences will come: but woe unto him, through whom they come! It were better for him that a millstone were hanged about his neck, and he cast into the sea, than that he should offend one of these little ones.' (Luke 17: 1–2)

Nothing could better apply to the persons responsible for stage-managing this outburst of 'wrath', the seducers of 'these little ones' who adopted a cowardly anonymity, or, rather, concealed themselves behind the names of the innocents duped by them in such outrageous fashion—Vasiltsev and others, who had 'not read' Pasternak but in the opinion of their seducers were entitled by social status to speak in the name of the 'ordinary people' and condemn him out of hand.

'The newspapers', said the excavator operator, 'are talking about someone called Pasternak. He's supposed to be a writer. I had never heard of him before and I have never read any of his books . . .' But this public admission of ignorance about the matter under discussion did not prevent him from going on to speak his mind in very categorical fashion: 'This is not a writer, but a White Guardist . . . I have not read Pasternak, but I know that literature is better off without frogs.'

This was, I believe, the first time—at least in my recollection—that avowed ignorance was actually made into a virtue, giving people the right to condemn and pillory a writer.

'Who is Pasternak? What has he written?' asked the oil worker R. Kasimov sternly, going on to explain that Pasternak was the author of 'aesthetic verse in obscure language incomprehensible to the people'.

These were not just isolated utterances, but amounted to something symptomatic of the times. In her memoirs Nadezhda Mandelstam tells of a conversation she had about Pasternak in 1963 with a fellow passenger in a train who said to her: 'How could they have allowed him to send it [Doctor Zhivago] abroad like that? What a blunder.' The man had not read Pasternak and had no intention of doing so: 'Who reads him? I keep up with literature—I have to—but I'd never heard of him.' When Nadezhda Mandelstam said she bet he had never heard of Tiutchev or Baratynski either, he took out a notebook and asked: 'Who did you say? I must find out about them.'

But to continue with the well-organized 'wrath of the people': Kolkhoz chairman G. Sitalo, to give him his due, did not take it on himself to judge the literary side of the matter, but reeled off a lot of farm production figures—1,250 thousand *poods* of grain . . . 200 thousand *poods* of oil cake, and so on. But the general conclusion to be drawn from these figures was unambiguous: 'We were glad to hear the news that Pasternak . . . has been expelled from the Union of Soviet Writers.'

One would not wish to hang millstones round the necks of 'these little ones' whose seducers were so careful to keep out of sight. But what is one to say of the intellectuals who made statements differing little from those ascribed to workers and collective farmers? An intellectual is by definition someone capable of thinking for himself. (The word literally means one who 'understands'.) An intellectual might well not accept Pasternak, but at least he should not condemn him outright, without bothering to try and understand him. Such people, as distinct from 'these little ones', cannot evade responsibility for their words and one may legitimately ask whether they could continue to call themselves 'intellectuals' after this.

An engineer, for example, put BL in 'the category of those who sell themselves cheaply', and concluded that his place was 'on the garbage heap'. A woman pianist writing from Riga declared that 'the mannered abstruseness of Pasternak has always left me cold'— from which it was clear to her that the 'Nobel Prize was awarded to him for his anti-Soviet act'. A woman geologist Maria Filippovich asked in a tone of great profundity: 'Is not Doctor Zhivago the spiritual heir of Klim Samgin?* Gorki exposed Klim Samgin. In Zhivago, Pasternak exposes himself.'†

The teacher A. Masitin used a well-tried method by suggesting that 'Bukharin's panegyric of him many years ago was not accidental.'

Then there was the voice of the old-age pensioners: '. . . a rabid cur, he is not even Mister Pasternak, but simply . . . emptiness and gloom.'

A salesgirl in a bookshop in Vilnius, who proved to be no sibyl, prophesied that 'his name will be forgotten, and no honest person will touch his books.'

Needless to say, un-named representatives of the non-Russian literatures of the Soviet Union—and who better qualified to judge the poetry of Pasternak?—joined their imprecations to those of all the rest. The writers of Kiev denounced the novel as 'untalented hackwork' and described the award of the Nobel Prize, in approved fashion, as 'payment for treason'. Connoisseurs of Russian poetry in Uzbekistan and Azerbaidzhan declared that they could no longer 'tolerate the renegade Boris Pasternak in the ranks of Soviet writers'.

Everybody knows of the personal and literary bonds between BL and many writers in Georgia,[40] so a telegram appropriate to the purpose was sent from there—though the only writer who signed it by name was Irakli Abashidze.

---

* Hero of Gorki's long, unfinished novel *The Life of Klim Samgin*; see Gorki in the Biographical Guide. (Tr.)

† I have in my possession a photograph of this same Maria Filippovich who had been a friend of my sister Tania since they were in secondary school together. She used to come and see me in the first happy days after I had got to know BL, and she gave me this photograph of herself inscribed: 'To the happiest woman in the world . . .'—'happiest' because of BL's love for me.

After this there was a list of other non-Russian regions of the country which had sent their expressions of indignation, though without a single signature. Even the Chechens, Ingush, and Kalmyks, who had experienced at first hand the wisdom of Stalin's policies towards the minorities (they were deported, men, women, and children, to remote areas of the country), joined in the chorus of indignation . . .

And finally, under the heading 'A Challenge to All Honest People', there was a statement from Nikolai Rylenkov: 'Boris Pasternak has published a novel preaching . . . the ideas of a policy based on nuclear weapons . . . He has become a slanderer, and the people turn away from him with contempt . . . ' One is touched by the modesty which enabled Rylenkov to sign these words in the name of all the progressive writers of the world, of the whole country, and of 'all honest people' in general.

These things were published in all seriousness by the official newspaper of the Union of Soviet Writers on November 1, 1958. As I sit and look at it now, I wonder why it never occurred to the editors that it could all have been reduced to one single phrase: '. . . I have not read Pasternak, but . . .'

Also, I cannot help remembering the lines of Marina Tsvetayeva:

> For 'news'—read 'lies'
> For 'news'—read 'trash'
> Each line—a libel
> Each word—a lash . . .

'. . . along trails of cats and foxes'

We now began to get sixty or seventy letters a day. Since I do not wish to compete for the laurels which could have been awarded to the *Literary Gazette* for its 'impartiality' in the selection of letters for publication, I should say at once that although the overwhelming majority were friendly, there were some which were not only critical, but also downright abusive. There is no point in talking about these, but it would be wrong not to mention the critical comments of some of BL's fellow writers.

I have quoted the letter from Selvinski in full, but cannot do the same in the case of one from Galina Nikolayeva—though I still have it—since it consisted of twelve pages written in pencil. It begins with a declaration of love: she loved the Pasternak who wrote *Lieutenant Schmidt* but, she goes on, she could '. . . put a bullet through a traitor's head. I am a woman who has known much sorrow and I am not a spiteful person, but for treachery such as this, I would not flinch from it.'

In case BL did not wish to accept her services as his executioner (in the literal, physical sense of the word) she proposed that he should travel round the country, get to know the people he had slandered, and have a look at the collective farms and the 'great construction sites of communism'—to which, she hoped, the author of *Lieutenant Schmidt* would not remain indifferent.

On the day the *Literary Gazette* published its expressions of the 'people's wrath', BL wrote the following reply to Galina Nikolayeva:

November 1

Thank you for being so frank. I have been changed by the years of Stalin's atrocities—at which I guessed before they were exposed.*

In your place, however, I would moderate my tone. Remember Vereshchagin and the scene of the 'just wrath of the people' in *War and Peace*.[41] However much independence you might claim for your words and their tone, they merge with this 'just indignation' and drown in it.

I should like to reassure you in your righteous outspoken protest: You are younger than I, and you will live to see a time when people will take a different view of what has happened.

I renounced the prize prior to the advice and prophecies contained in your letter. I am writing only so that it will not seem that I am evading a reply.   B.P.

On a separate piece of paper, he wrote this note for me:

Oliusha: should I reply to Galina Nikolayevna? Read this and think about it. If it isn't necessary, destroy the letter. I kiss you. If it weren't for my shoulder, I would be in a state of perfect bliss. And you?

* By Khrushchev in his 'secret speech' at the Twentieth Party Congress (February 1956). (Tr.)

I did not send the letter, and Ira still has it in her keeping. I do not remember him writing any other replies of this kind.

Every day brought new expressions of sympathy and support. BL was sometimes moved to tears by the most artless and simple of them —as, for example, this one:

Dear Boris Leonidovich,
Today I am sending out greetings cards and letters [i.e. for the anniversary of the October Revolution], and I thought I would write to you as well.

The whole of the week I have been reading the newspapers with great sadness, and I feel ashamed of our writers . . . But I do not believe those writers who have spoken out against you. Their behaviour is disgusting . . . One of them said that nobody would ever shake hands with you now. He was wrong. I shake hands with you warmly, and wish you good health, and the strength to stand up to all these trials.

Remember that the only judgment that matters is one's own—the judgment of one's conscience.

You must not feel lonely. You have probably never before in your whole life had so much sympathy from people unknown to you as at the moment.

Be happy. Yours sincerely, G. Zinchenko (Cutter at the Indposhiv clothing factory). Kiev, November 4, 1958

Somebody on the staff of *Pravda* sent on to us a letter to the editor from an engineer in Leningrad:

Dear Comrade Editor,
I have worked all my life in industry, and am not a critic, but I love and appreciate poetry. When I read V. Yermilov's article 'For Socialist Realism' in *Pravda*, No. 154, I thought to myself: if we who work in industry were to criticize each other like *this*, if each of us *gloated* like this over somebody else's mistakes and tried to make so much of them—then we shouldn't get very far in what we are doing . . .

And he went on to contradict all Yermilov's arguments about Pasternak's work.

From Latvia, P. Yantsevichus sent BL a copy of a long article, in which he said, among other things:

Pasternak has withstood the hardest test of time. The number of his readers is not large, but those who have entered into the inimitable world of his poetry will always remain faithful to it.
It is the fashion nowadays to give a writer credit for being sincere and honest. Pasternak was one of the few who preferred silence to insincerity. The most hazardous part of the journey is behind him, and before him is the time when he will cease to be a 'poet's poet' to become a poet for everybody.

There was also this letter:

To the poet Boris Pasternak,
I bow down low to you (down to the ground) for all the happiness and joy you have given me through your poetry since I first became acquainted with it. My life is nearing its end, but I leave it with your poetry—which I have given to many others who will also come to know it and never forget it.
K. Prutskaya.

Some of these letters were anonymous, like this one which arrived at the height of the campaign against BL:

Dear Boris Leonidovich,
Millions of Russian people are happy at the appearance in our literature of a truly great work. History will not treat you harshly.
The Russian People.

Apart from letters of this type we received many others from abroad—the post delivered them in bundles every day. They came from many parts of the world and were written by people of the most varied walks of life.

I remember BL being very moved by a letter he received from a man in Hamburg who ran a puppet theatre. He wrote about all the difficulties he was having, though he did not ask for help. All the same, however, BL sent instructions to Feltrinelli to give the man a large sum of money for Christmas out of the royalties on the novel.

I believe that in a short time he gave away over a hundred thousand dollars to his translators, to people who showed an interest in him or simply asked for help.

Reading and answering all these letters took up a lot of BL's precious time. But he felt it was essential and most important for him to do so. He replied to almost every letter if he thought it was written out of genuine human feeling. A good idea of his attitude is given at the end of a letter he wrote to E. D. Romanova:

... I break off my letter here not for lack of feeling but for lack of time, being snowed under by work, cares, and letters from abroad— to a part of which I reply for the same reason as to you: not because I am forced to by the authorship of the letter, by the dictates of politeness, or by some natural and pre-determined sense of obligation, but because the letter itself, breathing life, provokes rapture and astonishment...

To Boris Zaitsev* he wrote in a letter dated July 29, 1959:

... it has fallen to me as a great and undeserved piece of good fortune that towards the end of my life I have entered into direct personal relations with many estimable people in the vast and distant world, and have begun an intimate, informal, and important conversation with them. Unfortunately this has come late in the day.

According to Gerd Ruge's estimate BL received between twenty and thirty thousand letters from the moment he was awarded the Nobel Prize up to the day of his death.

He had very little time left for writing verse, and one of his last poems was about all these letters that poured in:

> ... along trails of cats and foxes
> I walk back with piles of mail
> To the house where I'll sit and read it,
> Revelling in it all—
>
> Countries, frontiers, mountains, lakes,
> Continents, peninsulas,

* Boris Konstantinovich Zaitsev (1881–1972): Russian writer who emigrated in 1922 and lived in Paris from 1924. (Tr.)

Views, reviews, reflections,
Children, young people, old.

Men's letters, so sober, so grave
—Every single one of them
Earnestly attesting
To careful thought and sense!

How precious the letters from women!
—I've fallen from the clouds myself
And swear you my allegiance
For now and evermore . . .

For two or three days before our visit to the Central Committee all delivery of letters to BL was held up on higher orders—something that depressed him more than any other aspect of the campaign against him. The first thing he demanded from Polikarpov as a condition for reaching any 'agreement' was that his correspondence should not be interfered with. The very next morning the postwoman brought two bags full of mail which had piled up during the previous few days, and BL was very pleased. Among it were foreign newspapers and magazines which contained first reactions to the hounding of him:

Ernest Hemingway: 'I shall give him a house to make his life in the West easier. I want to create for him the conditions he needs to carry on with his writing. I can understand how divided Boris must be in his own mind just now. I know how deeply, with all his heart, he is attached to Russia. For a genius such as Pasternak, separation from his country would be a tragedy. But if he comes to us, we shall not disappoint him. I shall do everything in my modest power to save this genius for the world. I think of Pasternak every day.'

Halldór Laxness: 'I do not understand Khrushchev or our Soviet colleagues. Tolerance is the only important qualification needed to judge the merits of such a great writer as Boris Pasternak.'

Albert Camus: 'The whole world knows that the Union of Soviet Writers would much rather have seen the Nobel Prize go to Sholokhov than to Pasternak. But this was not something that could influence the Swedish Academy, which was bound to take a detached view of the literary merits of both these writers. In this sense its choice, which is by no means a political one, is simply a recognition of Pasternak's achievement as a writer. It is a long time since Sholok-hov has produced anything new, while *Doctor Zhivago* has appeared everywhere in the world . . . as an incomparable work greatly superior to the bulk of the world's literary production. This great novel about love is not anti-Soviet, as some people say—it has nothing to do with any particular party; it is all-embracing.'

Alberto Moravia: 'Pasternak creates the impression of a youth with grey hair . . . Only his dark eyes and sad, penetrating expression give away his origins. These are the eyes of a man who has been mercilessly treated and whom life has subjected to cruel ordeals.'

Nehru: 'We believe that if a well-known writer expresses views which conflict with the dominant ones in his country, he should be respected rather than subjected to any kind of restrictions.'

Henri Troyat: 'A man of extraordinary courage, very modest, and of very high principles; a lone defender of constantly threatened spiritual values. His image rises high above the petty political squabbles of our planet.'

Georges Altman: 'I make bold to suggest that Pasternak is a much better representative of the great Russia of yesterday and today than is Mr Khrushchev.'

A 'Leader' on the Line

Polikarpov had promised us that we should be left in peace during the holidays and then, in a couple of weeks' time, he would invite me to go and see him so we could draft some new letter or other. It was clear that they did not intend to stop at the humiliation already inflicted on us, but at least we thought we could look forward to spending two weeks unmolested.

But we were wrong.

On Tuesday, November 4, Boria, Mitia, and I were sitting at Potapov Street going through the latest large batch of mail. Boria was terribly pleased when Mitia slit open one envelope and some pages torn from a book fell out. It was Kuprin's story 'Anathema'. There was no word of explanation—none was necessary!

Suddenly the telephone rang. We asked Mitia to say we weren't at home—we just wanted to sit together quietly for a while, shutting ourselves off for an hour or so from the hostile world around us. But we heard Mitia say sorrowfully in a half-whisper, as he covered the receiver with his hand: 'Mother, one of the leaders on the line!'

I went to the phone.

'This is the Central Committee, Olga Vsevolodovna—Dmitri Alexeyevich speaking. It's time we met again. We must ask Boris Leonidovich to write an open letter to the people . . .'

It would have been so much simpler to rest content with the letter to Khrushchev, but they had neither the brains nor the elementary humanity. So the same thing began all over again.

Boria immediately sat down to write a draft of a letter to *Pravda*. He said that he had thought that the award of the Nobel Prize to him would have been a matter for pride on the part of the people, and if he had renounced it, this was not because he felt himself to have done something wrong or because he was afraid for himself personally, but under pressure from persons close to him and out of fear for them . . . The letter would obviously be unacceptable to Polikarpov.

The next day I went to the Central Committee with this draft written by BL. As was to be expected, Polikarpov said that he and I would 'have to do a little work ourselves on this letter'. We 'worked' on it in fact like a pair of professional counterfeiters. We took isolated phrases written or said by BL on various different occasions and placed them together in such a way that white was turned into black.

In return we were offered our 'reward' right there and then: Polikarpov promised me quite definitely that he would see to it that BL's translation of *Faust* came out in a second edition, and also that the ban on BL and me in *Goslitizdat* be removed so that we would again be offered translating work.

When I went back to Boria with this new version of the letter, in which practically all the words but none of the sentiments were his, he simply waved his hand. He was tired. He just wanted an end to the whole abnormal situation. He needed money for his two households and for all the other people he was in the habit of giving aid to. (Once he had said, '. . . a whole financial dependency has grown up around me—there are many people who look to me for help, and I have to earn a lot of money . . .') Polikarpov's promise that we would again be given translating work offered some hope that we could resume our previous way of life. So BL, doing irreparable violence to himself, signed this second letter. It was published on Thursday, November 6:

I am addressing the editors of the newspaper *Pravda* with a request to publish my statement.

I am impelled to do so by my respect for the truth.

Just as everything that has happened to me is a natural consequence of my own acts, so all the steps I have taken in connection with the award to me of the Nobel Prize have been free and voluntary.

I regarded the award of the Nobel Prize as a literary distinction and was delighted by it, as I made clear in a telegram to the secretary of the Swedish Academy, Anders Østerling.

But I was mistaken. I had some reason for this mistake, since my candidature had been proposed on earlier occasions—five years ago, for instance, before my novel had come into existence.

After a week had gone by, when I saw the dimensions of the political campaign occasioned by my novel, and I realized that the award was a political move which had led to monstrous consequences, I sent my voluntary renunciation on my own initiative and without being forced to by anyone.

In my letter to Nikita Sergeyevich Khrushchev I stated that I am bound to Russia by my birth, by my life and work, and that it is unthinkable for me to leave her and go abroad into exile. Speaking of this bond I had in mind not only my sense of kinship with the land and countryside, but also of course with her people, her past, her glorious present, and her future. But obstacles to this bond, created through my own fault by the novel, rose up before me like a wall.

I never had any intention of doing harm to the State or to my people.

The editors of *Novy Mir* had warned me that the novel might be understood by readers as a work directed against the October Revolution and the foundations of the Soviet system. I was not conscious of this, and now regret it.

If one bears in mind the conclusions arising from a critical examination of the novel, it does indeed appear as if I maintain the following erroneous propositions. I seem to be saying that every revolution is a historically illegitimate occurrence, of which the October Revolution is an example, and that it has brought misfortunes on Russia, and led to the destruction of the traditional Russian intelligentsia.

It is clear to me that I cannot subscribe to propositions taken to such lengths of absurdity. Yet my work, awarded the Nobel Prize, has given rise to just such a regrettable interpretation, and this is the reason why in the final resort I renounced the prize.

If the publication of the book had been stopped, as I asked my publisher in Italy (editions in other countries were produced without my knowledge), it is possible that I might have been able to put this right, at least partially. But the book has been printed, and it is now too late to talk of this.

In the course of this turbulent week I have not been subjected to persecution, and neither my life, freedom, nor anything else at all have been at stake. I wish to emphasize once more that all my actions have been voluntary. People closely acquainted with me know very well that nothing on earth can force me to play the hypocrite or go against my conscience. This has also been the case now. It does not need to be said that nobody has tried to compel me to do anything and that I make this statement of my own free will, with bright faith in the common future and my own, with pride in the age I live in, and in the people around me.

I believe that I shall find the strength to restore my good name and the trust of my comrades.

November 5, 1958   B. Pasternak.

Perhaps it was about this kind of letter that BL had once said: '. . . when a person one suspects is being martyred says that he is flourishing one begins to wonder whether he may not have been forced to make such statements by the torments inflicted on him.'

Side by side with tragedy, as is usually the case, there was also farce.

After this second 'penitential' letter we began going to Moscow less and less, spending most of our time in Peredelkino. Our landlord, Kuzmich, was an amusing, sly old man, and a great scoundrel. Boria liked to sit and talk with him from time to time, and was delighted by his earthy way of speaking. Once or twice, he drank *samogon*★ with him, hugely enjoying his company and conversation. Kuzmich occasionally came home from the 'Fadeyev tavern' rather drunk and singing the old song: 'May I be punished by the grave because I love her so, but of the grave I'm not afraid . . .' Realizing that it gave us

★ Home-distilled vodka, 'moonshine'. (Tr.)

pleasure, he always sang when BL came to the house, and particularly when he wanted to cajole me into giving him his rent in advance. We were touched by the conversations we could hear through the wall between him and his wife, who was paralyzed. She was frightened he might leave her, and he was always playing her up. When he came home the worse for drink she would try to flatter him by singing a little ditty about a falcon on the wing ('Where's he been, my handsome falcon?'), and, making a great commotion as he brought in firewood, Kuzmich would threaten to bring home a 'Turkish girl in a turban' from the 'festival'* and boast loudly about how he had been 'a real devil with the women' in his day and could once easily have got me to leave BL for him!

In general, however, he stood in awe of BL, his generosity and jokes—although he did find fault with him on one occasion. It happened to be March 8 (International Women's Day). BL and I had quarrelled about something and spent a long time having things out. Kuzmich was expecting the traditional present of a bottle of vodka, but BL left, slamming the door behind him. 'Did he bring it?' Kuzmich asked me, putting his head in its fur hat round the door. In no mood to talk, I just waved my hand at him. 'A difficult custo-mer . . .' he said with a sigh. That same evening BL and I laughed at the way the poor man had been thwarted.

In summer Kuzmich wore a wide-brimmed straw hat of mine. Whenever we ran into him on the bridge it was hard not to laugh at the sight of the tall, stooping figure, his large nose and moustache sticking out comically from under the hat.

He had always been very gratified by the fact that we had found refuge in his house.

But now every loudspeaker in the country was blaring out the news that Pasternak had sold himself to world capitalism. The old man decided, with good reason, that the capitalists of the world must have a lot of money. Through the wall dividing our room from his we could hear him holding forth on the subject: 'Fancy that—it turns out he's a millionaire, our friend! Who would have thought it—he wears such poor shoes, worse than mine. And just to look at him you'd never know he had all those millions . . .'

I laughed, but Boria quite unexpectedly grew very angry. He jumped up and, rushing headlong round the verandah to the back,

* i.e. the International Youth Festival held in Moscow in 1958. (Tr.)

burst into Kuzmich's part of the house. Through the wall I heard him say: 'What millions, Kuzmich? Don't you know I gave up the prize? Now people will go on talking about millions and completely forget what happened to them. I've given them up, I tell you!'

Not wanting to spoil his relations with BL, Kuzmich immediately fell in with what he was saying: 'Yes, yes, that's right—of course we've heard you gave them up...'

BL came back through the verandah, still fuming: 'Just imagine his saying that! He doesn't want to hear that I gave the prize up—all he cares to know about are those millions I'm supposed to have...'

I tried to calm him down, but Kuzmich was still sceptical about what had happened and we could clearly hear him muttering on the other side of the wall: 'Now who would give up all that money, I'd like to know?... Given it up indeed!...'

Later on, in 1959, we moved to another small house nearby where our landlady was called Marusia—I have already mentioned her once before. She was a healthy, good-looking girl of about thirty with large, brown eyes of a Mongol cast, firm breasts, a dark complexion and glowing cheeks. She was quite often visited by her uncle, a small bald man, always very cheerful, and with a lot to say for himself. The window of her room—to which there was a separate entrance and porch, looked out on the 'Fadeyev tavern', where there were always a lot of drunks hanging around. Our three windows, on the other hand, overlooked the ravine through which the river Setun ran into the lake not far away—the Izmalkovo lake so often mentioned in BL's verse of the end of the 'fifties.

The tavern has now been demolished, the river is overgrown with reeds, and the whole area where the tavern stood is covered with wormwood and other weeds; the drunks have vanished, and Marusia has gone away, I don't know where. In those days we used to clamber up to the house over the roots of trees, but now steps have been built. Only my memories haunt the place—only mine are still alive there...

There is no hiding the fact that on his frequent visits Marusia's uncle used to distill *samogon* in the shed. Marusia was always inviting me to try some of it—which I did, not to offend her, though I found it revolting. Our relations with Marusia and her uncle were excellent. Instead of Kuzmich, it was now Marusia who kept the stove going in our room when we were away—I always left the key with her. Boria was very kind and generous to her, and I believe she would have wanted no other tenants but us.

One nice, damp, spring-like day in April we suddenly saw two men we had not seen before near Marusia's porch. They were bringing out some basins and wooden boxes. They politely introduced themselves as relations of Marusia. Marusia looked somehow embarrassed and said, as though apologizing for them, that they would only be staying with her for a short time.

The next morning I was awakened by a terrible drilling noise.

'What have you been up to so early in the morning?' I asked Marusia later.

Looking round anxiously at her door, she said that the two men were not relatives at all, but that they had told her to say this, supposedly to avoid alarming people. In fact they were detectives and had drilled a hole in her wall so as to keep watch on some important criminal who frequented the tavern—they said they were on the track of a whole gang. Marusia begged me not to tell any one, and at first I mentioned it to no one except BL.

After staying a short while, the two men went away, but then they came back again—and more than once. When one of my friends warned me that a microphone had been installed somewhere in our house, even telling me its serial number (he had learned about it from a drunken member of the relevant organization who lived with him), I became quite alarmed and began to pester BL with my worries. But in his usual way he just laughed at me, and asked how on earth I could imagine that the hole in Marusia's wall (which I had shown him once when Marusia was out) could possible have any connection with us. The only person who really shared my concern was Heinz Schewe. He told us all kinds of hair-raising stories about modern techniques of listening in to people at a distance—which did little to set my mind at rest. A Russian friend told us he knew someone 'reliable', an electronics expert, who could come and inspect the walls of our room and the cellar—if we managed to find the 'infernal device', 'they' would not be able to accuse us of anything, but, on the contrary, we should have a case against them, since putting such things in people's walls was supposedly not allowed any more.

This friend—though not immediately, but after quite a long time —did send along the electronics expert. I remember how I cleared everybody out of the house on a day when Marusia was away, and he sounded out all the walls, and climbed down into the cellar, which we let our tom cat use in winter. He clambered back out of there, covered in cat mess, dust, and cobwebs, earning every penny of his money, but unable to find anything. Our agreement was to pay him a thousand roubles if he found something and half that if nothing turned up. In the end, it was five hundred roubles down the drain, and Boria had all the more reason for making fun of me.

But the hole drilled in Marusia's wall remained, her 'relatives' continued to visit her from time to time, and I went on worrying about it as before. Then one day, as we were all sitting drinking tea —Boria, my mother, Sergei Stepanovich, and I—the business of the hole in the wall suddenly seemed to be cleared up. It was, I remember, just at sundown, as the sky had turned all pink, when Marusia came racing in and made me go with her to the hole in the wall. I looked through and saw somebody being hustled into a black police van parked in the roadway opposite: 'Look!' she shouted, 'they've caught him, they've found him.'

Once again, I was a laughingstock. 'Do you really think,' BL asked ironically, 'that they sent this police van and rounded up a thief all specially for your benefit? They wouldn't take so much trouble over us! Particularly since they know exactly what we think anyway. Why should they waste their money? We're not hiding anything from them, after all!'

Later on, at a party with some friends on New Year's Eve, I told this whole story, laughing at myself for being so over-suspicious. Among those present was a well-known lawyer, who was later to defend me at my trial. To my surprise he listened to my story in all seriousness, and then said: 'But perhaps it *was* all done for your sake. Do you really believe you are not worth the expense involved?'

I reported this conversation to Boria, but he dismissed it indignantly—it was all nonsense, and I was going out of my mind again!

In fact, however, as we were soon to discover, 'they' were not at all interested in tracking down an imaginary gang of thieves, but were concerned only with watching us. They thought we *were* well worth all the effort and expense: the hole drilled in the wall, the staging of a bogus 'arrest', and the installation of a microphone—this too was found in the end.

I was touched and astonished at the way in which BL, who was totally indifferent to the opinions of the powerful, put such great store by the attitude of the post-woman and the silent devotion of his domestic help Tatiana, and was overjoyed to find that Kuzmich greeted him 'just as before'.

Once, returning from a walk, he told me with tears in his eyes—as though it were a shining event of great significance—that he had met the Peredelkino militiaman, whom he had known for a long time, and the militiaman had greeted him just as if nothing had happened...

There was a tacit agreement between us in those days that we must keep our sense of humour, seeing the funny side of things wherever we could, and it seems that we managed to infect BL with our 'light-hearted' view of events. Ira recalls how well and amusingly he told stories about various things that happened to him at the time. Once, for instance, he recounted the following incident:

... *Doctor Zhivago* and the Nobel Prize are something so much out of the ordinary that all the lunatics have begun to look upon me as their leader. Various madmen lie in wait for me, and gain entry to the house in one way or another. There is one who has offered to put the novel in a secret code. Another—his name, I think, was Gitilin—told me that he and his mother have apocalyptic dreams by which they can determine the future course of my life, and in order to tell me what it is—so I won't unwittingly depart from it—Gitilin climbed up to our loft, and from there managed to penetrate into the upstairs part of the house. He described his own and his mother's dreams, and then went away. A little while later there was a knock on the front door. It was Gitilin again—he had left his galoshes in the loft. So Lionia clambered up the ladder to the loft and got them for him...

He told many more such comic stories, and I have quoted one of them here as an example simply because they played a by no means negligible role at that moment in his life. I realized that to a large extent he was only putting it on, and that in reality it was all very painful for him. But on the surface everything seemed well enough: we were constantly laughing, and an outside observer might have thought we hadn't a care in the world.

Our tension and anxiety disappeared in the evenings when Ira brought her young friends to see BL. It was very important for him to learn from them that they still loved and respected him, that he still inspired admiration and pride in them. Among these students I remember Yura Pankratov, who later became well known as a poet, Vania Kharabarov (now dead), and the young Chuvash poet Gennadi Lisin (Aigi).

Whenever they came, BL loved to sit and talk with them in our room in Kuzmich's house. When he left they went with him along the path which led between our window and the fence, and over the long bridge across the Izmalkovo lake, under the old willows. BL was always in high spirits, talked a great deal and did not disguise his child-like pleasure at this display of affection. He became particularly attached to Irina in those days.

It was then that he presented her with a small movie camera. Although none too skilfully, she made a film of one of these walks. Part of it has fortunately survived. BL looks so close and so alive that it is hard for me to look at it without crying.

'She is a very clever girl,' he used to say of Irina. 'She is just the kind I have dreamed of all my life. So many children have grown up around me, but I love only her . . .' When I reproached him for spoiling Irina, not always for good reason, he replied: 'Olia, you mustn't criticize her. The truth always speaks out of her mouth. You always say yourself that she's more mine than yours, so listen to what she says! She's very clever and she understands everything. It will be a lucky man who understands what a subtle spirit she is, how special she is. It's not something you can make out straightaway, but when she reveals herself in all her charm . . . no, no—I have yet to see the person who is worthy of her.'

When he gave her a copy of his translation of *Faust*, he wrote in it:

Irochka, this is your copy. I trust you and I believe in your future. Be bold in your soul and mind, in your dreams and purposes. Put your faith in nature, in the spirit of your destiny, in events of significance—and only in such few people as have been tested a thousand times, and are worthy of your confidence.

Almost like a father, your B.P.
November 3, 1955, Peredelkino.

The affair of the novel was not over with the ending of the official campaign of persecution. There were still various other preposterous attacks on him, such as a rhymed lampoon by Mikhalkov, an article by Kochetov, and a feature in the magazine *New Times* entitled 'The Case of Pasternak—Provocation of International Reaction'. But all this had no further effect on him. The only thing now of importance was that the violence he had done to himself by signing those two letters was irreparable and began to take its toll. The main falsehood in them had been the assertion that no violence was supposedly being done to him, when in fact violence of this very kind played a major part in the whole of his existence—particularly during those days when he was hounded so relentlessly over the novel.

Till the very end of his days, he of course continued to stand by every single line of what he had written in his novel—the novel in which he had indeed shown that he knew beforehand exactly what was in store for us:

. . . the great majority of us are required to live a life of constant, systematic duplicity. Your health is bound to be affected if, day after day, you say the opposite of what you feel, if you grovel before what you dislike and rejoice at what brings you nothing but misfortune. Your nervous system isn't a fiction, it's part of your physical body, and your soul exists in space and is inside you, like the teeth in your head. You can't keep violating it with impunity . . .

There is probably some limit in every man beyond which he cannot be driven. By the time BL found himself being forced to go against all his inclinations and desires, and constantly to violate his own nature, he had evidently already passed beyond this limit.

The violence done to him was overwhelming. It broke and then killed him. Slowly but surely his strength was undermined, and his heart and nervous system began to fail. The psychological climate in which he was forced to live was too much for him. His sense of his own worth and his pride were only enhanced by the flow of malevolent letters and the well-orchestrated 'anger of the people', but all the same these loathsome outpourings of official abuse and falsehoods inevitably overstrained his nerves and had their fatal effect.

Many years before, at the beginning of the 'twenties, Marina Tsvetayeva had written to him: 'You will never spend yourself, but you will suffocate.' Somebody else* said of him very aptly: 'All people lose their powers in their declining years, repeat themselves,

* Emmanuil Kazakievich, as reported by Ariadna Efron.

and outlive themselves. But this man, having lived one creative life, strode on into a second one.'

But it is all too true, as the Russian proverb says, that people can live when you pen them in, but die when you offend them

I shall describe the last year of Pasternak's life in Part Four.

PART IV
August

'I shall speak about that strange thing
—repeated through the ages—which may
be called the last year of a poet's
life . . .'

Boris Pasternak

'Farewell, years of tribulation.
Farewell, woman who braved
a bottomless pit of indignities!
I am the field on which you fight.'

Boris Pasternak

It seemed that we had survived our ordeal, and now we did everything we could to return to our usual way of life. Never before had
we felt so close and been so at one with each other. It was just as BL
says in the novel about Yuri and Lara:

It was not out of necessity that they loved each other, 'consumed by
passion'—in the conventional phrase used of lovers. They loved each
other because everything around them willed it, the trees and the
clouds and the sky over their heads and the earth under their feet.
Perhaps their surrounding world, the strangers they met in the street,
the landscapes unfolding before them on their walks, the rooms in
which they lived or met, were even more pleased with their love than
they were themselves.

Whenever I went into Moscow for any length of time, BL would
start to fret at the 'big house', and come out post-haste to join me in
the Potapov Street apartment. Here we entertained those people who
were not afraid to come and see us. We almost always had the stern,
calm and very strong-minded Ariadna with us, as well as the generous
and self-sacrificing Koma Ivanov.

The daily routine—almost a ritual—that BL had evolved over the
years was gradually renewed. Part of this ritual was his habit of
always making his telephone calls at nine in the evening, in accordance with a list of names drawn up beforehand, and a note of the
matters he wanted to speak about. It could be a question of calling an
elderly female admirer, for instance, or one of the young poets who
worshipped him. Sometimes he used the phone to reply to letters of a
personal or business nature, or to negotiate with publishers. He often
rang Ira from Peredelkino to say such things as the following: 'I am
coming to Moscow on Tuesday—can you buy me a hundred plain
envelopes, and also a selection of various stamps—particularly those
with squirrels on them, do you remember?' (For his replies to people
he didn't like he asked her to buy stamps of some particular issue
with what he thought was 'a nasty face' on them.)

Even in the days when not only his regular mode of life but also
his very existence was in jeopardy, he had still tried to stick to his
usual schedule. He felt that by so doing he could keep chaos and fear

at bay, not allowing them to get the better of him. He had continued, for example, to work on his translations of Słowacki and Calderón during those hours of the day allotted to the task. In working on Calderón he received help from Nikolai Mikhailovich Liubimov, a shrewd and enlightened person who understood very well that all the mud-slinging and commotion over the novel would be forgotten, but that there would always be a Pasternak. I took finished bits of the translation with me to Moscow, read them over with Liubimov at Potapov Street, and then went back to Peredelkino, where I would tactfully ask BL to change passages which in Liubimov's view departed too far from the original. Very soon after the 'scandal' was over, BL received a first payment for his work on Calderón. But the new edition of *Faust* promised by Polikarpov still seemed only a distant prospect glimmering on the horizon.

During the uproar over the novel we had also kept to our ritual of taking a stroll together in the evening. He and I (and sometimes Ira as well) would walk over to the office of the Peredelkino Writers' Club from which he made his traditional evening telephone calls. We could see very well that these calls had now become a torment for him, but he could not give them up, much as he dreaded hearing someone at the other end of the line speak to him in a cold or offensive way. It was sometimes a bitter or terrifying experience, but he always steeled himself to go through with it.

Once, when all three of us walked to the office together, BL went in while Ira and I waited on the steps outside the half-open door. It was a dark, dank autumn evening. The wind was sighing in the pine trees and we could hear electric trains hooting in the distance. It was the sort of moment at which we felt terribly afraid for ourselves—but particularly for this one man, who seemed the most lonely and defenceless of all in the vast, hostile world around us. As we stood there with our gloomy thoughts, we suddenly heard loud, unrestrainable sobs. Rushing in we saw BL crying by the phone. He wanted to tell us something but couldn't. At last he put down the receiver and told us through his tears that he had just phoned Lili Brik, who had exclaimed, as though she had been waiting to hear from him: 'Boria, my dear, what is all this? What are they doing to you?'

This was so unexpected that he was too overcome to get out a single word in reply, and had to phone her back a little while later . . .

Foreigners were always turning up to see us, as was now quite inevitable. Shortly after the publication of the novel in Italy, and then throughout the world, we were both of us summoned separately by the authorities 'at a high level'. The gist of what they had to say to both of us was: 'No foreigners'. Time was to show that there could have been no more absurd and impracticable demand.

The first to be summoned in this way was BL. Actually, he was not so much summoned as hauled off bodily—they came for him quite unexpectedly and took him away in a car, almost by force, in order to give him a talking-to. That day was very nearly the worst in my life. The evening before, I had gone up to Moscow with the intention of spending the whole of the next day there. But scarcely had I arrived in the apartment than BL phoned from Peredelkino to ask me to drop everything and return the next morning by nine o'clock to the 'little house'. I did as he asked, but when I got there, he was nowhere to be seen. I waited anxiously, racking my brains to think what might have happened. If he had asked me to come and wasn't here, something dreadful must have happened!

Only towards five in the evening, quite ill with worry by now, did I have the bright idea of going to the office of the Writers' Club and phoning my apartment to see if they knew anything there. I had guessed right: Mitia was waiting by the phone to pass on a message. 'Classoosha', he said, had called twice to say that he had unexpectedly come to Moscow, and that if I phoned, I was to be told to wait for him in Peredelkino. My despair gave way to indignation. On my way back from the office, I was quite astonished to see BL get out of an official car just by the bridge over the lake and walk towards me. I started giving him a piece of my mind, but he seemed hardly to listen, and told me how they had swooped on him out of the blue as he was standing on the steps in front of our house and carted him off. 'Don't be angry, Olia,' he said, stopping in the middle of the road to give me a kiss, 'but just wait to hear what I have to tell you! Do you know that I've been talking to a man without a neck? . . .'

If I remember rightly, 'the man without a neck' was the Prosecutor General, Rudenko. He had tried to get BL to sign a prepared statement undertaking not to meet foreigners.

'Cordon me off and don't let foreigners through, if you want,' BL told him, 'but all I can say in writing is that I have read your piece of paper. I can't make any undertakings. And altogether, it is strange to expect me to kiss the hand that beats me, but to forbid me even to say hello to people who want to pay their respects to me . . .'

'All I can say, Boris Leonidovich, is that you're a double-dealer,' the prosecutor replied crossly.

Boria cheerfully agreed with him: 'Yes, yes, you've found the right word—a double-dealer is what I am . . .'

When he returned to the 'big house', BL put up a notice in English, French, and German on the front door: 'Pasternak does not receive, he is forbidden to receive foreigners.'

Before very long I had my 'revenge': about ten days later it was BL's turn to wait at Potapov Street and worry about me. Ira and Mitia told him that two strangers had taken me away in a black ZIM. By way of a special favour I was allowed to ring home in the middle of the day to say that I would soon be back. I had been driven to the Lubianka, where a small, wizened general gave me tea, and then tried to get me also to sign a statement promising not to have dealings with foreigners. Following BL's example, all I agreed to do was sign a declaration that I had taken note of his demand, but I refused to enter into any undertakings. The general then told me that they had given up BL and myself as a bad job, but thought it necessary to try and save the children—who, he said, were getting the wrong kind of ideas into their heads.*

'Fancy that—they now worry about the education of children. How they've softened up,' Boria said in astonishment as he listened to my account of the conversation. 'I was beginning to think you were not coming back, and was getting ready to kick up a terrific rumpus.'

After these two incidents we did, however, agree that it would be better to exercise discretion and keep our meetings with foreigners to the minimum for the time being. But no sooner had we agreed on this than Boria sent one to see me at the Moscow apartment—a young West German student of literature, Gerd Ruge, who had just visited him in Peredelkino. I was terribly upset when Boria told me over the phone that the man was on his way.

'But, Olia,' he said, trying to justify himself, 'how could I refuse? He is writing a book about me. He has the first version of it with

* Not long before this, at a party, Mitia had broken the chair under a youth who made an offensive remark about BL. And Ira had acquired a French fiancé. All this, it appeared, had immediately become known in the Lubianka.

him. He wants to meet Lara and Katia! I couldn't say no—he's so handsome, with such blond hair!'

Ira immediately laid the table (without a tablecloth, 'in the Western manner'), and warned me not to bring out vast quantities of things to eat, but to give our guest only champagne and pineapple with icing sugar sprinkled on it.

Very soon Ruge rang from somewhere nearby in order to make sure how to find us. My attempts to explain were so confusing that at last I said Ira would meet him between the Pokrov and Kirov Gates. Amazingly she recognized him on sight, and brought him along. He really was very handsome, with brown eyes and fair hair, very spick and span, and looking even younger than Mitia—though Mitia was then only sixteen, and Ruge was twenty-seven.

We ate the pineapple, but our visitor showed no sign of wanting to leave the table. When BL rang to find out how he was getting on, I told him about Ira's insistence on entertaining him in such a grand manner. He asked me to get her to the telephone and told her not to be silly. She now gave way, and Gerd was soon happily tucking into Kiev cutlets,* sausages, and potatoes. He stayed till three in the morning ...

On a subsequent visit, Gerd asked whether he could bring a friend of his to see us, also a West German—the Moscow correspondent of *Die Welt*, Heinz Schewe. Schewe came to see us soon afterwards. He was a tall friendly man, still young, who spoke Russian badly, but not without humour. He introduced himself to BL as a fellow student. It was quite true: after serving in the Luftwaffe, Schewe had studied at Marburg University—where forty-five years earlier BL had attended a course by the famous Professor Hermann Cohen. Another very important thing about Schewe was that he was a close friend of Giangiacomo Feltrinelli, from whom he brought some money in Soviet currency for BL. He had also been entrusted by Feltrinelli with the delicate mission of asking BL to have as little as possible to do with d'Angelo and his friends, and to maintain contact through himself alone.

To anticipate a little, I may say that Schewe became our devoted and selfless friend. He had brought a draft contract from Feltrinelli, but when BL proposed to sign it without more ado, Schewe stopped him and said: 'Do not be in a hurry. Giangiacomo is in Milan, but

* Rolled breast of chicken cooked in butter. (Tr.)

you are here in Moscow, and he doesn't see the dangers for you. It needs thought.'

It soon became clear that Heinz Schewe was by no means indifferent to Ira. BL was even rather pleased, but around this time Ira became friendly with Georges Nivat. Seeing the sad look in Schewe's eyes when Ira stopped coming to our Sunday lunches at Peredelkino —clearly in order to avoid him—BL gave him a copy of his translation of *Faust* with the inscription: 'However life may turn out, you will always be a member of our family'.

Later, on June 2, 1960, when dozens (if not hundreds) of journalists from all over the world were taking photographs of every moment of BL's funeral and recording their impressions into dictaphones or writing them down in notebooks, Heinz Schewe stayed at my side the whole time, quite heedless of his professional interests. When one of his fellow journalists chided him about this, Heinz said: 'I know—I am taking no photographs and making no notes—but, you see, I am burying a friend . . .'

This is only one typical example. From the moment Schewe entered our lives we clearly understood that he was a real friend of the kind one rarely meets. Unfortunately, owing to circumstances (and at times through our own folly) we disregarded the message he had brought from Feltrinelli about d'Angelo, to whom we continued to write. We were to pay dearly for this.

D'Angelo had just translated BL's 'An Essay in Autobiography' into Italian, and had decided it was time to start his own publishing business instead of working for Feltrinelli.

When d'Angelo's official appointment in Moscow came to an end he had introduced us, before he left, to his successor, Garritano. I cannot say that we took an instant liking to Garritano. At a moment when Schewe was absent from Moscow, I had gone to see him on a peculiar errand from BL, namely to give him two blank pieces of paper with BL's signature on them, as well as certain important documents and instructions which he wanted passed on to Feltrinelli. Garritano then left Moscow—not, as we later discovered, for Italy, but for the Caucasus. When he returned—which was after BL's death—his wife Mirella told me that the basket in which they had put the documents had got soaking wet during one of the rainstorms for which the Caucasus is so famous, and had then disappeared.

I appealed to Heinz for help—he was by now back in Moscow.

Whatever grievance he might have felt, he came straightaway. I also asked Garritano and his wife to come to the Potapov Street apartment, although the Italian, as a Communist, was at first reluctant to meet a West German. During the meeting I became hysterical and Heinz had to calm me down. After hearing the story about the basket and the rainstorm, he commented icily: 'Even such things have been known to happen . . .' Then, rubbing his fingers together, he asked politely: 'And how is the weather in Rome?'

Heinz was in every way a true friend. He did everything he could to keep me from making unwise moves. 'A foolish woman,' he was later to say of me in a Russian-language broadcast from abroad, 'and too much fell on her shoulders at once.' It was not his fault if there was much he failed to protect me from . . .

But I have run on too far ahead. I must return to the beginning of the last year of BL's life.

'The Nobel Prize'

Tuesday, January 20, 1959, unexpectedly proved to be an important date for BL.

It was something that had been brewing quietly for a long time. Boria's relations with his family had settled into a rut of cold mutual antagonism. I was regarded at the 'big house' as the cause of the whole trouble, but at the same time they made no attempt to understand BL's position and had no wish to.

At last he could stand it no longer and decided to break with the 'big house' for good. He made arrangements with Paustovski for us to go to Tarusa and spend the winter with him there. But from the outset I did not believe Boria would actually be able to face the storm his departure would provoke—and how indeed could one expect it from a man of sixty-nine? But he had apparently made up his mind, and seemed completely set on it.

It was the time of the January blizzards, and I was full of gloomy forebodings.

On January 20, the day he had fixed for our departure to Tarusa, BL came early in the morning, very pale, and announced that he couldn't go through with it. 'What more do you need,' he asked, as though the initiative for the move had come from me, 'when you know that you are my right hand, and that I am entirely with you?' But it was impossible, he went on, to hurt people who were not at fault and now wanted only to preserve the appearance of the life they were used to. There was just nothing for it but to put up with things as they were, and he would have to go on living in two homes. He said a lot more, all on the same lines.

I was very angry indeed. I felt intuitively that I needed the protection of Pasternak's name more than anybody else. I had certainly done everything to deserve it. One and a half years later my worst forebodings came true. His name helped me in 1949, and it could just as surely have warded off disaster in 1960—if I had borne it officially . . .

But at that moment, on January 20, 1959, I could have had such thoughts only vaguely at the back of my mind, and the main cause of my fury was simply my resentment as a woman. Without intending to, BL had unleashed the spirit of protest in me. I accused him of wanting to preserve his own peace of mind at my expense, and I declared my intention of leaving immediately for Moscow.

Not knowing what to say, he kept repeating that now, of course, I could easily drop him altogether, when he was an outcast.

I called him a poseur. He went pale, and saying quietly that I would soon understand everything, he left. I did not try to stop him.

I went back to Moscow, and that evening he phoned and began with his usual 'Oliusha, I love you . . .' but I hung up on him.

The next morning I had a call from the Central Committee. It was Polikarpov: 'What Boris Leonidovich has done now,' he said indignantly, 'is even worse than the business of the novel.'

'I know nothing about it,' I replied, 'I have spent the night in Moscow and left Boris Leonidovich yesterday afternoon.'

'Have you quarrelled?' he asked in a tone of exasperation. 'A fine time to do that! Every foreign radio station is broadcasting a poem he handed to a foreigner here. All the fuss had died down, but now it has started all over again. Go out there and make things up with him—do everything you can to stop him committing some new act of madness . . .'

As I started getting dressed, the phone rang again. It was Boria calling from the office of the Writers' Club in Peredelkino:

'Oliusha, don't put the receiver down,' he began, 'let me tell you

everything. When you so rightly lost your temper with me yesterday
and went away, I just didn't want to believe it. I went over to the 'big
house' and wrote a poem about the Nobel Prize. Here it is:

> I am caught like a beast at bay.
> Somewhere are people, freedom, light,
> But all I hear is the baying of the pack,
> There is no way out for me.
>
> Over there is the dark wood, the lake-shore
> And the trunk of a felled fir tree,
> Everywhere my road is barred.
> Let it be so. I care no more.
>
> How dare I write such stuff
> —I, scoundrel and evil-doer,
> Who made the whole world weep
> At the beauty of my native land?
>
> The pursuit draws ever closer,
> And now I'm guilty of another thing:
> My right hand is no longer with me—
> My dear friend is with me no more.
>
> As the noose tightens round my neck,
> At the hour when death is so near,
> I should like my right hand near me
> To wipe away my tears.

'I wrote this poem, Oliusha, and went back to our house,' Boria
now went on to tell me. 'I could not believe you had gone away. On
the way I ran into a foreign journalist. He came along after me, and
asked if I had anything to tell him. I said I had just lost the person I
loved, and I showed him the poem I was taking to you. And now the
fuss has started all over again . . .'

I went out to Peredelkino and told him of Polikarpov's telephone
call. Peace was now restored in our little house by the Izmalkovo
lake: 'Surely you don't imagine I would ever leave you, whatever
you did? My poor dunderhead . . .'

The following day, as I was walking along the snow-covered road
from the Peredelkino shop, Yuri Olesha ran after me shouting,
'Wait a moment!' When I stopped, he came up and said to me with

a pleading look in his eyes: 'Do not leave him! You're a good woman, I know. Do not leave him!'

Although it was not written for publication, BL's poem 'The Nobel Prize' thus also became known to the whole wide world. The falling of a small stone sometimes precipitates an avalanche, and it was only in this sense that our quarrel was the cause of 'The Nobel Prize' being published. The real reason was the hounding of BL, the fact that he had been put in the situation of a 'beast at bay'. With this poem he cancelled out all the efforts of his persecutors to deceive posterity into believing that his renunciation of the prize had been 'completely voluntary', and that he had 'repented' . . . In this way he got his own back in appropriate fashion for the two letters he had been forced to sign out of concern for those close to him, and in the face of a threat to expel him from the country.[43]

On the Sunday of that same week, BL found among his papers two lithographs which had been produced by the Stroganov School in a hundred copies in 1903 from Leonid Pasternak's well-known sketch of Leo Tolstoi sitting at his writing desk. BL presented one of these lithographs to my step-father Sergei Stepanovich, and the other to my son Mitia. On Mitia's copy he wrote: 'To dear Mitia Vino-gradov, an impulsive and gifted young man, with the wish that the steep and checkered path of his youth may become easier—with love, and faith in him. B. Pasternak, January 25, 1959.'

In a word, peace and harmony reigned again. But this was not our last quarrel. If only it had been!

At the beginning of February, Polikarpov summoned me once more. He said that the British Prime Minister, Harold Macmillan, was coming to Moscow* and that a meeting between BL and any member of the party accompanying the Prime Minister would be undesirable. He might give some ill-considered interview which—in Polikarpov's words—could later do harm to BL himself. It would therefore be a good thing if BL would go away somewhere during this time.

As I expected, Boria was indignant, and said he had no intention of going anywhere. But at this moment he happened to get an invitation from Nina Tabidze in Tbilisi, and Zinaida Nikolayevna, who was a great friend of Nina's, took BL off to Tbilisi with her. When he

* Macmillan was in the Soviet Union from February 21 to March 3, 1959. (Tr.)

phoned me to say goodbye before leaving, all he could do in reply to
my expression of outrage was to keep on repeating: 'Oliusha, it's not
you, it's not you saying these things. This is something out of a bad
novel. It's not you and me.'

In a cold fury I then left for Leningrad. Ira forwarded to me there
the letters which Boria wrote to me from Tbilisi, but I did not reply
to them. To this very day the misery of this last quarrel in our life
still gnaws at me. On all other occasions when he had pleaded with
me like this, his voice and hands shaking, I had rushed to his side,
covering his hands, his eyes, his cheeks with kisses. How defenceless
he was, and how lovable . . .

He stayed in Tbilisi from February 20 to March 6, 1959, and sent
me eleven superb letters from there.*

Shortly after arriving back in Moscow, on March 15, he wrote to
Boris Zaitsev in Paris:

I cannot tell you . . . what joy your letter gave me. I doubt whether
anyone realizes how often I wish my life were quite different, how
often I am overcome with misery and horror at myself, at my
unfortunate temperament which demands freedom for the spirit and
its expression such as perhaps exists nowhere, at all the vicissitudes of
fate which bring so much suffering on those near to me. Your letter
reached me at one of these moments of gnawing anguish—thank you.

And almost a year later, on February 7, 1960, not long before his
death, he wrote (in English) to George Reavey[44] in New York:

To speak the truth, I should disappear and hide, as Knut Hamsun did
towards the end of his life, and write in secret whatever I can still
do—but in Russian conditions this is impossible.

* Letters 10–20 in Appendix A. (Tr.)

'Friends, family, dear good-for-nothings . . .'

BL could never bear to be alone. In the days when he was under pressure, not only I but many other people, all loving him in their own way, spoke with him, gave him advice or tried to tell him what to do. But like the cat in Kipling that 'walked by himself', BL did things in the way he wanted to, whatever anybody else may have thought. He always had his own ideas as to what he should or should not do.

It often happened that people who failed to understand this side of him, and, imagining themselves to be on the closest terms with him, tried to influence his behaviour or his thinking, would find that they did not in fact enjoy his confidence.

On September 30, 1958, he wrote to Renate Schweitzer:

. . . I have this matchmaking side to me—I like to bring together and introduce to each other all my most select and dearest friends. They meet each other more often than they meet me—these are mostly the ones I see together with Olga. Our usual guests, that is, the family guests, mean very much less to me. These are the ones who come on Sunday and they do not know Olga at all—they are prominent, well-to-do people connected with the arts and the theatre—my soul belongs not to them, but to the young, unknown people who gather round Olga.

During the dark days in which he was hounded, the 'family guests' at the 'big house' not only meant little to him, but often now got on his nerves as well. ('His friends had become strangely dim and colourless. Not one of them had kept his own outlook, his own world. They had been much more vivid in his memory. He must have over-estimated them in the past.')*

BL generally expressed agreement with any advice or criticism: 'Yes, yes, yes—you are quite right, it is very bad . . .', he would say, nodding his assent impatiently, but from then on he would think none too kindly of the person who had offered it. Marina Tsvetayeva once wrote of him: 'His trustfulness was equalled only by his mistrustfulness. He would trust—entrust himself to!—the first person who came along; yet part of him mistrusted even his best friend.'

* *Doctor Zhivago*, Chapter 6. (Tr.)

In the early autumn of 1959, Mikhail Astangov, an actor at the Vakhtangov Theatre, invited BL and myself to a performance of Gerhart Hauptmann's *Before Sunset* in which he was appearing. Boria liked Astangov, both as a person and as an actor. He gladly accepted the invitation and, little suspecting the distress it would cause, we set off for the theatre.

BL watched the play in brooding silence, hardly taking his eyes off the stage. I could see that behind this intense concentration there was something which affected him in a deeply personal way, that it was not just a matter of interest in a work of art. My suspicion was borne out when he said to me, as we were leaving the theatre: 'Astangov played me brilliantly, but Tselikovskaya was very poor as you.'

Everybody who knows Hauptmann's play will understand why BL identified himself with Matthias Clausen, and me with Inken Peters. The wall of incomprehension and malevolence surrounding the last love of the ageing scholar estranges him from all those close to him, and leads to tragedy . . . BL was beset by forebodings of something similar. For this reason any stone cast at me, no matter by whom, angered him, and aspersions on the novel—these were also often levelled at me by implication—roused him to fury. When this happened, BL, usually so benign and friendly, suddenly became sharp-tongued, impatient, and at times even downright rude.

Not all of his close friends understood this or took account of it in their relations with him. The Moscow Arts Theatre actor Boris Livanov, gently but quite pointedly, was always trying to suggest to BL that he was first and foremost a lyric poet and had therefore been unwise to spend so much time and effort on the novel—and, in particular, to put up such a fight for its right to exist.

But for BL the novel was something towards which he had been working all his life. It embodied all his reflections on human destiny, on the tragedy of existence, on nature and the meaning of art. Any sly attempts by certain of his friends to detract from its role and importance were always bound to lead to an explosion.

On September 13, 1959, during a Sunday lunch at the 'big house', Livanov once again began to say something on the subject of *Doctor Zhivago*, but this time Boria could stand it no more, and told him to shut up, silencing him with the words: 'You always wanted to play Hamlet, but how did you set about trying to?' (Livanov had dreamed of this all his life and used to tell people how once, at a reception in the Kremlin, he had asked Stalin himself what he thought the best way to play the part would be. Stalin had replied that Livanov should ask Nemirovich-Danchenko, but that he personally—Stalin—would never want to act the part, since the play was a pessimistic and reactionary one. At this Livanov gave up his attempts to appear in *Hamlet*, but continued to dream of it—as BL now cuttingly reminded him[45] . . .

I do not know what happened after this, but the next morning Boria came to me and wrote out on the spot the following short poem:

> Friends, family, dear good-for-nothings,
> You are so suited to this age of ours!
> Oh, the new disgrace I'll bring upon you
> One of these days, poltroons and liars.
>
> Providence has surely willed it so
> That you hang about and beg for favours
> —Having nowhere else to go—
> In ministerial antechambers . . .'

There was another stanza which I do not remember.

At the same time he sat down and wrote a long letter to Livanov:

September 14, 1959

Dear Boris, that time when you and I argued about Pogodin and Anna Nikandrovna,* there was no breach between us, but now there is, and will be.

For almost a year I have been in excellent health, and had forgotten what insomnia is, but last night, after you had been to see us, I could find no rest out of revulsion for life and for myself, and even a double dose of a sleeping drug had no effect.

The trouble is not wine, nor your departure from the rules of decent conduct, but the fact that I long ago broke away from and have left behind the grey, sickening, boring past, and I thought I had forgotten it—but you are a living reminder of it, an embodiment of it from tip to toe.

I begged you a long time ago not to get up at table and make speeches proposing my health. This is something you do not know

---

* Evidently Pogodin's wife. (Tr.)

how to do. I cannot stand your encomiums. I hate it when you trace my origins from refinement, from conscience, from my father, from Pushkin, from Levitan. Things that exist in their own absolute right have no need of a pedigree. And I can well do without your influential proposals to confer immortality on me. I shall manage somehow or other without your patronage. You are, perhaps, used to hearing exaggerations about yourself, but I am not a frog that needs to be blown up to the size of an ox. I realize what a lot I am putting at risk, but I would be happier to die than to breathe the same fumes of deceit as you. I have often seen how you have taken it out with your tongue on people who have broken with you—the Ivanovs, the Pogodins, the Kapitsas, and others.

May God help you. Nothing has happened. You are entirely in the right.

It is I, on the contrary, who am being unjust to you—I do not believe in you. And you will do very well to have no further truck with me. I am a treacherous friend. I have always said such nice things to you, Neigaus, and Asmus, and might go on doing so. But what I would most like to do, of course, is to hang the lot of you.

Yours, Boris.

Needless to say, he found it impossible to go on being angry with anyone, and before long he rang Livanov and invited him to come to the 'big house' again—'if, of course, you are able to overlook my letter'.

One is inevitably reminded by all this of the passage in which Yuri Zhivago mentally addresses his friends: 'Dear friends, how desperately commonplace you are—you, your circle, the names and the authorities you quote, their brilliance and the art you so much admire! The only bright and living thing about you is that you are living at the same time as myself and are my friends!' (And in an earlier passage he says: 'I . . . don't give a damn for any of you. I don't like you and you can all go to the devil.')

When I look back on this last year of his life, it always seems to me that BL felt much closer to a child, or to someone like Kuzmich, than to all the celebrities who visited him at the 'big house'.

Liusia Popova's seven-year-old son wrote to BL wishing him many happy returns on his birthday and at the same time sent him a drawing he had done showing BL as he saw him. On February 16, 1959, BL thanked the boy in the following words:

My dear Kiriusha,

I thank you from the bottom of my heart for your good wishes. How well you write already! And you draw very well too. Good for you. But you have enormously improved on my looks—I have never been so handsome in all my life.

Kiriusha, you are a marvel, and you have given me great joy. I wish you lots of success, happiness, and good luck in life. And long life and health to your grandmother, your mother, and everybody else in your house. Give them my greetings.

I send you a big kiss.

Yours, B. Pasternak★

To my step-father, Sergei Stepanovich, he wrote on October 20, 1959:

Dear Sergei Stepanovich,

Congratulations on your angel's day.† I remember that evening when we celebrated it at your old apartment, and I'm sorry we shan't be able to repeat it today. But for some time, it seems to me, Maria Nikolayevna‡ should see to it that you live a rather more uneventful life, without too many excitements and celebrations. Such need for rest is of course only temporary and soon passes, as I know in my own case.

I am very glad that we have been brought together by the circumstances of life. I have little belief in kinship based on ideas and convictions (I probably have none), but I attach great importance to the closeness of neighbours brought together by fate, by life. I am happy to greet such a neighbour in your person, and I embrace you warmly. Congratulations also to Maria Nikolayevna, the chief angel on the present occasion.

Yours, B. Pasternak

And now a much earlier example of the same kind of thing. Shortly before my arrest in 1949, I had happened to mention quite in

★ This letter is written in the second person plural—normally used only in addressing adults. (Tr.)

† Russians celebrate not only their birthday, but also the day of the saint—hence 'angel's day'—after whom they are named. (Tr.)

‡ The author's mother. (Tr.)

Boris Pasternak, 1958

Boris Pasternak and Ira, 1959

Boris Pasternak and Ira, 1960

passing to BL that Ira (then only eleven) was writing a poem, and also something resembling a story. He at once said he would like to see them, but before he could do so we were overtaken by the catastrophe of my imprisonment. Later, during my last but one winter in Potma, on one of his visits to my family in the Potapov Street apartment, Boria happened to come across some specimens of these childish attempts of Ira's at writing. He subsequently described how deeply affected he was by the whole situation—the mother had gone to prison because of him, and the daughter was left without anyone to help her develop what might well have been a natural talent. And some time later he wrote her a postcard:

Dear Irochka,
Whenever I come to see you I am always in such a hurry and have no time. So that I can read that verse of yours we talked about in the winter and your story, you must copy it all out (by hand, of course), and I'll take it with me to look at. Please try to do this when you have a spare moment. Then I will write and say what I think, or tell you when I see you. I am sure it is all very interesting and good.
Yours, BL. May 3 ,1952

The evident success of the novel in the outside world was very gratifying, but it also brought causes for complaint. In the first place Boria was irritated by the spate of articles containing endless—often quite ludicrous—conjectures about who the characters were based on, and particularly about the novel's 'symbolism'. On May 14, 1959, he wrote on this subject to Renate Schweitzer:

Various false interpretations are being placed on what I say (ostensibly as a way of paying me a compliment), and you may have been misled by them to some extent. In America, for instance, the book is being studied as though it were written in a secret code. The names of streets and people, the situations described, everything down to individual syllables must, they think, be allegorical, or symbolic, or have some deeper hidden meaning. But even if it were possible for me to have offended against art by writing such unnatural stuff, why on earth should I be complimented on it?
The whole of my symbolism, if it is possible to talk of any such

Boris Pasternak, Gustaf Gründgens (Director of the Hamburg Drama Theatre), actors Ehmi Bessel and Werner Hintz, after a performance of *Faust*, December 1959

Boris Pasternak and Heinz Schewe before a performance of the Hamburg Drama Theatre in the Central Children's Theatre, Sverdlov Square, December 1959

A specimen of Boris Pasternak's handwriting

thing, consists in the fact that despite the realism essential to me and inseparable from me, despite all the detail, I have tried to describe life in movement, at a high pitch of intensity, as I have always observed, seen, and known it.

And six days later he wrote (in French) to Jacqueline de Proyart:

People are searching for a hidden meaning in every syllable of my novel, deciphering words and proper names as though they were allegories or cryptograms. There is nothing of this in me. I do not accept the possibility that there can be symbols—comprehensive, partial, or isolated ones—even in the work of others, of anybody at all with claims to be a true artist. If a genuine work of literature contains something more than is written or printed in the text then this can only be a matter not of a hidden meaning that has to be puzzled out like a rebus but of its underlying general quality, of the spirit, dynamic, or aspiration to something infinite which pervades it and makes it what it is—just as the soul, in our conception of it, fills the whole body and cannot be abstracted from it.

If the 'soul' of French Impressionist painting is air and light, what is the 'soul' of this new prose represented by *Doctor Zhivago*? In its origin, in its preparatory stages, in its intention it is a realist work. It is supposed to depict the particular reality of a particular period of time—namely, Russian reality of the last fifty years. Beyond this there seemed to be something else worth defining and describing. What is this something else? It is reality as such, reality as a phenomenon or category in philosophy—the very fact of the existence of some particular reality or other.

One should not imagine there is anything new about this, that nobody had ever before attempted such a thing. On the contrary, art of a major kind has always aimed at conveying an overall sense of life as a whole, but has done so in various ways, depending on the prevalent philosophy, and hence from differing approaches . . .

My 'symbolism', my approach to reality is this: I describe characters, situations, details, and particulars with a single higher purpose—namely, with a view to undermining the idea of iron causality, the idea of absolute inevitability, and to depicting reality instead as a manifestation of inner impulses embodied in individuals, as a spectacle whose motive force is choice and freedom, and which

exists as one of a number of possibilities, taking place not just because
it simply so happens, but because it is so willed . . .

Publishers from all over the world began to pester BL with a
multitude of hare-brained schemes and proposals for the re-publica-
tion of his poetry and earlier prose. One American publisher tried to
get BL's agreement to the publication of a collection of the 'best'
articles on the novel, to be entitled *Homage to Zhivago*.

Most of all BL was irritated by new editions in the West of his
early verse and prose. I believe that in the longing for simplicity that
came to him in his later years, he clearly underestimated the appeal of
his early work—its lasting qualities were overshadowed, in his view,
by its complexity. Already in December of the previous year (1958),
he had written to Renate Schweitzer:

. . . After the success of *Zhivago* they are seizing on everything—my
early work, or anything at all that can be translated and published,
whether verse or prose. But almost all of it is no good at all. It is all
tarred with the brush of the expressionist era, of the disintegration of
form, of half-baked content abandoned to the mercies of a manner
which was adventitious, poorly understood, weak and empty. The
reason *Zhivago* rises above all this is because there is a concentration
of the spirit in it, because it is a labour of the spirit . . . And now they
want to water down this triumph of concentration with bucketfuls
and barrelfuls of nothing but water. The publishers have derived
much advantage and joy from *Zhivago* and one really might think
they could allow themselves a breathing space now until I am able to
write something more accomplished and of greater value. And then
there is another, quite baffling thing: after the prose, which has been
well translated, they reproduce the verse at the end, against all the
rules, in a formless, non-poetic rendering, which in fact is simply bad
prose. I fail to see the point of tacking this on at the end. Yet at the
same time there are excellent, rhymed translations of the verse to
hand, but of these nobody knows . . .[46]

On July 29, 1959, he wrote to Natalia Borisovna Sologub:

In the years of turmoil which we all went through together, I
managed, through lack of seriousness, to commit very many errors

and sins. How terrible and irredeemably sad that not only Russia, but the whole 'civilized world' was afflicted by this disintegration of forms and concepts during several decades . . . The success of the novel, with its evidence of my wish to contribute to the belated work of bringing our age to its senses, has meant that everywhere people are rushing to translate and publish all the stuff put out by me in those very years when we lapsed into folly and barbarism, when I was not only still incapable of expressing myself, but even, out of a feeling of comradeship and in deference to the prevailing tastes, refused to learn. How empty and verbose it is, how devoid of anything at all except worthless balderdash of the purest water . . . Almost more distressing to me now than anything else is the horror and despair I feel at the way people are everywhere dragging out into the light of day and voicing their approval of things I had gladly forgotten and thought were consigned to oblivion.

Finally, this is how he put it in a letter of December 10, 1959, to George Reavey in New York:

It is a cause of indescribable sadness and pain to me that I am again and again being reminded of these grains of life and truth buried among a vast quantity of dead, schematic rubbish and lifeless things. I am surprised that you and Kayden are making such efforts to resurrect things justly condemned to moulder away and be forgotten.

On my last birthday before his death Boria presented me with a copy of the American edition of *Doctor Zhivago* and wrote in it: 'To Oliusha on her birthday, June 27, 1959, with all my poor life. B.P.'

'The Blind Beauty'

The idea of a play had evidently come to BL a long time before, at the beginning of the war. In the poem 'Old Park' (written at the end of 1941), he speaks of writing a play 'inspired by the war', of describing in it the 'unimaginable course' of a kind of life never before experienced.

He began work on *The Blind Beauty*, a play about the unseeing

Russia of the days of serfdom, in the last autumn and winter of his life. He was much preoccupied by it, but complained he was unable to spend more than two hours a day actually writing it. He kept saying to me: 'I must work, I must work . . . I must finish it this year!'

In *The Blind Beauty* BL intended to show what he understood by freedom and the country's cultural tradition. At the beginning of the play—the time is just before the abolition of serfdom in 1861—there is much talk among the characters about freedom, particularly the problems of social freedom, as seen from the point of view of Russia's history and the situation at the time. After the reform, it soon becomes clear that the whole idea of social freedom is in general an illusory one, and that, as before, man is only truly free in art. These ideas were to be conveyed in the play by the serf actor Grigori.★

BL often told me it didn't really matter at the moment whether he wrote the play well or badly: 'I am writing for myself, as I did the novel. I am fascinated by that period—slavery, and at the same time emancipation somewhere in the offing, and against this background, the fate of an artist, an actor, at that turning point when serfdom was coming to an end and a new life beginning.'

Apart from the actor, BL intended to portray a private tutor who would eventually become a member of the 'People's Will'.[47] The play was to have reflected the actual events of the period (e.g. the attempted assassination of Alexander II), and there would also have been the story of a great love.

But much time would have been needed to complete the play, and BL's vast correspondence with people almost all over the world stood in the way of it. Sometimes he sighed and said in a completely childlike way: '. . . if only I could wake up one day and find the play was already written . . .'

Whenever he was asked how it was coming along, he used to reply: 'Before putting wallpaper up, you first lay a foundation by pasting over the surface with newspaper. That is all the play is at the moment—a foundation of newspaper.'

All he managed to get done was the prologue and scenes three and four of the first act. This came to 169 large pages written in standard

★ In the days of serfdom, many large landowners (e.g. the Sheremetyev family) maintained their own theatres, choosing talented young serfs to be trained as actors. (Tr.)

purple ink. (BL liked most of all to write with an ordinary pencil or, better still, with a small stub of a pencil, but if needs be, he would write with a school pen and nib; he had no time at all for fountain pens.)

On October 4, 1959, he wrote to Boris Zaitsev in Paris: 'Let it be your wish that nothing unforeseen should come to prevent the completion—still very far away—of the work in which I am now absorbed. Since the time when I first lukewarmly toyed with the idea of the play, it has turned from an idle whim or a trial shot into a cherished ambition, it has become a passion.'

On December 22, he wrote to Jacqueline de Proyart in Paris: '. . . if only I could get to the end of my play. I am staggering under an ever-increasing burden of things which often get in the way of my work. It has come so late—all these links with the outside world . . .'

And again, in a similar vein, the day after his seventieth birthday on February 11, 1960, to Boris Zaitsev: '. . . But I would like to swear to you personally, to make a solemn and binding oath by all that is holy, that from tomorrow everything else will be put aside, things will change out of all recognition, the work will fairly hum and start moving again.'

Around this same time, in a letter to Feltrinelli on practical matters concerning the need to iron out the complicated relations between BL and his French and Italian publishers, I had this to say about the play:

Now I would like to tell you something pleasant. I had always taken a sceptical view of BL's new work—his play about Russia under serfdom. For one thing I thought he would find the genre itself restricting, and for another I was worried by the choice of subject matter. But I can now confidently assure you that the new play will be a work just as bound up with his own life and artistic nature as the novel was. At present it is a vivid and dynamic dramatic narrative which will be trimmed down to make a stage-play. The language is colourful and every word is alive, the story is full of action and will make good theatre. For me, who was the first to hear him read it aloud, this was a very pleasant surprise. He needs about another two months to finish it, so he must be allowed to devote himself entirely to the work, without being distracted by wrangles over business matters.

And a little earlier I had written to Sergio d'Angelo:

BL has read me bits of his play. I am glad to be able to tell you that he has not been in the least constricted by the genre, there are simply extraordinary passages which show his gifts to the full. I listened, open-mouthed, with unflagging attention. There is no question of blind acceptance on my part—I did not believe in the play and was afraid of what might come of it . . .

When he wrote the following note to me, on April 7, 1960, I did not know that it was only a matter of days before the onset of his fatal illness, and that within little over a month he would be dead:

. . . I am very interested by the truthful and sensible things that you, Ira, Koma, and Kostia [Bogatyrev] have to say about the first half of the play, which still needs a lot of work . . . There is so much unnatural chit-chat, which must either be cut out or re-done . . .

And already mortally ill, on May 5, he still showed his concern about the play in another note to me:

Everything I have of value I am passing on to you: the manuscript of the play, and now the diploma . . .* Please staple together the pages of the notebook with the play in it, so people won't mix them up if they fall out as they read.

The previous year, on June 15, he had written to Renate Schweitzer:

What torments me and gnaws at my heart is that I receive so much from Olga Vsevolodovna and you, and benefit by it all, and the only thing I can offer in return to show my gratitude is the new work—but it is going so slowly, so sluggishly. I am unworthy of you both. But the play is already alive, and I have faith in it . . .

* He was already very ill by the time he received the diploma of the American Academy of Arts and Letters, to which he had been elected as an honorary member in February 1960 'in recognition of creative achievement in the arts'. He immediately sent the diploma to me with Kostia Bogatyrev. 'Only don't let anyone see it, keep it out of sight,' he said to Kostia. There was little hope of carrying a stiff folder measuring 32 by 42 cm without its being noticed. But he ran into nobody on the way, nor did anyone leave with him, as usually happened on these Wednesday visits of his to BL.

Last Meeting

When 1960, the last year of BL's life, came round, our life seemed to go on much as before. I often went into Moscow on business, and when I returned to Peredelkino, BL, as always, would be there to meet me, walking up and down in front of our new house, or sometimes coming there the moment after I arrived, just as I had closed the door behind me and started to light the stove.

On Sundays I and others (but not Boria, of course) would sometimes go out on skis. After that we generally had lunch with friends and relatives.* My mother and step-father, Sergei Stepanovich, would walk over from the *dacha* they now rented nearby. Kostia Bogatyrev would come in from Moscow, and sometimes Heinz Schewe, Georges Nivat, and Irina. Just as before, Boria was his usual lively, high-spirited self at table.

On Wednesday, February 10, he celebrated his seventieth birthday. It was astonishing how young and trim he still was at this age. His eyes shone as brightly as ever, he was just as easily carried away, and he was as spontaneous and unreflecting as a child.

Everybody who knew him was struck by this youthfulness, which remained with him till the hour of his death. Liusia Popova, for instance, writing in recent years about her first meeting with him, describes it like this:

The thing about him that made an extraordinary impression on me was that while his appearance was in no way different from what I had expected, he was at the same time quite incredible in some way, absolutely unlike anyone else. It seemed impossible that one could ever imagine such a person, yet he was exactly as I had always pictured him to myself. And so young! My goodness, how young he always looked! He was young right up to his death. Later, when I got to know him better, I saw him not only in public, when he was at the top of his form . . . I also saw him in poor health, depressed, tired, and even in despair, but he never looked like an old man . . .

On the morning of his seventieth birthday, I remember, we drank brandy together and exchanged fond kisses by the crackling stove

* Sometimes BL lunched at the 'big house' on Sundays, sometimes with me— there was no hard and fast rule about it.

and then, looking at his handsome face in the mirror, he said with a sigh: 'How late everything has come for me . . . But we did get through all our troubles together, Oliusha. And everything is all right now! If only we could live forever like this. Only I'm ashamed of those Polikarpov letters. What a pity you got me to sign them.'

I protested indignantly—how soon he had forgotten the state of desperate anxiety we had been in! To this he replied: 'We only took fright out of politeness, you must admit!'

He then sat with me reading with huge enjoyment the birthday greetings which had reached him from all over the world, and looking at his presents—among them souvenirs in Marburg earthenware, a little statuette representing Lara, some decorative candles, and delicate images of saints from Germany.

Many of these presents were preserved by Ira after BL's death. There was, for instance, an alarm clock in a leather case sent by Nehru. I still have a note written by BL about two others: 'The earthenware pots are from the proprietress of a filling station in Marburg, Frau Becker. The red, heart-shaped thing is a candle from R. Schweitzer, which Ira should light some time on a suitable occasion.'

A couple of months or so before this (in the middle of December 1959), the Hamburg Drama Theatre had visited Moscow with Gustaf Gründgens as its director. BL wanted to invite members of the cast to the 'big house' in Peredelkino, and on December 14 he wrote (in German) to Schewe:

Dear Herr Schewe,

I would be most grateful if you will kindly help us in the matter which O.V.* will ask you about. If you see the members of the Hamburg Theatre again, I should like to confirm my wish to invite them to my house at Peredelkino. The best thing for me would be if they had a free Sunday during their stay in Moscow. Only the hour I suggested—around three o'clock in the afternoon—is on the late side. I had forgotten how many important and absorbing things we have to talk about. I would now rather they come at two, or even at one. If they have no free Sunday left, then it could be any other day that suits them. If the worst comes to the worst, they could come late in the evening, after their performance. In any case, I should be

* Olga Vsevolodovna Ivinskaya. (Tr.)

informed in good time. The woman interpreter from the Ministry at the theatre knows Konstantin Petrovich Bogatyrev and (if there is no other way of contacting me from the theatre) he could serve as an intermediary. It could be ten to twelve of the actors playing leading parts in the production—the magnificent Gründgens could decide exactly who. Apart from the charming Ella Büchi—this goes without saying—it would be good if Fr[auen] Bessel and Goebel, and Herr Lowitz, who played Wagner so brilliantly, could do me the honour.

I must now take my leave of you, dear friend. Kindly give your mother my highest regards and best wishes for Christmas and the New Year. I wish you a good journey, and hope you are able to spend your winter vacation both profitably and happily, undarkened and undisturbed by anything or anyone.

Yours, B. Pasternak

I have already mentioned in a previous chapter why it was that BL was not able, in the event, to hold this reception as he had planned. But we had touching meetings with the members of the cast at the theatre. Schewe, who knew all of them, managed to get us tickets. We went to see *Faust* and Kleist's *Broken Jug*. On the first evening the actors hauled Boria out onto the stage, and then we went behind the scenes to meet the whole assembled company. Spellbound and beside himself with happiness, Boria was photographed together with Gründgens, whom he called 'a truly Satanic Mephistopheles'. He gave the actor a photograph of himself and wrote on the back of it in German:

One may say of this performance: 'Here, the inadequate/ To fullness groweth;/ Here is wrought the ineffable ...'*

The actress who played Margarita gave me a package with presents. BL was showered with praise and invitations and complimented on his good looks and youthfulness. It was all very gratifying to him. The whole atmosphere was joyful, simple, and carefree. We stayed until three o'clock in the morning talking about the theatre and everything under the sun ...

Not long after this I noticed the first signs that Boria was not well. We would sit down to go through some translation or other, but he

* From Goethe's *Faust*, Act 5 (as translated by Sir Theodore Martin). (Tr.)

at once began to feel tired and I would have to do most of the work by myself.

As before, we went out for walks, sometimes for a long one all the way round the Bakovka woods. But I could see that he was no longer so full of life. More and more often I began to notice a certain greyness about his complexion that had never been there before, and it frightened me. Once, seeing his head resting on a pillow—it was sunk deep down in it—I had a sudden feeling that it was the head of a dead man. I was aware of this peculiar thing about myself: I would have a momentary impression that some perfectly healthy person was dead—and shortly afterwards he would indeed die. I immediately put the terrible thought out of my mind.

He began to complain about a pain in his chest, and he was having trouble with his leg again. We suddenly had the feeling that all his treatment in hospital had not been entirely successful. It was all very disturbing and ominous.

In the evenings he put on a show of being in better spirits, fooling both himself and me. Three times in December and January, he read from his play at great length. He spoke the lines with great expression, imitating popular speech with gusto and lingering over the passages he thought funny. He corrected and added things in pencil as he went along.

On one of these occasions, when his family had gone into Moscow to a performance of the Hamburg Theatre, he devoted the whole evening to *The Blind Beauty*. He was reading it as much to himself as to me, listening to his own voice, and marking the manuscript here and there with jerky movements of his pencil. Suddenly he said: 'You know, Olia, I think we shall have to publish it in the same way as we published the novel. They certainly won't do it here.'

A month or two after this, in March, I slipped on our staircase in Moscow and pulled a muscle in my leg. It was put in plaster and I had to stay at the apartment. Boria was very upset. It meant a change in our routine—he had to come out from Peredelkino to see me.

When I returned there at the beginning of April, I felt that Boria seemed in rather better shape. He talked to me at length and with great animation about his meetings with Liubimov, and about all kinds of other matters.

April was blissful—as any April always is. Particularly splendid was our small garden with its pine trees, bushes coming into flower,

and pale-green birches. Dappled with spots of sunlight it seemed such
a safe and splendid haven for us.

BL looked to be well and in good heart, and the days resumed
their normal measured pace. I was overjoyed that my black mood of
March had lifted—March is always a terrible month for me.

At Easter, Renate Schweitzer finally arrived for her first (and only)
meeting with BL. Earlier in the year (on January 25) he had written
to her:

... you will meet my wife Z., you will see my house and what life in
it is like. When you come there, you may see people and relationships
that typify me in some way or another; or you may see people and
relationships that do not typify me in the least. It is a matter of chance.
Then later on I shall take you to see Olga ...

Just as he had promised, he first entertained Renate at the 'big
house' and then brought her over to me where I lived in our new
room with its three windows looking across to the 'Fadeyev
tavern'.

On a bright Easter day Renate sat with us at table. She was beside
herself with joy at seeing Pasternak, with whom she had corresponded
for more than two years. She spoke in her native language, but
deliberately mispronouncing it 'in the Russian way'. She said we were
exactly as she had imagined us—BL and me, 'Lara'.

The room was filled with the fragrance of the hyacinths Renate
had brought with her; we had a large plate of painted eggs on the
table,* and outside there was a young, translucent spring.

Boria, dressed in his favourite blue-grey jumper, was extraordinarily charming, fresh, and genial. He was very funny as he
awkwardly warded off Renate's affectionate advances.

After seeing Renate off at the station, BL came over to my
mother's house where I had gone to watch television, and called me
out on to the verandah. Falling on his knees and sobbing, he said:
'Oliusha, God will never forgive me for upsetting you by being so
nice to Renate. I don't wish to see her again. If you want, I'll stop
writing to her.'

But the only thing that upset me was his overwrought state—a
sure sign of approaching illness. I was worried about him and tried to
calm him as best I could.

* It is the Russian custom to paint eggs—generally red—at Easter. (Tr.)

On the first morning after Easter, he felt quite unwell, and again said to me: 'Oliusha, don't you think I may be falling ill as a punishment for what I did to you over Renate? Everything was all right, but now I have this pain in the chest again. I should have myself looked at by someone.'

However, it was not till past the middle of April that I again thought there was something disturbing about BL's appearance. He was generally fresh and rosy-cheeked in the mornings, but suddenly he began to look distinctly sallow.

I then asked a woman doctor he knew to come and see him at our little house in Peredelkino. This was a certain Baroness Tiesenhausen, who had an excellent manner with her patients and was very good at raising their spirits. She talked in a bass voice and looked so much like a man that the children on Sobinov Street (she used to come there to see my mother) always shouted: 'Auntie, why are you an uncle?'

The Baroness examined Boria at length, expressing amazement at the youthfulness of his physique. She assured us that she could find nothing seriously wrong with him.

BL was on top of the world. He said it must simply be exhaustion from overwork and nervous strain, and that perhaps he should put the play aside for a time. But at once he contradicted himself: 'I must work, I must work . . .'

On Wednesday, April 20, he suddenly felt really bad. A doctor whom the Ivanovs knew came to see him at the 'big house' and said he suspected angina.

Despite this, BL came to see me at the usual time that day.

'Oliusha,' he told me in a quiet voice, 'I shall have to stay in bed for a while. I will bring the play to you—don't let me have it back until I am well again.'

He stayed only a short time and before leaving he said: 'I do not want you to interrupt our normal mode of existence. I shall get messages to you as often as I can send them with someone. If I have to stay in bed for any length of time, we will find a way of communicating regularly. There may be some suitable opportunity for you to come to the house, but for goodness' sake don't try to see me there until I tell you. I must get better and come back to you healthy, so that I can earn the right to you. Perhaps this really is a punishment from God!'

Such was his mood as he left me. I stayed in Peredelkino all that day and the next, but I did not feel particularly alarmed. I even thought that the greyness about his face I had noticed in March was no longer there. And then I knew that he was occasionally given to hypochondria, and could also be genuinely superstitious about his health. Once he began to talk about death, partly in jest, but also half-seriously, when a plasticine sculpture of him made by Zoya Maslennikova began to lose its shape in the hot sun.

In general, however, he did not often talk about death, and then always with philosophical calm:

. . . art has two constant, two unending preoccupations: it is always meditating upon death, and it is always thereby creating life . . .*
. . . life is like a large meeting at which everybody may say his piece. But you can't go on speaking forever—you have to give the floor to others. I have said what I have to say, and am not frightened by the thought of death.
. . . in the same way that I have several times surrendered myself to life or to a serious piece of work, it now only remains for me, as a major undertaking, to surrender myself to death.

I had resigned myself to being separated from him for ten days or so at least, and was quite astonished when only a couple of days later, on Saturday April 23, I saw him coming down the road with his dilapidated briefcase in his hand. I ran out joyfully to meet him: 'Boria,' I said, 'why are you up—you promised to stay in bed! I am not anxious about you, I can wait. And if there's any news for you, I'll get someone to come and tell you.'

He was expecting some money and was worried at the delay in its arrival. He had ten people, if not more, living in the house at that moment, and he needed a good deal of it. He had asked Schewe to do something, but Schewe had gone away. He had left a special 'pass' to the 'big house' with me, in case Schewe or any of the Italians should turn up.

My joy at seeing him so unexpectedly was premature. He looked pale and haggard, a sick man. We went inside into the room, where it was cool and shaded.

Without replying to all my anxious questions, he kissed me—as

* *Doctor Zhivago*, Chapter 3. The following quotation is from a transcript of a private conversation, and the third from a letter.

though by this he could regain his health, as though it would give him back his strength, courage, and will to live ...

I thought of the very first time, this had happened—it was also in April, in 1947, now so far in the past ...

I saw him part of the way back. We stopped at the ditch beyond which I usually never went.

Suddenly he remembered: 'Oliusha, I almost forgot—I've brought you the manuscript.' He took a rolled-up sheaf of paper from the briefcase—he had wrapped it up in his usual neat way—and handed it to me. It was the manuscript of *The Blind Beauty*.

'Keep it,' he said, 'and do not let me have it back until I get better. I am going to attend to nothing now except my illness. I know you love me, I have faith in it, and our only strength is in this. Do not make any changes in our life, I beg you ...'

This was the last time we spoke with each other.

'*I am finished, but you are still alive ...*'

On May 2, Koma Ivanov came into the garden of the 'little house' in a state of some agitation. He had brought me a package from BL which contained a number of notes written in pencil in his hand. Koma told me that at best he might have had a minor heart attack but that treatment was difficult because of asthmatic breathing caused by some other condition.

These were anxious days. I sat waiting for people to bring word from BL, and someone came every day—he sent notes with Kostia Bogatyrev, Koma Ivanov, or anybody else who had been to visit him.*

His illness took a turn for the worse on Friday, May 6. The day had begun well enough. He had got out of bed and washed, and had even thought of going for his usual walk. Suddenly he took it into his head to wash his hair, but the consequences were catastrophic—he immediately felt very unwell and a doctor had to be called urgently. Unfortunately it took some time to discover that he had had another heart attack—which, as later turned out, had produced lesions of the tissue over a large area, even though not deep ones.

---

* After my return from the camp, only part of these notes were given back to me. See Appendix A, items 21–27.

After an anxious night had passed, I received a note from him in an unsteady hand, quite unlike his usual writing.

I went into Moscow and made contact with certain medical people there. The *Litfund* and the subsidiary branch of the Kremlin Hospital sent help in the shape of a doctor and two nurses who took turns keeping watch at his bedside.

One of the nurses, Marina Rassokhina (who was only sixteen years old) came to see me. From her I learned that as soon as BL was able to speak again, he had told her of the tragic state of affairs that had arisen because of our love for each other. He had now sent her to tell me that she would come and see me every day after her turn of duty was over.

If she had been on duty during the day, Marina often stayed the night with me. She told me that BL had asked her time and time again to arrange for me to see him—even though nobody was now being allowed to his bedside. He had been put in a downstairs room after falling ill, and his idea was that Marina should bring me up to the window there. Our meeting was being put off only because his false teeth had been taken away from him after the heart attack, and he was terribly upset at the effect this had on his appearance—he couldn't bear me to see him without them! In childlike fashion—but with very unchildlike tears in her eyes—Marina told me his exact words: 'Oliusha won't love me any more. It's bound to happen, I tell you—I look such a fright now.'

Soon after this I ceased to get any further notes from him—he was no longer allowed a pencil. I begged Marina to let him have the pencil stub she said still lay on the table, but she couldn't bring herself to—and there was nobody apart from her I could ask.

In the middle of the month I went to Moscow again to invite a well-known heart specialist, Professor Dolgoplossk, to come and examine BL and tell me what the real state of his health was.

When I brought Dolgoplossk to the 'big house', BL's brother, Alexander Leonidovich, told me that any kind of excitement was bad for him, and the elder son Zhenia said there was no question of my seeing him, because every time the slightest thing was said about me, he became upset and began to weep.

After some time, Professor Dolgoplossk came outside and told me that BL had to all intents and purposes got over the heart attack. His tone was so confident that it gave me hope.

I lived from one visit of Marina's to the next. I knew that on returning to him from me she passed on my words of encouragement, tenderness, and love—which were vitally important to him now.

Once, while the older nurse, Marfa Kuzminichna, was on duty, Boria suddenly felt worse and, as I learned from her later, began to tell her, haltingly and breathing with difficulty, about his relations with me.

Marfa Kuzminichna had been a nurse at the front during the war and had a high sense of her own worth. She came to see me because, as she put it, she felt it her moral duty.

She spoke a good deal about the courage with which BL was standing up to the pain. Ira made some notes at the time of some of the things she told us he had said to her:

BL was full of praise for his younger son Lionia—'a rare and unmodern person' and 'hers'. 'Will she forget me?'—to which he replied himself: 'No, no.' And 'Will she be happy without me?' . . . 'Do something for me, Marfa Kuzminichna, I so much want to live. Don't hurry, just sit and think, and do what you did the last time.'

Once Marfa Kuzminichna said to him: 'I don't seem to have read much of your work. Just a few poems.' And he replied: 'There's no need to. Don't read it. It's all nonsense. I have written other things, not published here.'

After a bad bout was over, he said to her: 'What can I do for you? I can't fall down on my knees before you—you see I can't. I already felt the breath of the other world on me, but you brought me back. When I get better, I won't write about politics or about art. I'll write about the work of nurses. Oh yes, you are real workers. The world is in such a muddle, everything people do has become so difficult and involved, but what you do is so straightforward, so genuine and selfless. That's what I want to write about.'

'Life has probably not been too kind to you, Marfa Kuzminichna, but you have a good heart, and you are so strong-willed and determined that you can do anything if you set your mind to it . . . Oh, if only you knew her, you would not condemn me. I live a double life. Have you ever lived a double life?'

'It doesn't matter—they will go on fussing for another five years or so, and then recognize [me].'

'This illness has made me so apathetic—I can't even smile at you.'

Watching the preparations being made for a blood transfusion, he said: 'Oh, you are like Tibetan lamas at their altars.'

Marfa Kuzminichna, who had seen everything imaginable during the war, spoke with astonishment of the remarkable courage, endurance, and dignity he displayed in his fight with death. For Ira and me this was simply a revelation. As Ira commented in her notes made at the time:

His hypochondria had always been a subject for our jokes—at which he took offence in the most comic way. I remember how he really got us all down over some quite unimportant growth between his toes. He started off every conversation, whether with a foreign correspondent or a high Soviet official, by talking about it. And once he had some trouble with the skin on his face—he was not supposed to wash or shave until it cleared up. Goodness, the way he went on about it! 'I know just how horrible it must be for you to talk to me,' he kept saying to people. Or: 'Irochka, you are a good girl, but for heaven's sake, you don't have to prove it by kissing me', and: 'Oliusha, how ashamed you must feel to be seen walking in the street with me . . .' And then suddenly Marfa Kuzminichna, whom it is impossible not to believe, talks with such respect of his physical endurance and patience. We were so surprised that I asked her to tell us the whole story a second time.

I had arranged to keep in touch with Zhenia [Pasternak] on practical matters. When I phoned him at his apartment in Moscow, he told me there was no improvement, but that, on the contrary, BL's blood was showing an alarming and rapid decrease of haemoglobin. After a consultation between the doctors he later told me there was a suspicion of something much worse than heart trouble and that it could be cancer of the blood, leukaemia.* In this case there would be a fatal issue in a matter of days, or even hours.

On the 27th, as Zhenia told me, BL was X-rayed by means of a portable unit, and it was discovered that the cancer had spread to a

* I believe Solzhenitsyn once said, with great truth, that 'cancer is the fate of all those who become prey to a consuming mood of black and bitter depression'.[48]

lung. He was given blood transfusions, and improved slightly, so that I continued to hope.

On the 28th Marina came to my house in a more cheerful mood to tell me on behalf of BL that I should get ready to go and see him—he would soon call me over for the meeting we had been planning earlier.

Against all logic, my hopes again rose up—this time even higher.

On the morning of the 29th I met Zoya Maslennikova on the main road. She told me the cancer was still spreading and there was no hope.

For the previous two years she had been doing a bust of BL, and she loved him dearly. After he fell ill she kept going to the house with things she thought would give him a little pleasure—such as books that might interest him, and once she brought a live fish in a bowl. She also relayed bits of news that were important for him. In this way she kept abreast of what was happening and passed on the latest bulletins to me. This time she was shaken and distressed, and said nothing could save him now.

I saw Lipkin by the fence of the house. He had tears in his eyes. 'Is it really very bad?' he asked. 'No, no, not at all,' I replied, 'there is hope.' I don't know why I went on hoping so stubbornly like this.

About what happened the next day, May 30, I learned from Marfa Kuzminichna. She told me that BL had called his two sons and told them they must take it on themselves to look after me. And then, speaking to Marfa, he said: 'Who will suffer most because of my death? Who will suffer most? Only Oliusha will, and I haven't had time to do anything for her. The worst thing is that she will suffer.' Marfa Kuzminichna wept as she repeated these words of his to us.

In the evening he became much worse.

As he fought for breath, Marfa Kuzminichna held his head in her large, kind hands. He spoke his last words to her: 'I can't hear very well. And there's a mist in front of my eyes. But it will go away, won't it? Don't forget to open the window tomorrow.'

At twenty minutes past eleven on the night of May 30, 1960, Boris Leonidovich died.

'They carried him not to bury him:
They carried him down to crown him.'[49]

It was only early the next morning that I learned Boria was no longer alive. I went out at six o'clock to meet the nurse coming off duty and ask how he was.

I saw Marfa Kuzminichna at a crossroads. She was walking quickly, with her head bowed low. I caught up with her and, barely able to get out the words, asked how he was. I knew the answer before she could reply: he was dead.

I don't remember how it happened, but I suddenly found myself in the 'big house'. Nobody stopped me at the door.

Boria was lying there still warm, and his hands were soft. He lay in a small room, with the morning light on him. There were shadows across the floor, and his face was still alive—not at all inert, like a sculpture, as it became after his body had been refrigerated.

I could hear his prophetic voice in my ears:

> Just as it promised, without deceit,
> The sun came in the early morning hour,
> A slanting saffron streak that reached
> Right from the curtains to the sofa.

> It covered with its burning ochre
> The nearby woods, the village houses,
> My bed, the soaking pillow-slip
> That patch of wall there by the books.*

Yes, it had all come true. The very worst had come true. Everything had been marked out beforehand, stage by stage, in the fateful novel—which had indeed played a tragic part in our life, and at the same time totally embodied it:

And now she began to take leave of him in the simple, everyday words of robust, familiar talk, the kind that bursts the framework of reality and makes no sense—no more sense than the choruses and monologues in tragedies, or the language of poetry or music or any other convention which is only justified by the circumstances of heightened emotion. The justification in this case, the circumstance which strained

* From 'August', in the *Zhivago* cycle. (Tr.)

the tone of her swift, unpremeditated speech, were her tears, in which the prosaic, unexalted words bathed and swam and drowned.

It seemed as if these tear-drenched words clung together of themselves and connected into a soft, quick, gentle patter, as when silky, moist leaves rustle, tangled by the wind.

'So here we are together once more, Yurochka. The way God has let us meet again! How terrible, just think of it! Oh, I can't bear it! Oh, Lord! I cry and cry! Just think: something so much like us again, right up our street. Your going, and the end of me. Again something big, inescapable . . .

Goodbye, my big one, my dear one, my own, my pride. Goodbye, my quick, deep river, how I loved your day-long splashing, how I loved to bathe in your cold, deep waves . . .'

And in response his farewell to Lara:

Goodbye, Lara, until we meet in the next world, goodbye my love, my inexhaustible, everlasting joy. I'll never see you again. I'll never, never see you again!

For me the events of that day and the two following ones (Tuesday, Wednesday, Thursday) seemed veiled by a mesh of fine, autumn rain —though in actual fact it rained only on the Thursday, towards the end of the funeral. Things went on not only outside my field of vision, but beyond the bounds of my consciousness. There was, for instance, the clash which took place between Liusia Popova and Anastasia Zuyeva right next to BL's coffin on the day of the funeral.* It was about Fedin. Zuyeva said Fedin was ill and did not even know about BL's death—nobody had told him out of concern for his health, because he loved BL so much . . . Liusia could not restrain herself: 'We know from the newspapers just how much Fedin loved Pasternak—and he can see perfectly well from his windows what is going on here at the house.'

Later on Kaverin wrote to Fedin: '. . . Who can forget the senseless and tragic affair of Pasternak's novel—an affair which did so much damage to our country? Your part in this business went so far that you even felt compelled to pretend you had not heard of the death

* In accordance with Russian custom, the body was displayed in an open coffin in the house before the funeral. (Tr.)

of the poet who was your friend and lived next door to you for twenty-three years. Perhaps you could see nothing from your window as people came in their thousands to take their leave of him, and as he was carried in his coffin past your house?'*

I remember, as in a haze, the sad, troubled faces of my family and friends who stayed at my side: my mother, the children, Ariadna, Koma, Sergei Stepanovich...

And then there were the two nurses in their white uniforms. Marina said that from now on, after she had come to know Pasternak, her life would be quite different. Marfa Kuzminichna, a real Russian woman, in whose kindly arms he had died, moulded an image of his face in modelling wax. The artist Yuri Vasilyev made a death mask of him.

He was to be buried at four o'clock on Thursday, June 2. On that day the *Literary Gazette* published the following notice:

The Board of the Literary Fund of the USSR announces the death of the writer and member of *Litfund*, Pasternak, Boris Leonidovich, which took place on May 30 in the seventy-first year of his life after a severe and lengthy illness, and expresses its condolences to the family of the deceased.[50]

There was not a word about the time and place of the funeral. But notices, written by hand on large sheets of paper, or on pages torn from exercise books, were posted in electric trains and near the ticket offices for the surburban lines at the Kiev railway station,† and in other places. I still have one of these notices in my possession:

'Comrades! On the night of May 30–31, 1960, one of the great poets of modern times, Boris Leonidovich Pasternak, passed away. The civil funeral service‡ will take place at 15.00 in Peredelkino.'

---

* Gladkov adds another detail: 'Fedin, we heard, had pleaded illness and was sitting it out in his house nearby, ordering the curtains to be drawn so that the murmur of voices from the funeral crowd would be muffled.'

† The Moscow station from which trains run south-west to Kiev. The electric train to Peredelkino—about twenty kilometres down the line—runs from here. (Tr.)

‡ The term for a non-religious service. The adjective 'civil' is used, because the word for funeral service (*panikhida*) is the one used in the Russian Orthodox Church. (Tr.)

People who arrived in Peredelkino early in the morning on the day of the funeral told us that militiamen, commanded by very senior officers, were already stationed at the approaches to the village. Everybody who arrived by car a few hours later was made to get out and walk the last stretch.

The doors of the house, now without its master, were thrown wide open. The apple trees were a mass of pink and white, and the lilac trees were also in blossom. Almost everybody wandering around was unknown to me.

As I walked by, people exchanged whispered remarks, and half-turned to cast curious glances. But hardly even aware of this, I went into the house. People were filing in through the verandah, past the coffin, and out at the front entrance.

The coffin, almost buried in flowers, had been put in the large room. There were wreaths at the foot of it: from the Ivanovs, from Kornei Chukovski and from the *Litfund*.

BL was in the formal dark-grey suit which had belonged to his father and which he liked more than any other. He was handsome, young, with a face carved in marble. To think he had reached the age of seventy, an age at which people die!

Without him or any of us noticing, it seemed, all his anxieties had done their work. Who could say when the last fatal illness had taken hold in his blood, making its terrible inroads furtively and unseen, in order to rob me of him? And now here I was saying goodbye to him—he would live on, and I would make my mistakes as if he were still at my side, paying the same high price, and understood by very few. There he was, looking alive and young, and I spoke with him as with a living person. *He* understood it all so well. How could he die and leave me on my own? . . .

Artists were making drawings of him. In a neighbouring room, taking it in turns, Sviatoslav Richter, Andrei Volkonski, and Maria Yudina played the piano. Yudina had aged very much and could no longer get about unless someone led her by the arm.

The stream of people coming into the house had swollen, and I couldn't go on standing there in the way. I went out through the front entrance.

Almost immediately Paustovski came up to me. Ever since the morning of that terrible summer's day, with its hot sun and wind, there had been a kind of haze in front of my eyes, but through it I now saw his lean and austere profile as he suddenly appeared next to the bench on which I had sat down under the window of the Pasternak house. Inside, people were still taking leave of my beloved, who lay there quite impassive now, indifferent to them all, while I sat by the door so long forbidden me.

Paustovski bent down to me, and I began to cry. It was the first time I had cried that day, and it slightly eased my pain. All at once everything that had happened seemed utterly improbable, and this too had a calming effect.

Konstantin Georgievich must have thought I had been unable to take my leave of BL because of my awkward situation as regards the family. He knew only too well how complicated my life with BL had been—as I have mentioned, he had offered to put us up in his house when BL had conceived his abortive plan, over a year before this, of moving to Tarusa . . .

Spare, of medium height, with a proud, sharply etched face (I suddenly remembered the story about how he was once supposed to become Hetman of the Ukraine), this gentle and kindly man found exactly the right words to say to me at that moment—they showed he had no doubt as to how genuine my grief was: 'I want to go past the coffin with you,' he said, taking me by the elbow and helping me up from the bench.

We went through once again, past the table, and the coffin with the inert, handsome man lying there—utterly aloof now from the world. He had turned to stone already and gone away from us, receding further and further with every second.

'I have already said a proper goodbye,' I remarked absurdly to Paustovski, 'he's no longer the same now. He was still warm then.'

We came out again and, like a sleep-walker, I went back to my bench. Paustovski stood beside me with his companion, a young-looking woman with a dark, rosy complexion and bright, shining eyes. He began to say what an authentic event the funeral was—an expression of what people really felt, and so characteristic of the Russia which stoned its prophets and did its poets to death as a matter of long-standing tradition. At such a moment, he continued indignantly, one was bound to recall the funeral of Pushkin and the Tsar's courtiers—their miserable hypocrisy and false pride. 'Just think how rich they are, how many Pasternaks they have—as many as there were Pushkins in the Russia of Tsar Nicholas . . . You might

think they were very rich indeed in poets to see what little they do
to preserve them, and how they stone them to death . . . Not much
has changed. But what can you expect? They are afraid . . .' (I now
remember that not very long after BL's funeral, there was an article
in one of the newspapers, on some appropriate date, recalling the
details of Pushkin's death in an oddly indignant tone—it was clearly
intended to evoke obvious associations. But I don't remember who
the author was.)

I was still in the dazed state into which I had been thrown by
Marfa Kuzminichna's first words to me two days before: 'He is
dead'. I had been distracted a little only by the trivialities of everyday
existence—such as trying on a dress for the funeral, or going to the
shops with Ariadna—and I found salvation in sheer tiredness,
plunging into a sleep which brought hope of waking up to discover
that none of it had really happened. I had dreams that Boria was still
alive, that he was tapping on my window with a twig. Perhaps I was
also dreaming this terrible day with the wind and hot sun?

No, this was not a dream. Through my daze I could clearly hear
the words of this man whose profile was etched against the deep-blue
sky over the house, a man who understood everything. I was looking
up at him, and he was saying to me: 'I want you to know that you
are very dear to me, and that, whenever you need me, I shall always
be with you.'

The dark woman next to him smiled at me with her bright eyes.
She loved him—as he of course loved her—and I felt that through
this love of theirs they had a true understanding of me and were
really mourning the man so dear to me not only as a great poet, but
as someone now parted from his love for ever.

Although there was still a long time to go before the body was
carried out for burial, the garden was already crowded. I recognized
only a few faces, and it would in any case have been impossible to
memorize everybody among the four to five thousand—according
to the most modest estimates—who attended the funeral. None of
them had been forced to come, or been ordered to do so at their
place of work. Not only were they here of their own free will, but
they had taken the risk of being blacklisted as 'unreliable' for their
pains. As Alexander Gladkov writes in his account of the funeral:

Very noticeable among the crowd were certain individuals who were looking round them with more than just idle curiosity. They were eavesdropping on conversations and clicking away with cameras. I picked out one of them in particular and watched him for quite a while. He pretended to be waiting to get into the house with the rest of the crowd, but he was just marking time, his eyes constantly darting from side to side. His open-necked sports shirt, low forehead, and distinctive expression made him unmistakable. Types such as this —as well as the foreign journalists who had also come only to do their job—were the sole alien element in the crowd which, with all its diversity, was united in its shared feelings.

The swarms of foreign correspondents were there with all their equipment. In their business-like way they improvised platforms to stand on. One of these, made from boards used to keep snow off the road, collapsed with a great crash, sending cameras and people flying to the ground . . .

Among all these thousands of faces the absence of some of our leading writers was acutely obvious—Nikolai Aseyev was not there, nor were Leonov, Katayev, Fedin . . . To quote Gladkov again: 'I began to think of what a wide range of different types of cowardice there are: from the staid, almost decorous variety to the hysterical, breast-beating kind; from the shamelessly unconcealed to the hypo-critically furtive.'

The sorrowful moment now arrived for the body to be brought out of the house. When Voronkov and Ari Davidovich Ratnitski, who were in charge of the funeral arrangements, gave the word, people began passing flowers by the armful through the window, now flung wide open, to others standing in the garden. The wreaths and the lid of the coffin were brought out through the door . . . Then the open coffin appeared, swaying slightly as it was carried down the steps.

A bus had drawn up outside and the two men in charge busily began to give instructions, but the young people handling the coffin ignored them and carried it off on their shoulders, while others piled the flowers and wreaths into the bus. Thousands of people followed along behind in procession. It was a display of genuine popular sorrow.

I had got separated from my family in the crowd, and only a friend of Ira's called Nanka, Liusia Popova, and Heinz Schewe managed to stick with me all the time. Heinz extricated me from the crowd, and took me across a field of potatoes direct to the grave, which had been dug on a hillock under three pine trees—BL had admired them from his window for many years.

In the middle of the field we were waylaid by two journalists, one French and the other Italian. Heinz squeezed my elbow and told me not to speak to them. 'She is so upset that you should be ashamed to ask questions,' he said to them in his broken Russian.

But as soon as we reached the road a third foreign correspondent came up. He said he wanted only 'very little'—would I please tell him where the manuscript of *The Blind Beauty* was, or better still, let him read it. Was this some kind of crude provocation?

Soon the procession arrived. The coffin was placed on top of baskets of flowers. Here as well the foreign correspondents had managed to set up some kind of platform, and their movie cameras whirred away furiously. Nearly every one of them had a tiny microphone worn on the wrist like a watch.

The graveside proceedings now began. It was hard for me in my state to make out what was going on. Later I was told that Paustovski had wanted to give the funeral address, but it was in fact Professor Asmus who spoke. Wearing a light-coloured suit and a bright tie, he was dressed more for some gala occasion than for a funeral.

'A writer has died,' he began, 'who, together with Pushkin, Dostoyevski, and Tolstoi, forms part of the glory of Russian literature. Even if we cannot agree with him in everything, we all none the less owe him a debt of gratitude for setting an example of unswerving honesty, for his incorruptible conscience, and for his heroic view of his duty as a writer.'

Needless to say, he mentioned BL's 'mistakes and failings', but hastened to add that 'they do not, however, prevent us from recognizing the fact that he was a great poet.'

'He was a very modest man,' Asmus said in conclusion, 'and he did not like people to talk about him too much, so with this I shall bring my address to a close.'

Then Golubentsov stepped forward and read BL's poem 'O Had I Known It Would Be So'. After that, in a very young and deeply anguished voice, someone read 'Hamlet', the first poem in the *Zhivago* cycle. The effect of the last stanza on everybody there was electric:

But the order of the acts is planned
And the end of the way inescapable.
I am alone; all drowns in the Pharisees' hypocrisy.
To live your life is not as simple as to cross a field.

At this point the persons stage-managing the proceedings decided the ceremony must be brought to an end as quickly as possible, and somebody began to carry the lid towards the coffin.

For the last time I bent down to kiss Boria on the forehead, now completely cold. And suddenly the dazed, prostrated feeling of the last few terrible days gave way to tears. I cried, and cried and cried. I cried without caring about appearances, about what people might say . . .

But now something unusual began to happen in the cemetery. Someone was about to put the lid on the coffin, and another person in grey trousers (was it Voronkov?) said in an agitated voice: 'That's enough, we don't need any more speeches! Close the coffin!'

But people would not be silenced so easily. Someone in a coloured, open-necked shirt who looked like a worker started to speak: 'Sleep peacefully, dear Boris Leonidovich! We do not know all your works, but we swear to you at this hour: the day will come when we shall know them all. We do not believe anything bad about your book. And what can we say about all you others, all you brother writers of his who have brought such disgrace on yourselves that no words can describe it. Rest in peace, Boris Leonidovich!'

The man in grey trousers seized hold of other people who tried to come forward and pushed them back into the crowd: 'The meeting is over, there will be no more speeches!'

A foreigner expressed his indignation in broken Russian: 'You can only say the meeting is over when no more people wish to speak!'

Now another voice—again a young one—was heard: 'God marks the path of the elect with thorns, and Pasternak was picked out and marked by God. He believed in eternity and he will belong to it . . . We excommunicated Tolstoi, we disowned Dostoyevski, and now we disown Pasternak. Everything that brings us glory we try to banish to the West . . . But we cannot allow this. We love Pasternak and we revere him as a poet . . .'

And then suddenly he shouted out in a loud voice: 'Glory to Pasternak!'

The crowd took up these last words and they echoed over the fields, like waves rolling over the sea: 'Glory to Pasternak! Hosanna! Glory! Glory!...'

At this moment, quite unexpectedly, the bells of the nearby Church of the Transfiguration suddenly began to peal. It may be that it was coincidence, and they were simply ringing for the evening service. But it may just as well not have been a coincidence—particularly since an Orthodox mass had been said for BL the day before at the 'big house'.

The man in the grey trousers was now scared out of his wits: 'Close the coffin, this demonstration is undesirable,' and he took hold of the coffin lid himself.

Tatyana Matveyevna, the domestic help who was devoted to BL and loved him dearly—she had been standing with me all this time next to the coffin—placed a prayer for the dead on his forehead, and then the coffin was closed.

As soon as it was lowered into the grave and the first lumps of earth thudded down on it, the crowd began to chant 'Glory to Pasternak', and its cries rose up again and again, surging like waves over the cemetery and the surrounding fields: 'Goodbye, the greatest of all!... Goodbye, Boris Leonidovich!... Goodbye... Glory!... Hosanna!... Glory!...'

For a long time a group of young people remained near the grave. They recited poetry and lit candles. Soon there was a crash of thunder and a violent downpour began. People put their hands over the candles to protect them from the heavy raindrops, and still went on and on, reciting one poem after another... Nature gave of its all that day: the luxuriant blossom in the garden, wind and sun, and even a thunderstorm.

Ever since, young people have gathered at the grave on every anniversary of BL's death. They read poetry, both their own and his, and light candles.

Once I heard someone there singing the words written by Yevtushenko to the 'Lara theme' from the film of Doctor Zhivago:

> ... Though the darkness be never-ending,
> Like two candles glowing in the night
> Pasternak and Lara
> Shed their gentle light...

We went from the cemetery to my house where the table had been laid for fifty people. Heinz showed me a telegram which had arrived from Feltrinelli: 'Arriving to embrace you, to be with you and near you, your friend Giangiacomo.' 'Your government won't like this,' said Heinz, 'we should tell Feltrinelli there is no point in coming here and that he shouldn't try.'

I agreed, and Heinz went off to put a telephone call through to Feltrinelli. By the time he came back, people were sitting at table, the room was full of cigarette smoke and I was in a state of trance.

Two days later I left to go to my apartment in Moscow. I had not even had time to take off the black dress in which I had gone to the funeral, when the phone rang. It was my old friend Khesin, the director of the department of authors' rights. He was calling from Peredelkino—he had gone there specially to see me but had just missed me. He demanded to see me straightaway and said he was bringing 'a highly placed person' with him. When it became clear that all my attempts to fend off this unwelcome visit were to no avail and they would come to see me whether I wanted or not, I rang the Bannikovs and asked them to be present at this strange meeting.

Polina Yegorovna (Bannikov's wife) was pouring out tea for us at my apartment when the phone rang again—it was Khesin, calling now from the pharmacy in our street.

He arrived with someone I had never seen before—a thick-set man with black eyes, who was wearing a brown suit. He said he was acting on behalf of Voronkov at the Union of Writers, and asked me to let him see the manuscript of *The Blind Beauty*. I put him in Ira's room and gave him one of the typewritten copies to look at—it was a messy, uncorrected version (and the one, incidentally, which in 1969 was published by Lev Ozerov in *Prostor*, supposedly from the 'original manuscript').

A few minutes later, Mitia came running in and said the visitor wanted to see me. When I went into Ira's room, he produced the red identity card of a KGB operative* and told me he wanted not a copy, but the manuscript itself—just to have a look at and leaf through.

* The term for agents of the KGB (Committee of State Security, i.e. secret police) who go out on active 'operations' or investigations. Roughly the equivalent of a detective in the ordinary criminal police. (Tr.)

I went downstairs to a neighbour's apartment, where I kept the manuscript. As soon as I handed it to the 'operative', he said he would have to take it away with him. I made such a violent scene that I managed to get the manuscript back from him and take it into another room.

Khesin now informed me, as if producing a trump card, that there was another person 'of the highest rank' waiting in the car outside the building with whom it would be impossible for me to argue. (Polina decided it must be none other than Nikita Sergeyevich Khrushchev in person, and began to lament that the refrigerator was empty—we had already eaten everything up—and there would be nothing to offer our exalted visitor!)

The man who now appeared in the doorway was wearing a mauve suit, with a mauve tie to match, and his hair was neatly parted down the side. He looked for all the world like a foreign diplomat.

'May I come in? How do you do, Olga Vsevolodovna. Forgive me for intruding like this,' he said in a suave and courteous tone of voice.

'Anybody who wants comes to see me at the moment,' I replied, very much less politely.

He showed me a document identifying him as one of the highest officials of the KGB, and then in a polite but quite categorical manner demanded that I hand over the manuscript to him.

To this I replied that I was not in sole possession of it and would have to consult my children.

The two of them came into the room. Mitia was pale and all braced to leap into action. Ira, as usual at critical moments, was as firm as a rock and said without the slightest quaver in her voice: 'Mother, the manuscript doesn't belong to you alone, and you mustn't think of giving it up. Let them show what right they have to it.'

'But don't you understand, Irochka,' said the newcomer with a smile, 'that we're only doing this for your own good?'

'I am not "Irochka"', she replied angrily, 'but Irina Ivanovna, and I don't know whether what you're doing is good or bad, but my mother mustn't give you the manuscript—it's not only hers, but ours as well.'

To this the high KGB official replied: 'I should not like to have to invite Olga Vsevolodovna to come with us to a place which will certainly be more traumatic for her than this conversation in a private apartment'. And his colleague added: 'And you should bear in mind that there are six of us in the car—we can take the manuscript by force if needs be.'

There was nothing to be done. They went away with the manuscript, and for a long time we remained sitting, quite shaken, in the dining room. I have no memory of the Bannikovs leaving or of how that day ended. But this was only a taste of things to come . . .

July 24 was my name-day.* I had just returned to Peredelkino from Tarusa where I had been staying with Ariadna for four days. Heinz Schewe came with gifts, from Feltrinelli and from himself. 'And here is a "present" from me,' I said, handing him a copy of *The Blind Beauty* which I had prepared for him beforehand, and he put it in his briefcase. Needless to say, I was giving it to him only for safe-keeping, not for publication.

After my other guests had gone, I went out to see Heinz part of the way to the railway station (he was without his car). About halfway through the Bakovka woods, I said goodbye to him and turned back towards the house. But when I happened to look round, I saw that Heinz had stopped for some reason. I ran back to him, and he motioned with his eyes to a place under some bushes where a man was lying on his stomach. We both felt very alarmed and set off back together. We could see the man crawling behind us in the undergrowth, his straw-coloured hair fairly bristling, and after a moment he got to his feet and, without any further attempt at concealment, ran across the path ahead of us, brazenly stomping his feet as he went.

We went back to my mother's house, where she and Sergei Stepanovich were watching television. My mother was startled to see how pale I was. Heinz stayed outside by the gate, but when I went out to call him inside, he had disappeared.

As luck would have it, I suddenly saw a green light moving along the main road—it was a taxi! Without even pausing to marvel at such a miracle—a taxi so late at night in our deserted parts!—I hailed it, and was soon speeding on my way into Moscow. I got no sleep that night in the apartment. Every few minutes or so, Mitia and I phoned the Hotel Berlin†, but there was no reply from Schewe's

* See footnote on p. 328. (Tr.)

† One of the three or four older hotels in the centre of Moscow, formerly the Savoy. (Tr.)

Heinz Schewe, Boris Pasternak and Olga Ivinskaya. Izmalkovo, 1960

Olga Ivinskaya with Boris Pasternak and Ira. Izmalkovo, 1959

Boris Pasternak and Olga Ivinskaya. Izmalkovo, 1960

Giangiacomo Feltrinelli and an
unidentified woman

Ariadna Sergeyevna Efron (Tsvetayeva's
daughter), 1964 (?)

Peredelkino, Thursday, June 2, 1960

room. Where on earth could he have got to? God knows the thoughts that went through my mind—I could already picture the report in the newspapers the next day: 'Body of unidentified man found in Bakovka woods', and then later it would turn out to be the correspondent of the newspaper *Die Welt*, my friend Schewe, 'killed by unknown hooligans'.

At eight in the morning the doorbell rang. It was Heinz.

'A car came by,' he explained calmly, with a smile. 'I went to put the manuscript in a safe place. I thought you would guess what had happened.'

He found it hard to understand why I was so furious with him . . .

Two weeks later Schewe brought me a letter from Feltrinelli promising not to publish *The Blind Beauty* without my permission.

A little over three weeks later, on August 16, I remember vividly, as though it were now, how I was sitting by myself in the house in Peredelkino. It was a sunny day, but not too hot. I was brooding gloomily, thinking about my recent name-day (the first without Boria), on which I had handed *The Blind Beauty* to Heinz and spent the whole night worrying because of his sudden disappearance.

I also thought of other events that had happened in the period since Boria's death. I had been visited by some friends of d'Angelo, an Italian couple by the name of Benedetti, who had come to the Soviet Union as tourists, bringing a letter from d'Angelo—and also a rucksack filled with packets of banknotes which, it struck me, bore a dismal resemblance to oblong blocks of confectionery. I had already spent the money and the Benedetti couple, having played this fateful role in my life, had departed on a carefree journey to the south.

Georges Nivat had said goodbye to us, sobbing into the phone at Sheremetyevo airport, after being prevented from marrying Ira. All his pleas to Khrushchev had gone unanswered. Unhappy and ill (he had broken out in a rash as the result of an unsuccessful vaccination), he had been forced to fly home to France, leaving a bewildered Ira to weep in her small room at the Potapov Street apartment. (Years later, in December 1966, Georges, in a letter to my friend Rimma Dunder* in Helsinki, wrote of his experiences in Moscow: 'It was a fabulously beautiful, painful, and feverish time. I went through a

---

* This is someone I got to know at the camp at Potma. She subsequently married a Finn, and went to live in Helsinki.

great deal, and the wound did not heal for a long time afterwards.')

In order to make it easier to understand the events of Tuesday, August 14, and what followed, I must go back again to the dark days when BL was being persecuted over the novel.

This is not a pleasant matter, but I cannot pass it over in silence, if only on account of all the false and malicious rumours which circulated about it at the time. Pasternak was a man to whom material gain meant nothing, but after our contracts were cancelled and our money ran out, the question arose: what were we to live on? Meanwhile, huge royalties on the novel were piling up abroad, and one day BL was summoned to the Foreign Legal Collegium.[52] I went there with him. He wrote out a request that any sums remitted to him by a Norwegian or Swiss bank should be divided equally between Zinaida Nikolayevna and myself so that 'in case anything happens'—as he put it—he need have no anxiety about our material situation. However, while he was discussing the matter with Volchkov, the president of the Collegium, I interrupted him and, calling him aside, persuaded him not to make any kind of financial arrangements until I had spoken with Polikarpov.

Needless to say, Polikarpov advised us against taking money for a novel not published in the Soviet Union, but—as I have mentioned earlier—he promised us work and the republication of some of BL's translations. When I complained that we now had nothing to live on, he replied somewhat ambiguously: 'It wouldn't be so bad if they even brought you your money in a sack as long as Pasternak quietens down.'

I told BL about this 'hint', and he interpreted it as meaning that he could receive his royalties with the blessing of the authorities, without going through the Foreign Legal Collegium.

At about this time it so happened, quite unexpectedly for him, that several sums of money reached him from abroad—'the first swallows', as it were. Some French tourists came to see him at the 'big house' and brought him 20,000 roubles in Soviet currency (equivalent to 2,000 roubles at the present day). He brought part of this money to me, and there was an immediate improvement in our financial situation. Next, we had a visit from Gerd Ruge, of whom I have already written, and he brought us some money in Soviet banknotes. Heinz Schewe also gave BL several remittances from Feltrinelli.

Something then happened which eventually, after BL's death, was to lead to the arrest of Ira as well as myself. The circumstances were as follows:

One morning BL came to the Potapov Street apartment, and was upset to find me lying there with my leg in plaster after falling down through sheer carelessness and severely spraining it. This had meant a disruption in his usual routine—something that irritated him more than anything. Suddenly the phone rang and a woman speaking in a foreign accent asked me to meet her at the post office and collect some books that had been sent for BL. It was Mirella, the wife of Garritano (who had succeeded d'Angelo in Moscow).

This upset Boria even more. I was, of course, unable to go, and it was our policy not to expose BL to any personal meetings of this kind with strangers. There was nobody else at home who could go, and he was very anxious to get the books. At this moment Ira and Mitia arrived. Naturally, I supported BL when he asked Ira to go and pick them up. She was the only one of us who knew Mirella by sight. But since she was in a hurry to get to the Institute* BL suggested that Mitia should go with her as well so she wouldn't have to come back with them. They could not refuse anything he asked, and off they went together. At the post office, Mirella handed a small suitcase to Ira, and Mitia brought it to Boria and me at Potapov Street.

When we opened the suitcase, we gasped with astonishment: instead of books, it contained bundles of Soviet banknotes in wrappers, all neatly stacked together—row upon row of them!

BL gave me one bundle to cover some expenses I had, and took the rest with him in the suitcase to Peredelkino. Ira, who had no inkling of what the suitcase really contained, was sent to a forced labour camp for 'transmitting' it ... Fortune is unjust in the way it distributes its favours, but who can call it to account? The simple fact is that we were less protected than those who legally bore Pasternak's name ...

The last of such episodes involving money from abroad—this time brought by the Benedetti couple, as I have mentioned—took place shortly after BL's death. They came to see me at Potapov Street, but as we had no common language, I phoned Irina, who knew French, and asked her to come out from Peredelkino to interpret for us. She came unwillingly, as though sensing the disaster to come.

The Benedettis gave me a letter from d'Angelo in which he said he was sending half the money he owed to Pasternak (500,000 in old

* The Gorki Literary Institute, at which Ira was a student. (Tr.)

roubles) and then they produced a rucksack full of money out of their suitcase. I begged them to take it away, but it was simply beyond them how I could refuse to accept money that belonged to me.

'You have no right to refuse it,' they said, 'you must use this money to put up some fitting monument to Pasternak's memory, and to help people he would have helped. And then, this is a personal debt and we promised d'Angelo to bring it to you without fail—which was not at all easy for us.'

Bidding us farewell, the Benedetti couple then departed, leaving Ira, Mitia, and myself to gaze in horror at the rucksack . . .*

'Now we are really done for,' Heinz Schewe said prophetically next day when he came to see us and I told him about the Benedettis' visit.

But we still clung to the thought that the authorities must surely realize it was in fact they themselves who had prompted us to settle for this way of receiving royalties on *Doctor Zhivago*. At the same time, although there was absolutely nothing illegal about it (and what could be more legitimate than literary earnings?), it nevertheless left a bitter taste in the mouth simply because it had been forced on us by circumstances: we had to have something to live on. Beyond all this, however, I saw no reason to question the arrangements made by the man with whom for fourteen years I had shared the joys of work, the hostility of ill-wishers, and the humble roof of my home near his in Peredelkino . . .

But to return to the events of August 16, 1960.

My mother and step-father, Sergei Stepanovich, had agreed to

---

* After my arrest, d'Angelo himself arrived in Moscow on a tourist visa, and came to see Mitia. He had two large bags with him. Mitia naturally suspected they might well contain more money. The arrest of Ira and myself was still being kept secret by the KGB—they had even put a woman with a voice just like Ira's in the apartment to answer the telephone and they warned Mitia to keep his mouth shut, saying we would be released only on this condition. But Mitia was no fool, and he managed to indicate to d'Angelo that we were under arrest, and got him to clear out of the apartment taking one of the two bags with him. When the KGB men who had been lying in wait burst into the room and swooped on the bag d'Angelo had left behind, they found, much to their fury, that there was nothing in it except some nylon skirts and lipstick sent to me by Giulietta (d'Angelo's wife). It later emerged that the other bag had contained the second instalment of the money d'Angelo owed Pasternak—another 500,000 roubles . . . I should emphasize (this is very important) that all the money brought to us was, without exception, in *Soviet* banknotes. We never saw a penny in foreign currency.

stay on for the rest of this melancholy summer in the comfortable little house they had rented near mine, on the hill opposite the 'Fadeyev tavern'. I had decided, on this beautiful, cool morning, to look in on them and then return to Moscow. Before I set out, I remember, Mitia came running in to ask me for 100 roubles—he wanted to treat some friends with whom he said he had 'business'.

I took ages going over to the other house, and then sat on and on there, completely forgetting about the time, until suddenly it was the mournful hour when the sun begins to go down—its slanting rays were already falling across the steps at the front of the terrace. I sat down at the table there to pour myself a cup of tea. As I did so, I saw several men come up to the garden gate and stop there for a moment. The one in front was a fat man in a light-coloured mackintosh.

'They've lost their way, by the look of it,' said my mother, and indeed, they started to move off uncertainly past my mother's gate towards the next one, which was mine. But from there they turned back again, and the fat man now came hurrying up the rickety steps —the same steps by which Boria had entered the house so many times to look for me when I was here drinking tea with my mother and step-father, or watching television... This man in the mackintosh running up the steps with the purpose of rudely—and for a long time—intruding into my life by brute force, would leave his mark on me. Pink and fat, like a good-natured porker, he was my future interrogator, Vladilen* Vasilyevich Alexanochkin.

'You were expecting us to come, of course, weren't you?' he said with a self-assured smile. 'You didn't imagine, did you, that your criminal activities would go unpunished?'

As I have said, I certainly had not thought what Boria and I had done was 'criminal'. It had been hinted to me by Polikarpov at the Central Committee that BL could receive payment for the novel in this manner, and what else *could* we have done? It looked as though the authorities—and what else was there for *them* to do?—had accepted the notion that we should exist on royalties paid out like this in Soviet roubles by the foreign publishers of *Doctor Zhivago*, and we had naturally not thought it an offence punishable by law...

But the fact is that the whole situation had changed with Boria's death. I soon began to realize that the authorities, who had been

* The first name Vladilen is a 'revolutionary' one made up in the Soviet period. It is derived from *Vladimir Lenin*. (Tr.)

gravely embarrassed by the affair of the novel, had now conceived the happy idea of putting the entire responsibility for it on me. (Later on it became apparent that some of the people dealing with my case —such as the very high official described below—were so ignorant as to take the notion of my responsibility quite literally: they believed I had actually written the criminal and anti-Soviet novel, which I had then cunningly brought out under Pasternak's name!)

Pasternak was too outstanding a figure to be permanently labelled as an 'enemy'. And after his death, therefore, when there was no longer any fear that he might spring some new surprise on them (as he had with the 'Nobel Prize' poem), the powers-that-be decided it would be better to elevate him to the pantheon of Soviet literature. Surkov did a complete about-turn and declared that Pasternak himself had always been an honest poet whom he personally respected, but that Pasternak's friend Ivinskaya was 'an adventuress who got him to write *Doctor Zhivago*, and then to send it abroad, so that she could enrich herself.' Trading on the good name of Pasternak, who supposedly knew nothing of my evil deeds, I had sold the 'criminal' novel (virtually concocted by me in the first place) to foreign publishers, and had then collected the royalties on it. This formula provided a convenient disguise for Surkov's envy—the envy, accumulated over the years, of a hack and a time-server for a great poet whose tragic lot was to be in opposition simply by virtue of the fact that true art is incorruptible and truthful by its very nature. Now all the blame could be put on an 'adventuress', and that would be the end of the matter!

But why all the hurry? It was not quite two and a half months since Boria's death, and sums of money had been coming in from abroad for more than three years.

The calamity that now struck had been in the air for some time already. Once again, strange groups of young people had begun hanging around the entrance to our apartment building. They trailed along behind us when we went out shopping or to make calls from phone booths, and got on trains with us. But even so it seemed odd to think we could be punished for any kind of wrong-doing, and many of our friends found it utterly inconceivable that I could be held criminally responsible for something calmly—and legally, or so it seemed—acquiesced to by BL.

Now, on August 16, several KGB cars were drawn up outside our small house. A search was carried out simultaneously in both my mother's house and mine. While it was going on, Mitia suddenly came home. His main worry was that I would learn about the mischief he had been up to—he had been detained and questioned in a shop while trying to buy a couple of bottles of spirits with the money I had given him to settle his 'business' with some friends. He sat there with bowed head, looking guilty. But my heart ached with pity for him at the thought that we might be parted for a long time. I remembered how he had witnessed my first arrest when he was only a small boy. Just as then, they were going through all my letters and other papers, looking for money, and taking away everything they could lay their hands on. I had the sudden thought that at least they might not find the suitcase I had asked my neighbours to keep for me in the apartment below us at Potapov Street. It contained what was left of the money, and, most important of all—letters concerning the novel, as well as manuscripts. My neighbours did not know what was in the suitcase. (For their sake, I had deliberately not told them, and they assumed it was material I wanted made up—the wife was a dressmaker. Since they really did know nothing of the contents of the suitcase, they suffered no ill consequences.)

When the search of our houses was almost over, I was put in a car and driven off to Moscow, to the Lubianka. This was my last ride through Moscow in an ordinary car—even though wedged in between two 'comrades' in plain clothes—for a long time. The streets were gay with flowers: it was the August 'Day of Flowers'.

At the first session with my interrogator I learned that the search had been conducted simultaneously in several places. The KGB's spy system had done its work very well: by listening in to our telephone conversations they had managed to pinpoint all our contacts and locate the money. The mere existence of it, even though it had been brought into the country on the instructions of BL, was quite sufficient for them: completely divorcing my alleged 'actions' from the arrangements originally made by BL (it was as if they had simply never been), they had no difficulty in making me out to have been the one who had 'smuggled in' all this currency.

At first I felt so sick at heart that I would have given anything simply to lose consciousness and not be aware of anything. But soon I was overcome by a peculiar feeling of indifference. Now that Boria was in his grave, perhaps it was just as well I had been plucked out of the hopeless dead-end of my existence without him and made to tread the path of new torments which would at least distract me from my sense of irreparable loss.

From the very first, I was interrogated about the foreigners in my 'case': Feltrinelli, d'Angelo, Schewe, Benedetti, Ruge, and others. Each of them by himself constituted a whole indictment against me...

My interrogator, Alexanochkin, visited our apartment in Potapov Street to pick out clothes to be brought to me in prison. He won the heart of our cleaning woman, Polia, by smiling enchantingly at her as he tried on some of my brassières. In the meantime, Ira, still feeling quite ill, was going the rounds of the lawyers to find someone to defend me when I was tried. The first one she saw was the brilliant V. A. Samsonov, who was then still very young. Samsonov agreed to take on my case—it promised to be a most interesting and scandalous one, if only for the reason that people in the West, already disturbed by the recent tragedy of Pasternak, were not inclined to dissociate him from the woman who had been destined to play a part in the story of *Doctor Zhivago*.

But in the end it was not Samsonov who defended me. About a month after she had been to see him (I think it was September 5), Ira was herself arrested and brought to the Lubianka. As she later told me, it was even a relief when the door of the Lubianka 'box'* clanged shut behind her. She had become sick and tired of the young thugs who dogged her footsteps whenever she went to her friends, to a shop or a telephone booth. The same 'romantic' methods were being used as before—including young men, for some reason dressed as women, who loitered in the stairway on the sixth floor of our apartment building. If ever our phone, which so faithfully served the interests of the Lubianka, went out of order, repair men immediately raced to put it right again.

There was now a change of plan as regards lawyers. Since Samsonov had already made the acquaintance of Ira, he decided to take on her case, and passed mine to Victor Adolfovich Kosachevski.

For a long time, I had no idea that Ira had been arrested. Perhaps Alexanochkin wanted to spare my feelings? Perhaps . . . but on the other hand, he had no hesitation in trying to unnerve me by going through my suitcase in my presence. Later on, however, he did do us

* See footnote on p. 97. (Tr.)

the extraordinary favour of arranging a 'confrontation' in his office
between Ira and me in connection with some quite trivial point of
difference between her evidence and mine. God, when I think of my
poor, sick Ira in prison, and the reason she was there—all because she
had accepted a suitcase from Mirella Garritano, believing it to contain
books for BL!

The only thing for which she could possibly have been held guilty
under our laws was her contact with a foreigner—the wife of an
employee of Moscow Radio, and a member of the Italian Communist
Party. As regards the foreigners who were always coming to see BL,
there was no way in which she could have avoided meeting them—
they were constantly in our house, and Boria often sent her to them
with messages. Her offence was quite simply that as a member of the
Komsomol and a student of the Literary Institute, she had failed to
report on BL's activities and made no attempt to try and get him to
mend his ways—it was her duty as a Komsomol member to 'educate
backward elements' such as him! In addition, she was made out to
have been actively concerned in 'smuggling' operations as the
daughter of an 'adventuress' whom BL, in the weakness of old age,
had allowed to run his financial affairs.

I shared a cell with a woman accountant who had worked in the
tailoring enterprise which made clothes for Khrushchev and his
family. During the exercise period in the enclosed prison courtyard,
or whenever I was taken to the toilets, I would fancy I could detect
the sound of Ira's footsteps, or in some other way sense her presence
beyond the stone walls dividing us. I made up a poem about her:

> ... Somewhere there, behind these stone walls,
> Perhaps to the left of me, perhaps to the right,
> Sits the girl with auburn hair in braids
> Whose life is ruined by my fault ...

Towards the end of my interrogation I was taken at one point to
Tikunov. He was not at all like Abakumov.* BL would have described him as 'a man without a neck'. He consisted of three spheres:
his back-side, his belly, and his head. When I was led in, he nodded
grandly towards a chair opposite his huge desk, on which he had

* The minister of State Security who briefly interrogated the author during her
first imprisonment. See p. 105. (Tr.)

For Tikunov, see the Biographical Guide. (Tr.)

spread out in front of him various letters of BL's and a copy of *Zhivago*.

'You disguised it very cleverly,' he said darkly, 'but we know perfectly well that the novel was written not by Pasternak, but by you. Look, he says so himself . . .'

Suddenly, I saw Boria's 'cranes' sailing in front of my eyes: 'It was you who did it all, Oliusha! Nobody knows that it was you who did it all—you guided my hand and stood behind me, all of it I owe to you.'

The fat carcass in front of me was looking at me maliciously through tiny slits of eyes buried in puffy rolls of flesh.

'You have probably never loved a woman,' I said, 'so you don't know what it means, and the sort of things people think and write at such a time.'

'That has nothing to do with the matter,' the carcass replied. 'The point is that Pasternak himself admits he didn't write it! It was you who put him up to it all. He was not so embittered until you came along. You have committed a criminal offence and established contact with foreigners . . .'

'Who was that idiot who interrogated me,' I asked Alexanochkin, when I was returned to him.

'Sh! That was Tikunov himself,' he hissed at me, but I thought I saw a twinkle in his eyes. (Luckily, I was not deserted by my sense of humour, and when Ira and I were being taken back to prison in a Black Maria after our trial, I told her what Tikunov had accused me of. 'He paid you a compliment, Mother,' she said with a laugh, 'and for that you ought to forgive him.')

Alexanochkin pretended he was trying to help me and made it sound so plausible that I was easily taken in by him—he almost succeeded, for example, in getting me to do without a lawyer to defend me at the trial. Whenever Victor Adolfovich Kosachevski came to see me, Alexanochkin would smile indulgently and say, making a pun on his name: 'Here comes your Hitlerovich. He's no good to you. Get rid of him before it's too late! He'll make a mess of things. Everything is quite clear enough. The worst thing would be if you went back on your evidence in court!' Another tack was: 'Your interrogator will defend you better than anyone else!' Or: 'Ah, Olga Vsevolodovna, if only I had known you earlier! People gave you bad advice, and you are too trusting!'

My 'friendship' with Alexanochkin reached its height towards the end of my interrogation. He even asked me to sign, 'as a memento' for him and his wife, one of my favourite books—a volume of Tsvetayeva's prose that had been confiscated from me during the search!

I remember the astonished look in the eyes of Victor Adolfovich when Alexanochkin and I exchanged 'knowing' smiles above his head—what a touching meeting of minds, he must have thought!

Ira was so much more intelligent: she demanded a meeting with me and told me I had no right to dispense with a lawyer, if only in her interests. And so I kept Victor Adolfovich on as my defence counsel. After reading all the documents in the case—two fat volumes of them—and examining the material evidence, he told me he could find nothing to substantiate the charges against me . . . It had been a very different story with my 'friend' Alexanochkin:

'We'll make it a charge of smuggling—which is a minor offence,' Alexanochkin had assured me on one occasion, smiling sweetly at me.

'But why smuggling?' I had asked in astonishment. 'Neither Pasternak nor I ever saw a single dollar, or a single franc, and we brought nothing into the country!'

'But you received Soviet currency, and you knew how it was brought into the country, didn't you?'

'We knew nothing at all about it! The arrangements were made by Boris Leonidovich several years ago. Why should Ira and I be guilty? Boris Leonidovich received money for all of us, in the way he wanted—he simply drew on it as he wished!' And I told him how none other than Polikarpov had advised us not to go through the Foreign Legal Collegium, on the grounds that it would be awkward for us to receive the money officially in view of the scandal over the novel, and had hinted that it would be better if we received it 'in a bag'. BL had agreed to this, and, relying on Polikarpov's word, I had persuaded him not to be in any hurry about making 'official' arrangements to get the money, but to leave it in the lap of the gods. And now poor Ira and I were paying the price for it all!

When the examination of our case was over, we were transferred to Lefortovo,[53] where prisoners are sent after signing the charges brought against them.

We were no longer 'under investigation', but 'under indictment', and theoretically only our defence counsel had the right to come and see us here. Imagine my surprise, then, when I was suddenly summoned by the head of the prison while I was walking during an exercise period and found myself face to face again with my 'dear friend' Alexanochkin. He was evidently worried that in court I might withdraw various statements he needed from me. Laughable as it may seem, I believed he really had come to see me in breach of the rules, perhaps risking his career, in order to keep my spirits up. I still looked at everything through the rose-coloured spectacles inherited from Boria—he could never conceive of anybody not loving me . . .

Victor Adolfovich also came to see me. These visits of his were red letter days for me—they brought a breath of fresh air from the outside world, where people walked around at liberty, went to the cinema in the evening, or drank tea with their friends whenever they took it into their heads.

Victor Adolfovich was a large, handsome and amiable man, with a gentle, cosy manner. His kindly brown eyes were full of sympathy and encouragement. We talked in a half-whisper, and often preferred to exchange notes scribbled on bits of paper about even the most innocent matters. I remember being very concerned over Heinz Schewe. From certain things said by Alexanochkin right at the beginning of my interrogation it had seemed reasonable to assume that he too must have been arrested.

In recent times Schewe—'Shavochka'* as we had nicknamed him affectionately in Russian—had been the trusted intermediary between Pasternak and Feltrinelli, helping them to correspond without interference from the Soviet censor by taking letters back and forth across the frontier in his red Volkswagen. For Boria he had become a member of the household. As I have already mentioned, when Ira transferred her affections from Heinz to Georges Nivat, Boria felt particular sympathy and tenderness towards him and wrote a dedication in one of his books assuring him that, whatever happened, he would always be a member of our family. And this is what he indeed became. Nobody could have been more understanding about our whole situation, and during Boria's illness. It gave him tremendous pleasure to do nice things for us—he quite simply loved us, in the way that a kind, homely German like himself would love his own family.

And now, if you please, 'Shavochka' might have been arrested

* In Russian a usual affectionate nickname for a small dog. (Tr.)

too! Lord preserve us! And again it would all be my fault, I had no doubt!

When Victor Adolfovich came to see me, I wrote down on a crumpled piece of paper a poem I had composed in my head about it all (I have forgotten some of the lines):

> ... You stood my world on its head—
> How can I ever lose my reason
> If I worry only when there is no cause to,
> And feel at home in utter hell?
> Life in this charmed circle, surely,
> Must be a waking dream, meant to confuse,
> If an airman who bombed Moscow*
> Is our most trusted friend and ally,
> And if the master of your fate (and mine)
> Who trumpets dissent from the enemy camp
> Tirelessly around the globe
> Was a madcap Milan publisher ...
> And so, subject to no one's will,
> We lived in a village outside Moscow.
> My daughter dreamed of marriage to a Frenchman,
> Of Paris 'in a lilac mist.'
> . . . . . .
> That was all.
> But here the film breaks off
> We are plunged abruptly into darkness ...
> You are in the grave, and I pay
> With my child's happiness for insane dreams!
> Faces dissolve in a haze around me,
> No one can help us now.
> . . . . . .
> What it is for a mother to know
> Her daughter is nearby—in the same prison.
> I always talked 'like a child', you said,
> Henceforth I'll try to hold my tongue!
> . . . . . .
> In my mind's eye I see that German airman
> At dusk in Peredelkino, by our garden gate ...

* See Schewe in the Biographical Guide. (Tr.)

The accusing finger points at him as well,
And in the heart of *such* confusion,
One ill-judged word from me
Could send him to his doom . . .
Well, there it is—there can be no excuses,
And, 'prey to the world's vain cares',
Alas, I cannot weep at the graveyard wall
Behind which you lie concealed.

Victor Adolfovich assured me that Alexanochkin was making things up—much as he might have liked to arrest Schewe as well, he did not have the power to, and in any case Schewe had now simply left the country. (Victor Adolfovich and Schewe were, incidentally, extremely unhappy with each other. Schewe had driven up in his Volkswagen to the office where Victor Adolfovich worked, and offered him 5,000 dollars to defend me in the best possible way. He also asked to be called as a witness. It appears that Feltrinelli had reproached him for not doing more to protect my interests. Victor Adolfovich explained to the naïve German that this was 'not done' in the Soviet Union and he refused the money, saying he would do his job in any case. Heinz went away discouraged—and later on he kept saying that Kosachevski must be a poor lawyer, if he wasn't interested in money . . . And when Kosachevski came to see me—I think this was while I was still at the Lubianka—he was indignant that Heinz, during the whole of his long stay in Russia, had learned so little about our ways.)

At this same meeting Victor Adolfovich, I remember, told me there had been a demonstration in London over Ira's and my arrest, and also that Surkov, in replying to the protests of P.E.N., had had the effrontery to describe himself as having been a 'friend of Pasternak's'. (When he had gone to see Feltrinelli in October 1957, trying by hook or by crook to get him to give up the manuscript of the novel, Surkov had used the same approach, but Feltrinelli was not deceived by his claim to be acting as a 'friend' of Pasternak's—under a large portrait of whom he had made Surkov wait before receiving him.)

Now, when so many years have gone by, and our good friend, the eccentric millionaire and adventurer Feltrinelli—with whom I corresponded over many years and who figured so prominently in the two fat volumes of my 'case' in the Lubianka—is dead, I should like to say a few words in his memory.

In the early hours of the morning of March 15, 1972, two peasants in a Milan surburb, alerted by the frantic barking of a dog, found the body of a bearded man at the base of an electric pylon, to which several charges of dynamite had been attached. In the pocket of the man's khaki trousers of a military type, they found papers in the name of 'Vincenzo Magiani'. The papers were false, and by the evening of the same day, the dead man had been identified by representatives of his publishing firm as Giangiacomo Feltrinelli. They alleged that he had not died as the result of an accident, but had been murdered.

Except during the years when I was in the forced labour camp, my correspondence with Giangiacomo went on uninterruptedly. Long before his death, I had formed the impression that he was a highly emotional man who had been carried away by his secret 'revolutionary' activities as an extreme left-wing underground conspirator. He was constantly afraid of reprisals against himself. It is known that not long before his death, he said to a trusted friend: 'If a mutilated corpse is discovered somewhere before long, think of me.' And also: 'I do not like to have my back to the woods—there could easily be a gun there ready to shoot me down.'[54]

The last things I received from him were some copies of a slim ultra-revolutionary magazine published by him, and a long letter written in German. In it he voiced concern about my financial situation and informed me that he was living in hiding in Austria— the Italian police were hunting him on account of his revolutionary activities. He denounced imperialism and expressed his faith in the victory of world revolution.

And so the poor, poor millionaire Giangiacomo Feltrinelli gave his life for the cause of world revolution at the early age of forty-six . . . It would have been so simple for him to live a life of ease and luxury, but peace is something we see only in dreams—and do we see it even in them?

But I must go back to the time when I was sitting in my prison cell in Moscow waiting to go on trial, and the 'madcap Milan publisher' was still alive.

The Trial

The day of the trial was foggy, and there was a driving sleet coming down—it was neither rain nor snow. As I was taken in the Black Maria through the gates of the Kalanchevski court, I caught a glimpse of some familiar faces—mostly girl friends of Ira, as well as students from the Institute. They stood there waiting.

The trial was to be held not in the usual courtroom, but in a more intimate room, circular in shape. Ira and I were put in armchairs not far from the assessors,* our defence lawyers, and the prosecutor. They all sat comfortably at an oval table unlike the usual official-looking one. Our guards stayed outside by the door.

Ira and I were so overjoyed at being together again, and had so much to say to each other, that we quite forgot about the friendly witnesses and admirers waiting outside in the vain hope that we might have the sense to ask to go to toilet—there we could at least have exchanged kisses! . . . But we could not stop talking, silly creatures.

Needless to say, no unwanted persons were admitted to the trial—in fact, nobody at all was let in. Not only was the case itself a sham, but even the actual proceedings were bogus—the whole thing was based on falsehood from beginning to end. They wanted to rush the trial through in a day, before foreign journalists got wind of it. They tried to make out that it was public, but there was nobody in court except the judge and assessors, counsel for the defence, and our interrogators (who had now exchanged their uniforms for civilian clothing).[55]

Our two lawyers were most impressive to look at. Well turned out and urbane, they seemed to belong to a different species from the others. The judge was quite frightful in appearance—his cheeks were all wrinkled, and he had huge ears which looked as if made of wax. I glanced over in consternation towards my counsel, the amiable and altogether delightful Victor Adolfovich who had assured me that Gromov (such was his name)† was the best of the judges, and that this was a 'piece of luck' for us. There was, he said, another

* In the Soviet Union the judge is flanked by two so-called 'people's assessors', whose role is in theory similar to that of a jury in some Western countries. (Tr.)

† The name derives from *grom*—'thunder' or 'destroy' (*pogrom* is from the same root). (Tr.)

one called Klimov who was a real monster. God knows what Klimov was like, but Gromov was also a pretty fine specimen, I must say!

Gromov got it into his head from the start that since I had translated poetry by people of various nationalities* I must know at least ten languages—which of course left absolutely no doubt in his cultivated mind what I was: clearly a spy! The names Pasternak and Feltrinelli were quite beyond him, and he pronounced them 'Pistirnak' and 'Fintrinelli'. And he was never really able to fathom why it was that the evidence in this 'Pistirnak case' consisted entirely of my correspondence with an Italian publisher—two whole volumes of it.

As I sat there in this alien place and people held forth around me, I was busy with my own thoughts. My mind went back to the beginnings of my friendship 'by correspondence' with Feltrinelli. After BL had already signed contracts with him, he suddenly received a visit from a certain French woman. She had come from Paris where she was supervising the work of the French translators of the novel. At that moment, it so happened, BL was very upset about the large number of misprints in the Russian edition of the novel just brought out in Italy. Whether for this reason, or because he in general felt closer in spirit to the French, he suddenly took it into his head to make over the rights in the novel to Gallimard†, and when his French vistor put a contract with them in front of him, he signed it, thereby causing great offence to the Italians. Heinz Schewe, clearly very put out by it all, came to see me and explained at great length what the consequences for BL would be of switching to another publisher like this. 'It won't be at all good,' he kept on saying. He then brought us a letter from Feltrinelli, who was very upset and asked me to try and get BL to understand—he knew I now looked after all BL's business matters—how wrong it was to do this. Feltrinelli made a particular point of the fact that in the whole affair of the publication of Doctor Zhivago, he had acted not only as a publisher, but as a friend, and he said he would now be put in the position of having to sue Gallimard.

I thought Feltrinelli was entirely in the right in the whole matter,

* As is common practice in the Soviet Union, the author translated from literal Russian versions supplied by experts in the various languages. (Tr.)

† Leading French publishing firm. (Tr.)

and with the support of Heinz (who at that time was empowered to sign papers on BL's behalf abroad),* I tackled Boria on the subject, explaining how badly he had behaved, and what unpleasant publicity there would be if new editions of the novel gave rise to a law suit between two 'capitalist sharks'. BL, very embarrassed, asked me to write to the French and the Italians, and 'sort out' the whole business.

The matter ended in a compromise: Feltrinelli arrived at a financial settlement with Gallimard, but retained all rights in the novel for himself. A conflict was thus averted—which Feltrinelli, quite justly, attributed entirely to my influence with BL.

Giangiacomo's taste for adventure had put me in a very difficult situation. In the last letter I had received from him before the trial he expressed surprise that I had asked certain obscure acquaintances of d'Angelo to take out some letters written by BL in the last days of his life. He enclosed in the letter half of an Italian banknote which he had torn in two, and told me that in future I should entrust things meant for him only to a person who would come to me with the other half. It was this celebrated banknote which really made it possible to make me out to be an 'adventuress'.[56] I remember how funny I thought it was when it arrived. There was in fact no need to make use of this romantic ploy right out of a bad thriller—for one thing Schewe had come back to Moscow again, and for another, I had no intention in any case of sending Feltrinelli all BL's remaining manuscripts, as had been his hope in sending me the unfortunate banknote.

The prosecutor was now telling the court how he had been convinced by his examination of the voluminous correspondence between myself and Feltrinelli that the manuscript of the novel had been sent abroad by me, not by Pasternak (though he too had sold himself to the Western war-mongers and was completely under my thumb). He was not certain, the prosecutor continued, who had actually *written* the novel, but he was not in any case going to press any charges on this score: we were being prosecuted only for receiving Soviet currency which had been smuggled into the country.

When the prosecutor had finished presenting his case on these primitive lines, the two lawyers acting for Ira and me gave the arguments for our defence with great eloquence and expertise.

* Particularly in view of what BL himself thought of Feltrinelli—in a letter to George Reavey (February 7, 1960) he described him as: 'My executor in practical matters, my producer, a man of enterprise who carries through what I begin.'

First of all, they pointed out, there was the fact that long before his death Pasternak had sent written instructions to Feltrinelli in which he had said: '. . . I empower Olga Vsevolodovna Ivinskaya, both during the rest of my life and after my death to handle all my royalties . . .' (The royalties in question were those for *Doctor Zhivago*, and any that might accrue for *An Essay in Autobiography* and *The Blind Beauty*.) This statement existed in more than one copy, and even in several different versions—all of which had reached Feltrinelli. Feltrinelli, therefore, had been carrying out the direct instructions of Pasternak in asking people on several occasions to bring money into the country for us while Pasternak was still alive and after his death. In every single case the money had been handed to us in Soviet currency. The prosecution, however, based its case against Ira and me on the absurd allegation that this Soviet money had first been illegally exported from the Soviet Union to Italy, and then smuggled in again and given to us.

Our lawyers reminded the court that anybody could go to the State Bank, hand any sum in foreign money to the cashier, and receive the equivalent in Soviet roubles at the current rate of exchange, without any questions being asked. Furthermore, it was not necessary in modern times to transport money from one country to another in suitcases now that there were such things as travellers' cheques, letters of credit, and so forth. It was also entirely to the advantage of the Soviet Union to receive foreign currency like this in return for roubles.

The final point was that the money had been brought to us not by carrier pigeons, but by persons who had come to us on instructions from Feltrinelli. We had been under close surveillance all the time, our every movement had been watched, and on each occasion when money had been handed to us, the fact had been noted. So why had none of the foreigners involved been detained and questioned, if only as witnesses? If the prosecution was to be believed, and the Italians had brought money into the country in the form of Soviet roubles, then they, clearly, were the ones who were actually guilty of smuggling. Was it not odd that those who had received these allegedly smuggled roubles were on trial, while the persons who had brought them across the frontier had not even been called as witnesses? The reason was all too obvious: if any of these foreigners had been questioned, he would immediately have been able to prove that he had obtained the roubles from the State Bank, and the whole wicked farce would have burst like a soap-bubble. But not only had the 'real' smugglers not been brought to trial, not only had they not been required at the very least to give evidence, they had not even been named by the prosecution. The prosecution's contention that the roubles had been brought from abroad, our lawyers maintained, had simply not been proved, and they were bound to conclude, therefore, that if any persons had really been guilty of smuggling, they were not present in this courtroom. There were, in fact, no charges to answer.

This blank denial that any crime had been committed, this outright rejection of the case clumsily fabricated during the preliminary investigation, was not to be taken lightly. Samsonov and Kosachevski must have been absolutely convinced of the truth of what they were saying—both, after all, were Party members specially licensed to take on 'political' cases (though, according to Khrushchev, there had long been no such thing as a 'political' case in the Soviet Union—and indeed we were nominally being tried only as 'smugglers', not for our real offence of having been the persons closest of all to Pasternak . . .).[57]

I could not take my eyes off Ira. She looked so touching and funny, with her pale, still child-like face, her almond eyes and her hair done up in two little braids. She told me that as a special favour they had given her an extra mattress in prison—the hard bunk in the cell was excruciating for her and she had come out in an allergic rash.

The hearing was still going on. By now the whole comedy was nothing more in our eyes than an opportunity for seeing people dear to us after several months' separation. Some of them were called as witnesses—Polina Yegorovna, our grumpy domestic help, whom we loved dearly, was brought in, looking stern and composed, but obviously frightened out of her wits. As she went by, hardly able to keep back her tears, she touched each of us on the head, and tried to kiss us. Then my beloved Masha* came in, also looking pale, almost green. I no longer remember what questions they were made to answer.

During the recess, Samsonov and Kosachevski talked to our family, friends and well-wishers outside the courtroom and told them there

* Maria Yefremovna Struchkova, an editor at *Goslitizdat* and my close friend.

was nothing to worry about: Ira would soon be back home with her grandmother, and I would get some nominal sentence for not having reported to the authorities about this money of Pasternak's which the Italians had brought in—just as they had several times in the last few years while he was still alive.

But the mood changed as soon as the recess was over. The judge returned with a sealed envelope in his hand containing the verdict and the sentences that had been laid down for us. When they were read out, the astonished guards at the door (they were all fine fellows, particularly the chief one, a young Ukrainian) passed on the news to the crowd waiting in the corridor outside: eight years' forced labour for the mother, and three for the daughter . . .

There was utter bewilderment. We walked out, and—although it was against the rules—the guards stood aside, and I threw myself into the arms of Sergei Stepanovich, who was crying, and of Masha, and my cousin Militsa . . . Ira, for some reason, tried to rush out as fast as she could ahead of her guards, but they stopped her—for her own sake, so she could say goodbye to her friends. On the way to the court, as she later told me, the Ukrainian guard had asked her whether she was yet fifteen.

The Bedlam of Un-persons

Now we were put in the Black Maria again, and people crowded round as it drove away. This time Ira and I were together. There was no longer any formal reason for keeping us separate, and we now learned that as a special favour we were to be taken to the same forced labour camp—to Taishet.

The journey to Siberia was long and terrible. It was January, when the frosts are at their most severe, and the stops on the way, during which we had to spend the night in the cold, damp 'boxes'* which serve as 'hotels' for prisoners in transit, were a great torment. Ira was wearing only a light coat intended for spring or autumn (it was made of dark-blue English bouclé) and with her silly mania for keeping in fashion, she had had it shortened. My heart bled for her now when I saw her arms sticking way out of her sleeves.

* See footnote on p. 97. (Tr.)

During the whole journey the only other prisoners around us were common criminals who cursed us and the guards in the foulest language. We were all crammed in together like sardines behind the bars of the coach,* and we kept an anxious eye on the guards. Some of them were decent enough, but there were some really nasty louts among them as well. In cases of trouble with our fellow prisoners, however, they were our only hope. At least, we thought, they would probably not stand by idly if the criminals tried to slit our throats.

To this very day I still do not understand why we were taken all the way to the truly fearful camp in Taishet just a month before it was due to be closed down and everybody there transferred to Mordovia.† Whether it was because of the usual confused state of the camp system, or out of sheer sadism, the fact is that we were taken to Siberia only to be brought back to the notorious Potma camp for major 'political' offenders—who are, of course, made out to be ordinary criminals.

The journey back across the continent to Mordovia was also an ordeal, but by no means as bad as the one to Taishet and our arrival there. The only thing to be said about Taishet is that we met some intellectuals there who had still not been released from ten- or twenty-five-year sentences imposed on them as a measure of 'temporary isolation'⁵⁸ and although their numbers had diminished, they provided much more congenial company for us than the cut-throats with whom we had been caged together on the train.

I still cannot think without horror of the final stage of our journey to the camp in Taishet, which we were forced to do on foot, late at night, and in 25° (centigrade) of frost. It was a silvery, Siberian night with a full moon. The pine trees cast their squat, deep-blue shadows across the snow. On either side of the road the grizzled northern fir trees with their spreading branches were bathed in ghostly moonlight, which made them look improbably vast. We were in the middle of a real Taishet forest, ominous and dazzlingly beautiful at the same time. Looking over our shoulders, we could see the horse on which

---

* The coach was of the usual type for the transport of prisoners in the Soviet Union: the prisoners are herded in a 'cage' separated by bars from the corridor, where the guards keep watch on them. (Tr.)

† In the Khrushchev years, as the huge labour camp complexes of Siberia and the Far North were wound down, the camps in Mordovia became the main centre for the detention of 'political' prisoners. See footnote on p. 95. (Tr.)

our things were being carried. Its shadow seemed the size of a camel's under the moon. The sleigh which should have been waiting for us at the rail junction had not been sent, and our two escort guards had refused to wait, so they had marched us off into the night, to our unknown destination. The two spectral shadows with rifles followed behind us as we stumbled along, shaking all over in this frost which would have seemed nothing very much to native-born Siberians, but was unbearable for Muscovites like us who were quite unused to such bitter cold. It penetrated to the marrow of our bones.

All of a sudden—rather as in a fairytale—we saw lights twinkling somewhere in the snowy waste ahead. When we got there, we went up some ice-covered steps and found ourselves in the comparative warmth of a cow-shed where prisoners from the camp were on night duty. We were greeted by a young Lithuanian woman called Yadia Zerdinskaite, who had been sentenced to ten years for sympathizing with the Lithuanian 'forest brotherhood'.* She was a nurse by training, but here in Taishet, she looked after the cows.

We were given some watery *lapsha*† which seemed very tasty to us and, even more important, it was hot and warmed us up. We travelled the last lap to the camp in the luxury of a large sleigh.

We soon found that there were three categories of 'political' prisoners at Taishet. By far the largest consisted of women who belonged to various religious sects disapproved of by our régime. After them came women who had been sentenced for collaboration with the Germans on occupied territory during the war, for serving in the Bandera and Vlasov‡ movements, or for 'spying'. The third and smallest group was made up of 'special' prisoners who had been found guilty of 'sedition'—that is, who on their own initiative, or on behalf of husbands already jailed as troublemakers, had written statements calling for the observance of the illusory rights we are supposed to enjoy. Among these was Anna Barkova, a writer whose name was familiar to me from the poetry anthology of Yezhov and Samurin. With her was her friend Valentina Sanagina who, although

---

* i.e. partisans who took refuge in the dense Lithuanian forests, and continued resistance against the Soviet authorities. 'Forest brotherhood' is the phrase used in Chapter 11 of *Doctor Zhivago* to describe the Bolshevik partisans in the Urals during the Civil War. (Tr.)

† A common dish resembling noodles. (Tr.)

‡ See Bandera and Vlasov in the Biographical Guide. (Tr.)

a woman of little education, was the author of some distinctly talented memoirs. Both of them were now serving a second term, after being sentenced together on the same kind of charge as before. Barkova had written vitriolic satirical verse denouncing Stalin and other Soviet rulers in a vivid style all her own. Sanagina had put down the story of her life in her awkward, uneven handwriting. She came from a working-class family and her father—long since dead—had taken part in the Revolution in 1917: for this she heaped curses on his memory. Both she and Barkova had passed on their writings to others, and were sitting out another ten years in Taishet as a result.

Ira and I listened in fascination to Barkova's savage comments on the world. She seemed an intelligent person to talk to, and it also emerged that she had once worked as a secretary for Lunacharski. She managed to continue to write sitting in her bunk in the camp—she was incapable of work or of fending for herself, even though she had been here so long, and she was looked after by Sanagina, who got food and made clothes for her, and in general treated her as though there were a family relationship between them. Very clever with her hands, Sanagina had the cunning of a peasant, and a natural intelligence.

It should not be thought that the inmates of the camps under Khrushchev were without exception worthy persons, nothing more than innocent victims of a denunciation, or of a 'political' indiscretion. There were among them some very bad types, real scum whose mean and petty natures were brought out by misfortune. They may not have been guilty of the charges for which they had received long sentences. but this did not alter the fact that they could be thoroughly vicious—in a way which might never have come out in normal conditions of life. It is said that people become worse in the camps, but I think the truth is simply that latent qualities of any kind come to the surface. In other words, the camps, like war, make a good person better and a bad one worse. There were many informers, actual or potential, and toadies always ready to sell themselves.

Barkova, for example, was not quite the person we took her for. At first she seemed genuinely attached to me. She recited her old poems to me, and composed new ones impromptu for my benefit—epigrams and whole ballads on Yezhov, Yagoda, and Beria. Ira and I would walk around the compound with her, talking about our favourite poets, and reciting Blok, Pasternak, or Tiutchev. This was a delight and a comfort after all our tribulations among the criminals on the journey to the camp.

But not for nothing do people speak of the face as the 'mirror of the soul'. The whole aspect of Barkova was unutterably fearsome. She was a frail, flat-chested dwarf of a woman with a large pasty face. Wicked little eyes shone out from under her simian brows, and the skin of her lantern jaws was all wrinkled, completing the resemblance to a monkey. From the very first moment she attached herself to me and stuck to me with the tenacity of a bulldog, and for a time was very jealous of anybody else I got to know in the camp. Through our friends and relations in Moscow, Ira and I arranged for her to receive food parcels, but before long she began to accept them as no more than her due.

It was only after our transfer to Potma that I got to understand her true nature. In Potma I was put in the CES, where my job was to edit the 'wall newspaper'.* Barkova brought me something she had written on the religious sectarians—after having wormed her way into their confidence, she now exposed their 'secrets' with great venom and sarcasm, calculating that she could buy her own freedom at the expense of the poor simpletons. I refused to take the stuff and, as I remember, threw her out of the CES. This was a declaration of war between us. That July, during the terrible summer heat, I had severe haemorrhages, and one day, while I was being helped to the camp infirmary, more dead than alive, Barkova gathered together all the local 'intelligentsia', and began to jeer and mock, and make faces at me. I can still see her standing there, with her evil leer, like a grotesque carnival mask.

I went through more than enough experiences of this kind in the Potma bedlam for 'un-persons'.

Another fellow prisoner I got to know well there was a certain Lida S. She was an honest woman, a good worker, who kept very much to herself. Her story was an unusual one. As a girl of seventeen, during the war, she had quarrelled with her step-mother and run away from home to volunteer for service at the front. After only two weeks she was captured by the Germans and spent two years in

* CES: Cultural and Educational Section, a 'recreation room' where prisoners can read newspapers, borrow books, etc. Like all Soviet institutions, the camps have a 'wall newspaper' a kind of bulletin or 'house magazine'. (Tr.)

a P.O.W. camp. The women were taken out to work in the fields. At the end of the war, she took part in a rising of the prisoners, just before the arrival of the Americans. It might have been possible for her after that to stay in some Western country, but she wanted to go nowhere except home to the Soviet Union. After coming back she met and fell in love with a pilot called L. who had fought almost all through the war. He had been awarded many medals for distinguished service, and was a member of the Party. But just before the war was over, he had to make a brief forced landing on Turkish territory—only for a couple of hours, but it was sufficient to cancel out the whole of his previous record. He was interrogated for eight months by those methods which were later* to be described as 'strictly forbidden', but they were unable to break him, and eventually he was released, and his Party card, his medals, and his officer's rank were given back to him.

Lida and he decided that, come what may, they must escape to the West. In January 1953 they managed to get hold of a pistol and boarded an IL-12.† During the flight they tried to force the crew to change course and head west, or to hand over the controls to L. But they were not sufficiently determined, and L. was hesitant about using the gun—it went off without his meaning to shoot, and the radio operator was severely wounded . . . During his interrogation L. took all the blame on himself, insisting that Lida had known nothing about the plan and was completely innocent. He was sentenced to death by firing squad, and she was given twenty-five years' forced labour.

A month later, the prosecutor demanded a retrial, and Lida was also sentenced to death. But she was pardoned after spending two months in the death cell. By the time I met her in 1961 she had already spent seven years in various camps, and was to spend another ten years and one month in them before her release in February 1971.

But enough about 'Bedlam' and its inhabitants . . . I shall now say a little more about my own situation.

Many people, both in the Soviet Union and abroad, who loved and appreciated Pasternak, made efforts to try and obtain my release and rehabilitation. D'Angelo, for example, writes in the article already quoted: '. . . in order to help Ivinskaya and her daughter, I

---

* i.e. after Stalin's death. (Tr.)
† Standard Soviet passenger plane. (Tr.)

made public, in the newspapers of a number of countries, the letters
in which Pasternak had informed me of his financial difficulties and
asked me to send him money by unofficial means, and also a receipt
signed by Pasternak for one sum that I sent him. Then I challenged
Surkov—admittedly without success—to give his reply, and I addressed a letter to Khrushchev calling on him to correct this miscarriage of justice.'

It is said that Feltrinelli also tried to prove our innocence by
publishing facsimiles of letters written to him by Pasternak in which
he said that I was inseparable from him, his *alter ego*, and that anything
done by me was virtually done by himself.

In a number of countries all over the world there were indignant
protests against our imprisonment on a charge of smuggling, as
something contrary both to commonsense and to elementary justice.

But it was all of no avail.

One thing that hampered the efforts on our behalf was the total
lack of sympathy for me in influential Soviet literary circles. Defama-
tory stories about me that were passed down from the high official
quarters dominated by Surkov and certain of his colleagues had
their effect not only on people who did not know me, but also—
what was particularly distressing—on some who had been close to
me. It still pains me to think that even Lidia Chukovskaya took one
of these slanders at its face value. It is, alas, true—as people say—that
if you throw enough mud at anybody, some of it is bound to stick.

During the years when we both worked on *Novy Mir*, Lidia and
I had been brought together by our common love of poetry—
particularly of Pasternak's. At difficult times I shared my hopes,
sorrows, and disappointments with her. I still have a photograph of
her which she gave me then, with the inscription: 'To Olia, as
demanded by the memory of a happy occasion.' She was referring
here to a moment when BL and I once met in her presence, in the
days not long after we had first fallen in love. He had come to pick
me up at her father's luxurious Moscow apartment in which Lidia
had a tiny room, living there in Spartan simplicity, like the poor
relation of a rich family. Next to it, in the opulent dining room with
chandeliers of glittering cut glass, the walls were hung with the
originals of famous Russian paintings, among them a portrait of a
beautiful young woman in lace. This was Lidia's mother, Maria
Chukovskaya. (BL once told me that she was the Maria to whom

Mayakovski cries out in his 'Cloud in Trousers'[59]: 'Maria! Maria! Maria!') And now, on this occasion on 1949, it was this same Maria who announced to me and Lidia that BL had arrived in the apartment: 'Pasternak is here to see you!' We could already hear him intoning in the corridor. He kissed the ladies' hands—hers and Lidia's and then hastened to get me out of the place as quickly as possible. In those days he was not fond of visiting the Chukovski apartment. There was something about the famous Maria he didn't like. Perhaps she had made the mistake of growing old . . .

The unfortunate fact is that by means of his filthy insinuations Surkov succeeded in poisoning my relations with Lidia. It would have been easy enough for me to rebut all the malicious lies put about by Surkov and others, but one of the most important pieces of advice given to me by BL was: never try to justify yourself if people accuse you of something or other. Those who know you will never believe you capable of the theft or murder, or whatever it is. If some slander is going the rounds, say nothing . . .

And so I simply kept my peace.

'Find my song alive! . . .'

Times change, life reclaims its due, old scores are forgotten. Over the years, more and more material relating to BL has appeared in Soviet publications: memoirs and learned articles about him, hitherto unpublished poems and letters. Both *An Essay in Autobiography* and *The Blind Beauty* have appeared in Soviet journals. This 'outstanding lyric poet', as he has been described in an article that came out in 1972, is not only being published, but even, after a fashion, canonized. Since his death three collections of BL's poetry have been published in large editions totalling 170,000 copies. A volume of his translations has been issued under the title *Starry Sky*. More than eighty of his letters have been published. Major Soviet journals, such as *Novy Mir*, *Questions of Literature*, and *Literary Georgia*, have turned their attention to the work of a poet not so long ago denounced as an outcast whose memory would be consigned to oblivion. I rejoice at this. I rejoice when I read a note published in *Literary Russia* by Galina Serebriakova about something Pasternak wrote in a book he once gave her.

She now recalls this with pride, even appending a photograph of the inscription to her in Boria's hand. But I cannot forget, it is more than I can do to bring myself to forget, that terrible meeting of October 31, 1958, when Boria was expelled from the Union of Writers, and Serebriakova—God help her!—was one of those present who put herself down to speak.

I rejoice when I read the following in an article by the influential Alexander Dymshitz: 'We will, of course, be able to give an objective appraisal of such complicated writers . . . as Pasternak . . . whose best works belong to us by right of inheritance.'

I am genuinely glad to read this, but all the same one cannot help wondering whether a cannibal has the right to speak in the name of those he has eaten, claiming to be their rightful heir. What particularly concerns and troubles me is that Pasternak's most important works have still not been published in his native country. The crowning achievements that made him world-famous are unknown here. Again and again I ask myself why this should be so, but can find no answer to the question.

In the winter of 1955 (or it may have been 1956), at a meeting of the editorial board of *Goslitizdat* called to discuss future publications, each of those present had in his hands a list of the proposals that had been put forward. One of them was for a four-volume collected edition of the works of Pasternak, to include even *Doctor Zhivago*. If this project had come about, we should have had a Soviet edition of Pasternak more complete and authoritative than the four volumes put out by the University of Michigan Press.[60] If . . .

When the editorial board came to this item on the agenda, there were cries of approval from many of those present: 'Yes, yes . . . it's high time . . .', and so forth. But then Surkov spoke. It was the same old Surkov. In a calm, quiet voice, and with a nasty little smile, he asked how it was possible: only a few years ago they had said one thing, and now here they were taking such a very different line . . . His heavy irony, the leering expression on his face, his whole manner were so full of hatefulness and spite that people were quite sickened.

I don't know at what level, whether in the Central Committee or lower down—it scarcely matters anyway—but the proposal was killed, and nothing more has been heard of it since.

At the same time, when the author of the article on Pasternak in the *Short Literary Encyclopaedia*[61] tried to take a calmer view of the novel, he was immediately attacked in *Oktiabr* and *Ogoniok*.★ How preposterous that our critics still go on condemning and heaping abuse on a novel which has never been published here, and which the ordinary reader has therefore never read and can have no way of judging for himself. What is he to make, for example, of the words of A.Ovcharenko, a professor and doctor of philology, who in a book published in 1972 described the hero of the novel, Yuri Zhivago, as 'a rabid philistine' who serves as the mouthpiece of the author? Who is to check the truth of what the professor says? How many will believe him? This is exactly the sort of thing that was written about BL while he was still alive. I cannot help thinking of the words BL addressed to his fellow writers in October 1958: 'Do what you like with me, only one thing I beg of you: do not be in too great a hurry, because it will bring you no increase either of glory or of happiness.'

I understand why people should engage in literary politics, but that they should stoop to such low levels of petty intrigue is quite beyond my comprehension. I only have to go over the whole long and terrible story of the novel in my mind again to realize how far some people still are from being able to take a calm and sober view of Pasternak, and how stubbornly they continue to distinguish between a poet who is 'one of ours', and a poet who is 'unacceptable'. 'Unacceptable' to *whom*, I always wonder?

Now that his name again appears in the pages of Soviet publications, the uninitiated might imagine that Pasternak has been completely 'rehabilitated', but this would be jumping to conclusions. The cycle of poems on Gospel themes from *Doctor Zhivago* has still not been published, and nor has 'Hamlet'—though every lover of Pasternak's poetry knows it by heart, and it is even recited on the stage of the Taganka Theatre as a prologue to Liubimov's production of Shakespeare's tragedy, and also read in *The Fallen and the Living*, but it has still not been published under Pasternak's own name.[62] It goes without saying that poems such as 'My soul is in Mourning', 'Nobel Prize', and others written during the scandal over the novel have also never appeared here. 'An Essay in Autobiography[63]' was eventually published, but only with cuts which distort and impoverish the text.

In 1965 a one-volume edition of Pasternak's selected poetry

★ *Oktiabr* (October) is a literary monthly journal which has consistently taken an anti-liberal line, as has *Ogoniok* (The Flame), a popular illustrated weekly. (Tr.)

appeared in the 'Large Series' of the 'Poet's Library'. BL would have
been pleased by this volume if he had lived to see it, but it still falls
short of what he was hoping for in 1957, when he was preparing the
abortive edition which now exists only as the 'Proof Copy'. The
selection of the poems is biased in a way that suggests a deliberate
flouting of BL's wishes, as clearly expressed by him in his numerous
notes to the 'Proof Copy'; the dating of many of the poems is in-
correct, and the variants given are not always the best.

There was something unsavoury about the circumstances in which
The Blind Beauty came to be published by Lev Ozerov in the journal
Prostor in October 1969. In a note accompanying the text, Ozerov
says that the 'manuscript of *The Blind Beauty*★ was put at my disposal
by the widow of the poet, the late Zinaida Nikolayevna Pasternak'.
Now, as I have described, the *manuscript* of *The Blind Beauty*,
together with all the rights in it, was given to me by BL at our
last meeting. When I was arrested, a typewritten *copy*, which had
been neither corrected nor signed by the author, was taken away
from me and never returned. It is probably this copy that came—
through K. Voronkov of the Writers' Union—into the hands of
Zinaida, who then gave it to Ozerov. What is astonishing is that a
literary scholar apparently so experienced as Ozerov should have
accepted as the original manuscript what was in fact a third or fourth
uncorrected carbon copy of a typescript. (Yet he could not but have
known of the existence of the manuscript as corrected by the
author.)[64]

Even on quickly reading through the *Prostor* version and com-
paring it with the manuscript, I discovered no less than ninety
errors, all of them serious distortions of the text, not to mention
innumerable 'emendations' to the original punctuation—which, though
unusual, had its point. It might even have been the lesser evil—I find
it hard to say—to have continued to withhold the play from the

---

★ At the end of 1969 I managed to get through on the telephone to the high
KGB official who had taken the manuscript away from me in 1960, and demanded
that he return it to me. After lengthy negotiations I was informed that I could go
and collect it from the deputy head of the State Archives of Literature and Art,
V. Chernykh. But, alas, Chernykh refused to return the original to me. Instead,
he handed me a photocopy accompanied by a piece of paper certifying that the
original (which he allowed me to see), 'the property of O. V. Ivinskaya', was
deposited 'for safekeeping' in the Archives.

public, rather than to bring it out in this careless, garbled form which breaks all the rules normally applied in editing a text, quite apart from the questions of literary, and simply human, ethics involved.

None of this, however, is very important compared with the overriding fact that the supreme work of Pasternak's life, *Doctor Zhivago*, has not only never been published in his own country, but is still under a ban. Here I should like to dwell on this matter a little further. The essential point is that Pasternak could only be 'rehabilitated' on condition that all the 'unacceptable', 'awkward', or 'unsuitable' parts of his work be expunged from the memory. Somehow or other the novel, which still sticks like a huge bone in the gullet of his latterday, self-appointed 'friends', had to be explained away and 'neutralized'.

'. . . the chief element in art,' Chekhov once wrote, 'is the feeling of personal freedom.' However paradoxical it may seem to anyone who remembers the atmosphere at the end of the 'forties and the beginning of the 'fifties, *Doctor Zhivago* was written out of a totally unclouded sense of boundless personal freedom. BL created the novel without taking account of any literary or political canons, and without regard for any accepted definition of the genre itself. It incorporated the experience of a whole generation. As someone has written of him: '. . . he understood everything at a glance and was able to express ideas in the form in which they first come into the mind, while they are still fresh and retain their meaning to the full.'

BL was well aware that in every age men who seek the truth are condemned as heretics. In his first version of his translation of Goethe's *Faust*, there is one passage which, significantly, he rendered as follows:

> The few who strove to pierce the core of things
> And reveal to all the tablets of the soul
> Were burned at the stake and crucified
> By the will of the mob from earliest days.*

And in his first version of Hamlet's soliloquy 'To be or not to be', which is very far from the original, he was also talking for himself:

> And who could bear the false greatness
> Of rulers, the ignorance of grandees,

---

* After the violent attack on his translation by T. Motyleva in *Novy Mir* (August 1950),[65] he changed the words 'by the will of the mob' to 'as you well know'.

The universal sham, the ban on pouring out
One's heart, unhappy love,
And the worthlessness of merit in mediocrity's eyes . . .

Before Pasternak could be received into Soviet literature again, a
scapegoat had to be found for the 'indecency' committed in the shape
of the novel, and the blame for it was put on me.

If I had not actually written the novel (so it was now said), I had
certainly put BL up to it, and it was also I who had sent it abroad—
and what was I, according to Surkov, but a common criminal? Even
my first arrest in 1949, he insinuated, had been on ordinary criminal
charges.*

Surkov had by now climbed to the top of the ladder in the Union
of Writers and become a very powerful figure indeed. But I always
think of a line from Rabindranath Tagore which has stuck in my
mind from the days when I was engaged in translating him into
Russian: 'Though becoming mighty, untruth still never grows up
into truth.' While I was still in the camp, this whole strategy of
dealing with the problem of Pasternak had its logic and seemed to
make sense: I had no way of giving the lie to Surkov, and there was
nobody else to do it for me. But now the situation is different, and
times have changed: new ways have to be found of glossing everything over, of squaring the circle . . .

The roots of Pasternak's art are deeply Russian, but his talent and
his courage, his struggle for the freedom of the personality make him
an honorary citizen of the whole world—which is why his work and
his destiny have aroused such a universal response.

In his address given on receiving the Nobel Prize, speaking of the
'beautiful and tragic works of the first years of the Russian Revolution', Albert Camus said: 'At that moment the Russia of Blok and of
the great Pasternak, of Mayakovski and Yesenin, of Eisenstein and

* The story he told was that I had been involved in a huge swindle uncovered
in the editorial offices of the magazine *Ogoniok*. In fact, my only connection with
this case was that I was summoned, together with forty other people, and asked to
give evidence confirming that a member of the staff there had received payment
for a certain piece of work. My arrest by the MGB (Security police) took place six
months later and had nothing whatsoever to do with this—otherwise I would
hardly have been taken to the Lubianka, or been charged under Article 58.[66] (Even
Surkov might have heard that common criminals—including slanderers—are
prosecuted under other articles.)

the first novels about steel and cement, was a magnificent laboratory for new forms and themes, and was gripped by a creative fever, by a frenzy of experiment.'

Interest in Pasternak's work is as great as ever, and the treatment of his novel in his own country continues to exercise the leading writers of Europe. Soviet officials—not least our Minister of Culture—have constantly been questioned about it, and the time will come when the issue can no longer be evaded.

I believe that eventually the calm, wise words of Konstantin Paustovski, Veniamin Kaverin, and of many other of this country's most outstanding writers and artists will be heard. Here is what some of them have said in open (but never published) letters:

Konstantin Paustovski:
'. . . it was we ourselves, with our own hands, who ill-advisedly set in motion the scandal over Pasternak. It did nothing to raise our standing in the world, or to strengthen and enhance our ties of friendship with other nations, particularly with the intellectuals, but only damaged us in their eyes. It is impossible to forget this sad and instructive tale. What was the point of humiliating and hounding this magnificent poet—magnificent, that is, for anyone who has the slightest understanding of what poetry is about? What sort of brains did you need to slander a man who was the pride of Russian poetry and of the Russian nation? Who fabricated the 'Pasternak affair'— which destroyed this utterly honest man, this man of transparent integrity? There is nothing hostile to the Soviet system in *Doctor Zhivago*. The book could easily be brought out here in a mass edition. But certain people evidently thought it to their advantage, through this persecution of Pasternak, to undermine the prestige of the Soviet system and make us into a laughing-stock. Or perhaps they thought they were proving their loyalty by mounting the whole affair. The fate of literature should not be decided by people with the mentality of a Sergeant Prishibeyev★ . . . Must we always view any criticism of our shortcomings as a calumny or a crime? Writers have an absolute right to participate in the life of the country as citizens able to use their critical faculties constructively. Must they really be condemned and punished for this?'

(February 5, 1966)

★ An ignorant martinet in a story by Chekhov. (Tr.)

Veniamin Kaverin: '. . . Who can forget the senseless and tragic affair of Pasternak's novel, which caused such harm to our country?'

(January 25, 1969)

Mstislav Rostropovich: 'I remember with pride how I failed to turn up at the meeting of representatives of culture which was held in the Central House of Workers in Art to denounce Pasternak, and at which I was supposed to speak—I had been charged with the task of criticizing *Doctor Zhivago*—though at that time I had not even read it . . .' (October 13, 1970)

Neither *Doctor Zhivago* nor the poems on Gospel themes which go with it can be taken away from Russia—people read and love them, and copy them out.

Eleven years after BL's death, one night in the late autumn, more than a thousand young people gathered in the woods near the village of Sofrino* outside Moscow. Under an autumn rain, they listened intently to an extraordinary recital consisting of the poems from *Doctor Zhivago* interspersed with passages from some of the abusive attacks—including Semichastny's speech—made against BL at the height of the campaign against him. 'The Miracle', 'Gethsemane', 'Mary Magdalene', and 'Hamlet' were read. Two girls sang 'Winter Night', accompanying themselves on a guitar, and the words so familiar and precious, floated up to the tops of the pine trees:

> . . . and two small shoes fell down
> With a clatter to the floor,
> And from the night-light waxen tears
> Dropped on a dress.
> And all was lost in a haze of snow,
> Silver and white.
> The candle on the table burned,
> The candle burned . . .

Oh, if BL could have been there that night in the Sofrino woods, I know what tears he would have wept.

> How it blows from the north! How
> The cold bristles! O storm-wind

* Village forty-six kilometres north east of Moscow, on the railway line to Zagorsk. (Tr.)

Search each dell and hollow tree,
Only find my song alive!

Your song is alive, my love—and it will live as long as people
know what poetry is!

All the attempts to make him out as nothing more than a lyric
poet remote from the political life and concerns of his times would
have been indignantly rejected by BL himself. ('Don't you think
you'd have to be a hopeless nonentity to play only one role all your
life, to have only one place in society, always to stand for the same
thing?'*)

Through his portrayal of the daily round of private existence, the
ordinary life of the world around us, he clearly brings out his revolt
against 'the power of the glittering phrase', his belief in the need to
restore faith in the value of personal opinions, to revive people's
instinctive sense of right and wrong, to refuse to live by alien ideas
imposed from without, and to acknowledge the uniqueness of each
individual human personality.

BL is still thought of as an 'unpolitical poet', but in some of his
superb lyric poems written long before *Doctor Zhivago*, there are
already prophetic notes about the age. Everybody knows, for
instance, and can quote by heart such lines as:

A genius comes as a harbinger of betterment,
And his going is avenged with tyranny.†

Or:

O, graven image of the State,
Liberty's perpetual threshold!
Uncaged, the centuries steal forth,
Wild animals prowl the Coliseum,
And the hand of a preacher, raised
In fearless blessing, tames with faith
A panther in its dank confinement.
And so, the selfsame step from
Roman circuses to a Roman church
Is endlessly repeated: in this sign
We too inhabit catacombs and mines.'‡

* *Doctor Zhivago*, Chapter 9. (Tr.)   † From 'A High Illness', 1928. (Tr.)
‡ From *Lieutenant Schmidt*, 1926. (Tr.)

And then, what more concise and telling comment on the times could there be than this fragment of a sentence: '. . . the collective squandering of thousands for the sake of earning a copeck's worth of living . . .'

Like one of the characters created by him, 'he craved for an idea, inspired yet concrete, which would show a clear path and change the world for the better, an idea as unmistakable even to a child or an ignorant fool as a flash of lightning or a thunderclap . . .'*

My love! I now come to the end of the book you wanted me to write. Forgive me for writing it as I have. It was beyond me to do it in a manner worthy of you.

When we first met at *Novy Mir* I was only just thirty-four years old. Now, as I write these final lines, it is my sixtieth birthday . . . The greater part of my conscious life has been devoted to you—and what is left of it will also be devoted to you.

Life, as you know, has not been kind to me. But I have no complaint against it: it bestowed on me the great gift of your love, of our friendship and closeness. You always used to say to me that life treats us more gently, with more compassion, than we generally expect. This is a great truth, and I never cease to be mindful of your words to me: '. . . one must never, in any circumstances, despair. In misfortune it is our duty to hope and to act.'

You were right also in saying that we never learn from the lessons of others, and are always fatally drawn to the hollow and perilous vanities of life. But through all my follies and misfortunes, through all the emptiness and futility of my present lonely existence, I stretch out my hands to you, and say:

> . . . now, as life begins to fade
> And I stand by my dear ones' graves
> I know I may knock at heaven's gate,
> For wasn't I loved by you?

June 27, 1972[67]

* Both quotations are from *Doctor Zhivago*. (Tr.)

APPENDIX A

Letters of Boris Pasternak to Olga Ivinskaya

This is a very small part (besides others quoted in the text) of the letters written to me by BL. Most of our correspondence was confiscated at the time of my arrest and has disappeared.*

1.

Dear Oliusha,

Whatever position I lie in, I cannot write without pain. I shall certainly ask you to visit me—I need it—but after I have got to know the people here better. The doctor treating me is Valentina Nikolayevna Bystrova. I shall tell her about you and ask her to phone you. When I send for you I will do it through her. Today I no longer believe it's radiculitis.† Either it's a tumour spreading rapidly in all directions, or a tumour in the part of the spinal cord which controls the lower extremities and everything in their neighbourhood. The thought itself doesn't frighten me—what is terrifying is that the end will come through torments protracted by treatment. I will tell you when to visit me. I must see you one last time, give you my blessing for the long years of life you will live in me and without me, and see you make your peace with all the others and look after them. I kiss you.

Night of 1–2 April.

Thank you for an infinity of things.

Thank you. Thank you. Thank you.

2.

April 6, 1957

Oliusha dear,

Again I have nothing very cheerful to tell you. Yesterday's improvement, brought about by Blokhin, went for nothing during the night and now everything is the same as before. The night was appalling. I couldn't sleep a wink and just twisted and turned, unable to find any position at all bearable. It can't go on like this of course. We have behaved liked spoiled children—I am an idiot and a scoundrel without

---

* Letters 1–9 were written during the spring of 1957 while BL was undergoing treatment in a branch of the Kremlin Hospital. In the later stages he was transferred to Uzkoye, just outside Moscow.

† Inflammation of a spinal nerve root. (Tr.)

equal, and now I have been given the punishment I deserve. Forgive me, but what else is there I can say? I have a pain in my leg, I feel weak and sick. You really can't imagine how ill I am—not in the sense of danger, but of suffering. If I feel better on Tuesday, I'll send for you, but in my present state life is not worth living, and the idea is unthinkable. I kiss you. Don't be cross with me. Thank Irochka for her letter.

3.

Oliusha, yesterday evening was nice and quiet, and I could even lie on my back for a while. But the night was awful, just as it always is—from dusk until dawn.

Tell your mother and all the others: I'm not afraid to die—I want it terribly, and the sooner the better. Everything is getting worse and worse and more and more difficult all the time. All my vital functions are dying away—except for two: the capacity to suffer pain and the capacity not to sleep. Whatever position I lie in I get no rest. Even you can't imagine what a misery it is.

Keep calm. Don't come here [unannounced]. I'll send for you again out of the blue—when, I don't know.

I kiss you.

Yesterday you saw for yourself!

I have no strength left from pain.

4.

[On the envelope: For Olga Vsevolodovna Ivinskaya, to be collected.]
Dear Nina* and Oliusha,

I am suffering untold physical pain (my leg, knee, back, and everything else), and get no sleep. Pray God to send me a quick death, to deliver me from this torture, the like of which I have never known before.

Thank you, Ninochka, for coming to see me, thank you for your letter, thank you for being part of my life and for bringing Olechka with you. Oliusha my angel, what can I do? You can see, my love—I have to die in order not to go out of my mind from pain. Perhaps later on we can do what you say in your letter and I'll ask you to come [and stay], but there's not much likelihood—it's not that sort of hospital. And they haven't even yet really begun to give me any treatment to speak of. Carry on as you are and attend to things for me exactly as you see fit—find support and consolation in this. I kiss you, and weep without end. What have I done to deserve this? Such unspeakable physical suffering, which gets worse all the time. Christ be with you,

* Nina Tabidze, who twice went with me to see BL in the hospital.

my treasures. How right and what a joy that you both came together!

Perhaps later on things will be as you say, but not at once.

I kiss you both.

5.

Oliusha, my treatment is getting more complicated and difficult all the time. I have no strength left to deal with your anxieties, to calm you down. You saw how glad I was to see you. But not during this week. Perhaps at the end of it, or after Sunday the 14th. The nights are completely unspeakable . . .

I kiss you and beg you to calm down. I'll send for you when it's possible. The pain at night is excruciating and there is nothing to draw on for the will to live. I kiss you. Forgive me. I can't help it.

6.

April 18, 1957

Dear Oliusha,

They're very strict about visits during the week. They certainly won't allow a third one, and they're even grumbling about the second. Write me a letter on Saturday about how all our business has turned out and leave it at the reception. In my letter to Al. Iv.* I should have asked him to speed up the publication of the poetry volume—that would be very important. Alia has been enquiring through Zina† when she can come and see me. I have told her Wednesday the 24th. If there is the slightest chance that two people, not just one, are allowed to come on a weekday and you could come with her, it would be splendid, and I shall ask Val. Nik. [the doctor] about it, but I think it's not possible— it's against the regulations here.

It really would be marvellous if you could phone and find out when Val. Nik. is going to *Maria Stuart*‡ and manage by hook or by crook to get a ticket yourself for the same evening, so you can meet her and have a talk with her.

Today they got me out of bed for the first time and made me sit and walk a little. I was as helpless as a year-old baby. During this test it emerged that the main centre of the pain—quite unbearable when I walk, but always there at other times as well—is in the knee. It seems to weigh like lead and to have become all stiff and swollen up from the pain. Another thing: perhaps by some inexplicable witchcraft, but

---

* Alexander Ivanovich Puzikov, the senior editor of the State Publishing House for Literature.

† Alia: Ariadna Efron; Zina: Zinaida Nikolayevna, BL's wife.

‡ Pasternak's translation of Schiller's play, then being performed in Moscow. (Tr.)

for whatever reason it may be, my ability to [. . .]* by myself has gone without even leaving a memory and I have no faith that it will gradually come back. I think I will have to request an operation if its success would really ensure the normal working of this elementary function at the expense of losing the others. Because of this unexpected misfortune everything has changed with terrifying abruptness during the month. It's no joke. Please write and tell me calmly about the arrangements you have made with d'Ang[elo] and *Goslitizdat*, and what you have achieved. Thursday and Sunday are already taken. If you can get permission to come with Alia, that will be terrific.

I kiss you,

Your B.

7.

April 22

Dear Oliusha,

I have read A. I.'s [Puzikov's] letter. My warmest thanks to him. I don't like the place in his letter where he says: 'I'm working, redoing it, adding things.'† My real wish is that the verse should come out (so there is something which will earn plenty of money for the house next month), and that this mutual bluffing game—now so complicated—over the novel‡ should be terminated by its publication somewhere in the original form and then come to an end and be forgotten in this country, leaving no trace. Do you really think that after the unlikely miracle of an early recovery I want nothing better than to sit in Peredelkino rewriting the novel from beginning to end? And of course the idea that one might have any doubts about Marxism or criticize it is absolutely unacceptable [to the authorities]—and will remain so as long as we live. This is what Zina Livanova§ was saying when she came to see me yesterday: 'We have the dictatorship of the proletariat here, Boria—didn't you know, or have you gone out of your mind?' This was apropos of the fact that their friend Kozyrev, the Soviet ambassador in Italy, has read the novel.

I am returning Puzikov's letter to you.

What did you talk about with Zelinski?

There is no more talk on the urological theme here. Perhaps interest

---

* Word omitted; evidently: urinate. (Tr.)

† Puzikov was editing *Doctor Zhivago*. (Tr.)

‡ i.e. the official pretence that it might be published after editing, and Pasternak's apparent agreement to this—though in fact he was determined to have it come out in full abroad. (Tr.)

§ The wife of the actor Boris Livanov. (Tr.)

in it will revive, but for the time being it has lapsed completely. And I am absolutely against coming back to it, calling in someone, etc. There's no point in it at all.

It's too bad that arthritis of the knee-cap always takes on such acute forms. My leg hurts intolerably, unbelievably, almost all the time. Every night, if I doze off for half an hour—so they tell me—I groan and shout out from pain in my sleep. If there is ever any question of calling in other specialists for a consultation, then only in connection with surgery—on the leg, that is. But there is no necessity for it. I understand what they are trying to do—to disperse the salt deposits in the knee by exercise and massage—and it is sensible and correct, but they have no idea of the suffering caused by any attempt at movement.

Today I was washed in a bath, and for the first time I was able to hobble over to it by myself. If I have the strength to get to the phone, I will ring you today or tomorrow evening.

Yesterday, the first day of Easter, I had a lot of letters, including two remarkable ones from the Arts Theatre.

When should you come? Alia will be here on Wednesday. After her, on Thursday, they'll say it's too soon [to receive another visitor], so you should try on Friday. I'm weak and tire terribly quickly, and am all in a sweat from writing this answer.

I kiss you.

Your B.

8.

April 27, 1957

Dear Oliusha,

What possessed you to talk in such definite terms to Val. Nik. about Uzkoye? She's now got it into her head that they've already arranged for me to go there—which will make it easier for her to have me discharged from here in ten days' or two weeks' time, before my leg is better, so the treatment can be completed in Uzkoye, as though this had already been decided on. But I was so much hoping to stay on here till my leg is all right, and then go home to Peredelkino. Now they will shorten my time here with a perfectly easy conscience. But I'm not blaming you—only this devilish business with my leg, and I give you a big kiss.

I have written everything for *Goslitizdat*.

9.

Sunday, May 26

My dear, the leg has got worse today. I shall try to stay in bed today and tomorrow, and perhaps it will come all right again. I probably shan't be able to phone you during the next day or two. If I'm not better by Tuesday and can't manage to get to you, please don't worry. I now understand what brings all this on—it's an attack of sciatica (inflammation of the sciatic nerve in the hip-joint). I hope I'll get over it and keep it from becoming worse by staying in bed.

[When I say:] don't worry, it also means: don't disrupt your established routine. Stay out in Izmalkovo and try to work until I arrive—and if I don't turn up by Friday, then arrange with Andriusha* for him to come and see me here next Sunday during lunchtime. I will then give him a message for you, and he will tell me your news.

On no account must you take any unforeseen or unexpected initiative of your own. Don't send anybody over to the *dacha*† and in particular don't try to go there yourself. Any departure from the established routine we are used to would upset our whole way of life, and this would be worse than breaking both arms and legs—something I just wouldn't have the strength to face.

But I know you won't do this, my treasure. I think everything will turn out all right and I'll be with you in a couple of days at the most. If the worse comes to the worst, then just wait till Friday (till you can send Andriusha). But I don't think it will come to that. I give you endless hugs, my angel. There can be no question of Shchupletsov‡ of course.

10.§
    Oliusha my dear, I'm writing to you at the post office. I am depressed by all the life going on around, by the [airplane] flight, by the huge number of decent people who live in the right way, as demanded by the times, while only I am suspect to myself, and am not about to mend my ways, and will just go on living more and more badly. I don't know whether I'll be able to phone you from here. Everybody round me is so blameless and so right—you first of all. But I cause distress to everybody—to you most of all, as I understood before I left.

Oliusha, life will go on as it did before. I wouldn't even know how to live in any other way. Nobody thinks badly of you. Only just now N.A.'s daughter‖ was rebuking me for taking such risks and then evad-

* Andrei Voznesenski.   † i.e. to the 'big house'. (Tr.)

‡ Boris Vsevolodovich Shchupletsov: senior editor of the 'Foreign Literature' Publishing House.

§ Letters 10–20 were sent to me from Tbilisi, where BL stayed from February 20 to March 6, 1959.

‖ Nita, the daughter of Nina Alexandrovna Tabidze.

ing responsibility, leaving you to bear the brunt—this [she said] is
unworthy of me and ignoble.

I give you a big hug. How extraordinary life is. How much we need
to love and think. Nothing else should concern us.

Your B.

11.

February 22

Dear Oliusha

Idleness and the break from the fixed habits of my working day are
having their effect. N.A. has put me in her own room and moved with
Zina into her grandson's room—from which he has been thrown out.
All the people here are extraordinary, full of self-sacrifice and devotion.
I wrote to you yesterday from the post office. At the airport, where she
came to see us off, Livanova said a few nice words in my ear about you.
As I told you, I want to spend these two weeks reading the rest of
Proust—I am gradually getting to the end.

I shall try to phone you today (Sunday, 22nd) from the post office.
I am beginning to feel that quite apart from the novel, the [Nobel]
prize, the articles,* scares and scandals, I am also to blame in some other
way for our life having recently turned into a bad dream, and that it
needn't have been like this. I suppose, as D.A.† said to you, I really
should draw in my horns, calm down and write for the future. Yesterday—when I was reproached for it—I clearly understood for the first
time that by involving you in all these terrible affairs, I am casting a large
shadow on you and putting you in awful danger. It's unmanly and
contemptible. I must try to see that it doesn't happen again and that as
time goes on only good, joyful, and easy things come your way. I love
you and send you lots of kisses. On the assumption that you are in
Leningrad (although I would rather you were not) please give my
regards to Zin. Ivanovna, and Fiod. Petrovich.‡ I kiss you. Forgive me.

Your B.

12.

February 24

My dear Oliusha,

Something very silly has happened. When I was leaving I expected
I would be keeping in touch with you by phone rather than by writing,

* i.e. press attacks on Pasternak. (Tr.)
† Dmitri Alexeyevich Polikarpov.
‡ Fiodor Petrovich: the nephew of my step-father, F. P. Kostko, and his wife,
Zinaida Ivanovna.

but it has turned out the other way round. Before departing I made quite sure of your Leningrad telephone number, but not of your address there. I now find that it's very difficult to phone Leningrad from here because it can't be done directly, only via Moscow, and you can get through only after one o'clock at night. I am sending my letters to Irochka in Moscow in the hope that she is keeping in touch with you by phone and will pass on what I write. The worst is that I have no news of you and no way of knowing if you are well and how you are off for money—whether you were able to borrow some from anybody.

The writers here have evidently been given to understand how to behave towards me—quietly, with reserve, without any banquets, so I am living at Nina's in complete obscurity and isolation, reading Proust, eating, sleeping, walking round the town to exercise my leg, whiling away the time and occasionally writing you these empty, vacuous notes which tell you nothing.

During the short time I shall be away there will probably be a huge accumulation of the letters I so much prize, and some of which will require an answer. All the habitual and familiar things which have made up my life and given me joy will continue, God willing, but there must be a few changes in these set ways. We must put our financial affairs, both yours and mine, in order, and make a real attempt, as D.A. said to you (I have written about this already) to live at a slower pace, with our thoughts on the future—a more distant one.

As always, I love you terribly, but I'm sure you're neither aware of it, nor see any proof of it, and simply don't notice. For my part, if I could hope that everything will remain as it was before our recent exchange of words, I would be in a state of perfect bliss. To imagine anything better than this would be inconceivable, beyond my power. I fancy I see something very, very good ahead of me—something indefinable and undeserved, a part of which I experience in advance as I embrace and kiss you in my thoughts.

13.
February 26

Oliusha my dear, my treasure, my darling Oliusha! How I miss you! The sadness I feel in the mornings—the same inexplicable sadness I know so well from childhood! Outside a gust of pure, fresh air smelling of spring, the twittering of birds and the voices of children, and this sudden twinge of sadness comes over me. What causes it? I must try to understand it and do something about it. How strange—my position has never been so doubtful and precarious, the future has never been so uncertain, but for some reason I have never felt so clear in my mind and calm—just as though you and all the rest of us, our houses, our children, our work and our health were in perfect order and unthreatened by anything, as though I had something very good in store for me. Never has the urge to put certain ideas into final shape and the desire to go home and concentrate [on my work] been so great or seemed so all-important, and never have I been so firmly convinced that nothing will stand in the way of satisfying this need.

Oliusha my love, my treasure and my angel, I am writing you such senseless letters, forgive me. I have nothing to tell you. What am I doing here? Mainly lying low. While so doing I read Proust, go for walks to keep my leg in shape, eat and sleep. N.A. lavishes attention on me at every step—to take advantage of this is swinish, I don't deserve it from anyone, least of all from her. Nobody here is hostile to you. She and I have talked about nothing else. But I have a feeling that many people love me without any good reason, and loving me, they love you as well. This atmosphere of tacit acceptance and agreement emanates even from Zina.

I give you a big, big hug. I can't wait for this interval of animal idleness to come to an end and for us to return home. How nice it would be if you were in Moscow, and Irochka didn't have to forward my letters.

14.
February 27, 1959

Oliusha, for some reason I feel so sad at the moment of waking up in the morning! I am in complete ignorance about where you are and what's happening to you, and also what to expect on my return, what my situation is. When I walk round the town all by myself on the grey, cold days we are having just now, I feel at peace in a sad kind of way, and all seems so clear in my mind. I have a steady glimmer of hope and faith that they are not going to do any more bad things to me, and that the mysteries of the Foreign Legal Department* will enable me to improve both your and my financial position. Assuming I and my activities are not overtaken by some disaster which would spell the end of everything, allow me to believe that my life will go on as before, that you won't leave me and turn your back on me. There is really no disagreement of any kind among us all. You were wrong when, as you thought, you put the question 'fair and square' and insisted I make a

---

* The reference is to Pasternak's negotiations with the Foreign Legal Collegium on the possibility of transferring his foreign earnings through official channels. See p. 362. (Tr.)

choice and come to a firm decision. All this is quite different with us, and outsiders are just as little able to judge it as they are my place in contemporary life—a place so painfully unassuming and unobtrusive, so unique and so fraught with both sorrow and the happiness of freedom. There is no drama or tragedy as far as we are concerned, my darling girl—I am alive and breathing, and this suffices for me to go on thinking my thoughts and loving you, but to recall and bring up for discussion incidental and attendant circumstances is—in our case—false and artificial. I send you a big kiss. Don't be angry with me. It's sad and strange to be without you.

15.

February 28, 1959

Oliusha my precious girl, I give you a big kiss. I am bound to you by life, by the sun shining through my window, by a feeling of remorse and sadness, by a feeling of guilt (oh, not towards you of course, but towards everyone), by the knowledge of my weakness and the inadequacy of everything I have done so far, by my certainty of the need to bend every effort and move mountains if I am not to let down my friends and prove an impostor. And the better all those around me are than we two, and the nicer I am to them and the dearer they are to me, the greater and deeper my love for you, the more guilty and sorrowful I feel. I hold you to me terribly, terribly tight, and almost faint from tenderness, and almost cry.

16.

March 1, 1959

Dear Oliusha,

The whole ten days we have been here it has been windy and cold, but today for the first time it is warm and sunny outside. Only ten days have gone by and it's just as hard for me to imagine that it may be given to me to hear your voice and see you, as it is to imagine the house in Peredelkino still standing in its place. The thought that my settled way of life and ordinary daily routine of work will go on as before, and that I shall come back to it, receiving and replying to letters, asking your advice, sharing all the new things that will come into both our minds, putting in order, with your help, our joint affairs, the thought that the happiness you give, concentration and work await me in the fairly near future—all this seems like a presumptuous, undeserved, and unfulfillable dream. Oh, how Il ove you and how much I shall owe you for ever and ever!

17.

March 2, 1959

Dear Oliusha,

They never let me go out walking alone—N.A.'s daughter Nita always comes with me, and on the way she tells me the story of all the houses and places we pass, and of her friends, whom we run into in large numbers. These are whole sagas about moral exploits, about people with hearts of gold who gave much help to each other during the terrible years of tribulation and hardship, about miracles of self-sacrifice, self-denial, and compassion. I have become such a convinced and conscious egotist in recent years that it shames me to hear all this. Walking around Tiflis* is not the same as it was on my previous visits, and I look at it with different eyes than Mitia probably did a little while ago. This time I have come not to admire, to seek inspiration, to make speeches and be feted at banquets.† I have come now to be silent and to hide, pursued by public execration and by the equally just reproaches you have heaped on me, and in such a state of mind, downcast and sad, that it is best to sit and gently occupy myself with something slow-moving and un-demanding. I am getting to the end of the endless Proust—whom I had made it my aim to finish off when I came here. And, as always, I feel very sad in the mornings, once I wake up. Why is this? Probably because you often come to me in my dreams without my remembering anything about it—just as I very often have dreams about you which remain vividly in my mind. I have already written to you several times about this feeling. Another reason, I dare say, is that our last conversations in Moscow had a bad effect on me. You were wrong, it seems to me. I am in no way guilty towards you—or rather, I am guilty towards everybody, towards the age we live in, towards my family—but least of all towards you. Even if your fears for yourself were well-founded—well, that would of course be terrible, but no danger hanging over you arises from the circumstances of my [private] life, any more than my being permanently together with you could ward it off. We are joined together by subtler ties, by higher and more powerful bonds than those of the intimate existence we lead in full view of the world—and every-body is well aware of this. My life with you proceeds not at all in the sphere to which your recent demands and reproaches referred, but in another one so entirely dedicated to the highest and purest concerns that no misfortunes can destroy it or detract from it, for the simple reason that it transcends all obstacles and adversities.

* The old name for the capital of Georgia; now officially called Tbilisi. (Tr.)

† Pasternak visited Georgia as part of a delegation of Russian writers in November, 1933, and went there again early in 1944. (Tr.)

I cannot change my way of life not only for fear of causing suffering to those around me, but also for fear of the unnatural effect which would be created by such an unneeded and abrupt step. Even in this present accustomed state of affairs your and my situation is both hazardous and blatantly provocative. Just pull one thread and the whole fabric will unravel and come apart.

Today is the first day this year on which I feel I have some good reason to believe and to promise you that as soon as I get home I will, I think, be able to start on a long and major new work of the same kind as *Doctor Zhivago*—a novel which in some small part will be a sequel to it.

I give you a great big hug and must end this letter now—someone is coming in a moment.

18.

March 3, 1959

Oliusha my treasure,

I think—I am afraid of tempting fate—I think we shall try to fly back to Moscow (Vnukovo) on Sunday the 8th. If this comes off, and if you are alive, still out of prison, and in Moscow, and if you have not washed your hands of me and agree to speak with me and see me, I hope to phone you as usual (O bliss!) at your apartment on Sunday evening at 9 (between 9 and 10), and on the morning of Monday the 9th, if you are willing to grant me this joy, this ecstasy, I shall hope to see you in Izmalkovo, as always. (How afraid I am to anticipate events, how afraid I am to write these words!)

Could there be new blows of fate waiting for me, some unpleasant surprise or visitation? Am I making a fatal mistake in thinking to come back only to good things? This is the last letter I'll be writing you from here. I have already written you a good many, hastily and in pencil. Have they reached you? They are all worthless. Don't keep them but just note in your diary that in 1959, at the end of the winter, I left you all alone for two weeks and wrote to you every day.

As I write this last letter, I am just reading the last hundred pages (out of the total of three thousand five hundred) of Marcel Proust. I didn't like him very much, you remember. But these final pages ('Time Regained') are infinitely human and brilliant, like Tolstoi. I send you kisses without end. Forgive this hurried scrawl—I am writing standing up at the post office.

19.

March 3, 1959

My darling Oliusha,

I have already written to you once today and now I'm writing again. I am with you all day long. I feel you are so much part of me—it's like writing letters to myself. I shall soon be back. What am I to expect? Surely not some new threat, demand, or unpleasantness? Surely nothing could have happened to you? Although I'm not superstitious, I am so used to treating feelings, premonitions, and mere appearances as realities that I lend more credence to states of mind than I do to hard facts—which is why I believe I can look forward to nothing less than the improbable and scarcely imaginable joy of seeing you again, and to the happiness of getting back to work and once more seeing my friends in the world far away. If only we are left in peace—everything else we can manage by ourselves. I made a terrible mistake when I asked you that time—after we handed in the Słowacki* to clarify the financial situation and find a way of settling it more quickly. It was probably wrong to do this. We should keep quiet, lie low, and let them forget about us—which is what we'll do now, a little late and under less favourable conditions.

But of course I have no idea what's happening. As I write I am overcome by tenderness for you, but this makes me feel that you and I are favoured by fate and fortune, whereas in actual fact you could long ago have run out of money and might be going frantic in vain attempts to get some. Oh, what joy it is to kiss you if only in words and on paper! Stay well, I hug and kiss you countless times, my dear heart, my beloved darling!

20.
March 4
Oliusha my treasure,

Yesterday I wrote you my last letter in the evening at the post office. It was raining, deep puddles were gathering in the potholes in the almost dark streets, reflections from the lamp posts spread in gleaming patches over the pavements, and it seemed to me that I was saying goodbye to this hospitable town in a fitting way. But now, in the morning, here I am writing to you once more, my joy and love, without any hope that this letter will arrive in advance of me, before I have flown back (the verbs we use nowadays, thanks to air travel!). My joy, my delight, what incredible good fortune that you are there, that there exists in the world this hardly believable possibility of finding you and seeing you, that you bear with me, that you let me pour out to you all the thoughts and feelings accumulated and pent up between our meetings,

* A translation of the Polish writer Słowacki. This sentence appears to refer to negotiations with the Foreign Legal Collegium about the transfer of Pasternak's royalties. (Tr.)

that you have given me as a gift this precious right to plunge self-obliviously into the deepest depths of my admiration for you, for your talents and—over and over and over again—for your goodness.

One day things may be as you (perhaps mistakenly and wrongly) want them to be. But meanwhile, my beloved and adored one, for the very reason that I am pampered by the happiness you give me and lit by the light of your angelic sweetness, for the sake of the charity in which you yourself are always unwittingly instructing me, let us be generous to others—and if needs be, let us be even more generous and forbearing than before—in the name of everything warm and bright that so inseparably and permanently joins us together.

I kiss you, my white marvel, my fond love, you drive me to distraction by making me so grateful to you.

21.*

April 23, 1960

Oliusha, be patient, I must stay in bed for a few days. Don't be alarmed if I can't come this evening, or can't get to the phone perhaps for a day or two. It seems I must stay in bed till I'm well. I give you a big kiss. Everything will be all right.

22.

Monday, April 25, 1960

Oliusha dear, the doctor will be coming today. Things are no better —neither in the places where I expect pain nor in those where it is starting up. If Shavochka† gets in touch and wants or needs to see me, then on the Sunday when he comes out to you, let him bring everything he may have for me, and after he has learned what you think and decide, let him come over here to the house and ask to see me alone. He will be shown in and left alone with me. I am enclosing a kind of 'pass' for him with this note. But if he has nothing important, he can put off his visit until I am well.

23.

Monday, 25, evening

The doctor has been—you probably know already—and found I have high blood pressure, badly shaken nerves, and a heart condition he says is responsible for these infernal pains I have in the left side of the back. I find it hard to imagine that such a constant pain, as firmly embedded as a splinter, should be due only to something wrong with my heart, very over-tired and in need of attention as it is.

* Letters 21–27 were written to me by BL during his last illness.
† Heinz Schewe.

24.

April 27, 1960, morning

I have moved to the ground floor, so as not to have to use the stairs, and I keep to my bed all the time. The day before yesterday, on Sunday evening, despite the terrible pain, I was still able to get over to the office* and phone you. Today, not for all the tea in China or even on doctor's orders could I possibly stand on my legs or remain sitting for more than five minutes. I am writing to you lying down. Unless this clears up earlier in some other way, we shall have to cross off (it seems to me) two weeks, at the very least, of our life. Work, do some writing of your own. It will calm you down. Let's keep in touch through Kostia Bogatyrev on Wednesdays, and through Koma Ivanov on Sundays. For the time being don't take any active steps to see me. The waves of alarm set off by it would impinge on me and at the moment, with my heart in this condition, it would kill me. Z.† in her foolishness would not have the wit to spare me. I have already taken soundings on the subject.

If there is any money due to me from 'Art'‡ let them pay it into my savings account. Copy out the particulars from the authorization I gave you for *Faust*—they are written down there.

I'm very interested in the true and sensible things you all (you, Ira, Koma, Kostia) have to say about the first half of the play, which still needs a lot of work. You needn't return it to me, but don't make a copy either. There is so much unnatural chit-chat, which must either be cut out or re-done.

If you begin to feel particularly cheated and unhappy in the situation arising from this new complication, take a firm hold of yourself and remember: everything, everything crucial that gives meaning to my life is in your hands alone. So be brave and patient.

Give Shavochka Renate's address—I enclose it on a separate piece of paper. Let him write and tell her that I am ill with something painful (that is, accompanied by great pain) which will evidently last for some time, and that she shouldn't expect any letters from me but can get news of my health from him—let him give her his address too for this purpose. In case of any particularly urgent matters he should come and see me. You know how well I think of him. It is very difficult to write, and I have to do it in a hurry as well. I kiss you and hug you endless times. Don't upset yourself. We have come through worse things than this.

Your B.

* The office of the nearby club belonging to the Writers' Union. (Tr.)
† Zinaida Nikolayevna.
‡ Moscow publishing house which brought out Pasternak's Shakespeare translations. (Tr.)

25.
April 30. Saturday

Oliusha my dear, just think what a disaster!* I have some hope that Koma will come today and that I'll get some news of you and your health. How is your leg? My illness is now at its height. I am terribly weak. The effect on my heart of the slightest movement is instantaneous and horribly painful. All I can do that is relatively painless is lie flat on my back. The behaviour of everyone here is such that they evidently believe I am going to get well again. I see no panic round about. But it's all very, very painful. Oliusha, my sweet, I've done nothing but cause you sorrow! I also suspect this illness is God's judgment on me for showing too much affection to Renate. Oliusha my joy, occupy yourself with some major piece of work. Start writing an account of your life—concisely, in proper literary form, as though for publication. This will take your mind off things. I kiss you endless times—you and yours.

If it becomes necessary to make some decisive move to surmount all the obstacles,† you will learn about it in good time. I am writing to you in defiance of the doctor's orders—he has forbidden me to fret.

Your B.

26.
Thursday, May 5

Oliusha my dear, I was taken aback by your fantasies‡ yesterday about a sanatorium. That is all utter and rather heartless nonsense. I haven't got the strength to shave myself, the razor falls out of my hand from the stabs of pain in my shoulder-blade, and the elementary functions of the body are impeded for the same reason—and now, in this condition, when I can't be taken into town for an X-ray, you want me to be hauled off to some sanatorium near Moscow! And all for what? All because you fear you won't have the patience to wait until I'm well and our life comes back to normal again? But thank goodness that we have this to look forward to, that it now seems probable!! Only a few days or two ago one could well have had doubts. The fact that it is not fatal, that it is an inflammation of the nerve and muscle doesn't mean, you know, that it's a figment of my imagination, or all nonsense and 'literature'. While it was humanly possible to fight this pain, I did so—for the sake of our meetings, of our life and work. But then this became unthinkable, impossible. I can't understand why you are so alarmed. The factual evidence (the cardiogram and so forth) make

* There is no indication of what this refers to. (Tr.)
† i.e., in the way of a meeting at the 'big house'. (Tr.)
‡ Evidently in a message to Pasternak. (Tr.)

it possible to believe I shall recover. I already feel a little better. Everything I possess of value I am passing on to you: the manuscript of the play, and now the diploma.* Everybody is being so helpful to us. Surely it is possible to put up with this brief separation, and even if it requires a certain sacrifice, surely this sacrifice can be borne? I have awful palpitation as I write this—it started the moment I wrote the first few words. I don't believe I shall die of it, but why ask for it? If I were really near to death, I should insist that you be called over here to see me. But thank goodness this turns out to be unnecessary. The fact that everything, by the looks of it, will perhaps go on again as before seems to me so undeserved, fabulous, incredible!!!

Have you heard anything about the money for *Faust*? Is it true that something is due from 'Art' (for Shakespeare)? Have you met Yevg. Mikh. Morozova? Please staple together the pages of the notebook with the play in it, so people won't mix them up if they fall out as they read.

I give you a big hug and beg you to calm down.

I must stop now, the palpitation has got much worse.

* The diploma of the American Academy of Arts and Letters which Pasternak sent to the author with Kostia Bogatyrev. See p. 335. (Tr.)

APPENDIX B

Letter to Boris Pasternak from Sergei Spasski

'. . . from the very first one has a feeling that the rhythm of the narrative
has been established once and for all: the precise and sparing sequence
of the phrases, the compact and finished quality of each segment. There
is an immediate sense of standing on firm ground, of being in the hands
of a narrator whose skill has matured and who has now conquered new
territory, making himself completely at home in it—it is the sort of
prose which will not let you down by falling to pieces, which will take
you to the end of the story without fail, and force the reader to listen all
the way. It seems ridiculous to congratulate you on having achieved
such mastery of form, since for you it was a foregone conclusion, but
the nature of art is such that there is never any limit to its growth, and
every new stage of development thus comes as a happy surprise. And
if one thinks of the general loss of a sense of style, this is particularly
refreshing. There is, incidentally, not even a question of making any
comparisons [i.e. with other current prose-writing]—they would be
pointless unless made with real examples of great art. But I should like
to stress that the descriptive power is by no means confined to those
passages where similes and metaphors suddenly flare up so brightly
that one cannot help smiling with pleasure at their brilliance, at their
playful freshness. The same strength is present even in the most
deliberately restrained and muted places, where it is simply, as it were,
a question of communicating information to the reader in a matter-of-
fact way, without artifice, or concern for literary effects of any kind.
Here too one always finds the same precision in hitting the mark—and
eventually it dawns on one that it is just such ostensibly straightforward passages which demand the most effort on the part of the
writer, since real prose is created only by blending them with the more
brightly coloured surfaces of neighbouring passages. And it may be
that these [latest] parts are such a success mainly because there is a
'matter-of-fact' narrative here which is just as essential and strong as
the description, growing directly out of it, of the fragrance of night or
of a rain-storm. This is a success for you as a prose-writer—the kind of
success you always aimed at in your earlier attempts at prose, but where
the riot of metaphors was sometimes not contained within the necessary
limits and the outlines of the narrative became blurred.

Now I would like to write a little about other 'formal' aspects of what I have just read—and this will, of course, apply to the novel as a whole. Incidentally, I may say that it gives me great pleasure to dwell on what might seem to be purely matters of technique. How one longs to talk about the professional side of literature, and how few occasions there are for doing so! But now we have your novel—which will inevitably invite discussion of its structure.

There are no hard and fast rules about how a novel should be composed, or about what comes within the compass of the genre, and you need not concern yourself with what other people may have to say on this score. In the final resort, a writer writes in the way that suits him. You have hit on this particular form which is marked—in contrast to the intricate, labyrinthine periods of the verse you used to write—by a succession of short episodes, as well as of short sentences. Proust astonished the world by an incessant flow of detail which seemingly lacked any firm framework, and Tolstoi was quite capable of injecting disquisitions on topical, philosophical or historical themes into his novels. In form, *A la Recherche du Temps Perdu* and *War and Peace* are at first sight simply grotesque or monstrous, yet each of them in its own way is as inevitable and 'right' as some natural process or other. In what way is this less true of the continuous pulsation of the successive short episodes in your novel? They have their own rhythm, just as Tolstoi has, or any great work. It is this rhythm that binds the whole thing together—the reader only has to breathe at the same rate. This is really all that any author may insist on—provided of course that he himself knows how to breathe and move. Unity of rhythm, unity of breathing—this is the essence of a work's composition; and it is the inner rhythm, as perceived by the author, which—serving perhaps as the first creative impulse—compels the characters in the novel to fall into place in a certain way, thus giving rise to the externals of plot and theme. It indeed is the inner necessity—the unobtrusive, sublimated necessity of art, enhancing and transcending necessity as we know it in everday life—by virtue of which the encounters between Zhivago and Lara come about in the novel. It constantly makes their paths cross, forcing them to live, as it were, in the same magnetic field, even though they are kept apart by distance and circumstances, and it is not clear what they need from each other. Thus, cautiously at first, the theme is set—the theme of human destiny, something not immediately recognized for what it is but only foreshadowed as it draws people together or sends them in different directions. This theme of destiny is delineated through the lives of the people in the novel—it is the theme of any novel, and wherever it is present, the work's composition or structure comes into being *ipso facto*. And once this sense of an integrated whole, of a rhythmic entity complete in itself has been established, then there is nothing unnatural about all the minor 'coincidences'—such as Zhivago's meeting with his half-brother Yevgraf on the corner of Silent and Silver Streets,★ and in general all the other meetings at this same place, for the whole novel thereby becomes, in effect, a 'bewitched crossroads'—as does indeed any other real work of art of its kind.

Destiny—in other words, the things that are fated to happen somewhere at some time in the future and already permeate the past and present—is hence the deeper background, and it is good that it is not contrasted in simplistic fashion with what at first stands in the foreground, namely, the story of Zhivago's relations with Tonya—for whom one feels real sympathy, hoping that all the troubles brewing around her may be staved off. But wherever the theme of destiny comes to the fore, even the most personal experiences cease to be purely personal, merging into something common to everybody: the approaching confrontation with the future. The theme of individual destiny thus becomes identical with that of the country as a whole, of the times, and of the question put by each to the epoch: Why am I here, and what should I do?

This, then, is the theme around which the whole novel revolves.

But before saying more on this subject, it would be a pity not to mention a few points of detail. How well the rain is described, and the expectation of Lara's return which does not take place† though it seems so likely—and how good that it does not happen at this point, and what a poignant contrast between this and the vague rumour that Zhivago hears about her later on‡ in dark, typhus-ridden Moscow, with its 'house committees'§ and the slums off the Sadovaya Boulevard! The rain seems like a key to all the events of that period, as does also the smell of lime trees (on which many people must have commented to you already). The encounter with Yevgraf‖ in an entry-way seems to come at an astonishingly appropriate moment—and this Yevgraf is an extraordinarily interesting figure. I don't know what you intend to do with him later, or even whether he will re-appear at all, but at this moment, at this turning point in history, he is a very telling figure—one who somehow seems tragic to me, suddenly linked with death, and recovery, and having connections with the new authorities into the

★ *Doctor Zhivago*: Chapter 8 (Tr.)
† *Doctor Zhivago*: Chapter 5 (9). (Tr.)
‡ *Doctor Zhivago*: Chapter 6 (12). (Tr.)
§ Which managed apartment buildings in place of the former owners, dispossessed by the Revolution. (Tr.)
‖ *Doctor Zhivago*: Chapter 6 (8). (Tr.)

bargain. This assortment has something piquant and intriguing about it—and was characteristic of the times. I should say, incidentally, that I have a very good picture of that crossroads—and specifically in connection with those days. At the height of the fighting* I made my way over to the Arbat from Silent Street, and I still remember hearing the tinkle of the glass in a streetlight right above my head as it was smashed by a stray bullet just at that corner. I remember how I stopped for a moment to look up in surprise at the light and then down at the broken glass at my feet. This is not in itself interesting, but the point is that probably anyone of our generation who reads your novel will recall a good deal of his own life and will take it as an account of something he has lived through himself. And this will be sufficient answer to the question as to whether the novel reflects reality or not.

I realize that people will be able to say: the author has ignored the things that matter most. But in fact, as I said at the beginning, the very reason why one reads the novel with such interest is that while descriptions of strategy and tactics are all too familiar, there is a panic fear of showing life at the ordinary everyday level, as it is lived in the home and on the street. Day-to-day existence was not of course a matter of rhetoric, but did in actual fact consist of such things as lighting stoves and sealing up windows with putty† for the winter—and indeed this was what real life was primarily about. In any case, Zhivago's feelings as he reads the news-sheet‡ announcing the formation of the new government—feelings almost wearisomely familiar, and you will understand how one is involuntarily irked by them—are convincing only because they come together with descriptions of stoves, the sealing of windows, the fetching of firewood from the Vindava Station, and the delirium brought on by typhus. So let such 'trivialities'—which would otherwise vanish from memory—be preserved, and let us be thankful to writers who recall and reproduce them. Indeed, as I read these parts, I thought how gratefully someone might accept them for publication—provided, of course, that he took them for what is in them and did not worry about what is not there.

People will in fact probably say that what is shown is secondary . . . But an author has every right to give prominence to the secondary. And in any case, can even a faultfinder say that there is not a great deal that was truly characteristic of the period? The description of life in Melyuzeyevo and in Moscow is full of the most authentic detail. And then, is there any reason why a book should be written not about those

* i.e. the fighting during the Bolshevik seizure of Moscow in October 1917. (Tr.)
† *Doctor Zhivago*: Chapter 6 (5). (Tr.)
‡ *Doctor Zhivago*: Chapter 6 (8). (Tr.)

who direct the course of history, but about all of us—a not insignificant group—who are ruled by them? . . . A constant, unswerving, unimaginable faithfulness to art is boundlessly rewarded, and it cannot but lead to results which justify one's existence, and all the great sacrifices made in the course of it. At the same time art does not forgive betrayal of it. Your manuscript is the best proof of the first proposition . . .'

Letter to Boris Pasternak from Mikhail Alpatov

'In our days of universal disarray and mental confusion—even on the part of those undaunted by the ardours of the road—your novel is stirring first and foremost because it gives faith in the possibility of doing something genuine if one remains true to the way of looking at things which is given to a man once in life, and which may be debased or adapted to circumstances only on pain of losing what is most important in oneself.

I imagine I am not the only one to be attracted by a number of features present in your novel: its almost all-embracing scope and autobiographical approach in dealing with our age, the absorbing narrative thread, the historical background, the local colour and variety of modes of speech and, lastly, your rare and happy gift of noticing those things in life which people generally pass by with indifference, and of speaking about them in such a way that everyone begins to feel he sees them for the first time, discovering them for himself and coming to love them—not even suspecting (what ingratitude!) that all this has been vouchsafed him by the skill of a major artist.

In our age, when the collapse of beliefs of every kind has such an overpowering effect on people's lives, some are forced to their knees by it, losing their pride and human dignity, while others are driven, as a last resort, to retreat into some bleak world of lost illusions. What is particularly precious in your novel is the balance—the classical balance, one might say—between man's *dentro* and his *fuori*, between what rages all around him like a blizzard, and those antibodies so feverishly secreted by his mind in the form of myths, epics and intuitions of various kinds.

For this reason, what I find most affecting of all, if I may be permitted to give a quite personal view, is the way in which the narrative really hinges not so much on external events, as on those moments in the characters' lives when the scales fall from their eyes, they become aware of the sounds and smells of the life around them, and harken to "the growing of the vine in the valley"; when a transfigured world appears to their senses more clearly than ever before in all its minute particulars—such as the sheets of blotting paper suddenly wafted off the desks in a schoolroom by a gust of air as a storm approaches,* or a flock of wild geese starting up from the waters of a creek in spring— these lovingly conveyed tokens of truth to life, as in the paintings of the old Dutch and Flemish masters, provide assurance that everything in our world is indeed holy.

With all my heart I wish that nothing may stand in the way of your completing this remarkable work. Yours, M. Alpatov.'

* *Doctor Zhivago*: Chapter 3 (5).(Tr.)

NOTES AND COMMENTS

1. page 7 Pasternak took part in a poetry reading in early February 1948, together with a number of other Soviet poets. It was his last public appearance during the Stalin years. The occasion is described in the Introduction to *Meetings with Pasternak* by Alexander Gladkov (London and New York, 1977).

2. page 8 This is an allusion to Gumilev's poem 'Tsaritsa' (1909).

3. page 13 Although identified only by her initial in *Safe Conduct*, the young lady's name was Ida Vysotskaya, who came from the well-known Moscow family of tea merchants. Pasternak had first met her when they were both in the last class of high school, and he had coached her for her final examinations. When she suddenly arrived in Marburg in the summer of 1912, while he was studying there, he declared his love for her—as he describes in the poem 'Marburg' (1917).

4. page 17 Sukho-Bezvodnaya (literally 'Dry-Waterless') is the rail junction for a forced labour camp known as Unzhlag, east of the Volga in the Gorki (formerly Nizhni Novgorod) Province. There is a description of it in Lev Kopelev's *Khranit Vechno* (Keep for Ever, Ann Arbor, Michigan, 1975).

5. page 19 This poem was written by Pasternak as a dedication to Mayakovski in a copy of *My Sister Life* in 1923. The first and last stanzas are quoted by Pasternak himself in his *An Essay in Autobiography*, but the full text has never been published in the Soviet Union. Ira had probably read it in a manuscript copy in the author's possession. The poem is an interesting indication of how early Pasternak had become sceptical of Mayakovski's self-imposed commitment—instead of roaming the seas of poetry freely, like the 'Flying Dutchman', as he had before the Revolution, he was now writing about the political and economic concerns of the new order. (The S.C.P.E. was the 'Supreme Council of the People's Economy', set up in 1917.)

6. page 24 The reference is to one of the very earliest of Chekhov's stories, 'A Fiasco' (*Neudacha*, 1886). It is about the parents of a girl who burst into the room where they believe a young man has just made a proposal to her, in order to give their blessing in the traditional way by holding an icon over the couple. But in their haste they snatch from the wall not an icon, but a picture of a popular writer of historical novels, Ivan Lazhechnikov, so that their blessing is invalidated (much to the relief of the young man).

7. page 36 The theme of cruelty to women, or of women as victims, was something that always preoccupied Pasternak. In his *An Essay in Auto-*

biography he says that as a result of the walks on which his nanny took him as a child—when they sometimes passed through squalid slum areas near the Pasternak home—he was 'filled too early and for life with a compassion for women so terrible that it was hardly to be borne . . .' In one of the poems of *Second Birth* (see Introduction, p. XXVI), he mentions how, from his earliest childhood years, he was 'wounded by the lot of women'. This, in part at least, is the key to his constant interest in the story of Mary Queen of Scots, with which he first became acquainted, apparently, through Swinburne's dramatic trilogy on her (1865–81). During the First World War, when Pasternak spent a good deal of time travelling to various places in the Urals and along the river Kama in connection with his civilian war service, he translated the first part of this trilogy, *Chastelard*, but—as he reports in *An Essay in Autobiography*—he subsequently lost the manuscript, and it was never published. By an extraordinary 'Zhivago-esque' coincidence, as appears from an article published by Pasternak in 1922, one of the towns on the Kama where in 1916 or 1917 he worked on his translation of *Chastelard*, during a snowstorm, was none other than Yelabuga—the place where a quarter of a century later Marina Tsvetayeva was to hang herself. From the way he wrote about his work on the translation in his article in 1922, it is clear that he felt an almost mystic link between himself and Mary Queen of Scots: he fancied that the Yelabuga blizzard spoke 'Scottish' that day. He eventually paid his homage to her (and, perhaps, implicitly, to Marina Tsvetayeva, as well as to 'Lara') by completing his version of Schiller's *Maria Stuart*, which had a triumphant reception at its première in the Moscow Arts Theatre in 1957. In the very last years of his life, Pasternak began to translate yet another version of the tragedy of Mary Queen of Scots—*Marja Stuart* by the Polish poet Juliusz Słowacki.

8. page 44 In *An Essay in Autobiography* Pasternak describes how these letters were lost by a friend to whom he gave them for safekeeping during the war: travelling home in a state of utter exhaustion, the friend left them in a suburban train. Fortunately, Tsvetayeva kept copies of her letters, and these have been preserved. (They are published in the volume of her letters edited by G. and N. Struve, Paris, 1972.)

9. page 48 The general title of Pasternak's last collection of poems. Several of them (including 'August') have never been published in the Soviet Union, but they are all available in the bi-lingual edition *Boris Pasternak: Poems 1955–59* (English versions by Michael Harari), London, 1960, and in the Michigan edition of Pasternak's works edited by Struve and Filippov.

10. page 63 The first of the 'Two Poems' is not reproduced in the translation, but the full text of the original may be found in the University of

Michigan edition of Pasternak's works (vol. III, pp. 138-9 and 256). It is in the same 'conciliatory' (or 'propitiatory') tone as the second poem, and mentions Stalin by name.

11. page 65 It was widely believed among Russians that Stalin was not a true Georgian but actually came from Ossetia, a region to the north of Georgia, where the people are of Iranian stock, and were generally held in low regard by neighbouring Caucasian peoples and by the Russians—as may be seen, for example, from Lermontov's *A Hero of Our Time.*

12. page 68 In 1927 there were still several more or less independent, and sometimes mutually hostile, literary organizations, such as Mayakovski's LEF (Left Front of Art), to which Pasternak belonged until that year, and FOSP (Federation of Writers' Organizations), to which most relatively moderate, non-political writers adhered. To some extent these various organizations stood up for their members' differing viewpoints, and also for their material interests. But in 1927 the militant Association of Proletarian Writers (RAPP) began to press for greater ideological conformity. By 1929 the other writers' organizations had only nominal independence, and having been 'purged', became unable to prevent witch hunts against their members. In 1932 RAPP was suddenly disbanded by Party decree and the present Union of Soviet Writers was set up as the sole literary organization. At first this seemed less intolerant than RAPP, but it was soon clear that it was nothing more than an instrument in the hands of the Party, concerned not to protect its members but to police them.

13. page 72 In 1932 all the various writers' organizations and groupings which had arisen more or less spontaneously after the Revolution were abolished by Party decree, and the Union of Soviet Writers established in their stead. At the First Congress of Soviet Writers in 1934, the statutes of the new Union were adopted and the doctrine of 'Socialist realism' officially promulgated. Although Soviet literature became increasingly regimented after 1934, the atmosphere at the First Congress was still relatively 'liberal'. The Second Congress was held only after Stalin's death in 1954.

14. page 75 Tsvetayeva was mistaken in thinking that Pasternak flew to Paris. Because of the state of his health, and even though he had been ordered to go at the last moment by Stalin personally, he in fact made the journey by train. During a stop-over in Berlin he was able to see his sister Josephine (who was alarmed by his nervous condition), but his parents were too ill to travel from Munich for this last chance (as it turned out) of a meeting with him. The Congress in Paris met from June 21 to 25, 1935, but Pasternak arrived only on the twenty-third. (For further details of his visit to Paris, see Guy de Mallac, *Pasternak: His Life and Art*, Norman, Oklahoma, 1978.)

15. page 80 For individual cases mentioned in this paragraph, see the relevant entries in the Biographical Guide.

A more or less open campaign against Jews was launched at the end of 1948 with the publication of an article in *Pravda* entitled 'On a Certain Group of Anti-Patriotic Theatre Critics'. Most of the critics in question were Jewish, and were labelled 'homeless cosmopolitans' and 'persons without kith or kin'. At the same time there were widespread dismissals and arrests of Jews in universities and other institutions, the Jewish anti-Fascist Committee (set up during the war) was liquidated and its chairman, Mikhoels, was murdered; during this and the following year all Jewish publications and the Jewish theatre were closed down. Most of the leading Yiddish-language writers (Fefer, Bergelson, Kvitko, Markish, and others) were executed in 1952. In January 1953, *Pravda* announced the arrest of a large group of Kremlin doctors (nearly all Jewish) on charges of having conspired to assassinate Soviet leaders by medical malpractice on the orders of foreign intelligence services, which were alleged to have operated through the Jewish international charity organization, the Joint Distribution Agency (JOINT). Except for some who evidently did not survive their interrogation, all the accused were released shortly after Stalin's death.

The 'Leningrad Affair' (for which Abakumov—see in the Biographical Guide—was made the scapegoat after Stalin's death) was one of many purges of regional Party organizations carried out in 1949–51 on Stalin's orders. All the leaders of the Leningrad Party apparatus were arrested and N. A. Voznesenski, a Politburo member formerly associated with it, was summarily executed; thousands of lower-ranking officials were swept away with them. (See Roy A. Medvedev: *Let History Judge*, New York, 1972.)

The peoples deported to Siberia and Central Asia were the Chechens, Ingush, Karachai, and Balkars from the Caucasus; the Crimean Tartars; the Kalmucks; the Volga Germans; The Black Sea Greeks.

16. page 86 This collection, published in 1943, included some poems written in 1936 (the two *Izvestia* poems, and a cycle inspired by Pasternak's second visit to Georgia), a series of nature poems entitled 'Peredelkino' written in 1940 (the ones referred to here), and the 'Poems on the War'.

17. page 103 The book in question was evidently *The Collected Prose Works*, arranged, with an introduction, by Stefan Schimanski, London, 1945. It contained translations of *Safe Conduct*, *The Childhood of Luvers*, and other prose writings by Pasternak.

18. page 134 The letters to Tabidze and his widow quoted on this and the following page ('. . . rely only on yourself . . .'; 'My thoughts about him . . .'; 'Titian is for me . . .'; '. . . I have long since ceased . . .'; '. . . poor

poor Titian . . .') have been published in a collection of Pasternak's correspondence with a number of his Georgian friends. The Moscow publication of this material (in *Questions of Literature*, January 1966) is deficient, since it omits all 'sensitive' items, including those quoted here. Almost simultaneously, however, the letters appeared—evidently in their entirety and uncensored—in *Literary Georgia* (nos. 1 and 2, 1966), a Russian-language journal which comes out in Tbilisi and was notable in the mid-sixties for the way in which it sometimes succeeded—clearly thanks to bold local initiatives—in publishing Russian works turned down by the censors in Moscow. An edition in English translation (*Letters to Georgian Friends*, London and New York, 1967) is based on the complete text. It is a fact worthy of note that though the collection was denied publication in full in Moscow, it was sold by an official Soviet agency to Western publishers.

19. page 137 Pasternak met Tsvetayeva in Paris in 1935, when he attended the International Writers' Congress in Defence of Culture. He described this meeting himself in his *An Essay in Autobiography* (English translation, London, 1959):

'In the summer of 1935, when I was on the verge of mental illness after almost twelve months of insomnia, I found myself at an anti-Fascist congress in Paris. There I met Tsvetayeva's son and daughter and her husband, an enchanting, sensitive, and steadfast being of whom I grew as fond as of a brother.

Tsvetayeva's family were pressing her to return to Russia. It was partly that they were homesick, partly that they sympathised with communism and the Soviet Union; and partly that they thought Tsvetayeva had no sort of life in Paris and was going to pieces in loneliness and isolation from her readers.

She asked me what I thought about it. I had no definite opinion. It was hard to know what to advise them; I was afraid that these remarkable people would have a difficult and troubled time at home. But the tragedy which was to strike the whole family surpassed my fears beyond all measure.'

20. page 144 A quotation from Pushkin's *Mozart and Salieri* (1831), a short drama in verse based on the story that Salieri supposedly poisoned Mozart because he was envious of his genius. These words are spoken in the play by Mozart: '. . . Genius and villainy
           Are two things that never go together . . .'

21. page 144 Pasternak used this phrase in conversation with Alexander Gladkov (see Gladkov's *Meetings with Pasternak*, p. 78). The same idea occurs in a slightly disguised form in *Doctor Zhivago*, Chapter 1:
    '. . . history as we know it began with Christ . . . There was no history

in this sense in the classical world. There you had blood and beastliness and cruelty and pockmarked Caligulas untouched by the suspicion that any man who enslaves others is inevitably second-rate . . .'

22. page 150 'Nightglow' (*Zarevo*) was conceived as an ambitious narrative poem which, if it had been completed, would have reflected in more or less open fashion the widespread expectations which arose after the Battle of Stalingrad that with final victory over Germany there would be a general relaxation of the Draconian régime imposed before the war. The hero of the poem is a returning Red Army soldier who is depicted in such a way as to suggest that if his hopes were thwarted, then the atmosphere in the country could become mutinous. The title 'Nightglow', refers to the gun salutes which then greeted every new Soviet victory in the night sky of Moscow, and is intended to stand for the approach of better times. (Pasternak harks back to his sanguine mood of that time in a passage on the last page of *Doctor Zhivago*: 'Although the enlightenment and liberation which had been expected to come after the war had not come with victory, a presage of freedom was in the air throughout these post-war years, and it was their only historical meaning.')

The Introduction to the poem was published in *Pravda* in October 1943, but the remaining completed part, 'Chapter One' (from which the quotation given here is taken), was published only in the 1965 edition of Pasternak's poetry. For a more detailed discussion of the poem's significance, see Alexander Gladkov's *Meeting with Pasternak*, pp. 192–4.

23. page 155 In *The Possessed* (1871–72), Shigalev, an underground radical conspirator, embodies Dostoyevski's prophetic vision that absolute freedom could lead to absolute despotism, and that in claiming to set men free, the Russian revolutionaries would eventually enslave them as never before. Shigalev envisages a future society in which all will be bound together by mutual denunciation and complicity in common crimes. Dostoyevski's accurate prediction of what Russian society could become under a revolutionary tyranny led to his major works (particularly *The Possessed*) being virtually put under a ban in the late Stalin years.

24. page 161 Timur was the young hero of a tremendously popular book for children, *Timur and his Team*, published in 1940 by Arkadi Gaidar (1904–41). Timur is a member of the Pioneers (a Soviet organization for children) who organizes a group to give material and moral support to the families of soldiers fighting at the front.

25. page 162 From the river Donets. The Donets basin is one of the largest coal-mining areas in Russia, and the image evoked is similar to that conveyed by the two following adjectives.

26. page 166 In the poem 'At the Top of My Voice' (1930), written not long before his suicide, Mayakovski spoke of the way he had deliberately put his commitment to the cause of Party propaganda before the personal, lyrical side of his poetry:

'Agitprop sticks in my teeth too,
And I'd rather compose romances for you—
More profit in it, and more charm.
But I subdued myself,
Setting my heel on the throat
Of my own song.'

(Translation by George Reavey)

27. page 165 After Russia's disastrous defeats in East Prussia at the beginning of the First World War, General Samsonov (although by no means to blame for them and depicted sympathetically by Solzhenitsyn in his *August 1914*), committed suicide. In his book *The Oak and the Calf*, published in the West in 1975, Solzhenitsyn describes his relations with Tvardovski, who first published some of his work in *Novy Mir* and, as editor of the journal in the Khrushchev years, fought many battles with the censorship to get prose and poetry by other liberal or dissident writers into print. In *The Oak and the Calf*, while often speaking of him in warm and friendly terms, Solzhenitsyn suggests that Tvardovski, owing to a basically defeatist attitude, ultimately always capitulated in the face of overwhelming odds.

28. page 173 These four lines are from the semi-autobiographical narrative poem *Spektorski*. There is no overt reference to Tsvetayeva, but the woman in the poem called 'Maria Ilyina' (to whom these lines refer) is clearly Tsvetayeva. It is interesting to note that the first letters of the lines of the dedication to *Lieutenant Schmidt* (the other long poem on which Pasternak was working at that period) formed an acrostic of Marina Tsvetayeva's name. (See Olga R. Hughes, *The Poetic World of Boris Pasternak*, Princeton, 1974, p. 105–6.)

'Pushkin's miller' is a character in the short play in verse, *Rusalka* (1832).

29. page 176 Several translations by Tsvetayeva were published in Soviet journals in 1941—'The Ballad of Robin Hood'; and 'Biblical Motif' by the Hebrew and Yiddish writer Isaac Leib Peretz (1851–1915). Other translations, such as that of the Georgian Vazha Pshavela, were published only posthumously.

30. page 179 The writers' organization is distinct from the Union of Writers and is a much less important and prestigious body, whose members are translators, editors and others engaged in minor kinds of literary work, but not recognized or accepted as Soviet writers—to emphasize the distinction, a different word is employed for the former (*literatory*), whereas the latter are called *pisateli*.

31. page 188 These lines are the last in Tsvetayeva's 'Poem of the End' (1924) and refer to Tsvetayeva's final parting from Rodzevich.

32. page 223 For the full text of this letter in English translation, see Robert Conquest, *Courage of Genius*, London, 1961, p. 136.

33. page 225 Only two volumes of *Literary Moscow* appeared, both in 1956. The second one came out just at the time of the uprising in Hungary (November 1956) after which the climate in the Soviet Union rapidly changed for the worse, and all the 'liberal' tendencies and initiatives (such as *Literary Moscow*) made possible by Khrushchev's revelations about Stalin at the Twentieth Party Congress (February 1956) were abruptly ended. The almanac was edited by a group of liberal writers, such as Margarita Aliger, Veniamin Kaverin, Emmanuil Kazakievich, and Konstantin Paustovski, and, despite a judicious 'balance' in the selection of materials for both volumes, the intention was clearly to create a relatively independent forum for the liberal Moscow writers. Several very outspoken stories were published in the second volume (notably Alexander Yashin's *Levers*), and some verse of Marina Tsvetayeva with an introduction by Ilya Ehrenburg. The first volume had verse by Nikolai Zabolotski, Akhmatova, and Pasternak's long essay on translating Shakespeare's tragedies. A third volume, which was to have included Pasternak's *An Essay in Autobiography*, never appeared.

Pasternak was all too justified in his scepticism as to the possibility of establishing anything resembling an independent writers' journal. In later years, Tvardovski's remarkable and partly successful attempt to achieve independence for *Novy Mir* also eventually foundered with his removal from the editorship.

34. page 228 The publication of the Russian text of *Doctor Zhivago* was attended by odd circumstances. It first appeared in a 'pirated' edition, a short time before Feltrinelli's official edition came out in Milan. The 'pirated' version, however, bore Feltrinelli's imprint and had apparently been produced by the reputable firm of Dutch printers with whom he was negotiating, and to whom he had sent the manuscript. What seems to have happened is that a number of copies were run off and distributed prematurely—perhaps in accordance with instructions that only purported to come from Feltrinelli. Another possibility is that the manuscript was somehow intercepted and photocopied on the way from Italy to Holland, and the unauthorized edition made from it. The main point of the operation seems to have been to get the book out earlier than Feltrinelli had planned, so that it would be available for the large number of Soviet visitors expected to attend the International Fair in Brussels in 1958. Soviet visitors were able to get it from a Russian-speaking priest at the Vatican Pavilion, and a number apparently did so: there were stories at the time that the ground round about was littered with the dark-blue binding, which was torn off so that the book could be divided in two halves, one for each pocket. Whatever the truth of the matter, copies of this edition were probably the first to be smuggled into the Soviet Union, where the novel soon began to circulate on the underground book market.

35. page 228 To this list one may add Indonesian and Maltese (an abbreviated edition translated by Fr. Dionysius Mintoff, the brother of the present Prime Minister of Malta). In some languages (Arabic, Persian, and Turkish) there were rival versions.

36. page 275 *An Essay in Autobiography* was first published in a New York émigré newspaper and only later in the Paris Russian newspaper, *Russkaya Mysl*. It was eventually published in the Soviet Union, with a number of substantive cuts, in *Novy Mir* (January 1967) under the title *Liudi i polozhenia* (People and Circumstances). It had originally been completed by Pasternak in May–June 1965, and had been intended by him as the introduction to the one-volume edition of his poetry planned to appear in 1957, but never published.

Pasternak's letter to Stalin thanking him for having called Mayakovski 'the best, most talented poet of our epoch . . .' was, of course, ironical. This 'canonization' of Mayakovski in 1936 (after which he 'began to be introduced forcibly, like potatoes under Catherine the Great') protected Pasternak, as he put it, 'from the inflation of my role'.

37. page 278 It is interesting that this same term was later used in the Soviet press with reference to Solzhenitsyn, at the time of his expulsion from the Soviet Union in 1974. (For Vlasov see the Biographical Guide.)

38. page 288 In the memoirs of Khrushchev, published in the West, he denies actually having read *Doctor Zhivago*, but expresses regret that it was not published:

'To this day I haven't read [Pasternak's] book and therefore cannot judge it. People who've spoken to me about it say that they don't have any special admiration for the artistic aspect of the work, but that's beside the point. To judge an author and to judge his work are two different matters. If the book was really of low artistic quality, then that judgment should be left to the reader. If a work fails to touch a responsive chord in a reader— then the writer will have to draw the necessary conclusions. Naturally, he'll be morally shaken, but he will have nobody to blame but himself for the failure of his work to embody and communicate some idea worth the reader's attention. The main point is: readers should be given a chance to make their own judgments; and administrative measures, police measures, shouldn't be used. A sentence should not be pronounced over our creative intelligentsia as though they were on trial.

In connection with *Doctor Zhivago*, some might say it's too late for me to express regret that the book wasn't published. Yes, maybe it is too late. But better late than never.' (*Khrushchev Remembers*, translated by Strobe Talbot, London, 1974).

39. page 289 These are the words spoken in the poem (first published in 1926–27) by Lieutenant Schmidt on the eve of his execution for mutiny (he was a historical figure in the Russian Revolution of 1905). They seem to have been widely quoted in Moscow during the campaign of persecution against Pasternak. They were so remarkably apposite to his plight that some people apparently took them to be a *new* poem written by him in 1958.

40. page 292 Pasternak first visited Georgia in 1931, with his second wife, Zinaida Nikolayevna, and as had become traditional for Russian writers since Pushkin and Lermontov, he was immensely impressed not only by the Caucasian landscape, but also by the sense of freedom among the people. Pasternak referred to Georgia as the 'country which has become my second motherland', and he had close personal relations with a number of Georgian poets and intellectuals (particularly Paolo Yashvili and Titian Tabidze, both of whom fell victim to the Terror of 1937). He published several volumes of translations of Georgian poetry and his passionate interest in the country is reflected in some of his own work (such as the cycle of poems called *Travel Notes*, 1936—significantly, perhaps, a major part of the small amount of original verse he published in the second half of the 'thirties). His correspondence with Georgian friends, stretching from the time of his first visit until almost the year of his death, was published posthumously in 1966. (It came out in English translation in 1967. See Note 18) Perhaps his finest tribute to Georgia (and simultaneously to Poland, as another symbol of proud independence) is the poem 'Grass and Stones', written in the summer of 1956.

41. page 294 The reference is to a lynching scene in Book 3 (Part 3) of *War and Peace*. The incident, as described by Tolstoi, was based on historical fact. A merchant's son, M. N. Vereshchagin, had been accused by the Governor-General of Moscow, Count Rastopchin, of spreading seditious broadsheets in support of Napoleon in 1812. Vereshchagin admitted having composed certain things on his own initiative, but the basis of the accusation—that he had translated Napoleon's letter to the King of Prussia and another similar document—was false. He was condemned to forced labour but, on the eve of Napoleon's entry into Moscow, Rastopchin had him brought from the jail, and incited the mob to lynch him. What makes Pasternak's use of this analogy with his own case particularly apt is that the crowd was at first apathetic and felt no animus against Vereshchagin—their anger and bloodlust had to be artificially aroused by the Governor-General.

42. page 313 The phrase is taken from a passage in *Doctor Zhivago* (Chapter 2) about Christ's parables having explained the truth in the 'light of everyday existence'.

43. page 322 Some details in this account of the circumstances in which the 'Nobel Prize' poem came to be published cannot be squared with events as perceived in the West at the time. The poem actually first appeared in English translation, in the London *Daily Mail* of February 11, 1959; it had been brought out by a British journalist, Antony Brown, recently returned from the Soviet Union, and it does not have the two final stanzas relating to the quarrel between Pasternak and the author. The full Russian text, including these two stanzas, was published for the first time only three years later, in the University of Michigan edition of Pasternak's work (1961). It makes perfect sense from the psychological point of view that Pasternak should have written this belated reaction to his hounding in October of the previous year under the emotional stress of his quarrel with Madame Ivinskaya on January 20, 1959. The poem is dated (in the Michigan edition) 'January–March'—which indeed suggests that it was not written, as was always assumed, at the height of the campaign against him in October 1958, but over two months later, under the impact of a different kind of crisis. It would also have been understandable that, as a kind of despairing gesture, he should have handed it to a foreign journalist (though minus the last two stanzas, which must have been added later—perhaps in March 1959, after a further quarrel with the author and temporary separation from her). But since the poem, in its shorter form, was published for the first time only on February 11 by the *Daily Mail*, it can hardly have been the reason for Polikarpov's urgent summons to the author on January 20. A most likely explanation of this discrepancy is that two separate, but very similar, events have understandably, with the passage of time, merged into one in the author's recollection. Polikarpov's anger on January 20 was undoubtedly provoked by an interview with Pasternak which had been published in the London *News Chronicle* the previous day and which expresses total defiance, undoing all of Polikarpov's efforts to present him as a 'penitent'. In the interview (given to another British journalist, Alan Moray Williams—evidently a week or two before its publication in the *News Chronicle* on January 19), Pasternak said, for example: 'The writer is the Faust of modern society, the only surviving individualist in a mass age. To his orthodox contemporaries he seems a semi-madman . . . The Union of Writers would like me to go down on my knees to them—but they will never make me.' One can imagine the consternation in the Central Committee when this statement was beamed to the Soviet Union in Western Russian-language broadcasts. There is no record of Pasternak having repudiated it, whatever pressure may have been put on him. On the other hand, when the 'Nobel Prize' poem was published in the *Daily Mail* nearly three weeks later (again arousing the fury of the Central Committee, and no doubt causing the outraged Polikarpov to summon Madame Ivinskaya a second time), Pasternak issued a strongly-worded denunciation of the journalist who he felt had abused his confidence by unauthorized publication of the poem, and vowed that he would receive no more correspondents, 'who only hinder my work and cause harm'. It is noteworthy that this statement (given to the U.P. correspondent in Moscow, and published in the New York *Herald Tribune* of February 14 –15) contained no hint of a repudiation of the poem itself— only indignation at what Pasternak clearly regarded as its premature publication. (For further details, see the careful record of the events of those days in Robert Conquest's *Courage of Genius*, London, 1961.)

44. page 323 George Reavey (1907–76), the English poet and translator, was one of the first to appreciate and call attention to Pasternak's work in the West. He read Pasternak as an undergraduate at Cambridge, and published an essay on him, together with some translations, in a Cambridge review called *Experiment* (1930). When Reavey sent Pasternak a copy of the article, he received a reply from him, and this was the beginning of an intermittent correspondence between them that went on until a few months before Pasternak's death in 1960. Nine letters from Pasternak to Reavey were published in the *Harvard Library Bulletin*, October 1967.

45. page 326 In his *Meetings with Pasternak*, Alexander Gladkov mentions an almost identical incident supposedly involving Vsevolod Vishnevski, a well-known playwright: 'There were now stories in literary circles about brusque behaviour that would have been unthinkable previously. This was a different Pasternak from the one I had known. The earlier one would scarcely have reacted so crossly to V. Vishnevski's vulgar and offensive toast' (p. 152). It has proved impossible to obtain any details of a scene with Vishnevski or indeed to confirm that it ever took place. It seems, therefore, very likely that Gladkov was mistaken in mentioning Vishnevski in this context (he is reporting the incident from hearsay, and it would be natural to confuse two theatrical personalities of roughly similar standing) and that the 'vulgar and offensive toast' was actually pronounced by Livanov on the occasion described here by Madame Ivinskaya, i.e., that the toast in question was the one alluded to below at the beginning of the fourth paragraph of Pasternak's letter to Livanov.

46. page 331 It is hard to say which 'excellent, rhymed translations' are referred to here. In so far as it is a question of translation into English, Pasternak may well have had in mind the versions of the *Zhivago* poems (and many others) done by his sister, Lydia Pasternak-Slater, in Oxford. One of these ('Fairy Tale') appears among the *Zhivago* poems in the

British edition of the novel, and others were published in a small volume brought out in London in 1958—Pasternak had perhaps received it by the time he wrote this letter to Renate Schweitzer.

47. page 333 Populist organization of the 1870s which believed in terror as the only means of radical social and political change in Russia; in psychological terms, though not in strictly doctrinal ones, it prepared the way for Lenin and the Bolshevik Revolution. Many of its members came from the déclassé intelligentsia which vastly expanded its ranks after the Great Reform of 1861 and the resulting growth in social mobility.

48. page 346 Solzhenitsyn wrote this about Alexander Tvardovski, the editor of *Novy Mir*, in the autobiographical work quoted earlier (*The Oak and the Calf*).

49. page 348 From Voznesenski's poem, 'Leaves and Roots', published in the newspaper *Literature i zhizn* (Literature and Life) on November 20, 1960—that is, five months after Pasternak's death. This date happened to be the fiftieth anniversary of the death of Leo Tolstoi—to whom the poem is nominally dedicated, but there is no question that it was in fact intended as a poetic tribute to Pasternak. The full text is as follows:

> They carried him not to bury him:
> They carried him down to crown him.
> Greyer than granite,
> More reddish than bronze,
> Steaming like a locomotive,
> The poet flourished here, dishevelled,
> Who would not bow before votive lamps
> But to the common spade.
>
> The lilac at his doorstep burned . . .
> A fountain of falling stars soaked in sweat,
> His back steamed
> Like a loaf in the oven.
>
> Now his house gapes, vacant,
> tenantless;
> There is nobody in the dining room,
> There is not a soul in Russia.
>
> It is the way of the poet to search
> For sanctuary. He goes hatless, as people do in church,
> Through the murmuring fields
> To the birch grove and the oaks.
>
> In his flight is his victory;
> In his retreat, an ascent

To pastures and planets
Far from lying ornament.

Forests shed their crowns of leaves,
But powerfully underground
Roots twist and thrust
Like a gnarled hand.

(Translated by Stanley Kunitz: in *Antiworlds: Poems by Andrei Voznesensky*, published by Oxford University Press 1967. Reprinted by permission of the publisher.)

Yevgeni Yevtushenko also had to resort to a subterfuge in order to publish a tribute to Pasternak. His poem 'The Fence' (*Ograda*) appeared with a dedication to Vladimir Lugovskoi, a poet who had died almost exactly three years before Pasternak. This 'false' dedication (dated '1959', to make it appear that it had been written in the year before Pasternak's death) was made with the knowledge and agreement of Lugovskoi's widow, and was removed from the poem as published in a collection of Yevtushenko's verse which came out in 1969.*

50. page 350 On the death of a leading Soviet writer, it is the Union of Writers which makes the announcement, usually accompanied by an obituary signed by friends and colleagues. Since Pasternak had recently been expelled from the Union, and was still technically in disgrace, the only formula which suggested itself to the authorities (who were evidently sufficiently concerned by the judgment of the outside world and of posterity not to let the event go totally unrecorded) was that of this brief statement by *Litfund*—of which Pasternak remained a member. (See footnote on p. 178). Although this would not have occurred to those responsible, there was something appropriate about this solution. Pasternak had never, in spirit, been a member of the Union of Soviet Writers, an instrument of Stalin's cultural policy created in 1932. *Litfund*, on the other hand, is one of those very few bodies in the Soviet Union, which in name and substance has some tradition of continuity with pre-revolutionary times. The Literary Fund (at first known in full as the Society for Aid to Needy Writers and Scholars) was founded in Petersburg in 1859—among the original members were Tolstoi and Turgenev. Although in abeyance for nearly ten years after the Revolution, it was re-created in 1927, and then, in 1934, was affiliated to the Union of Soviet Writers, though still retaining a nominal autonomy. The old Literary Fund even used to intervene on behalf of its members when they were in trouble with the

* This information is given by Madame Ivinskaya in a note accompanying the full text of 'The Fence' which appears, together with other poetic tributes to Pasternak, in an appendix to her manuscript not included in this translation.

government (e.g. in 1905, when Gorki was arrested), instead of actively assisting in their persecution, like the Union of Soviet Writers.

The *Litfund* announcement of Pasternak's death in the *Literary Gazette* did not, of course, constitute an obituary and none ever appeared in the Soviet press. The only eulogies to be published were those by Voznesenski and Yevtushenko. Yet it is impossible not to be struck by a curious feature of the make-up of the back page of the issue of the *Literary Gazette* in which the curt item about Pasternak's death appears. Directly opposite the modest eight-line announcement (set in notably small type) there is a bold headline, in large characters, over an article by Semion Kirsanov about the Czech poet Vitězslav Nezval: A MAGICIAN OF POETRY. It thus seems possible that some sub-editor responsible for the make-up of the page was able to record an indirect tribute in a way which would no doubt have been appreciated by Pasternak more than the usual kind of obituary signed by fellow members of the Union of Writers.

51. page 358 This chapter heading is suggested by a line of Akhmatova's.

52. page 362 Legal consultants—defence lawyers, etc.—are organized in the Soviet Union in so-called collegia, and private citizens requiring legal aid or counsel in criminal or civil cases can only turn to them. The Foreign Legal Collegium (*Inyurkollegia*) deals with private matters involving international law. Its main business is probably concerned with the transfer of money to Soviet citizens from abroad (inheritances, etc.). In the present case, there had evidently been an attempt or proposal by Feltrinelli to transfer money to Pasternak 'legally', i.e. by sending remittances to him via the State Bank in Moscow—which evidently referred the matter to the Collegium. From the context it is clear that Pasternak must have been asked to discuss the question with the latter some time between the author's first and second visits to Polikarpov.

53. page 371 Lefortovo is one of the three main Moscow jails, together with the Lubianka and Butyrki. Political prisoners, or other prisoners of major importance, are first taken to the Lubianka where they are interrogated, often over a long period of time, by the investigation official (*sledovatel*) whose function is to 'make the case' for the prosecution at the trial. In the years since Stalin's death, which was followed by many pronouncements on the need to 'restore socialist legality', procedures have become less arbitrary, and blandishments, rather than direct physical or psychological maltreatment, are the preferred methods of winning a prisoner's 'co-operation'—at least in the more sophisticated conditions of Moscow. While prisoners, just as before, are held virtually incommunicado from their arrest until trial (which is often only nominally 'public', even in Moscow, attendance being effectively denied to all independent witnesses, foreign journalists, etc.), there is greater observance of legal formalities and—most importantly—defence lawyers are no longer always mere adjuncts to the prosection, as they invariably were in Stalin's day. In recent years certain lawyers have been notably courageous in defending clients charged with political offences, and have sometimes suffered ostracism, or worse, as a result. These improvements have come about largely because of an increased sensitivity to public opinion inside and particularly outside the country, but have not been embodied in effective constitutional guarantees or legal institutions. Defence counsel now has access to his client in Lefortovo, where prisoners are held pending trial. (After trial they are transferred to the third prison, Butyrki, to await transportation to a forced labour camp or enforced residence—'exile'—in a remote part of the country.) It is interesting to note that the interrogator may now be genuinely concerned that the case he has made in the Lubianka could be 'unmade' by a defence counsel in Lefortovo—with the possibility of an embarrassing retraction in court of earlier admissions. Such blows to the professional pride of the interrogator were inconceivable in Stalin's day.

54. page 375 The death of Feltrinelli led to much speculation in Italy that he had been the victim of right wing assassins, but despite various odd, unexplained circumstances, no conclusive evidence ever came to light that he died other than as the result of a bungled attempt to blow up a pylon in a field a few miles outside Milan. The post-mortem revealed nothing suspicious. His fears of assassination were, however, certainly justified in view of his involvement in ultra-left activities during the years before his death. He had decided to stay away from Italy since December 1969, after a bomb outrage in a Milan bank, on the grounds that he would be held responsible for it (though there was no evidence that he was). After this, his journeys to Italy—mainly from Austria, where he had a house—were clandestine. Before that he had attracted attention by his attempt to secure the release of Regis Debray from prison in Bolivia. His name later cropped up in connnection with the assassination in Hamburg of the Bolivian consul—who was shot with a pistol which had apparently belonged to Feltrinelli, though here again, there was no proof of his direct participation.

55. page 376 The trial was kept completely secret both from the Soviet and the Western public. The first report on it from Moscow came well over a month and a half after the one-day trial had taken place—on the night of Jan. 21, 1961 in a broadcast in the English-language service of Moscow Radio. This broadcast (which incongruously referred to the trial as having been 'public') was clearly intended as a response to the very considerable disquiet about the case—of which the details were so far known only from unofficial sources—in the West. As the facts filtered through, various enquiries and requests for futher information were made by P.E.N., and other Western bodies and individuals. These enquiries (e.g. David Carver's telegrams of January 19 and 23 on behalf of P.E.N. to Surkov) elicited the first admissions that a trial had indeed taken place, but they were followed by systematic attempts to blacken the character of Ivinskaya and her daughter—as, notably, in Surkov's long letter to Carver of April 3, 1961. Despite reiterated requests in the West, however, no transcript of this 'public' trial was ever made available.

56. page 378 The Italian bank-note figured prominently in attempts to discredit Madame Ivinskaya abroad: 'In February 1961, Mr Alexei Adzhubei, editor of *Izvestia*, and son-in-law of Khruschchev, came to Britain (together with Surkov, Mr Georgi Zhukov, and others) on a delegation to a conference on 'peaceful co-existence', organized by the Great Britain-USSR Association. He brought a set of documents supposedly proving Ivinskaya's guilt, and attempted to get a number of leading British newspapers to publish these. He wanted them published 'without any comment whatsoever' . . . and complained of censorship when this was not found acceptable—though, as British journalists pointed out to him, the documents had not been published, nor the case referred to, in the papers of the USSR itself! The documents consisted of: (a) photographs of bundles of Russian banknotes; (b) photographs of Italian banknotes [*sic*] cut in two; (c) a photostat of a letter in German said to have been sent to Mrs Ivinskaya by Signor Feltrinelli; (d) a confession written by Mrs Ivinskaya in the Investigation Section of the Committee of State Security.' (Robert Conquest, *Courage of Genius*, London, 1961)

57. page 380 There seems no doubt that some if not all of the roubles handed to Madame Ivinskaya by d'Angelo's emissaries *were* brought in from abroad and not obtained in the Moscow State Bank in exchange for foreign currency. In a letter published in *Avanti* on January 28, 1961, Feltrinelli wrote as follows about the money taken to Moscow by d'Angelo's friends after Pasternak's death:

'I myself know that the 100,000 dollars, *converted entirely or in part into roubles* [My italics. M.H.] and transmitted to Moscow came from funds at the disposal of Boris Pasternak in the West. The amount in question was withdrawn on a written order in the author's [i.e. Pasternak's] own hand, dated 6th December, 1959. This order arrived in the West in March 1960 . . . I know that the sum was duly withdrawn [i.e., by d'Angelo from the Pasternak royalties held by Feltrinelli] on 10 March, 1960. As for the delay of some months between the date of withdrawal and consignment to Moscow, I maintain this was due as much to the understandable difficulty which Pasternak's emissary experienced in finding the *rouble equivalent* [My italics. M.H.], as to the actual transfer of the currency

. . . It is my opinion that Olga Ivinskaya is not responsible either for the transfer of the sum or for its eventual destination. In the first place the transfer order was given, I repeat, by Pasternak himself; secondly it was Pasternak himself who wished that the sum converted into roubles should be sent, without distinction, either to himself or to Madame Ivinskaya.' (Quoted from *Courage of Genius*. Robert Conquest, London, 1961.)

It is forbidden to take roubles out of the Soviet Union, but they do find their way abroad and can be acquired (no doubt cheaply) in Western capitals by people prepared to run the risk of taking them back into the Soviet Union. It is significant that the lawyers acting for Madame Ivinskaya and her daughter based their defence on the claim that the roubles were *not* smuggled in. This suggests that the prosecution refrained from presenting any material evidence on this score: such evidence would certainly have incriminated the Italian emissaries, not the defendants, and would thus only have strengthened the already overwhelmingly obvious conclusion that the Soviet authorities were not interested in bringing a case against the Italians who under their eyes (and with their acquiescence) were in actual fact committing an offence indictable under Soviet law.

Years later, during a complicated lawsuit between Feltrinelli and d'Angelo over the rights in Pasternak's remaining royalties, Feltrinelli expressed his conviction that d'Angelo's action in conveying this vast sum to Moscow after Pasternak's death was the cause of the disaster that overtook Madame Ivinskaya and her daughter, and he asked whether the whole thing was not, 'unknown to d'Angelo, a cleverly-set trap to discredit Pasternak and Mrs Ivinskaya'. (See the interview with Feltrinelli in *The Sunday Times Weekly Review*, London, May 31, 1970.)

58. page 382 Under Stalin ten-or twenty-five-year sentences were the standard ones for imaginary or trivial' political' offences, and although by 1960 most people unjustly sentenced before 1953 had been released, some still remained, largely thanks to the vagaries of the system (just as later, long after the fall from power of Khrushchev, there were reported still to be people in the camps who had been sentenced for making derogatory remarks about him).

59. page 388 Mayakovski's poem, published in 1915, is a denunciation of contemporary society, but its lyrical anguish came from disappointment in love. The 'Maria' of the poem was probably a composite figure, of whom Maria Chukovskaya could well have been part. Mayakovski completed the poem while staying in the Chukovskis' summer home on the Gulf of Finland.

60. page 389 The University of Michigan Press edition of Pasternak's poetry and prose in the original Russian came out in 1961, and is edited by

Gleb Struve and Boris Filippov. It is the most complete edition to appear so far, and probably contains almost everything available up to the time of publication, including many rare items from early Soviet periodicals, and several poems or variants of poems received by private channels and never previously published. The fourth volume (sometimes thought of as separate from the three volumes of prose and poetry) consists of *Doctor Zhivago* and came out earlier, in 1959. Although the Michigan edition is not, needless to say, available in the Soviet Union, it is interesting to note that it is listed in the bibliography to the article on Pasternak in the *Short Literary Encyclopedia*.

61. page 389 The entry on Pasternak in the *Short Literary Encyclopedia* (Vol. 5, 1969) by Z. Paperny, a noted scholar and critic, is perhaps exceptional in its relative objectivity: 'After the war Pasternak decided to return to a novel in prose conceived a long time previously. The poet attached great importance to it. The novel centres around Doctor Zhivago, an intellectual akin to Spektorski [the hero of Pasternak's unfinished narrative poem of this name, 1931] who stands at a tragic crossroads between his personal world and active involvement in the life of society. The novel conveys deep disillusionment in the idea of revolutionary violence or a self-sacrificing submission of the personality to revolutionary destiny. The pages in the novel about nature and love are written with great power. The sending of the novel abroad, its publication there in 1957, and the award of the Nobel Prize [to Pasternak] in 1958 provoked sharp criticism in the Soviet press and ended with Pasternak's expulsion from the Union of Writers and his renunciation of the Nobel Prize . . . '

The *Short Literary Encyclopedia* (in eight volumes, Moscow, 1962-75) is in general distinguished by a tone of scholarly detachment in its entries on modern authors, both Soviet and foreign, and has consequently often been under attack by more 'conservative' critics.

62. page 390 It is true that the 'Hamlet' poem has never been published in the Soviet Union under Pasternak's name, but it has appeared there under Shakespeare's! In January, 1968, in the monthly periodical *Foreign Literature*, Andrei Voznesenski reviewed a collection of Pasternak's translations from various languages which had appeared posthumously in 1966 in a volume entitled *Starry Sky*. Discussing Pasternak's Shakespeare translations, Voznesenski at one point quotes the whole of the 'Hamlet' poem in a context where it might appear to be a quotation from Pasternak's translation of Shakespeare's play.

Since then—a typical example of the vagaries of Soviet censorship in recent years—it has become possible to recite the poem in public, even though it is still theoretically under a ban. (It will be interesting to see whether it will at last be passed for publication in a forthcoming new collection of Pasternak's poetry in the Poet's Library series, intended to replace the 1965 volume, now 'unacceptable' because of the association of Andrei Siniavski with it.) The poem is declaimed from the stage in the production of *Hamlet* (as translated by Pasternak) at the 'Theatre on the Taganka' in Moscow, directed by Yuri Liubimov (see the Biographical Guide). In 1976 the Taganka Theatre visited Belgrade and the production has been described as follows:

'It opens on a bare stage; a black-clad balladeer-Hamlet (played by the famous Soviet folksinger Vladimir Visotski) stands at an open grave singing the haunting lines from the 'Hamlet' poem in Pasternak's *Doctor Zhivago* (whose publication is still banned in Russia). Then a huge hemp curtain, the only scenery, falls from the ceiling. The actors come out dressed in heavy turtleneck sweaters and suede boots. Modern in its looks, the court is Byzantine in texture, so evil and ridden with intrigue that the slightest mistake Hamlet makes will worsen his already precarious position...' (Margaret Croyden, *The New York Times*, October 31, 1976)

The Fallen and the Living was also put on by the Taganka Theatre (in 1965). It was a composite production about the war and its aftermath, with music by Shostakovich, and readings from many poets, including Pasternak.

63. page 390 *An Essay in Autobiography* (American title: *I Remember*) appeared in full in the West, both in the original and in English translation, in 1959. When it eventually came out in *Novy Mir* (January 1967) under the title *People and Circumstances*, the censorship cuts were indicated in an unusually demonstrative way by means of the three dots of omission in parentheses.

64. page 391 The publishing history of *The Blind Beauty* has been no less complicated in the West. It first appeared early in 1969 in the Italian journal *Il Dramma*, edited by Giancarlo Vigorelli, who claimed copyright in it. It seems, however, that the Italian translation was made in Moscow from an original that was unavailable in the West. As a result of the Italian publication, a copy of the original, which had been in England for some time in the possession of a young scholar, was offered to Collins/Harvill Publishers in London, who had in the meantime acquired rights from Vigorelli. Collins/Harvill published this original text in a limited edition, recognizing Vigorelli's copyright (which, needless to say, could not be protected). The English translation of the play published in London and New York in the same year was made from this original which appears to have derived from the same copy as was used a few months later by Lev Ozerov in *Prostor* (October 1969).

65. page 392 Motyleva's review was of the selected works of Goethe in one volume, edited by Pasternak's relative by marriage, Nikolai Vilmont, which came out in 1950. This contained Pasternak's translation of Part One of *Faust*, but his translation of the whole work was published only in 1953.

66. **page 393** Article 58 was the notorious section of the Soviet Criminal Code which laid down Draconian penalties for 'crimes of sta.e', i.e. for a wide and loosely-defined range of 'political' offences—'propaganda and agitation' against the Soviet régime, 'counter-revolutionary activity', espionage, etc. In 1958 a new criminal code was issued, and the old Article 58 became Article 70—which has now achieved similar notoriety, since the basic principles remain unchanged.

67. **page 397** This is the date on which the first draft of the book was completed. It now contains some material which was added in later years.

BIOGRAPHICAL GUIDE

Most of the persons mentioned in the text, except when they are identified by the author and occur only once, have been included in this Guide. Many of the entries amount only to a bare identification (full name, and dates, etc.), since nothing more is needed; in other cases, additional information has been given, as a general rule, only in so far as it might help in a better understanding or appreciation of the text. The long entry on Marina Tsvetayeva is intended as background to the chapter on her relations with Pasternak (pp. 170–192). Nicknames or diminutive forms used in the text have been given in brackets after the first names of the persons concerned. Cross references to other persons mentioned within entries are indicated by the use of capital letters.

ABAKUMOV, Victor Semionovich (1894–1954): Minister of the MGB (State Security) 1946–52; he was tried in secret and summarily executed in December 1954 charged with having used 'criminal methods of investigation' on the orders of BERIA, who had appointed him to his post. More specifically, he was accused of having fabricated the 'Leningrad Affair' (see note 1).

ABASHIDZE, Irakli Vissarionovich (1909–): Georgian poet.

ADAMOVICH, Georgi Victorovich (1894–1972): émigré poet and critic.

AGAPOV, Boris Nikolayevich (1899–): prose-writer.

AIGI, (Lisin) Gennadi Nikolayevich (1934–): a poet in Russian and Chuvash, also well-known for his translations into both languages (particularly from French). He was a student at the Gorki Literary Institute, 1953–8.

AKHMADULINA, Bella Akhatovna (1937–): popular woman poet; once the wife of YEVTUSHENKO.

AKHMATOVA, Anna Andreyevna (1889–1966): great Russian poet virtually condemned to silence for much of the Soviet era. Her reputation was firmly established already before the Revolution by several volumes of verse published then. Although she herself was never directly touched, her first husband, Nikolai GUMILEV was shot, her third husband was arrested during the purges in the 'thirties, and her son, Lev GUMILEV, was imprisoned three times. In 1946 she and Mikhail ZOSHCHENKO were singled out as the special targets of a violently worded Party decree which signalled the beginning of the massive post-war persecution of the Soviet intelligentsia as a whole. She was denounced by Stalin's henchman for cultural affairs, Andrei ZHDANOV, as 'half-nun, half-whore', and expelled from the Union of Writers. She bore her ordeal stoically, but when her son was arrested for a third time in 1949 she published some verse in praise of Stalin, evidently in the (vain) hope of obtaining clemency for him. Her true feelings about her times are contained in two long poems which have still not been published in full in the Soviet Union: *Requiem* (written 1935–40), occasioned by the imprisonment of her third husband, Nikolai PUNIN, and her son, but also a lament for the country as a whole; and *Poem Without a Hero* (1940–42), an extraordinary attempt to come to terms with her memories of the era of war and revolution. Her last years, under the Khrushchev régime, were comparatively peaceful. She was accorded a certain measure of cautious recognition (e.g. some of her poetry was republished, and she was restored to membership in the Union of Writers). In 1964 she was allowed to go to Italy to receive the Taormina Literary Prize (her first visit abroad since 1911), and in the following year went to Oxford where she was awarded an honorary degree. (For her biography see Amanda Haight, *Anna Akhmatova*, Oxford 1976; samples of her work, including part of *Poem Without a Hero*, are available in *The Poetry of Anna Akhmatova*, translated by Stanley Kunitz, Boston and London, 1973.)

ALIGER, Margarita Iosifovna (1914–): poetess who achieved wide popularity during the war, particularly for her long poem *Zoya* (1942) about a war-time heroine.

ALPATOV, Mikhail Vladimirovich (1902–): leading art historian; author of works on Western European and Russian art.

ALTMAN, Georges: editor-in-chief of the French newspaper *Franc-Tireur*.

ANDRONIKOV, Irakli Luarsabovich (1908–): literary scholar, well-known for his studies of LERMONTOV.

ANISIMOV, Ivan Ivanovich (1899–1966): literary scholar.

ANTOKOLSKI, Pavel Grigoryevich (1896–): poet.

ANTONOV, Sergei Petrovich (1915–): prose-writer.

ANTONOVSKAYA, Anna Arnoldovna (1886–1967): poet, playwright, and novelist.

ARDOV, Victor Yefimovich (1900–): writer of humorous stories, sketches, and scenarios.

ARSKI, Pavel Alexandrovich (1886–1967): poet and prose-writer.

ASANOV, Nikolai Alexandrovich (1906–): poet and prose-writer; he spent some time in a forced labour camp in the post-war years (this may well have been connected with the fact that he had translated poetry of the Chechens and Ingush, two small Caucasian peoples deported by Stalin in 1944).

ASEYEV, Nikolai ('Kolia') Nikolayevich (1889–1963): poet who was briefly linked with Pasternak in a group of Futurist poets, *Centrifuge*, which was formed in 1913. He wrote an introductory article to Pasternak's first published collection of verse *A Twin In Clouds* (1914). After the Revolution he became a close associate of MAYAKOVSKI.

ASMUS, Valentin Ferdinandovich (1894–1975): philosopher and logician; a friend of Pasternak's.

ASTANGOV, Mikhail Fiodorovich (1900–65): actor; played Matthias Clausen in Hauptmann's *Before Sunset*.

ATAROV, Nikolai Sergeyevich (1907–   ): prose-writer.

AZARKH, Raisa Moiseyevna (1897–   ): prose-writer.

AZHAYEV, Vasili Nikolayevich (1915–68): author of a documentary novel *Far from Moscow* (awarded the Stalin Prize in 1948) about the exploits of the workers in the construction of a pipe-line. The project in question was completed by forced labour, but this is not mentioned.

BABEL, Isaac Emannuilovich (1894–1941): Russian-Jewish short story writer, author of *Red Cavalry* (1923). He was arrested in 1939 and presumably died in prison.

BALTRUSHAITIS, Yurgis Kazimirovich (1873–1944): poet of Lithuanian origin who was associated with the Symbolists. He wrote in both Russian and Lithuanian. Pasternak worked as a tutor to his son in the summer of 1914. After the Revolution he settled in newly independent Lithuania and served as its first and only ambassador to the Soviet Union (1921–39). As such he played a part in the efforts to save MANDELSTAM from death in 1934. (See Nadezhda Mandelstam, *Hope Against Hope*, p. 27). He died in Paris.

BANDERA, Stepan (1909–59): Ukrainian nationalist leader whose forces continued to operate against the Soviet régime in the Ukraine for several years after the war. He was assassinated in Munich. Captured followers of Bandera, together with those of VLASOV, formed a numerous category in the Soviet forced labour camps in the post-war years.

BANNIKOV, Nikolai Vasilyevich: editor at *Goslitizdat* (State Publishing House for Literature); author of the afterword to a small volume of Pasternak's verse which appeared in 1966.

BARANOVICH, Marina Kazimirovna (1898–   ): see author's footnote on p. 96.

BARATYNSKI, Yevgeni Abramovich (1800–44): poet, one of the best known of PUSHKIN's contemporaries.

BARKOVA, Anna Alexandrovna (1901–76): poetess of working-class origin. Her first volume of verse was published in 1923, with a preface by LUNACHARSKI. Seven poems by her appeared in the anthology

Russian Poetry of the Twentieth Century, compiled by Yezhov and Samurin, Moscow, 1925.

BARUZDIN, Sergei Alexeyevich (1926–): prose-writer.

BATALOV, Alexei ('Aliosha') Vladimirovich (1929–): cinema actor.

BEBUTOV, G. V.: see author's footnote on p. 76.

BEDNY, Demyan (1883–1945): writer of vigorous propaganda verse, very popular in the 'twenties.

BELY, Andrei (pseudonym of Bugayev, Boris Nikolayevich, 1880–1934): leading Symbolist poet, novelist, critic, and (after the Revolution) writer of important memoirs on literary and intellectual life in the first years of the century. His novels (notably *Petersburg*, 1913) were a new departure in Russian prose and their experimental manner influenced several writers in the early Soviet period.

BERGGOLTS, Olga Fiodorovna (1910–75): poet and prose-writer, known for her long poems on the siege of Leningrad.

BERIA, Lavrenti Pavlovich (1899–1953): head of the NKVD (secret police) after the fall of YEZHOV in 1938. He was ousted in the struggle for power after Stalin's death and executed together with some of his associates (he was accused of having been a British agent, of fomenting national antagonisms within the Soviet Union, and of planning to disrupt the system of collectivized agriculture).

BEZYMENSKI, Alexander Ilyich (1898–1973): poet.

BLOK, Alexander Alexandrovich (1880–1921): by common consent Russia's greatest twentieth-century poet and an all-pervasive influence. Pasternak met him only once, not long before his death in 1921—the occasion is described in *An Essay in Autobiography*—and wrote a cycle of four poems about him which are included in his last collection, *When the Weather Clears*.

BLOKHIN, Nikolai Nikolayevich (1912–): eminent surgeon.

BOBROV, Sergei Pavlovich (1889–1971): poet, critic, and translator (of Voltaire, Stendhal, Victor Hugo, G. B. Shaw). He was for a time associated with Pasternak in a literary group *Centrifuge*. After the Revolution he wrote several futuristic novels. He is also the author of popular books on mathematics for children.

BOGATYREV, Konstantin ('Kostia') Petrovich (1925–76): translator (of Rilke, Erich Kästner, and others). In April 1976 he was found severely injured outside his apartment in Moscow and died in hospital nearly two months later. He was buried near Pasternak in Peredelkino. (See the letter of Gleb Struve in the *Times Literary Supplement* of August 13, 1976). His father, Piotr Grigoryevich Bogatyrev (1893–1973), was a well-known ethnographer and authority on the popular theatre.

BORODIN, Sergei Petrovich (1902–74): a historical novelist, who also wrote under the pseudonym 'Amir Sargidzhan'. (The incident mentioned in the author's footnote on p. 170 is also referred to in Nadezhda MANDELSTAM's *Hope Against Hope*.)

BRIK, Lilia ('Lili') Yuryevna: widow of Osip Brik (a literary critic associated with MAYAKOVSKI) and sister of Elsa TRIOLET; her publication in 1968 of Mayakovski's intimate letters to her provoked controversy in the Soviet press.

BRIUSOV, Valeri Yakovlevich (1873–1924): leading Symbolist poet.

BUDBERG, Baroness Marie ('Moura') *née* Zakrevskaya, Maria Ignatyevna (1892–1976): born in Kharkov, the daughter of Count Ignat Zakrevski; married a Russian diplomat called Benckendorff in 1911 (who was killed by his peasants in 1918) and then a Baron Budberg, whom she later divorced. She was successively mistress of Sir Robert Bruce Lockhart (whom she met in Moscow in 1918. See his *Memoirs of a British Agent*), of Maxim GORKI (with whom she lived first in Moscow and then, from 1921, in Capri), and, after Gorki's departure for Russia in 1933, of H. G. Wells. She lived in London for nearly forty years. Her translation of Pasternak's story *The Childhood of Luvers* (mentioned on p. 54), for which Gorki wrote a preface, was never actually published.

BUGAYEVA, Claudia Nikolayevna: widow of BELY.

BUKHARIN, Nikolai Ivanovich (1888–1938): Old Bolshevik; member of the Politburo from 1919 to 1929, when he was defeated by Stalin over the issue of collectivization. He was editor of *Izvestia*, 1934–7. After his arrest in 1937 he was tried at the last great Moscow 'show trial' in 1938 and sentenced to be shot. Bukharin, more cultivated and moderate than most of the other Bolshevik leaders, took a genuine interest in poetry. At the end of the 'twenties he helped Osip MANDELSTAM to get published, and in 1934 exercised his vestigial influence with Stalin to obtain a reprieve for him. At the First Congress of the Union of Writers he went out of his way to praise Pasternak. (See Stephen F. Cohen, *Bukharin and the Bolshevik Revolution*, New York, 1973.)

BULGAKOV, Mikhail Afanasyevich (1891–1940): major Russian prose-writer and playwright; the author of an outstanding philosophical-satirical novel, *The Master and Margarita*, which was only published a quarter of a century after his death, first with cuts in the journal *Moskva* (1966–7), and later in full as a book (1973). His play *Flight* (1928), mentioned on p. 183, is a relatively sympathetic study of the Whites in defeat and was for a long time banned by the Soviet censorship.

BULGAKOV, Sergei Nikolayevich (1871–1944): priest and religious thinker; lived as an émigré in Paris, where he died.

BULGARIN, Faddei Benediktovich (1789–1859): journalist and writer who also worked as an informer for the 'Third Department' (the secret police department under Nicholas I). He wrote articles attacking PUSHKIN, LERMONTOV, and others in his newspaper *The Northern Bee* (1825–57).

BUNIN, Ivan Alexeyevich (1870–1953): poet and novelist who emigrated in 1918 and settled in Paris; he was awarded the Nobel Prize in 1933, the first Russian writer to receive the honour. In the years since Stalin's death he has come to be recognized as a Russian classic in the Soviet Union, and his collected works have been published there.

CHAGIN, Piotr Ivanovich (1898–1967): editor and director of several Soviet publishing houses.

CHARENTS, Yegishe Abgarovich (1897–1937): Armenian poet and translator.

CHORNY, Osip Yevseyevich (1899–): novelist; author of a *samizdat* work, *The Book of Destiny*, published in Holland in 1974.

CHIKOVANI, Simon Ivanovich (1902–66): Georgian poet; some of his work was translated into Russian by Pasternak.

CHUKOVSKAYA, Lidia Korneyevna (1907–): daughter of Kornei CHUKOVSKI; a literary critic, editor and prose-writer; the author of two short novels published abroad, *The Deserted House* (*Sofia Petrovna*) and *Going Under*, both about the persecution of the intelligentsia under Stalin. In recent years she has been a prominent defender of human rights and literary freedom in the Soviet Union.

CHUKOVSKI, Kornei Ivanovich (1882–1969): leading man of letters; critic, literary scholar, writer of books for children, and translator (of G. K. Chesterton, Mark Twain, Arthur Conan Doyle, Rudyard Kipling, Walt Whitman, O. Henry, and others; he also did adaptations for children of *Robinson Crusoe*, Raspe's *Baron von Münchhausen* stories, and others).

CHUKOVSKI, Nikolai Korneyevich (1904–65): prose-writer and translator (son of Kornei CHUKOVSKI).

CLODT VON JURGENSBURG, Nikolai Alexandrovich (1865–1918): painter.

COHEN, Hermann (1842–1918): founder of the 'Marburg School' of philosophy; author of commentaries on Kant, and of original treatises on neo-Kantian lines.

D'ANGELO, Sergio (1922–): Italian journalist and translator.

DOLMATOVSKI, Yevgeni Aronovich (1915–): poet.

DUDINTSEV, Vladimir Dmitrievich (1918–): novelist whose *Not by Bread Alone* provoked fierce controversy in 1956 because of its outspoken portrait of a Stalinist bureaucrat. It was passionately defended by PAUSTOVSKI at a closed meeting in the Union of Writers but, after the Hungarian uprising in November 1956, its opponents prevailed; it was, however, never banned, and in later years came to be accepted (by Khrushchev himself, among others) as a legitimate critique of bureaucratic highhandedness under Stalin.

DYMSHITZ, Alexander Lvovich (1910–75): critic.

EFRON, Ariadna ('Alia') Sergeyevna (1913–): daughter of Marina TSVETAYEVA; returned to the Soviet Union from Paris in 1937; arrested in August 1939 and sent to Siberia, she came back to Moscow only after Stalin's death. She helped to edit the volume of her mother's poetry published in Moscow in 1965.

EFRON, Georgi ('Moor') Sergeyevich (1925–42?): son of Marina TSVETA-YEVA. After his mother's suicide in 1941, he appears to have made his way to Central Asia, volunteered for service at the front, and to have been killed in action.

EFRON, Sergei Yakovlevich (1893– ?): Marina TSVETAYEVA's husband, whom she married in 1912. He came from a Jewish family well known for its publication of the Brockhaus-Efron encyclopaedia. He served in the White Army and emigrated to Prague, then to Paris. Forced to flee France in 1937 as a suspected Soviet agent, he was arrested in Moscow in late 1939, and died or was executed in prison.

EHRENBURG, Ilya Grigoryevich (1891–1967): novelist and journalist of prolific output; originally hostile to the Bolshevik régime, he became a fervent propagandist for it in later decades, but after Stalin's death he played an important part in the 'liberal' movement, first by his novel *The Thaw* (1954), and then in his memoirs, published in 1960–65, *People, Years, Life*. Despite censorship cuts, these gave a franker account of the fate of the intelligentsia under Stalin than had ever before appeared in print.

EISENSTEIN, Sergei Mikhailovich (1898–1948): famous film director (*The Battleship Potemkin*, 1925, *Alexander Nevski*, 1938, and others). The second part of his *Ivan the Terrible* was denounced in a special Party decree in September 1946 because of alleged 'ideological' distortions: Stalin was displeased by a failure to idealize Ivan the Terrible as unconditionally as demanded by his own self-identification with the 'strong' Tsars of the past—from the late 'thirties historians and writers (such as Alexei TOLSTOI) had brought out works glorifying Ivan the Terrible and Peter the Great as Stalin's predecessors. Pasternak's remarks about Eisenstein's *Ivan the Terrible*, quoted on p. 131, refer to the first part of the film, which was released for public showing; the second part was banned before it could be shown, and was released only after Stalin's death.

ERDMAN, Nikolai Robertovich (1902–70): playwright and writer of many film scenarios. There is an interesting portrait of him in Nadezhda MANDELSTAM's *Hope Against Hope*.

FADEYEV, Alexander Alexandrovich (1901–56): Soviet novelist whose book *The Rout* (1927) was regarded as a classic of 'Socialist Realism'.

He was secretary general of the Union of Writers 1946–53. He shot himself after Khrushchev's revelations about Stalin at the Twentieth Party Congress in 1956.

FEDIN, Konstantin ('Kostia') Alexandrovich (1892–1977): veteran Soviet novelist; in 1959 he succeeded SURKOV as secretary of the Union of Writers and held the post until 1971, when he was appointed to the honorific post of President.

FET, Afanasi Afanasyevich (1820–92): lyric poet.

FIGNER, Vera Nikolayevna (1852–1942): veteran populist revolutionary; author of memoirs.

FIRSOV, Vladimir Ivanovich (1937–   ): poet who identified himself with the 'conservatives' in the Khrushchev years.

FRANK, Victor Semionovich (1909–72): critic, journalist, and broadcaster; (his father was the religious thinker Semion Ludvigovich Frank, 1877–1950, who was expelled, together with other prominent Russian intellectuals, from the Soviet Union in 1922 and eventually settled in England.) Seven essays by him on Pasternak have been published (in Russian) in *Selected Articles*, London, 1974.

FRENKEL, Ilya Lvovich (1903–   ): poet.

GAFUR GULIAM (1903–66): Uzbek poet and prose-writer.

GALICH, Alexander Arkadyevich (1918–77): poet and playwright best known for his songs—such as the one mentioned on p. 244 which has been published abroad under the title *Oblaka* (Clouds). He often sang his songs at private gatherings in Moscow, and they circulate widely on 'unofficial' recordings. He emigrated to the West in 1974, after being expelled from the Union of Writers.

GAMARNIK, Yan Borisovich (1894–1937): head of the Political Directorate of the Red Army, editor of the Army newspaper *Red Star* and Deputy Minister of Defence; committed suicide during the terror of 1937.

GAMSAKHURDIA, Konstantin Simonovich (1891–   ): Georgian novelist, critic, and translator (e.g. of Dante's *Divine Comedy* into Georgian).

GERASIMOVA, Valeria Anatolyevna (1903–70): prose-writer.

GERMAN, Yuri Pavlovich (1910–67): novelist.

GLADKOV, Alexander Konstantinovich (1912–76): playwright who once worked with MEYERHOLD; his memoir *Meetings with Pasternak* (published in English in 1977) throws important light on Pasternak's life and attitudes during and after the Second World War.

GOLOVINA, Alla Sergeyevna (1911–   ): émigré poetess.

GOLUBOV, Sergei Nikolayevich (1894–1962): novelist.

GONCHAROV, Andrei Dmitrievich (1906–   ): artist noted particularly for his book illustrations (e.g. to Pasternak's translation of Goethe's *Faust*).

GORKI, Maxim (1868–1936): his most significant work after the Revolution was an epic novel, *The Life of Klim Samgin* (begun in 1925 and unfinished at the time of his death), whose hero is often held to typify the vacillating liberal intelligentsia so much scorned by the Bolsheviks. Gorki was acquainted with Pasternak's father, who drew a portrait of him. (During the 'twenties Pasternak wrote to Gorki a number of times in Capri, and these letters, together with several replies from Gorki, were published in Moscow in 1963.)

GOTOVITSKAYA, Militsa: See p. 45.

GRIBACHEV, Nikolai Matveyevich (1910–): poet and prose-writer.

GUCHKOV, Alexander Ivanovich (1862–1936): prominent businessman and politician who became Minister of Defence in the Provisional Government; emigrated to France after the Bolshevik seizure of power.

GULIA, Georgi Dmitrievich (1913–): novelist from Abkhazia in the Caucasus.

GULIAM: see GAFUR GULIAM.

GUMILEV, Lev Nikolayevich (1911–): son of Nikolai GUMILEV and Anna AKHMATOVA; historian and Orientalist (author of books on the Huns, and Prester John). He was arrested three times (in 1934, 1937, and 1949).

GUMILEV, Nikolai Stepanovich (1886–1921): leading Russian poet; founder of the Acmeist movement; first husband of Anna AKHMATOVA. His travels in remote parts of the world, particularly in Africa, lent an exotic flavour to some of his poetry. He was shot as a 'counter-revolutionary' in 1921.

HERZEN, Alexander Ivanovich (1812–70): revolutionary thinker and publicist who together with his childhood friend, the poet OGAREV, founded a Russian free press in London, where he began to publish his newspaper *The Bell* in 1857.

INBER, Vera Mikhailovna (1890–1972): prose-writer.

IVANOV, Viacheslav Ivanovich (1866–1949): leading Symbolist poet; emigrated to Italy in 1924, and died in Rome.

IVANOV, Viacheslav ('Koma') Vsevolodovich (1929–): son of Vsevolod IVANOV; a linguist specializing in semantics. (He was appointed deputy editor-in-chief of *Questions of Linguistics* in 1956, but lost the post in 1959—no doubt as a result of his association with Pasternak.)

IVANOV, Vsevolod Viacheslavovich (1895–1963): prose-writer famous for his colourful novels and stories about the Civil War; a friend of Pasternak and his neighbour in Peredelkino.

JASIENSKI, Bruno (1901–41): Polish Communist writer who settled in the Soviet Union in 1929; arrested in the purges, he apparently died in a camp.

KALININ, Mikhail Ivanovich (1875–1946): Old Bolshevik who, as President of the Central Executive Committee (and then, from 1938, of the Presidium of the Supreme Soviet), was titular head of state from 1922 to 1946. He never had any real power, particularly in the later Stalin years, but his avuncular appearance made him a useful figurehead, and there was an assiduously fostered myth of his supposed ability to intervene on behalf of ordinary citizens—for which reason he was sometimes styled the 'All-Union *starosta*' (*starosta* was the village elder who before the Revolution represented the community in its dealings with authority).

KAMENEV, Lev Borisovich (1883–1936): Old Bolshevik and member of the ruling triumvirate (with Stalin and ZINOVYEV) after Lenin's death. He was executed after his confession at a show trial in 1936.

KAPITSA, Piotr Leonidovich (1894–): eminent physicist; worked with Rutherford in Cambridge, and returned to the Soviet Union in 1934.

KARAMZIN, Nikolai Mikhailovich (1766–1826): historian and man of letters, important for his influence on the development of the modern Russian literary language.

KARAVAYEVA, Anna Alexandrovna (1893–): prose-writer.

KATANIAN, Ruben Pavlovich (1881–1966): Assistant Prosecutor General of the Soviet Union, 1933–37. Arrested in 1938.

KATAYEV, Ivan Ivanovich (1902–39): prose-writer; arrested during the purges.

KATAYEV, Valentin Petrovich (1897–): well-known novelist.

KAVERIN, Veniamin Alexandrovich (1902–): novelist who in the post-Stalin years played an important part in trying to obtain greater freedom of expression for writers. He was one of the editors of *Literary Moscow* (see note 33), and has written several novels and stories about the persecution of scientists under Stalin.

KAYDEN, Eugene (1886–): Russian-born American scholar and translator; his translations of Pasternak's poems were published by the University of Michigan Press in 1959.

KAZAKIEVICH, Emmanuil Genrikhovich (1913–62): novelist; originally a Yiddish writer, he began to write in Russian only after the War. He was chief editor of the two volumes of the almanac *Literary Moscow* (see note 33), in one of which he published his own short novel, *The House on the Square*, about the persecution of innocent people under Stalin.

KHARABAROV, Ivan ('Vania') Mitrofanovich (1938–69): poet; a fellow student of Madame Ivinskaya's daughter at the Gorki Literary Institute, from which he graduated in 1960.

KHESIN, Grigori ('Grishka') Borisovich: at one time head of V.U.O.A.P., the All-Union Commission for the Protection of Authors' Rights, an agency of the Union of Soviet Writers, which handles legal matters involving royalties, etc.

KHITAROVA, Sofia: editor at *Goslitizdat* (State Publishing House for Literature).

KIROV, Sergei Mironovich (1886-1934): member of the Politburo and Party chief of Leningrad. His assassination was probably engineered by Stalin, who then used it as a pretext for the mass terror that followed later.

KIRSANOV, Semion Isaakovich (1906-72): poet, much influenced by MAYAKOVSKI.

KOCHETOV, Vsevolod Anisimovich (1912-73): author of novels attacking the liberal intelligentsia.

KOLTSOV, Mikhail Yefimovich (1898-1942): writer and journalist, best known for his *feuilletons* in *Pravda* (for which he worked from 1922), and his *Spanish Diary* (1938). Like many of the Soviet citizens who were in Spain during the Civil War, he was arrested during the purges on returning to Moscow. He evidently died in a camp.

KORNILOV, Boris Petrovich (1907-38): poet who was arrested during the purges.

KORZHAVIN (MANDEL), Naum Moiseyevich (1925-): poet who suffered reprisals under Stalin for writing anti-régime verse; was able to publish several volumes of poetry after Stalin's death. In 1973 he emigrated to the United States.

KOTOV, Anatoli Konstantinovich (1909-56): literary scholar and editor; head of *Goslitizdat* (State Publishing House for Literature) from 1948 until his death; he was one of the editors of *Literary Moscow* (see note 33).

KOZHEVNIKOV, Vadim Mikhailovich (1909-): novelist; editor, since 1949, of the monthly literary journal *Znamia* (The Banner), which published some of the verse from *Doctor Zhivago* in 1954.

KOZYREV, Semion Pavlovich (1907-): Soviet career diplomat and a Deputy Minister of Foreign Affairs (since 1966), who has served in London, Paris, and Cairo, and was ambassador to Italy, 1957-66, at the time of the publication there of *Doctor Zhivago*.

KRIVITSKI, A. Y.: editor (member of editorial board of *Novy Mir*).

KRUCHENYKH, Alexei Yeliseyevich (1886-1968): Futurist poet.

KUGULTINOV, David Nikitich (1922-): Kalmuck poet; graduated from the Gorki Literary Institute in 1960.

KULMANOVA, Zinaida: editor in *Goslitizdat* (State Publishing House for Literature).

KUPRIN, Alexander Ivanovich (1870-1938): well-known prose-writer who emigrated in 1919 but returned to the Soviet Union in 1936. The story referred to on p. 299 is about a priest who revolts against the anathema pronounced on Leo Tolstoi by the Holy Synod in 1901, and which had to be read out in the churches every year in the first week of Lent; the story was banned and confiscated by order of the censorship when it first appeared just before the Revolution.

LAVRENEV, Boris Andreyevich (1891–1959): poet, prose-writer, and playwright.

LAXNESS, Halldór (1902–   ): Icelandic novelist; awarded the Nobel Prize in 1955.

LERMONTOV, Mikhail Yuryevich (1814–41): great Russian poet and author of a famous novel, *A Hero of our Times*; killed in a duel at the age of twenty-seven.

LEVITAN, Isaac Ilyich (1860–1900): famous Russian landscape painter, a friend of Chekhov's.

LEZHNEV, A. (pseudonym of Gorelik, Abram Zelikovich, 1893–1938): critic and theoretician of literature who wrote on Pasternak and others. He was arrested in 1938 and died in prison.

LIPKIN, Semion Izraelevich (1911–   ): poet and translator.

LISIN: see AIGI.

LIUBIMOV, Nikolai Mikhailovich (1912–   ): translator from Spanish and French (of Cervantes, Rabelais, Flaubert, Maupassant, and others); collaborated with Pasternak on a translation of Calderón.

LIUBIMOV, Yuri Petrovich (1917–   ): theatre director who in 1963 founded his own group: the Moscow Theatre of Drama and Comedy on the Taganka; usually known simply as the 'Theatre on the Taganka', after the district where it is situated, it has revived the best traditions of the Russian theatre in the 'twenties, and is noted for its bold and lively productions. For the production of *Hamlet* in Pasternak's translation (first staged in 1972) see note 62; in 1977 he put on a stage version of BULGAKOV's *Master and Margarita*.

LIVANOV, Boris Nikolayevich (1904–72): famous actor.

LIVSHITZ, Benedict Konstantinovich (1889–1939): poet and translator (of Mallarmé, Valéry, the Georgian poets TABIDZE and YASHVILI); the author of an outstanding literary memoir, *The One-and-a-half-eyed Archer* (1933). He was arrested in the purges.

LO GATTO, Ettore (1890–   ): eminent Italian scholar of Russian literature; professor at Rome and Naples; author of a standard history of Russian literature.

LOZINSKI, Mikhail Leonidovich (1886–1955): translator, noted particularly for his Russian version of Dante's *Divine Comedy*.

LUGOVSKOI, Vladimir Alexandrovich (1901–57): poet.

LUKACZ, General: see ZALKA.

LUKNITSKI, Pavel Nikolayevich (1900–73): prose-writer.

LUKONIN, Mikhail Kuzmich (1918–76): poet.

LUNACHARSKI, Anatoli Vasilyevich (1875–1933): publicist, playwright, translator (of Sándor Petöfi, Friedrich Hölderlin and others); as People's Commissar of Public Enlightenment (1917–29) he was responsible for educational and cultural policies in the first years of the Bolshevik régime.

MAKARENKO, Anton Semionovich (1888–1939): educationalist and prose-writer best known for his *Pedagogic Poem* (1933–5).

MANDELSTAM, Nadezhda ('Nadia') Yakovlevna (1899–   ): widow of Osip MANDELSTAM and author of memoirs on him (in English translation: *Hope Against Hope*, 1970; *Hope Abandoned*, 1974).

MANDELSTAM, Osip Emilyevich (1891–1938): great Russian poet associated with AKHMATOVA in the Acmeist movement. The story of his life and of the ordeal which ended in his death in a camp near Vladivostok in 1938 has been told by his widow. The Acmeists opposed the formal innovations of the Futurists (with whom Pasternak was briefly associated) and were thought to be more conservative, both in poetry and in general outlook. Mandelstam's last book of poetry, *The Voronezh Notebooks*, was written in his place of exile.

MARKOV, Georgi Mokeyevich (1911–   ): novelist; appointed secretary of the Union of Writers in 1971 in succession to FEDIN.

MARSHAK, Samuil Yakovlevich (1887–1964): poet noted as a children's writer and translator (of Wordsworth, Burns, William Blake, Keats, Kipling, Edward Lear, Shakespeare's sonnets).

MARTYNOV, Leonid Nikolayevich (1905–   ): poet.

MARYAMOV, Alexander Moiseyevich (1909–   ): prose-writer and critic.

MASLENNIKOVA, Zoya: see footnote on p. 71.

MAYAKOVSKI, Vladimir Vladimirovich (1893–1930): in many ways the antipode of Pasternak, Mayakovski combined powerful poetic gifts with a romantic anguish which could find relief only in total service to the Revolution—at the cost of suppressing in himself the urgent personal emotions evident in his pre-revolutionary work (such as *The Cloud in Trousers*, 1913. See notes 26 and 59). After the Revolution he wrote many *agitprop* jingles on topical themes, as well as long epic glorifications of the new order, such as *Mysteria-Bouffe* (1918), *150,000,000* (1921), and *Vladimir Ilyich Lenin* (1924). His concern at the loss of revolutionary momentum is reflected in two plays, *The Bedbug* and *The Bathhouse*, written not long before his suicide. Before the Revolution he had been one of the leading figures of the Futurist movement, and after the Revolution, from 1922, he headed a group known as LEF ('Left Front of Art'), with which Pasternak was also associated—at least nominally—until 1927, when he broke with it. Rather incongruously, Mayakovski was 'canonized' in 1936 by Stalin who proclaimed that he 'was and remains the best and most talented poet of our Soviet epoch', adding that 'indifference to his memory and to his work is a crime'. The ensuing cult of him prompted Pasternak's famous comment in his *An Essay in Autobiography*, that 'Mayakovski began to be introduced forcibly, like potatoes under Catherine the Great'. (For an outline of Mayakovski's life and work, and samples of his poetry, see: *The Bedbug and Selected Poetry*, edited, with an introduction, by Patricia Blake, New York, 1960.)

MECHNIKOV (generally spelled METCHNIKOFF in the West), Ilya Ilyich (1845–1916): eminent Russian biologist and physiologist; awarded the Nobel Prize (together with Paul Ehrlich) in 1908.

MEYERHOLD, Vsevolod Emilyevich (1874–1940): famous actor and producer; a friend of Pasternak's, who wrote a poem ('To the Meyerholds', 1929) about him and his wife, the actress Zinaida Raikh. After Meyerhold's arrest in 1939, his wife was brutally murdered in their apartment by 'unknown persons'. Meyerhold himself died in prison the following year, and was 'posthumously rehabilitated' after Stalin's death.

MEZHIROV, Alexander Petrovich (1923–): poet.

MIKHALKOV, Sergei Vladimirovich (1913–): poet and playwright noted for his satirical verse on topical themes, often written to order (e.g. his poem denouncing Pasternak after the award of the Nobel Prize).

MIKHOELS (VOVSI), Solomon Mikhailovich (1890–1948): leading actor who created the State Jewish Theatre in Moscow. He was assassinated on Stalin's orders while on a visit to Minsk—he was run down on the street by a truck-driver supposedly 'by accident'. A fulsome obituary appeared in *Pravda*, but a year later the theatre founded by him was closed, together with all other Jewish cultural institutions. The brother of Mikhoels was one of those arrested in the anti-Semitic affair of the 'Doctors' Plot' in 1953. (See note 15.)

MINDLIN, Emil Lvovich (1900–): author of literary memoirs entitled *Neobyknovennye Sobesedniki* (Unusual Interlocutors), Moscow, 1958.

MOLOTOV, Viacheslav Mikhailovich (1890–): now (1977) the only surviving 'Old Bolshevik' leader. His real name was Scriabin, and he was distantly related to Alexander SCRIABIN. Appointed Foreign Minister in succession to Litvinov, he negotiated the Soviet pact with Nazi Germany in August 1939. Ten years later he fell into disfavour with Stalin and was replaced as Foreign Minister by VYSHINSKI. After Stalin's death he again become Foreign Minister (1953–6), but in 1957 he fell foul of Khrushchev as a member of the so-called 'anti-Party group', and though expelled from the Party, was allowed to hold minor diplomatic posts (in Mongolia and Vienna) until his retirement.

MOTYLEVA, Tamara Lazarevna (1910–): literary critic.

NAROVCHATOV, Sergei Sergeyevich (1919–): poet and critic.

NEDOGONOV, Alexei ('Aliosha') Ivanovich (1914–48): poet.

NEIGAUS, Genrikh ('Garrik') Gustavovich (1888–1964): eminent pianist and teacher of music. Pasternak first met him at the end of the 'twenties, when Neigaus was a professor at the Moscow Conservatory. After Pasternak's divorce from his first wife, Yevgenia Vladimirovna, he married Neigaus's wife, Zinaida Nikolayevna, in 1934, but later resumed friendly relations. His son, Stanislav Neigaus, is also a concert pianist.

NEKRASOV, Nikolai Alexeyevich (1821–78): populist poet and editor; author of long narrative poems, often of 'social significance.'

NEMIROVICH-DANCHENKO, Vladimir Ivanovich (1858–1943): famous theatre director; founder, with Stanislavski, ot the Moscow Arts Theatre in 1898.

NEZVAL, Vitězslav (1900–58): well-known Czech poet.

NIKOLAYEVA, Galina Yevgenyevna (1911–63): novelist.

NILIN, Pavel Filippovich (1908–): prose-writer.

NILSSON, Nils Åke: head of the Institute of Slavic Studies, Stockholm.

NIVAT, Georges (1935–): Professor of Russian language and literature at the University of Geneva since 1972; studied at Moscow University in the late 'fifties under the academic exchange programme between the Soviet Union and France, and made the acquaintance of Pasternak, Madame Ivinskaya and her daughter, Irina YEMELYANOVA. In January 1960 he became engaged to Irina, with the blessing of Pasternak. (Irina was then a student at the Gorki Literary Institute.) But after Pasternak's death on May 30, 1960, is became clear that the Soviet authorities were determined to prevent the marriage, which had been fixed for August 20, in a Moscow Registry office. On August 10, Nivat was forced to leave the Soviet Union, despite an appeal to Khrushchev. Irina was arrested less than a month later. None of Nivat's pleas from abroad, nor the many made on his behalf (including one from Mrs Eleanor Roosevelt in a personal letter to Khrushchev), ever received any response.

OGAREV, Nikolai Platonovich (1813–77): poet and journalist; co-editor with HERZEN of the Russian émigré newspaper *The Bell.*

OKUDZHAVA, Bulat Shalvovich (1924–): Soviet poet and prose-writer best known as a *chansonnier*. Many of the songs he has composed (and performs himself, often at semi-private gatherings) have not been published in the Soviet Union.

OLESHA, Yuri Karlovich (1899–1960): novelist and playwright, author of one of the best early Soviet novels, *Envy* (1927). His autobiographical notes, *Not a Day without a Line*, appeared posthumously in 1961.

OSHANIN, Lev Ivanovich (1912–): poet.

ØSTERLING, Anders: Secretary of the Nobel Prize Committee, Stockholm.

OTSUP, Nikolai Avdeyevich (1894–1958): Acmeist poet who emigrated to France after the Revolution; his memoirs, *Contemporaries*, were published posthumously in 1961.

OVCHARENKO, Yevgeni Ivanovich (1922–): professor of Moscow University; author of books and articles on 'Socialist realism'.

OZEROV, Lev Arnoldovich (1914–): poet; translator, and literary scholar.

PANFEROV, Fiodor Ivanovich (1896–1960): novelist and editor.

PANKRATOV, Yuri ('Yura') Ivanovich (1935–): poet, graduated in 1961 from the Gorki Literary Institute (where he was a fellow-student of Madame Ivinskaya's daughter).

PANOVA, Vera Fiodorovna (1905–73): novelist.

PASTERNAK, Alexander Leonidovich (1893–): younger brother of Boris Pasternak; an architect, he lives in Moscow.

PASTERNAK, Josephine (Zhosefina Leonidovna 1900–): elder of Pasternak's two sisters; lives in Oxford.

PASTERNAK, Leonid ('Lionia') Borisovich (1937–76); Pasternak's younger son by his second marriage.

PASTERNAK, Leonid Osipovich (1862–1945): the father of Boris Pasternak; a painter noted for his portraits (e.g. of members of his family, Leo Tolstoi, Rilke, Lenin, Einstein, and others) and book illustrations (of Tolstoi's *Resurrection*). He was a professor at the Moscow College of Painting, Sculpture, and Architecture. In 1921 he was given permission —through the good offices of LUNACHARSKI—to travel to Germany with his wife and two daughters for medical treatment, and did not return to the Soviet Union (although he never officially became an émigré, and contemplated going back, particularly after the rise of Hitler). After living some years in Berlin and Munich, he settled in England in 1938, and died in Oxford. His wife, Rosalia Isidorovna; died in 1939. Some memoirs by him were published in Moscow in 1975.

PASTERNAK, Yevgeni ('Zhenia') Borisovich (1923–): elder son of Boris Pasternak by his first wife.

PASTERNAK, (*née* Yeremeyeva), Zinaida ('Zima') Nikolayevna (?–1966): second wife of Boris Pasternak; previously married to Genrikh Neigaus.

PASTERNAK-SLATER, Lydia Leonidovna (1902–): Pasternak's sister; lives in Oxford.

PAUSTOVSKI, Konstantin Georgievich (1892–1968): novelist, playwright and memoirist who played a prominent part in the liberal movement among writers in the post-Stalin years. He was one of the editors of

BIOGRAPHICAL GUIDE 459

Literary Moscow (see note 33) and brought out a literary miscellany, *Pages from Tarusa* (1961), which caused a stir at the time.

PAVLENKO, Piotr Andreyevich (1899–1951): novelist who was awarded a Stalin prize for his anti-Western *Happiness* (1947).

PAVLOV, Ivan Petrovich (1849–1936): famous physiologist and experimental psychologist; awarded the Nobel Prize in 1904.

PERTSOV, Victor Osipovich (1898–): critic and literary scholar; specialist on MAYAKOVSKI.

PETÖFI, Sándor (1823–49): the greatest Hungarian poet.

PIATNITSKI, Mitrofan Yefimovich (1864–1927): founder of a popular choir, which still exists and is named after him.

PISMENNY, Alexander ('Sasha') Grigoryevich (1909–): prose-writer.

PLATONOV, Andrei Platonovich (1899–1951): outstanding prose-writer; neglected and virtually under a ban in the later Stalin years, he has now been partially reprinted in the Soviet Union.

POGODIN, Nikolai Fiodorovich (1900–62): leading playwright.

POLEVOI, Boris Nikolayevich (1908–): novelist.

POLEZHAYEV, Alexander Ivanovich (1805–38): a poet of radical and atheist views ordered by Nicholas I to serve as a private in the Army.

POLIKARPOV, Dmitri Alexeyevich (1904–65): Party official who was appointed head of the Cultural Department of the Central Committee in 1955 and, as such, was responsible for the political supervision of literature.

POPOVA, Olga ('Liusia') Ilyinichna (1926–): artist; friend of Pasternak's.

POZHENYAN, Grigori Mikhailovich (1922–): poet.

PROKOFYEV, Alexander Andreyevich (1900–71): poet.

PROYART, de Baillescourt, Comtesse Jacqueline de: Professor of Russian language and literature at the University of Poitiers; author of a book on Pasternak (*Pasternak*, Paris, 1964) which incorporates important letters to her written in the last years of his life.

PUNIN, Nikolai Nikolayevich (1888–1953): art historian and critic; the third husband of Anna AKHMATOVA, he was imprisoned for a time in the mid-thirties.

PUSHKIN, Alexander Sergeyevich (1799–1837): acknowledged in his lifetime as Russia's greatest poet, he was a constant object of attention from the Third Section, Nicholas I's secret police. He was twice exiled from the capital, and briefly detained for questioning after the Decembrist uprising of 1825. Although the Tsar to some extent protected him, he never ceased to be subject to censorship and surveillance, and was never allowed to travel abroad. His death in a duel was widely thought by the Russian public at the time to have been the result of slander and intrigues originating in court circles, and these suspicions found powerful expression in a poem ('The Death of a Poet') by his younger contemporary LERMONTOV.

PUZIKOV, Alexander Ivanovich (1911–   ): literary scholar; authority on French literature; since 1951, senior editor of *Goslitizdat* (State Publishing House for Literature).

RADISHCHEV, Alexander Nikolaevich (1749–1802): a forerunner of the Russian liberal intelligentsia; his *Journey from Petersburg to Moscow* (1770) described the evils of serfdom. Though the book had been passed by the censor, Catherine the Great ordered his arrest and he was condemned to death, but this was commuted to ten years' exile in Siberia; he was pardoned by Paul I a few years later, and appointed to a legislative position by Alexander I, but he committed suicide soon afterwards.

RADLOVA, Anna Dmitrievna (1891–1949): poetess and translator (of Shakespeare, Christopher Marlowe, Guy de Maupassant, and others).

RAGIMOV, Suleiman (1900–   ): Azerbaidzhan prose-writer.

RANEVSKAYA, Faina Grigoryevna (1896–   ): famous actress.

RASKIN, Alexander Borisovich (1914–71): writer of humorous prose and verse.

RATNITSKI, Ari Davidovich: employee of *Litfund* (see note 50), with special responsibility for funeral arrangements.

REAVEY, George: see note 44.

REISS, Ignace: see TSVETAYEVA.

RIABININA, Alexandra Petrovna: editor at *Goslitizdat* (the State Publishing House for Literature).

RICHTER, Sviatoslav Teofilovich (1914–   ): famous pianist.

RILKE, Rainer Maria (1875–1926) Austrian poet, born in Prague. He visited Moscow in 1900 when Pasternak's father painted a portrait of him. (*Safe Conduct* opens with a childhood recollection of him during a train journey to see Leo Tolstoi.) In the few years before Rilke's death, Pasternak corresponded with him through the intermediary of Marina TSVETAYEVA.

RIPELLINO, Angelo Maria (1923–   ): Italian writer, translator and critic; professor of Russian at University of Rome.

RODZEVICH, Konstantin Borisovich: friend of TSVETAYEVA's; her relations with him are the subject of her *Poem of the Mountain* and *Poem of the End*. (See also the author's footnote on p. 183).

ROMANOVA, A. D.: see author's footnote on p. 200.

ROSTROPOVICH, Mstislav ('Slava') Leopoldovich (1927–   ): famous cellist; in 1974 he was allowed to leave the Soviet Union (after being subjected to various restrictions there because of his help to SOLZHENITSYN) on a two-year exit visa, and now lives in the West.

ROZANOV, Vasili Vasilyevich (1856–1919): critic and religious thinker.

RUDENKO, Roman Andreyevich (1907–   ): Prosecutor-General of the USSR (and, hence, its highest 'law' officer) since 1953; he represented the USSR at the Nuremberg trial of the Nazi war criminals.

RUGE, Gerd (1928–   ): West German journalist. He was stationed in Moscow as bureau chief of the West German television network, ARD, from 1956 to 1959. He subsequently served as a correspondent in Washington and Peking. His book on Pasternak (English title: *Boris Pasternak—A Pictorial Biography*, New York, 1959) appeared. simultaneously in several languages.

RUMIANTSEV, Count Nikolai Petrovich (1754–1826): statesman, diplomat, and bibliophile whose collection of manuscripts, books, and coins formed the basis of the Rumiantsev Museum, founded in Moscow in 1861 (after the collection had been transferred from St. Petersburg), and now called the Lenin Library.

RYLENKOV, Nikolai Ivanovich (1909–69): poet.

SAKHAROV, Academician Andrei Dmitrievich (1921–   ): eminent physicist and now leading champion of human rights in the Soviet Union.

SAMARIN, Dmitri: friend of Pasternak's at high school and the University; a student of philosophy (it was on his advice that Pasternak went to Marburg), he was the grandson of a prominent leader of the Slavophile movement, Yuri Fiodorovich Samarin (1819–76). According to Pasternak's account of him in *An Essay in Autobiography* he died of typhus at the beginning of the 'twenties. The family estate was at Peredelkino and the adjacent Izmalkovo. Dmitri Samarin evidently served, at least in some externals, as the prototype of Yuri Zhivago.

SCHEWE, Heinz (1921–   ): West German newspaper man; served in the Luftwaffe as a radio operator in the Second World War and in 1943 twice took part in reconnaissance missions over Moscow, and in strafing raids on the approaches to it. He has published a book on his wartime experiences on the Russian front and in *Pasternak Privat* (Hamburg, 1974), he tells the story of his relations with Pasternak and Olga Ivinskaya.

SCHMIDT, Piotr Petrovich (1867–1906): lieutenant of the Black Sea fleet who was executed for his part in a naval mutiny at Sebastopol in 1905.

SCHWEITZER, Renate: German writer; has published her correspondence with Pasternak: *Freundschaft mit Boris Pasternak. Ein Briefwechsel*, 1963.

SCRIABIN, Alexander Nikolayevich (1872–1915): composer; as a young man Pasternak was very much under his influence for a time, but eventually broke free of it. 'I took him for my supreme authority, not realising that he alone could afford his own egocentricity, that his teaching was right only for him.'—*An Essay in Autobiography*

SEDYKH, Konstantin Fiodorovich (1908–   ): novelist.

SELVINSKI, Ilya Lvovich (1899–1968): well-known poet; leader of the so-called 'Constructivists' in the 'twenties.

SEMICHASTNY, Vladimir Yefimovich (1924–   ): Party official, who rose up through the Komsomol to become head of it in 1950. In 1961 he was put in charge of the KGB (secret police). He made his attack on Pasternak in the course of a speech before a plenary session of the Komsomol Central Committee. (For the relevant extract, see Robert Conquest, *Courage of a Genius*, London, 1961)

SEMIONOV, Nikolai Nikolayevich (1896–   ): Soviet chemist; received the Nobel Prize in 1956.

SEREBRIAKOVA, Galina Iosifovna (1905–   ): author of biographical novels on Marx and Engels.

SERGOVANTSEV, Nikolai Mikhailovich (1934–   ): critic associated with the 'conservative' Journal *Oktiabr*; a member of the editorial board of *Ogoniok* (see footnote on p. 390).

SHAGINYAN, Marietta Sergeyevna (1888–   ): novelist.

SHAKHOVSKAYA, Zinaida Alexeyevna (1906–   ): émigré poetess, who now edits the Russian newspaper *Russkaya Mysl* in Paris.

SHALAMOV, Varlam Tikhonovich (1907–   ): poet and prose-writer who spent seventeen years in forced labour camps. His stories of life in the notorious camps of Kolyma in the far north east of Siberia, have been published only abroad.

SHCHEPKINA-KUPERNIK, Tatyana Lvovna (1874–1952): granddaughter of the famous nineteenth-century Russian actor Shchepkin; a playwright and translator (of Sheridan, Goldoni, Lope de Vega, Molière). In her memoirs, *The Theatre in My Life* (1948), she recalls her friendship with Chekhov and Stanislavski.

SHCHERBINA, Vladimir Rodionovich (1908–   ): critic, and editor (of *Novy Mir*, 1941–6).

SHCHIPACHEV, Stepan Petrovich (1899–   ): poet.

SHKLOVSKI, Victor Borisovich (1893–   ): critic and literary theorist; a leading member of the Formalist movement in the 'twenties.

SHOLOKHOV, Mikhail Alexandrovich (1905–   ): author of *Quiet Flows the Don*, (1928–1940) regarded as a classic in the Soviet Union, and of which the earlier parts are relatively objective in the treatment of the Civil War—both Reds and Whites are shown to have committed atrocities. In the years since Stalin's death he has emerged as an anti-liberal, chauvinist 'hardliner', and has sometimes made disparaging or intemperate remarks about fellow writers (including Pasternak); he was awarded the Nobel Prize in 1965.

SHOSTAKOVICH, Dmitri Dmitrievich (1906–75): famous composer; he was attacked for 'formalism', first in 1934, after Stalin walked out of the première of his opera *A Lady Macbeth of the Mtsensk District*, and then in 1948, together with other Soviet composers, during the purges of the intelligentsia conducted by ZHDANOV in the post-war years. The outward appearance of almost grovelling conformity which he adopted as a result of the attacks on him sometimes seemed exaggerated, but it apparently masked a spirit of independence which continued to find expression in his music.

SIMONOV, Konstantin Mikhailovich (1915–): poet and novelist who became well known during the war for his lyrical poems (such as the cycle *With You and Without You*), and a novel on the battle of Stalingrad, *Days and Nights*. He was editor of *Novy Mir* from 1946 to 1950, and again from 1954 to 1958.

SIZOVA, Magdalina Ivanovna: writer for children; author of a novel on Lermontov.

SLONIM, Mark Lvovich (1894–1976): prominent émigré critic and editor. His articles about Marina Tsvetayeva, whom he knew well, appeared in *Novy Zhurnal* (New Review), New York, in 1970 and 1971.

SŁOWACKI, Juliusz (1809–49): major Polish poet; author of many poetic dramas (including *Marja Stuart*, 1830).

SLUTSKI, Boris Abramovich (1919–): poet.

SMELIAKOV, Yaroslav Vasilyevich (1912–72): well-known poet.

SMIRNOV, Sergei Sergeyevich (1915–76): prose-writer.

SMIRNOV, Sergei Vasilyevich (1913–): poet.

SMOLICH, Yuri Korneyevich (1900–): Ukrainian prose-writer.

SOBOLEV, Leonid Sergeyevich (1898–1971): novelist and functionary of the Union of Writers.

SOFRONOV, Anatoli Vladimirovich (1911–,): poet and playwright.

SOLOGUB, Natalia Borisovna (1912–): the daughter of Boris ZAITSEV; lives in Paris.

SOLOUKHIN, Vladmir Alexeyevich (1924–): poet and prose-writer.

SOLOVYEV, Boris Ivanovich (1904–): literary critic and scholar.

SOLOVYEV, Vladimir Sergeyevich (1853–1900): major religious thinker and poet.

SOLZHENITSYN, Alexander Isayevich (1918–): after his forcible expulsion from the Soviet Union in 1974, he published (in Paris) an autobiographical work, *The Oak and the Calf*, in which he describes his emergence as a writer in the Soviet Union, and where he speaks of his feelings on hearing that Pasternak had renounced the Nobel Prize.

SPASSKI, Sergei Dmitrievich (1898–1956): poet and prose-writer; at one time close to the Futurists. He was arrested in the late 'forties—probably in 1949—and returned from a camp in 1954 (some of Pasternak's letters to him were published in *Questions of Literature*, September 1969, and in the last of them, dated November 5, 1954, there is a reference to his 'return'). In her memoirs, Nadezhda MANDELSTAM implies that Spasski was also arrested in the pre-war terror, but he was certainly at liberty again by 1939).

SPASSKI, Yevgeni Dmitrievich (1900–   ): an artist, brother of Sergei SPASSKI.

STANIUKOVICH, Konstantin Mikhailovich (1843–1903): a novelist who wrote many popular stories about the life of sailors.

STAROSTIN, Anatoli Vasilyevich: editor of *Goslitizdat* (State Publishing House for Literature).

STAVSKI, Vladimir Petrovich (1900–43): prose-writer and journalist; appointed Secretary General of the Union of Writers after GORKI's death in 1936 and, as such, was active in the purges of writers in the late 'thirties. He was killed at the front as a war correspondent.

STETSKI, Alexei Stepanovich (1896–1938): Party functionary. He was head of the Central Committee's department of Agitation and Propaganda (*Agitprop*), 1930–8.

STROGANOV, Count Sergei Grigoryevich (1794–1882): founder of the Technical School of Drawing in Moscow.

STRUCHKOVA, Maria ('Masha') Yefremovna: See author's footnote on p. 380.

STRUVE, Nikita Alexeyevich (1931–   ): literary scholar and editor, resident in Paris. His article on AKHMATOVA, referred to in the author's footnote on p. 158, is in Vol. 2 of Akhmatova's *Works* edited by Gleb Struve and Boris Filippov.

SURKOV, Alexei Alexandrovich (1899–   ): poet and editor. Secretary General of the Union of Writers, 1953–59.

SVIRIDOV, Yuri Vasilyevich (1915–   ): composer who has put works by several Russian poets to music.

SYTIN. Victor Alexandrovich (1907–   ): prose-writer.

TABIDZE, Galaktion Vasilyevich (1892–1959): Georgian poet.

TABIDZE, Nina Alexandrovna: widow of Titian TABIDZE.

TABIDZE, Titian Yustinovich (1895–1937): Georgian poet, and friend of Pasternak who translated him into Russian; arrested during the Great Terror, he died or was executed in prison. Part of his correspondence with Pasternak has been published (in *Letters to Georgian Friends*, London and New York, 1967).

TESKOVÁ, Anna (1872–1954): Czech translator from Russian, and friend of TSVETAYEVA, who dedicated a cycle of poems to her. Their correspondence was published in Prague in 1969.

TIKHONOV, Nikolai ('Kolia') Semionovich (1896–   ): poet noted for the romantic flavour and themes of his ballads in the 'twenties. He was secretary of the Union of Writers, 1944–46. From 1950 he was chairman of the Soviet 'Peace Committee'.

TIKUNOV, Vadim Stepanovich (1921–   ): a Party functionary who began his career in the Komsomol. He held a post in the 'apparatus of the Central Committee', 1953–59, and from 1959–61, the period in which the encounter with Olga Ivinskaya described on p. 369–70 took place, he was deputy chairman of the Committee of State Security (KGB), that is, second in charge of the secret police. He was Minister of Internal Affairs of the RSFSR (the Russian Republic of the Soviet Union), 1961–2, and Minister for the Protection of Public Security of the RSFSR, 1962–66. In 1969 he was appointed Counsellor-Minister of the Soviet Embassy in Bucharest, and in 1974 was sent as Ambassador to the Republic of Upper Volta.

TIMIRIAZEV, Kliment Arkadyevich (1843–1920): plant physiologist. He was one of the few established Russian scientists to give his support to the Bolsheviks after the October Revolution in 1917.

TIUTCHEV, Fiodor Ivanovich (1803–73): lyric poet.

TOKOMBAYEV, Aaly (1904–   ): Kirghiz poet and prose-writer.

TOL, Count Karl Fiodorovich (1777–1842): Russian military leader.

TOLSTOI, Count Alexei Nikolayevich (1883–1945): novelist distantly related to Leo Tolstoi; at first anti-Bolshevik, he emigrated in 1919, but then returned to the Soviet Union in 1923, where his outstanding skill as a writer of narrative fiction made him immensely popular. As ideological pressures on literature mounted in the 'thirties and 'forties, he adapted himself to what was required with a gusto matched only by his taste for high living—which earned him the sobriquet of 'The Red Count'. His epic trilogy on Peter the Great, written between 1929 and 1945, has considerable merit from a literary and historical point of view, even though it reflects the 'cult' of Peter which Stalin began to encourage in the later 'thirties. His two-part drama on Ivan the Terrible (1941–3), on the other hand, is a flattering portrait frankly intended to appeal to Stalin: it avoids the 'error' of EISENSTEIN, who in the second part of his *Ivan the Terrible*—according to the Party decree condemning it—had turned the *oprichnina* (Ivan's ferociously cruel special force, the instrument of his terror) into something as sinister-looking as the Ku-Klux-Klan. Tolstoi's success in striking the right note was recognized by the award to him of the Stalin Prize in 1946, but the play is now acknowledged by Soviet critics to have idealized the Tsar and in particular the *oprichnina*.

TRAIL, Vera (*née* Guchkova, Vera Alexandra): daughter of GUCHKOV; now lives in England.

TRETYAKOV, Sergei Mikhailovich (1892–1939): poet and playwright, best known for his *Roar, China!*, a play based on a visit to China in the mid-thirties. He translated Brecht into Russian. He was arrested during the purges and died in prison.

TRIOLET, Elsa (1896–1970): French writer of Russian origin; she was the sister of Lili BRIK and the wife of Louis Aragon. She wrote a book on MAYAKOVSKI, and edited an anthology of Russian poetry.

TROYAT, Henri (pseudonym of TARASOV, Lev, 1911–): French writer of Armenian origin, born in Moscow; author of biographies of Tolstoi, Pushkin, Dostoyevski, Gogol, and Catherine the Great.

TSELIKOVSKAYA, Liudmila Vasilyevna (1919–): actress; played Inken Peters in Gerhart Hauptmann's *Before Sunset*.

TSVETAYEVA, Anastasia ('Asia') Ivanovna (1894–): sister of Marina TSVETAYEVA; author of memoirs which were published as a book in Moscow in 1971.

TSVETAYEVA, Marina Ivanovna (1892–1941): born in Moscow, where her father was director of the Alexander III (now Pushkin) Museum of Fine Arts. Her mother was of Baltic-German origin, and half-Polish. Tsvetayeva's first privately-printed volume of verse (1910) immediately attracted attention, and by the time of the Revolution, her reputation as a poet of unmistakable power and originality was well-established. Her husband, Sergei EFRON, whom she married in 1912, became an officer in the White Army and after the Bolshevik victory in the Civil War, he made his way to Prague (1921). Marina spent these years in Moscow with their two young daughters, Ariadna and Irina, suffering great material hardship. The younger daughter, Irina, died of starvation in a children's home in 1920. Marina was bitterly opposed to the new order (less on directly political grounds than because it offended her romantic sensibilities) and wrote verse in support of the White Army. In 1922 she was granted permission to emigrate and went to join her husband in Prague (despite several passionate, but short-lived attachments to other men, she always remained basically loyal to him). After a few years in Prague, she settled in Paris (1926), where for a time her husband helped to edit a literary journal which published her verse. In the 'thirties the material difficulties of living as an émigré in Paris (her husband suffered from chronic TB, could not get regular work, and was sometimes reduced to hiring himself out as a film extra) were compounded by the hostility towards her of several leading émigré critics and writers—not only on aesthetic grounds, but also because her characteristic independence of judgment went against the grain of important sections of received émigré opinion. Although not in a meaningful sense 'pro-Soviet', she refused to join in the chorus of condemnation of MAYAKOVSKI in the émigré press after his suicide in 1930, and wrote a cycle of poems dedicated to him (she recognized a certain affinity in their poetic temperaments). In the later 'thirties she wrote poems denouncing the Nazis, particularly their seizure of Czechoslovakia and may gradually have come to see the Soviet Union as the lesser evil. In the meantime her husband and daughter, Ariadna, had developed clear-cut and unconcealed Communist sympathies. Some time in the early 'thirties Efron was apparently recruited by the Soviet intelligence service. In early 1937 Ariadna, now aged about twenty-five, returned to the Soviet Union. In September of the same year Efron was forced to flee France and return to the Soviet Union by a clandestine route because he was wanted by the French police for suspected complicity in the assassination of a Soviet intelligence agent, Ignace Reiss (real name: Poretsky), who had defected to the West. (For an account of this bizarre affair, see the book by Reiss's widow, Elizabeth K. Poretsky, *Our Own People, a Memoir of 'Ignace Reiss' and His Friends*, London, 1969.) Efron was also thought to have been involved in the murder of Trotski's son, Andrei Sedov. Although Marina was undoubtedly innocent in these matters and had no knowledge of them, she was ostracized by the emigration. At the same time, her adolescent son Georgi ('Moor') began to urge her to return to Moscow. It was not, however, until almost two years after her husband's flight that Marina and her son left for Moscow (in June 1939). Contrary to what was believed for many years, and to what EHRENBURG suggests in his memoirs (published in Moscow, 1960–5), her husband and daughter were still at liberty at the moment when she arrived in Moscow. Ariadna was arrested only in August 1939, and Efron a little later. After working for a while as a translator (from Georgian and Yiddish) in Moscow, Marina went to Yelabuga with her son, where she hanged herself. Some of her letters to Pasternak have been published in Russian in the volume *Unpublished Letters* (edited by Gleb and Nikita STRUVE, Paris 1972), which also contains valuable information about her life in the Soviet Union before her death. There is a comprehensive account of her life and work in English by Simon Karlinsky, *Marina Cvetaeva, Her Life and Art*, Berkeley and Los Angeles 1966. The first Soviet edition of some of her work came out in 1961, and a further one in 1965. Elaine Feinstein has translated some of her poetry into English (London 1971).

TUKHACHEVSKI, Mikhail Nikolayevich (1893–1937): Commander-in-Chief of the Red Army, executed with YAKIR and other leading military figures in 1937.

TURSUN-ZADE, Mirzo (1911–): Tadzhik poet.

TUSHNOVA, Veronika Mikhailovna (1915–65): poet.

TVARDOVSKI, Alexander Trifonovich (1910–71): poet and editor. An epic poem about a Soviet soldier, Vasili Tiorkin, won him great fame during the war, and a daring satirical sequel, *Vasili Tiorkin in the Other World*, was published in 1963, by special dispensation of Khrushchev, after first circulating in *samizdat*. As editor of the monthly *Novy Mir* (1958–70), he skilfully and courageously took advantage of the vagaries of cultural policy in the Khrushchev years to publish many works (such as Solzhenitsyn's *One Day in the Life of Ivan Denisovich*) which otherwise would hardly have appeared in print. His narrative verse is written in an expressive, colloquial manner.

USPENSKAYA, Yelena Borisovna (1916–66): prose-writer.

VAKHTANGOV, Yevgeni Bagrationovich (1883–1922): director who at first worked with Stanislavski, but founded his own theatre (still called after him) in 1922.

VASILYEV, Pavel Nikolayevich (1910–37): poet who became well known in the late 'twenties and 'thirties; died in a forced labour camp.

VASILYEV, Sergei Alexandrovich (1911–75): poet.

VAZHA-PSHAVELA (1861–1915): Georgian prose-writer and poet (some of his work has been translated by Pasternak).

VENCLOVA, Antanas (1906–71): Lithuanian poet and prose-writer.

VERTINSKI, Alexander Nikolayevich (1889–1957): popular singer who returned to the Soviet Union in 1943, via the Far East, after many years in emigration. His songs were frowned on in the Soviet Union as 'decadent', but he achieved some success in film parts (e.g., in the screen version of Chekhov's *Lady With a Dog*.)

VIGDOROVA, Frida Abramovna (1915–65): writer and journalist; as a member of the Moscow district Soviet she used her influence in the 'sixties to help various people in practical ways. Nadezhda MANDEL-STAM obtained a permit to reside in Moscow in 1964 thanks to her. Her transcript of the proceedings at the trial of Joseph Brodski in the same year played a vital part in arousing public opinion abroad on his behalf —he was released in 1965 and allowed to emigrate to the United States in 1972.

VILMONT (VILLYAM-VILMONT), Nikolai ('Kolia') Nikolayevich (1901–   ): critic, literary scholar, and translator (mainly of German literature): his sister is the wife of Pasternak's brother.

VINOGRADOV, Dmitri ('Mitia') Alexandrovich (1942–   ): Olga Ivinskaya's son by her second marriage.

VINOKUROV, Yevgeni Mikhailovich (1925–   ): poet.

VLASOV, Andrei Andreyevich (1900–46): Soviet general who, after distinguishing himself in the defence of Moscow, was later (in 1942) encircled by the Germans on the Volkhov front and captured. He agreed to form a 'Russian liberation army' under the supervision of German military intelligence, but the idea never met with approval by the higher Nazi leadership, and the army was not seriously committed to combat on the Eastern front. At the end of the war Vlasov was handed over to the Red Army by the Americans and taken back to the Soviet Union, where he was hanged. The many hundreds of thousands of Soviet POW's who joined the Vlasov movement (often simply in order to avoid starvation) were sent to Soviet camps after being captured by the Red Army or handed over by the Western Allies. (For an account of Vlasov's career, and of the fate of the men who served under him, see SOLZHENITSYN's *The Gulag Archipelago*, Part 1, Chapter 7.)

VOLCHKOV, A. F.: lawyer; head of *Inyurkollegia* (see note 52).

VOLKONSKAYA, Princess Zinaida Alexandrovna (1792–1862): writer (in French, Russian, and Italian), famous for her salon in Pushkin's time; emigrated to Italy (where she was born) in 1829 and died in Rome.

VOLKONSKI, Andrei Mikhailovich (1933–): Russian composer born in Switzerland, a student of Nadia Boulanger in Paris, 1944–7; moved to the Soviet Union and continued his studies there; has now re-emigrated to the West.

VORONKOV, Konstantin Vasilyevich: playwright and prose-writer; he was a member of the board of the Union of Writers during the campaign against Pasternak. Now Deputy Minister of Culture of the USSR.

VOROSHILOV, Kliment Yefremovich (1881–1969): veteran military leader and associate of Stalin. He became President of the Supreme Soviet (i.e. titular head of state) in 1953, and in this capacity went to India on an official visit in January/February 1960. Shortly after this he was ousted by Khrushchev for his alleged involvement with MOLOTOV and others in the so-called 'anti-Party group', and was expelled from the Central Committee in 1961.

VOZNESENSKI, Andrei ('Andriusha') Andreyevich (1933–): lyric poet who attracted considerable attention by his originality and freshness of form, when he first began to publish in 1958. Together with YEVTU-SHENKO he played a major part in the revival of poetry which began in the years after Stalin's death. For his poem in memory of Pasternak see note 49.

VYSHINSKI, Andrei Yanuaryevich (1883–1954): originally a professor of law, was appointed Prosecutor General by Stalin in 1935. He became notorious during the 'show trials' of the Old Bolsheviks, whom he denounced as 'mad dogs'. In 1949 he was made Soviet Foreign Minister (in succession to MOLOTOV) and died in New York while representing the Soviet Union at the United Nations.

WEISSMAN, Boris Savelyevich: editor at *Goslitizdat* (State Publishing House for Literature).

YAGODA, Genrikh Grigorievich (1891–1938): head of the NKVD (secret police) from 1934. He was replaced by YEZHOV in 1936 for his alleged lack of determination in destroying the 'opposition'. He was tried together with BUKHARIN and others, and executed in 1938.

YAKIR, Iona Emmanuilovich (1896–1937): Soviet army commander; tried on false charges and executed in June 1937, together with TUKHACHEVSKI and six other leading military figures.

YASHIN, Alexander Yakovlevich (1913–68): poet and prose-writer whose story 'The Levers', 1956 (in *Literary Moscow*; see note 33), was a major contribution to the post-Stalin 'thaw'.

YASHVILI, Paolo Dzhibrielevich (1895–1937): Georgian poet and translator; friend of Pasternak. He committed suicide during the Terror.

YEMELYANOVA, Irina ('Ira', 'Irochka') Ivanovna (1938–): daughter of Olga Ivinskaya by her first husband. She is married to Vadim Markovich Kosovoi, an outstanding young specialist in modern French literature, who has translated many French writers into Russian. They have a son called Boris.

YENUKIDZE, Abel Sofronovich (1877–1937): old comrade of Stalin who was expelled from the Party in 1935. He was secretly tried and executed in 1937.

YERIKEYEV, Akhmed Fazylovich (1902–67). Tartar poet.

YERMILOV, Vladimir Vladimirovich (1904–70): critic.

YERSHOV, Vladimir Lvovich (1896–1948): leading actor, associated with the Moscow Arts Theatre.

YESENIN, Sergei Alexandrovich (1895–1925): major lyric poet; hanged himself in December 1925.

YEVTUSHENKO, Yevgeni ('Zhenia') Alexandrovich (1933–): lyric poet who made his mark in the Khrushchev years with his poems on the evils of the Stalin era and its legacy (e.g. *Babi Yar*, 1961, about anti-Semitism; and *The Heirs of Stalin*, 1962); he has also written several epic poems, sometimes with strong libertarian undertones. His *Precocious Autobiography*, in which he vividly describes the effect on him of Stalin's death and funeral, was published in the West in 1963 but has never appeared in the Soviet Union. The collection *Bow and Lyre* (referred to on p. 159) was published in 1959 and contained translations from the Georgian, as well as original verse on Georgian themes.

YEZHOV, Nikolai Ivanovich (1894–1939?): chief of the NKVD (secret police) 1936–38 in succession to YAGODA. He carried out on Stalin's orders the mass purges of those years, which are often referred to as the 'Yezhov terror' (*yezhovshchina*). He was later made the scapegoat for its 'excesses', and presumably executed in 1939. He was succeeded by BERIA.

YUDINA, Maria Veniaminovna (1899-1970): famous pianist, and professor at the Moscow Conservatory.

ZABOLOTSKI, Nikolai Alexeyevich (1903-58): one of the most original and distinctive poets of the Soviet period. He was arrested in Leningrad in 1938 and, after being brutally maltreated in jail, was sent to forced labour camps in Magadan and then in Central Asia but was released in 1946 and allowed to settle in Moscow. His poem on the signs of the Zodiac (mentioned on p. 4) was written in 1933. His experiences as a prisoner in a forced labour camp are graphically described in his poem 'Somewhere in a Field near Magadan' (published in Russian in the collection of his poems edited by Gleb Struve and Boris Filippov, Washington, D.C. and New York, 1965 (p. 129).

ZAITSEV: see author's footnote on p. 297.

ZAKREVSKAYA: see BUDBERG.

ZALKA, Maté (1896-1937): a Hungarian who fought on the side of the Bolsheviks during the Civil War. In the 'twenties and 'thirties he published short stories and a novel. During the Spanish Civil War he commanded the 12th International Brigade under the name of 'General Lukacz', and was killed in action.

ZAMIATIN, Yevgeni Ivanovich (1884-1937): prose-writer and playwright; author of a celebrated anti-Utopian satire *We* (1924) whose publication abroad led to a campaign of persecution against him in the late 'twenties. In 1932, apparently with the help of Maxim GORKI, he was able to emigrate to France, where he died a few years later.

ZAMOSHKIN, Nikolai Ivanovich (1896-1960): critic and editor.

ZARYAN, Nairi (1901-69): Armenian poet and playwright.

ZASLAVSKI, David Iosifovich (1880-1965): journalist noted for his vituperative *feuilletons*, generally published in *Pravda*. He was originally a Menshevik and was violently attacked by Lenin in 1917 for his articles in the Menshevik press. In 1919 he 'recanted' and declared his allegiance to the Bolsheviks. In 1929 he wrote a scurrilous attack on Osip MANDELSTAM, provoking a strong reply by a group of leading writers, including Pasternak.

ZELINSKI, Korneli Lucianovich (1896-1970): critic and literary scholar.

ZHDANOV, Andrei Alexandrovich (1896-1948): associate of Stalin and member of the Politburo from 1939; he implemented the tough ideological line of the post-war years, both in promoting Communist militancy abroad (the founding of the Cominform, 1947) and in a savage campaign intended to terrorize the intelligentsia at home—this found expression in the series of Party decrees (the 'Zhdanov decrees') condemning alleged deviations in literature, the cinema, philosophy, and music. In each case, scapegoats were chosen and made examples of (AKHMATOVA and ZOSHCHENKO in literature, EISENSTEIN in the cinema, SHOSTAKOVICH, Prokofyev and Muradeli in music, etc.)

ZHIVOV, Mark (1890?–1963): a translator from Polish and a specialist in Polish literature; a friend and near contemporary of Pasternak, he helped him with his translations of the Polish poet Juliusz Słowacki.

ZINOVYEV, Grigori Yevseyevich (1883–1936): Old Bolshevik leader; tried and executed, together with KAMENEV, in 1936.

ZOSHCHENKO, Mikhail Mikhailovich (1895–1958): short-story writer immensely popular in the 'twenties and 'thirties for his humorous treatment of the incongruities of life in post-revolutionary Russia. Together with AKHMATOVA, he was violently denounced by ZHDANOV in 1946—he had incurred the wrath of the Party authorities for the first part of an autobiographical story *Before Sunrise*, published in 1943, which betrays clear influence of Freudian doctrine, and most of all for an innocuous-seeming tale *The Adventures of an Ape* (1946) which was implausibly alleged to be a slur on the Soviet people. He was expelled from the Union of Writers and for a time suffered great material hardship but in the last years of Stalin's life was able to make a living by translating.

ZUYEVA, Anastasia Platonovna (1896–   ): actress, about whom Pasternak wrote a poem ('The Actress', 1957). In May/June 1958 she went to London with the Moscow Arts Theatre and played in Chekhov's *The Three Sisters* at Sadler's Wells.

SOURCES OF QUOTATIONS

An attempt has been made here to indicate the original—and, in some cases, the translated—sources of most of the numerous quotations in the text, in so far as this has not already been done by the author. As a general rule (and, notably, except in the case of *Doctor Zhivago*) it has not been thought necessary to give additional information where the poem or prose work concerned is named in the text.

The page references to *Doctor Zhivago* (DZ)—including those of the poems in it not yet published in the Soviet Union—are to the edition in the original Russian as published by Feltrinelli (Milan, 1957).

Quotations from poems by Pasternak are identified by reference to the page on which they occur in the fullest edition of his verse so far to have been published in the Soviet Union: *Stikhotvorenia i poemy*, Moscow, 1965, with an introductory article by Andrei D. Siniavski, and edited with notes by L. A. Ozerov (OZ). For poems not hitherto published in the Soviet Union, and for prose works other than *Doctor Zhivago*, the references are to the three-volume University of Michigan Press edition (Ann Arbor, 1961) of Pasternak's poetry and prose in the original Russian, edited by Gleb Struve and Boris Filippov (SF).

Quotations from other writers (whose names are given in brackets immediately after the opening words of the passages in question) are identified by the transliterated Russian titles, or occasionally by the title of a translation published in English, of the works from which they are taken.

page xxxix 'You are eternity's hostage...': OZ 463
page 1 'I am not writing my own...': *Safe Conduct*, SF 11 213
 'And I shall say to myself...': from an unpublished poem by the author.
page 8 'With his lips' brass': OZ 198
page 11 How one begins to live by Poetry: allusion to a line in a poem: OZ 179
 'This is not the right city...': OZ 85
 'god of detail'; 'god of love': OZ 151
page 12 'Poet, you are granted...' (N. Gumilev): *Vosmistishye* (1916).
 'little bundle of laundry...': OZ 187
 'Those candle-drippings....': OZ 88
 'the aspen leaf without lips...': OZ 85
 'piles of gardens...': OZ 66

page 13 A Forlorn God: OZ 149
    'off by heart . . .'; 'how beautiful you are! . . .': OZ 108
page 19 'You, so concerned . . .': full text only in SF *111* 134 (See note 5)
page 20 'Like gauze butterflies . . .' OZ 428
page 21 'He did not believe in "free love" . . .': DZ 312
page 22 'Beckoned by the passion . . .': OZ 431
    'I have let my family . . .': OZ 435
    'lack of sleep': OZ 432; 'helmeted woman': OZ 431
page 23 'under high tension': OZ 431
page 24 '. . . Again I rehearse . . .': OZ 430
page 26 'A man stands . . .': OZ 440
    'When the snow covers . . .': OZ 442
page 27 'living sorcery . . .': OZ 480
page 33 'But who are we . . .': OZ 443
page 40 'like a dish' OZ 455
page 41 'I'll stay here with you till the spring': OZ 609
page 42 'fiery skin': OZ 449
page 46 'Miss Touch-me-not's on fire . . .': OZ 449
page 47 'The world is ruled by pity . . .': OZ 570
    'What is the hour? . . .' OZ 569
page 48 'Farewell the counsel . . .': this stanza of *August* is published here
for the first time.
page 49 'Now I walk along the highroad . . .' (F. Tiutchev): *Vot bredu ya
vdol bolshoi dorogi* . . . (1865)
page 50 'Powdered silver by the frost . . .' (A. Pushkin): *Eugene Onegin*,
I/xvi, 4
    'the princess sleeping in her tomb . . .': OZ 400
    'a dead woman of white plaster': OZ 473
page 52 'I don't like people who have never fallen . . .': DZ 409–10
page 54 'Tall, graceful, and slim . . .' (A. Tsvetayeva): *Vospominania*
(Memoirs), Moscow, 1971, pp. 515–17
page 56 'When he looks at you, his eyes . . .' (A. Tsvetayeva): *op. cit.*,
p. 520
page 57 'I cannot for the life of me understand . . .' (M. Tsvetayeva): letter
published in *Novy Mir*, Moscow, May 1969.
page 63 'And in these same days . . .': SF *111* 241
    'some later historian . . .' (A. Blok): *Druzyam* (1908)
page 64 '. . . there is a whole folklore . . .': *Listki iz dnevnika* (Leaves from a
Diary), published in the Russian-language *Vozdushnye puti* (Aerial
Ways), No. 4, New York, 1965.
    'We live, deaf to the land . . .' (O. Mandelstam): *My zhiviom pod
soboi ne chuya strany* . . . (In this translation from: N. Mandelstam,

Hope Against Hope, London and New York, 1970, p. 13)

page 68 'Pasternak was called to the phone . . .' (N. Mandelstam): *op. cit.*, p. 146ff.

page 71 'The only person who . . . visited . . .' (N. Mandelstam): *op. cit.*, p. 131

page 73 'Pasternak sat on the platform . . .' (I. Ehrenburg): *Liudi, gody, zhizn* (People, Years, Life), *Novy Mir*, Moscow, 1960–5

page 76 'Thus one begins . . .': OZ 178

page 77 '. . . the pavement underneath . . .': OZ 559

page 79 'Gordon, recently promoted . . .': DZ 516

page 80 '. . . And for all our laurels . . .' (unnamed author): unpublished.

page 82 'In our days political denunciation . . .': A. Gladkov, *Meetings with Pasternak*, London and New York, 1977, p. 90
'If things remain the same . . .'; 'We could do with a new Tolstoi . . .': A. Gladkov, *op. cit.*, p. 56 and p. 90

page 85 'power of the lie'; 'spell of the dead letter'; 'I think that collectivization . . .': DZ 519
'I started to work on my novel again . . .': A. Gladkov, *op. cit.*, pp. 136–7

page 87 'Resurrection: in the crude form . . .': DZ 67–8

page 88 '. . . Art has two constant . . .': DZ 91

page 89 'only a dead man . . .' (A. Akhmatova): *Requiem* (1935–40)

page 109 'martyred'; 'graveyard mould': SF *111* 63–4
'. . . the sentries will no longer . . .' (N. Zabolotski): *Gde-to v pole vozle Magadana* (See note on Zabolotski in the Biographical Guide)

page 111 'As though a rasp . . .': OZ 443

page 124 'When the snow covers . . .'; '. . . Trees and fences . . .': OZ 442

page 128 '. . . In years of tribulation . . .': OZ 441

page 132 'I threw in my lot . . .': SF *111* 66–7

page 133 'Fame is the pull . . .': OZ 362
'Like a songbird . . .': OZ 482

page 135 'Yevgeni Dmitrievich . . . was recently here . . .': letter published in *Questions of Literature*, Moscow, September 1969.
'Thank you for telling me . . .'; 'If ever something prevented me . . .': A. Gladkov, *op. cit.*, pp. 121 and 145

page 138 'My soul, you are in mourning . . .': SF *111* 63

page 143 '. . . he could have no possible illusions . . .': A. Gladkov, *op. cit.*, pp. 157–8

page 144 'remembrance of all that . . .': DZ 413
'paint a Russian version . . .': DZ 81

page 145 'I think a little philosophy . . .': DZ 418
'tragically typical . . .' DZ 406

page 145 '... he would not have made ...': DZ 257
page 146 'It's so strange that these people ...': DZ 310
    'You can't imagine ...': DZ 122
page 147 'I was baptized as a child ...': letter in French quoted in
Jacqueline de Proyart, *Pasternak*, Paris, 1964, p. 40
    '... he listened to the ...': DZ 88–9
page 148 'The Bible is not so much ...': *Safe Conduct* SF 11 263; 'In this
most Christian ...' (M. Tsvetayeva): *Poema Kontsa* (1924)
page 149 '... Why do I avoid giving ...': J. de Proyart, *op. cit.*, p. 38
page 150 'In Peredelkino Fadeyev ...': A. Gladkov, *op. cit.*, p. 75
page 152 'The roads have turned to mire ...': OZ 482
page 154 'In days when great councils ...': OZ 199
    'The noise is stilled ...': DZ 532
page 155 'Men who are not free ...': DZ 494
page 156 'There are few of us ...': OZ 179
    'More and more poets ...' (V. Mayakovski): from *Poslanie
proletarskim poetam* (1926)
    'all-powerful god of detail': OZ 151
    'purple-grey circle' (A. Blok): *K muze* (1912)
page 158 'In the birch wood's very throat' (N. Zabolotski): *Ustupi mne,
skvorets, ugolok* (1946)
page 159 'rhyme summertime with Lermontov ...': OZ 362
page 160 'Even if this is only a part ...': OZ 202
page 161 'unheard-of simplicity': OZ 351
page 162 'In a world where ...' (M. Tsvetayeva): *Dvoye* (1924)
page 163 'I've always liked Mayakovski ...': DZ 180
    'These verses and odes ...' (V. Mayakovski): *Razgovor
s fininspektorom o poezii* (1926)
page 165 '... it turns out that those who inspired ...': DZ 306–7
page 166 'It was ... as if a living human face ...': DZ 412
    'He is a doomed man ...': DZ 306
    '... for us life was a campaign ...': DZ 471
page 170 'Oh allow me to be ...' (O. Mandelstam): *Vozdukh pasmurny ...*
(1911)
page 172 'Soon this world will perish! ...' (M. Tsvetayeva): quoted in
Unpublished Letters, Paris, 1972, p. 407
page 174 '... I am indifferent ...': OZ 201
    'In the silence of your going ...': OZ 567
page 177 'Today I came back ...' (A. Akhmatova): *Nevidimka, dvoinik,
peresmeshnik* (1940)
page 181 'equal loneliness' (M. Tsvetayeva): *Neizdannye pisma* (Unpublished Letters), Paris, 1974, p. 256

page 183 'Friend, rain beats . . .' (M. Tsvetayeva): *Russkoi rzhi ot menia poklon* (1925)

'. . . Love is flesh and blood . . .' (M. Tsvetayeva): *Poema Kontsa* (1924)

page 184 'Do not hasten . . .' (M. Tsvetayeva): *Suda pospeshno ne chini* (1920)

page 186 'Winter—all for the first . . .': OZ 399

'And at noon the skies . . .': OZ 454

'The City. A winter sky . . .': OZ 474

page 188 'into hollow waves . . .' (M. Tsvetayeva): *Poema Kontsa* (1924)

page 189 'The gold of my hair . . .' (M. Tsvetayeva): *Zoloto moikh volos* (1922)

'Actually, winter was still far off . . .': A. Gladkov, *op. cit.*, p. 77

page 190 '. . . a bleak entrance' (Y. Yevtushenko): part of an apparently hitherto unpublished poem

page 192 'Your face turned to God . . .': OZ 568

page 195 'This is not the right city . . .': OZ 85

page 198 'What can compare with woman's strength? . . .': OZ 216

page 199 'Daughter of a small landowner . . .': DZ 535

'I have noticed how quick . . .': DZ 290

'. . . ever since his schooldays': DZ 65–6

'considered that art was no more . . .': DZ 65

page 200 'It's a good thing when a man . . .': DZ 306

page 202 'And life itself is only . . .': OZ 435

'It was as if there was something . . .': DZ 412

page 207 'It had been the dream of his life . . .': DZ 451–2

'I am not by any means saying . . .': A. Gladkov, *op. cit.*, p. 133

'parables from everyday life'; 'communion between mortals . . .': DZ 42

page 222 'The whole world will make way for me . . .': OZ 482

page 228 'They want to make a new Zoshchenko out of me . . .': A. Gladkov, *op. cit.*, pp. 149–50

page 233 'Only real greatness . . .': DZ 199

page 235 'But can devotion to the Motherland . . .' (F. Schiller): from *Maria Stuart* (here translated from Pasternak's version published in Moscow in 1958. The two lines quoted are on p. 42)

page 240 '. . . Like a beast at bay . . .': SF *111* 107

page 243 'That is the reason why . . .': OZ 445

page 244 'Ordinary people are anxious to test . . .': DZ 268

page 247 'A kinsman of all that is . . .': OZ 351

page 253 'It was a bleak, rainy afternoon . . .': DZ 339

page 261 'Victory through renunciation' (M. Tsvetayeva); *Neizdannye pisma* (Unpublished Letters), Paris, 1974, p. 450

page 266 'unwavering attachment...': DZ 198
'cynic fascinating...'; 'the great gift...' (I. Bunin): *Collected Works*, Moscow, 1967, Vol. 9, p. 433

page 267 'Stavrogin in Dostoyevski's...' (A. Tolstoi): *Izvestia*, June 14, 1937
'The whole of life...'; 'I have a whole estate...' (A. Tolstoi, as quoted by Bunin): I. Bunin, ibid., p. 443 and p. 445

page 271 'Manikins and Men': DZ 188. In the original this phrase is literally 'playing at people' (*igra v liudei*).

page 279 'when they appeared...' (Y. Yevtushenko): hitherto unpublished.
'prose and verse, and every kind of odds and ends...': DZ 188

page 280 'The great misfortune, the root of all the evil...': DZ 414–15

page 289 'In vain, in years of turmoil...' OZ 302

page 293 'For "news"—read "lies"...' (M. Tsvetayeva): *Chitateli gazet*, 1935
'... along trails of cats and foxes': OZ 487

page 309 '... the great majority of us...': DZ 494–5

page 311 'I shall speak about that strange thing...': *Safe Conduct*, SF 11 285
'Farewell, years of tribulation...': DZ 549

page 313 'It was not out of necessity...': DZ 513

page 321 'I am caught like a beast at bay...': SF 111 107–8

page 324 'His friends had become strangely dim...': DZ 177
'Friends, family, dear good-for-nothings...': hitherto unpublished.

page 327 'Dear friends, how desperately...': DZ 493
'I... don't give a damn for any of you...': DZ 348

page 330 'People are searching for a hidden meaning...': J. de Proyart, *op. cit.*, pp. 235–6

page 342 '... art has two constant, two unending...': DZ 91

page 343 'I am finished, but you are still alive...': OZ 432

page 346 'cancer is the fate of all those...' (A. Solzhenitsyn): *Bodalsia telionok s dubom*, Paris, 1975, p. 309

page 348 'Just as it promised...': DZ 548
'And now she began to take leave...': DZ 513–14

page 349 'Goodbye, Lara, until we meet...': DZ 462–3

page 353 'Very noticeable among the crowd...' (A. Gladkov): *op. cit.*, p. 179

page 388 'Find my song alive!...': OZ 197

page 395 'How it blows from the north! . . .': OZ 197

page 396 'Don't you think you'd have to be . . .': DZ 308
          'the power of the glittering phrase': DZ 414-15
          'A genius comes as a harbinger . . .': OZ 244
          'O, graven image . . .': OZ 277-8

page 397 'the collective squandering . . .' DZ 247
          'he craved for an idea . . .': DZ 7

page 418 'bewitched crossroads': DZ 196

page 421 'the growing of the vine in the valley . . .' (A. Pushkin): *Prorok*
  1826

INDEX